Traveling the Select Registry Way

IMAGINE FOR JUST A MINUTE the perfect hideaway. Imagine, that yours is a well-deserved vacation, a special occasion or perhaps an anniversary getaway. Imagine this is your opportunity to discover a quality experience and—just perhaps—a bit of that side of yourself that quests for adventure or romance. We, the Innkeepers of the Select Registry, invite you to follow the *Select Registry* as it leads you into the sanctuary of quality Inns and quality experiences. Let's allow your story to unfold now, beginning in the Atlantic Provinces, Quebec and New England, the seat of the American colonies, then expanding the story as you travel with us across North America, into the rich and diverse regions represented by the *Select Registry*. A Sioux salutation *"Metakuyu Oyasin."* We are one family.

"This guidebook is your Innkeeper's gift to you when you stay at a Select Registry property."

Welcome!

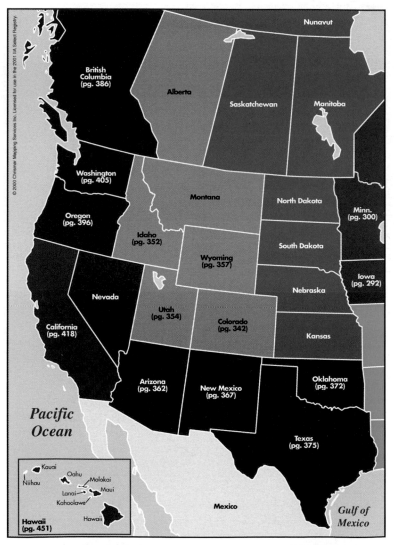

Nunavut
British Columbia (pg. 386)
Alberta
Saskatchewan
Manitoba
Washington (pg. 405)
Montana
North Dakota
Minn. (pg. 300)
Oregon (pg. 396)
Idaho (pg. 352)
South Dakota
Wyoming (pg. 357)
Iowa (pg. 292)
Nevada
Nebraska
Utah (pg. 354)
California (pg. 418)
Colorado (pg. 342)
Kansas
Arizona (pg. 362)
New Mexico (pg. 367)
Oklahoma (pg. 372)
Pacific Ocean
Texas (pg. 375)
Kauai
Niihau
Oahu
Molokai
Maui
Lanai
Kahoolawe
Hawaii
Hawaii (pg. 451)
Mexico
Gulf of Mexico

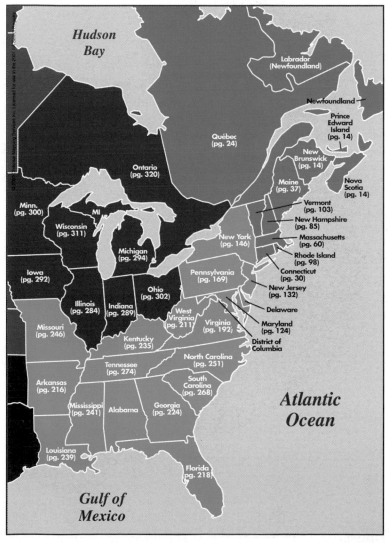

Hudson Bay
Labrador (Newfoundland)
Newfoundland
Québec (pg. 24)
Prince Edward Island (pg. 14)
New Brunswick (pg. 14)
Ontario (pg. 320)
Maine (pg. 37)
Nova Scotia (pg. 14)
Minn. (pg. 300)
MI
Vermont (pg. 103)
New Hampshire (pg. 85)
Wisconsin (pg. 311)
New York (pg. 146)
Massachusetts (pg. 60)
Michigan (pg. 294)
Rhode Island (pg. 98)
Iowa (pg. 292)
Pennsylvania (pg. 169)
Connecticut (pg. 30)
Ohio (pg. 302)
New Jersey (pg. 132)
Illinois (pg. 284)
Indiana (pg. 289)
Delaware
West Virginia (pg. 211)
Missouri (pg. 246)
Virginia (pg. 192)
Maryland (pg. 124)
Kentucky (pg. 235)
District of Columbia
North Carolina (pg. 251)
Tennessee (pg. 274)
Arkansas (pg. 216)
South Carolina (pg. 268)
Atlantic Ocean
Mississippi (pg. 241)
Alabama
Georgia (pg. 224)
Louisiana (pg. 239)
Florida (pg. 218)
Gulf of Mexico

How to Use This Book

Different Lodging Plans

THE WORLD IS A DIVERSE PLACE, and there are probably as many lodging alternatives as there are beds to rent. Putting that aside, the SELECT REGISTRY would like to define some of the more common alternatives offered by our association.

B&B Plan: Breakfast included (a few inns charge for breakfast but tell you this in their listing). The morning repast might consist of an elegant Continental breakfast, or a four-course extravaganza.

American Plan (AP): Breakfast, lunch, and dinner are included in this rate. The words "full-service" jump out.

Modified American Plan (MAP): This plan includes breakfast and dinner in the guest's tariff. Some of the best food in the US and Canada comes forth from these Inns.

European Plan (EP): A guest pays for the guestroom and those amenities, but breakfast, lunch and dinner are billed separately. There is a nice opportunity to shape a personal dining experience with this plan.

Taxes and gratuities: We may or may not include service charges, state and local taxes and gratuity in these plans. Please ask your Innkeeper in advance if they have tax & gratuity policies.

Price changes: Please call the Inn to verify all prices and services. They are subject to change during the lifetime of this book.

Type

HOTEL • *Generally 50 rooms or more with a range of amenities and services often associated with hotels.*

INN • *Generally less than 40 rooms with an emphasis on personal, professional hospitality. Breakfast available daily, dinner four or more nights a week.*

BREAKFAST INN • *Typically six to 15 rooms, with a full morning meal offered.*

RANCH • *An inn, often in multiple buildings, located in a ranch setting with compatible recreational activities available. Ranches are most often located in the country but may be mountain or seaside.*

RETREAT/LODGE • *An inn or hotel where guests' privacy is emphasized, often in a setting of solitude, with an abundance of recreational opportunities.*

RESORT • *An inn or hotel offering, on the premises or on adjacent ground, a variety of organized recreational activities, such as golf, tennis or health and fitness facilities.*

Style

ELEGANT • *Emphasis is on high-style furnishings and service.*

TRADITIONAL • *Eclectic but comfortable and well-appointed. Furnishings can often be from several periods. Attentive but relatively informal service.*

RUSTIC • *Emphasis on natural, straightforward presentation in buildings, furnishings and service. An ambiance of informal comfort. Rustic, however, does not mean spare or primitive.*

CONTEMPORARY • *Modern to stiking furniture and décor. Service tone ranges from stylish to relatively informal.*

Location

IN TOWN • Larger town or city where a range of cultural and other facilities exist. Inns in smaller towns may offer access to natural attractions, too.

VILLAGE • Community with a population range of a few hundred to a few thousand, the smallest could be relatively isolated. Many villages offer historic, natural or specialized cultural attractions.

COUNTRY • Rural setting where the conveniences of cities may be miles away. These inns may offer access to recreation opportunities such as fishing, skiing and bird watching.

MOUNTAIN • A country location near mountains or hill country.

WATERSIDE • River, lake or oceanside locations with related recreational opportunities. May or may not be near cities or towns.

Quality Assurance Program

There is no sense skirting the issue: the Select Registry Quality Assurance Program is tough. Just ask any of our Innkeepers.

The inspection process proceeds like this: An anonymous man, woman or couple checks into the Inn to spend the night. Let's choose a woman and call her Lucille.

Lucille talks with the Innkeeper at the front desk. She is friendly but inquisitive. She scouts the Inn like a raccoon with night eyes, scooping out the minute details: How's the hospitality, cleanliness, room quality? She might even run a linen napkin into the places most of us miss. It better come up clean.

Lucille has dinner. She eats slowly and seems to savor every bite. Her eyes dart around the room. Are the other guests happy? Is the service impeccable? How about that dessert tray? Nice wine list. Is the wait staff educated about the varietals, the vintages? Does the white Chardonnay match the fish? What about the Merlot? Yakima Valley! Delicious! Lucille asks lots of polite questions.

She visits with the guests the next morning. Asks about their experience. Lucille chooses carefully from the breakfast entrees. She is the master of the nuance. She walks through the garden, then around the building. Later, she checks out.

"May I talk with the Innkeeper," she inquires. "Hi, I'm the Quality Assurance Inspector. I'd like to tell you what I found."

Recently, an Innkeeper confessed an appreciation for the inspection process. That surprised some of his peers. Wasn't the process a bit intimidating, they asked? "No," the Innkeeper explained. "This is the surest way to keep myself and my staff on their toes. This is my assurance program."

In the Select Registry, we aim for the best. We are professionals. The Quality Assurance program guides us, along the way.

Web site
selectregistry.com
For more detailed information about the rooms, the innkeepers, and the many attractions in an area you can find our Inns at *SelectRegistry.com.* You can also look-up availability of many SELECT REGISTRY Inns on the web site. This is a tremendous convenience when you are planning a trip and don't want to make dozens of phone calls, only to find out an Inn is full.

About the Inns' Policies

Cancellation Policy

Most Country Inns of the SELECT REGISTRY are middle-sized Inns or B&Bs. Most are run by couples, many by families. Most are small enough that they cannot absorb a last minute cancellation. Unlike some big hotels or the airlines, we refuse to overbook. Often, we turn other people away because we have guaranteed your reservation. Unless the Innkeeper can re-rent the room, a last-minute default will generally cost revenue vital to that business's survival.

Cancellation fees are nothing new to the industry. We guarantee your room, your arrival. That is our deal. We will not sell that room to anybody else. That is our guarantee. However, the Innkeeper must be given adequate time to re-rent the room if you, the customer, has a change of plans. It's kind of like a handshake that consummates a deal. The Inn will likely state its policy in your confirmation letter. So please, pay attention to the cancellation policies of those hard-working families that exist to serve you through the *Select Registry*.

Children and Pets

Unlike that famous actor and comedian W.C. Fields, we, the Innkeepers of the SELECT REGISTRY, love most all of those two-and four-legged creatures. A sensible gambler would wager that 90 percent of our Innkeepers have, or have had one or more cuddly cats or dogs or-believe it or not-rabbits. Some of our Innkeepers raise goldfish or carp, and one, in Washington state, salmon. All that aside, not all of our Inns allow children or pets. Many of those Inns are filled with priceless carpets or period antiques, and some of our customers are allergic to pets. Sure there probably are a few curmudgeons among us. Let's say two out of 400, but those aren't bad odds. And a good number of our guests are escaping the little ones for a weekend of-how to say this so the little ones don't suspect—-a romantic interlude.

If you run into a problem, chances are, the Innkeeper will find you an accommodation nearby that will be the cat's meow. Remember, we exist to please.

Associate Members

SELECT REGISTRY is proud to present the following companies as Associate Members:

InnStyle, *supplier of fine linens to our member Inns. 215-348-5689.*

The RobeWorks, *supplier of quality robes to our member Inns. 213-687-1177.*

Arndt-McBee Insurance, *supplier of insurance to our member Inns. 800-548-8857*

Third Millennium Marketing, *supplier of Internet services to our member Inns. 860-521-5151.*

Seasonal Concepts, *supplier of miniature porcelain lighted houses to our member Inns. 612-546-8887.*

NC Inn Brokers, Munden & Associates, *property sales to potential member Inns. 800-963-4197.*

MunsenWare, *supplier of reservation software to our member Inns. 763-441-7512.*

Blizzard B&B Internet Marketing, Inc. *supplier of Internet skills to member Inns. 970-928-7875.*

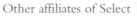

Other affiliates of Select Registry include Endorsed Providers:

James W. Wolf Insurance, *supplier of insurance to our member Inns. 800-488-1135.*

LPC Group of Olmstead Press, *Select Registry cookbook publisher & bookstore distributor of guidebook,* 312-432-7650

Web Developer, *Select Registry Webmaster and web site designer – David Swain, American Dreams, Inc. 740-385-5555.*

Being Selected for Select Registry

Any Inn that displays this logo as having been selected or recommended by SELECT REGISTRY – Distinguished Inns of North America, has achieved a high pinnacle of success.

SELECT REGISTRY Inns are excellent Inns that travelers can depend upon for an enjoyable lodging experience in unique, stylish, and tasteful surroundings with warm hospitality.

Inns recommended by *Select Registry* have gone through a gauntlet of reviews and inspections by some of North America's leading hospitality professionals, including a full property visit by incognito inspectors who evaluate the Inn and the hospitality of it's Innkeepers before the Inn is chosen to be a Select Registry Inn.

The quality control inspections continue even after the Inn has been recommended, to assure that high standards remain in place for all guests.

SELECT REGISTRY
DISTINGUISHED INNS OF NORTH AMERICA

Contents

SELECT REGISTRY™
DISTINGUISHED INNS OF NORTH AMERICA

THE ROCKY MOUNTAINS

THE SOUTHWEST

THE PACIFIC NORTHWEST

THE PACIFIC COASTLINE

Traveling New England to Quebec and the Atlantic Provinces

This is the Atlantic Coast. Stretching from Quebec and the Atlantic Provinces all the way south into Connecticut, this region of the Select Registry is large and diverse and as well represented by quality Inns and hospitality as any travel destination in the world.

THIS IS THE ATLANTIC COAST, where broad skies fluctuate from steely gray during those famous-and beautiful-white winters, to royal-blue under summer skies, and always here, history remains palpable. If a line separates Canada from the United States, hospitality and cuisine know no borders. A French tradition of hauté cuisine inundated Quebec with the arrival of the first settlers, and today food is an extension of diverse cultures defined best by the word "pride." Begin your travels in the Atlantic Provinces, known for the splendid beauty of its coastline.

Just across the border, New England manners and Yankee integrity are keystones of another cultural mecca.

Maine is synonymous with lobster, Vermont with maple syrup, as are parts of Quebec in Canada. Today, the cuisine is diverse and spectacular. Imagine a splendid five-course meal served on wide-brimmed plates decorated with colorful sauces and delicate floral presentations.

A traveler might sip an after-dinner wine while scanning a dessert tray laden with delectables. In either country, taste and hospitality will constitute the foundation of your visit.

The aroma of a rich New England chowder wafts from the antiques appointed kitchen. The scent of fresh-baked blackberry scones wafts up a 18th century staircase greeting guests as they rise from under goose-down comforters. It is snowing. Coffee is on, and a fire blazes in an antique fireplace. Cranberries are prime in Massachusetts. They simmer in a batch of slow-cooked oatmeal on an antique wood stove. Maple-cured bacon sputters on a grill.

Waiting for you in Rhode Island and New Hampshire, are more of those famous Innkeepers' smiles. Many of our Innkeepers are second and third generation. They know that where history and cuisine are a commonality, hospitality trumps.

Winter, summer, spring and fall, a smile is the calling card of the *Select Registry*. You can count on it here, where the Atlantic skies beckon.

"This Inn has beautiful grounds, garden, and tiered ocean view with outdoor seating. We'll be back. This kind of romance is hard to find. One of a kind!"—John Edwards,

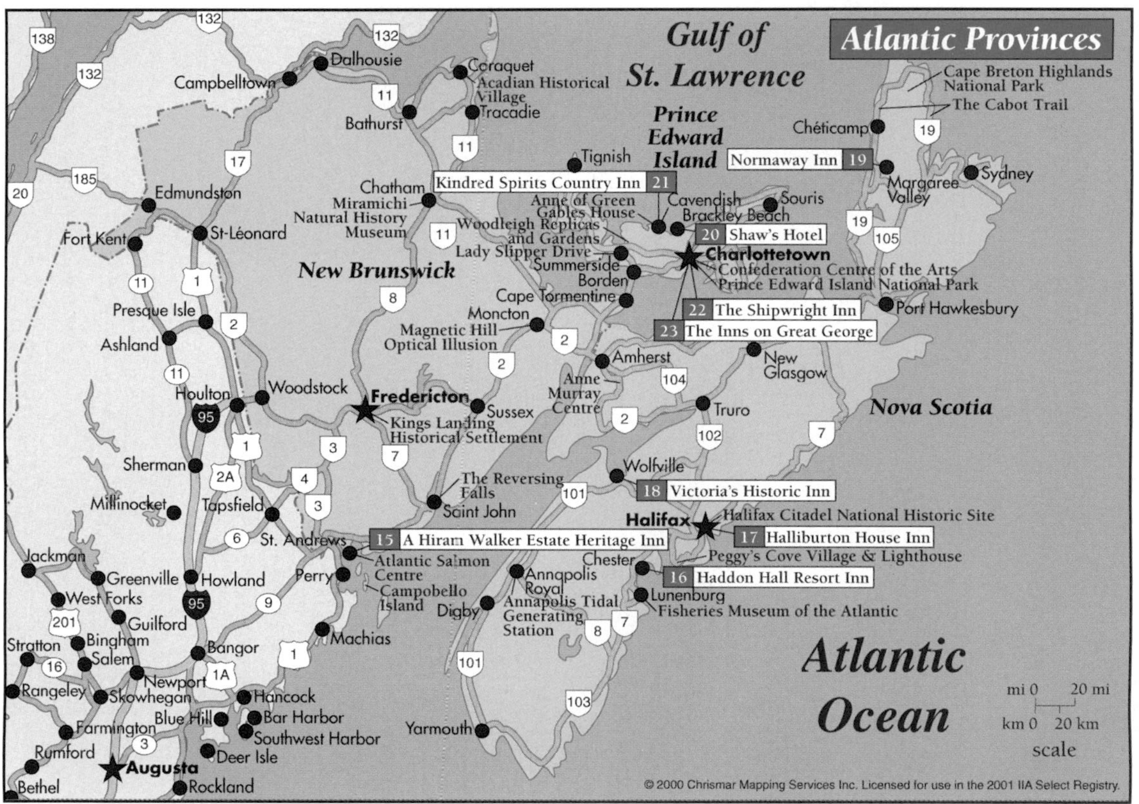

Atlantic Provinces
Gulf of St. Lawrence
Prince Edward Island
New Brunswick
Nova Scotia
Atlantic Ocean
Cape Breton Highlands National Park
The Cabot Trail
Chéticamp
Normaway Inn 19
Margaree Valley
Sydney
Port Hawkesbury
Tignish
Kindred Spirits Country Inn 21
Anne of Green Gables House
Cavendish
Brackley Beach
Souris
20 Shaw's Hotel
Woodleigh Replicas and Gardens
Lady Slipper Drive
Summerside
Borden
Charlottetown
Confederation Centre of the Arts
Prince Edward Island National Park
Cape Tormentine
22 The Shipwright Inn
23 The Inns on Great George
Dalhousie
Campbelltown
Coraquet
Acadian Historical Village
Tracadie
Bathurst
Chatham
Miramichi Natural History Museum
Edmundston
St-Léonard
Fort Kent
Presque Isle
Ashland
Houlton
Woodstock
Fredericton
Kings Landing Historical Settlement
Moncton
Magnetic Hill Optical Illusion
Sussex
Amherst
Anne Murray Centre
New Glasgow
Truro
Wolfville
18 Victoria's Historic Inn
Halifax
Halifax Citadel National Historic Site
17 Halliburton House Inn
Peggy's Cove Village & Lighthouse
Chester
16 Haddon Hall Resort Inn
Lunenburg
Fisheries Museum of the Atlantic
The Reversing Falls
Saint John
15 A Hiram Walker Estate Heritage Inn
St. Andrews
Atlantic Salmon Centre
Campobello Island
Perry
Annapolis Royal
Annapolis Tidal Generating Station
Digby
Machias
Yarmouth
Sherman
Millinocket
Tapsfield
Jackman
Greenville
Howland
West Forks
Guilford
Stratton
Bingham
Salem
Bangor
Newport
Rangeley
Skowhegan
Hancock
Bar Harbor
Blue Hill
Southwest Harbor
Farmington
Deer Isle
Rumford
Augusta
Rockland
Bethel
138
132
132
132
11
11
11
11
11
17
185
20
1
1
1
2
2
2
2
8
7
7
7
3
3
4
2A
6
9
95
95
201
16
1A
104
102
101
101
103
19
19
105
mi 0 20 mi
km 0 20 km
scale
© 2000 Chrismar Mapping Services Inc. Licensed for use in the 2001 IIA Select Registry.

St. Andrews, NB Canada

A Hiram Walker Estate Heritage Inn

Voice 506-529-4210 Fax 506-529-4311
800-470-4088
www.walkerestate.com
walkest@nb.sympatico.ca
109 Reed Avenue, St. Andrews, NB Canada E5B 2J6

Select Registry Member *Since 1998*
Innkeeper/Owner
ELIZABETH COONEY

PLANNING A HOLIDAY DESTINATION to the US Eastern Seaboard or Canada's Maritimes? Canada's newest ★★★★★ inn is situated on 11 acres in St. Andrews By-The-Sea, New Brunswick, only two hours from Bar Harbor, Maine. Millionaire's mansion offers 12 luxury air-conditioned guestrooms, king canopy beds, fireplaces, Jacuzzis for two, ocean championship golf course, sea/sail day adventures, unique shopping, galleries and antiques. U.S. guests—enjoy an international experience where $2 US is worth $3 CDN. Canadian Guests—enjoy a truly Canadian experience where $1.00 CDN is always worth $1.00 CDN.

ELEGANT WATERSIDE RESORT

RATES
12 rooms (dbl. occ.).
High-season rates from $125/$350 U.S. INN. All private en suite baths, 7 dbl. Jacuzzis. Breakfast available but not included in daily rate.
Open year-round.

ATTRACTIONS
On-site swimming pool, hot tub, golf, nearby tennis, whale watching, ocean swimming, kayaking, yachting, historic tours.

CUISINE
Breakfast and dinner served. Licensed bar. Wine, liquor and beer served.

DIRECTIONS
US 1-95 N exit 45 A (Bangor) to Rte 9 E to Calais/St. Stephen to Hwy 1 E to Hwy 127 (exit 14) to St. Andrews, first driveway past golf course.

Suitable for Children Over 12 • Conference Facilities for 40
Non-Smoking Inn • Credit Cards Accepted
Reservations Accepted Through Travel Agents

Chester, NS Canada

Haddon Hall Resort Inn

902-275-3577
Fax 902-275-5159
www.haddonhallinn.com
haddon@tallships.ca
P.O. Box 640, 67 Haddon Hill
Chester, NS Canada B0J 1J0

Select Registry Member *Since 1998*
Manager/Innkeeper
CYNTHIA O'CONNELL

AWARD WINNING exclusive small resort inn designed for ten couples with discriminating tastes. Haddon Hall provides luxuriously appointed guest suites and exquisite fine dining overlooking the spectacular Mahone Bay and its many islands. Choose from elegant or rustic ambience for your stay. A complete ensuite bath, whirlpool and fireplace add to the luxury. Leisure activities include on site pool, tennis court, mountain biking and birding. The surrounding village of Chester offers a world class 18-hole golf course, sailing, local theatre, and shopping. Whether you wish to wear you golf clothes or "dress" for dinner, is your choice. Your table dhote meal is sumtuously presented on our outdoor deck, or indoors in the traditional dining room.

1 Guestroom Handicap Accessiable • Suitable for Children Over 12
Non-Smoking Inn • Conference Facilities for 25 • Visa, MC Accepted
Reservations Accepted Through Travel Agents

ELEGANT WATERSIDE RESORT

RATES

Rates include breakfast and dinner (MAP) $175/$320 US per night plus tax, based on double occupancy.
Open May to October 31, 2001.

ATTRACTIONS

ON-SITE: pool, tennis court, mountain bikes and canoes.
NEARBY: summer theater, sailing and golf.

CUISINE

Evening dinner service is offered in our elegant dining room from June 16, 2001, until October 11, 2001. The menu changes frequently and the price is included in the room rate, plus tax and gratuity for a three-course meal.

DIRECTIONS

From Halifax: S on Hwy 103, take exit #8. Turn L towards Chester. Drive 2 miles, stop at red light. Turn L towards Chester, Haddon Hall Rd. within 100 yds. Inn at top of hill on R.

Halifax, NS Canada

Halliburton House Inn

902-420-0658
Fax 902-423-2324
www.halliburton.ns.ca
innkeeper@halliburton.ns.ca
5184 Morris Street, Halifax, NS Canada B3J 1B3

Select Registry Member *Since 1998*
Innkeeper
ROBERT PRETTY

ELEGANT IN TOWN INN

LOCATED ON A QUIET STREET in historic Halifax, Halliburton House Inn offers the charm and elegance of a four-star country inn with the convenience of a central downtown location. Our twenty-nine gracious guest rooms are tastefully furnished with period antiques and all have a private bath. Three beautifully appointed one-bedroom suites are complete with working, wood-burning fireplaces.

RATES

29 guest rooms including 3 one-bedroom suites. Rates from $130 CDN, plus tax.
Open year-round.

ATTRACTIONS

Halliburton House Inn was built in 1809 as the home of Sir Brenton Halliburton, Chief Justice of the Nova Scotia Supreme Court. Today, this registered heritage property is Halifax's finest inn. Historic attractions, shopping and the Halifax waterfront are all close by.

CUISINE

Our dining room offers relaxed and elegant surroundings for dinner. Our chef's specialties are local game such as boar, pheasant and venison, also tempting selections of fresh Atlantic seafood. Private dining rooms are available for special occasions.

DIRECTIONS

Downtown Halifax, Barrington at Morris.

Non-Smoking Inn • Visa, MC, AMEX, Diners/EN Accepted
Reservations Accepted Through Travel Agents

Wolfville, NS Canada

Victoria's Historic Inn

Voice 902-542-5744 Fax 902-542-7794
800-556-5744
www.valleyweb.com/victoriasinn
victoria.inn@ns.sympatico.ca
Box 308, Wolfville, NS Canada B0P 1X0

Select Registry Member *Since 1998*
Innkeepers/Owners
THE CRYAN FAMILY

'NOW PERHAPS THE FINEST Victorian home in Nova Scotia, the Cryan family has worked tirelessly to achieve the first B&B five-star *Canada Select* rating in the province. The professionally decorated rooms lend an intimate and first-class atmosphere, some offering double Jacuzzi baths and fireplaces with balcony or sweeping view. It is the attention to detail and the softly decorated rooms, as well as the sincere care of the innkeepers, that draw people back to Victoria's again and again for peace and relaxation in a pampered environment.'—*Travel Writers.*

ELEGANT VILLAGE
BREAKFAST INN

RATES
14 rooms, $105/$195.
2 suites, $225 CDN B&B.
Open year-round.

ATTRACTIONS
Hiking, bird-watching, antiquing, dyke walks, live theatre, historic sites, golf, ocean beaches all nearby.

CUISINE
Fine selection of wines available. Hot breakfast included in room rate. Award-winning restaurants within walking distance.

DIRECTIONS
From Halifax: 101 W to exit #10.
From Yarmouth: 101 E to exit #11.

Non-Smoking Inn • Visa, MC, AMEX, Diners/EN Accepted
Reservations Accepted Through Travel Agents

Margaree Valley, NS Canada

Normaway Inn

Voice 902-248-2987 Fax 902-248-2600
800-565-9463
normaway@atcon.com
www.selectregistry.com
Box 138, Margaree Valley, NS Canada B0F 2C0

Select Registry Member *Since 1972*
Innkeepers/Owners
DAVID M. MACDONALD AND THERESA O. LEARY

NESTLED IN THE HILLS of the Cape Breton Highlands, near the beginning of the spectacular Cabot Trail, this 250-acre property offers a 1920s inn and cabins, most with woodstove fireplaces and some with Jacuzzis. Enjoy superb food service and choice wines. Guests often relax by the fieldstone fireplace after dinner and enjoy films or traditional entertainment nightly.

TRADITIONAL COUNTRY RETREAT/LODGE

RATES
9 rooms, $85/$139 EP.
19 cabins, $99/$199 EP.
$45 CDN per person, MAP.
$99/$199 CDN per person, EP.
Open year-round.

ATTRACTIONS
Tennis, hiking trails, library, mountain bikes, lawn games, fiddle concerts, animals. Nearby: canoeing, salmon fishing, whale cruise and airstrip.

CUISINE
Dinner nightly 6-9 pm, June 15 to October 15. Picnic lunches. Wine list, spirits, scotch list.

DIRECTIONS
Trans-Canada Hwy Jct. 7 at Nyanza, N on Cabot Trail 17 miles. Turn off between NE Margaree and Lake-O-Law on Egypt Rd.; 2 miles to inn.

Suitable for Children • Pets Allowed
Conference Facilities for 50 • Credit Cards Accepted
Reservations Accepted Through Travel Agents

Prince Edward Island, PEI Canada

Shaw's Hotel

902-672-2022
Fax 902-672-3000
www.peisland.com/shaws
shaws@auracom.com
Brackley Beach
Prince Edward Island, PEI Canada C1E 1Z3

Select Registry Member *Since 1975*
Innkeeper/Owner
ROBBIE SHAW

WE ARE THE OLDEST family-operated inn in Canada. The Shaw family continues the tradition which began in 1860. Shaw's Hotel is located on a 75-acre peninsula overlooking glistening Brackley Bay. It provides an ideal setting for its 17 antique-furnished rooms and suites, plus its 19 charming cottages ranging in size from one to four bedrooms. Our seven deluxe chalets featuring whirlpools and fireplaces are open year-round. Shaw's Hotel provides superb meals in their daily rates. We also have many recreational activities and a children's program. We are 600 yards from Brackley Beach and minutes away from great golf. *Canada Select* ★★★ 1/2.

TRADITIONAL WATERSIDE RESORT

RATES

10 rooms.
7 suites, $85/$140 pp CDN MAP.
Cottages $100/$170 pp CDN MAP.
Open year-round, cottages only.

ATTRACTIONS

Great golf, walking paths, canoeing, theatre, Anne of Green Gables, children's program, bicycling, scenic sightseeing and ocean fishing.

CUISINE

Full country breakfast, picnic lunches and fine evening dining featuring fresh seafood. Our dining room is fully licensed.

DIRECTIONS

Fly or drive to PEI Trans-Canada Hwy 1 to Charlottetown. Follow signage to airport and Rte 15. Then 10 miles N to Brackley Beach.

2 Cottages Handicap Accessible • Suitable for Children • Pets Allowed
Conference Facilities for 75 • MC, AMEX, Visa, Diners/EN Accepted
Reservations Accepted Through Travel Agents

Cavendish, PEI Canada

Kindred Spirits Country Inn

902-963-2434
Fax 902-963-2434
www.kindredspirits.pe.ca
info@kindredspirits.pe.ca
Route 6, Memory Lane, Cavendish
PEI Canada C0A 1N0

Select Registry Member *Since 2001*
Innkeepers
Al James
Sharon James

Kindred Spirits Country Inn is a friendly, informal, family-owned country inn and resort. It is located beside Green Gables House and Golf Course. The spacious Victorian country inn rooms and suites, all with private baths and air conditioning, are beautifully furnished with antiques and hospitality. Both inn rooms and the charming housekeeping cottages combine all the modern amenities with the elegance and ambiance of a yesteryear. The spacious six-acre estate also includes a large outdoor heated pool, family whirlpool and playground.

Traditional Country Breakfast Inn

RATES
39 rooms, $140/$300 CDN
18 rooms, 14 cottages, 7 suites individually styled in country Victorian design with private baths.
Open May 15 - October 15.

ATTRACTIONS
Green Gables House, Cavendish Beach, birthplace and home of Lucy Maude Montgomery, world-class golf courses, live theatre.

CUISINE
Buffet breakfast, evening tea.

DIRECTIONS
From Charlottetown Airport: Sherwood Rd. to Rte 13N to Rte 6. Turn L to Memory Lane. From Bridge: Rte 1 E to Rte 13N to Rte 6 (as above).

1 Guestroom Handicap Accessible • Suitable for Children
Conference Facilities for 40 • Non-Smoking Inn • MC, Visa Accepted
Reservations Accepted Through Travel Agents

Charlottetown, PEI Canada

Shipwright Inn

Voice 902-368-1905 Fax 902-628-1905

888-306-9966

www.shipwrightinn.com

shipwright@isn.net

51 Fitzroy Street

Charlottetown, PEI Canada C1A 1R4

Select Registry Member *Since 1999*

Innkeepers/Owners

JORDAN AND JUDY HILL

THE SHIPWRIGHT INN is an elegant early Victorian 'Anne of Green Gables' style house built in the 1860s by shipbuilder, James Douse. This 'award-winning' heritage inn is located in 'Olde' Charlottetown, within a three-minute walk of all the historic, cultural, waterfront, dining and shopping facilities. In keeping with the nautical theme, Jordan and Judy have carefully collected antiques and artwork for your enjoyment. All guest rooms have private baths, wood floors, AC, duvets, Victorian memorabilia, amenities, TV, desk and phone. Some with fireplaces, balconies, whirlpools as additional features. Free parking, safe environment, interesting, comfortable, quiet, *Canada Select* five-star, *Frommer's* favorite on PEI.

3 Guestrooms Handicap Accessible • Suitable for Children Over 8
Conference Facilities for 15 • Visa, MC, AMEX, Diners/EN Accepted
Designated Smoking Areas • Reservations Accepted Through Travel Agents

ELEGANT IN TOWN BREAKFAST INN

RATES

4 premium/2 apartment style units, 3 conventional units.
$95.00/US $200.
Breakfast included. Parking, amenities, air-conditioning, fireplaces.
Open year-round.

ATTRACTIONS

Province House, waterfront boardwalk, Confederation Theatre, beaches only 30 minutes away, golf, nature sites, Celtic events, fine dining, pubs, scenic drives, shopping, museums, geneology, entertainment. seal tours. Walk to most! Safe environment.

CUISINE

Judy's 'memorable' full hot breakfast daily. Homemade bread, quiche, waffles, pancakes, muffins, coffee cakes, fresh fruit and our own blend of coffee. Box breakfasts for early departures. Breakfast in bed for lazybones.

DIRECTIONS

TransCanada Hwy E Rte 1A from Confedration Bridge into center of Charlottetown. Turn R onto Fitzroy St., go 1.5 blocks. We are on your R before Pownal St. Watch for the lighted red and gold sign with a black ship model on top.

Charlottetown, PEI Canada

The Inns on Great George

Voice 902-892-0606 Fax 902-628-2079

800-361-1118

www.innsongreatgeorge.com

innkeeper@innsongreatgeorge.com

58 Great George Street

Charlottetown, PEI Canada C1A 4K3

Select Registry Member *Since 2000*

Innkeeper/Owner

MICHAEL CASSIDY

WHILE ENJOYING THE STREETSCAPE SPLENDOUR of Charlottetown's National Historic District, experience the ambiance of the district's four-star inn—The Inns on Great George, a unique cluster of tastefully restored heritage properties offering guests a choice of accommodations. Choose from the elegant 24-room Pavilion, the intimate five-room Wellington and Carriage House, the Witter-Coombs loft suite or the J.H. Down spacious flats. Charlottetown is the birthplace of Confederation and the 'inns' have become a landmark destination, symbolizing the area's spirit of innkeeping dating back to 1811. Our historical charm and classic elegance awaits you.

ELEGANT IN TOWN INN

RATES

40 rooms/suites, $165/$300 B&B CDN. Off-season rates and packages available. Stylishy appointed air-conditioned rooms with antiques, all amenities, some with fireplace, Jacuzzi or claw-foot tub. *Open year-round.*

ATTRACTIONS

Shops, restaurants, Confederation Waterfront, live theatre, Province House, all within strolling distance. Famous PEI lobster suppers, beaches and golf within a 30-minute drive.

CUISINE

Complimentary 'Season's Best' breakfast served in the lobby. Afternoon coffee, tea and 'treats'.

DIRECTIONS

Downtown historic Charlottetown on Great George St. Two blocks from Province House, The Confederation Centre and The Confederation Landing Historic Waterfront.

Handicap Access Available • Suitable for Children Over 12
Conference Facilities for 30 • Credit Cards Accepted
Reservations Accepted Through Travel Agents

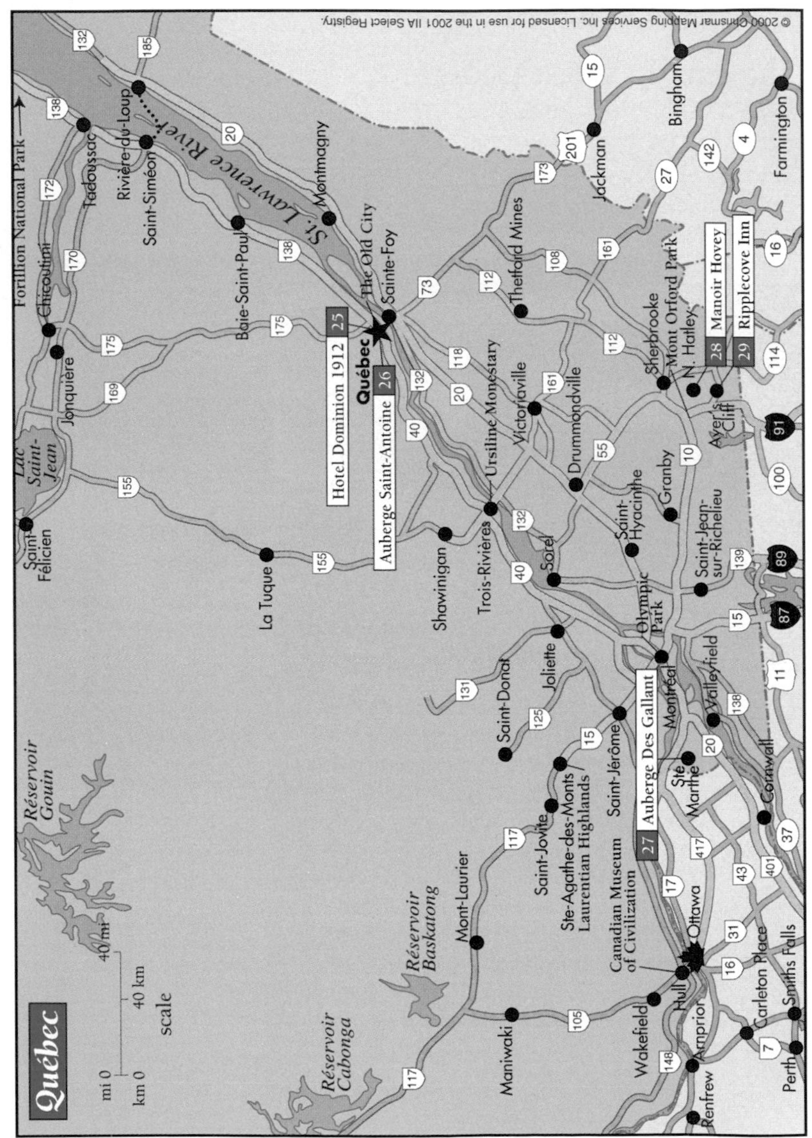
Québec
mi 0
km 0
40 km
40 mi
scale
Réservoir Gouin
Réservoir Cabonga
Réservoir Baskatong
Lac Saint-Jean
St. Lawrence River
Forillon National Park
© 2000 Chrismar Mapping Services Inc. Licensed for use in the 2001 IIA Select Registry.
25 Hotel Dominion 1912
26 Auberge Saint-Antoine
27 Auberge Des Gallant
28 Manoir Hovey
29 Ripplecove Inn
Québec
The Old City
Sainte-Foy
Montmagny
Baie-Saint-Paul
Saint-Siméon
Rivière-du-Loup
Tadoussac
Chicoutimi
Jonquière
Saint-Félicien
La Tuque
Shawinigan
Trois-Rivières
Ursiline Monestary
Victoriaville
Drummondville
Thetford Mines
Jackman
Bingham
Farmington
Sherbrooke
Mont Orford Park
N. Hatley
Ayer's Cliff
Granby
Saint-Hyacinthe
Sorel
Saint-Jean-sur-Richelieu
Olympic Park
Montréal
Joliette
Saint-Donat
Saint-Jérôme
Ste-Agathe-des-Monts
Laurentian Highlands
Saint-Jovite
Mont-Laurier
Maniwaki
Wakefield
Hull
Ottawa
Canadian Museum of Civilization
Ste Marthe
Valleyfield
Cornwall
Arnprior
Renfrew
Perth
Carleton Place
Smiths Falls

Quebec, QUE Canada

Hotel Dominion 1912

Voice 418-692-2224 Fax 418-692-4403
888-833-5253
www.hoteldominion.com
reservations@hoteldominion.com
126 Saint-Pierre, Quebec, QUE Canada G1K 4A8

Select Registry Member *Since 1999*
Innkeeper/Owner
RICHARD GERMAIN

SURROUNDED BY AN ECLECTIC MIX of antique shops, art galleries, cafes and gourmet restaurants, the Hotel Dominion 1912 is a boutique-style hotel designed for discriminating travelers who expect the best. The hotel, which takes its name from the building's first owners, Dominion Fish and Fruit Limited, has 40 luxuriously-appointed rooms with exceptional quality of fabrics and bedding. River scapes, cityscapes and comfort everywhere. At the Dominion, spectacular views and high-ceilinged elegance go hand in hand. Immense windows flood every room with light adding to the delight and comfort of guests.

CONTEMPORARY
IN TOWN HOTEL

RATES

Low-season, $149/$219 CDN.
High-season, $199/$289 CDN.
Duvet quilt, fresh fruits minibar, bathrobes, coffeemaker, hair dryer, air-conditioning.
Open year-round.

ATTRACTIONS

Old Quebec, Place Royale, Citadelle, Old Port, Montmorency Falls, Parliament, Museum of Civilisation and of Quebec, Ile D'Orleans, Royal Battery Rue Du Tresor, evening cruises.

CUISINE

Complimentary continental breakfast served in the lobby. Cocktail lounge and outside terrace. Packages offered with Laurie and Raphael Restaurant.

DIRECTIONS

From Hwy 20: Pont Pierre LaPorte Bridge, exit blvd. Champlain 8 km, L on St. Andre St., L on St. Pierre St. From Hwy 40: Follow signs for blvd. Charest E, 10 km which becomes St. Paul St., R on St. Pierre St.

Designated Smoking Areas
Conference Facilities for 25 • Visa, MC, AMEX, Diners/EN Accepted
Reservations Accepted Through Travel Agents

Quebec, QUE Canada

Auberge Saint-Antoine

Voice 418-692-2211 Fax 418-692-1177

888-692-2211

www.saint-antoine.com

info@saint-antoine.com

10, Rue Saint-Antoine

Quebec, QC Canada G1K 4C9

Select Registry Member *Since 1999*

General Manager

MR. LLEW PRICE

STAYING AT AUBERGE SAINT-ANTOINE is like stepping back in time, a stylish retreat from everyday worries. Classic, romantic, historic, avant-garde...We've created a succession of stunning rooms, each one designed for your pleasure and comfort. Many offer a view on the Saint-Lawrence River. Hidden amongst this charm are all the amenities you expect in a luxury hotel. Each morning guests may treat themselves with homemade muffins, breads and jams, as well as many other fresh delights, all complimentary. Whether on business or enjoying a weekend getaway, Llew Price and his staff will make you wish your stay were permanent!

ELEGANT IN TOWN HOTEL

RATES

31 rooms incl. 7 luxury suites. Low-season, $159/$299 CDN. High-season, $279/$499 CDN. River view, whirpool bath, terrace, minibar, kitchenette.
Open year-round.

ATTRACTIONS

Historical and cultural attractions, museums, strolling within the old city. Antique shops and art galleries. NEARBY: biking, in-line skating, golf, downhill and cross-country skiing, ice-skating.

CUISINE

Hearty complimentary breakfast including many homemade delicacies. Refreshments always available at no charge. Fine selection of wine and liquors for an evening drink, renowned restaurants close by.

DIRECTIONS

By Rte 20: Pont Pierre-Laporte-exit Boul Champlain-12 km-turn L at Saint-Antoine St. By Rte 40: Exit Vieux-Quebec-follow Musee de la Civilisation signs-on Dalhousie St., turn R at Saint-Antoine St.

2 Guestrooms Handicap Accessible • Suitable for Children
Conference Facilities for 90 • Visa, MC, AMEX, Diners/EN Accepted
Designated Smoking Areas • Reservations Accepted Through Travel Agents

Ste-Marthe, Rigaud, QUE Canada

Auberge Des Gallant (The Gallant Inn)

Voice 450-459-4241 Fax 450-459-4667
800-641-4241
www.gallant.qc.ca
gallant@rocler.qc.ca
1171 St-Henry Road
Ste-Marthe, Rigaud, QUE Canada J0P 1W0

Select Registry Member *Since 1998*
Innkeepers/Owners
LINDA AND GERRY GALLANT

ELEGANT MOUNTAIN RESORT

RATES
25 rooms with fireplace and balcony. From $125 CDN/$90 US, MAP P.P. (gratuities included). *Open year-round.*

ATTRACTIONS
Bird/deer watching, cross-country and walking trails, sleigh rides, factory outlets, antiques, summer theater, golf, maple sugar shack, fall foliage, sauna.

CUISINE
Breakfast, lunch, gourmet dinner, Sunday brunch. Extensive wine list and liquor.

DIRECTIONS
Between Montreal and Ottawa, Rte 40 W, exit 17, L on Rte 201, 3 miles and R on St-Henri 5 miles.

NATURE LOVERS WILL ENJOY THIS ROMANTIC INN nestled in the heart of a bird and deer sanctuary. Enjoy award-winning cuisine while dining with your 'dear' and our 'deer,' as attentive staff cater to your every wish. Elegant spacious rooms with real wood-burning fireplace and balcony overlook our cedar and maple forest or our beaver and trout ponds. In summer, our gardens attract a multitude of birds and butterflies, while winter promises sleigh rides and skiing on-site. Fall foliage is at its best in October, and maple sugar shacks open from March to May. Only 45 minutes from Montreal and one hour from Ottawa. Why not stay an extra night and visit?

2 Guestrooms Handicap Accessible • Suitable for Children Over 6
Conference Facilities for 100 • Visa, MC, Diners/EN, AMEX, Debit Accepted
Designated Smoking Areas • Reservations Accepted Through Travel Agents

North Hatley, QUE Canada

Manoir Hovey

800-661-2421
819-842-2421 Fax 819-842-2248
www.hoveymanor.com
manhovey@hoveymanoir.com
Lake Massawippi
North Hatley, QUE Canada J0B 2C0

Select Registry Member *Since 1973*
Innkeepers/Owners
STEVE, KATHY AND JASON STAFFORD

ELEGANT WATERSIDE RESORT

FORMERLY A PRIVATE ESTATE modeled on Mount Vernon, this gracious manor is nestled on 25 acres of prime lakeshore amongst spectacular English gardens. Most of the lakeside rooms offer combinations of fireplaces, Jacuzzis, canopy beds and balconies. Acclaimed French cuisine, wine cellar and a full range of on-site, year-round recreational facilities included in our rates make this charming and romantic inn a destination in itself. We're only twenty minutes from Vermont, four hours from Boston and six hours from NYC, on route to Montreal and Quebec City. *Quebec Lodging* ★★★★★ AAA ◆◆◆◆ for inn and dining room.

RATES

39 rooms US $75/$200, MAP/person/day. Mostly on the lake. Many with fireplaces, balconies, Jacuzzis and canopy beds.
Open year-round.

ATTRACTIONS

HERE: Beaches, heated pool, kayaks, canoes, pedalos, wind-surfing, waterskiing, cruises, tennis, touring bikes, fishing, cross-country ski trails, skating, ice fishing, massage/exercise/games rooms.
NEARBY: skiing, golf, riding, theatre, concerts, antiquing.

CUISINE

Breakfast, lunch, dinner, cream teas (Quebec 'Table de Prestige'). Winner: *Gourmet* Top Tables Poll; in Quebec, #1 in Ambiance and Romantic Dining. World-class wine list and sommelier. Pool lunches and garden cocktails. Historic colonial pub.

DIRECTIONS

VT I-91 to Canadian border. Continue on Rte 55 N for 29 km to N Hatley exit. Follow Rte 108 E and Manoir Hovey signs to the inn (9 km). Only 25 minutes from the border.

Suitable for Children Over 12 + Designated Smoking Areas
Conference Facilities for 50 • Visa, AMEX, MC, JCB, Diners/EN Accepted
Reservations Accepted Through Travel Agents

Ayer's Cliff, QUE Canada

Auberge Ripplecove Inn

Voice 819-838-4296 Fax 819-838-5541

800-668-4296

www.ripplecove.com

info@ripplecove.com

700 Ripplecove Road

Ayer's Cliff, QUE Canada J0B 1C0

Select Registry Member *Since 1995*

Innkeepers / Owners

DEBRA AND JEFFREY STAFFORD

SINCE 1945 Ripplecove Inn has been chosen by sophisticated travelers from around the world to get away from it all in an atmosphere of privacy, unsurpassed service and luxury. The inn resides on a beautifully landscaped peninsula alive with English gardens and century-old pines. Choose from 26 designer-decorated rooms and suites; many with fireplace, TV, lakeview balcony and double whirlpool. Enjoy refined French cuisine with sterling service in our romantic Victorian-style dining room and lakeside terrace. American visitors don't forget, a Canadian exchange rate of 48 percent means extra value for you! An AAA ◆◆◆◆ Award Inn.

ELEGANT WATERSIDE RESORT

RATES

26 rooms, suites and houses.
$260/$600 MAP CDN.
$159/$405 MAP U.S.
Includes dinner and breakfast.
Open year-round.

ATTRACTIONS

12 golf courses, horseback riding, Alpine skiing nearby. Tennis, heated pool, private beach, all water sports, cross-country skiing and skating on-site.

CUISINE

Award-winning French cuisine in our Victorian dining room and lakeside terrace. Extensive wine cellar and pub. "Award of Excellence" *Wine Spectator Magazine.*

DIRECTIONS

From New England take I-91 N to the Canadian border then follow Rte 55 N to exit 21. Follow signs to inn which is 3 miles from exit 21. Only four hours from Boston. 75 minutes from Montreal via Rte 10 E.

Suitable for Children • Conference Facilities for 40
2 Guestrooms Handicap Accessible • Visa, MC, AMEX Accepted
Designated Smoking Areas • Reservations Accepted Through Travel Agents

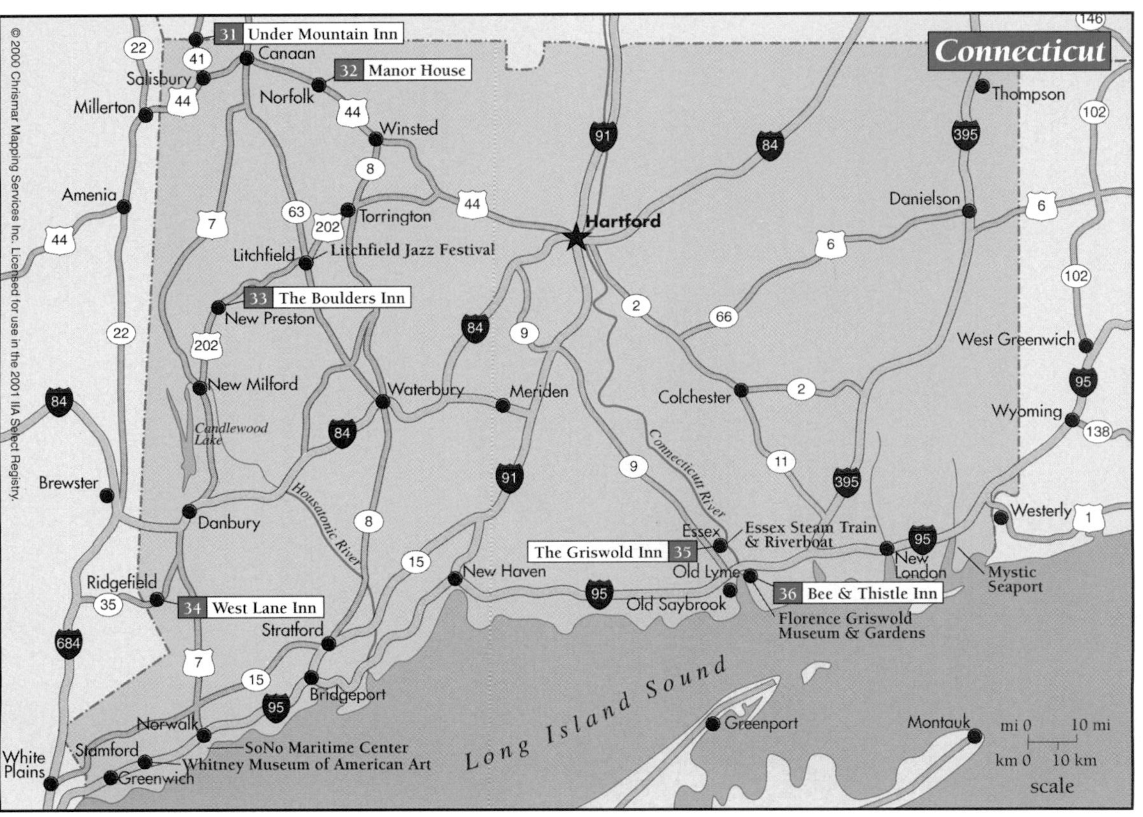
Connecticut
31 Under Mountain Inn
Canaan
32 Manor House
Salisbury
Norfolk
Millerton
Winsted
Amenia
Torrington
Hartford
Litchfield
Litchfield Jazz Festival
33 The Boulders Inn
New Preston
New Milford
Waterbury
Meriden
Candlewood Lake
Brewster
Danbury
Housatonic River
Ridgefield
34 West Lane Inn
Stratford
Bridgeport
Norwalk
SoNo Maritime Center
Whitney Museum of American Art
Stamford
Greenwich
White Plains
New Haven
Long Island Sound
Thompson
Danielson
West Greenwich
Colchester
Wyoming
Connecticut River
Essex
Essex Steam Train & Riverboat
The Griswold Inn 35
Old Lyme
Old Saybrook
36 Bee & Thistle Inn
Florence Griswold Museum & Gardens
New London
Westerly
Mystic Seaport
Greenport
Montauk
mi 0 10 mi
km 0 10 km
scale
© 2000 Chrismar Mapping Services Inc. Licensed for use in the 2001 IIA Select Registry.

Salisbury, CT

Under Mountain Inn

860-435-0242
Fax 860-435-2379

482 Undermountain Road (Route 41)
Salisbury, CT 06068

Select Registry Member *Since 1991*
Innkeepers/Owners
PETER AND MARGED HIGGINSON

TRADITIONAL COUNTRY INN

SAMPLE OLDE ENGLAND in New England in an 18th century farmhouse in the Litchfield/Berkshire hills. British library and videos, English ales, full English breakfast, enjoy our picnic for Tanglewood. Try Manchester-born owner-chef Peter's steak and kidney pie. Stroll around the lake or hike the mountain. Be amused by wild turkeys. Enjoy Dicken's weekend, horse-drawn sleigh rides. *Travel and Leisure* raved, "This is the country getaway we all wish we had." "Kettle's on...want a cuppa?"

RATES
7 rooms, $180/$225 per room, dbl. occ. MAP.
Open year-round by reservation.

ATTRACTIONS
Hiking, boating, Alpine/Nordic skiing, rafting, horseback riding, golf, tennis, antiquing, museums, historic sites, music, theater and dance festivals.

CUISINE
Breakfast, dinner, tea, British, American, Tanglewood picnics. English ales, wine, spirits. We serve a full English breakfast most mornings.

DIRECTIONS
Mass. Tpk. exit 2. 102 W, 7 S, 23 W in Gt. Barrington, MA, 41 S 9 miles on R. From NYC: Taconic Pkwy. N, 44 E, 41 N 4 miles.

Non-Smoking Inn • Suitable for Children Over 6
Conference Facilities for 15 • Visa, MC Accepted
Reservations Accepted Through Travel Agents

Norfolk, CT

Manor House

860-542-5690
Fax 860-542-5690
www.manorhouse-norfolk.com
tremblay@esslink.com
69 Maple Avenue, Norfolk, CT 06058

Select Registry Member *Since 2000*
Innkeepers / Owners
HENRY AND DIANE TREMBLAY

TREAT YOURSELF TO A GETAWAY at an historic 1898 Victorian Tudor estate described by *Gourmet* as 'quite grand with its Tiffany windows' and designated Connecticut's 'Most Romantic Hideaway,' by *The Discerning Traveler*. Featured in *National Geographic Traveler*, '20 Best Weekend Getaways' in *Good Housekeeping* and in the top 25 Inns by American Historic Inns. All guestrooms overlook the spacious grounds and are furnished with antiques. Savor a full breakfast in the elegant dining room, relax by the baronial fireplace in the living room, retreat to the sunporch or browse in our library, then stroll around the grounds to enjoy the perennial gardens.

ELEGANT VILLAGE BREAKFAST INN

RATES

8 rooms, 1 suite, $115-$250 B&B. All guest rooms have private baths. 4 have wood or gas fireplaces, 2 have Jacuzzis and 2 have private balconies.
Open year-round.

ATTRACTIONS

Music, theater and dance festivals, antique and craft shops, vineyards, historic homes and museums, gardens, Alpine and Nordic skiing, hiking, biking, tennis, golf, riding stable, water sports, carriage and sleigh rides, bird-watching, sports car racing.

CUISINE

Full country breakfast. Complimentary coffee, hot or iced tea, hot chocolate available all day, BYOB, glassware, refrigerator and ice machine also available.

DIRECTIONS

NYC: I-84 E to exit for Rte 8 N in Waterbury. At terminus of highway in Winsted take Rte 44 W R to Norfolk. Boston: I-84 W to exit for Rte 4 Farmington to Rte 179 to Rte 44 W to Norfolk.

Suitable for Children Over 8 • Non-Smoking Inn
Conference Facilities for 50 • MC, Visa, Disc, AMEX Accepted
Reservations Accepted Through Travel Agents

New Preston, CT

The Boulders Inn

860-868-0541
800-55boulders Fax 860-868-1925
www.bouldersinn.com
boulders@bouldersinn.com
East Shore Road (Route 45)
New Preston, CT 06777

Select Registry Member *Since 1990*
Innkeepers/Owners
ULLA AND KEES ADEMA

THE BOULDERS, built in 1895, is a charming Victorian mansion nestled spectacularly into the base of a mountain overlooking Lake Waramaug. The inn offers private guest rooms furnished with period antiques. The glass-enclosed lake room houses the widely renowned restaurant, which delivers the best of new American cuisine with polished service. Behind the main inn are individual guest houses offering comfortable country decor, private decks, fireplaces, lake views and double whirlpool baths. The carriage house has traditionally furnished rooms with antiques and fireplaces. A wide variety of recreational options are available on property.

ELEGANT COUNTRY INN

RATES
17 rooms total.
6 guestrooms/suites.
3 carriage house rooms.
8 guest house rooms.
$210/$380 B&B.
Open year-round.

ATTRACTIONS
Beach, boating and hiking on-site. Downhill and cross-country skiing, antiquing, golf, music festival, art galleries, antique bookshops, fishing, bicycling, bird-watching.

CUISINE
Country breakfast for guests only, dinner a la carte, alfresco dining in summer. Award-winning wine list. Full-service bar.

DIRECTIONS
Rte 84 E exit 7 to Rte 7 N to New Milford; Rte 202 E to New Preston; L on Rte 45 (E Shore Rd.) to Lake Waramaug (85 miles from NYC).

Handicap Access Available
Conference Facilities • Credit Cards Accepted
Reservations Accepted Through Travel Agents

Ridgefield, CT

West Lane Inn

203-438-7323
Fax 203-438-7325
www.westlaneinn.com
westlanein@aol.com
22 West Lane, Ridgefield, CT 06877

Select Registry Member *Since 1979*
Innkeepers/Owners
Maureen M. Mayer and
Deborah L. Prieger

Elegant In Town Inn

The West Lane combines the charm of an intimate country inn with every convenience of a luxurious hotel. *Zagat's* considers it a "Great Getaway." Judged by *USA Today* as one of America's finest inns. Rated "Excellent" by *American Bed & Breakfast*. Individually appointed climate-controlled rooms, some with fireplaces, all with queen-sized four-poster beds, full private baths, remote cable TV, modem jacks, voice mail, 24-hour phone service, one day laundry/dry cleaning and free continental breakfast. Weekend packages with the Bernards Inn at Ridgefield available during the winter months—overnight and dining. "The Inn For All Seasons". AAA ◆◆◆ and Mobil ★★★.

RATES
14 rooms, $125/$195.
2 with fireplaces.
3 with kitchens.
Open year-round.

ATTRACTIONS
Exceptional dining selection, antique shopping, cross-country ski, tennis, hiking, museums, ice-skating and horseback riding.

CUISINE
Dining next door at Bernards Inn at Ridgefield.

DIRECTIONS
Henry Hudson Pkwy (W side Hwy) to Saw Mill Pkwy. Both Saw Mill Pkwy and Rte 684 exit 6 = Rte 35 E 12 miles. Hutchinson Pkwy to Merritt Pkwy. Both Merritt Pkwy and Rte 95 exit for New Canaan, Rte 123 N to Rte 35 - R 1 mile. Rte 91 to Rte 84 exit 3 = Rte 7 S to Rte 35. NYC 1 1/2 hrs., Boston 3 hrs.

Suitable for Children Over 1 • Conference Facilities for 15
Designated Smoking Areas • AMEX, Visa, MC, Disc, Diners Accepted
Reservations Accepted Through Travel Agents

Essex, CT

The Griswold Inn

860-767-1776
Fax 860-767-0481
www.griswoldinn.com
griswoldinn@snet.net
36 Main Street, Essex, CT 06426

Select Registry Member *Since 1974*
Innkeeper/Owner
DOUGLAS PAUL

THIS HISTORIC 1776 LANDMARK is located in the "storybook" seaport village of Essex, selected as the best small town in America. Recommended for its superb cuisine, it also houses a renowned maritime art collection. In its historic Tap Room, called the most handsome barroom in America, you'll find a long-standing tradition of sea chanteys, banjo and more. Riverboat cruises, antiquing, hiking, museums and historic homes are just outside the door, while Mystic Seaport, Goodspeed Theatre and Foxwoods casino are within easy reach.

TRADITIONAL VILLAGE INN

RATES
14 rooms, $90/$120 B&B.
16 suites, $145/$195 B&B.
Open year-round.

ATTRACTIONS
Steam train, riverboats, antiquing, museums, historic homes, theatre, hiking, swimming, golf, tennis and bicycling.

CUISINE
Free continental breakfast, lunch, dinner, Sunday brunch/hunt breakfast. Wine and liquor available.

DIRECTIONS
I-91 S to exit 22 S. Rte 9 S to exit 3 Essex. I-95 (N&S) to exit 69 to Rte 9 N to exit 3 Essex.

Suitable for Children • Conference Facilities for 70
Non-Smoking Inn • MC, Visa Accepted

Old Lyme, CT

Bee and Thistle Inn

800-622-4946
860-434-1667 Fax 860-434-3402
www.beeandthistleinn.com
info@beeandthistleinn.com
100 Lyme Street, Old Lyme, CT 06371

Select Registry Member *Since 1984*
Innkeepers/Owners
PHILIP & MARIE ABRAHAM

THIS LOVELY 1756 INN is located in the Historic District and along the Lieutenant River. Its English gardens, sunlit porches, fireplaces, beautiful carved staircase, canopied and four-poster beds, antique quilts and furnishings reflect a gracious lifestyle. Widely commended for its cuisine and wine list, it has been voted the Best Restaurant and Most Romantic Place to Dine in Connecticut. It also received one of only three "Excellent" reviews in Connecticut 1996-98 from *The New York Times.* AAA ◆◆◆.

TRADITIONAL VILLAGE INN

RATES
11 rooms, $85/$165.
1 cottage, $225 EP.
Open year-round.

ATTRACTIONS
English and herb garden, river, museums, Art Academy, Gillette Castle, Goodspeed Opera House, Mystic Village, Rocky Neck State Park and beach.

CUISINE
Breakfast, lunch, dinner, brunch, English tea. Voted best restaurant in CT. Full-service bar with excellent wine list.

DIRECTIONS
I-95 S exit 70 turn R off ramp to 3rd building on L - I-95 N L off ramp to 2nd light, turn R to end of road, turn L - 3rd building on L.

Non-Smoking Inn • Conference Facilities for 10
MC, Visa, AMEX, Diners, Disc Accepted
Reservations Accepted Through Travel Agents

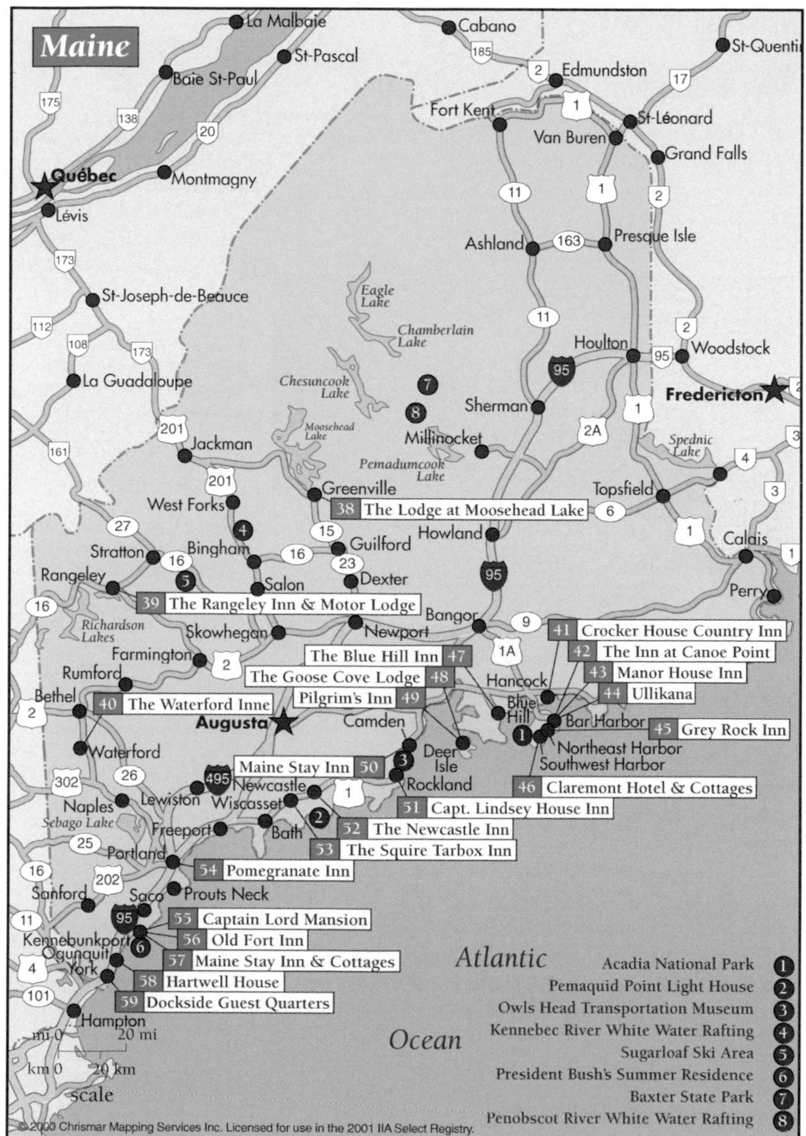

Maine
La Malbaie
Cabano
St-Pascal
Baie St-Paul
Edmundston
St-Quentin
Fort Kent
St-Léonard
Van Buren
Grand Falls
Québec
Montmagny
Lévis
Ashland
Presque Isle
St-Joseph-de-Beauce
Eagle Lake
Chamberlain Lake
Houlton
Woodstock
La Guadaloupe
Chesuncook Lake
Sherman
Fredericton
Moosehead Lake
Millinocket
Jackman
Pemadumcook Lake
Spednic Lake
Greenville
Topsfield
West Forks
38 The Lodge at Moosehead Lake
Howland
Stratton
Bingham
Guilford
Calais
Rangeley
Salon
Dexter
Perry
39 The Rangeley Inn & Motor Lodge
Bangor
Richardson Lakes
Skowhegan
Newport
41 Crocker House Country Inn
Farmington
The Blue Hill Inn 47
42 The Inn at Canoe Point
Rumford
The Goose Cove Lodge 48
Hancock
43 Manor House Inn
Bethel
40 The Waterford Inne
Pilgrim's Inn 49
Blue Hill
44 Ullikana
Augusta
Camden
Bar Harbor
45 Grey Rock Inn
Waterford
Deer Isle
Northeast Harbor
Southwest Harbor
Maine Stay Inn 50
Rockland
46 Claremont Hotel & Cottages
Naples
Lewiston
Newcastle
Wiscasset
51 Capt. Lindsey House Inn
Sebago Lake
Freeport
Bath
52 The Newcastle Inn
53 The Squire Tarbox Inn
Portland
54 Pomegranate Inn
Sanford
Saco
Prouts Neck
55 Captain Lord Mansion
Kennebunkport
56 Old Fort Inn
Ogunquit
57 Maine Stay Inn & Cottages
York
58 Hartwell House
59 Dockside Guest Quarters
Hampton
Atlantic Ocean
Acadia National Park 1
Pemaquid Point Light House 2
Owls Head Transportation Museum 3
Kennebec River White Water Rafting 4
Sugarloaf Ski Area 5
President Bush's Summer Residence 6
Baxter State Park 7
Penobscot River White Water Rafting 8
mi 0 20 mi
km 0 20 km
scale
© 2000 Chrismar Mapping Services Inc. Licensed for use in the 2001 IIA Select Registry.

Greenville, ME

The Lodge at Moosehead Lake

207-695-4400
www.lodgeatmooseheadlake.com
innkeeper@lodgeatmooseheadlake.com
Upon Lily Bay Road, Box 1167
Greenville, ME 04441

Select Registry Member *Since 1995*
Innkeepers / Owners
ROGER AND JENNIFER CAUCHI

OVERLOOKING THE BROAD WATERS and islands of Moosehead Lake in rustic Greenville, the lodge marries the amenities of a luxury hotel with the casual intimacy of a country inn. Each accommodation includes unique beds, Jacuzzi, TV/VCR and fireplace which create a quiet retreat. Guests often prefer the expansive pleasures of the great room with its well-padded chairs and sofas set before a massive stone fireplace. This is a comfortable way to regard the wilds of the great northwoods of Maine. An outdoor person's paradise—roughing it in comfort. AAA ◆◆◆◆ and Mobil ★★★★ Johansen's Award of Excellence—first one in USA.

ELEGANT COUNTRY RETREAT/LODGE

RATES
5 rooms, \$175/\$325.
3 suites, \$250/\$425B&B.
Open late December to mid-March and mid-May to early November.

ATTRACTIONS
Summer: Moose safaris, fly and canoe, hiking, fly-fishing, mountain biking, plane tours, white-water rafting. Winter: cross-country and downhill skiing, dogsledding, snowshoeing, snowmobiling.

CUISINE
Breakfast. In season-dinner served two nights. Off season-dinner served Saturday night. 24-hour pantry. Full liquor license.

DIRECTIONS
I-95 to Newport, 7 N to Dexter, 23 N to Guilford, 15 N to Greenville. 1.5 hrs drive from Bangor airport 2.5 hrs. from Portland and 4.5 hrs from Boston.

5 Guestrooms Handicap Accessible • Suitable for Children Over 14
Non-Smoking Inn • Conference Facilities for 25
Visa, MC, Disc Accepted

Rangeley, ME

The Rangeley Inn & Motor Lodge

800-666-3687
207-864-3341 Fax 207-864-3634
www.rangeleyinn.com
rangeinn@rangeley.org
P.O. Box 160, Main Street, Rangeley, ME 04970

Select Registry Member *Since 1989*
Innkeepers
DAVID AND REBECCA SCHINAS

THE RANGELEY INN is a waterfront country Inn, with sweeping veranda, acres of lawns and gardens, and beautiful turn-of-the-century decor. Dine fireside in our tavern or enjoy the elegance of our fine dining room. Experience the spectacular beauty of our four season mountain lake resort. We have been welcoming guests since 1907. Share your vacation moments with us.

TRADITIONAL COUNTRY INN

RATES
50 rooms.
$69/$119 in-season.
$60/$95 off-season.
MAP PP $75/$98.
Open year-round.

ATTRACTIONS
Moose-watching, fly fishing, hiking, canoeing, mountain biking, golf, tennis, antiquing. Snowmobile or cross country from our door. Saddleback and Sugarloaf downhill skiing.

CUISINE
Fine dining. Extensive wine collection. Hearty country breakfasts. Pub open nightly with pub menu.

DIRECTIONS
ME tpke, exit 12. Then Rte 4 to Rangeley; From VT and NH to ST. Johnsbury E on Rte 2 to Gorham and Rte 16 N to Rangeley.

Handicap Access Available • Suitable for Children • Pets Allowed
Conference Facilities for 200 • Credit Cards Accepted
Reservations Accepted Through Travel Agents

Waterford, ME

The Waterford Inne

207-583-4037
Fax 207-583-4037
www.waterfordinne.com
inne@gwi.net
Box 149 Chadbourne Road, Waterford, ME 04088

A 19TH CENTURY FARMHOUSE on a country lane midst 25 acres of fields and woods, distinctively different, a true country inn offering uniquely decorated guestrooms, a charming blend of two centuries—the warmth of early furnishings combined with contemporary comforts. Outside—rolling terrain, a farm pond, an old red barn and a bird-watcher's paradise. Inside—an air of quiet simple elegance, antiques and art, barnboard and brass, pewter and primitives. Country chic cuisine to pamper your palate. A place to relax, to re-create one's spirit.

Select Registry Member *Since 1979*
Innkeeper/Owners
BARBARA VANDERZANDEN

TRADITIONAL COUNTRY INN

RATES
8 rooms, $85/$125 B&B.
1 suite, $120 B&B.
Open year-round.

ATTRACTIONS
Library on premises. Nearby: downhill and cross-country skiing, swimming, boating, hiking, bicycling, antiquing, rock hunting and summer musical events.

CUISINE
Breakfast included. Fine dinners available with advance reservation. BYOB.

DIRECTIONS
From ME Tpke: Take Exit 11 to Rte 26 N for 28 miles into Norway, then Rte 118 W for 9 miles to Rte 37. Then turn L, go 1/2 mile to Springers Store. Take immediate R go 1/2 mile up hill.

Suitable for Children • Pets Allowed
Conference Facilities for 15 • AMEX Accepted
Reservations Accepted Through Travel Agents

Hancock Point, ME

Crocker House Country Inn

207-422-6806
Fax 207-422-3105
www.maineguide.com/downeast/crocker
crocker@acadia.net
HC 77 Box 171, Hancock Point, ME 04640

BUILT IN 1884, this restored inn is sequestered on Hancock Point. The carriage house, converted in 1992, adds two spacious guestrooms, an additional common room and a spa. The restaurant, open to the public, continues to draw guests from distant places for its extraordinary cuisine and live jazz piano on Friday and Saturday nights. A three-minute walk to Frenchman Bay and public moorings. An ideal location for wedding receptions, family reunions and small business retreats.

Select Registry Member *Since 1987*
Innkeepers
RICHARD AND ELIZABETH MALABY

TRADITIONAL COUNTRY INN

RATES
11 rooms, B&B.
$100/$145 in-season.
$75/$100 off-season.
Open year-round.

ATTRACTIONS
Spa, croquet, library, clay tennis courts, antiquing, golf, Acadia National Park, kayaking and biking.

CUISINE
Breakfast, dinner. Sunday brunch July 1 thru Labor Day. Wine list and full bar.

DIRECTIONS
From Ellsworth go 8 miles N on U.S. Rte 1, turn R on Point Rd. Continue 5 miles to inn on R.

Suitable for Children • Pets Allowed • Non-Smoking Inn
Conference Facilities for 36 • AMEX, Disc, MC, Visa Accepted
Reservations Accepted Through Travel Agents

Bar Harbor, ME

The Inn at Canoe Point

207-288-9511
Fax 207-288-2870
www.innatcanoepoint.com
canoe.point@juno.com
P.O. Box 216, Bar Harbor, ME 04609

Select Registry Member *Since 1991*
Innkeepers / Owners
TOM AND NANCY CERVELLI

THIS SECLUDED WATERSIDE INN situated among the pines on two secluded acres tucked into a quiet cove, is only moments away from lively Bar Harbor and next door to the unspoiled natural attractions of Acadia National Park. Located directly on Frenchman's Bay, you can walk among the trees, sit on the rocks and watch boats sail by, or relax in front of the granite fireplace in the ocean room where you can enjoy a 180-degree view of the sea and mountains beyond. From the surrounding deck, you can look out over the ocean while listening to the rolling surf.

TRADITIONAL WATERSIDE BREAKFAST INN

RATES

5 rooms/suites.
IN-SEASON, $170/$285 B&B.
Off-season, $90/$175 B&B.
Open year-round.

ATTRACTIONS

Adjacent to Acadia National Park, hiking, biking, sailing, kayaking, mountain climbing, golf, whale watching, cross-country skiing and snowshoeing.

CUISINE

Full breakfast, afternoon refreshments, BYOB.

DIRECTIONS

From Ellsworth: Rte 3 E approx 15 miles toward Bar Harbor, through Hulls Cove. Continue past Acadia National Park entrance 1/4 mile to inn on L.

Suitable for Children Over 16
Non-Smoking Inn • Visa, MC, Disc Accepted

Bar Harbor, ME

Manor House Inn

800-437-0088
207-288-3759 Fax 207-288-2974
www.barharbormanorhouse.com
manor@acadia.net
106 West Street, Bar Harbor, ME 04609

Select Registry Member *Since 1998*
Innkeepers
MAC NOYES, JIM DENNISON

BUILT IN 1887 AS A 22-ROOM MANSION, Manor House Inn has been authentically restored to its original splendor and is now on the National Register of Historic Places. The moment you step into the front entry a romantic Victorian past becomes the present. Enjoy comfort, convenience and privacy while staying within easy walking distance of Bar Harbor's fine shops, restaurants and ocean activities. Each morning wake up to a delicious home-baked breakfast such as baked stuffed blueberry French toast. Then spend your day exploring Acadia National Park. AAA ◆◆◆.

TRADITIONAL VILLAGE BREAKFAST INN

RATES
17 rooms/suites.
$95/$205 B&B.
Off-season, $65/$155.
Open year-round.

ATTRACTIONS
Acadia National Park, hiking, biking, mountain climbing, kayaking, whale watching, swimming, golf and schooner rides.

CUISINE
Full breakfast, afternoon tea and cookies.

DIRECTIONS
Turn L onto West St. as you enter town. Manor House Inn will be 3 blocks down, on your R.

Suitable for Children Over 12 • Non-Smoking Inn
Conference Facilities for 20 • Visa, MC, Disc, AMEX Accepted
Reservations Accepted Through Travel Agents

Bar Harbor, ME

Ullikana

207-288-9552
Fax 207-288-3682
www.ullikana.com

15 The Field, Bar Harbor, ME 04609

THE ULLIKANA is one of the few early cottages still remaining in Bar Harbor. Although only a minute from the center of town, our quiet location offers a haven of hospitality. Watch the sails of ships in the harbor from the garden or the patio where sumptuous breakfasts are served every morning. Relax in the casual elegance of this historic Tudor Inn where art is an important part of the decor. We invite you to share the history and hospitality of Ullikana with us.

Select Registry Member *Since 2000*
Innkeepers/Owners
HELENE HARTON AND ROY KASINDORF

TRADITIONAL IN TOWN BREAKFAST INN

RATES

16 rooms.
High-season: $135/$250.
Low-season: $90/$200.
All our rooms have king or queen beds. All have private baths. Some porches overlooking harbor, some fireplaces.
Open year-round.

ATTRACTIONS

Acadia National Park, hiking, biking, whale watching, kayaking, sailing.

CUISINE

Full breakfast, afternoon refreshments.

DIRECTIONS

Rte 3 to Bar Harbor. L onto Cottage St. R onto Main St. L after Trust Company building. Take gravel road towards water.

MC, Visa Accepted • Non-Smoking Inn
Reservations Accepted Through Travel Agents

Northeast Harbor, ME

Grey Rock Inn

207-276-9360 summer
207-244-4437 winter Fax 207-276-9894
www.greyrockinn.com

Select Registry Member *Since 1998*
Innkeepers
Janet, Karl and Adam Millett

Harbourside Road, Northeast Harbor, ME 04662

THIS BEAUTIFULLY SITUATED MANSION on seven acres overlooks the harbor, lighthouse and outer islands off Mount Desert. Built in 1910 as a private residence, Grey Rock has been a gathering place, hosting many of the famous families that built their summer homes in Northeast Harbor. With warmth and charm, Grey Rock offers elegant rooms that are pleasingly decorated. To assure your pleasure and relaxation, fireplaces are featured throughout the public rooms and many of the bedrooms. Grey Rock is a seven-minute walk to the picturesque village of Northeast Harbor with its quaint old-fashioned shops and to our marina, a popular yachting basin. Elegant, cottage-style, country inn with breakfast.

Suitable for Children Over 7 • Visa, MC, Disc Accepted
Non-Smoking Inn • Reservations Accepted Through Travel Agents

Elegant Country Breakfast Inn

RATES

7 rooms, 1 suite.
May to July, $110/$275.
July thru Oct., $165/$375.
Mid-May through the end of October

ATTRACTIONS

Bordering Acadia National Park. Hiking, horse and carriage rides, biking, swimming, tennis, golf, sailing, whale watching, museums, flower gardens, naturalist tours, bird watching, kayaking and canoeing.

CUISINE

Breakfast only; 110 restaurants on this island. We make reservations for you. BYOB. We supply ice and glassware.

DIRECTIONS

Follow Rte 198 on Mount Desert Island. We are the first property bordering the National Park as you approach the village.

Southwest Harbor, ME on Mount Desert Island

Claremont Hotel & Cottages

800-244-5036

207-244-5036 Fax 207-244-3512

www.theclaremonthotel.com

clmhotel@post.acadia.net

P.O. Box 137, Southwest Harbor, ME 04679

Select Registry Member *Since 1974*

General Manager

JOHN MADEIRA JR.

A SHOREFRONT HOTEL, listed on the National Register of Historic Places, offering classic Maine summer refuge since 1884. Located on the shore of Somes Sound, America's east coast fjord, our five-acre resort offers privacy, as well as panoramic views of Mount Desert Island's mountains and seascape. In addition to the historic main building, we offer memorable dining, cottages, tennis court, dock, moorings, glorious sunsets and, of course, croquet.

TRADITIONAL WATERSIDE HOTEL

RATES

24 rooms in main hotel.
6 rooms in the Phillips House.
2 suites.
12 cottages.
2 large houses.
Open May to October.

ATTRACTIONS

Hike and bike through Acadia National Park. Tennis, rowboats, bicycles, croquet and badminton on property.

CUISINE

Breakfast and dinner. Lunch served July-August only. Wine and liquor available. Tea in the afternoon in July and August.

DIRECTIONS

ME tpke, (Augusta) Rte 3 E thru Ellsworth to Mt. Desert Island. Take Rte 102 to SW Harbor-follow signs.

Handicap Access Available

Suitable for Children • Conference Facilities for 125

Blue Hill, ME

The Blue Hill Inn

800-826-7415
207-374-2844 Fax 207-374-2829
www.bluehillinn.com
bluehillinn@hotmail.com
P.O. Box 403, Union Street, Route 177
Blue Hill, ME 04614

Select Registry Member *Since 1994*
Innkeepers / Owners
MARY AND DON HARTLEY

THE SMALL VILLAGE OF BLUE HILL wraps around the head of Blue Hill Bay and is centrally located for exploring Acadia National Park, Deer Isle, Castine and the Down East and mid-coast areas. The multi-chimneyed, clapboarded inn has been the village hostelry since 1840 and is a short walk from the village center, art and antique galleries and Kneisel Chamber Music Hall. Down comforters, fireplaces, afternoon tea, hors d'oeuvres, extensive wine list and attentive service, create an intimate atmosphere for relaxation. Kayaking, lighthouse and foliage cruises, music, wine dinners and custom packages take the guess work out of vacation planning. Recipient of The *Wine Spectator's* Award of Excellence.

TRADITIONAL VILLAGE INN

RATES

11 rooms, $125/$185 B&B.
1 luxury suite, $190/$260 B&B, plus 7% tax.
Inn open mid-May through Thanksgiving. The Cape House is open year-round.

ATTRACTIONS

Cooking classes, wine dinners, sailing, kayaking, art, weaving, pottery, antiques, tennis, hiking, lighthouse and foliage cruises, biking, birding, chamber music and whale watching. Easy drive to Acadia, Bar Harbor, Castine, Deer Isle, island ferries.

CUISINE

Multi-course breakfasts with several entrees, afternoon tea, hors d'oeuvres. After dinner, cheese and dessert courses. Special event dinners by arrangement. Wine dinners June, July, Sept, and Oct.

DIRECTIONS

I-95 to Augusta, Rte 3 E to Belfast and continue E to Bucksport. Follow 15 S toward Blue Hill. From 15 S bear R at Blue Hill Inn sign and continue on 177 E. From the sign it is 4 1/2 miles to the inn.

---

1 Guestroom Handicap Accessible • Suitable For Children Over 9
Conference Facilities for 15 • Visa, MC, AMEX Accepted
Non-Smoking Inn • Reservations Accepted Through Travel Agents

Sunset, ME

The Goose Cove Lodge

800-728-1963
207-348-2508 Fax 207-348-2624
www.goosecovelodge.com
goosecove@goosecovelodge.com
Deer Isle Goose Cove Road, Sunset, ME 04683

OVERLOOKING THE MAJESTIC BEAUTY of Penobscot Bay sits the secluded paradise of Goose Cove Lodge. Nestled on a gently sloping hillside, the lodge is a highly informal and unhurried place ruled by the restorative rhythms of nature. With its inspiring vistas, warm hospitality and celebrated cuisine the lodge offers a perfect blend of rusticity and sophistication to discerning guests. Goose Cove Lodge offers secluded lodging, sand beaches, superb sailing and kayaking, hiking on moss-covered trails and magnificent ocean vistas. Tennis courts and golf are nearby. Cabins have fireplaces, sundecks and ocean views.

Non-Smoking Inn • Suitable for Children
Conference Facilities for 25 • Visa, MC, AMEX, Disc Accepted
Reservations Accepted Through Travel Agents

Select Registry Member *Since 1981*
Innkeepers / Owners
DOM AND JOANNE PARISI

RUSTIC WATERSIDE RESORT

RATES

23 cabin suites and rooms, $120/$250 B&B.
May-Oct. cabins yr. round. The accommodations are rustic and tastefully decorated. All have private baths. Most have fireplaces and private sundecks.
Open year-round.

ATTRACTIONS

Sea kayaking, sailing, nature trails, hiking, biking, golf and tennis. Kayaking and sailing lessons. Guided nature walks for adults and children, childrens program nightly during July and August. Acadia National Park, astronomy, birdwatching. Haystack School of Fine Arts and Crafts.

CUISINE

Superb, innovative, regional American fare. Breakfast, brunch, lunch, dinner. Full bar with an excellent wine list.

DIRECTIONS

From Rte 1 N in Bucksport, turn R onto Rte 15 S to Deer Isle. Follow 15 S for 25 miles over Deer Isle bridge and then 5 miles to Deer Isle Village. Upon reaching the village turn R on the main st. Go 3 miles to Goose Cove Rd.; turn R to lodge.

Deer Isle, ME

Pilgrims Inn

207-348-6615
Fax 207-348-7769
www.pilgrimsinn.com
dudhe@ctel.net
P.O. Box 69, Deer Isle, ME 04627

Select Registry Member *Since 1980*
Innkeepers / Owners
JEAN AND DUD HENDRICK

OVERLOOKING NORTHWEST HARBOR and a picturesque millpond, the 1793 colonial is surrounded by the unspoiled beauty of remote Deer Isle in Penobscot Bay. Glowing hearths, colonial colors, pumpkin pine floors, antique furnishings, combined with warm hospitality and gourmet meals in the charming barn dining room have pleased many contented guests. Easy access to Haystack School of Crafts, the busy fishing village of Stonington, Isle au Haut. Day-trips to pleasant coastal villages. On the National Register of Historic Places.

TRADITIONAL COUNTRY INN

RATES
13 rooms, 2 cottages, MAP (B&B avail), $165/$235, double MAP, single rate available. *Open mid-May to mid-October. Cottages open year-round. EP*

ATTRACTIONS
Haystack School of Crafts, Acadia, Isle au Haut, hiking, biking, boating, galleries, tennis and golf nearby.

CUISINE
Breakfast and dinner—creative American cuisine. Wine list, full liquor license.

DIRECTIONS
I-95 N to Augusta Rte 3 N to Belfast, thru Bucksport to Rte 15 S, thru Blue Hill. Over bridge to Deer Isle Village. Turn R, inn on L.

Suitable for Children Over 10
Conference Facilities for 35 • Visa, MC Accepted
Reservations Accepted Through Travel Agents

Camden, ME

Maine Stay Inn

207-236-9636
Fax 207-236-0621
www.mainestay.com
innkeeper@mainestay.com
22 High Street, Camden, ME 04843

Select Registry Member *Since 1995*
Innkeepers / Owners
PETER AND DONNY SMITH AND DIANA ROBSON

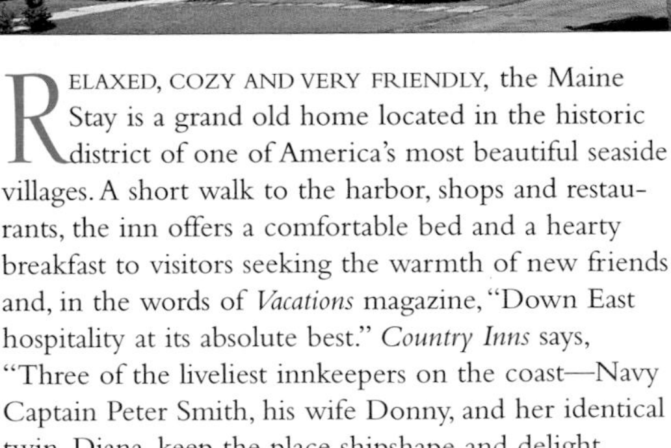

TRADITIONAL VILLAGE BREAKFAST INN

RATES
8 rooms, $100/$150.
Open year-round.

ATTRACTIONS
Sailing, sea kayaking, hiking (Camden Hills State Park), golf, downhill and cross-country skiing, fishing.

CUISINE
Full breakfast.

DIRECTIONS
US Rte 1 (High St.) 3 blocks N of the village.

RELAXED, COZY AND VERY FRIENDLY, the Maine Stay is a grand old home located in the historic district of one of America's most beautiful seaside villages. A short walk to the harbor, shops and restaurants, the inn offers a comfortable bed and a hearty breakfast to visitors seeking the warmth of new friends and, in the words of *Vacations* magazine, "Down East hospitality at its absolute best." *Country Inns* says, "Three of the liveliest innkeepers on the coast—Navy Captain Peter Smith, his wife Donny, and her identical twin, Diana, keep the place shipshape and delight guests with their enthusiasm."

Suitable for Children Over 10 • Non-Smoking Inn
Conference Facilities for 16 • Visa, MC, AMEX Accepted
Reservations Accepted Through Travel Agents

Captain Lindsey House Inn

800-523-2145
207-596-7950 Fax 207-596-2758
www.lindseyhouse.com
lindsey@midcoast.com
5 Lindsey Street, Rockland, ME 04841

Select Registry Member *Since 1998*
Contact
KEN AND ELLEN BARNES

ELEGANT IN TOWN INN

LOCATED IN THE HEART of Rockland's Historic Waterfront District, this "in-town" inn offers up old world charm with all the modern amenities in a comfortably elegant setting. Antiques and artifacts from around the world grace our spacious guest rooms, cozy parlor and library. Afternoon refreshments are served fireside or outside on our garden terrace and a sumptuous dinner awaits you in our Waterworks Restaurant. Close by you'll enjoy the Farnsworth Art Museum, fine galleries and "Down East" coastal life. Come, relax, and experience your comfort zone. AAA ◆◆◆.

RATES
9 rooms.
$65/$110 off-season.
$120/$175 in-season.
Packages available.
Open year-round.

ATTRACTIONS
Windjamming, hiking, skiing, day sailing, picnicking, swimming, museums, antiquing, theatre, concerts, ferry to North Haven Vinalhaven, and Monhegan.

CUISINE
Lunch and dinner in our Waterworks Restaurant. Pub favorites, local fare and seafood. Microbrewed beers, wines and spirits.

DIRECTIONS
From Boston: Rte I-95 N to Rte I-295 N to Rte I-95 N to exit 22(Coastal Rte 1) into Rockland, Main St. to L on Summer St.(by Ferry terminal), L on Union, 1st L to Lindsey.

1 Guestroom Handicap Accessible • Suitable for Children Over 10
Conference Facilities for 40 • Visa, MC, AMEX, Disc Accepted
Non-Smoking Inn • Reservations Accepted Through Travel Agents

Newcastle, ME

The Newcastle Inn

800-832-8669
207-563-5685 Fax 207-563-6877
www.newcastleinn.com
innkeep@newcastleinn.com
60 River Road, Newcastle, ME 04553

A ROMANTIC COUNTRY INN located in Maine's Mid-Coast, famous for its beaches, lighthouses and rocky shore. The Inn's living rooms and special sunporch are a quiet, peaceful and relaxing place from which to enjoy the wonders of Coastal Maine. Overlooking the harbor, the Inn's gardens abound in lupines and other perennials. Renowned for its cuisine, the Inn offers fine dining choices changing daily. Many of the Inn's rooms feature king or queen canopy or four-poster beds, fireplaces, Jacuzzis and other special treats. Winner of the prestigious *Waverly/Country Inns* magazine Room of the Year Award for 1997. AAA ◆◆◆ and Mobil ★★★.

Suitable for Children Over 12
Conference Facilities for 34 • Credit Cards Accepted
Reservations Accepted Through Travel Agents

Select Registry Member *Since 1990*
Innkeepers/Owners
HOWARD AND REBECCA LEVITAN

TRADITIONAL VILLAGE INN

RATES

14 rooms including four suites. Nine rooms with fireplaces and two with Jacuzzis. 2001 rates $100 to $260 B&B. Dinner by reservation. *Open year-round. We are a completely non-smoking property.*

ATTRACTIONS

Walk trails, beaches, lighthouses, bicycling, antiquing, birding, boating, touring, xc-skiing, hiking, swimming, kayaking, sailing, whale watching. For a complete description see The Ten Days on our website www.newcastleinn.com.

CUISINE

Breakfast is multi-course served from 8-9:00 am. Innkeeper's Reception at 6:00 pm on dinner nights. Four-course gourmet dinner by reservation each night except Mondays (weekends only in winter season). Our dinner menu changes daily.

DIRECTIONS

Rte 95 N to the Maine Turnpike. Exit 6 A Rte 295 N to Rte 95 N and take Exit 22 Coastal Rte 1, Brunswick. Rte 1 N approx. 30 miles over two bridges. Six miles N of Wiscasset Bridge take R to River Rd. Inn is 1/2 mile on R.

Wiscasset, ME

The Squire Tarbox Inn

207-882-7693
Fax 207-882-7107
www.squiretarboxinn.com
squiretarbox@ime.net
Box 1181, Westport Island, Wiscasset, ME 04578

Select Registry Member *Since 1974*
Innkeepers/Owners
KAREN AND BILL MITMAN

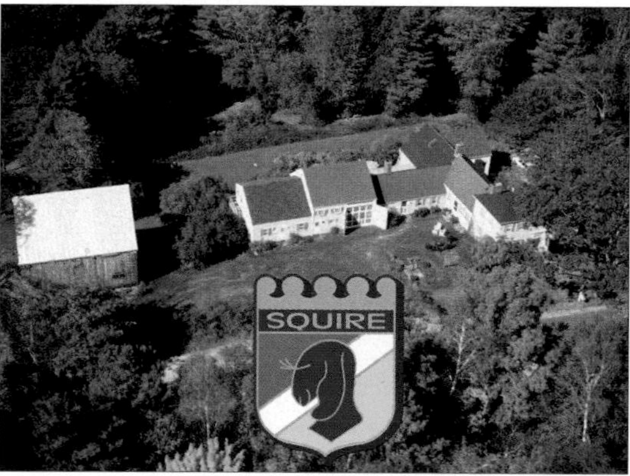

ONCE UPON A TIME, there was a country inn conspicuous from all others. After a restoration for your comfort, this colonial farm created an alternate luxury, the splendor of nature. Set within fields, stone walls and woods, and with kindness to all creatures great and small, pristine barns were filled with gentle, refined animals who help make a fresh goat cheese for your nourishing pleasure. With four-star fireside dining, the inn offers you a savory journey into countryside simplicity. Away from tourist crowds, but convenient to coastal adventures. On the National Register of Historic Places.

TRADITIONAL COUNTRY INN

RATES

11 rooms, $90/$189, B&B.
$160/$251, MAP.
Open May thru October and winter weekends.

ATTRACTIONS

Walking path, rowboat, birding and mountain bikes on premises. Beaches, harbors, antique shops, museums, lobster shacks, scenic day-trips, hiking and L.L. Bean nearby.

CUISINE

Full breakfast served buffet style for inn guests only. Dinner to inn guests and public by reservation. Our fresh goat cheese served at cocktail hour. Liquor license and wine list. Chocolate chip cookies available at any hour of the day.

DIRECTIONS

I-95 or Maine Turnpike to Brunswick; Rte 1 N thru Brunswick and Bath; from Bath Bridge go another 7 miles on Rte 1; turn R on Rte 144 and take it 8.5 miles, it makes turns but is well marked; all you will see is us—rambling Colonial farmhouse on R.

Suitable for Children Over 14 • Disc, Visa, MC, AMEX Accepted
Designated Smoking Areas • Reservations Accepted Through Travel Agents

Portland, ME

Pomegranate Inn

800-356-0408
207-772-1006 Fax 207-773-4426
www.pomegranateinn.com

49 Neal Street, Portland, ME 04102

PORTLAND'S BEAUTIFUL Western Promenade Historic Residential District is the location of this special city inn. It is a small sophisticated hotel which offers a quiet haven from the tensions of travel. The bustle of downtown is forgotten when you step through the Pomegranate's doors. Antiques and art abound. For real seclusion the carriage house offers a lovely suite upstairs. Downstairs is a guestroom with its own private terrace. The Inn has a lovely urban garden. A lot of elegance with a touch of panache. Chosen by *Travel & Leisure Magazine* as one of the top ten favorite Inns in the country, June 2000.

Select Registry Member *Since 1995*
Owner
ISABEL SMILES
Innkeeper
CHRISTOPHER MONAHAN

ELEGANT IN TOWN
BREAKFAST INN

RATES
8 rooms, 1 suite, 1 garden room
$95/$135 B&B off-season
$135/$205 B&B in-season
Open year-round.

ATTRACTIONS
Museums, art galleries, historic homes, boat rides, nature walks, fine restaurants, shopping, tennis, golf and fitness club nearby.

CUISINE
Complimentary wine and tea upon arrival.

DIRECTIONS
From S: I-95 N exit 6A to I-295 exit 4 exit 1A immediate L Danforth St. 1st L Vaughan R on Carroll 1 block. From N: Exit 6A Rte 77 State St. R on Pine L on Neal.

Non-Smoking Inn • MC, Visa, AMEX Accepted
1 Guestroom Handicap Accessible

Kennebunkport, ME

Captain Lord Mansion

207-967-3141
Fax 207-967-3172
www.captainlord.com
innkeeper@captainlord.com
P.O. Box 800, Kennebunkport, ME 04046

Select Registry Member *Since 1975*
Innkeepers/Owners
BEV DAVIS AND
RICK LITCHFIELD

ENJOY AN UNFORGETTABLE romantic experience here. Both your personal comfort and intimacy are assured by large, beautifully appointed guest rooms, luxurious amenities such as oversize four-poster beds, cozy gas fireplaces, heated marble/tile bathroom floors, several double Jacuzzis, as well as fresh flowers, full breakfasts, afternoon refreshments and lots of personal attention. The Inn is situated at the head of a sloping village green, overlooking the Kennebunk River. This picturesque, quiet, yet convenient, location affords a terrific place from which to walk to enjoy the shops, restaurants and galleries in this historic village. AAA ◆◆◆◆.

ELEGANT VILLAGE
BREAKFAST INN

RATES
15 rooms, $175/$349 B&B.
1 suite, $249/$399 B&B.
Open year-round.

ATTRACTIONS
Scenic walks, bicycling, fine dining, shopping, beaches, sailing, tennis, golf, whale watching, fishing and antiquing.

CUISINE
Full three-course breakfast.
Afternoon tea and sweets. BYOB.

DIRECTIONS
Exit ME Tpke at exit 3, L onto Rte 35 for 5.5 miles to Rte 9 E, L, go over bridge, 1st R in square, onto Ocean Ave., at .3 mile, L onto Green St.

Non-Smoking Inn
Conference Facilities for 16 • Visa, MC, Disc Accepted
Reservations Accepted Through Travel Agents

Kennebunkport, ME

Old Fort Inn

207-967-5353
Fax 207-967-4547
www.oldfortinn.com
ofi@ispchannel.com
8 Old Fort Avenue, P.O. Box M
Kennebunkport, ME 04046

Select Registry Member *Since 1976*
Innkeepers/Owners
SHEILA AND DAVID ALDRICH

ONE OF KENNEBUNKPORT, MAINE'S exceptional country inns and secret treasures. The unique combination of yesterday's charm and today's conveniences entice many guests to return to the inn year after year and recommend it to friends. The Old Fort Inn features antique appointed rooms with first-class amenities(TV, A/C, phones and wet bars), buffet breakfast, free parking, heated pool, tennis court and antique shop. The location is residential a block from the ocean, 1 1/4 miles from the village and five minutes from two 18-hole golf courses. AAA ◆◆◆◆ Award.

ELEGANT WATERSIDE BREAKFAST INN

RATES
16 rooms, $155/$350 B&B.
Open mid-April to mid-December.

ATTRACTIONS
Tennis, pool, beaches, jog, boat, walk, bike, golf, fish, sight-see, antique, shop, playhouse, paint, write, whale watching, dine in style, relax and rejuvenate.

CUISINE
Buffet breakfast, fresh fruit, cereals, homemade breads, quiche, waffles and croissants. BYOB or special order.

DIRECTIONS
I-95 Exit 3 (Kennebunk exit), turn L on Rte 35 for 5 1/2 mi. L at light on Rte 9 for .3 miles. R on Ocean Ave. for .9 miles to Colony Hotel. L. Follow signs .3 miles to Inn.

Suitable for Children Over 12 • Designated Smoking Areas
Conference Facilities for 32 • Visa, MC, Disc, Diners, AMEX Accepted
Reservations Accepted Through Travel Agents

Kennebunkport, ME

Maine Stay Inn & Cottages

800-950-2117
207-967-2117 Fax 207-967-8757
www.mainestayinn.com
innkeeper@mainestayinn.com
34 Maine Street, P.O. Box 500A
Kennebunkport, ME 04046

Select Registry Member *Since 1996*
Innkeepers / Owners
LINDSAY AND CAROL COPELAND

A BEAUTIFUL 1860 VICTORIAN, distinguished by its suspended staircase, wraparound porch and cupola. The Maine Stay offers charming inn rooms, suites and cottage rooms, several with fireplaces and whirlpool tubs. Guests staying in most of our cottage rooms may choose to have a breakfast basket delivered. The wraparound porch is a wonderful place to enjoy breakfast and afternoon tea. The grounds offer a peaceful respite amid gigantic pines. The Maine Stay is perfectly situated in the historic district, a short walk to shops, galleries, restaurants and the harbor. AAA ◆◆◆.

TRADITIONAL VILLAGE BREAKFAST INN

RATES
4 inn rooms, $105/$195.
4 suites, $135/$250.
9 cottage rooms, $105/$250.
Open year-round.

ATTRACTIONS
Beaches, bicycling, antiquing, shopping, boat cruises, whale watching, golf, tennis, museums and historic architecture.

CUISINE
Sumptuous full breakfast and afternoon tea and sweets. BYOB.

DIRECTIONS
ME. Tpke., exit 3. L on Rte 35, 6 miles to Rte 9. Turn L on Rte 9, Go over bridge, thru village to stop sign. Turn R on Maine St. Go 3 blks.

Suitable for Children
Non-Smoking Inn • MC, Visa, AMEX Accepted
Reservations Accepted Through Travel Agents

Ogunquit, ME

Hartwell House

800-235-8883
207-646-7210 Fax 207-646-6032
www.hartwellhouseinn.com
hartwell@cybertours.com
118 Shore Road, P.O. Box 393, Ogunquit, ME 03907

PERFECT FOR A ROMANTIC GETAWAY or business function, this country inn is ideally situated. It is just outside of Perkins Cove, where lobster boats depart each morning and shops and restaurants overlook the ocean. The scenic Marginal Way footpath, winding along the rocks at water's edge, is only moments away. Ogunquit's sandy beaches, quaint shops, art and antique galleries and renowned Playhouse Theatre are also within walking distance. Begin each day with a full gourmet breakfast, enjoy afternoon tea on the sunporch and explore our gardens. Dine in an award-winning area restaurant and retire in an elegant, antique-filled guestroom or suite.

Select Registry Member *Since 1981*
Innkeepers
JAMES AND TRISHA HARTWELL
CHRISTOPHER AND TRACEY ANDERSON

ELEGANT VILLAGE BREAKFAST INN

RATES
11 guest rooms, $100/$180 B&B.
2 studios, $130/$160 B&B.
3 suites, $145/$200 B&B.
Open year-round.

ATTRACTIONS
Atlantic Ocean, beach, sailing, fishing, whale watching, swimming, golf and tennis privileges, hiking, walking, shopping, horseback riding, restaurants, art galleries, antiquing, theatre, movies, museums, xc-skiing.

CUISINE
Complimentary full gourmet breakfast, afternoon tea with sweets and pastries. Dinner packages and gourmet dining series available in off-season.

DIRECTIONS
I-95 N: Exit 4, in Maine, L on northbound Rte 1, 4.4 miles, R on Pine Hill to end, L on Shore, .2 miles to inn on L. From I-95 S: Exit 2, L on eastbound Rte 109, R on Rte 1 S, 6 miles, L on Shore, .6 miles to inn on R.

Handicap Access Available • Suitable for Children Over 14
Conference Facilities for 65 • Credit Cards Accepted

Dockside Guest Quarters

800-270-1977
207-363-2868 Fax 207-363-1977
www.docksidegq.com
info@docksidegq.com
P.O. Box 205, York, ME 03909

Select Registry Member *Since 1975*
Innkeepers/Owners
THE LUSTY FAMILY

THE DOCKSIDE captures the essence of Maine with its natural beauty, gracious hospitality, abundant sights, recreation and activities. Uniquely situated on a private peninsula, each room has a panoramic water view. Accommodations are in the Maine House, a classic 'New England cottage,' furnished with antiques and marine art, and multi-unit buildings at the water's edge. Warmth and charm are found throughout. The Dockside Restaurant boasts a water view from every table. A creative menu specializes in fresh Maine seafood.

TRADITIONAL WATERSIDE INN

RATES
19 rooms, $82/$150.
6 suites, $120/$200.
Off-season rates and packages EP.
Most with private decks and water views.
Open year-round.

ATTRACTIONS
On-site: river cruise, boat rentals, fishing, lawn games, bikes. Nearby: whale watching, deep-sea fishing, sailing, golf, tennis, outlet shopping, Ogunquit playhouse, four beaches, nature trails and preserves, lighthouses, scenic tourist destinations.

CUISINE
Dining on porch overlooking harbor with complete and varied menu. Specialties: roast duckling, bouillabaisse, lobster dublin lawyer, grilled salmon maison. Lunch and dinner are served in the restaurant. Breakfast is available in the Maine House.

DIRECTIONS
From I-95 exit at York, ME (exit #4). Go S on Rte 1. At the first traffic light, turn L on Rte 1A. Follow 1A through York Village and turn R on Rte 103. Take the 1st L immediately after crossing York River. Follow signs from there.

2 Guestrooms Handicap Accessible • Suitable for Children
Non-Smoking Inn • Conference Facilities for 65 • MC, Visa Accepted
Reservations Accepted Through Travel Agents

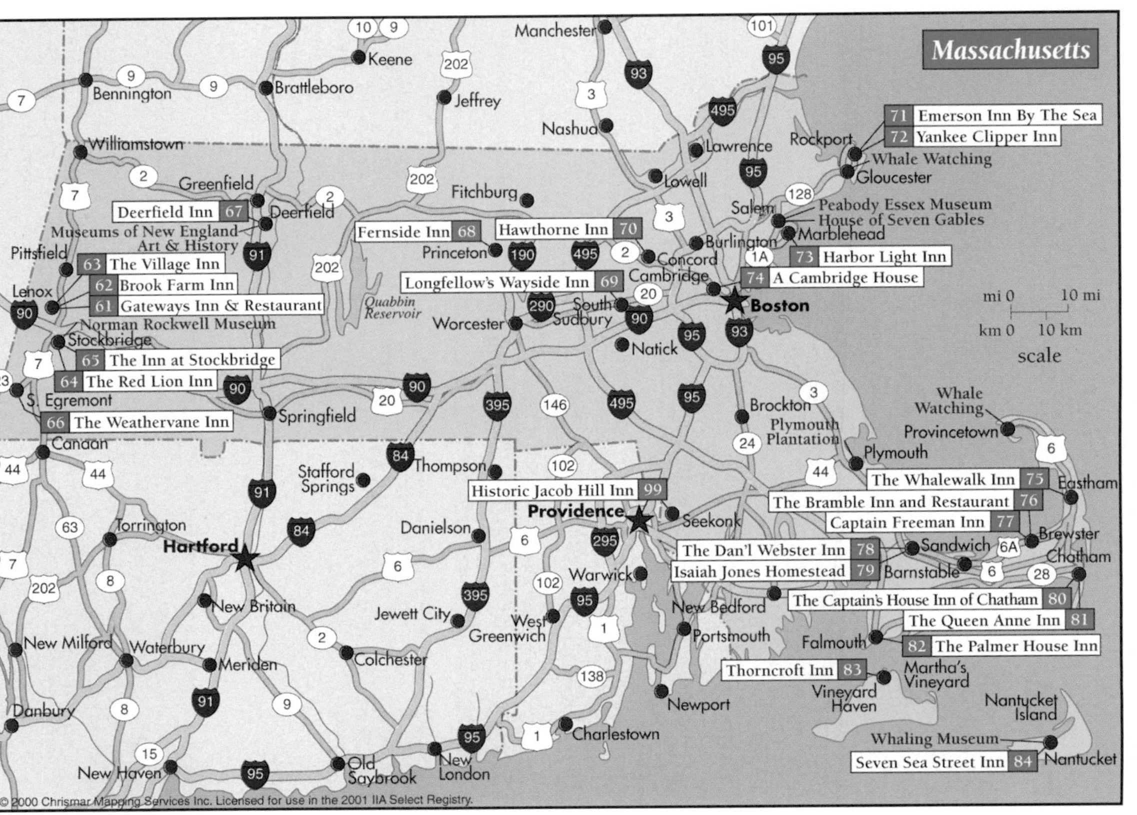

Massachusetts
71 Emerson Inn By The Sea
72 Yankee Clipper Inn
Whale Watching
Peabody Essex Museum
House of Seven Gables
73 Harbor Light Inn
74 A Cambridge House
mi 0 10 mi
km 0 10 km
scale
Whale Watching
75 The Whalewalk Inn
76 The Bramble Inn and Restaurant
77 Captain Freeman Inn
78 The Dan'l Webster Inn
79 Isaiah Jones Homestead
80 The Captain's House Inn of Chatham
81 The Queen Anne Inn
82 The Palmer House Inn
83 Thorncroft Inn
Whaling Museum
84 Seven Sea Street Inn
99 Historic Jacob Hill Inn
68 Fernside Inn
70 Hawthorne Inn
69 Longfellow's Wayside Inn
67 Deerfield Inn
Museums of New England Art & History
63 The Village Inn
62 Brook Farm Inn
61 Gateways Inn & Restaurant
Norman Rockwell Museum
65 The Inn at Stockbridge
64 The Red Lion Inn
66 The Weathervane Inn
Keene
Manchester
Bennington
Brattleboro
Jeffrey
Nashua
Williamstown
Lawrence
Rockport
Gloucester
Lowell
Greenfield
Fitchburg
Deerfield
Salem
Marblehead
Burlington
Pittsfield
Princeton
Concord
Cambridge
Lenox
Quabbin Reservoir
Worcester
South Sudbury
Boston
Stockbridge
Natick
S. Egremont
Springfield
Brockton
Plymouth Plantation
Provincetown
Canaan
Plymouth
Thompson
Stafford Springs
Eastham
Providence
Seekonk
Torrington
Danielson
Brewster
Sandwich
Hartford
Chatham
Barnstable
Warwick
New Britain
Jewett City
New Bedford
West Greenwich
Portsmouth
Falmouth
New Milford
Waterbury
Colchester
Meriden
Martha's Vineyard
Vineyard Haven
Newport
Nantucket Island
Danbury
Charlestown
Nantucket
New Haven
Old Saybrook
New London
© 2000 Chrismar Mapping Services Inc. Licensed for use in the 2001 IIA Select Registry.

Lenox, MA

Gateways Inn & Restaurant

888-492-9466
413-637-2532 Fax 413-637-1432
www.gatewaysinn.com
gateways@berkshire.net
51 Walker Street, Lenox, MA 01240

GATEWAYS INN, a turn-of-the century neoclassical mansion, built for Harley Procter, offers European hospitality in an elegant setting. A relaxing atmosphere, in the center of town. The beauty of Stanford White's staircase and Tiffany style rose windows enhance the building. Charming rooms each uniquely decorated with antiques many with fireplaces, with modern amenities including centralized air-conditioning, TV, phones with dataport and voice mail. The aroma of fresh-brewed coffee and warm croissants fills the air each morning as guests awake to breakfast and to another day of being pampered by the owners and staff.

Suitable for Children Over 12 • Conference Facilities for 90
Non-Smoking Inn • AMEX, Visa, MC, Diner, Disc Accepted
Reservations Accepted Through Travel Agents

Select Registry Member *Since 2001*
Innkeepers / Owners
FABRIZIO & ROSEMARY CHIARIELLO

ELEGANT IN TOWN INN

RATES

11 rooms, \$95/\$180 (\$120/\$250 peak)
1 suite, \$225/\$315 (\$275/\$400 peak)
Peak season premium apply.
Individually decorated, each in a distinctive style. Many antiques, 4-poster canopy or sleigh beds. All with new private baths.
Open year-round.

ATTRACTIONS

HERE: tennis. NEARBY: concerts, ballet, opera, theater, scenic tours, biking, golf, hiking, fly fishing, shopping, antiquing. Visit several museums and galleries as well as historical residences.

CUISINE

Full breakfast. Elegant yet casual dining Tuesday through Sunday. Extensive selection of American and Italian wines and a fully stocked bar. After theater desserts and light meals available. Open to the general public.

DIRECTIONS

From Boston: I-90 W to Lee Exit 2, Turn R on Rte 20 W stay on until intersect Rte 183 S. Turn L onto Rte 183 S (Walker St.) One mile on R. From New York: Taconic Pkway to I-90E Exit 2 Lee (Same as above).

Lenox, MA

Brook Farm Inn

800-285-7638
413-637-3013 Fax 413-637-4751
www.brookfarm.com
innkeeper@brookfarm.com
15 Hawthorne Street, Lenox, MA 01240

Select Registry Member *Since 2001*
Innkeepers / Owners
JOE AND ANNE MILLER

THERE IS POETRY HERE. Nestled in a wooded glen, Brook Farm has been welcoming guests for over 50 years. Just a short walk to historic Lenox village, this country Victorian is tucked away on a quiet side street surrounded by gardens. Built in 1870, and furnished with antiques, period pieces and family treasures, some guestrooms feature canopy beds and fireplaces and all have air conditioning and phones. Close to Tanglewood and all the Berkshire cultural attractions, seasonal activities include downhill and xc-skiing, hiking, antiquing and museum tours. Special winter packages are offered AAA ◆◆◆, Mobil ★★★.

TRADITIONAL VILLAGE BREAKFAST INN

RATES
12 rooms, $90/$205 B&B
Individually decorated with antiques, period pieces, canopy beds. Six with fireplaces and all with air conditioning and phones.
Open year-round.
Weekends only November – March.

ATTRACTIONS
Pool on premises. Close to Tanglewood, summer theater, Norman Rockwell Museum, Clark Art Institute, Hancock Shaker Village. Outdoor activities include downhill and xc-skiing, hiking, biking, golf, tennis. Antiquing, fine dining, galleries and shops.

CUISINE
Full breakfast and afternoon tea with homemade scones.

DIRECTIONS
Mass. Tpke. (I-90), exit 2, R on Rte. 20W 5 miles, to L on Rte. 183, 1 mile to L on Old Stockbridge Rd., then R on Hawthorne Street.

Suitable for Children Over 15 • Non-Smoking Inn
Visa, MC Accepted

Lenox, MA

The Village Inn

800-253-0917
413-637-0020 Fax 413-637-9756
www.villageinn-lenox.com
villinn@vgernet.net
16 Church Street, P.O. Box 1810, Lenox, MA 01240

Select Registry Member *Since 1977*
Innkeepers/Owners
CLIFFORD RUDISILL AND RAY WILSON

TRADITIONAL VILLAGE INN

IN THE HISTORIC DISTRICT of the Berkshire village of Lenox, this colonial inn, built in 1771, is near shops, galleries, library, churches, parks, wooded trails, Tanglewood, summer theatre, dance festivals, winter downhill and cross-country skiing, fall foliage and spring flower excursions. Year-round museums: Norman Rockwell, Grandma Moses, Hancock Shaker Village and Clark Art Museum. Every room is individually furnished with country antiques and reproductions, many four-posters and fireplaces, all with private baths with hairdryer and magnifying mirror and many with whirlpool tub, telephones with voice mail, TV/VCR with complimentary video library and air-conditioning in summer. Special winter and spring packages.

RATES
32 rooms, $55/$255 B&B.
1 suite, $345/$530 B&B.
Rates change seasonally.
Open year-round.

ATTRACTIONS
Near downhill and cross-county skiing, golf, riding, tennis, swimming, hiking, bicycling, antiquing, Rockwell and Shaker Museums, Tanglewood and summer stock.

CUISINE
Breakfast, afternoon English tea, dinner (June-Oct ex. Mondays). Light fare served in the downstairs tavern. Full bar service in the dining room.

DIRECTIONS
Mass. Tpke.(I-90): Exit 2, Rte 20 W to Rte 183 S. Turn L for 1 mile to R on Church St. and Inn. From Rte 7 take Rte 7A to Church St. in Lenox.

---

2 Guestrooms Handicap Accessible • Suitable for Children Over 6
Conference Facilities for 50 • AMEX, MC, Visa, Disc, Diners Accepted
Reservations Accepted Through Travel Agents

Stockbridge, MA

The Red Lion Inn

413-298-5545
Fax 413-298-5130
www.redlioninn.com
innkeeper@redlioninn.com
30 Main Street, P.O. Box 954
Stockbridge, MA 01262

Select Registry Member *Since 1967*
Owners
THE FITZPATRICK FAMILY
Innkeeper
BROOKS BRADBURY

TRADITIONAL VILLAGE INN

RATES
84 rooms, $102/$189.
26 suites, $179/$400.
7 annex buildings.
Open year-round.

ATTRACTIONS
Tanglewood, Norman Rockwell Museum, Chesterwood, Berkshire Theatre Festival, antiquing, skiing and golf nearby. Outdoor activities abound.

CUISINE
Breakfast, lunch and dinner served daily. MAP available for groups. Wine and liquor available.

DIRECTIONS
I-90 to exit 2 at Lee, to Rte 102 W to Main St., Stockbridge.

FOR OVER TWO CENTURIES, this renowned antique-filled Inn has welcomed guests with old-fashioned charm and a longstanding tradition of New England hospitality. As one of the few American inns in existence since the 18th century, The Red Lion Inn has 110 individually decorated rooms and suites, and serves contemporary New England cuisine in the elegant main dining room, cozy Widow Bingham's Tavern and flower-filled courtyard in season. The Lion's Den Pub offers nightly entertainment (never a cover). Shop in the Pink Kitty Gift Shop and the flagship Country Curtains Store, both at the Inn.

Limited Handicap Access Available • Suitable for Children
Conference Facilities for 100 • Credit Cards Accepted
Designated Smoking Areas • Reservations Accepted Through Travel Agents

Stockbridge, MA

The Inn at Stockbridge

888-466-7865
413-298-3337 Fax 413-298-3406
www.stockbridgeinn.com
innkeeper@stockbridgeinn.com
RTE 7N, Box 618, Stockbridge, MA 01262

Select Registry Member *Since 1986*
Innkeepers/Owners
ALICE AND LEN SCHILLER

CONSUMMATE HOSPITALITY and outstanding breakfast distinguish a visit at this turn-of-the-century Georgian Colonial estate on 12 secluded acres in the heart of the Berkshires. Close to the Norman Rockwell Museum, Tanglewood, Hancock Shaker Village, summer theatres and four-season recreation. The inn has a gracious, English country house feeling, with two well-appointed living rooms, a formal dining room and a baby grand piano.

ELEGANT VILLAGE
BREAKFAST INN

RATES
8 rooms.
4 suites.
B&B rooms, $115/$255.
Suites, $180/$280.
Open year-round.

ATTRACTIONS
Pool on premises, golf, tennis, nearby horseback riding, downhill and cross-country skiing, Norman Rockwell Museum, Tanglewood and cultural activities.

CUISINE
Complete gourmet breakfast is included. Complimentary wine.

DIRECTIONS
Mass Pike: Take exit 2, W on Rte 102 to Rte 7 N 1.2 miles to inn on R. NYC: Taconic Pkwy to Rte 23 E and Rte 7 N past Stockbridge 1.2 miles.

1 Guestroom Handicap Accessible • Suitable for Children Over 12
Conference Facilities for 25 • Visa, MC, AMEX, Disc Accepted
Non-Smoking Inn • Reservations Accepted Through Travel Agents

South Egremont, MA

The Weathervane Inn

800-528-9580
413-528-9580 Fax 413-528-1713
www.weathervaneinn.com
innkeeper@weathervaneinn.com
P.O. Box 388, Route 23, South Egremont, MA 01258

NESTLED IN THE QUAINT AND HISTORIC VILLAGE of South Egremont, this charming landmark country inn has been offering gracious hospitality to visitors to the Berkshires for over 18 years. The Lome family invites you to enjoy all the Berkshires has to offer in the comfort of our 10 charming and beautifully-appointed guestrooms. We offer a bountiful country breakfast to start your day and a fireside tea for your relaxation after a full day of activities. The Berkshires offer four seasons of cultural and recreational activities including Tanglewood summer stock, historic homes, hiking, skiing and antiquing. Rekindle your romance and get away from it all at the Weathervane.

Suitable for Children • Conference Facilities for 40
Non-Smoking Inn • Visa, MC, AMEX Accepted
2 Guestrooms Handicap Accessible

Select Registry Member *Since 1984*
Innkeepers
JEFFREY AND MAXINE LOME

TRADITIONAL VILLAGE BREAKFAST INN

RATES
8 rooms and 2 suites, $115/$245 B&B.
Open year-round.

ATTRACTIONS
Pool on site, golf, tennis, skiing, Tanglewood summer theater, dance festivals, antiquing, historic homes, museums, fall foliage, hiking, horseback riding, fine dining, outlet shopping, fly-fishing.

CUISINE
Dinner served for parties of 10 or more. Wine and liquor available.

DIRECTIONS
From NYC: Taconic Pkwy to Rte 23 E 13 miles to inn on R. From Mass Tpke: Exit 2 to Rte 102 to Rte 7 S to Rte 23 W to inn on L.

Deerfield, MA

Deerfield Inn

800-926-3865
413-774-5587 Fax 413-775-7221
www.deerfieldinn.com
SR@deerfieldinn.com
81 Old Main Street, Deerfield, MA 01342-0305

Select Registry Member *Since 1996*
Innkeepers
KARL AND JANE SABO

ELEGANT VILLAGE INN

RATES
23 rooms, $188/$255 B&B.
Open year-round.

ATTRACTIONS
14 museums on the street, old books, antiquing, cross-country skiing, arts and crafts, boating, fishing, hiking, white-water rafting, craft fairs, shopping, golf.

CUISINE
Our casual but elegant restaurant serves breakfast and dinner year-round, featuring new American cuisine with an international flair. The Terrace Cafe is open for lunch, and in warm weather you can enjoy dining outside on the garden terrace.

DIRECTIONS
I-91 exit 24 going N exit 25 going S. Deerfield Village is just off Rte 5 and 10 N.

ONE OF THE FEW ORIGINAL country inns in the region, this classic hostelry opened its doors in July 1884, despite a plague of grasshoppers devouring its way across a drought-stricken county! Located along a charming mile-long way known simply as "The Street", the Deerfield Inn is still the centerpiece of Old Deerfield with 11 rooms in the main inn, and 12 in the south wing. A National Historic Landmark, this unspoiled 330-year-old village is a perfect destination for those looking for the real New England. Enjoy Deerfield's farms, museums, events, country walks, friendly folk and beautiful scenery. We look forward to welcoming you here.

2 Guestrooms Handicap Accessible • Suitable for Children
Conference Facilities for 30 • MC, Visa, AMEX, Diners Accepted
Non-Smoking Inn • Reservations Accepted Through Travel Agents

Princeton, MA

Fernside Inn

800-545-2741
978-464-2741 Fax 978-464-2065
www.fernsideinn.com
innkeeper@fernsideinn.com
162 Mountain Rd, PO Box 303, Princeton, MA 01541

Select Registry Member *Since 2001*
Innkeepers
JOCELYN AND RICHARD MORRISON

BUILT ON THE SECOND HIGHEST MOUNTAIN IN MASSACHUSETTS, this historic 1835 federal mansion offers breathtaking sunrises and views of Boston, 55 miles to the East. Discover the natural beauty of central Massachusetts, enjoy a quiet, romantic retreat, relax in the tranquility and understated elegance of the three sitting rooms with fireplaces, or watch hummingbirds and deer from the porch. Large and luxurious guestrooms, many with working fireplaces and four-poster beds, have been decorated with down comforters, fine fabrics, antiques, and oriental rugs on original heart pine floors. A full breakfast and afternoon refreshments are provided.

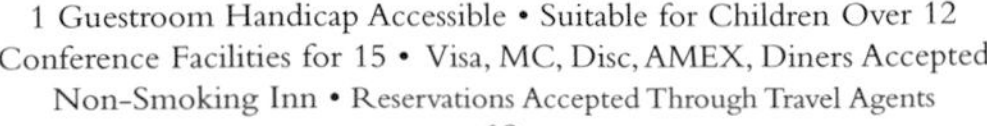

1 Guestroom Handicap Accessible • Suitable for Children Over 12
Conference Facilities for 15 • Visa, MC, Disc, AMEX, Diners Accepted
Non-Smoking Inn • Reservations Accepted Through Travel Agents

ELEGANT COUNTRY BREAKFAST INN

RATES

6 rooms; 2 suites, $120/$175 B&B
Corporate rates.
4 rooms with fireplaces and four-poster beds. Handicap accessible suite. All private baths. Smoke-free environment. Good views.
Open year-round, except 2 weeks in March.

ATTRACTIONS

Hiking, fall foliage, downhill and cross-country skiing, bird watching, canoeing, biking, and fine-dining within 5 miles. Golf, fishing, antiquing, museums, shopping, Lexington & Concord, Old Sturbridge Village within 30 miles. One hour to Boston.

CUISINE

Three course, New England style gourmet breakfast consisting of seasonal fresh fruit, homemade baked goods, and a hot entree served in an elegant, yet relaxed atmosphere. Afternoon refreshments.

DIRECTIONS

Princeton is approximately one hour West of Boston. From the Princeton town common, located at the blinking light at the intersection of Rte 31 and Rte 62, take Mountain Road North 1 1/2 miles to Fernside.

Sudbury, MA

Longfellow's Wayside Inn

800-339-1776
978-443-1776 Fax 978-443-8041
www.wayside.org
longfelo@wayside.org
Wayside Inn Road, Sudbury, MA 01776

Select Registry Member *Since 1967*
Innkeeper
ROBERT H. PURRINGTON

STEP BACK IN TIME to the inn that represents the glory of Colonial New England. Immortalized in 1863 by Longfellow in his *Tales of a Wayside Inn*, this 280 year-old landmark continues today as an inn, restaurant and museum. Enjoy antique-filled guest rooms and full-course Yankee fare. Take a stroll—you could see a wedding at our white-steepled chapel or an artist sketching our working Grist Mill. Visit the "Little Red Schoolhouse" (of Mary's lamb fame), that attracts children worldwide (seasonal). Reservations (dining and lodging) well in advance.

TRADITIONAL COUNTRY INN

RATES

10 rooms, B&B.
Jan-Mar: $98/$112.
Apr-Aug: $112/$122.
Sept-Dec: $130/$145.
Open year-round.

ATTRACTIONS

Historic landmarks and museum rooms on-site. Quaint local shops, antiquing, golf, cross-country skiing, historic Walden Pond, Lexington, Concord, Boston.

CUISINE

Lunch and dinner daily in seven dining areas. Breakfast to house guests only. Wine and liquor available.

DIRECTIONS

Just W of Boston. Between Boston and Worcester off Rte 20. 11 miles W of Rte 128 and seven miles E of Rte 495. Sign on R for Wayside Inn Rd.

Handicap Access Available • Suitable for Children
Conference Facilities for 56 • Credit Cards Accepted
Reservations Accepted Through Travel Agents

Concord, MA

Hawthorne Inn

978-369-5610
Fax 978-287-4949
www.concordmass.com
inn@concordmass.com
462 Lexington Road, Concord, MA 01742

Select Registry Member *Since 1980*
Innkeepers
GREGORY BURCH AND MARILYN MUDRY

BESIDE THE BATTLE ROAD the Minutemen marched in 1775 to face the British Regulars, the Hawthorne Inn (circa 1870), was constructed on land once owned by Emerson, Hawthorne, the Alcott family, and surveyed by Thoreau. Amidst aged trees and bountiful gardens this colorful inn beckons the traveler to refresh the spirit in a winsome atmosphere abounding with original artworks, antique furnishings and archaic artifacts. With a copy of *Walden* or *Little Women* in hand, bask near the whispering fire or be led by the resident cat, to a garden seat for a spot of tea.

TRADITIONAL VILLAGE BREAKFAST INN

RATES
7 rooms (double and queen), $150/$275 B & B.
Open year-round.

ATTRACTIONS
Homes of: Emerson, Alcott and Hawthorne. Walden Pond of Thoreau fame. Old North Bridge where "the shot heard round the world" was fired in 1775.

CUISINE
Expanded continental breakfast offered each morning. BYOB, set-ups provided.

DIRECTIONS
From Rte 128-95, exit 30 (Rte 2A W) for 2.8 miles. Bear R, at fork toward Concord for 1.2 miles. Inn directly across road from Hawthorne's home.

Suitable for Children • Visa, MC, AMEX, Disc Accepted
Non-Smoking Inn • Reservations Accepted Through Travel Agents

Rockport, MA

Emerson Inn By The Sea

978-546-6321
Fax 978-546-7043
www.emersoninnbythesea.com
info@emersoninnbythesea.com
1 Cathedral Avenue, Rockport, MA 01966

Select Registry Member *Since 1973*
Innkeepers / Owners
BRUCE AND MICHELE COATES

RALPH WALDO EMERSON called the inn, "Thy proper summer home." Today's vacationers enjoy the relaxed 19th century atmosphere from our broad oceanfront veranda, but can savor the 20th century amenities of a heated saltwater pool, room phones, air-conditioning and private bath; sauna, whirlpool and a recreation room featuring a TV and VCR. Nearby are hiking trails along the oceanfront, tennis, golf and the always popular whale watches. Halibut Point State Park features the history of the Rockport Quarries and downtown Rockport is famous for shops and art galleries.

TRADITIONAL WATERSIDE INN

RATES

35 rooms, $95/$295 B&B.
Rooms with ocean views.
Open year-round.

ATTRACTIONS

Heated saltwater pool, private whirlpool and sauna. Also, a day spa with massage services, whale watching, shopping, sightseeing, golf, tennis, deep-sea fishing and nature walks nearby.

CUISINE

Outdoor oceanfront dining and elegant turn-of-the-century dining room, serving breakfast daily; dinner seasonally. BYOB. Ideal location for weddings and conferences.

DIRECTIONS

Rte 128 N to traffic light in Gloucester L on Rte 127 to Pigeon Cove. R at our sign on Phillips Ave. (just past sign for Rockport Marina and Yacht Club).

Limited Handicap Access Available • Suitable for Children
Conference Facilities for 50 • Credit Cards Accepted
Reservations Accepted Through Travel Agents

Rockport, MA

Yankee Clipper Inn

800-545-3699
978-546-3407 Fax 978-546-9730
www.yankeeclipperinn.com
info@yankeeclipperinn.com
96 Granite Street, P.O. Box 2399
Rockport, MA 01966

Select Registry Member *Since 1973*
Owners
Bob and Barbara Ellis

Fresh ocean breezes and sweeping views have greeted guests here for 54 years. The Inn, the Quarterdeck, the 1840 Bulfinch House and a three-bedroom villa all offer country inn amenities. Historic sites abound here on Cape Ann as well as in Boston, Salem, Concord, Lexington, Southern Maine and New Hampshire—all within easy reach. A heated outdoor saltwater pool on a landscaped terrace overlooks the gardens and ocean. Our Veranda Restaurant features New England gourmet cuisine. 1994 Romantik Hoteliers of the Year, AAA, Mobil. Featured on 'Great Country Inns' on Learning Channel.

Traditional Waterside Inn

RATES
26 rooms, $119/$309 B&B. Rooms w/ocean view, 5 suites, 6 Jacuzzis, 1-3 bedroom and bathroom villa. TVs, AC, telephones. *Open March – November.*

ATTRACTIONS
Saltwater swimming pool, tennis, golf, whale watching, deep-sea fishing, hiking, biking, river cruises, kayaking, island cruises, theater, music.

CUISINE
Breakfast and gourmet dinner by candlelight in our oceanfront Veranda Restaraunt. BYOB.

DIRECTIONS
Rte 128 N to traffic light in Gloucester. L on Rte 127 for 4 miles to Rockport's 5 Corners and sharp L and Pigeon Cove sign. Continue 1 mile to inn.

Suitable for Children • Conference Facilities for 35
Non-Smoking Inn • MC, Visa, AMEX, Disc Accepted
Reservations Accepted Through Travel Agents

Marblehead, MA

Harbor Light Inn

781-631-2186
Fax 781-631-2216
www.harborlightinn.com
hli@shore.net
58 Washington Street, Marblehead, MA 01945

Select Registry Member *Since 1996*
Innkeepers
PETER AND SUZANNE CONWAY

©Jim McElholm

WINNER OF NUMEROUS NATIONAL AWARDS for excellence, including *Vacation* magazine's "America's Best Romantic Inns". The inn offers first-class accommodations and amenities found in the finest of lodging facilities. Elegant furnishings grace these two connected Federalist mansions. Formal fireplaced parlors, dining room and bed chambers, double Jacuzzis, sundecks, patio, quiet garden and outdoor heated pool combine to ensure the finest in New England hospitality. Located in the heart of historic Harbor District of fine shops, art galleries and restaurants. AAA ◆◆◆ and Mobil ★★★.

ELEGANT IN TOWN INN

RATES
21 rooms, $105/$195.
Suites, $150/$275 B&B.
Open year-round.

ATTRACTIONS
Salem museums, Harbor District of fine shops, galleries, historic homes and locations, 30 minutes north of Boston.

CUISINE
Extensive continental breakfast buffet. Seven restaurants within two blocks of inn. Wine and liquor within two blocks of inn.

DIRECTIONS
From Boston and airport: Take Rte 1A N to Rte 129 E to Marblehead. Take first R after Texaco station, 1/4 mile to Inn.

Suitable for Children Over 7
Conference Facilities for 15 • Credit Cards Accepted
Reservations Accepted Through Travel Agents

Cambridge, MA

A Cambridge House

800-232-9989
617-491-6300 Fax 617-868-2848
www.acambridgehouse.com
innACH@AOL.com
2218 Massachusetts Avenue
Cambridge, MA 02140-1846

Select Registry Member *Since 1998*
Innkeeper
Ellen Riley

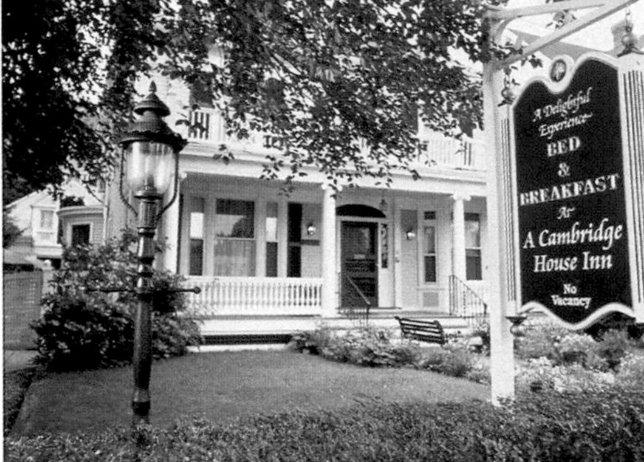

A CAMBRIDGE HOUSE is a unique turn-of-the-century property. Guests of the inn—lovingly renovated to include modern amenities, tastefully emerged with period charm—enjoy personalized attention, sumptuous breakfasts, and in the evening—complimentary hors d'oeuvres and beverages by a crackling fire with jazz music. Each guestroom contains color cable TV, a telephone with voice mail and air-conditioning or heat. Fax service is available and the subway is a five-minute walk away. We do, however, provide off-street parking. To quote *Country Inns* magazine, A Cambridge House is 'Boston's Finest Gem.' AAA .

Elegant In Town Inn

RATES
15 rooms.
10 w/fireplaces, $129/$275 B&B.
Open year-round.

ATTRACTIONS
Area attractions: all that Boston and Cambridge have to offer.

CUISINE
No restuarant on premises. Casual to elegant dining within walking distance and top Boston restaurants only a 15-minute subway ride away.

DIRECTIONS
Direction sheet available

---

1 Guestroom Handicap Accessible • Non-Smoking Inn
Suitable for Children Over 7 • AMEX, Visa, MC, Disc, Diners Accepted

Eastham, Cape Cod, MA

The Whalewalk Inn

800-440-1281
508-255-0617 Fax 508-240-0017
www.whalewalkinn.com
whalewak@capecod.net
220 Bridge Road, Eastham, Cape Cod, MA 02642

Select Registry Member *Since 1993*
Innkeepers/Owners
CAROLYN AND RICHARD SMITH

THE OWNERS OF THIS INN promise you an unspoiled environment on outer Cape Cod, one of the country's most beautiful areas. Located on a back road only minutes by car or bike to beaches, bike trails or Orleans Village. This 1830s sea captain's home has been restored and furnished with antiques from around the world. There are 16 very special accommodations located in five buildings on a three-acre compound of lawns and gardens. All are beautifully decorated and air-conditioned. Most have fireplaces and some have whirlpool baths for two. An imaginative full breakfast is served each day. Come and enjoy our service and heartfelt hospitality.

TRADITIONAL VILLAGE
BREAKFAST INN

RATES
11 rooms, 5 suites,
$165/$300 B&B.
Off season rates available.
Open mid February - mid December.

ATTRACTIONS
Cape Cod National Seashore, Wellfleet Wildlife Sanctuary, Cape Cod Rail Trail Bike Path, whale watching, boating, fishing, golf, tennis, antiquing and theatre.

CUISINE
Breakfast, afternoon refreshments and evening hors d'oeuvres.

DIRECTIONS
Rte 6 to Orleans Rotary, Rock Harbor exit off Rotary, L on Rock Harbor Rd., R on Bridge Rd. Driving time, Boston or Providence—2 hours.

Suitable for Children Over 12 • 1 Guestroom Handicap Accessible
Conference Facilities for 12 • MC,Visa,AMEX Accepted
Non-Smoking Inn • Reservations Accepted Through Travel Agents

Brewster, MA

The Bramble Inn and Restaurant

508-896-7644
Fax 508-896-9332

Select Registry Member *Since 1977*
Innkeepers
Ruth and Cliff Manchester

2019 Main Street, P.O. Box 807, Brewster, MA 02631

WELCOMING GUESTS FOR OVER FIFTY YEARS, The Bramble Inn is nestled in the heart of Historic Brewster village, just a short stroll to Cape Cod Bay and many attractions. Canopy beds, wide pine floors, antique cottage bureaus and lovely art and collectibles adorn guestrooms reminiscent of yesteryear with a bow to the twenty-first century. A complimentary buffet breakfast is served in the elegant dining rooms, or outside in the secret courtyard garden. Dine superbly with chef-owner Ruth Manchester and her talented kitchen for some of the Cape's most innovative cuisine. Featured in the *NY Times, Gourmet, Bon Appetit and Travel & Leisure.*

Suitable for Children Over 8 • AMEX, Visa, MC, Disc Accepted
Reservations Accepted Through Travel Agents

Elegant Village Inn

RATES
8 rooms, $125/$175 B&B.
Open year-round.

ATTRACTIONS
Swimming, biking, horseback riding, tennis, hiking, sailing, whale watching, antiquing, museums and summer theatre.

CUISINE
Complimentary buffet breakfast, prix fixe dinner by reservation. Full liquor.

DIRECTIONS
Rte 6, exit 10 and bear L on Rte 124 to R on 6A for .8 mile. Inn on L.

Brewster, Cape Cod, MA

The Captain Freeman Inn

800-843-4664
508-896-7481 Fax 508-896-5618
www.captainfreemaninn.com
visitus@capecod.net
15 Breakwater Road
Brewster, Cape Cod, MA 02631

BUILT JUST A SHORT STROLL from beautiful Breakwater Beach, The Captain Freeman Inn is a lovingly restored Victorian sea captain's mansion furnished with canopy beds and period antiques. Luxury accommodations include fireplace, two-person whirlpool, garden and pool views. Breakfast is served poolside on the wraparound porch overlooking lush perennial gardens. In cooler winter weather you will dine fireside in the garden-view dining room. Bicycles, badminton and croquet are provided to while away the hours. Venture out to watch humpback whales at play or bike miles of wooded trails. See sunset on Cape Cod Bay. Sail, surf, fish, golf, or rock on our wrap-around porch.

Suitable for Children Over 10 • Non-Smoking Inn
Conference Facilities for 30 • Visa, MC, AMEX Accepted
Reservations Accepted Through Travel Agents

Select Registry Member *Since 1998*
Innkeepers / Owners
CAROL AND TOM EDMONDSON

ELEGANT VILLAGE BREAKFAST INN

RATES
12 rooms, 6 w/fireplaces, $125/$250 B&B.
Open year-round.

ATTRACTIONS
AT THE INN: pool, gardens, croquet, badminton, bicycles. NEARBY: beaches, bike trails, museums, golf, fishing, theatre, gourmet food, antique shops, galleries, hiking, sailing, bird-watching, whale watching, tennis.

CUISINE
Full gourmet breakfast, afternoon tea, winter weekend cooking school with wine-tasting and dinner.

DIRECTIONS
From Rte 6 (Mid Cape Hwy) take exit 10 (Rte 124) toward Brewster. At the end of 124 go R on Rte 6 A, then L on Breakwater. Our driveway is the first one on the L.

Sandwich, MA

Dan'l Webster Inn

800-444-3566
508-888-3622 Fax 508-888-5156
www.danlwebsterinn.com
dwi@capecod.net
149 Main Street, Sandwich, MA 02563

Select Registry Member *Since 1994*
Innkeepers / Owners
THE CATANIA FAMILY

THIS AWARD-WINNING INN in historic Sandwich Village offers guests the romance of the past with conveniences of today. Canopy beds, fireplaces and whirlpool tubs await your arrival. Enjoy a romantic dinner in one of the intimate dining rooms or the warm and friendly tavern. Savor the delicious cuisine, complemented by an award-winning wine list. "Outstanding-worth a special trip."

TRADITIONAL VILLAGE INN

RATES
37 rooms, $109/$199.
17 suites, $179/$369.
Open year-round.

ATTRACTIONS
Heated outdoor pool and gift shop on premises. Antique shops, museums, golf, tennis and health club nearby.

CUISINE
Breakfast, lunch, dinner and Sunday brunch. Tavern on premises. Fine and casual dining menus available.

DIRECTIONS
From Boston, MA: Rte 3 S to Rte 6 to exit 2 turn L on Rte 130 approx. 2 miles, R at fork. Inn will be on L.

---

2 Guestrooms Handicap Accessible • Suitable for Children
Conference Facilities for 125 • Credit Cards Accepted
Designated Smoking Areas • Reservations Accepted Through Travel Agents

Sandwich, MA

Isaiah Jones Homestead

800-526-1625
508-888-9115 Fax 508-888-9648
www.isaiahjones.com
info@isaiahjones.com
165 Main Street, Sandwich, MA 02563

Select Registry Member *Since 1989*
Owners, Innkeepers
JAN AND DOUG KLAPPER

RELAX IN PAMPERED ELEGANCE in this 1849 Italianate Victorian Inn. Exquisitely appointed guest rooms with private baths feature queen beds, antique furnishings, oriental carpets, fireplaces and oversize whirlpool tubs. Two new guest suites have been added to the Carriage House. Located in the heart of Sandwich, you are within easy walking distance of many attractions of the Cape's oldest town. Unwind by strolling the meandering garden paths or relaxing by the original antique-tiled fireplace in the gathering room. A full breakfast, served by candlelight sets a warm tone to start your day. AAA ◆◆◆ and Mobil ★★★.

ELEGANT VILLAGE BREAKFAST INN

RATES
7 rooms, $95/$175 B&B.
Open year-round.

ATTRACTIONS
Museums, antiques, gift shops, beach, whale watching, fishing, golf, tennis, biking and historic sites. Heritage Plantation, the Boardwalk, Sandwich Glass Museum, Thornton Burgess Museum, Dexter Grist Mill, Hoxie House.

CUISINE
Full multi-course breakfast and complimentary beverages.

DIRECTIONS
Rte 6 (Mid-Cape Hwy.) exit 2, L on Rte 130 and bear R at fork for .2 mile, inn on L.

Non-Smoking Inn • Conference Facilities for 10
MC, Visa, Disc, AMEX, Diners Accepted
Reservations Accepted Through Travel Agents

Chatham Cape Cod, MA

The Captain's House Inn of Chatham

800-315-0728
508-945-0127 Fax 508-945-0866
www.captainshouseinn.com
info@captainshouseinn.com
369-377 Old Harbor Road
Chatham Cape Cod, MA 02633

Select Registry Member *Since 1989*
Innkeepers / Owners
JAN AND DAVE MCMASTER

PERHAPS CAPE COD'S FINEST SMALL INN, this historic 1839 sea captain's estate on two acres is the perfect choice for a romantic getaway or elegant retreat. Country breakfasts, afternoon teas, beautifully decorated rooms, all air-conditioned; king and queen four-poster beds, telephones, most with fireplaces and TV/VCR's; some with whirlpool tubs, mini refrigerators, coffeemakers. Enjoy uncompromising service from our enthusiastic international staff and savor the scenic beauty of Chatham Village and the ocean. Mobil ★★★ and AAA ◆◆◆◆.

ELEGANT VILLAGE
BREAKFAST INN

RATES
15 rooms, $165/$325 B&B.
3 suites, $225/$375.
Open year-round.

ATTRACTIONS
Cape Cod National Seashore, antiquing, beaches, boating, bicycling, golf, fishing, tennis, theatre, whale watching, museums, lawn croquet.

CUISINE
Breakfast, afternoon tea, evening snacks.

DIRECTIONS
Rte 6 (Mid-Cape Hwy) to exit 11 S Rte 137 to Rte 28, L approx. 3 miles to rotary. Continue around rotary on Rte 28 toward Orleans 1/2 mile on L.

1 Guestroom Handicap Accessible • Suitable for Children Over 12
Conference Facilities for 18 • AMEX, MC, Visa, Disc Accepted
Non-Smoking Inn • Reservations Accepted Through Travel Agents

Chatham Cape Cod, MA

The Queen Anne Inn

800-545-4667
508-945-0084 Fax 508-945-4884
www.queenanneinn.com
info@queenanneinn.com
70 Queen Anne Road
Chatham Cape Cod, MA 02633

Select Registry Member *Since 1981*
Innkeepers/Owners
DANA AND GUENTHER WEINKOPF

ELEGANT COUNTRY RESORT

WELCOME TO THIS ROMANTIC PLACE of timeless tranquility and complete relaxation. Discover its charm and character of more than 150 years. Find delight in the privacy of your lodgings and the excellent cuisine served by the inn. Enjoy a set of tennis or dip in the large heated pool. Unwind with a relaxing massage in the tranquility of the spa, or just watch the sunset from your balcony or dream in front of a warm fire. Leisurely stroll down the quaint main street, or watch the fishing boats coming in. Let us be your home away from home, while discovering Cape Cod.

RATES

31 rooms, $125/$300 B&B.
Open year-round.

ATTRACTIONS

Private clay tennis courts, garden, heated outside pool. NEARBY: golf, biking, beaches, boating, whale and seal watching, theatre and concerts.

CUISINE

Intimate top-rated dining, poolside snacks, full breakfast. Full selection of wine and liquors.

DIRECTIONS

Rte 6 E to exit 11, L on Rte 137. L on the Rte 28 for 3.5 miles to traffic light. Turn R on Queen Anne Rd. Inn is first R.

Suitable for Children • Conference Facilities for 30
AMEX, Visa, MC, Disc Accepted
Reservations Accepted Through Travel Agents

Falmouth, MA

The Palmer House Inn

800-472-2632
508-548-1230 Fax 508-540-1878
www.palmerhouseinn.com
innkeepers@palmerhouseinn.com
81 Palmer Avenue, Falmouth, MA 02540-2857

ON A TREE-LINED STREET in the heart of the historic district, the Palmer House Inn is an elegant Victorian home. Stained-glass windows, rich woodwork, gleaming hardwood floors and antique furnishings create an overall sense of warmth and harmony. Beautiful beaches, quaint shops, ferry shuttles, and excellent restaurants are only a short stroll away. The innkeepers pamper you with meticulous housekeeping, fresh flowers, extra pillows, fluffy robes, fine linens and good reading lights. The Palmer House Inn is the perfect place to stay, in splendid comfort and gracious care. AAA ◆◆◆◆.

Select Registry Member *Since 2001*
Innkeepers / Owners
KEN AND JOANNE BAKER

ELEGANT VILLAGE BREAKFAST INN

RATES
16 rooms, $90/$225.
1 cottage suite, $165/$250.
Rooms feature king, queen, or double beds, and have a/c, cable TV and phones. Some rooms have whirlpool tubs and fireplaces.
Open year-round.

ATTRACTIONS
Beach activities and water sports, sailing, fine dining, theater, shopping, museums, historical sites, biking, scenic walks, tennis, golf, fishing, whale watching. On-Site: beautiful flower and herb gardens, complimentary bikes.

CUISINE
Full gourmet breakfast served with candlelight and classical music. Afternoon and evening refreshments. Early morning coffee.

DIRECTIONS
After crossing the Bourne Bridge, follow Rte 28 S for approximately 15 miles. A half-mile past the only traffic light, Rte 28 turns L into Falmouth Village. The Inn is on the L just after the turn.

1 Guestroom Handicap Accessible • Suitable for Children Over 10
Conference Facilities for 20 • Non-Smoking Inn • Credit Cards Accepted
Reservations Accepted Through Travel Agents

Martha's Vineyard, MA

Thorncroft Inn

800-332-1236
508-693-3333 Fax 508-693-5419
www.thorncroft.com
innkeeper@thorncroft.com
460 Main Street, P.O. Box 1022
Martha's Vineyard, MA 02568

Select Registry Member *Since 1994*
Innkeepers / Owners
LYNN AND KARL BUDER

THORNCROFT INN is situated in two restored buildings on 3 1/2 acres of quiet, treed grounds on the Island of Martha's Vineyard. It is secluded, exclusively couples-oriented and first-class, with AAA ◆◆◆◆ ratings for 11 consecutive years. Most rooms have working, wood-burning fireplaces and canopied beds. Some have two-person whirlpool bathtubs or private in-room 300-gallon hot tubs. Several offer private exterior entrances. Thorncroft Inn is an ideal honeymoon, anniversary or special couples getaway with seriously sensual surroundings.

ELEGANT VILLAGE
BREAKFAST INN

RATES
14 rooms, 10 with fireplaces, \$180/\$500 B&B.
Open year-round.

ATTRACTIONS
Beaches, boating, golf, tennis, fishing, bicycling, hiking and theatre.

CUISINE
Breakfast in dining room, breakfast in bed, afternoon tea and pastries. Delivery available from liquor store.

DIRECTIONS
Steamship Authority Ferry, Woods Hole, MA; Year-round car and passenger ferry; take R at first stop sign, next R onto Main St., inn 1 mile on L.

1 Guestroom Handicap Accessible • Non-Smoking Inn
MC, Visa, AMEX, Disc, Diners Accepted
Reservations Accepted Through Travel Agents

Nantucket, MA

Seven Sea Street Inn

508-228-3577
Fax 508-228-3578
www.sevenseastreetinn.com
seast7@nantucket.net
7 Sea Street, Nantucket, MA 02554

Select Registry Member *Since 1996*
Innkeepers/Owners
MATTHEW AND MARY PARKER

ENJOY THE WARMTH of our beautiful post and beam Inn, located on a quiet street, in the heart of historic Nantucket. A charming early American ambiance combined with modern comforts creates the perfect atmosphere for you to relax and unwind. Most guestrooms have fishnet canopied beds while our suites have beautiful gas stove fireplaces. We'll serve you an elegant continental breakfast on fine china and suggest you take in a spectacular view of Nantucket Harbor from our widow's walk deck or relax in our Jacuzzi spa. Treat yourself to a truly special accommodation in a very special place...Nantucket. AAA ◆◆◆.

TRADITIONAL VILLAGE BREAKFAST INN

RATES
9 rooms, $75/$225 B&B.
2 suites, $155/$295 B&B.
Open year-round.

ATTRACTIONS
Beaches, bicycling, boating, fishing, tennis, golf, fine shopping and museums.

CUISINE
Breakfast available.

DIRECTIONS
Flights from Boston, NYC, Newark, Providence, New Bedford, and Hyannis. Ferry service from Hyannis to Steamboat Wharf in Nantucket. Three-minute walk from wharf to inn.

Suitable for Children Over 5 • MC, Visa, AMEX, Disc Accepted
Non-Smoking Inn • Conference Facilities for 10

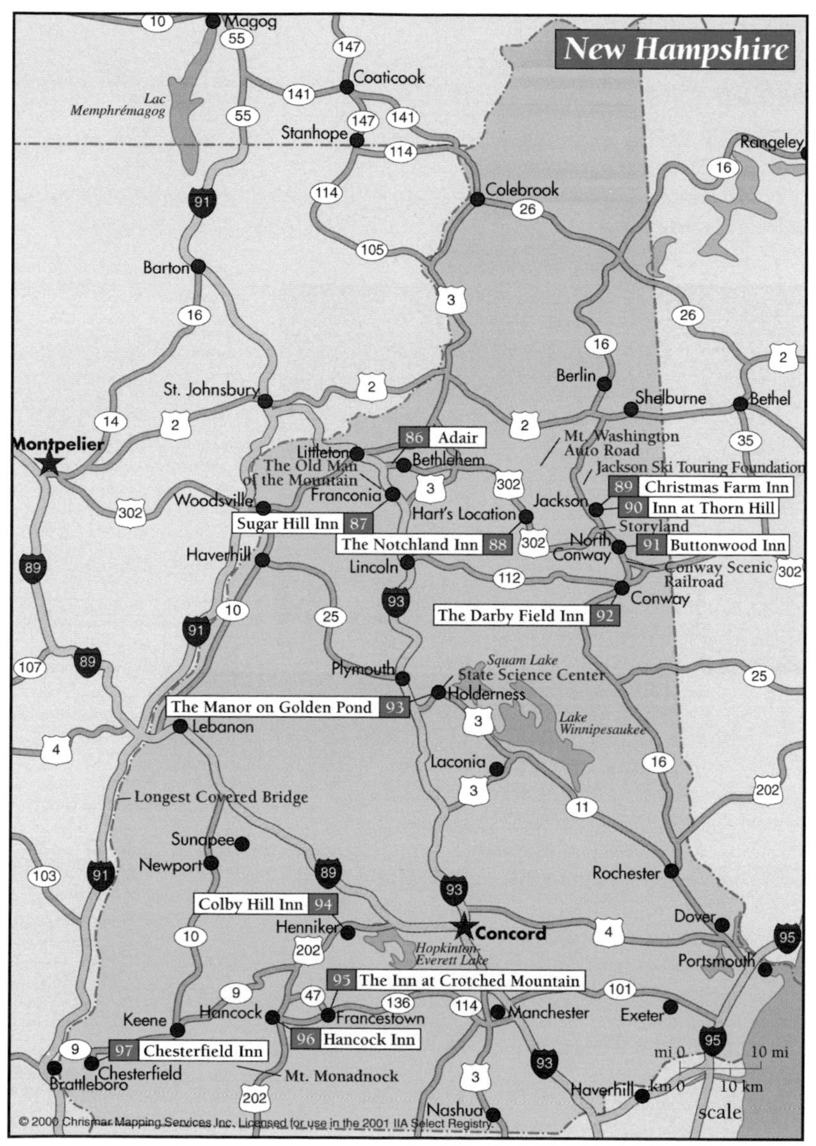
New Hampshire
86 Adair
87 Sugar Hill Inn
88 The Notchland Inn
89 Christmas Farm Inn
90 Inn at Thorn Hill
91 Buttonwood Inn
92 The Darby Field Inn
93 The Manor on Golden Pond
94 Colby Hill Inn
95 The Inn at Crotched Mountain
96 Hancock Inn
97 Chesterfield Inn
Magog
Coaticook
Stanhope
Lac Memphrémagog
Rangeley
Colebrook
Barton
Berlin
Shelburne
Bethel
St. Johnsbury
Montpelier
Littleton
Bethlehem
The Old Man of the Mountain
Franconia
Woodsville
Hart's Location
Jackson
Mt. Washington Auto Road
Jackson Ski Touring Foundation
Storyland
North Conway
Conway Scenic Railroad
Conway
Haverhill
Lincoln
Plymouth
Squam Lake State Science Center
Holderness
Lake Winnipesaukee
Lebanon
Laconia
Longest Covered Bridge
Sunapee
Newport
Rochester
Dover
Portsmouth
Henniker
Concord
Hopkinton-Everett Lake
Hancock
Francestown
Manchester
Exeter
Keene
Chesterfield
Brattleboro
Mt. Monadnock
Nashua
Haverhill
mi 0 10 mi
km 0 10 km
scale
© 2000 Chrismar Mapping Services Inc. Licensed for use in the 2001 IIA Select Registry.

Bethlehem, NH

Adair

888-444-2600
603-444-2600 Fax 603-444-4823
www.adairinn.com
adair@connriver.net
80 Guider Lane, Bethlehem, NH 03574

Select Registry Member *Since 1995*
Innkeepers / Owners
JUDY AND BILL WHITMAN

DOWN A LONG WINDING DRIVE surrounded by rock walls, ponds, gardens and 200 acres, sits a country estate called Adair. Relax in elegance at this White Mountain retreat. It offers spacious public rooms with fireplaces, comfortably appointed guest rooms with antiques, reproductions, air-conditioning, most with fireplaces and fine dining. Enjoy wonderful views of the Presidential Range, stroll through perennial gardens, originally designed by the Olmsted Brothers, or curl up with a good book from the extensive library. Personal attention, cleanliness, flavorful food and proximity to White Mountain activities are hallmarks of Adair. AAA ◆◆◆◆. Editor's Pick, *Yankee Magazine*.

Suitable for Children Over 12
Conference Facilities for 16 • Visa, MC, AMEX, Disc Accepted
Non-Smoking Inn • Reservations Accepted Through Travel Agents

ELEGANT COUNTRY INN

RATES
9 rooms/suites, most with fireplaces and/or mountain views; several with two-person tubs.
$165/$285 B&B
Spacious 2 bdrm/1 bath cottage with fireplace & deck. $345 B&B
Open year-round. One week closures possible in April & November.

ATTRACTIONS
Nearby White Mountains offer countless hiking trails in summer and both cross-country and downhill skiing in winter. Within 1/2 hour are seven golf courses, Mount Washington/Cog Railway, Franconia and Crawford Notches, summer theaters and sleigh rides.

CUISINE
Full breakfast includes cold buffet with granola, yogurt, fruit juices, as well as fresh fruit cup, steaming popovers and hot entree. Afternoon tea at 4 pm with scratch-baked sweets. Fine, new American dining at Tim-bir Alley (Wed-Sun) seasonally.

DIRECTIONS
From I-93 N or S, take exit 40 onto Rte 302 E; take sharp L at the Adair sign and follow the signs to the inn. From the E, take Rte 302 W 3+ miles past Bethlehem and make a R at the Adair sign.

Franconia, NH

Sugar Hill Inn

800-548-4748
603-823-5621 Fax 603-823-5639
www.sugarhillinn.com
info@sugarhillinn.com
SCENIC ROUTE 117, FRANCONIA, NH 03580-0954

Select Registry Member *Since 2001*
Innkeepers/Owners
JIM AND BARBARA QUINN

TRADITIONAL COUNTRY INN

AMBLE UP A SCENIC BYWAY to find the Sugar Hill Inn nestled into the hillside, on 16 acres of woodland, rolling lawns and well tended gardens. A warm welcome awaits guests to this classic Inn. Each guestroom and cottage are tastefully appointed with antiques and reproductions and are impeccably kept. The Inn has earned a reputation for exceptional meals. Guests can enjoy two spacious common rooms with fireplaces or a large veranda with inviting wicker chairs to relax while savoring the mountain views. The surrounding villages are steeped in history and unspoiled beauty, so put away your daily stress and rejuvenate at this quintessential Inn.

RATES
10 rooms, $115/$215
6 cottages, $125/$250
2 suites, $225/$325
Open year-round, except April.

ATTRACTIONS
Hiking, golf, swimming, canoeing, bike trails, nature walks, Franconia Notch State Park, Cog Railway, summer theater, chamber concerts, museums, antiques, craft shops, festivals. Close to three ski resorts, XC touring.

CUISINE
Full breakfast and afternoon refreshments daily. Dinner by reservations. Wine and liquor available.

DIRECTIONS
From I-93 N or S take exit 38 to Rte 18 N. Travel .05 miles L at bridge Rte 117. The Inn is .05 miles up the hill on R. From I-91 N or S take exit 17 R onto Rte 302 E 13 miles on R is Rte 117. 8 miles on the L is the Inn.

Suitable for Children Over 12 • Non-Smoking Inn
Credit Cards Accepted
Reservations Accepted Through Travel Agents

Hart's Location, NH

The Notchland Inn

800-866-6131
603-374-6131 Fax 603-374-6168
www.notchland.com
notchland@aol.com
Route 302, Hart's Location, NH 03812

Select Registry Member *Since 1996*
Innkeepers/Owners
LES SCHOOF AND ED BUTLER

GET AWAY FROM IT ALL, relax and rejuvenate at our comfortable granite manor house, completed in 1862, within the White Mountain National Forest. Settle into one of 12 spacious guest rooms, individually appointed and each with wood-burning fireplaces. A wonderful five-course dinner and full country breakfast are served in a fireplaced dining room overlooking the pond and gardens. Visit with Coco and Abby, our Bernese Mountain Dogs, as well as our llamas. Shopping and four-season activities abound. Secluded, yet near to all the Mount Washington Valley has to offer. Notchland…a magical location.

TRADITIONAL MOUNTAIN INN

RATES

7 deluxe rooms, $230/$285 MAP.
5 suites, $260/$360 MAP.
B&B rates available.
Open year-round.

ATTRACTIONS

Hiking, bird-watching, river swimming, rock climbing, skating, cross-country and downhill skiing, canoeing, golf, antiques, crafts, shopping outlets, ice climbing.

CUISINE

Five-course distinctive dinners Tues-Sun, hearty country breakfast daily. Fully licensed: wine, spirits and beer.

DIRECTIONS

Take Rte 93 N to exit 35, Rte 3 N, go 10 miles to Rte 302, turn R, continue 17.5 miles E on 302 to inn on R.

Suitable for Children Over 12 • Non-Smoking Inn
Conference Facilities for 24 • MC, Visa, AMEX, Disc Accepted
Reservations Accepted Through Travel Agents

Jackson, NH

Christmas Farm Inn

800-443-5837
603-383-4313 Fax 603-383-6495
www.christmasfarminn.com
info@christmasfarminn.com
P.O. Box CC Route 16B, Jackson, NH 03846

IN A SETTING OF MAJESTIC MOUNTAINS, crystal-clear rivers and leafy woods, the cluster of buildings that make up this rambling inn invite you to share the good life. Our innkeepers will warmly welcome you to well decorated guest rooms or our deluxe cottages, many which romance guests with glowing fireplaces and Jacuzzis. Flower gardens, heated pool and sauna will refresh your senses after a day of exploring, or mingle with guests in the Mistletoe Pub before, or after, a masterfully prepared candlelit dinner. Enjoy homemade soups, breads and desserts. AAA ◆◆◆ and Mobil ★★★.

Select Registry Member *Since 1988*
Owner
MICHAEL TOLLEY
Innkeepers
DAVID RODGERS AND BARBARA HIRSCH

TRADITIONAL MOUNTAIN INN

RATES
22 rooms, $88/$145. MAP.
7 deluxe cottages, $110/$145 MAP.
per person rate/double occupancy.
Carriage House, $169/$189 MAP
Open year-round.

ATTRACTIONS
Shopping, hiking, golf, fishing, biking, cross-country and downhill skiing, skating and horse-drawn sleigh rides, all in the White Mountains.

CUISINE
Country breakfasts, candlelit dinners, home-baked breads and desserts. Mistletoe Pub-full bar available.

DIRECTIONS
Follow Rte 16 to Jackson. From Rte 16 to 16 B. Go through covered bridge. 5 miles to schoolhouse on R. Keep schoolhouse to R and go up hill 5 miles. Inn on R.

---

1 Guestroom Handicap Accessiable • Suitable for Children
Conference Facilities • MC, Visa, AMEX, Disc Accepted
Designated Smoking Areas

Jackson Village, NH

Inn at Thorn Hill

800-289-8990
603-383-4242 Fax 603-383-8062
www.innatthornhill.com
thornhll@ncia.net
P.O. Box A, Thorn Hill Road
Jackson Village, NH 03846

Select Registry Member *Since 1998*
Contact
JAMES AND IBBY COOPER

ELEGANT VILLAGE INN

THIS 1895 STANFORD WHITE INN, situated grandly on a knoll overlooking Jackson Village and the Presidential Mountain range, offers antique-filled rooms, three suites with fireplaces and Jacuzzis in the main Inn, a New England Carriage House, three deluxe cottages furnished with Jacuzzis and fireplaces. All rooms are smoke-free and air-conditioned, with sumputous dining by candlelight. Activities are available in all seasons at the Inn and throughout the White Mountains. Outdoor pool, cross-country skiing and tobogganing at the Inn—hiking, golf, tennis, shopping, skiing and sleigh rides are all nearby. Ideal for groups and weddings. Lodging and restaurant AAA ◆◆◆◆.

RATES
19 rooms, $190/$345.
3 deluxe cottages. 3 suites, MAP.
Open year-round.

ATTRACTIONS
HERE: Cross-country skiing, swimming, pool, tobogganing.
NEAR: Hiking, golf, tennis, fishing, horseback riding, ice-skating, snow-shoeing, antiquing, canoeing.

CUISINE
Three-course candlelit dinner, featuring New England Fusion Cuisine. Full bar included. *Wine Spectator* award.

DIRECTIONS
Boston I-95 to Spaulding Turnpike Rte 16 N to Jackson; Portland Rte 302 to Rte 25; Rte 113; Rte 302-16 N Montreal Canada-Can55-I-91/I-93; Exit 40; Rte 302; Rte 16 N-Jackson.

Suitable for Children Over 8 • Conference Facilities for 25
Non-Smoking Inn • Credit Cards Accepted
Reservations Accepted Through Travel Agents

North Conway, NH

The Buttonwood Inn on Mt. Surprise

800-258-2625
603-356-2625 Fax 603-356-3140
www.buttonwoodinn.com
innkeeper@buttonwoodinn.com
P.O. Box 1817, Mt. Surprise Road
North Conway, NH 03860

Select Registry Member *Since 1999*
Innkeepers / Owners
PETER AND CLAUDIA NEEDHAM

AN AMERICA'S FAVORITE INNS AWARD-WINNER, this 1820s farmhouse sits on seventeen secluded acres on Mt. Surprise, just two miles from the village of North Conway. Our guests enjoy a peaceful, rural setting and the convenience of being close to everything. Ten newly renovated guestrooms feature Shaker furniture, wide pine floors, stenciling, quilts and antiques. Breakfasts are second to none. Three-time award-winning perennial gardens surround the inn. Hike or cross-country ski from the backdoor. Borrow a backpack and venture off for the day with an individually prepared itinerary. We are a memorable blend of hospitality, laughter and kindness.

TRADITIONAL COUNTRY BREAKFAST INN

RATES

10 rooms, $95/$225 B&B.
All private baths; one with gas fireplace, two-person Jacuzzi.
Open year-round.

ATTRACTIONS

Mt. Washington, The Old Man in the Mountain, the Flume, the Kancamagus Highway. Find waterfalls and covered bridges. Golf, tennis, hike, bike, canoe, fish, shop, go antiquing. Alpine or nordic ski, snowshoe, ice-skating, take a sleigh ride or relax.

CUISINE

Full breakfast with choice of entree. Afternoon tea. Fine dining within minutes.

DIRECTIONS

I-95 N to Rte 16 N; Spaulding Tnpk to N Conway. In N Conway Village, at light by Horsefeathers Rest, turn R on Kearsarge St. 1.5 miles to stop sign. Straight across intersection, up Mt. Surprise Rd. From N: Rte 302 S. L onto Hurricane Mt. Rd. L onto Mt. Surprise Rd.

---

1 Guestroom Handicap Accessible • Suitable for Children Over 6
Conference Facilities for 25 • AMEX, MC, V, Disc Accepted
Non-Smoking Inn • Reservations Accepted Through Travel Agents

Albany, NH

The Darby Field Inn

800-426-4147
603-447-2181 Fax 603-447-5726
www.darbyfield.com
marc@darbyfield.com
185 Chase Hill Road, Albany, NH 03818

Select Registry Member *Since 1981*
Innkeepers/Owners
MARC AND MARIA DONALDSON

A T THE END OF AN UNWINDING ROAD, guests are beguiled with a spectacular view of the mountains in the White Mountain National Forest. Set at the forest's edge, this 1826 inn is well-known for its fine dining, relaxed atmosphere and friendly hospitality. The massive stone fireplace, the cozy pub, the terrace swimming pool and the well-groomed cross-country ski and walking trails through woods and meadows provide guests with distinctive New England charm during all seasons. Beautifully appointed guestrooms are available, some with fireplaces, Jacuzzis, steam room and balconies. A peaceful setting within easy distance of major ski areas and North Conway shopping. AAA .

TRADITIONAL MOUNTAIN INN

RATES
14 rooms.
\$120/\$240, B&B, dbl. occ..
\$160/\$280, MAP, dbl. occ.
Fireplace and/or Jacuzzi rooms are available.
Closed April.

ATTRACTIONS
Swimming pool, outdoor hot tub, walking and xc-skiing/snowshoe trails, croquet, canoeing, golf, hiking, fishing, rock climbing, downhill skiing, shopping, Mt. Washington Auto Road, Cog Railway and White Mountain National Forest.

CUISINE
Full country breakfast and candlelit gourmet dinner. Fine wines and local and regional microbrews available. Fully-stocked tavern.

DIRECTIONS
Rte 16 N. Turn L .5 mile before Conway on to Bald Hill Rd., 1 mile to inn sign, turn R and continue 1 mile to inn.

Suitable for Children Over 6 • Conference Facilities for 30
Designated Smoking Areas • Visa, MC, AMEX Accepted
Reservations Accepted Through Travel Agents

Holderness, NH

The Manor on Golden Pond

800-545-2141
603-968-3348 Fax 603-968-2116
www.manorongoldenpond.com
manorinn@lr.net
Box T, Route 3, Holderness, NH 03245

SET ON 15 HILLSIDE ACRES AND OVERLOOKING SQUAM LAKE, this turn-of-the-century estate exudes the warmth and charm of a country home. Beauty and allure are reflected in the individually decorated bedrooms; most have wood-burning fireplaces and views, and several have whirlpools for two. Magnificently carved moldings and rich wood paneling in the dining rooms provide a setting of classical elegance for the superb New American cuisine. The Manor on Golden Pond is an unforgettable romantic getaway. AAA ◆◆◆◆ Inn and Dining Room, *Wine Spectator* Magazine Award of Excellence, Editor's Pick - *Yankee Magazine*, Best of New England - Andrew Harper's *Hideaway Report.*

Suitable for Children Over 12 • Non-Smoking Inn
Conference Facilities for 30 • Visa, MC, AMEX, Disc Accepted
Reservations Accepted Through Travel Agents

Select Registry Member *Since 1995*
Innkeepers/Owners
BRIAN AND MARY ELLEN SHIELDS

ELEGANT COUNTRY INN

RATES
25 rooms
Summer/Fall/Holidays, $210-$375 B&B
Winter, $150-$375 B&B
Open year-round.

ATTRACTIONS
On Site: canoes, beach , pool, clay tennis court, lawn games. Nearby: fishing, hiking, golf, skiing, sleigh rides, horseback riding.

CUISINE
Dinner by reservation. AAA four-Diamond Award. Tea 4 pm. Full bar service; *Wine Spectator* Award.

DIRECTIONS
I-93, exit 24, E on Rte 3, proceed for 4.7 miles, turn R just in front of our sign (Less than two hours from Boston.)

Henniker, NH

Colby Hill Inn

800-531-0330
603-428-3281 Fax 603-428-9218
www.colbyhillinn.com
info@colbyhillinn.com
The Oaks, P.O. Box 779, Henniker, NH 03242

Select Registry Member *Since 1993*
Innkeepers / Owners
CYNDI AND MASON COBB
Innkeeper
LAUREL DAY MACK

TRADITIONAL VILLAGE INN

A WARM WELCOME AWAITS in an old fashioned lobby and the cookie jar beckons at this rambling 18th century Inn, a complex of farmhouse, carriage house and barns on five village acres. Sixteen antique-filled guestrooms, four with working fireplaces, each with private bathroom and phone with data port and private phone line. And the food is memorable—from the bountiful breakfasts to the acclaimed candlelit dinners served every night in the gardenside dining room. Chefs Dana Hansen and Steve Golder's creative cuisine continues to bring raves—classic New England scenery abounds around this village on the river.

RATES
16 rooms, $95/$185
Rates based on double occupancy.
Breakfast included.
3 room suite available.
Open year-round.

ATTRACTIONS
Relax with a good book by the fire or in the gazebo. Also swimming, walking, antiquing, tennis, antique books, skiing, birding, Canterbury Shaker Village. Or just enjoy the charm of New Hampshire.

CUISINE
Full breakfast for guests. Dinner every evening for guests and public. Full-service bar with fine wines, beers and spirits.

DIRECTIONS
17 miles W of Concord off Rtes 202/9. S 1/2 mile on Rte 114 to blinking light and village center. Turn R; Inn is 1/2 mile on the R.

Suitable for Children Over 7 • Conference Facilities for 30
Designated Smoking Areas • Visa, MC, AMEX, Disc, Diners Accepted
Reservations Accepted Through Travel Agents

Francestown, NH

The Inn at Crotched Mountain

603-588-6840
Fax 603-588-6623
perry-inncm@conknet.com

534 Mountain Road, Francestown, NH 03043

Select Registry Member *Since 1981*
Innkeepers
JOHN AND ROSE PERRY

THIS 175 YEAR-OLD COLONIAL HOUSE is located on the northeastern side of Crotched Mountain. An awe-inspiring setting and a spectacular view of the Piscatagoug Valley makes all the difference at this out-of-the-way colonial inn. Walking and ski trails through the woods, vegetable and flower gardens supply food and adornment for tables and rooms. Rose Perry's savory home cooking has the added zest of an occasional Indonesian dish. John and Rose, who have been operating the inn since 1973, and their three English Cockers, look forward to welcoming you.

TRADITIONAL MOUNTAIN INN

RATES

13 rooms, 3 with fireplaces, $70/$140 B&B.
Open year-round.

ATTRACTIONS

Swimming pool, two clay tennis courts, cross-country skiing, walking trails, antique and craft shops, summer theatres, ice-skating, hiking.

CUISINE

Full breakfast daily. Wine and liquor available.

DIRECTIONS

From Boston: I-93 N 101 W to 114 N to Goffstown 13 S to New Boston 136 W to Francestown 47 N 2.5 miles L onto Mountain Rd. .1 mile. From N.Y.: I-91 N to Brattleboro Rte 9 E to 31 S 47 4.5 miles. R onto Mountain Rd. 1 mile.

1 Guestroom Handicap Accessible • Suitable for Children
Pets Allowed • Conference Facilities for 13 • Non-Smoking Inn
Reservations Accepted Through Travel Agents

Hancock, NH

The Hancock Inn-1789-NH's Oldest Inn

800-525-1789
603-525-3318 Fax 603-525-9301
www.hancockinn.com
innkeeper@hancockinn.com
33 Main Street, P.O. Box 96, Hancock, NH 03449

Select Registry Member *Since 1971*
Innkeepers/Owners
LINDA, JOE AND CHRIS JOHNSTON
Chef
MICHAEL MACK

TRADITIONAL VILLAGE INN

SINCE 1789, the first year of George Washington's presidency, the inn has hosted rumrunners and cattle drovers, aristocracy and a U.S. President. Over time the inn has seen elegant balls, Concord Coaches and the first rider of the railroad. 'We are used to hearing the steepled clock sound as often as the village gets named one of the prettiest in New England', *Yankee Magazine,* '98. 'One of the top ten affordable luxury inns in the country,' *Country Inns,*'97. AAA ◆◆◆. 'Dinner may be enjoyed by anyone lucky enough to hold a reservation,' *Country Homes,* '97.

RATES
15 antique-appointed rooms with handmade quilts, cable, phone, a/c. 8 with fpl. $120/235 B&B. King/queen/double/twin.
Open year-round.

ATTRACTIONS
The natural beauty of the region is a mecca for outdoor enthusiasts with year-round opportunities to enjoy nature. The arts, inspired by the famous McDowell Art Colony include theater, galleries and music—ah, the music! Premier antiquing!

CUISINE
'...a restaurant known for its outstanding dining,' *Country Inns.* Amidst the glow of candles and a flickering fireplace you will dine in Colonial splendor. 'Shaker cranberry pot roast worth the trip alone,' *Recommended Country Inns.*

DIRECTIONS
From Boston: I-93 N to 293 N. 101 W to Peterborough. R on 202 to 123. Turn L at stop sign and drive down historic Main St. The Hancock Inn is on the R. From NY: I-91 to Brattleboro. Rte 9 toward Keene to 123. Turn R to inn.

1 Guestroom Handicap Accessible • Suitable for Children Over 12
Conference Facilities for 15 • AMEX, MC, Visa, Diners Accepted
Non-Smoking Inn • Reservations Accepted Through Travel Agents

Chesterfield, NH

Chesterfield Inn

800-365-5515

603-256-3211 Fax 603-256-6131

www.chesterfieldinn.com

chstinn@sover.net
Route 9, Box 155, Chesterfield, NH 03443

Select Registry Member *Since 1990*
Innkeepers
PHIL AND JUDY HUEBER

SERVING SINCE 1787 AS A TAVERN, a farm and a museum, the inn's guestrooms today are spacious; some with fireplaces or outdoor balconies, all with private baths, air-conditioning, TV and telephone. Outside, the meadow overlooks Vermont's Green Mountains. Unique, contemporary fine-dining served nightly. Chesterfield Inn is a wonderful place to relax in comfortable elegance.

ELEGANT COUNTRY INN

RATES
13 rooms, $150/$275 B&B.
2 suites, $200/$225 B&B.
Open year-round.

ATTRACTIONS
Arts, crafts and music in Brattleboro and Keene. Swimming and boating on Spofford Lake. Hiking and bicycling.

CUISINE
Breakfast and dinner daily. Wine and liquor available.

DIRECTIONS
From I-91, take exit 3 to Rte 9 E, continue on Rte 9 for 2 miles. Turn L onto Cross Road, then R into our driveway.

Suitable for Children • Pets Allowed • Non-Smoking Inn
Conference Facilities for 15 • MC, Visa, AMEX, Diners Accepted
Reservations Accepted Through Travel Agents

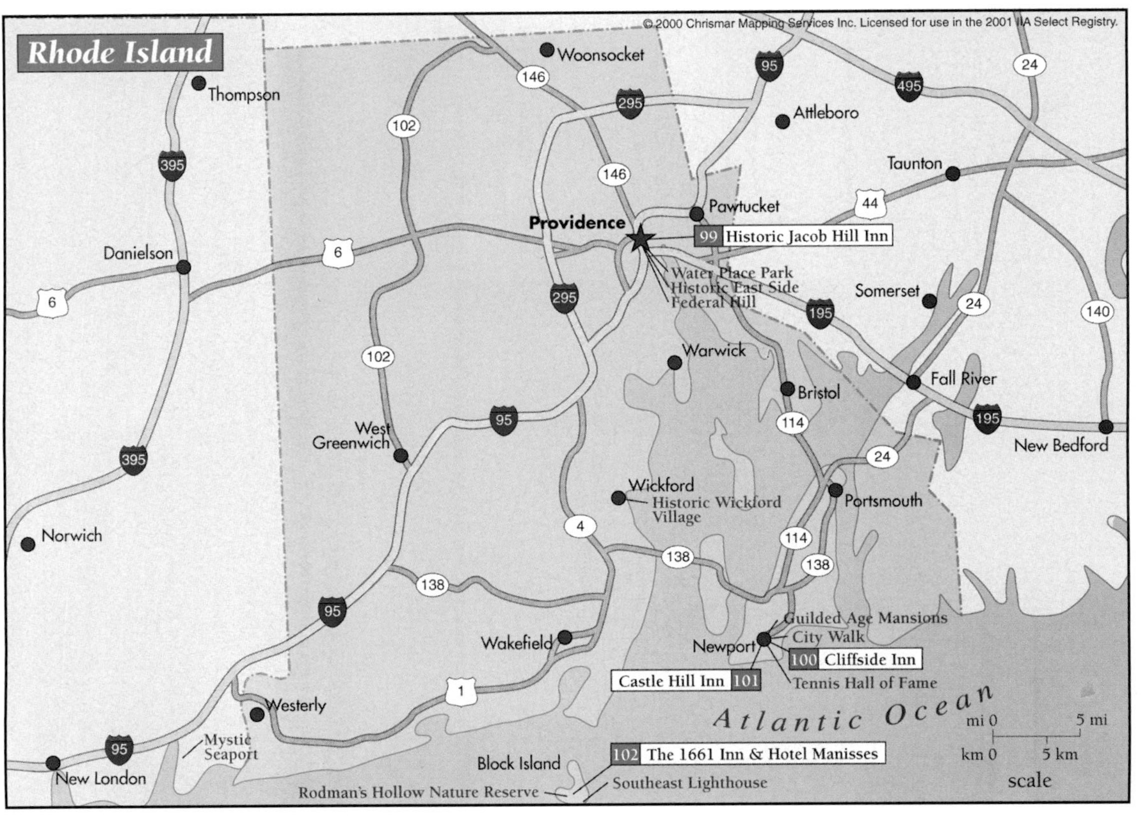
Rhode Island
© 2000 Chrismar Mapping Services Inc. Licensed for use in the 2001 IIA Select Registry.
Thompson
Woonsocket
Attleboro
Taunton
Pawtucket
Providence
99 Historic Jacob Hill Inn
Water Place Park
Historic East Side
Federal Hill
Danielson
Somerset
Warwick
Bristol
Fall River
New Bedford
West Greenwich
Wickford
Historic Wickford Village
Portsmouth
Norwich
Guilded Age Mansions
City Walk
Newport
100 Cliffside Inn
Castle Hill Inn 101
Tennis Hall of Fame
Wakefield
Westerly
Atlantic Ocean
Mystic Seaport
New London
Block Island
102 The 1661 Inn & Hotel Manisses
Southeast Lighthouse
Rodman's Hollow Nature Reserve
mi 0
5 mi
km 0
5 km
scale

Providence, RI

Historic Jacob Hill Inn

888-336-9165
508-336-9165 Fax 508-336-0951
www.Inn-Providence-RI.com
host@Jacobhill.com
P.O. Box 41326, Providence, RI 02940

Select Registry Member *Since 2000*
Innkeepers/Owners
BILL AND ELEONORA REZEK

LOCATED ON A COUNTRY ESTATE, just a ten-minute drive from the Providence Convention Center, Brown University or the Historic East Side. Built in 1722, Jacob Hill has a long history of hosting America's most prominent families, including the Vanderbilts. Recently updated rooms are spacious, all with private bathrooms; some have Jacuzzi tubs. King- and queen-sized canopied beds blend with hand-picked antiques, period wall coverings and Oriental rugs. The gleaming wood floors mirror the romantic flames from the original fireplaces. The elegant surroundings are complemented by the genuine warm hospitality that will make you feel at home.

TRADITIONAL COUNTRY BREAKFAST INN

RATES
5 rooms, 1 cottage $120/$295.
3 romantic whirlpool suites, king and queen-sized canopy beds, fireplaces.
3 multi-bedroom suites.
Phones, TV, A/C.
Open year-round.

ATTRACTIONS
On-site: pool, tennis, gazebo, beautiful sunsets. Nearby: antiquing, golf, nature walk, horseriding, bike path, canoeing, ice-skating, fine shopping, theatre, concerts, movies, State House, Brown University, RISD, museums, galleries, 'Water-Fire', Gondola ride.

CUISINE
Full breakfast, complimentary beverages and cheese plate on arrival. Many fine restaurants nearby for lunch and dinner.

DIRECTIONS
From I-95: Exit 20 Rte 195 E to Massachsetts exit 1 Seekonk Rte 114A. Turn L follow to Rte 44 E. Turn R follow 1.7 miles. Turn L on Jacob St. 120 Jacob St. on L.

Suitable for Children Over 12 • Non-Smoking Inn
Conference Facilities for 12 • AMEX, MC, Visa, Disc, Diners Accepted

Newport, RI

Cliffside Inn

800-845-1811
401-847-1811 Fax 401-848-5850
www.cliffsideinn.com
cliff@wsii.com
2 Seaview Avenue, Newport, RI 02840

THIS HISTORIC SECOND-EMPIRE MANOR HOUSE was built in 1876 by Maryland Governor Thomas Swann, and later owned by legendary artist Beatrice Turner. Located in a quiet neighborhood, it is steps from the famous Cliff Walk, a five-minute walk to the beach and near Newport's renowned mansions. Romantic interiors include 25 fireplaces, 14 whirlpool tubs, antiques, 100 Turner artworks and architectural surprises. Cliffside is noted for its gourmet breakfasts and afternoon Victorian tea served fireside.

Select Registry Member *Since 1997*
Innkeeper
STEPHAN NICOLAS

ELEGANT WATERSIDE
BREAKFAST INN

RATES
16 rooms including 3 cottage suites.
Rooms, $225/$345.
Suites, $315/$500.
Open year-round.

ATTRACTIONS
100 yards to Cliffwalk, one block from sand beach, half-mile from Newport mansions and harbor front shops and restaurants.

CUISINE
Morning coffee and juice, wake-up service to rooms. Full, hot gourmet breakfast. Afternoon Victorian tea served fireside. Handmade evening turn-down chocolates.

DIRECTIONS
From NY: 95 N to RI exit 3 for Rte 138 follow 138 into Newport. From Boston: 93 S to Rte 24 S to 138 S. Inn is on corner of Cliff and Seaview.

Suitable for Children Over 13 • Non-Smoking Inn
Conference Facilities for 16 • AMEX, Visa, MC, Disc Accepted
Reservations Accepted Through Travel Agents

Newport, RI

Castle Hill Inn & Resort

888-466-1355
401-849-3800 Fax 401-849-3838
www.castlehillinn.com
info@castlehillinn.com
590 Ocean Drive, Newport, RI 02840

Select Registry Member *Since 2000*
General Manager
CHUCK FLANDERS

SITUATED ON A PRISTINE 40-ACRE peninsula off Newport's famed Ocean Drive, Castle Hill offers the discriminating traveler the elegance and unparalleled beauty of a first-class resort. Marvel at panoramic views of the ocean and Narragansett Bay from each of the 25 guest rooms. Pamper yourself with luxurious amenities such as large whirlpool tubs with marble surrounds, fireplaces, king-sized down-laden beds with cotton damask linens, fine furnishings with antiques and oriental carpets. The exclusive beach house rooms are nestled on our private white sand beach. Complimentary gourmet breakfast served overlooking the bay and afternoon high tea, gracefully accent the guest's experience.

Handicap Access Available • Suitable for Children Over 12
Conference Facilities for 250 • Credit Cards Accepted

ELEGANT WATERSIDE RESORT

RATES
25 rooms and 2 suites.
$250/$495 in-season.
9 rooms with Victorian decor in the mansion.
6 cliffside harbor house rooms.
2 chalet bridal rooms.
8 beach house rooms.
Open year-round.

ATTRACTIONS
Newport mansions and museums, Newport Waterfront Festivals, Newport Classical, Jazz and Folk Festivals. World-class sailing, fishing and water sports. Beautiful beaches. Historic downtown Newport's great shopping and dining.

CUISINE
Castle Hill offers northeast regional cuisine from our award-winning chef. Lunch, dinner and Sunday jazz brunch. Dinner reservations required. We have received *Wine Spectator* magazine's Award of Excellence in 1996, 1997, 1999, and 2000.

DIRECTIONS
NYC: I-95 N to Rte 138 E. First exit off Newport Bridge. R to 2nd light. R on Americas Cup, 5th light, R on Thames to Wellington. R to Ocean Dr. 3 miles on R, Boston: Rte 93 S, Rte 245, Rte 114 S, to Americas Cup.

Block Island, RI

The 1661 Inn & Hotel Manisses

800-626-4773
401-466-2421 Fax 401-466-3162
www.blockisland.com/biresorts
biresorts@riconnect.com
PO Box I, Spring Street, Block Island, RI 02807

ENJOY THE NEW ENGLAND DECOR of The 1661 Inn and the romantic Victorian charm of the Hotel Manisses. Each room is individually decorated and many rooms feature a combination of whirlpool tubs, decks, ocean views or wood-burning fireplaces. Marvel at the spectacular views of the Atlantic Ocean from the covered porch of the inn. Enjoy fine dining in the casual elegance of the Manisses Dining Room as featured in *Gourmet* and *Bon Appetit* magazines. Stop by and visit the unique garden and farm with many exotic animals including llamas, emus, zebu and more. All rates include a full buffet breakfast, wine & nibble hour and a tour of the Island.

Select Registry Member *Since 1976*
Contacts
JOAN AND JUSTIN ABRAMS
RITA AND STEVE DRAPER

ELEGANT WATERSIDE INN

RATES

Rates $50/$370.
Rooms feature combinations of telephone, whirlpool tub, television, wood-burning fireplace, deck or ocean view.
Open year-round.

ATTRACTIONS

Wide sandy beaches, bicycling, nature walks on over thirty miles of conservancy trails, horseback riding, shopping, dining, yachting, freshwater and saltwater fishing, birdwatching, kayaking and historical lighthouses (featured by *National Geographic*).

CUISINE

Rates include full buffet breakfast, afternoon wine and nibble hour. Delight in a dinner at the award-winning dining room of the Hotel Manisses or enjoy the Bistro Menu of the Gatsby Room. Open seasonally.

DIRECTIONS

By ferry: Pt. Judith (year-round), New London, CT and Montauk, NY. By air: Newport, Westerly, Providence, RI or charters. Contact inn for schedules.

Handicap Access Available • Suitable for Children
Conference Facilities for 50 • Visa, MC Accepted
Designated Smoking Areas • Reservations Accepted Through Travel Agents

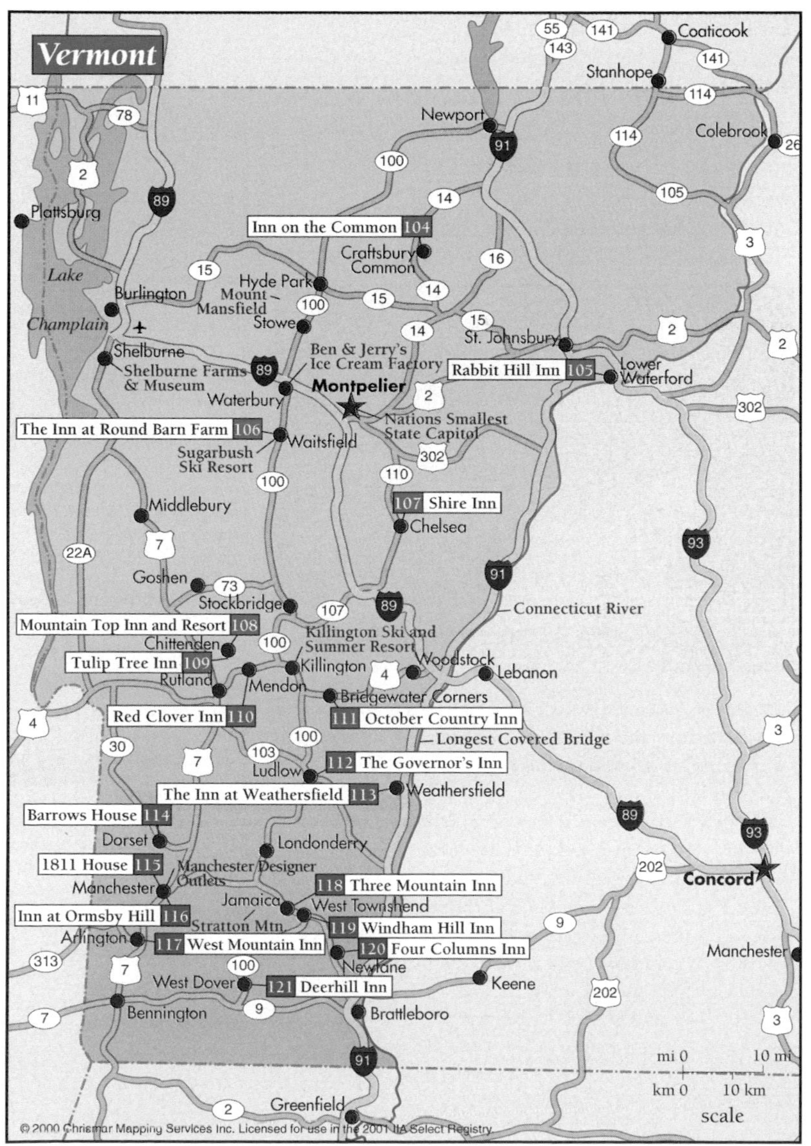
Vermont
Inn on the Common 104
Rabbit Hill Inn 105
The Inn at Round Barn Farm 106
107 Shire Inn
Mountain Top Inn and Resort 108
Tulip Tree Inn 109
Red Clover Inn 110
111 October Country Inn
112 The Governor's Inn
The Inn at Weathersfield 113
Barrows House 114
1811 House 115
Inn at Ormsby Hill 116
117 West Mountain Inn
118 Three Mountain Inn
119 Windham Hill Inn
120 Four Columns Inn
121 Deerhill Inn
Coaticook
Stanhope
Newport
Colebrook
Plattsburg
Lake Champlain
Burlington
Craftsbury Common
Hyde Park
Mount Mansfield
Stowe
St. Johnsbury
Shelburne
Shelburne Farms & Museum
Ben & Jerry's Ice Cream Factory
Montpelier
Lower Waterford
Waterbury
Nations Smallest State Capitol
Waitsfield
Sugarbush Ski Resort
Middlebury
Chelsea
Goshen
Stockbridge
Connecticut River
Chittenden
Killington Ski and Summer Resort
Killington
Woodstock
Lebanon
Rutland
Mendon
Bridgewater Corners
Longest Covered Bridge
Ludlow
Weathersfield
Dorset
Londonderry
Manchester Designer Outlets
Manchester
Jamaica
West Townshend
Stratton Mtn.
Concord
Arlington
Newfane
Manchester
West Dover
Keene
Bennington
Brattleboro
Greenfield
mi 0
10 mi
km 0
10 km
scale
© 2000 Chrismar Mapping Services Inc. Licensed for use in the 2001 IIA Select Registry

Craftsbury Common, VT

The Inn On The Common

800-521-2233
802-586-9619 Fax 802-586-2249
www.innonthecommon.com
info@innonthecommon.com
North Main Street, Craftsbury Common, VT 05827

Select Registry Member *Since 1976*
Innkeepers/Owners
MICHAEL AND PENNY SCHMITT

SET IN VERMONT'S unspoiled and lovely Northeast Kingdom, the inn offers sophisticated cuisine and an award-winning wine cellar. The inn is surrounded by some of New England's finest gardens, with spectacular views of the Green Mountains. Each elegant guest room is individually decorated with antiques and artwork, some with fireplaces. The inn consists of three restored Federal houses, in one of Vermont's most photographed hill towns. In the winter, there is some of the best cross-country skiing in New England—with special packages. An inn for all seasons. AAA ◆◆◆ and Mobil ★★★.

ELEGANT COUNTRY INN

RATES
14 rooms, 2 suites,
$250/$270. $280/$300. DO MAP.
Open year-round.

ATTRACTIONS
Pool, tennis court, lavish gardens, cross-country skiing, golf, canoes, biking, lakes, sightseeing, historic districts and birding.

CUISINE
Full breakfast, five-course gourmet dinner. Fully licensed, superb wine list.

DIRECTIONS
From I-91 N exit 21, Rte 2 W to Rte 15 W, in Hardwick, Rte 14 N 7 miles, turn R to inn. From I-91 S exit 26, Rte 58 W Rte 14 S 12 miles to marked L turn.

Suitable for Children • Pets Allowed
Conference Facilities for 40 • Visa, MC, AMEX Accepted
Reservations Accepted Through Travel Agents

Lower Waterford, VT

Rabbit Hill Inn

800-76-BUNNY
802-748-5168 Fax 802-748-8342
www.rabbithillinn.com
info@rabbithillinn.com
Route 18, Lower Waterford, VT 05848

Select Registry Member *Since 1990*
Innkeepers/Owners
Brian and Leslie Mulcahy

EXPERIENCE WHAT TIME COULD NOT CHANGE in this 1795 country inn classic. This is an enchanting romantic hideaway in a tiny hamlet set between the river and the mountains. Our inn features elegant and uniquely styled guest rooms, many with fireplaces, whirlpool tubs and private porches. We are recognized for award-winning candlelit dining, pampering service, attention to detail and hospitality unlike you have ever known. A true Vermont country home, complete with a swimming pond. AAA ◆◆◆◆ and Mobil ★★★★. Repeatedly voted one of America's 10 Best Inns. Air-conditioned.

Elegant Country Inn

RATES

20 rooms/suites, most w/fireplaces; many with porches and whirlpool baths; $220/$380 MAP (there is no tipping at RHI).
Closed early April and early November.

ATTRACTIONS

Downhill/cross-country skiing, sledding, skating, sleigh rides. Golf, hiking, biking, horseback riding, canoeing, swimming, fishing. Antiquing, shopping, sightseeing, craft/country stores, museums and galleries. Massage services available.

CUISINE

Full country breakfast, five-course gourmet candlelit dinner, afternoon tea and pastries.

DIRECTIONS

From I-91 N or S, exit 19 to I-93 S. Exit 1 R. on Rte 18 S 7 miles to inn. From I-93 N, exit 44, L on Rte 18 N, 2 miles to inn.

1 Guestroom Handicap Accessible
Non-Smoking Inn • Visa, MC, AMEX Accepted
Reservations Accepted Through Travel Agents

Waitsfield, VT

The Inn at Round Barn Farm

802-496-2276
Fax 802-496-8832
www.theroundbarn.com
roundbarn@madriver.com
1661 East Warren Road, Waitsfield, VT 05673

WE INVITE YOU to our elegant, romantic Bed & Breakfast inn, surrounded by lush green hillsides, flower-covered meadows, graceful ponds and extensive perennial gardens. This idyllic pastoral scene, in the heart of the Sugarbush/Mad River Valley, has offered a serene peaceful escape for travelers since 1987. The interior of the inn is memorable; the restoration impeccable. Reconstructed timbers, refurbished floors covered in oriental rugs, walls awash in a palette of rich tones, warm, relaxing gathering rooms and soothing music create an unpretentious atmosphere. Gracious and friendly innkeepers await your arrival.

Select Registry Member *Since 2000*
Owner
AnneMarie DeFreest

Elegant Country Breakfast Inn

RATES
12 rooms, 1 suite $135/$275. Guest rooms are tasteful and luxurious, with comforts of home, yet none of the demands…canopied beds, whirlpool tubs, fireplaces. *Open year-round.*

ATTRACTIONS
Sugarbush/Mad River Valley is pure Vermont! Snowshoeing and xc-skiing on premises, downhill skiing, mountain biking, paddling and canoeing nearby. Ben & Jerry's Ice Cream Factory (14 miles), Shelburne Museum (35 miles). Nearest traffic light 14 miles.

CUISINE
The Inn at the Round Barn Farm takes pride in serving creative breakfasts made with the best seasonal and local ingredients. Dinner is enjoyed at one of 15 area restaurants within 10 miles.

DIRECTIONS
I-89 S exit 10, Rte 100 S 14 miles. L on Bridge St., through covered bridge, R at fork up one mile. I-89 N exit 9, Rte 100B 14 miles. L on Bridge St., through covered bridge, R at fork, up one mile.

Conference Facilities for 200 • AMEX, MC, Visa, Disc Accepted
Suitable for Children over 15 • Designated Smoking Areas
Reservations Accepted Through Travel Agents

Chelsea, VT

Shire Inn

800-441-6908
802-685-3031 Fax 802-685-3871
www.shireinn.com
innfo@shireinn.com
P.O. Box 37, Main Street, Chelsea, VT 05038

Select Registry Member *Since 1986*
Innkeepers/Owners
KAREN AND JAY KELLER

VERMONT BEFORE SKI RESORTS and factory outlets? Come to Chelsea! Dairy farms, forests, picturesque villages, trout streams, covered bridges, birds, deer, friendly folks, unbelievable starry nights. Your own bright, comfortable room with a wonderful wood-burning fireplace in this 1832 mansion. Begin and end each day with fabulous meals. Between, enjoy our custom tours of vintage Vermont, hike the nearby hills, bike or cross-country ski this beautiful valley, swim or tube in the nearby White River. Or...just relax by the fire, on the porch or on our 23 acres with a rocky trout stream running through it. Experience the simpler life...as you'd expect it to be. Come explore—come unwind!

Suitable for Children Over 7 • Non-Smoking Inn
Conference Facilities for 10 • Visa, MC, Disc, AMEX Accepted
Reservations Accepted Through Travel Agents

TRADITIONAL VILLAGE INN

RATES

6 rooms w/pvt baths.
4 w/wood-burning fireplace.
$115/$165 B&B; $185/$225 MAP.
2 BR cottage,
$420/3-days, $575/625/week.
Open May 20-Oct. 23 and Christmas season. Weekends Dec. 15-Feb. 24. Other times on request.

ATTRACTIONS

HERE: Hiking, biking, fishing, sledding, cross-country skiing, just plain relaxing. NEAR: Swimming, boating, rafting, golf, antiquing, downhill skiing, horse riding and sleigh. Or, just explore the uniqueness of this unspoiled Vermont countryside!

CUISINE

Vermont country breakfast. Casual afternoon tea. Romantic five-course gourmet candlelit dinner - just for guests - available weekends, during Fall colors, on holidays or by special request. Our wine cellar of 1,000 bottles offers a fine selection, reasonably priced. Premium beers also available.

DIRECTIONS

I-89, VT exit 2 (Sharon) L, 150 yds. to STOP; R on 14, 7 miles, R on 110; 13 miles to Chelsea. I-91 exit 14; L on 113, 23 miles to end. L, 200 yds. to inn.

Chittenden, VT

Mountain Top Inn and Resort

800-445-2100
802-483-2311 Fax 802-483-6373
www.mountaintopinn.com
info@mountaintopinn.com
Mountain Top Road, Chittenden, VT 05737

Select Registry Member *Since 1987*
Innkeeper/Owner
MIKE AND MAGGIE GEHAN

SECLUDED IN THE HEART of Central Vermont's Green Mountain National Forest, Mountain Top Inn offers a complete resort experience. Summer activities include an outdoor heated pool, tennis, golf and golf school, boating, fly-fishing, hiking, claybird shooting and horseback riding with instruction. In winter, the resort offers cross-country skiing, horse-drawn sleigh rides, sledding, ice-skating and snowshoeing. Spectacular views, relaxing atmosphere and fine dining complete the picture. "A place of serenity with endless activities."

TRADITIONAL MOUNTAIN RESORT

RATES

35 rooms, $168/$226 EP (2), $252/$310 MAP (2).
Cottages and chalets also available.
Open year-round, except April and November.

ATTRACTIONS

Full resort—horseback riding, boating, golf, cross-country skiing, sledding, ice-skating. Museums, antiquing, summer theater and more all nearby.

CUISINE

Breakfast, lunch and dinner. Wine and liquor available.

DIRECTIONS

Chittenden is 10 miles NE of Rutland. N on Rte 7 or E on Rte 4 from Rutland. Follow state signs to "Mountain Top Inn".

16 Guestrooms Handicap Accessible • Suitable for Children
Conference Facilities for 40 • Visa, MC, AMEX Accepted
Designated Smoking Areas • Reservations Accepted Through Travel Agents

Chittenden, VT

Tulip Tree Inn

800-707-0017
802-483-6213 Fax 802-483-2623
www.TulipTreeInn.com
ttinn@sover.net
49 Dam Road, Chittenden, VT 05737

Select Registry Member *Since 1998*
Innkeepers / Owners
Ed and Rosemary McDowell

Just the way you have always pictured a country inn. Here is the Vermont for which you have been searching. We offer you more than a place to sleep and eat. Here you will find the chance to rekindle your affair with life. Relaxing in front of a fireplace or sitting on the front porch with a glass of wine, are the times when memories are made. Once the home of William Barstow, you can easily imagine the family entertaining their friends, the Fords, Firestones, and his partner, Thomas Edison. By earning our share of awards for food, wine and innkeeping, we have kept that tradition of entertaining alive for the past 15 years. This is backwoods elegance at its best.

Traditional Country Inn

RATES

9 rooms: 1w/fp+fp in dbl Jacuzzi,
2 w/fp, Jacuzzi,
3 w/Jacuzzi,
2 w/full bath,
1 w/shower.
$129/$319 B&B or
$159/$409 MAP.
Open year-round.

ATTRACTIONS

Hike the Long or Appalachian Trails, bike, alpine slide, swim, golf, ride horseback, canoe, fish, antique, shop, ski Killington, xc-ski, sleigh rides, relax. We are located in the center of Vermont, so nothing is very far from our doorstep.

CUISINE

Enjoy a very full Vermont country breakfast and a candlelit dinner. Choose from our ever-changing menu, featuring the freshest ingredients. See the difference between eating and dining.

DIRECTIONS

Chittenden is 10 miles NE of Rutland, Vermont. From Rutland take Rte 7 N or Rte 4 E, follow the state hospitality signs.

Conference Facilities for 18 • Visa, MC Accepted • Non-Smoking Inn
Reservations Accepted Through Travel Agents

Mendon, VT

Red Clover Inn

800-752-0571
802-775-2290 Fax 802-773-0594
www.redcloverinn.com
redclovr@vermontel.net
7 Woodward Road, Mendon, VT 05701

Select Registry Member *Since 1998*
Owners/Innkeepers
SUE AND HARRIS ZUCKERMAN

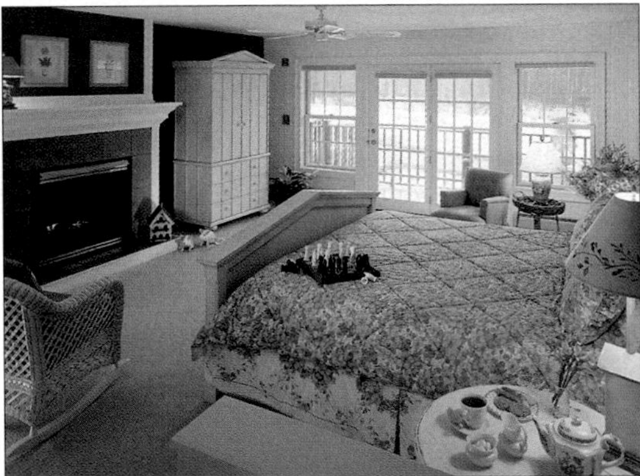

DOWN A TREE-LINED COUNTRY ROAD in the Green Mountains, this rambling 1840s farmhouse estate on 13 acres offers warmth, pampering by caring staff and attentive innkeepers and exceptional gourmet fare complemented by an award-winning wine list. Rooms are attractively furnished with thoughtful attention to detail. Many offer whirlpools for two, gas fireplaces and majestic views. From the inn, explore quaint villages and pastoral beauty, or choose from many seasonal activities. Later dine leisurely and sumptuously from an extensive menu featuring the freshest dairy, produce and game that Vermont offers, and savor this idyllic inn awarded AAA ◆◆◆ and Mobil ★★★.

Suitable for Children Over 12 • Pets Allowed in 3 rooms w/prior notice
Conference Facilities for 20 • Visa, MC, Disc Accepted • Non-Smoking Inn
Handicap Access Available • Reservations Accepted Through Travel Agents

TRADITIONAL MOUNTAIN INN

RATES

14 rooms.
6 w/gas fireplaces,
4 w/dbl whirlpools,
1 w/sgl whirlpool,
1 w/dbl soaking tub
6 w/TV, many a/c.
Summer, $175/$340.
Fall/Winter, $185/$450.
Open Memoiral Day Weekend through April 1st. Closed first 3 weeks in November.

ATTRACTIONS

Swimming pool, hiking, biking, golfing, horseback riding, summer theater, concerts, antiquing, microbrewery tours, farmer's markets, craft fairs, downhill skiing, cross-country skiing, snowshoeing, sleigh rides, ice-skating.

CUISINE

Candlelit four-course gourmet dining from extensive menu by nationally acclaimed chef. Over 370 wine selections from award-winning list and full bar; hearty country breakfast.

DIRECTIONS

5 miles W of Killington turn L from Rte 4 to Woodward Rd., 1/2 mile to inn on L, or 5 miles E of Rutland turn R from Rte 4 to Woodward Rd., 1/2 mile to Inn on L.

Bridgewater Corners, VT

October Country Inn

800-648-8421
802-672-3412
www.octobercountryinn.com
oci@vermontel.net
P.O. Box 66 Upper Road
Bridgewater Corners, VT 05035

RELAXED AND COMFORTABLE, this converted nineteenth century farmhouse near Woodstock offers warmth and intimacy in the finest innkeeping tradition. The scents of baking breads, fresh herbs and homemade desserts fill the inn as Patrick works magic in French Country, Mexican, Italian, Greek and even American cuisines. Swim in the pool, bicycle, hike, ski, shop, sightsee or simply relax by the fire—then dine by candlelight. Away from the crowds, yet close to Killington, Woodstock, Weston and Dartmouth. Bridgewater Corners and October Country Inn are always just around the corner.

Select Registry Member *Since 1992*
Innkeepers/Owners
RICHARD SIMS AND
PATRICK RUNKEL

TRADITIONAL COUNTRY INN

RATES

10 rooms,
$129/$166 dbl. MAP,
$75/$106 B&B.
Special rates for longer stays and single occupancy.
Open nearly year-round, closed April.

ATTRACTIONS

Swimming pool, downhill and cross-country skiing, hiking, cycling, fabulous summer theater, antiquing, shopping, Woodstock, Coolidge Homestead, Dartmouth College, golf, tennis, games and books.

CUISINE

Full breakfast. Family-style dinners, ethnic delights, homemade breads, muffins, desserts. Beer and wine license.

DIRECTIONS

From Woodstock, go 8 miles W on Rte 4 to junction of Rte 100A continue on 4 for 200 yards. Take 1st R (opposite Long Trail Brewery) then R again.

Suitable for Children • Conference Facilities for 20
Non-Smoking Inn • MC, Visa, Disc, AMEX Accepted
Reservations Accepted Through Travel Agents

Ludlow Village, VT

The Governor's Inn

802-228-8830
Phone 800-Governor
www.thegovernorsinn.com
kubec@thegovernorsinn.com
86 Main Street, Ludlow Village, VT 05149

Select Registry Member *Since 1987*
Innkeepers/Chef
JIM AND CATHY KUBEC

GOVERNOR STICKNEY BUILT THIS HOUSE for his bride, Elizabeth Lincoln, in 1890, and it retains the intimate feeling of an elegant country house furnished in the Victorian fashion. With its extraordinary slate fireplaces and antique-filled rooms, as well as afternoon tea, six-course gourmet dinners and full hot breakfasts, the Governor's Inn provides the perfect base from which to explore Vermont. Experience outstanding food, impeccable service and gracious surroundings. Mobil ★★★★...'You will love it here!'

ELEGANT VILLAGE INN

RATES
8 rooms, $95/$195 B&B.
1 suite, $200/275 B&B.
Dinner is available Thurs-Sun.
Open year-round except Dec. 23-26.

ATTRACTIONS
Summer and fall cooking classes, lake activities, Alpine and cross-country skiing, golf, hiking, Priory, theatre, bicycling and front porch rocking.

CUISINE
Full, hot cooked breakfast, tea time, dinner (all private tables), picnics. Wine and liquor available.

DIRECTIONS
Ludlow Village is located where Rte 100 and Rte 103 meet. Inn is S on Main St., just off village green.

Suitable for Children Over 12 • AMEX, MC, Visa Accepted
Non-Smoking Inn • Reservations Accepted Through Travel Agents

Perkinsville, VT

The Inn at Weathersfield

800-477-4828
802-263-9217 Fax 802-263-9219
www.weathersfieldinn.com

P.O. Box 165, Route 106, Perkinsville, VT 05151

Select Registry Member *Since 1982*
Innkeepers / Owners
TERRY AND MARY CARTER

SET BACK FROM A COUNTRY ROAD by a row of stately maples, our 204-year-old inn gently beckons you back to a time long forgotten. Nearby, Christmas card villages, country stores and covered bridges await. Return for tea and savor gourmet dining by candlelight and hearth while surrounded by the ethereal sounds of our Steinway grand. Come morning, delight in poetry while feasting on a hearty buffet. Canopy beds, clawfoot tubs and wood-burning fireplaces round out the ultimate inn experience. AAA ◆◆◆◆. Simply romantic!

TRADITIONAL COUNTRY INN

RATES
10 rooms, 2 suites.
$95/$185 B&B.
Open year-round.

ATTRACTIONS
Villages of Woodstock, Weston and Grafton. National Historic sites, golf, lake and hiking. Downhill and xc-skiing. Summer theatre and outlet shopping.

CUISINE
Five-course evening meal and full breakfast buffet. Full bar. Award-winning wine list.

DIRECTIONS
I-91 N exit 7, Rte 11 W to Rte 106 N. Inn 5 miles on L. I-91 S, exit 8, Rte 131 W to Rte 106 S. Inn is 3 miles on R.

Suitable for Children Over 12 • Non-Smoking Inn
Conference Facilities for 75 • Credit Cards Accepted
Reservations Accepted Through Travel Agents

Dorset, VT

Barrows House

800-639-1620
802-867-4455 Fax 802-867-0132
www.barrowshouse.com
Innkeepers@barrowshouse.com
Route 30, Dorset, VT 05251-0098

Select Registry Member *Since 1974*
Innkeepers / Owners
LINDA AND JIM MCGINNIS

BARROWS HOUSE IS A COLLECTION of nine white clapboard buildings on 12 acres in the heart of a small picture-book Vermont town. Guests have a choice of 28 accommodations in nine different buildings, each with a history and style of its own. All rooms and suites have their own private baths and air-conditioning. Dining at the Barrows House is an informal and delicious adventure in American regional cuisine. Whether with iced tea in the gazebo and English garden or mulled cider in front of a warm fire and historic stenciling, Barrows House extends its welcome. Weddings and family reunions are done with a very personal touch.

TRADITIONAL VILLAGE INN

RATES
18 doubles.
10 suites.
7 w/ fireplaces.
$140/$220 B&B.
$170/$280 MAP.
All with private baths and air-conditioning.
Open year-round.

ATTRACTIONS
Barrows House has two tennis courts, heated swimming pool, xc-skiing, bicycles. Golf and theater packages are available. NEARBY: Recreational areas, Green Mountain National Forest, outlets, craft shops, cultural landmarks.

CUISINE
Dining is relaxing and informal. The quality of your meal will impress you, especially in a village of less than 1,000 people. Speciality of the House is Maine crab cakes, Chesapeake style. Tavern is fully licensed.

DIRECTIONS
Boston: 3 hours.
New York: 4 hours.
Montreal: 4 hours.

Handicap Access Available • Suitable for Children • Pets Allowed
Conference Facilities for 20 • Credit Cards Accepted
Reservations Accepted Through Travel Agents

Manchester Village, VT

1811 House

800-432-1811

802-362-1811 Fax 802-362-2443

www.1811house.com

stay1811@vermontel.net

Route 7A , P.O. Box 39

Manchester Village, VT 05254-0039

THE 1811 HOUSE OFFERS UNEQUALLED AMBIANCE with English and American antiques and decor, in a nationally registered historic building that has been carefully and authentically restored to the Federal period of the early 1800s. Wood-burning fireplaces, oriental rugs, fine paintings and canopied beds are just some of the appointments you will encounter when you stay in the 1811 House. The inn sits on seven acres of lawn containing gardens and a pond, offering an exceptional view of the Green Mountains. The 1811 House is a place to visit in all seasons. Come make a cup of tea or sip a single malt. Relax and enjoy the beauty all around you. Fully air-conditioned.

Suitable for Children Over 16 • Visa, MC, AMEX, Disc Accepted
Non-Smoking Inn • Reservations Accepted Through Travel Agents

Select Registry Member *Since 1998*

Owners/Innkeepers

BRUCE AND MARNIE DUFF
CATHY AND JORGE VELETA

ELEGANT VILLAGE
BREAKFAST INN

RATES

14 rooms, $120/$230 B&B.
Open year-round.

ATTRACTIONS

Hiking, biking, fishing, canoeing, swimming, falconry, Range Rover driving, downhill and xc-skiing, summer theater, music, art, antiquing, museums and shopping.

CUISINE

Elegant full breakfast and award-winning cookies, complimentary sherry afternoons. Fully-licensed British Pub-70 single malts, English ale on tap, wine by the glass and premium liquors and cordials.

DIRECTIONS

In Manchester Center, at junction of Rtes 11/30 and 7A, take Historic Rte 7A S approx. 1 mile. Inn is on the L.

Manchester Center, VT

The Inn at Ormsby Hill

800-670-2841
802-362-1163 Fax 802-362-5176
www.ormsbyhill.com
stay@ormsbyhill.com
1842 Main Street, Manchester Center, VT 05255

Select Registry Member *Since 1996*
Innkeepers / Owners
TED AND CHRIS SPRAGUE

WHEN YOU VISIT THIS RESTORED 1764 manor house, listed on the Register of Historic Places, you will be surrounded with a spectacular setting. Be pampered in bed chambers with canopies, fireplaces and air-conditioning. Luxurious bathrooms with Jacuzzis for two. Indulge in '...the attention to detail, the romantic ambiance...' *Colonial Homes*. Nationally-acclaimed breakfasts served in the magnificent conservatory, with its wall of windows facing the mountains. A patio and porch, with breathtaking views of the Battenkill Valley and Green Mountains, just inviting you to relax and renew. Renowned for comfort, heartfelt hospitality and profound attention to detail. AAA ◆◆◆◆.

1 Guestroom, 3 Common Rooms Handicap Accessible
Conference Facilities for 12 • Visa, MC, Disc Accepted
Non-Smoking Inn • Reservations Accepted Through Travel Agents

ELEGANT VILLAGE BREAKFAST INN

RATES
10 rooms, all with fireplace and Jacuzzi for two, $180/$300 B&B. Peak season premiums apply.
Open year-round.

ATTRACTIONS
Hiking, fishing, golf, cross-country and downhill skiing, bicycling, skating, horseback riding, summer theatre, museums, antiquing, shopping, canoeing, swimming, arts and music.

CUISINE
'...a breakfast that'll knock your socks off...' *Yankee Magazine's Travel Guide*. '...perhaps the best breakfasts in Vermont.' *New England Travel*.

DIRECTIONS
In Manchester Center, at junction of Rtes 11/30 and 7A, take Historic Rte 7A S. Approx. 3 miles. Inn is on L.

Arlington, VT

West Mountain Inn

802-375-6516
Fax 802-375-6553
www.WestMountainInn.com
info@WestMountainInn.com
River Road & Route 313, Arlington, VT 05250

NESTLED ON A MOUNTAINSIDE overlooking historic Arlington and the Green Mountains, the century-old West Mountain Inn provides a perfect getaway. Distinctively decorated guest rooms and common areas, 150 woodland acres with wildflowers, a bird sanctuary and llamas provide space to relax and renew the body and spirit. Miles of hiking trails and the Battenkill River provide seasonal outdoor activities. A hearty country breakfast and an elegant six-course dinner in front of an open hearth complement your stay. The Inn also offers private dining, meeting rooms, unique celebrations of weddings, birthdays, anniversaries, reunions or business meetings.

1 Guestroom Handicap Accessible • Suitable for Children
Conference Facilities for 40 • AMEX, Disc, MC, Visa Accepted
Non-Smoking Inn • Reservations Accepted Through Travel Agents

Select Registry Member *Since 1984*
Innkeepers / Owners
THE CARLSON FAMILY

TRADITIONAL MOUNTAIN INN

RATES
12 rooms, $155/$230 MAP.
3 suites, $155/$281 MAP.
3 townhouses, $155/$261 MAP.
All rooms with private bath and A/C.
Open year-round.

ATTRACTIONS
Hiking, canoeing, tubing, swimming, fly-fishing available from the premises. Golf, tennis, cross-country and downhill skiing nearby. Hiking or wilderness cross-country skiing on inn's trails. Shopping, antiquing, theater, museums and art galleries all nearby.

CUISINE
Full country breakfast and elegant six-course dinner served daily. Sumptuous Sunday brunch throughout the year. Lunch by arrangement. Wedding and rehearsal dinners. Premium beers, fine wines and spirits available.

DIRECTIONS
Vermont Rte 7 N, exit 3, L off ramp, take access road to end, R on Rte 7A into Arlington. One mile then L on Rte 313 for .5 mile, L on River Rd., green bridge over river, inn's driveway on the L, inn at top of driveway.

Jamaica, VT

Three Mountain Inn

800-532-9399
802-874-4140 Fax 802-874-4745
www.threemountaininn.com
threemtn@sover.net
Route 30, Jamaica, VT 05343

Select Registry Member *Since 1982*
Innkeepers/Owners
DAVID AND STACY HILER,
BILL OATES AND
HEIDE BREDFELDT

ELEGANT VILLAGE INN

THE MISSION OF THREE MOUNTAIN INN is all about you—to exceed your expectations, and we hope to have the opportunity. The 21st Century is evident in our splendiferous in-room amenities, our Vermont-fresh cuisine, extensive wine selection and well-stocked pub. Three Mountain Inn is convenient to all of Vermont. Hiking, cross-country skiing, summer theater, Vermont Symphony are seasonal events; while fresh air, starry nights and mountain views are available year-round. Most of all we have innkeepers, chefs and staff devoted to the fulfillment of your desires, and the creation of pleasures and contentment you didn't know existed.

RATES

14 rooms and suites $115/$195.
1 cottage, $250/$295 B&B.
Open year-round.

ATTRACTIONS

Ten minutes to Stratton Skiing, twenty minutes to Manchester shopping, two minutes to West River fishing, seconds to our secluded swimming pool. Walk to Jamaica State Park and hiking, biking and kayaking. Golf, tennis and xc-skiing nearby. Antiquing everywhere!

CUISINE

Full breakfast/dinner. Wine and liquor available. Romantic dining by candlelight in two dining rooms. Wood-burning, 1790s fireplace in each dining room. Menus are diverse and change frequently. Fine wines. Pub lounge. Special dietary needs met. Conference room available for small meetings and functions.

DIRECTIONS

Jamaica is located on Rte 30, 1/2 hr. NW of Brattleboro (I-91 exit 2) and 1/2 hr. SE of Manchester (Rte 7 N to Rte 30 S).

---

3 Common Rooms Handicap Accessible • Suitable for Children Over 12
Conference Facilities for 40 • MC, Visa, AMEX Accepted
Reservations Accepted Through Travel Agents

West Townshend, VT

Windham Hill Inn

800-944-4080
802-874-4080 Fax 802-874-4702
windhamhill.com
windham@sover.net
311 Lawrence Drive, West Townshend, VT 05359

Select Registry Member *Since 1989*
Innkeepers/Owners
PAT AND GRIGS MARKHAM

ELEGANT COUNTRY INN

RATES
21 rooms, $200/$325 B&B.
Peak season premiums apply.
Open year-round except the week prior to the 27th of December.

ATTRACTIONS
HERE: Swimming pool, clay tennis court, hiking and cross-country ski trails, snowshoeing, tobogganing.
NEARBY: Biking, scenic day-trips, golf, downhill skiing, skating, shopping, theatre, horseback riding, antiquing.

CUISINE
Full breakfast and daily afternoon refreshments. Dinner by reservation. Wine and liquor available.

DIRECTIONS
I-91 N to Brattleboro exit 2, follow signs to Rte 30, 21.5 miles NW to West Townshend. Turn R onto Windham Hill Rd., 1.3 miles, follow sign to inn.

WINDHAM HILL INN SITS ON 160 ACRES at the end of a Green Mountain hillside country road, surrounded by rock-wall bordered fields and forests and breathtaking views. Friendly innkeepers and staff welcome you to this country estate with its sparkling rooms, memorable gourmet meals, relaxing ambiance and closeness to nature. Relax in four elegantly furnished common rooms with wood-burning fireplaces, an 1888 Steinway grand piano and an 800-disk CD library. Guest rooms feature antiques, locally crafted furnishings, hardwood floors and oriental rugs. Centrally air-conditioned throughout. Close to abundant Southern Vermont events and activities.

---

1 Guestroom Handicap Accessible • Suitable for Children Over 12
Conference Facilities for 35 • Visa, MC, AMEX, Disc Accepted
Non-Smoking Inn • Reservations Accepted Through Travel Agents

Newfane, VT

Four Columns Inn

800-787-6633
802-365-7713 Fax 802-365-0022
www.fourcolumnsinn.com
innkeeper@fourcolumnsinn.com
P.O. Box 278, Newfane, VT 05345

Select Registry Member *Since 2000*
Innkeepers/Owners
PAM AND GORTY BALDWIN

THE FOUR COLUMNS INN was lovingly built in 1832 by Pardon Kimball to replicate the childhood home of his southern wife. Today, that home is an elegant country inn with 15 stunning rooms and suites, many with fireplaces, two-person whirlpool and soaking tubs. All rooms have private baths. Situated on the historic Newfane Green (unchanged since the 1830s), the property includes 150 acres of rolling hills, an inviting stream, trout-filled ponds and exquisite gardens. The inn is rated Three Diamonds by AAA and the restaurant is rated Four Diamonds by AAA. The property also has a pool and wonderful hiking trails. Come and escape to southern Vermont!

ELEGANT COUNTRY INN

RATES

9 rooms, \$115/\$195.
6 suites, \$195/\$340.
All with private baths and showers.
Suites have whirlpool tubs.
Ten rooms have fireplaces.
Open year-round.

ATTRACTIONS

ON SITE: hiking, swimming.
NEARBY: biking, golfing, hiking, fishing, canoeing, kayaking, tennis, horseback riding, alpine and xc-skiing, sleigh rides, ice-skating, snowmobiling, snowshoeing, shopping, antiquing.

CUISINE

Four Diamond restaurant. Chef: Greg Parks. Cuisine: a combination of New American, Asian and French. Extensive wine list. Fully-stocked bar. Tavern and dining room handicap accessible. Awards: DiRona, James Beard House.

DIRECTIONS

I-91 to VT exit 2. Turn L at end of exit ramp onto Western Ave. Go 1/2 mile, turn L onto Cedar St. Go to 3rd stop sign. Turn L onto VT Rte 30 N. Go 11 miles. We are on the Newfane Green behind the county courthouse.

Suitable for Children • Pets Allowed • Non-Smoking Inn
Conference Facilities for 45 • Visa, MC, AMEX, Disc, Diners, CB Accepted
Reservations Accepted Through Travel Agents

West Dover, VT

Deerhill Inn

800-99DEER9
802-464-3100 Fax 802-464-5474
www.deerhill.com
deerhill@sover.net
P.O. Box 136 Valley View Road
West Dover, VT 05356

Select Registry Member *Since 1999*
Innkeepers / Owners / Chef
LINDA AND MICHAEL ANELLI

CHOSEN "one of the most romantic places in the world," the Deerhill Inn sits on a hillside overlooking a quintessential Vermont village and offers panoramic views of the Green Mountains. Guest rooms (including *Country Inn* Magazine's Room of the Year) have private baths, designer linens, terry robes, private porches and complimentary breakfast with newspapers. The inn's impressive art gallery, secluded 'grotto' pool and lush gardens complete the experience. Chef-owned and operated and only four hours from Manhattan and two and one-half hours from Boston.

ELEGANT MOUNTAIN INN

RATES
15 rooms and suites, $120/$285 B&B. $200/$365 MAP. Special packages and off-season discounts. Limited smoking. *Open year-round.*

ATTRACTIONS
Downhill and xc-skiing, pool, tennis, biking, fishing, state parks, historical sites, golf and airport close-by, horseback riding, sleigh rides, antiques, music and shopping. Personalized itineraries our forte!

CUISINE
Full menu at breakfast, award-winning dinner menu and *Wine Spectator* award-winning wine list. Full lounge featuring Vermont microbreweries. Chosen one of the 25 best chef-owned inns in the U.S. by *Conde Nast Traveler* April 1999.

DIRECTIONS
From I-91, VT exit 2 (Brattleboro) to Rte 9 W 20 miles to Rte 100 N 6 miles to Valley View Rd., up hill 200 yards.

Suitable for Children Over 8 • Designated Smoking Areas
Conference Facilities for 30 • MC, Visa, AMEX Accepted
Reservations Accepted Through Travel Agents

The Mid-Atlantic

The Mid-Atlantic is stunning in the springtime. In March and April the landscape is "greening up." You can drive leisurely through the soft rolling hills of the Virginias where the air is rich and fresh after brief spring showers. Travel on into New York, Pennsylvania, Maryland or New Jersey. Sunrays christen the landscape, and it's proper to move leisurely. It's slow-dance time, so don't push the river. You're in the countryside now. About you, the landscape is cloaked in history, and the promise of a great meal spurs you onward.

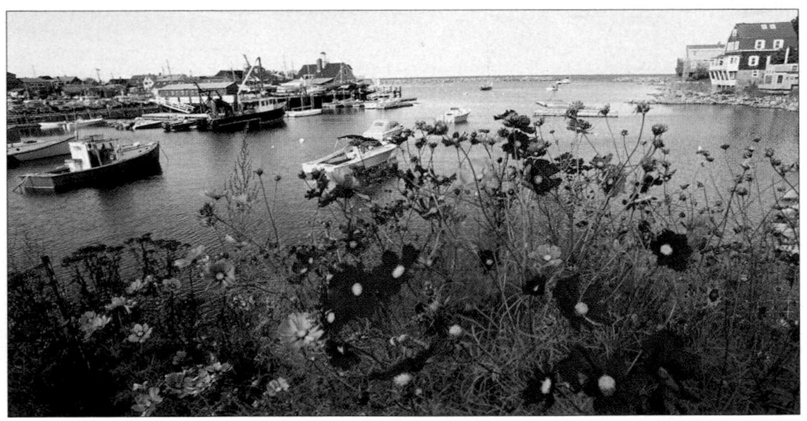

IF YOU—OUR GUEST—choose a Plantation Inn from the *Select Registry*, arrive early enough so that you can explore the neighborhood. Along the way, spacious estates are dappled with magnificent oaks that suggest another time and place. Monticello is nearby. Bright Atlantic sunshine trickles through the fat, lush branches. The front porch of the Country Inn is antebellum; the house speaks to Select Registry comfort. One can almost imagine the formal gowns and lavish parlors of another era. Romantics remember Rhett Butler and Scarlet O'Hara.

The red wines of New York are splendid, with fruity bouquets and deep ruby lusters. A chef has encrusted a rack of lamb with fresh herbs from the Inn's garden. A discerning guest might sip local cabernet. Wild greens grace a decorated plate, and a perfect sauce reduced from meat drippings and red wine curls gracefully beneath the entrée.

As you travel north you will find more of that famous Innkeeper's hospitality. A traveler is awestruck by the avalanche of rivers, weeping watertrails and waterfalls. At one of our Inns, you may choose to test local trout garnished with wild garlic greens and forest edibles. An Innkeeper in Pennsylvania even smokes his own meats. Oyster mushrooms are in season. Sautéed with homemade pasta, fresh herbs and a splash of wine and cream, they are delectable.

With regularity, the cuisine delights and surprises. Our Inns specialize in regional cuisine. Many have a story to tell that involves the earth and local custom and rich history. Many of the Innkeepers prepare their own cuisine. Ethnic specialties abound.

You've found a new friend in the *Select Registry*. Along the way, a familiar message beckons: Come to the Mid-Atlantic. Where you travel, the *Select Registry* leads the way.

"Friendliness and personality, surpassed their excellent rating. Hosts were so gracious—everything was fabulous. Can't wait to go there again."

—Sue Wells, Magnolia, TX

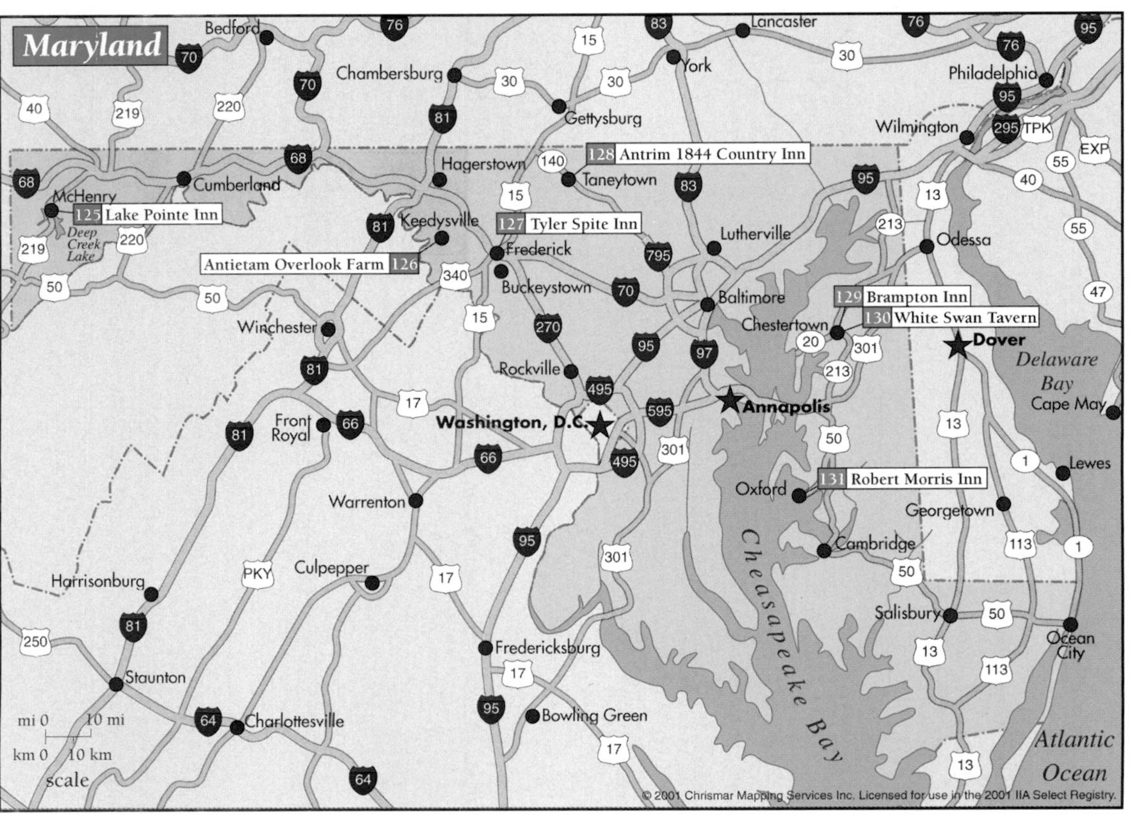
Maryland
125 Lake Pointe Inn
126 Antietam Overlook Farm
127 Tyler Spite Inn
128 Antrim 1844 Country Inn
129 Brampton Inn
130 White Swan Tavern
131 Robert Morris Inn
Bedford
Chambersburg
Gettysburg
York
Lancaster
Philadelphia
Wilmington
McHenry
Deep Creek Lake
Cumberland
Hagerstown
Taneytown
Keedysville
Frederick
Buckeystown
Lutherville
Odessa
Baltimore
Chestertown
Dover
Delaware Bay
Cape May
Winchester
Rockville
Annapolis
Washington, D.C.
Front Royal
Lewes
Oxford
Georgetown
Warrenton
Cambridge
Harrisonburg
Culpepper
Salisbury
Ocean City
Fredericksburg
Staunton
Charlottesville
Bowling Green
Cheasapeake Bay
Atlantic Ocean
mi 0 10 mi
km 0 10 km
scale
© 2001 Chrismar Mapping Services Inc. Licensed for use in the 2001 IIA Select Registry.

Deep Creek Lake, MD

Lake Pointe Inn

800-523-LAKE
301-387-0111 Fax 301-387-0190
www.deepcreekinns.com
info@deepcreekinns.com
174 Lake Pointe Drive, Deep Creek Lake, MD 21541

Select Registry Member *Since 2000*
Innkeeper
CAROLINE MCNIECE

THE LAKE POINTE INN, the oldest house on Deep Creek Lake in Western Maryland, is perched just 13 feet from water's edge and is located across from the Wisp Ski/Golf Resort. The Mission-style furnishings, ironwork and pottery are handcrafted—true to the Arts and Crafts tradition. Relax by the nine foot stone fireplace in the Great Room or rock in one of our chairs on our wraparound porch and take in the two-mile view down Marsh Run Cove. Enjoy the outdoor hot tub or the quiet cove with a private dock for swimming, boating or fishing. Tour the area with the Inn's complimentary bikes, canoes and kayak. Golf, tennis, hiking, downhill/xc-skiing are within walking distance.

Suitable for Children Over 16 • Non-Smoking Inn
Conference Facilities for 20 • Visa, MC, Disc Accepted
Reservations Accepted Through Travel Agents

TRADITIONAL WATERSIDE BREAKFAST INN

RATES

8 guestrooms, $118/$189 dbl. Each room has a private bath, individually controlled heat, telephone with private number, down comforter, television and VCR.
Closed Christmas Eve.

ATTRACTIONS

Garrett County is rich with state parks, forests, Amish farms, waterfalls, rushing rivers and swampy primeval glades. Summer temperatures are 70-85 with no biting insects and annual snowfall is 100 inches. Frank Lloyd Wright's *Falling Water* is nearby.

CUISINE

Full breakfast included, hors d'oeuvres served daily, special dinners served to Inn guests on three-day holiday weekends.

DIRECTIONS

From I-68 in Western Maryland, take Rte 219 S. Follow 219 S for 12.5 miles; R turn onto Sang Run Rd.; go 2 blocks to a L at Marsh Hill Rd.; 1/4 mile just past the Wisp Resort, L onto Lake Pointe Dr.

Keedysville, MD

Antietam Overlook Farm

800-878-4241
301-432-4200 Fax 301-432-5230
antietamoverlookfarm@erols.com
www.selectregistry.com
P.O. Box 30, Keedysville, MD 21756

©Roger Miller

OUR 95-ACRE MOUNTAINTOP FARM overlooking Antietam National Battlefield has extraordinary views of four states. The hand-hewn timber framing, rough-sawn walls and stone fireplaces juxtaposed to the softly flowered furnishings and fine crystal create a warm, comfortable atmosphere. Spacious suites include fireplaces, queen beds, sumptuous bubble baths and private screened porches. While our seclusion and tranquility are unparalleled, many guests also enjoy visiting the neighboring Civil War battlefields at Gettysburg, Bull Run and Harpers Ferry.

Select Registry Member *Since 1992*
Innkeepers/Owners
BARBARA AND JOHN DREISCH

TRADITIONAL MOUNTAIN RETREAT/LODGE

RATES
6 rooms, $115/$165 B&B.
Open year-round.

ATTRACTIONS
Walking tours, antiquing, Civil War sites, river recreation, hiking and bird-watching.

CUISINE
Memorable country breakfast, complimentary beverages, wine and liqueurs (not for sale).

DIRECTIONS
Located in the Western Maryland Mountains just over one hour W of Baltimore and Washington, D.C. Call for directions and availability.

Suitable for Children Over 12 • Visa, MC, AMEX, Disc Accepted
Non-Smoking Inn • Reservations Accepted Through Travel Agents

Frederick, MD

Tyler Spite Inn

301-831-4455
Fax 301-662-4185

Select Registry Member *Since 1993*
Innkeepers/Owners
BILL AND ANDREA MYER

112-114 West Church Street, Frederick, MD 21701

A ROMANTIC 1814 INN located in the heart of Frederick's Historic District. Spacious, beautifully appointed rooms with 14-foot ceilings, marble fireplaces, oriental carpets, comfortable antique furnishings and paintings captivate our guests who are looking for the ultimate in romanticism. Walled gardens replete with color, entice guests for a leisurely stroll. A stay is complete once you ascend from the carriage block located at the front door for a horse-drawn carriage tour through Frederick's quaint city.

ELEGANT IN TOWN BREAKFAST INN

RATES
3 rooms.
6 suites, $200/$250/$300 B&B.
Open year-round.

ATTRACTIONS
Swimming pool, hiking, tennis, biking, golf, museum, antiquing and performing arts theatre within one block at the Weinberg Center.

CUISINE
Full breakfast and tea. 20 restaurants 1.5 blocks away.

DIRECTIONS
Rte 70 to Market St., L on 2nd St., 2 blocks and L on Record St., 2 blocks at corner of Church St.

1 Guestroom Handicap Accessible
Conference Facilities for 25 • Visa, MC Accepted
Reservations Accepted Through Travel Agents

Taneytown, MD

Antrim 1844 Country Inn

800-858-1844

410-756-6812 Fax 410-756-2744

www.antrim1844.com

antrim1844@erols.com

30 Trevanion Road, Taneytown, MD 21787

Select Registry Member *Since 1993*

Innkeepers/Owners

DOROTHY AND RICHARD MOLLETT

General Manager

JAY KRAMER

ELEGANT COUNTRY INN

RATES

13 guest rooms.
9 suites, $150/$350.
Open year-round.

ATTRACTIONS

Gettysburg, antiquing, hiking, golf, tennis, swimming, croquet, bicycling, relaxing.

CUISINE

Five-course, fine dining, beginning with hors d'oeuvres party, gourmet breakfast, continental tray at your door with newspaper. Full bar and extensive wine list. $55.00 prix fixe.

DIRECTIONS

From Washington DC: I-495 to I-270 W; 15 N to 140 E to Taneytown through light; 1 block and bear R on Trevanion Rd. From Baltomore/BWI: I-695 N to 795 W to 140 W to Taneytown; L after the 2nd Farmers & Mechanics (F&M) Bank.

ONE OF THE MOST PRESTIGIOUS INNS in the country, Antrim 1844's antebellum ambience and nationally acclaimed cuisine has earned the inn a place in connoisseurs' hearts. Chef Lynn Kennedy-Tilyou, C.E.C., has been honored by the James Beard Foundation for her creativity and presentation. Guest rooms/suites are appointed with canopy featherbeds, antiques, fireplaces and/or Jacuzzis. Suites have private sitting rooms, decks and luxurious bathrooms and amenities. Endless special services spoil even the most discriminating traveler. If you are near Baltimore and Washington, D.C., stop by—we are Maryland's best-kept secret. Top Ten Inn *Country Inn, Zagat* Excellent, Dirona; Best of Excellence *Wine Spectator.*

Handicap Access Available
Conference Facilities for 50 • Credit Cards Accepted
Reservations Accepted Through Travel Agents

Chestertown, MD

Brampton Inn

410-778-1860
Fax 410-778-1805
www.bramptoninn.com
innkeeper@bramptoninn.com
25227 Chestertown Road, Chestertown, MD 21620

Select Registry Member *Since 2001*
Innkeepers/Owners
DANIELLE AND MICHAEL HANSCOM

BRAMPTON IS A MAGNIFICENT 1860 NATIONAL REGISTER PLANTATION house that sits in serene splendor amid towering trees on 35 acres of lush landscape, forest and fields just outside historic Chestertown, on Maryland's Eastern Shore. Guest and common rooms are spacious and feature original floors, windows, doors, and mantles and are appointed with antiques, oriental rugs and live plants. Wood burning fireplaces and whirlpools in most guestrooms assure a romantic and comfortable stay. Attention to detail, personal service and friendly innkeepers will make your visit a relaxed and memorable one. "Meticulously restored, in a pastoral setting…" *The New York Times.*

ELEGANT COUNTRY BREAKFAST INN

RATES

8 rooms, $135/$225
2 suites, $165/$250
Beautiful, spacious rooms featuring simple elegance and attention to detail. Romantic wood burning fireplaces and whirlpools.
Open year-round.

ATTRACTIONS

Historic Chestertown, fine-dining, antiquing, sailing, bicycling, horseback riding, canoeing, kayaking, bird-watching, golf, tennis, sporting clays, fishing, crabbing, beaches all nearby.

CUISINE

Full gourmet breakfast with individual table service. Afternoon high-tea buffet. Cookie jar!

DIRECTIONS

0.9 miles outside of Chestertown on Rte 20 South.

---

1 Guestroom Handicap Accessible • Suitable for Children
Conference Facilities for 16 • Non-Smoking Inn
MC, Visa, Disc Accepted

Chestertown, MD

The White Swan Tavern

410-778-2300
Fax 410-778-4543
www.chestertown.com/whiteswan/
whiteswan@vtechworld.com
231 High Street, Chestertown, MD 21620

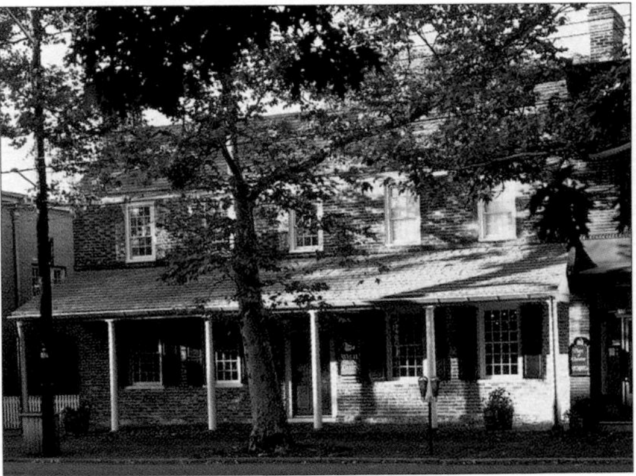

THE WHITE SWAN has been a familier landmark in Chestertown since pre-revolutionary days. Close to the great Eastern cities, yet quietly nestled in the history of Maryland's Eastern shore, the Inn is for those who treasure serene streets, birdsong mornings, impeccable service and the grace of New World tradition. All rooms are elegantly appointed with antiques, reproductions and artwork within a museum quality restoration. Guests enjoy working fireplaces in our common rooms, a lovely garden terrace and meadow, central heat, air-conditioning, and off-street parking.

Select Registry Member *Since 2001*
General Manager / Innkeepers
MARY SUSAN MAISEL
WAYNE MCGUIRE

ELEGANT IN TOWN BREAKFAST INN

RATES

4 Rooms $120/$160
2 Suites $180/$200
Charming rooms furnished with period pieces, each with private bath, combine authenticity with warmth and comfort.
Closed one week in mid-August.

ATTRACTIONS

HERE: museum, garden terrace, game room, afternoon tea.
NEARBY: historic tours, shops, antiques, biking, swimming, boating, fishing, horses, nature walks, birding, sporting clays, hunting, tennis, golf, concerts and plays.

CUISINE

Complimentary continential breakfast, afternoon tea, fruit basket and wine. Fine Restaurants and cafe's within walking distance.

DIRECTIONS

Rt. 213 to Chestertown. W on Cross St. L on High St. White Swan on R. Ring Doorbell.

Handicap Access Available • Suitable for Children
Non-Smoking Inn • Visa, MC Accepted

Oxford, MD

Robert Morris Inn

410-226-5111
Fax 410-226-5744
www.robertmorrisinn.com

314 North Morris Street, P.O. Box 70
Oxford, MD 21654

CHESAPEAKE BAY AND THE TRED AVON RIVER play a big part in the life of this Eastern Shore country-romantic 1710 Inn. Delicacies from the bay are featured in the nationally acclaimed seafood restaurant, and the Tred Avon offers lovely views from many of the rooms and porches. Main Inn rooms are quaint and charming including four original rooms dating back to 1710. Relaxing in a natural environment are here in the colonial waterside village of Oxford. James A. Michener, author of *Chesapeake*, rated the Robert Morris Inn's crab cakes the highest of any restaurant on the Eastern Shore.

(View from Sandaway property.)

1 Guestroom Handicap Accessible • Suitable for Children Over 10
Conference Facilities for 10 • MC, Visa, AMEX Accepted
Non-Smoking Inn • Reservations Accepted Through Travel Agents

Select Registry Member *Since 1970*
Owners
WENDY AND KEN GIBSON
Innkeeper
JAY GIBSON

TRADITIONAL WATERSIDE INN

RATES

35 rooms, $110/$280 EP.
Private bath. Many rooms are located on the waterfront Sandaway property. $40 savings midweek.
Open April-November.

ATTRACTIONS

Oxford is near the towns of Easton, St. Michaels and Tilghman Island. Experience antiquing, biking, golf, sailing, historic car ferry, Chesapeake Bay Maritime Museum and Blackwater Wildlife Refuge. Come see the wildlife, watermen and sailboats.

CUISINE

April-November, open daily. Breakfast, lunch, dinner. (Breakfast not included in rate). Dining areas include: dining room w/historic murals, rustic taproom and colonial tavern. James Michener rated our crab cakes the best on the shore. Wine and spirits available.

DIRECTIONS

Hwy 301 to Rte 50 E. Turn R on Rte 322 for 3.4 miles, turn R on Rte 333 for 9.6 miles to inn. 1 hour from Annapolis 1 1/2 hours from D.C. 1 3/4 hours from Baltimore 2 1/2 hours from Philadelphia. *Speed limit in town is 25 mph and is strictly enforced.

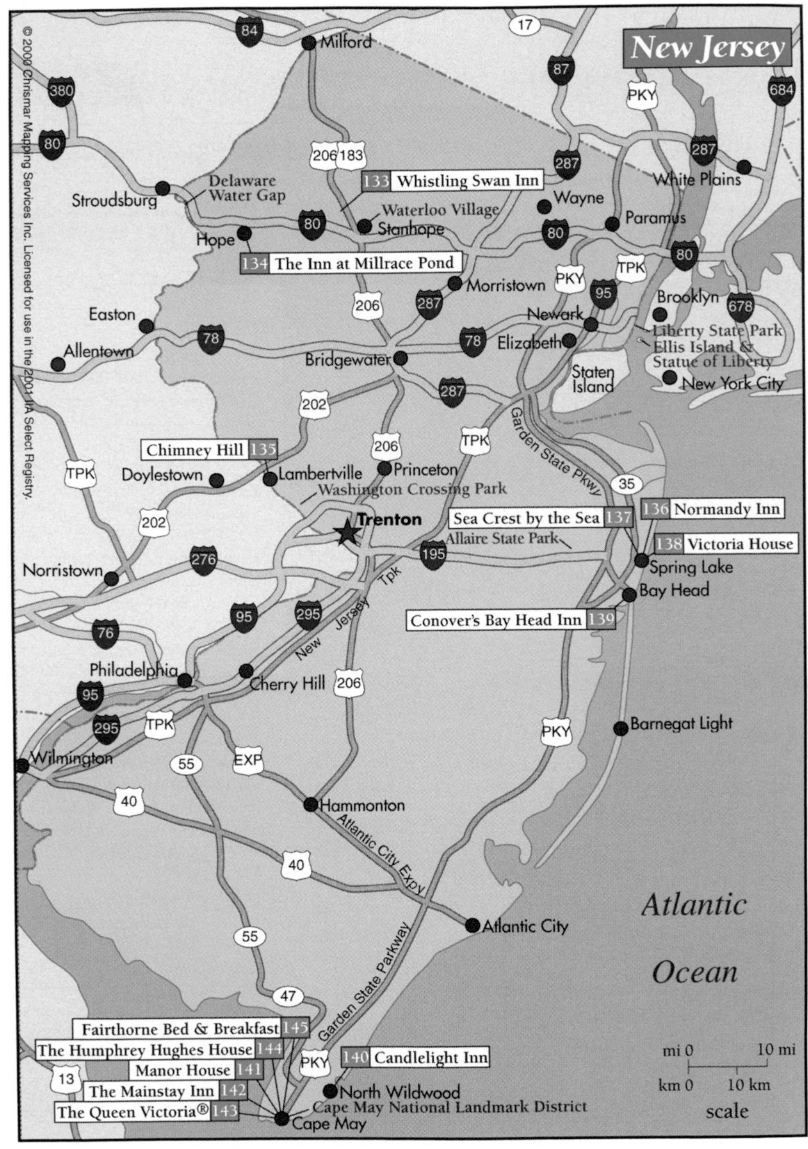
New Jersey
© 2000 Chrismar Mapping Services Inc. Licensed for use in the 2001 IIA Select Registry.
133 Whistling Swan Inn
134 The Inn at Millrace Pond
Chimney Hill 135
136 Normandy Inn
Sea Crest by the Sea 137
138 Victoria House
Conover's Bay Head Inn 139
140 Candlelight Inn
Fairthorne Bed & Breakfast 145
The Humphrey Hughes House 144
Manor House 141
The Mainstay Inn 142
The Queen Victoria® 143
Milford
Stroudsburg
Delaware Water Gap
Waterloo Village
Stanhope
Hope
Wayne
Paramus
White Plains
Morristown
Easton
Allentown
Newark
Brooklyn
Elizabeth
Liberty State Park
Ellis Island & Statue of Liberty
Staten Island
New York City
Bridgewater
Garden State Pkwy
Doylestown
Lambertville
Princeton
Washington Crossing Park
Trenton
Allaire State Park
Norristown
Spring Lake
Bay Head
New Jersey Tpk
Philadelphia
Cherry Hill
Barnegat Light
Wilmington
Hammonton
Atlantic City Expy
Atlantic City
Atlantic Ocean
Garden State Parkway
North Wildwood
Cape May National Landmark District
Cape May
mi 0 10 mi
km 0 10 km
scale

Stanhope, NJ

Whistling Swan Inn

973-347-6369
Fax 973-347-3391
www.whistlingswaninn.com
wswan@att.net
110 Main Street, Stanhope, NJ 07874

Select Registry Member *Since 1992*
Innkeepers/Owners
JOE AND PAULA WILLIAMS MULAY

TRADITIONAL VILLAGE BREAKFAST INN

RATES
10 rooms, $99/$150, B&B.
Corporate rate; govn't per diem.
Open year-round.

ATTRACTIONS
Near Waterloo Village, antiquing, wineries, winter sports, shopping, fairs, theatre, historic tours, baseball, lakes, horse rides, biking and flea markets and International Trade Center.

CUISINE
Full buffet breakfast, many fine-dining and casual restaurants nearby. Social drinking permitted.

DIRECTIONS
Bus and Train via NJ Transit to Netcong/Stanhope. Exit 27 off I-80 via Rte 183/206 one mile to Hess gas station. Turn on Main St. across from Hess.

NESTLED IN NORTHWESTERN New Jersey's Skylands Tourism region (only 45 miles west of NY City), this 1905 Victorian home has been converted to a B&B and renovated in three major segments of time. Each room has queen bed, TV/VCR, telephone, data ports, private bath and period furnishings. Many items are from Paula's family in Oklahoma. Enjoy the porch swing, hammock and picnic table. Or sherry, movies, parlor fireplaces, side-yard garden and tubs-for-two bathroom. The inn is centrally air-conditioned. We work with any dietary requirements. We specialize in business travelers, and are known for our friendliness and hospitality. The inn is rated ◆◆◆ by AAA.

Suitable for Children Over 12 • Non-Smoking Inn
Conference Facilities for 10 • Visa, MC, AMEX, Disc, Diners Accepted
Reservations Accepted Through Travel Agents

Hope, NJ

The Inn at Millrace Pond

800-746-6467
908-459-4884 Fax 908-459-5276
www.innatmillracepond.com
millrace@epix.net
Route 519N, P.O. Box 359, Hope, NJ 07844

THE MAIN INN BUILDING was a gristmill from 1770 until the early 1950s. Authentically decorated rooms, all with private bath, suggest the quiet elegance of Colonial America. In the fine-dining restaurant, gourmet dinners are served. The tavern is downstairs past the mill's old water wheel. In 1997, a fine 1830 home from the Moravian Village of Hope was moved onto the inn's property. It features large and small meeting rooms, a library and a parlor with fireplace. The inn has a tennis court and many major or minor walks and hikes are nearby. AAA ◆◆◆ and Mobil ★★★.

Select Registry Member *Since 1988*
Innkeepers
CORDIE AND CHARLES PUTTKAMMER.

TRADITIONAL VILLAGE INN

RATES
17 rooms, $130/$170. ($115 Sun-Thurs), continental breakfast included.
Open year-round.

ATTRACTIONS
Tennis court on premises, excellent antiquing nearby, two wineries, tour Morovian Village of Hope, hike and canoe in the Deleware Water Gap.

CUISINE
Dinner served Mon-Sat 5-9 pm, Sunday 4-7:30, Sunday Brunch 11-2, luncheon and dinner for groups. Tavern wine/liquor served with meals.

DIRECTIONS
From S: 31 N to 46 W to 519 N – R at blinker in Hope 1/10 mile to inn. From N, E or W: I-80 exit 12 1.25 mile S on 521 to blinker L 1/10 mile to inn.

3 Guestrooms Handicap Accessible • Suitable for Children
Pets Allowed • Conference Facilities for 40
MC, Visa, AMEX, Disc, CB, Diners Accepted

Lambertville, NJ

Chimney Hill Farm Estate & The Ol' Barn Inn

609-397-1516
Fax 609-397-9353
www.chimneyhillinn.com
chbb@erols.com
207 Goat Hill Road, Lambertville, NJ 08530

Select Registry Member *Since 1998*

Owners
TERRY ANNE AND RICHARD ANDERSON

ELEGANT IN TOWN BREAKFAST INN

RATES
8 rooms w/fireplace in main house.
4 suites w/fireplace in The Ol' Barn Inn.
$120/$225 Mon-Thurs.
$150/$325 Fri-Sun.
Open year-round.

ATTRACTIONS
New Hope, PA, Mule Barge ride, hiking, biking, fishing, skiing, river tubing, wineries, museums, horseback riding, antiquing mecca, golf, art galleries, kayaking, theater, outlet shops, peddlers' village.

CUISINE
Gourmet country breakfast served by candlelight, a guest butler pantry filled with cookies, goodies and sherry. Fine and casual dining at Lambertville and New Hope.

DIRECTIONS
From Philadelphia: I-95 N exit 1 (Lambertville) to Rte 29 N. Travel 7 miles; turn R onto Valley Rd., L on Goat Hill Rd.—1.5 miles on R. From New York: I-78 W to I-287 S to Rte 202 S to Rte 179 S (Lambertville exit). At traffic light go straight to 2nd L (SWAN St.) Go to 2nd R (Studdiford St.) to top.

ON A COUNTRY ROAD high in the hills above the charming historic riverside town of Lambertville, New Jersey, sits Chimney Hill Farm Estate and The Ol' Barn Inn. This gorgeous fieldstone house and barn, built in 1820, are surrounded by beautiful fields and gardens. The perfect spot for romantic getaways or corporate retreats, Chimney Hill is only 1/2 mile from the antique-filled towns of Lambertville and New Hope. Known for great country-style hospitality, Chimney Hill Farm Estate provides its guests with comfort and elegance. Featured as the cover for *Country Inns, New Jersey Country Roads* magazines, it is a connoisseur's choice—Come visit!

Suitable for Children Over 12 • Non-Smoking Inn
Conference Facilities for 10 - 75 • MC, Visa, AMEX Accepted
Reservations Accepted Through Travel Agents

Spring Lake, NJ

Normandy Inn

800-449-1888
732-449-7172 Fax 732-449-1070
www.normandyinn.com
normandy@bellatlantic.net
21 Tuttle Avenue, Spring Lake, NJ 07762

THE AUDENREID FAMILY OF PHILADELPHIA built the Normandy Inn as a summer home and rental property in 1888. The Italianate villa, with Queen Anne modifications, on the National Register of Historic Places, offers 17 guest rooms and a suite. Its present owners have undertaken extensive and authentic renovation of both the interior and the exterior of the house. Prized furnishings of the common rooms, as well as all of the guest rooms, are American Victorian antiques and are accented with reproduction wallpaper to reflect the elegance of the inn's origins.

Select Registry Member *Since 1996*
Owners
MICHAEL AND SUSAN INGINO
Innkeepers
JERI AND MIKE ROBERTSON

TRADITIONAL VILLAGE BREAKFAST INN

RATES

17 rooms,
high season, $116/$235;
quiet season, $96/$186.
1 suite,
high season, $325;
quiet season, $275 B&B.
Open year-round.

ATTRACTIONS

One-half block from beach, 6-8 blocks to shopping village and lakes; PNC Arts Center, Six Flags-Great Adventure, state parks, antiquing, shopping, local theater and bike riding.

CUISINE

Full country breakfast served here. Variety of restaurants locally.

DIRECTIONS

Garden State Parkway to exit 98. Follow Rte 34 S to traffic circle, 3/4 around to Rte 524 E. Take to ocean, turn R onto Ocean Ave. and then first R onto Tuttle. Fifth house on the L.

Suitable for Children • Conference Facilities for 25 • Non-Smoking Inn
Visa, MC, Disc, Diners, CB, AMEX Accepted
Reservations Accepted Through Travel Agents

Spring Lake, NJ

Sea Crest By The Sea

800-803-9031
732-449-9031 Fax 732-974-0403
www.seacrestbythesea.com
capt@seacrestbythesea.com
19 Tuttle Avenue, Spring Lake, NJ 07762

Select Registry Member *Since 1993*
Innkeepers/Owners
FRED AND BARBARA VOGEL

YOUR ROMANTIC FANTASY ESCAPE. A Spring Lake Bed & Breakfast Inn just for the two of you. Lovingly restored 1885 Queen Anne Victorian for ladies and gentlemen on seaside holiday. Ocean views, open fireplaces, luxurious linens, featherbeds, Jacuzzis for two, antique-filled rooms, sumptuous breakfast and afternoon tea. A *Gourmet* magazine "Top Choice", one of *Country Inns* magazine's "Top Inns". *Victoria Magazine* calls it "a perfect ocean refuge." Barbara and Fred Vogel welcome you with old-fashioned hospitality to an atmosphere that will soothe your weary body and soul. AAA ◆◆◆.

ELEGANT WATERSIDE BREAKFAST INN

RATES
9 rooms, $175/$255 B&B.
2 suites, $285/$305 B&B.
Open year-round.

ATTRACTIONS
Ocean beach, tennis, golf, year-round theater, antiquing, biking, fishing, sailing, walking, two miles noncommercial boardwalk and shopping.

CUISINE
Full breakfast and afternoon tea.

DIRECTIONS
From NY and N: GS Parkway to exit 98. 34 S to first traffic circle. 3/4 around to 524 E to Ocean, R 1 blk. R again to Tuttle Ave. 4th house on L. From S: Rte I-195 to 34 S then follow above.

Conference Facilities for 11 • AMEX, Visa, MC Accepted
Designated Smoking Areas • Reservations Accepted Through Travel Agents

Spring Lake, NJ

Victoria House

888-249-6252
732-974-1882 Fax 732-974-2132
www.victoriahouse.net
victoriahousebb@worldnet.att.net
214 Monmouth Avenue, Spring Lake, NJ 07762

Select Registry Member *Since 1998*
Innkeepers/Owners
ROBERT AND LOUISE GOODALL

NESTLED IN THE QUAINT SEASIDE VILLAGE of Spring Lake is the perfect retreat for relaxing, romancing and renewing one's spirit. Linger over a delightful breakfast served on the veranda overlooking a charming garden or cozy up by the fire in the parlor. The beautifully appointed rooms offer a vintage reflection with their 'Victorian Era' furnishings, some with fireplaces, whirlpool, all with select amenities. Walk the beach or bike the boardwalk, but save time to explore the unique shopping and antiquing or perhaps enjoy an evening of theatre. Louise and Robert offer you warm hospitality and pampered elegance at their 'Bed and Breakfast for all seasons.'

ELEGANT VILLAGE BREAKFAST INN

RATES

8 beautifully appointed guests rooms all PB.
Oct.1-May 10-$130/$275.
May 11-Sept. 30-$184/$335.
Open year-round.

ATTRACTIONS

We are a seashore Victorian village. Ocean Beach-two blks., biking, golfing, tennis, deep-sea fishing, antiquing, local theater, unique village shopping, horseback riding. NEARBY: diversified restaurants and free health club passes.

CUISINE

Gourmet-served breakfast with house specialties. Enjoy your breakfast on the veranda or sit at cozy tables for two in our European dining room. A perfect start to your day.

DIRECTIONS

From NY, CT and North Jersey: GS Pkwy S to exit 98, take 138 E to Rte 35 S, 3rd light L Warren Ave. Through next light, stop sign, turn R on 3rd Ave. (church on L), L on Monmouth Ave. From DC/DE/PA: Rte I-95 N to I-195 E into 138 E, then follow above dir.

Suitable for Children Over 14 • Non-Smoking Inn
Conference Facilities for 10 • AMEX, Visa, Disc, MC Accepted
Reservations Accepted Through Travel Agents

Bay Head, NJ

Conover's Bay Head Inn

800-956-9099
732-892-4664 Fax 732-892-8748
www.conovers.com
beverly@conovers.com
646 Main Avenue, Bay Head, NJ 08742

ONE OF SIX GEMS ON THE JERSEY SHORE, according to the "*Washintonian*," Conover's Bay Head Inn has been recognized for fine accommodations and hospitality since 1970. Each bed chamber has been uniquely designed with views of the ocean, bay, English gardens, or other shingle-style Victorians. Guests choose from 3 suites and 9 rooms, some with fireplaces and whirlpool tubs. Relax in our garden Jacuzzi or explore the 19th century seaside village of Bay Head. Conover's is ideal for a romantic getaway or as an executive retreat.

Select Registry Member *Since 1996*
Innkeepers/Owners
TAPLYNN DUGAN,
BERNIE MURPHY

ELEGANT VILLAGE
BREAKFAST INN

RATES
12 rooms, $145/$300 B&B.
Open year-round.

ATTRACTIONS
Ocean, beach, croquet, tennis, golf, antiquing, biking, fishing, windsurfing, on-lake sailing, weekly concerts in summer, racetrack, Six Flags Park, Island Beach State Park.

CUISINE
Breakfast, afternoon tea. No alcohol license.

DIRECTIONS
From NY and North: Garden State Parkway exit 98 to Rte 34 S to Rte 35 S to Bay Head. From PA and South: NJ turnpike to I-195 E to Rte 34 S to Rte 35 S to Bay Head.

Designated Smoking Areas • Conference Facilities for 12
AMEX, MC, Visa Accepted
Reservations Accepted Through Travel Agents

North Wildwood, NJ

Candlelight Inn

800-992-2632
609-522-6200 Fax 609-522-6125
www.candlelight-inn.com
info@candlelight-inn.com
2310 Central Avenue, North Wildwood, NJ 08260

COME VISIT A UNIQUE PART OF THE WILDWOODS. Enjoy the quiet elegance reminiscent of another era. The Candlelight Inn is a beautifully restored 1905, Queen Anne Victorian home. We offer rooms with private baths and suites with double whirlpool tubs and fireplaces. Sit on our veranda where cool ocean breezes delight you, relax in our hot tub while your stress melts away, or warm yourself by a roaring fire in our inglenook. Minutes away are beautiful beaches, fine dining, shopping, history, and amusements - something for everyone. The Candlelight is our small piece of the New Jersey Coast that we would like to share with you and your special someone.

Select Registry Member *Since 2001*
Owners
BILL AND NANCY MONCRIEF
EILEEN BURCHSTED

VICTORIAN VILLAGE
BREAKFAST INN

RATES
7 rooms, $85/$175.
3 suites, $120/$250.
Rooms have private baths, some with a double whirlpool tub. Suites with fireplaces and double whirlpool tubs. Air-conditioned. *Open year-round.*

ATTRACTIONS
Ocean beach, amusements, antique shopping, historic tours, lighthouses, zoo, birding, nature trails, fine dining, boating, biking, tennis, golf, hot tub, and relaxing on our wide veranda.

CUISINE
Full breakfast and afternoon refreshments.

DIRECTIONS
S-bound: G.S. Pkwy to exit 6; Rte 147 E; L on 2nd Ave.; R on Central Ave.; go to 24th Ave.; Inn is on R. N-Bound: G.S. Pkwy to exit 4 into Wildwood. After bridge, L at 6th light (Atlantic Ave.). L at 24th for 1 blk.

Suitable for Children Over 12 • Non-Smoking Inn
Visa, MC, Disc, AMEX Accepted
Reservations Accepted Through Travel Agents

Cape May, NJ

Manor House

609-884-4710
Fax 609-898-0471
www.manorhouse.net
innkeepr@bellatlantic.net
612 Hughes Street, Cape May, NJ 08204

Select Registry Member *Since 1991*
Innkeepers/Owners
Nancy and Tom McDonald

On a tree-lined residential street in the heart of Cape May's Historic District, Manor House offers guests an exceptionally clean and comfortable turn-of-the-century inn experience. Fluffy robes in the rooms and a generous cookie fairy are but a few of the fun touches found here. Relaxing on the porch, reading in the garden, or roaming the beaches and streets of Cape May occur with little effort. Traditional sticky buns, made-from-scratch full breakfasts and the innkeeper's good humor give the inn its reputation for fine food and character. AAA ◆◆◆.

Traditional Village Breakfast Inn

RATES
9 rooms, $100/$225 B&B.
1 suite, $150/$275 B&B.
Open year-round.

ATTRACTIONS
Ocean swimming, beach, walking, porch sitting, bird-watching, golf, tennis, biking, historic homes tours and napping.

CUISINE
Breakfast, afternoon tea.

DIRECTIONS
From Zero-mile mark on Garden State Parkway to Rte 109 S becoming LaFayette St., turn L on Franklin for 2 blks to R on Hughes -612 Hughes on L.

Conference Facilities for 10 • Visa, MC, Disc Accepted
Reservations Accepted Through Travel Agents

Cape May, NJ

The Mainstay Inn

609-884-8690
www.mainstayinn.com

Select Registry Member *Since 1976*
Innkeepers/Owners
Tom and Sue Carroll

635 Columbia Avenue, Cape May, NJ 08204

ONCE AN EXCLUSIVE GAMBLING CLUB, the Mainstay is now an elegant Victorian inn furnished in splendid antiques. Within a lovely garden setting, the inn and adjacent cottage feature wide rocker-lined verandas, and large, high-ceilinged rooms which are lavishly but comfortably furnished. The Officers' Quarters is more contemporary with many extras such as whirlpool tubs and fireplaces. The Mainstay is a landmark within a National Historic Landmark town, and is but a short walk to restaurants, shops, theater, concerts, nature trails and beaches.

Elegant Village Breakfast Inn

RATES
9 rooms, $105/$255 B&B.
3 suites, $125/$295 B&B.
4 luxury fireplace suites, $125/$345.
Open year-round.

ATTRACTIONS
Ocean beach, historic tours, birding, boating, unique shopping, hiking, biking, tennis, golf, lighthouse climbing and rocking on a wide veranda.

CUISINE
Breakfast and elegant afternoon tea. Excellent restaurants a short walk away. No liquor license.

DIRECTIONS
Take Garden State Parkway S. In Cape May, Parkway becomes Lafayette St. Take L at light onto Madison Ave. Go 3 blocks, R at Columbia. Inn on R.

1 Guestroom Handicap Accessible • Non-Smoking Inn
Suitable for Children Over 12 • Conference Facilities for 14

Cape May, NJ

The Queen Victoria®

609-884-8702
www.queenvictoria.com
qvinn@bellatlantic.net

Select Registry Member *Since 1992*
Innkeepers/Owners
JOAN AND DANE WELLS

102 Ocean Street, Cape May, NJ 08204-2320

©George W. Gardner

THE WELLS FAMILY WELCOMES YOU with warm hospitality and special services to two Victorian homes in the center of the historic district. Rooms are designed for comfort, featuring handmade quilts and fine antiques. Some have gas-log fireplaces and whirlpool tubs. Start your day with a hearty breakfast, then enjoy bicycling, antique shopping, historic tours and nature walks. Sip afternoon tea while relaxing on porches overlooking Victorian gardens. Dine at one of the many fine restaurants within walking distance. The Queen Victoria® offers you Victorian ambience with modern amenities such as air-conditioning, mini-refrigerators and clock radios.

TRADITIONAL VILLAGE BREAKFAST INN

RATES

15 rooms, $90/$230 B&B.
6 suites, $130/$290 B&B.
Weekday discounts fall, winter, spring.
Open year-round.

ATTRACTIONS

Fifty rocking chairs for relaxing on our porches. Free bicycles, beach chairs and showers. Ocean beach one block. Historic house and town tours, birding, nature trails, fishing, golf, tennis, shopping, antiques and fine dining nearby. Music festival.

CUISINE

Rates include full buffet breakfast and afternoon tea with sweets and savories. Complimentary soft drinks and sherry. Excellent restaurants within walking distance.

DIRECTIONS

Garden State Parkway to S end; continue straight over bridges, becomes Lafayette St. 2nd light turn L onto Ocean St. 3 blocks turn R onto Columbia Ave. Loading areas for check-in on R.

---

1 Guestroom Handicap Accessible • Suitable for Children
Conference Facilities for 10 • Visa, MC Accepted • Non-Smoking Inn

Cape May, NJ

The Humphrey Hughes House

800-582-3634
Voice 609-884-4428
www.humphreyhugheshouse.com

Select Registry Member *Since 1999*
Innkeepers/Owners
LORRAINE AND TERRY SCHMIDT

29 Ocean Street, Cape May, NJ 08204

NESTLED IN THE HEART of Cape May's primary historic district, The Humphrey Hughes is one of the most spacious and gracious inns. Expansive common rooms filled with beautiful antiques. Relax on the large wraparound veranda filled with rockers enjoying the ocean view and colorful gardens. Our large, comfortable guest rooms offer pleasant, clean accommodations. All rooms are air-conditioned with cable TV. Our location offers the visitor the opportunity to walk to the beach, restaurants, shops, theatre, concerts and nature trails. A full breakfast and afternoon refreshments are offered daily.
AAA ◆◆◆ .

TRADITIONAL VILLAGE BREAKFAST INN

RATES
$125/$290 per night, dbl.
Open year-round.

ATTRACTIONS
Ocean beach, historic tours, birding, boating, unique shopping, biking, tennis, golf, enjoying wonderful ocean views while rocking on our veranda.

CUISINE
Full breakfast and afternoon tea.

DIRECTIONS
Take Garden State Parkway S to end, follow Lafayette St. S. Turn L at second stop light; Ocean St. The Inn is on your L the corner of Ocean St. and Columbia St.

Non-Smoking Inn • Visa, MC Accepted

Cape May, NJ

The Fairthorne

800-438-8742
609-884-8791 Fax 609-884-1902
www.fairthorne.com
wehfair@aol.com
111 Ocean Street, Cape May, NJ 08204

Select Registry Member *Since 2001*
Innkeepers/Owners
ED AND DIANE HUTCHINSON

INNKEEPERS DIANE AND ED HUTCHINSON warmly welcome you to their romantic old whaling captain's home. This 1892 colonial revival-style Inn features a gracious wraparound veranda where sumptuous breakfasts are served on pleasant mornings and stress-relieving rockers offer afternoon relaxation. The Fairthorne is beautifully decorated in period style without being too frilly or formal. Guestrooms are appointed with a seamless blend of fine antiques and contemporary comforts, including air conditioning, mini fridges and TV, plus gas-log fireplaces in some rooms. Each day Diane and Ed invite you to gather for tasty snacks and fresh-baked cookies.

VICTORIAN IN TOWN
BREAKFAST INN

RATES

10 rooms, $145/$235
Antique furnishings, lace curtains, king or queen beds.
Open year-round.

ATTRACTIONS

Historic house tours, horse drawn carriage ride, birding, fishing, antiquing, sunbathing, zoo, golfing, lighthouse climbing, tennis.

CUISINE

Full breakfast and afternoon hot tea and coffee on cool days or iced tea and lemonade on summer days complimentary sherry. Excellent restaurants a short walk.

DIRECTIONS

Garden State Parkway S to end; continue straight over bridges, becomes Lafayette St 2nd light, turn L onto Ocean St. 3rd Block on L-111 Ocean Street.

Suitable for Children Over 10 • Conference Facilities for 16
Designated Smoking Areas • Visa, MC, Disc, AMEX Accepted
Reservations Accepted Through Travel Agents

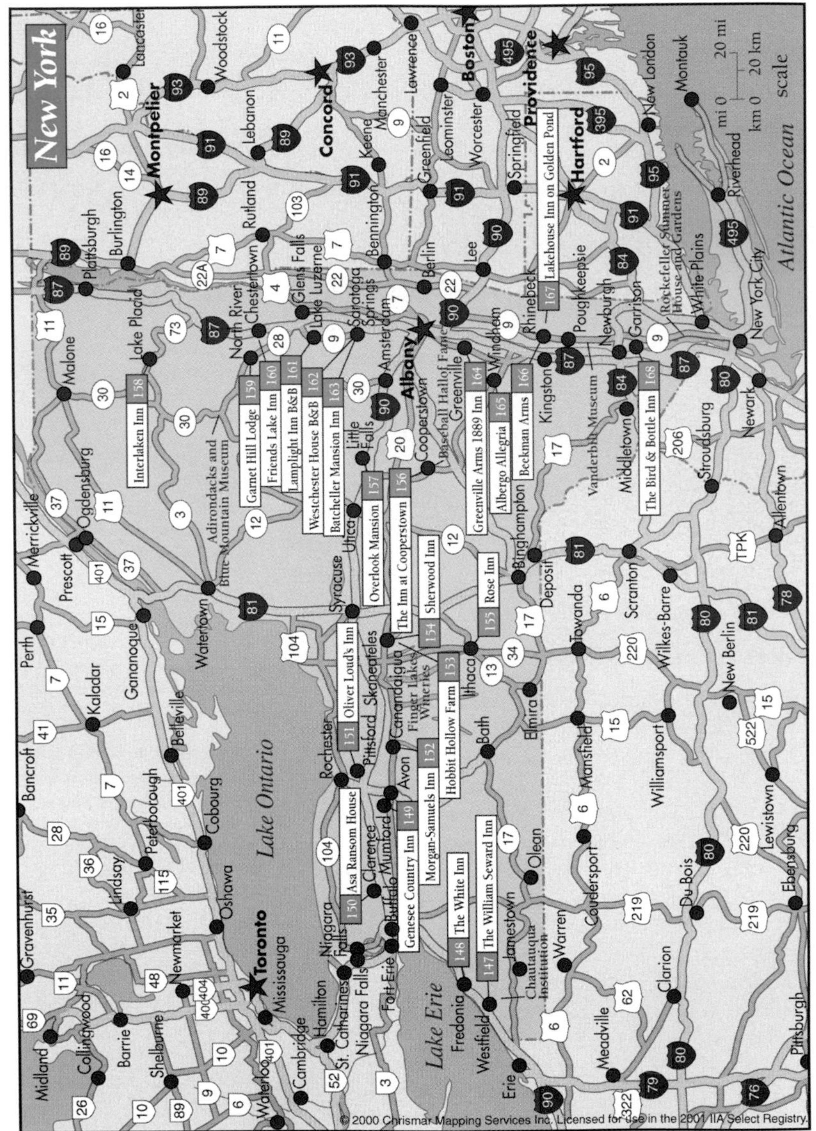
New York
147 The William Seward Inn
148 The White Inn
149 Genesee Country Inn
150 Asa Ransom House
151 Oliver Loud's Inn
152 Morgan-Samuels Inn
153 Hobbit Hollow Farm
154 Sherwood Inn
155 Rose Inn
156 The Inn at Cooperstown
157 Overlook Mansion
158 Interlaken Inn
159 Garnet Hill Lodge
160 Friends Lake Inn
161 Lamplight Inn B&B
162 Westchester House B&B
163 Batcheller Mansion Inn
164 Greenville Arms 1889 Inn
165 Albergo Allegria
166 Beekman Arms
167 Lakehouse Inn on Golden Pond
168 The Bird & Bottle Inn
Lake Ontario
Lake Erie
Atlantic Ocean
Toronto
Albany
Montpelier
Concord
Boston
Providence
Hartford
Adirondacks and Blue Mountain Museum
Baseball Hall of Fame
Vanderbilt Museum
Finger Lakes Wineries
Rockefeller Sumner House and Gardens
Chautauqua Institution
mi 0 20 mi
km 0 20 km
scale
© 2000 Chrismar Mapping Services Inc. Licensed for use in the 2001 IIA Select Registry.

Westfield, NY

The William Seward Inn

716-326-4151
Fax 716-326-4163
www.williamsewardinn.com
wmseward@cecomet.net
6645 South Portage Road, Westfield, NY 14787

ALTHOUGH CHAUTAUQUA INSTITUTION is a major attraction, many travelers come specifically to stay at this 1821 antique-filled inn for rest and relaxation. The inn is increasingly known for its fine dining, serving a four-course prix fixe dinner Wednesday through Sunday of each week, by advance reservation only. Recipient of upstate *New York Magazine* Fine Dining Award. AAA ◆◆◆ and Mobil ★★★.

Select Registry Member *Since 1992*
Innkeepers / Owners
JIM AND DEBBIE DAHLBERG

ELEGANT COUNTRY INN

RATES
4 rooms, double Jacuzzi, $160/$185 B&B.
2 rooms, fireplace, $120/$165 B&B.
8 rooms, $70/$125 B&B.
Open year-round.

ATTRACTIONS
The area boasts Chautauqua Institution, Lilly Dale, Panama Rocks, Roger Tory Peterson Institute, Lucy-Desi Museum and Amish area. Six wineries, antique and specialty shops. Skiing, hiking, bicycling, horseback riding, beaches, golf, boating nearby.

CUISINE
Dinner available Wednesday-Sunday, by advance reservation with a single seating at 7 pm. Guests pre-select their appetizer and main entree from our seasonal menu at least one day in advance of arrival. Wine available.

DIRECTIONS
4 miles S on Rte 394 from I-90, exit 60. 2.5 hrs. NE of Cleveland, OH; 2.5 hrs. N of Pittsburg, PA; 1.5 hrs. SW of Buffalo, NY; 3 hrs. SW of Toronto, Canada.

1 Guestroom Handicap Accessible • Suitable for Children Over 10
Conference Facilities for 14 • AMEX, Visa, MC, Novus Accepted
Designated Smoking Areas • Reservations Accepted Through Travel Agents

Fredonia, NY

The White Inn

888-FREDONIA (reservations)
716-672-2103 Fax 716-672-2107
www.whiteinn.com
inn@whiteinn.com
52 East Main Street, Fredonia, NY 14063

Select Registry Member *Since 1989*
Innkeepers/Owners
Robert Contiguglia and
Kathleen Dennison

EXPERIENCE THE WHITE INN as described by our guests: "...the perfect mix of old-fashioned charm and modern elegance." "I am fascinated by the quality of service, attention to detail and feeling of warmth conveyed by the staff and management of The White Inn." Built in 1868, the Inn lies at the center of a vibrant cultural and historical community. Our beautifully restored guest rooms and public spaces complement our award-winning American cuisine. The Inn offers fine dining and banquets, as well as cocktails and casual fare in the lounge or on the 100-foot-long veranda.

Traditional In Town Inn

RATES
12 rooms, $69/$119 B&B.
11 suites, $99/$189 B&B.
Open year-round.

ATTRACTIONS
Wineries, antique and specialty shops. Performing arts at Chautauqua Institution, Fredonia Opera House and SUNY Fredonia. Golf, skiing, parks nearby.

CUISINE
Full breakfast. Lunch and dinner daily. Banquet facilities for up to 150. Full-service cocktail lounge.

DIRECTIONS
NY Thruway (I-90) exit 59. At light, L onto Route 60 S. At second light, R onto Route 20 W (Main St. in Fredonia). Inn is 1.25 miles on R.

All Common Rooms Handicap Accessible • Suitable for Children
Conference Facilities for 150 • AMEX, Visa, MC, Disc, Diners Accepted
Designated Smoking Areas • Reservations Accepted Through Travel Agents

Mumford-Rochester, NY

Genesee Country Inn Circa 1833

716-538-2500
Fax 716-538-4565
www.geneseecountryinn.com
gbarcklow@aol.com
948 George Street, Box 340
Mumford-Rochester, NY 14511-0340

Select Registry Member *Since 1988*
Proprietor
GLENDA BARCKLOW
Innkeeper
KIM RASMUSSEN

TRADITIONAL WATERSIDE INN

STEP BACK IN TIME TO A QUIETER-GENTLER TIME as you enjoy our unique water setting and visit the nearby Genessee Country Village-Museum. A former plaster-paper mill during the 1800's, our Inn, with 2-1/2 foot thick stone walls, is located near Rochester, New York; just three hours from Toronto at the edge of the Finger Lakes. From our guest diaries: "A fine Inn indeed. You are on a par with the better country Inns of England. Your Inn and Hospitality are fabulous! The Inn is so beautiful – our fireplace, canopy bed, stenciled walls, waffles with cider sauce; I could go on and on... After a hectic day of traveling and sales calls, this is just the place I want to be! A wonderful change from run-of-the-mill hotels. Excuse the pun!"

Suitable for Children • Conference Facilities for 20
Non-Smoking Inn • Diners, Visa, MC, Disc Accepted
Reservations Accepted Through Travel Agents

RATES

9 rooms, $85/$150 B&B.
Historic getaways, romance pkgs., ladies weekends, winter specials. Some decks, fireplaces, canopy beds. *Open year-round, except Christmas week.*

ATTRACTIONS

Spring-fed, year-round trout fishing; 20 minutes to Rochester; walk to Genesee Country Museum. Day-trips: Letchworth Park, Erie Canal, antiquing, biking, museums, golfing, Lake Ontario. One and one-half hours to Niagara Falls, three hours to Toronto.

CUISINE

Full country gourmet breakfast served each morning by candlelight. Casual tea upon arrival. Several fine-dining restaurants nearby (including one within walking distance).

DIRECTIONS

I-90 exit 47 to Rte 19 S. Follow 'Genesee Country Museum' Green signs; turn L onto North Rd. Travel 4 miles Rte 36 and turn R into Mumford. At only light, turn R onto George St. (George St. changes to Flint Hill Rd). Go 1 1/2 block on George St. and the Inn is on the R at 948 George St.

Clarence, NY

Asa Ransom House

716-759-2315
Fax 716-759-2791
www.asaransom.com
innfo@asaransom.com
10529 Main Street, Clarence, NY 14031

Select Registry Member *Since 1976*
Innkeepers
Robert Lenz
Abigail Lenz

Traditional Village Inn

On the site of the first gristmill built in Erie County (1803), you will find intimate seclusion and gentle harmony. Guests are romanced in the winter by the glowing fireplaces in most rooms. Our spacious grounds, full of herbs and flowers, are enjoyed from many porches and balconies. Experience world-class cuisine and full country breakfasts with delicious regional accents. Often upon arrival you will find the aroma of fresh pies and breads lingering in the air! Clarence is known throughout the east for its antiques and treasures. Only 28 miles from Niagara Falls.

RATES

9 rooms.
$95/$145 B&B.
$150/$200 MAP.
$210/$275 MAP only Fri. and Sat.
Open year-round, except January.

ATTRACTIONS

Many antique shops within walking distance, Niagara Falls 28 miles away. Lancaster Opera House/live theater, Shea's Center for the performing arts, Albright/Knox Art Gallery.

CUISINE

Dinner-Tuesday thru Sunday. Monday-B&B only. Friday and Saturday prix fixe, fully licensed.

DIRECTIONS

Traveling E: I-90, exit 49, L on Rte 78 for 1 mile to R on Rte 5 for 5.3 miles. Traveling W: I-90 exit 48 A and R on Rte 77 for 1 mile to R on Rte 5 for 10 miles to inn.

Handicap Access Available • Suitable for Children Over 6
Conference Facilities for 40 • Credit Cards Accepted
Reservations Accepted Through Travel Agents

Pittsford, NY

Oliver Loud's Inn

716-248-5200
Fax 716-248-9970
www.frontiernet.net/~rchi
rchi@frontiernet.net
1474 Marsh Road, Pittsford, NY 14534

Select Registry Member *Since 1989*
Innkeeper
VIVIENNE TELLIER

FEEDING DUCKS, building snowmen, visiting nearby shops, or rocking on the porch overlooking the Erie Canal, are some ways to relax at this stagecoach inn (circa 1810). Authentically furnished with antiques and period artwork, guests are pampered with VIP welcome trays, as well as a breakfast hamper delivered to your room. King-sized and canopy beds available. AAA ◆◆◆◆.

ELEGANT COUNTRY INN

RATES
8 rooms, $135/$155 B&B.
Open year-round.

ATTRACTIONS
Erie Canal towpath for hiking, jogging, cross-country skiing, biking, boating. Golf, tennis, museums and sightseeing nearby.

CUISINE
Richardson's Canal House Restaurant on premises. Beverages available at Richardson's.

DIRECTIONS
NY Thruway I90 Exit 45 to I-490 W for 3 miles to Bushnell's Basin exit 27 turn R and continue to Marsh Rd. Signal and bear R to Inn.

1 Guestroom, 1 Common Room Handicap Accessible
Suitable for Children Over 12 • MC, Visa, AMEX, Diners Accepted
Non-Smoking Inn • Reservations Accepted Through Travel Agents

Canandaigua, NY

Morgan-Samuels Inn

716-394-9232
Fax 716-394-8044
www.morgansamuelsinn.com
MorSamBB@aol.com
2920 Smith Road, Canandaiqua, NY 14424

TRAVEL THE 2,000 FOOT TREE-LINED DRIVE to the secluded 1810 English-style mansion and sense the difference between ordinary and legendary. The inn sits like a plantation on a rise surrounded by 46 acres. Four patios, trickling waterfall, acres of lawn and gardens canopied by 250 noble trees. Three rooms with French doors and balconies, three Jacuzzi rooms, 11 fireplaces. Tea room with stone wall and 16-foot glass windows, pot-bellied stove. Library, common room, large enclosed porch/dining room, museum quality furniture, oil paintings. AAA ◆◆◆◆.

Select Registry Member *Since 1992*
Innkeepers/Owners
JULIE SULLIVAN AND
JOHN SULLIVAN

ELEGANT COUNTRY
BREAKFAST INN

RATES
5 rooms, $119/$225 B&B.
1 suite, $195/$295 B&B.
Open year-round.

ATTRACTIONS
Lake, tennis, golf, Hobart College, 50 wineries, outdoor symphonies, "Big Name" concerts, Sonnenberg Gardens, cross-country and downhill (2,100') skiing 11 miles.

CUISINE
Breakfast, dinner prix fixe by reservation, special request for eight or more. BYOB.

DIRECTIONS
I-90 from exit 43 R on 21 to 488; L 1st R on East Ave. to stop. Continue 3/4 mile to inn on R.

Conference Facilities for 15 • MC, Visa Accepted
Non-Smoking Inn • Reservations Accepted Through Travel Agents

Skaneateles, NY

Hobbit Hollow Farm, B&B

315-685-3405

800-374-3796   Fax 315-685-3426
www.hobbithollow.com

innkeeper@hobbithollow.com

3061 West Lake Road, Skaneateles, NY 13152

HOBBIT HOLLOW FARM has been painstakingly restored inside and out to recreate the casual comfort of an elegant country farmhouse. Hobbit Hollow serves a full, farm breakfast as part of the room price. Overlooking Skaneateles Lake, Hobbit Hollow Farm is situated on 320 acres of farmland with trails and ponds, as well as private equestrian stables. Spend time contemplating the lake on our east verandah. Enjoy afternoon tea or coffee and watch the light play on the water in the soft wash of dusk. Rediscover what it means to be truly relaxed in a setting of tranquility. This is the perfect spot for a quiet, romantic getaway.

Non-Smoking Inn • MC, Visa, AMEX, Disc Accepted

Select Registry Member *Since 1998*

Proprietor
NOREEN FALCONE

Innkeeper
RICHARD FYNN

ELEGANT COUNTRY BREAKFAST INN

RATES

Master Suite $250 off-season; $270 peak season
Lake View $200 off-season; $230 peak season
Chanticleer $150 off-season; $170 peak season
Meadow View $100 off-season; $120 peak season
Twin $250 off-season; $270 peak season

Five rooms elegantly decorated with master-crafted period furniture and antiques. Three rooms include four-poster beds.
Open year-round.

ATTRACTIONS

Antiques, wineries, boat rides, cocktail cruises on our antique Chris Craft, downhill and cross-country skiing, fishing, walks on the farm, enticing shops in the village.

CUISINE

Breakfast only. Find excellent dinner and lunches at the Sherwood Inn, Blue Water Grill, the Krebs.

DIRECTIONS

Located on the W side of Skaneateles Lake on 41A. Rte 20 (Genesee St.) to 41A S. In less than 2 miles the stone entrance to Hobbit Hollow Farm will be on the R.

Skaneateles, NY

The Sherwood Inn

800-374-3796

315-685-3405 Fax 315-685-8983

www.thesherwoodinn.com

info@thesherwoodinn.com

26 West Genessee St, P.O. Box 529, Skaneateles, NY 13152

Select Registry Member *Since 1979*

Innkeepers

LINDA B. HARTNETT

BUILT AS A STAGECOACH STOP IN 1807, The Sherwood Inn has always been a favorite resting place for travelers. The handsome lobby with fireplace, gift shop, antiques and orientals offers a warm reception. Each room has been restored to the beauty of a bygone era to create a relaxing harmony away from everyday cares. Many of our guestrooms overlook beautiful Skaneateles Lake. Fine dining and The Sherwood are synonymous, and we have been recognized by *Bon Appetit, Country Living, Harper's Bazaar* and *New Yorker* magazines. Our extensive menu offers American cooking with a continental touch, accompanied by an impressive wine list.

TRADITIONAL VILLAGE INN

RATES

14 rooms and 6 suites.
6 rooms have fireplaces and whirlpool baths. All have private baths, telephones and televisions.
Open year-round.

ATTRACTIONS

Swimming, boating, golf, downhill/cross-country skiing, fishing, bicycling, shopping, hiking, antiquing and touring wineries. Cocktail cruises on our beautifully restored, antique Chris Craft.

CUISINE

Tavern and dining room menus serving continental breakfast, lunch and dinner.

DIRECTIONS

From New York Thruway: Exit Weedsport (exit 40) Rte 34 S to Auburn. E on Rte 20, 7 miles to Skaneateles. From the S: 81 N to Cortland, Rte 41 N to Skaneateles Lake, L, W on Rte 20 for 1 mile.

Suitable for Children • Conference Facilities for 60
Designated Smoking Areas • MC, Visa, AMEX, Disc Accepted
Dining Rooms Wheelchair Accessible

Ithaca, NY

Rose Inn

607-533-7905
Fax 607-533-7908
www.roseinn.com
info@roseinn.com
Route 34 North, P.O. Box 6576
Ithaca, NY 14851-6576

A QUINTESSENTIAL COUNTRY INN in a park-like setting. Halfway between New York City and Niagara Falls, in the heart of Finger Lakes, this 1850 Italianate mansion is a gem of woodcraft, with a stunning circular staircase of Honduran mahogany. Large, high-ceiled rooms are luxuriously furnished with antiques from around the world accented by lush colors and fabrics. Extraordinary cuisine is romantically served in the Carriage House Restaurant. Charles and Sherry welcome you to New York's only Mobil ★★★★ and AAA ◆◆◆◆ country inn.

Select Registry Member *Since 1986*
Innkeepers / Owners
CHARLES AND SHERRY ROSEMANN

ELEGANT COUNTRY INN

RATES
10 rooms, $115/$200 B&B.
11 suites all with Jacuzzi, 7 with fireplaces $230/$320 B&B.
Open year-round.

ATTRACTIONS
Cayuga Lake sports, cross-country skiing near, downhill skiing, golf, fishing, wineries, Cornell University and antiques.

CUISINE
Breakfast, dinner served Tues-Sun. Wine and liquor available.

DIRECTIONS
10 miles N of Ithaca on Rte 34 N. From Rte 13, exit 34 N 6 miles to "T" (traffic light). R for .5 mile to fork, stay L, inn is 3.5 miles on R.

1 Guestroom Handicap Accessible • Suitable for Children Over 10
Conference Facilities for 70 • Visa, MC Accepted
Non-Smoking Inn • Reservations Accepted Through Travel Agents

Cooperstown, NY

The Inn at Cooperstown

607-547-5756
Fax 607-547-8779
www.innatcooperstown.com
theinn@telenet.net
16 Chestnut Street, Cooperstown, NY 13326

Select Registry Member *Since 1998*
Innkeepers
MICHAEL JEROME AND
MARIANNE BEZ

A WARM WELCOME AWAITS YOU at The Inn at Cooperstown. This award-winning structure was built in 1874 and fully restored in 1985. The inn has the warmth and comfort of a home. Spotless rooms are individually decorated with many charming touches. In a relaxing atmosphere, guests are invited to escape the hectic pace of the modern world. Unwind in a rocking chair or enjoy a cozy sitting room after exploring the lovely village of Cooperstown. Nearby streets are lined with historic buildings, interesting shops and restaurants. Cooperstown has many cultural, recreational and natural attractions to offer.

TRADITIONAL VILLAGE
BREAKFAST INN

RATES

17 rooms, $98/$275 B&B.
All private baths, wheelchair one room, smoking in restricted areas. TV/Phones in sitting room.
Open year-round.

ATTRACTIONS

Baseball Hall of Fame, golf, Glimmerglass Opera, art and history museums, shopping, art galleries, lake, boating, tennis, summer theater, dining, biking, porch sitting, antiquing.

CUISINE

Continental breakfast, afternoon refreshments, fine restaurants nearby.

DIRECTIONS

From I-88: Exit 17 to Rte 28 N, to 16 Chestnut St. From I-90: Exit 30 to Rte 28 S, to 16 Chestnut St. From I-87: Exit 21 to Rte 23 W to Rte 145 to Rte 20 W to Rte 80 W to 16 Chestnut St.

1 Guestroom Handicap Accessible • Suitable for Children
Conference Facilities for 12 • MC, Visa, AMEX, Disc, Diners Accepted
Designated Smoking Areas • Reservations Accepted Through Travel Agents

Little Falls, NY

Overlook Mansion

315-823-4222
Fax 315-823-4760
www.overlookmansion.com
info@overlookmansion.com
1 Overlook Lane, Little Falls, NY 13365

NESTLED ON A NATURAL BLUFF overlooking the picturesque city of Little Falls, the Overlook Mansion is an architectural treasure that recalls a time of grace and elegance. Stained-glass windows, hardwood floors, ceramic tiles, fruitwood trim and handcarved fireplaces are among the beautiful features to be found. Today, Overlook Mansion is a haven for guests seeking the quiet, warmth, hospitality and visual delights usually associated with a bygone era. "We will give you a wonderful welcome!"

Select Registry Member *Since 1997*
Innkeeper
CARIN CAROLINA MEI

ELEGANT VILLAGE INN

RATES
$100/$110/$120 B&B.
$195 MAP; 5 Rooms $87
Corp. rate.
Open year-round. Closed January.

ATTRACTIONS
Herkimer Diamond Mine, Cooperstown-Glimmerglass Opera, cross-country skiing, hiking, antiquing, bicycling, Turningstone casino, golfing, Saratoga, Adirondacks, Vernon Downs Racetrack. Herkimer Home, Leatherstocking country, Revolutionary War sites.

CUISINE
Full breakfast for our guests; Thurs-Sat. Buffet is served on major holidays.

DIRECTIONS
N.Y.S. I-90 exit 29 A, Rte 169 N to Little Falls, follow 169 N to W Monroe St., turn L. Turn R onto Lewis St. (cemetery), turn R on Douglas.

Suitable for Children • Conference Facilities for 100
Credit Cards Accepted
Reservations Accepted Through Travel Agents

Lake Placid, NY

Interlaken Inn

800-428-4369
518-523-3180 Fax 518-523-0117
interlkn@northnet.org
www.selectregistry.com
15 Interlaken Avenue, Lake Placid, NY 12946

AN ADIRONDACK VICTORIAN INN in the heart of Lake Placid, and site of both the 1932 and 1980 winter Olympics. A family-owned and operated inn featuring warm and friendly service and wonderful cuisine. Our chef and innkeeper, Kevin Gregg, is a CIA graduate. His menu features fine dining with seasonal menus. Specialties may include his wonderful rack of lamb with a rosemary-cabernet sauce, fresh fish or black-angus filet mignon. Enjoy the wonders of each season in these beautiful Adirondack Mountains.

Select Registry Member *Since 1992*
Owners/Innkeepers
ROY AND CAROL JOHNSON

TRADITIONAL VILLAGE INN

RATES
11 rooms, including 1 suite, MAP.
Double $160/$245, MAP.
Extra person $45
Single $110/$195, MAP.
Double $80/$165 B&B
Extra person $15.
Singles $70/$155, B&B.
7% sales tax, 3% room tax, 18% gratuity on food and beverage service.
Open year-round.

ATTRACTIONS
Golf, tennis, hiking, boating, fishing, down-hill skiing, cross-country skiing, olympic venues, bobsledding, horseback riding, arts and crafts.

CUISINE
Full breakfast and five-course gourmet dinner included in rates. Some entrees are surcharged. Full liquor and complete wine list.

DIRECTIONS
I-87 to Rte 73 to Lake Placid, L at 1st light (Main St.), to Mirror Lake Dr. to Interlaken Ave. 2nd St. on L.

Suitable for Children Over 5 • Designated Smoking Areas
Conference Facilities for 30 • MC, Visa, AMEX Accepted
Pets Accepted with Restrictions • Reservations Accepted Through Travel Agents

North River, NY

Garnet Hill Lodge

518-251-2444
Fax 518-251-3089
www.garnet-hill.com
mail@garnet-hill.com
13th Lake Road, North River, NY 12856

Select Registry Member *Since 1980*
Owners/Innkeepers
MARY AND GEORGE HEIM

WALKING INTO THE LOG HOUSE at Garnet Hill Lodge, you are greeted by the spaciousness of a great hotel, the warmth of a rustic mountain lodge and the friendly charm of a country inn. Once inside, you're drawn to the front windows and magnificant lake and mountain view, or the huge stone hearth and the welcome cheer of an ever-burning fire. Awake to the aroma of fresh pies and bread baking in our ovens. Enjoy full and hearty meals, including our lowfat, low-cholesterol menu and special vegetarian dishes.

RUSTIC MOUNTAIN INN

RATES
24 rooms, $140/$195 MAP.
Open year-round.

ATTRACTIONS
Beach, canoes, fish, hike, tennis, mountain-bike trails, cross-country skiing, snowshoeing. Nearby: Alpine skiing, Adirondack Museum, garnet mine tours, white-water rafting, maple sugar tours.

CUISINE
Full breakfast, lunch and dinner. Wine and liquor available.

DIRECTIONS
I-87 from Albany N to exit 23 N Rte 9 to Rte 28 W 22 miles to 13th Lake Rd. L for 5 miles. For directions from N or W please call.

Handicap Access Available • Suitable for Children
Conference Facilities for 60 • Visa, MC Accepted
Reservations Accepted Through Travel Agents

Chestertown, NY

Friends Lake Inn

518-494-4751
Fax 518-494-4616
www.friendslake.com
friends@netheaven.com
963 Friends Lake Road, Chestertown, NY 12817

Select Registry Member *Since 1998*
Innkeepers
Sharon and Greg Taylor

Experience the comfort and intimate ambiance of our handsomely restored inn, surrounded by the natural beauty of the Adirondacks. Guest rooms feature antiques, fine fabrics and featherbeds—some with Jacuzzis and fireplaces. Nationally acclaimed cuisine is served daily in the candlelit nineteenth century dining room, complemented by gracious service and a *Wine Spectator* Grand Award-winning wine list. Swim, canoe, or fish on Friends Lake. Ski or hike on 32 kilometers of trails. Come soon—we look forward to meeting you! AAA ◆◆◆. DiRoNa award of dining excellence.

Elegant Country Inn

RATES

17 guest rooms, many with private balconies, Jacuzzis and/or fireplaces. $235/$375. Dinner and breakfast included.
Open year-round.

ATTRACTIONS

In-ground heated swimming pool, hiking, canoeing, kayaking, fishing, swimming, bicycling, downhill and xc-skiing, golf, antique shops, horseback riding and museums nearby. White-water rafting on the mighty Hudson in the spring is a must!

CUISINE

Full country breakfast and candlelight dinner served daily. Banquets, luncheons, rehearsal dinners and weddings. Wide selection of wine and liquor. Wine, beer and scotch-tasting events monthly. Lighter Bistro menu available from 2 pm daily.

DIRECTIONS

I-87 (The Northway) to exit 25, follow Rte 8 W for 3.5 miles, turn L at Friends Lake Rd. Bear R at fork, continue for one mile, then turn R. .8 of a mile to inn, on the R.

Designated Smoking Areas • Conference Facilities for 17
MC, Visa, AMEX, Disc, CB Accepted
Reservations Accepted Through Travel Agents

Lake Luzerne, NY

The Lamplight Inn Bed & Breakfast

800-262-4668
518-696-5294 Fax 518-696-5256
www.lamplightinn.com
lamp@netheaven.com
231 Lake Avenue, P.O. Box 70
Lake Luzerne, NY 12846

Select Registry Member *Since 1996*
Innkeepers/Owners
GENE AND LINDA MERLINO

THE LAMPLIGHT INN is in the active Saratoga Springs/Lake George area. It was built in 1890 as a Victorian vacation home of a wealthy playboy/lumberman, on the southern edge of the Adirondack Park. The inn sits on 10 acres surrounded by towering white pines, just a short walk to crystal-clear Lake Luzerne. The Carriage House includes four Jacuzzi/fireplace suites w/TV and private deck and one wheelchair-accessible room w/fireplace, TV and private deck. A romantic getaway—a honeymoon location. Memorable full breakfast. Wine and beer, gift shop. 1992 Inn of the Year—*Laniers-Complete Guide to Bed & Breakfast.* Featured in the 1993 Christmas issue of *Country Inns* Magazine. AAA ◆◆◆ and Mobil ★★★.

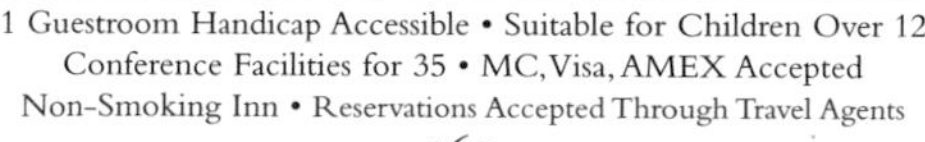
1 Guestroom Handicap Accessible • Suitable for Children Over 12
Conference Facilities for 35 • MC, Visa, AMEX Accepted
Non-Smoking Inn • Reservations Accepted Through Travel Agents

TRADITIONAL VILLAGE INN

RATES
17 rooms, 12 with fireplaces, 4 with Jacuzzis; 1 is wheelchair accessible. $95/$229—depending on season and type of room.
Open year-round.

ATTRACTIONS
One block-lake, one block-Hudson River. Pretty village midway between Lake George and Saratoga Springs. All year activity—swimming, kayaking and canoe rentals, white-water rafting, hiking, antiques, museums, horseback riding, golf, biking, skiing, snowmobiling.

CUISINE
Memorable full breakfast. Wine and beer licensed. Winter dinner packages.

DIRECTIONS
I-87 N from Albany to exit 21—Lake George/Lake Luzerne exit. 9N S 11 miles. Inn is on the R.

Saratoga Springs, NY

Westchester House Bed & Breakfast

518-587-7613
800-579-8368
www.westchesterhousebandb.com

102 Lincoln Avenue, P.O. Box 944
Saratoga Springs, NY 12866

Select Registry Member *Since 1996*
Innkeepers/Owners
BOB AND STEPHANIE MELVIN

WELCOME TO THE WESTCHESTER HOUSE B&B–Saratoga's hidden jewel. Nestled in a residential neighborhood of tree-lined streets and surrounded by exuberant gardens, this enticing Victorian confection combines gracious hospitality, old-world ambiance and up-to-date comforts. Lace curtains, oriental carpets, high ceilings, rich luster of natural woods, king- or queen-sized beds, tiled baths and luxury linens provide elegance and comfort. The charm and excitement of Saratoga is at our doorstep. After a busy day sampling the delights of Saratoga, relax on the wraparound porch, in the gardens or in the parlour, and enjoy a refreshing glass of lemonade. AAA ◆◆◆ and Mobil ★★.

Suitable for Children Over 10 • Non-Smoking Inn
Conference Facilities for 10 • AMEX, MC, Visa, Disc Accepted
Reservations Accepted Through Travel Agents

TRADITIONAL IN TOWN BREAKFAST INN

RATES

7 rooms.
Queen beds, $95/$225.
King beds, $115/$285 B&B.
Open Feb. through Nov.

ATTRACTIONS

Close to Saratoga Performing Arts Center, thoroughbred racing, tennis, golf, swim, boat, bike, hike, Skidmore College, museums and antiques.

CUISINE

A variety of excellent restaurants within easy walk of the inn.

DIRECTIONS

30 miles N of Albany: I-87 to exit 13 N. 4 miles N to 6th traffic light. Right, E on Lincoln to number 102.

Saratoga Springs, NY

Batcheller Mansion Inn

518-584-7012
Fax 518-581-7746
www.BatchellerMansionInn.com
BatMan5420@aol.com
20 Circular Street, Saratoga Springs, NY 12866

Select Registry Member *Since 2000*
Innkeeper
Sue McCabe

©1994 Robert Kerr

Designed by Nicols and Halcott of Albany in 1873, this High Victorian Gothic exhibits influences from the French Renaissance, Italian and Egyptian styles. The red and gray slate mansard roof is bifurcated by dormers, each accented by a huge clamshell arch. The ivory stucco facade is studded by a myriad of ornate bays and balustraded balconies, and as if that weren't enough to impress, its conical tower resembling a minaret is right out of Arabian Nights. That bit of exotica was the result of original owner George S. Batcheller. Selected as inn of the month in the April, 1999, issue of *Country Inns*.

Elegant In Town Inn

RATES
9 rooms, 5 suites.
Off-season $135/$275.
Racing season $250/$400.
Open year-round.

ATTRACTIONS
Saratoga Racetrack, Saratoga Performing Arts, Saratoga State Park, National Museum of Dance, National Museum of Racing, Saratoga Equine Sports Center, Skidmore College, Lake George, Saratoga Lake, Gore Mountain.

CUISINE
Continental breakfast Mon.-Fri. Full breakfast on weekends and racing season. Catered events available on request.

DIRECTIONS
From Albany take I-87 N exit at 13 N. Proceed for 3 miles to traffic light at Holiday Inn. Turn R 3rd building on R.

Suitable for Children Over 14 • Non-Smoking Inn
Conference Facilities for 20 • Visa, MC, AMEX Accepted
Reservations Accepted Through Travel Agents

Greenville, NY

Greenville Arms 1889 Inn

888-665-0044

518-966-5219 Fax 518-966-8754

www.greenvillearms.com

stay@greenvillearms.com

Route 32 South Street, P.O. Box 659

Greenville, NY 12083

Select Registry Member *Since 1975*

Innkeepers/Owners

ELIOT AND TISH DALTON

BUILT IN 1889 in the foothills of the Northern Catskills, this lovely Queen Anne Victorian Inn has welcomed guests for almost 50 years. Two buildings are set on six acres of lawns, shade trees and gardens. Antiques, original artwork and Victorian details add to an atmosphere of warmth and relaxed comfort. After a full country breakfast, guests enjoy hiking, biking, Hudson Valley sightseeing or relaxing by the inn's 50-foot outdoor pool. In the evening, guests are treated to delicious seasonal American cuisine, completing a memorable experience. Mobil ★★★.

TRADITIONAL VILLAGE INN

RATES

12 rooms, $115/$175 B&B.
1 suite, $175 B&B.
2 whirlpool rooms, $195 B&B.
Open May 1 - November 1.

ATTRACTIONS

Swimming pool, English croquet on premises. Tennis, golf courses nearby, bicycling, Catskill Mountains, hiking, Hudson Valley Historical sites, weekly art workshops.

CUISINE

A full country breakfast and afternoon tea is served in our brick-hearth dining rooms. Candelit dinners are available to houseguests Sunday through Friday. On Saturday night, accommodations are B&B with fine area restaurants recommended.

DIRECTIONS

From NYC: 2 1/2 hrs. N on I-87 to exit 21B, R 9W. S 2 miles to R 81, W 13 miles to Greenville. L at traffic light, inn is on R.

Suitable for Children Over 12 • Non-Smoking Inn
Conference Facilities for 40 • MC, Visa Accepted
Reservations Accepted Through Travel Agents

Windham, NY

Albergo Allegria

518-734-5560
Fax 518-734-5570
www.AlbergoUSA.com
mail@AlbergoUSA.com
43 Route 296, PO Box 267, Windham, NY 12496-0267

Select Registry Member *Since 2001*
Innkeepers / Owners
LESLIE AND MARIANNA LEMAN

ITALIAN FOR THE "INN OF HAPPINESS," Albergo Allegria is a circa 1892 inn set in the Northern Catskill Mountains. Situated on manicured lawns and country gardens, guests can relax under the 100 year-old oak tree or by the creek that is home to natural wildlife. The Inn's guestrooms offer beauty and history, while the carriage house suites are gracious and inviting with whirlpool and fireplace. In the sun-filled dining room an extended continental breakfast awaits on the marble sideboard. Chef Marianna then excites the pallet each morning with several hot breakfast entrees from the kitchen. Voted "2000 Inn of the year" by author Pamela Lanier.

VICTORIAN VILLAGE BREAKFAST INN

RATES

21 rooms, $73/$183 B&B.
6 suites, $153/$233 B&B.
Well-appointed guestrooms have down comforters and modern amenities. Suites are for those who desire privacy and indulgence.
Open year-round, except 2 weeks in April and November.

ATTRACTIONS

HERE: Old-fashion swimming hole, bird-watching, bountiful herb and country gardens, shuffle board and golf net. NEARBY: hiking, biking, kayaking, waterfalls, arboretum, golf, tennis, horseback riding, antiques, alpine and xc-skiing, snow tubing.

CUISINE

Hearty, full gourmet breakfast served each morning. 24-hour guest pantry with complimentary soft drinks, hot beverages and sweets. Afternoon tea served on Saturdays. Dinner restaurants nearby.

DIRECTIONS

I-87 Exit 21 (Catskill). Take Rte 23 W for 24 miles. L onto Rte 296. 1/10 mile on L.

2 Guestrooms Handicap Accessible • Suitable for Children Over 12
Conference Facilities for 14 • Non-Smoking Inn • Visa, MC Accepted
Reservations Accepted Through Travel Agents

Rhinebeck, NY

Beekman Arms

800-361-6517
845-876-7077 Fax 845-876-7077
www.beekmanarms.com
beekmanarm@aol.com
6387 Mill Street, Route 9, Rhinebeck, NY 12572

BEEKMAN ARMS is located in a historic walking village with exceptional attractions nearby: FDR Home and Library, Culinary Institute of America, Montgomery Place and a World War I air show. The 63 rooms are uniquely decorated, many with working fireplaces. The 1766 Tavern, rated excellent by the *New York Times,* offers American Cuisine by Larry Forgione, noted chef and author who has been a James Beard Chef of the Year. Wide plank floors, overhead beams and a stone hearth beckon guests as they enter the lobby. "What a perfectly lovely inn you have."—M.J.R. 5/31/96. AAA ◆◆◆ and Mobil ★★★

Select Registry Member *Since 1967*
Owner
CHUCK LA FORGE

TRADITIONAL VILLAGE INN

RATES
61 rooms, $85/$160.
2 suites, $125/$160.
Open year-round.

ATTRACTIONS
Golf, swimming, tennis, fishing, cross-country skiing, summer theatre, historic sites and antiquing nearby.

CUISINE
Breakfast, lunch, dinner. Banquet room (120). 1766 Tap Room—full-service bar.

DIRECTIONS
NY State Thruway (I-87) exit 19 to Rhinecliff Bridge. Go to Rte 9 G, S, then to Rte 9 S to Rhinebeck Village (2 miles). From Taconic Parkway Rte 199 W to Rte 308 W to Rhinebeck Village.

2 Guestrooms Handicap Accessible • Suitable for Children Over 10
Conference Facilities for 40 • AMEX, Visa, MC, Disc Accepted
Designated Smoking Areas

Stanfordville, NY

Lakehouse Inn on Golden Pond

845-266-8093
Fax 845-266-4051
www.lakehouseinn.com
judy@lakehouseinn.com
Shelley Hill Road, Stanfordville, NY 12581

A PRIVATE 22-ACRE LAKEFRONT ESTATE with spectacular views of the lake and woods. Rowboats and paddle boats await at a covered boat dock in warm weather and stacks of firewood feed blazing fireplaces when it is cold. The Lakehouse, built in 1990, is a contemporary cedar house that blends gently with the environment. The inside aura of the Lakehouse is subtle, elegant and serene. 'A trip to the Lakehouse on Golden Pond is like going to another world, the last word in luxury, from rare antiques to fireplaces and Jacuzzis.' *NY Times*. 'This idealized retreat offers what can only be called country luxury.' *NY Magazine*. Come spend a special time in splendid circumstances.

Select Registry Member *Since 2000*
Owner
JUDY KOHLER

ELEGANT WATERSIDE BREAKFAST INN

RATES
7 suites, $450/$675.
3 Maidens rooms, $125/$350.
Jacuzzis for two, woodburning fireplaces, private decks, views of the lake or woods. Color TV, VCR, CD tape player, mini-fridge.
Open year-round.

ATTRACTIONS
Historic mansions, wineries, golf, tennis, Hudson River cruises, horseback riding, summer theater, Dutchess County fairgrounds, Rhinebeck Aerodrome, antiquing and fine dining.

CUISINE
Breakfast delivered to guest rooms in covered basket. No other meals served.

DIRECTIONS
From Taconic Parkway and Rte 199: E on Rte 199, first R on Rte 53 3.5 miles, R on Shelley Hill Rd. Exactly .9 mile turn R into driveway which is just after the lake. Drive slowly, watch for deer. There is no sign.

Suitable for Children • Conference Facilities for 14
Credit Cards Accepted
Reservations Accepted Through Travel Agents

Garrison, NY

The Bird & Bottle Inn

800-782-6837
845-424-3000 Fax 845-424-3283
www.birdbottle.com
innkeeper@birdbottle.com
1123 Old Albany Post Road (Route 9)
Garrison, NY 10524

Select Registry Member *Since 1972*
Innkeeper/Owner
IRA BOYAR

A FAMED LANDMARK on the Old Albany-New York Post Road since 1761. This inn continues to welcome travelers with traditional Hudson Valley hospitality. An authentic old country inn, it is internationally renowned for its gourmet cuisine, served in three dining rooms with woodburning fireplaces. The Bird & Bottle Inn offers cozy overnight accommodations, also with working fireplaces, four-poster or canopied beds and colonial furnishings. *Hudson Valley Magazine* voted… "Most romantic Getaway, Hudson Valley, NY 1998," and "Best Restaurant Putnam County, 1999."

TRADITIONAL COUNTRY INN

RATES
2 rooms, $210/$220 MAP.
1 suite, $240 MAP.
1 cottage, $240 MAP.
Open year-round.

ATTRACTIONS
Hiking, nature walks, golf, cross-country skiing, boating.

CUISINE
Sun. brunch, dinner Wed. - Sun.
Wine and liquor available.

DIRECTIONS
From Rte I-84: Fishkill: S 8.5 miles on Rte 9 inn on L. From NYC and Westchester: N on Rte 9A/9, past Peekskill. Inn 8.5 miles beyond Peekskill on Rte 9.

Suitable for Children Over 12 • Conference Facilities for 40
Non-Smoking Inn • AMEX, Visa, MC, Diners, Disc Accepted
Reservations Accepted Through Travel Agents

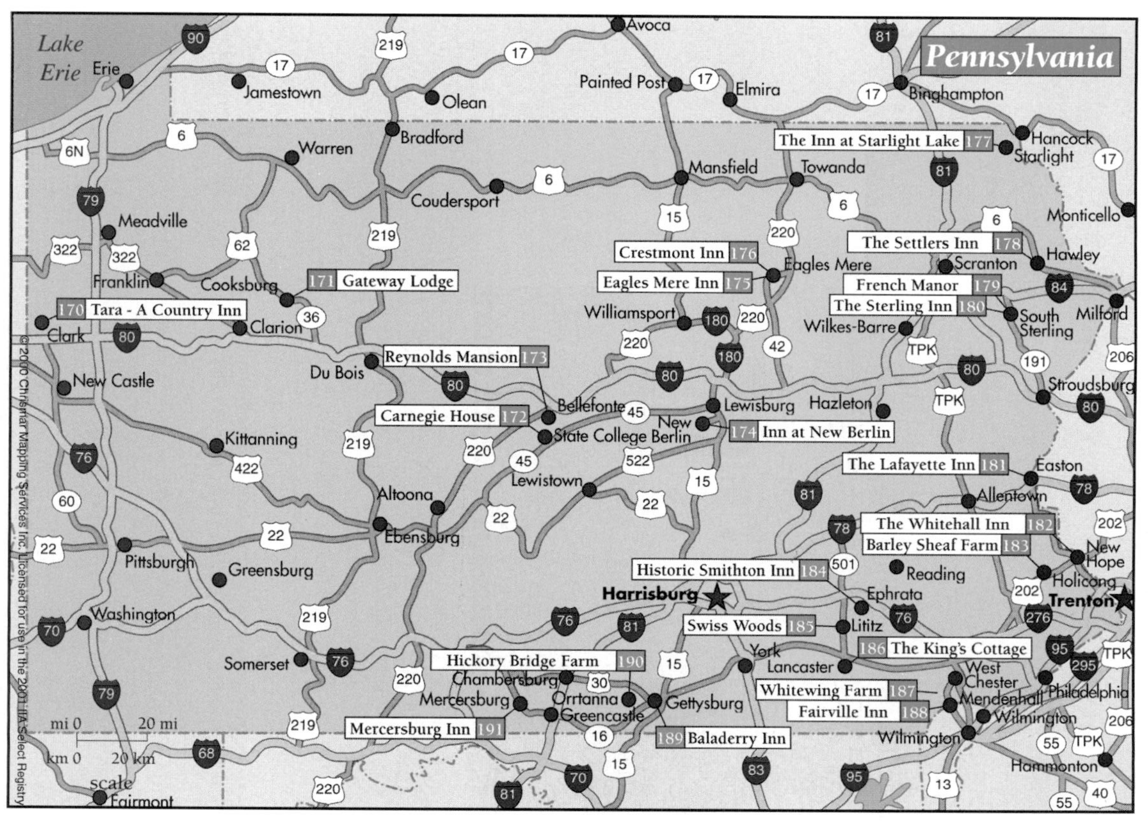

Pennsylvania
170 Tara - A Country Inn
171 Gateway Lodge
172 Carnegie House
173 Reynolds Mansion
174 Inn at New Berlin
175 Eagles Mere Inn
176 Crestmont Inn
177 The Inn at Starlight Lake
178 The Settlers Inn
179 French Manor
180 The Sterling Inn
181 The Lafayette Inn
182 The Whitehall Inn
183 Barley Sheaf Farm
184 Historic Smithton Inn
185 Swiss Woods
186 The King's Cottage
187 Whitewing Farm
188 Fairville Inn
189 Baladerry Inn
190 Hickory Bridge Farm
191 Mercersburg Inn
Lake Erie
Erie
Meadville
Franklin
Cooksburg
Clarion
Clark
New Castle
Pittsburgh
Washington
Fairmont
Kittanning
Greensburg
Somerset
Jamestown
Warren
Du Bois
Bradford
Olean
Coudersport
Altoona
Ebensburg
Bellefonte
State College
Lewistown
Williamsport
Eagles Mere
Lewisburg
New Berlin
Harrisburg
Chambersburg
Mercersburg
Orrtanna
Greencastle
Gettysburg
York
Lancaster
Lititz
Ephrata
Reading
Allentown
Easton
Hazleton
Wilkes-Barre
Scranton
South Sterling
Stroudsburg
Hawley
Milford
Monticello
Hancock
Starlight
Binghampton
Towanda
Mansfield
Elmira
Painted Post
Avoca
New Hope
Holicong
Trenton
Philadelphia
West Chester
Mendenhall
Wilmington
Hammonton
scale
mi 0 20 mi
km 0 20 km
© 2000 Chrismar Mapping Services Inc. Licensed for use in the 2001 IIA Select Registry

Clark, PA

Tara-A Country Inn

800-782-2803
724-962-3535 Fax 724-962-3250
www.tara-inn.com
info@tara-inn.com
2844 Lake Road, Clark, PA 16113

Select Registry Member *Since 1986*
Innkeepers/Owners
JIM AND DONNA WINNER

IF YOU LOVED THE MOVIE 'GONE WITH THE WIND', you will love *Tara,* a themed Inn, complete with costumed southern Belles, antiques, and the largest Civil War Gun and memorabilia collection west of Gettysburg. Built in 1854, this magnificent mansion reflects the golden days of the antebellum South, with rooms charmingly decorated to recall the grace and grandeur of yesteryear. Award-winning restaurants attract gourmet critics from many states. Seven-course/white glove service in Ashley's, renowned steakhouse tavern called Stonewall's and family-style dinners for groups. AAA ◆◆◆◆ and *Wine Spectators* award of excellence. Superior gardens, walkways, elaborate statuary, swans. Rooms all have gas fireplaces and many have whirlpool tubs.

14 Guestrooms Handicap Accessible • Suitable for Children
Conference Facilities for 100• AMEX, Visa, MC, Disc Accepted
Non-Smoking Inn • Reservations Accepted Through Travel Agents

ELEGANT WATERSIDE INN

RATES

24 rooms.
Sun.-Fri., $200/$375.
Sat., $275/$375.
3 suites.
Sun.-Fri., $375.
Sat., $450 MAP.
Open year-round.

ATTRACTIONS

Indoor and outdoor heated pools. Pool table, bikes available (no charge), gift shop, bocci, and croquet. NEARBY: art galleries, World's Largest Ladies Off-Price Fashion Store, World's Largest Shoe Store, World's Largest Candy Store, outlet shopping, and Winners Collectibles Store featuring antiques, bronzes, oriental carpets, and gifts. Boating on Lake Shenango.

CUISINE

Gourmet dining, steakhouse. Breakfast room (guests only). Package rates. Top-shelf bar full service, extensive wine list.

DIRECTIONS

From I-80: Exit 1 N, Rte 18 N for 8 miles, inn is located on E side overlooking Shenango Lake. Rte 258 Clark exit from 18.

Cooksburg, PA

Gateway Lodge–Country Inn

800-843-6862
814-744-8017 Fax 814-744-8017
www.gatewaylodge.com

Select Registry Member *Since 1983*
Innkeepers
Joe and Linda Burney

Route 36, Box 125, Cooksburg, PA 16217

AMID SOME OF THE MOST MAGNIFICENT FOREST scenery east of the Mississippi, this rustic log cabin inn has been awarded one of the top 10 best inns in the U.S. and *Money Magazine's* Top Travel Pick. The inn features a large stone fireplace in the common room, home-cooked meals by candlelight, air-conditioning, indoor heated pool and sauna, afternoon tea, nightly turn-down service. Cottages have fireplaces, Suites with king-sized beds, fireside whirlpool tubs and large private bath. Our conference complex has break-out kitchen, porches and reception area. Customized small weddings and retreats. All Gateway buildings and facilities are non-smoking.

2 Guestrooms Handicap Accessible
Conference Facilities for 50 • Non-Smoking Inn
Visa, MC, Disc Accepted

Rustic Mountain Inn

RATES
7 rooms, $90/$190.
8 cottages, $135/$280.
Suites, $135/$290 EP, B&B, MAP.
Weekly and mid-week specials, too.
Open year-round.

ATTRACTIONS
Hiking, biking, canoeing and inner-tubing, horseback riding, bird-watching, antiques, crafts, collectibles, cross-country skiing, hunting, ice-skating, snowmobiling, summer theatre, on-site pool, sauna and exercise room, old-fashioned game room/library.

CUISINE
Full service breakfast, lunch, dinner. Four- and seven-course dinners by reservation. Afternoon tea served daily. Five-star wine list offering over 350 selections.

DIRECTIONS
I-80 E: Exit 13, R on Rte 36 N, 17 miles. Lodge on R. I-80 W: Exit 9, L on Rte 68, go thru four stoplights to Main St. intersection for 10 miles. At stop sign turn R, go S on Rte 36 4 miles. Cross bridge. Go 1/4 mile and Lodge is on L.

State College, PA

Carnegie House

800-229-5033
814-234-2424 Fax 814-231-1299
www.carnegiehouse.com
carnhouse@penn.com
100 Cricklewood Drive, State College, PA 16803

Select Registry Member *Since 1997*
Innkeepers/Owners
PETER AND HELGA SCHMID

THIS OLD-WORLD STYLE COUNTRY HOUSE HOTEL overlooks the 17th green of Toftrees championship golf course; 20 large rooms and two suites are each uniquely decorated in its own way. The Carnegie House Library with fireplace and comfortable furnishings invites you to pause, enjoy a pleasant libation, read a good book, delight in gracious conversation with new-found friends. A complete food fare is served daily in full breakfasts, leisurely luncheons and elegantly unhurried dinners. Perfect for holidays, reunions, getaways, business retreats and meetings. AAA ◆◆◆◆.

ELEGANT IN TOWN INN

RATES

20 rooms, $150/$175/$195.
2 suites, $275 B&B.
Open year-round, except Christmas Day.

ATTRACTIONS

18-hole championship golf course, fitness trail, cross-country skiing, biking, touring historic villages, Penn State cultural and athletic events.

CUISINE

Full Breakfast, delightful Lunches. A la carte and table d'hôte dinner. Fine wines, Thistle Bar, single malts.

DIRECTIONS

Mt. Nittany Expressway (322 Bypass) to Toftrees exit. (Westbound turn R/ Eastbound turn L) to Toftrees Ave. Turn R onto Toftrees Ave., proceed to stop sign at Cricklewood Dr. Carnegie House on corner, enter from Toftrees Ave.

---

1 Guestroom Handicap Accessible • Non-Smoking Inn
Conference Facilities for 40 • AMEX, MC, Visa Accepted
Reservations Accepted Through Travel Agents

Bellefonte, PA

Reynolds Mansion

800-899-3929
814-353-8407 Fax 814-353-1530
www.reynoldsmansion.com
innkeeper@reynoldsmansion.com
101 West Linn Street, Bellefonte, PA 16823

Select Registry Member *Since 2000*
Innkeepers/Owners
CHARLOTTE & JOSEPH HEIDT, JR.

ESCAPE TO THE REYNOLDS MANSION and enter a romantic atmosphere of Victorian elegance and luxurious comfort. Enjoy a game of pool in the billard room or curl up by the fire in the snuggery with your favorite book. Relax in three elegantly furnished common rooms, each with a unique wood carved and tiled fireplace. Built in 1885, the mansion is a blend of the Gothic, Italianate and Queen Anne styles. Interior details include a marble vestibule, classic mirrors, Eastlake woodwork, stained glass windows and inlaid parquet floors. So whether you are looking for a romantic getaway, or a retreat from the stress of daily life, come visit us. A warm welcome awaits you.

VICTORIAN IN TOWN
BREAKFAST INN

RATES

6 Suites, $95 to $175
Spacious guestrooms feature fireplaces, and Jacuzzi or steam shower. Each beautifully decorated, provides A/C and private bath.
Open year-round.
Closed December 24 and 25.

ATTRACTIONS

Only 10 miles from cultural activities and events at Penn State. Enjoy our town's outstanding Victorian architecture, explore nearby parks. Golf or fish the area's many famous trout streams. Biking, hiking, antiquing, and scenic day-trips to Amish country.

CUISINE

Full breakfast included. Fine dining within walking distance. Award winning French cuisine nearby.

DIRECTIONS

I-80 exit 24. Take Rte 26 towards Bellefonte to 550. Go R at bottom of ramp and follow 550 into town. At third light turn R onto Allegheny St. At second light turn L on Linn. Enter through iron gates on R.

Just 4 miles from Rt. 80 and 10 miles from Penn State.

Suitable for Children Over 12 • Visa, MC, AMEX Accepted
Designated Smoking Areas
Reservations Accepted Through Travel Agents

New Berlin, PA

The Inn at New Berlin

800-797-2350

570-966-0321 Fax 570-966-9557

www.innatnewberlin.com

stay@newberlin-inn.com

321 Market Street, New Berlin, PA 17855-0390

Select Registry Member *Since 1997*

Innkeepers/Owners

JOHN AND NANCY SHOWERS

TRADITIONAL VILLAGE INN

INN MEMORIES ARE MADE from the inviting front porch swing to the herb garden where the restaurant's seasonings and garnishes are selected. Superb dining at Gabriel's Restaurant coupled with romantic lodging provide an uptown experience in a rural setting, and Gabriel's Gift Collection now features central PA's largest selection of Christopher Radko ornaments! Guests relay that they depart feeling nurtured, relaxed, and most of all inspired. Featured on two national PBS broadcasts hosted by Gail Greco (1998). "A luxurious base for indulging in a clutch of quiet pleasures" ... *The Philadelphia Inquirer.* AAA ◆◆◆ and Mobil ★★★.

RATES

7 rooms, 2 suites (2 bedrooms), $99/$169 B&B.
Open year-round.

ATTRACTIONS

Nearby state parks for hiking and biking, trout fishing in Penns Creek, Amish culture (shops, quilts), antiquing, museums, Knoebel's Amusement Grove.

CUISINE

Acclaimed Gabriel's Restaurant: brunch and dinner Wednesday through Sunday. Wine and liquor available.

DIRECTIONS

In central PA, take Lewisburg exit off Rte 80/Rte 15 S to Rte 45. Go W on Rte 45 for 4 miles. Turn L onto Dreisbach Mt. Rd. Continue 5 miles to Market St.; turn R. The inn will be the second home on your R.

Limited Handicap Access Available • Suitable For Children
Conference Facilities for 20 • MC, Visa, Disc Accepted
Non-Smoking Inn • Reservations Accepted Through Travel Agents

Eagles Mere, PA

Eagles Mere Inn

800-426-3273
570-525-3273
www.eaglesmereinn.com
relax@eaglesmereinn.com
Corner of Mary and Sullivan, Eagles Mere, PA 17731

Select Registry Member *Since 1993*
Innkeepers/Owners
SUSAN AND PETER GLAUBITZ

EAGLES MERE, 'THE LAST UNSPOILED RESORT,' sits on a mountain with a pristine lake surrounded by giant hemlock, rhododendron and mountain laurel. Built in 1887, restored in 1998, we are the last remaining inn built for guests of the 1800s. The inn has received many recognition awards, and is featured by numerous travel writers. Comments are: 'Wonderful food... friendly and accommodating staff...ultimate relaxation.' Guests enjoy genuine hospitality with personal attention. If you want a quiet, relaxing place to spend time together and enjoy warm hospitality and gourmet meals, call for our brochure or visit our web site at www.eaglesmereinn.com.

TRADITIONAL MOUNTAIN INN

RATES

16 rooms/3 suites.
All have summer AC and private baths. $139/$250 includes full country breakfast and gourmet dinner for two.
Open year-round.

ATTRACTIONS

Bike, boat, xc-skis available. Great hiking trails, 17 waterfalls, covered bridges, birding, ice toboggan, antiquing, tennis, golf, swimming, fishing, shopping, spectacular sunsets, Victorian cottages. Reading, fireplaces, hammock, porch rockers.

CUISINE

Our experience is in three and four-star restaurants. We have the area's best reputation for excellent five-course candlelit gourmet dinners. We also serve ample country breakfasts. We have a full liquor license, a cozy pub and an excellent wine selection.

DIRECTIONS

From E: Rte 80 W to Exit #34, Rte 42 N. From W: Rte 80 to Rte 220 N then Rte 42 N. In Eagles Mere turn at sign to Mary Ave. Go one block to inn on the corner.

1 Guestroom Handicap Accessible • Suitable for Children
Conference Facilities for 35 • Visa, MC Accepted
Designated Smoking Areas • Reservations Accepted Through Travel Agents

Eagles Mere, PA

Crestmont Inn

800-522-876
570-525-3519 Fax 570-525-35347
www.crestmont-inn.com
crestmnt@epix.net
Crestmont Drive, Eagles Mere, PA 17731

EXCLUSIVE TWO-NIGHT PACKAGE offered to our guests! This special package includes a two-night stay in one of our premium suites with a romantic dinner for two, evening of your choice, a full country breakfast each morning, and complimentary champagne upon your arrival. Our suites include queen bed, large private baths with clawfoot tubs, spacious sitting area with cable TV and refrigerator. All of our suites are tastefully decorated with your comfort in mind. During your stay at Crestmont Inn, you may enjoy golf, hiking, pool, tennis, lake activities, biking, shopping and sightseeing, or simply relax on one of our porches. AAA ◆◆◆.

Select Registry Member *Since 1989*
Owners
KATHLEEN AND ROBERT OLIVER
Innkeepers
KAREN AND DOUG

TRADITIONAL MOUNTAIN INN

RATES

EXCLUSIVE PACKAGE!
Two-night stay, breakfast, gourmet dinner one evening, complimentary champagne, tax $389. Other rates available.
Open year-round.

ATTRACTIONS

HERE: Har-tru tennis, heated swimming pool, shuffleboard.
NEARBY: 18-hole golf course, lake, state parks, hiking, biking, fishing, toboggan slide, cross-country skiing, shopping, antiquing, cultural activities in summer months.

CUISINE

Traditional country breakfast included in rate. Gourmet, candlelit dinners available in our two dining rooms. Bar and cocktail lounge with a fine selection of beer, wine and spirits.

DIRECTIONS

From 1-80, exit 34 to 42 N for 33 miles to Eagles Mere Village. Continue through town and follow Crestmont Inn signs.

1 Guestroom Handicap Accessible • Suitable for Children in family suites
Conference Facilities for 32 • Visa, MC Accepted
Designated Smoking Areas • Reservations Accepted Through Travel Agents

Starlight, PA

The Inn at Starlight Lake

800-248-2519
570-798-2519 Fax 570-798-2672
www.innatstarlightlake.com
theinn@unforgettable.com
P.O. Box 27, Starlight, PA 18461

Select Registry Member *Since 1976*
Innkeepers/Owners
JACK AND JUDY MCMAHON

SINCE 1909, GUESTS HAVE BEEN DRAWN to this classic country inn on a clear lake in the rolling hills of northeastern Pennslyvania. The atmosphere is warm, congenial and informal. Twenty-two main house and cottage rooms, one w/fireplace, suite w/whirlpool, and a family house and conference center complete this delightful little universe. Activities for all seasons are at your disposal. A menu that blends classic recipes with innovative touches gives added pleasure. But most important is the opportunity to get away from it all and enter into the comfort and quality of hospitality that the McMahons' provide.

TRADITIONAL WATERSIDE INN

RATES

22 main house and cottage rooms, $125/$165 MAP.
Suite, $185/$225 MAP.
Open daily for lodging and public dining except earylApril.

ATTRACTIONS

Swim, boat, fish, hike, cycle, play tennis, near xc and downhill skiing, ice-skate, near golf, near Delaware River, fly-fishing, canoeing, antiques, historic river towns.

CUISINE

Lakeside dining offers variety of fresh-made entrees, pastas and pastries. Full wine, beer and liquor service.

DIRECTIONS

From N.Y.: Rte 17 exit 87-Hancock N.Y. on Rte 191 S. 1 mile to Rte 370 W turn R 3 miles to sign on R. From I-81: Exit 62, local roads, map sent.

Common Rooms Handicap Accessible • Suitable for Children
Conference Facilities for 20 • Visa, MC Accepted
Designated Smoking Areas • Reservations Accepted Through Travel Agents

Hawley, PA

The Settlers Inn

800-833-8527
570-226-2993 Fax 570-226-1874
www.thesettlersinn.com
settler@ptd.net
4 Main Avenue, Hawley, PA 18428

Select Registry Member *Since 1992*
Innkeepers/Owners
JEANNE AND GRANT GENZLINGER

THIS TUDOR MANOR, of English arts and crafts design, surrounded by herb and flower gardens, lends visitors a sense of place and serenity. The Chestnut Tavern's bluestone fireplace beckons with large comfortable chairs to offer relaxation. Guest rooms are decorated with white wicker, flowered wallpapers and comfortable antique furnishings. The inn's tradition of fine dining is highlighted by the artisan breads and menus influenced by the seasons. Dine in the elegant dining room, casual tavern, or outdoor terrace. Experience the sense of comfort given by the blend of nature, gardens, art, fine food and personal service. AAA ◆◆◆ and Mobil ★★★.

TRADITIONAL VILLAGE INN

RATES
20 rooms and suites,
$95/$160 B&B.
Open year-round.

ATTRACTIONS
Lake Wallenpaupack, Delaware River, Promised Land State Park, golf, canoe, fishing, Glass Museum and antique shops.

CUISINE
Breakfast, lunch, dinner. Outdoor terrace dining. Wine, liquor and many microbrews.

DIRECTIONS
I-84 exit 7, Rte 390 N to 507 N to Rte 6 W. 2 1/2 miles to inn.

Suitable for Children• Designated Smoking Areas
Conference Facilities for 125 • Credit Cards Accepted
Reservations Accepted Through Travel Agents

South Sterling, PA

The French Manor

800-523-8200
570-676-3244 Fax 570-676-9786
www.thesterlinginn.com
thesterlinginn@ezaccess.net
Box 39 Huckleberry Road South Sterling, PA 18460

Select Registry Member *Since 1991*
Innkeepers
RON AND MARY KAY LOGAN
Chef
KEVIN CONROY

ELEGANT COUNTRY INN

RATES
6 rooms, $135/$210 B&B.
9 suites, $195/$275 B&B.
8 suites with fireplace and Jacuzzi.
Open year-round.

ATTRACTIONS
Beautiful scenery, hiking, croquet, cross-country skiing, sledding. Nearby: tennis, boating, ice-skating, indoor pool, golf, horseback riding, antiquing, 3 state parks.

CUISINE
Gourmet breakfast and French cuisine at dinner; breakfast in bed on request. Wine cellar, premium liquors and beer available.

DIRECTIONS
From NYC: I-80 W exit 50, 191 N to S Sterling (27 miles), turn L on Huckleberry Rd.
From Philadelphia: NE exit PA tpke. to exit 35; 940 E to 423 N to 191 N; from I-84: exit 5, 191 S to R onto Huckleberry Rd.

MODELED AFTER HIS CHATEAU in the south of France, Joseph Hirshhorn created a private retreat where he could enjoy the solitude of the mountains and the serenity of "Mother Nature". Having breakfast or tea on the veranda with a view to the surrounding hilltops, gives our guests this same feeling. The accommodations and cuisine are unmatched in the area. At the French Manor, old world charm and furnishings are seamlessly joined with all the modern conveniences. Midweek travelers can enjoy our "Enchanted Evening" package. Triple sheeting and turn down service along with complimentary sherry, cheese and fruit add to the romance.

2 Guestrooms Handicap Accessible • Designated Smoking Areas
Conference Facilities for 30 • AMEX, Visa, MC, Disc Accepted
Reservations Accepted Through Travel Agents

South Sterling, PA

The Sterling Inn

800-523-8200
570-676-3311 Fax 570-676-9786
www.thesterlinginn.com
thesterlinginn@ezaccess.net
Route 191, South Sterling, PA 18460

Select Registry Member *Since 1974*
Innkeepers
THE LOGAN FAMILY

A FRIENDLY, ROMANTIC, ATMOSPHERE with beautiful grounds, crystal clear streams, a waterfall, 106 acres of woods and trails, indoor pool and hot tub. "The country inn you've always looked for but never thought you'd find." Attractive accommodations include traditional country rooms, Victorian suites with fireplaces and cottage suites with fireplace and Jacuzzi. Attentive service and American country cuisine. Couples celebrating a special occasion may enjoy our "Innkeeping with Romance" package. Social and family gatherings can enjoy our lodge or guest house. The Logans are the third family to operate the inn in its 140-year history.

TRADITIONAL COUNTRY INN

RATES

38 rooms, $110/$140 B&B.
27 suites and cottages, $140/$240 B&B. Some with fireplace and Jacuzzi.
Open year-round.

ATTRACTIONS

ON SITE: private lake, fishing, indoor pool, tennis, hiking trails, cross-country skiing, skating, tobogganing. NEARBY: golf, horseback riding, rafting, biking, antiquing, three state parks within fifteen minutes.

CUISINE

Full country breakfast, luncheon and candlelit dinner. Packed lunches. Wine and cocktails available.

DIRECTIONS

From NY and NJ: I-80 W to PA exit 50, follow 191 N 25 miles to inn; from PA tpke (NE exit): take exit 35, 940 E to 423 N to 191 N .5 mile to inn; from I-84: take exit 5, 191 S to inn.

---

3 Guestrooms Handicap Accessible • Suitable for Children
Conference Facilities for 80 • AMEX, Visa, MC, Disc Accepted
Designated Smoking Areas • Reservations Accepted Through Travel Agents

Easton, PA

The Lafayette Inn

610-253-4500
Fax 610-253-4635
www.lafayetteinn.com
lafayinn@fast.net
525 West Monroe Street, Easton, PA 18042

Select Registry Member *Since 2000*
Innkeepers/Owners
SCOTT AND MARILYN BUSHNELL

THE ANTIQUE-FILLED ROOMS and landscaped grounds of The Lafayette Inn offer the most elegant and distinctive accommodations available to travelers in Pennsylvania's historic Lehigh Valley. Located just a few blocks from Easton's National Register Historic District and two blocks from the Lafayette College campus, our Inn offers a place to relax after enjoying the colors of the Crayola factory, the peacefulness of a mule-drawn canal boat ride, or exploring the historic Delaware and Lehigh River valleys. Our lounge, sunroom, garden patio, and wrap-around porch are ideal for a elegant party, celebrating a special event, or relaxing with friends.

TRADITIONAL VILLAGE BREAKFAST INN

RATES

16 rooms/suites, $99/$250. Antique-filled rooms, all with private bath, TV, phones. Suites with gas fireplace, balcony. Premier room with whirlpool tub.
Open year-round.

ATTRACTIONS

Antiquing, Crayola factory, National Canal Museum, mule-drawn canal boat rides, Musikfest, scenic Delaware River canoeing/tubing, Dorney Park, art galleries. Nearby: outlet shopping, skiing, or relax with a good book by the waterfall on the patio.

CUISINE

Breakfast, complimentary soft drinks, coffee, pastries available all day. Excellent restaurants within short distance. No liquor license.

DIRECTIONS

I-78, PA exit 22 N through Easton. N on Third St. toward Lafayette College. Up hill to corner of Cattell St. and Monroe St.

3 Common Rooms Handicap Accessible • Suitable for Children
Conference Facilities for 15 • MC, Visa, AMEX, Diners, Disc Accepted
Non-Smoking Inn

New Hope, PA

The Whitehall Inn

215-598-7945
Fax 215-598-0378
www.selectregistry.com

Select Registry Member *Since 1990*
Innkeepers/Owners
Mike and Suella Wass

1370 Pineville Road, New Hope, PA 18938

COME TO NEW HOPE—Bucks County—and experience our very special Inn! Indulge in a four-course candlelit breakfast set with heirloom sterling, European china, and beautiful crystal—called "Sumptuous" by *Bon Appetit.* Relax and enjoy afternoon tea. The culinary genius of Suella abounds! Rooms furnished with family antiques and top-of-the-line Sealy Crown Jewel mattresses. Most rooms with-fireplaces. Enjoy the pool, rose garden and horses—all situated on the grounds of our 1794 estate. Evening turn-down service with our own Whitehall chocolate truffles. "After years in their niche, the Wasses continue to stand above the rest."

Traditional Country Breakfast Inn

RATES
5 rooms, $150/$210.
Suite, $220 B&B.
Open year-round.

ATTRACTIONS
Pool and horses on property, antiquing, outlet shopping, hiking, biking, river activities, Washington Crossing, Michener Art Center and Mercer Mile.

CUISINE
Four-course candlelit breakfast, afternoon tea.

DIRECTIONS
Hwy 202, S from New Hope to Lahaska. L. onto Street Rd. to 2nd intersection, R onto Pineville Rd. Continue 1.3 miles to inn on R.

Conference Facilities for 12
Visa, MC, Disc, AMEX, Diners, CB Accepted
Reservations Accepted Through Travel Agents

Holicong, PA

Barley Sheaf Farm

215-794-5104
Fax 215-794-5332
www.barleysheaf.com
info@barleysheaf.com
5281 York Road (Route 202), Holicong, PA 18928

Select Registry Member *Since 1982*
Innkeepers/Owners
VERONIKA AND PETER SUESS

BARLEY SHEAF IS A 1740 BUCKS COUNTY FARM situated on 30 acres at the end of a long tree-lined drive. Once owned by the playwright George S. Kaufman, it was the gathering place for some of Broadway's brightest luminaries, ie. Dorothy Parker, Moss Hart, The Marx Brothers, etc. A park-like setting provides beauty and seclusion ideally suited for a romantic getaway. Lovely decorated guest rooms, some with working fireplaces or Jacuzzi, gracious common rooms, warm Swiss hospitality, and an outstanding breakfast are Barley Sheaf hallmarks. French and German spoken.

TRADITIONAL COUNTRY BREAKFAST INN

RATES
8 rooms, $110/$170 B&B.
5 suites, $155/$300 B&B.
Open year-round.

ATTRACTIONS
Pool, lawn games, antiquing, flea markets, galleries, theaters, shopping, historic touring, horseback riding, tubing and ballooning.

CUISINE
Full country breakfast, afternoon treat, dining close by. BYOB.

DIRECTIONS
On Rte 202 between New Hope and Doylestown, .5 mile W of Lahaska. From NJ use 202 S; from S take 276 to 611 N. In Doylestown take 202 N.

1 Guestroom Handicap Accessible • Suitable for Children Over 8
Conference Facilities for 50 • AMEX, Visa, MC, Diners Accepted
Non-Smoking Inn • Reservations Accepted Through Travel Agents

Ephrata, PA

Historic Smithton Inn

717-733-6094
www.historicsmithtoninn.com

Select Registry Member *Since 1987*
Innkeeper/Co-owner
DOROTHY GRAYBILL

900 West Main Street, Ephrata, PA 17522

THE HISTORIC SMITHTON INN, a restored romantic stone inn, open 235 years, is located in Lancaster County, the home of Amish and Pennsylvania Dutch people. It has large bright rooms, with working fireplaces, canopy beds, desks, leather upholstered and handcrafted furnishings, Pennsylvania Dutch bed quilts, and candlelight and chamber music. Fresh flowers and nightshirts all help to create the perfect setting, and we are small enough to provide individual attention to make yours the perfect trip. Common rooms are warm and inviting with fireplaces. Easy access to farmlands, museums, crafts and antiques help make our inn a most desirable stop. AAA ◆◆◆◆.

TRADITIONAL VILLAGE
BREAKFAST INN

RATES
7 rooms, $75/$155 B&B.
1 suite, $145/$175 B&B.
Open year-round.

ATTRACTIONS
Touring PA Dutch farmland (Amish, Mennonite, etc.), farmers markets, antiques, auctions, craft centers, museum, Smithton Dahlia Gardens, golf and hiking.

CUISINE
Full breakfast served (waffles, pancakes, etc.) Some rooms have refrigerators.

DIRECTIONS
From N: Take Route 222 S to 322 W. Exit Right. 2.5 miles to Inn.
From S: Exit 30 to 222 N to 322 W. 2.5 miles to Inn.

1 Guestroom Handicap Accessible • Suitable for Children
Pets Allowed by prior arrangement • Visa, MC Accepted
Non-Smoking Inn • Reservations Accepted Through Travel Agents

Lititz, PA

Swiss Woods

800-594-8018
717-627-3358 Fax 717-627-3483
www.swisswoods.com
innkeeper@swisswoods.com
500 Blantz Road, Lititz, PA 17543

SURROUNDED BY MEADOWS AND GARDENS, Swiss Woods is a quiet retreat on 30 acres in Lancaster's Amish country. All rooms feature patios or balconies, some with lake views, and are decorated with the natural wood furnishings typical of Switzerland. Fabulous breakfasts, complemented by our own blend of coffee, are served in our sunlit common room. Enjoy the views of extraordinary gardens, landscaped with a wide variety of annuals and perennials. Take a hike, watch the birds and relax! ...Where the cookie jar is always full! German spoken. AAA ◆◆◆ and Mobil ★★★.

MC, Visa, Disc, AMEX Accepted
Non-Smoking Inn • Reservations Accepted Through Travel Agents

Select Registry Member *Since 1993*
Innkeepers/Owners
WERNER AND DEBRAH MOSIMANN

TRADITIONAL COUNTRY BREAKFAST INN

RATES
6 rooms (2 with Jacuzzi), $110/$180 B&B.
1 suite, $150 B&B.
January-March, midweek discounts B&B.
Open year-round.

ATTRACTIONS
Convenient between the Hershey and Lancaster attractions. Hershey Park, Amish tours, farmers markets, pretzel and chocolate factories, canoeing, bird-watching, hiking, antiques, quilts, shopping outlets. NOAH at the Millenium Theater in Strasburg.

CUISINE
Every morning our guests are greeted with a breakfast to remember! Inn specialties include garden fritatta with our own fresh asparagus and freshly-baked breads from old world recipies with whole grains and unique flavors. Afternoon tea and sweets.

DIRECTIONS
From Lancaster: 11 miles N on 501 thru Lititz. L on Brubaker Valley Rd. 1 mile to lake. R on Blantz Rd. Inn is on the L.
From NYC: Rte 78/22 W to exit 3. S on Rte 501 1 mile beyond Brickerville. R onto Brubaker Valley Rd. 1 mile to lake.

Lancaster, PA

The King's Cottage, A Bed & Breakfast Inn

800-747-8717
717-397-1017 Fax 717-397-3447
www.kingscottagebb.com
kingscottage@earthlink.net
1049 East King Street, Lancaster, PA 17602-3231

Select Registry Member *Since 1995*
Innkeepers / Owners
KAREN AND JIM OWENS

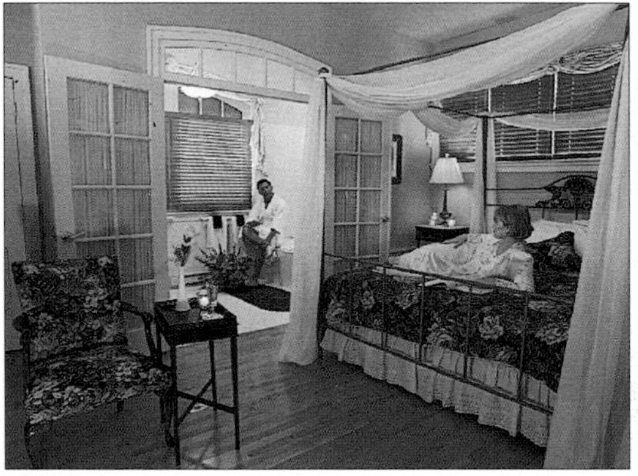

SNUGGLED IN THE MIDST OF HISTORIC LANCASTER, The King's Cottage, a Bed & Breakfast Inn, is an oasis of ultimate comfort and amenities, specializing in lavishly decorated rooms and personalized guest services. Our luxurious rooms feature king/queen-sized brass or canopy beds, antique armoires, private baths with oversized soaking tubs or whirlpools. After a delicious full breakfast, visit the scenic Amish farmlands, tour historic sites, or shop for handmade quilts and crafts, then return to a gourmet treat by the fireplace in the library. We'll help you make reservations for fine dining or dinner with an Amish family. On the National Register, AAA ◆◆◆ and Mobil ★★★. Spanish spoken.

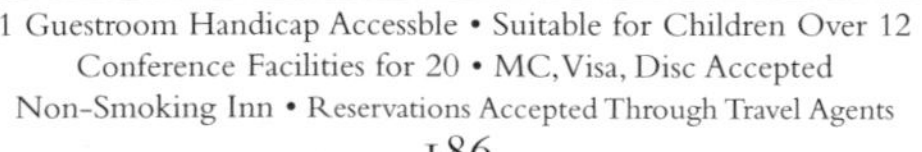

1 Guestroom Handicap Accessble • Suitable for Children Over 12
Conference Facilities for 20 • MC, Visa, Disc Accepted
Non-Smoking Inn • Reservations Accepted Through Travel Agents

TRADITIONAL IN TOWN BREAKFAST INN

RATES

7 rooms main building.
K/Q beds, $105/$195.
Honeymoon cottage, $205 B&B.
Open year-round.
Holiday and Special Event rates apply.

ATTRACTIONS

PA Dutch Country tours, historic homes and museums, theme parks, sports, theaters and good old-fashioned exploring. Ride steam locomotives, hot-air balloons, Amish buggies. Feast on gourmet food or smorgasbords. Antique capitol, quilts and Hershey!

CUISINE

We serve a full gourmet breakfast and afternoon tea. Breakfast features fresh local produce and meats. Most dietary restrictions accommodated if requested in advance. Near many fine restaurants. A small guest kitchen allows ice, coffee and tea any time.

DIRECTIONS

Rte 30 to Walnut St. exit. At second light turn L. At 2nd stop sign turn L. Go 1 block and turn R onto Cottage Ave. Inn is last building on R. Parking: Turn R before white wall.

West Chester, PA

Whitewing Farm B&B

Adjacent to Longwood Gardens

610-388-2664
Fax 610-388-3650
www.whitewingfarm.com
info@whitewingfarm.com
370 Valley Road, RD 6, West Chester, PA 19382

Select Registry Member *Since 1998*
Innkeepers / Owners
EDWARD AND WANDA DESETA

WHITEWING FARM is a 1700s Pennsylvania farmhouse with greenhouses, flower gardens, a barn and a carriage house, all situated on 43 rolling acres in historic southern Chester County. Breakfast is served in the Hay Barn, where the fireplace is lit on cold mornings. Guests are welcome to play tennis or a round of golf on our 10-hole chip-and-putt course, or relax in the pool and heated Jacuzzi. All of the rooms have private marble-floored baths and are decorated in the Hunt Country Elegance fashion.

ELEGANT COUNTRY BREAKFAST INN

RATES
7 rooms, $135/$179.
3 suites with fireplaces, $205/$259.
Open year-round. Closed December 23, 24, and 25.

ATTRACTIONS
Longwood Gardens, Winterthur Museum, Brandywine River Museum, canoeing on the Brandywine River, Franklin Mint, Historic Old New Castle, Brandywine Battlefield, Hagley Museum, Nemours.

CUISINE
Full country breakfast, afternoon tea. BYOB.

DIRECTIONS
8 miles S of West Chester off Rte 52; or 9 1/2 miles N on Rte 52 from I-95 (Exit 7), Wilmington, DE. At Rte 1 turn L 0.8 mile to red light. Turn right N on Rte 52, 1 1/3 mile to Valley Rd. Left on Valley Rd. 0.8 mile.

5 Guestrooms Handicap Accessible • Non-Smoking Inn
Suitable for Children • Conference Facilities for 15

Chadds Ford, PA

Fairville Inn

610-388-5900
Fax 610-388-5902
www.fairvilleinn.com
info@fairvilleinn.com
506 Kennett Pike (Route 52), Chadds Ford,PA 19317

Select Registry Member *Since 1995*
Innkeepers/Owners
TOM AND ELEANOR EVERITT

LOCATED BETWEEN Winterthur, Longwood Gardens and the Brandywine River Museum, The Fairville Inn is surrounded by scenes from the Wyeth family paintings and the year-round haunting beauty of the Brandywine Valley. Fifteen guest rooms in the Main House (circa 1820), Carriage House and Springhouse each have a private bath, TV/telephone and AC. Several have a canopy bed, fireplace, and private deck. Fresh flowers welcome you. Your room has all the comforts of a country house inn! Mobil ★★★ and AAA ◆◆◆.

TRADITIONAL VILLAGE BREAKFAST INN

RATES
13 rooms, $150/$185 B&B.
2 suites, $195/$205 B&B.
Open year-round.

ATTRACTIONS
Museums (Winterthur, Longwood Gardens, Hagley, Nemours, Brandywine River Museum), golf, canoeing the Brandywine, and polo (in season).

CUISINE
Breakfast and afternoon refreshments with homemade cookies. BYOB.

DIRECTIONS
Located on Rte 52 8 miles N from I-95 (exit 7 Wilmington DE); 2 miles S from U.S. Rte 1 at Hamorton (Longwood Gardens area), PA .

1 Guestroom Handicap Accessible • Non-Smoking Inn
Suitable for Children Over 17 • AMEX, Visa, MC, Disc Accepted
Reservations Accepted Through Travel Agents

Gettysburg, PA

Baladerry Inn at Gettysburg

717-337-1342
Fax Call First
www.baladerryinn.com
baladerry@blazenet.net
40 Hospital Road, Gettysburg, PA 17325

Select Registry Member *Since 1998*
Innkeeper/Owner
CARYL O'GARA

BALADERRY INN is located at the edge of the Gettysburg Battlefield near Little Round Top. This brick Federal-style home (circa 1812), served as a hospital during the War Between the States. A large two-storied great room dominated by a massive brick fireplace is both a dining and gathering area. A brick terrace provides an outdoor area for socializing, while a garden gazebo offers tranquil privacy. Private and spacious, the inn is an excellent choice for history buffs, leisure travelers, small business meetings and reunions. AAA ◆◆◆ and Mobil ★★★.

TRADITIONAL COUNTRY BREAKFAST INN

RATES
8 rooms, $115/$155 B&B.
$15 extra person in room.
Open year-round.

ATTRACTIONS
Tour Gettysburg Battlefield and Eisenhower National site. Excellent biking, horseback riding, golf, skiing, antiquing. Tennis on-site.

CUISINE
Full country breakfast. BYOB.

DIRECTIONS
From U.S. 15, exit at Baltimore St. N 1 mile, L at McAllister Mill Rd., L onto Blacksmith Shop Rd., L onto Hospital Rd.

Suitable for Children Over 12 • Non-Smoking Inn
Conference Facilities for 25 • Visa, MC, Disc, AMEX, Diners Accepted
Reservations Accepted Through Travel Agents

Orrtanna, PA

Hickory Bridge Farm

800-642-1766
717-642-5261 Fax 717-642-6419
www.hickorybridgefarm.com
hickory@innbook.com
96 Hickory Bridge Road, Orrtanna, PA 17353

Select Registry Member *Since 1976*
Innkeepers/Owners
ROBERT AND MARY LYNN MARTIN

A QUAINT COUNTRY RETREAT offering five-bedroom farmhouse accommodations (some with whirlpool baths), and four private cottages along a mountain stream (with fireplaces). Dinner is served in a beautiful Pennsylvania barn decorated with hundreds of antiques. All meals are farm-fresh and bountiful. Full breakfast is offered to overnight guests at the farmhouse and is taken to their cottage on Sunday morning. The farm is located nine miles west of Gettysburg, Pennsylvania, on 75 beautiful acres—a wonderful place to relax while visiting Gettysburg or antiquing in the nearby area. AAA ◆◆◆. Featured in *Taste of Home* magazine.

TRADITIONAL COUNTRY BREAKFAST INN

RATES
9 rooms, cottages and farmhouse, $85/$145 B&B.
Open year-round.

ATTRACTIONS
Gettysburg historical sites, golf, biking, hiking, fishing, skiing and antiquing.

CUISINE
Fine country dining in a beautiful Pennsylvania barn—Fri., Sat., Sun. Some weeknights.

DIRECTIONS
Gettysburg, Rte 116 W to Fairfield and R 3 miles N to Orrtanna. Or Rte 997 to Rte 30 E for 9 miles turn S at Cashtown for 3 miles.

Limited Handicap Access Available • Suitable for Children Over 6
Conference Facilities for 75 • MC, Visa, Disc Accepted

Mercersburg, PA

Mercersburg Inn

717-328-5231
Fax 717-328-3403
www.mercersburginn.com
walt@mercersburginn.com
405 South Main Street, Mercersburg, PA 17236

Select Registry Member *Since 1998*
Innkeepers/Owners
Walt and Sandy Filkowski

In 1909, Ione and Harry Byron embarked upon a dream—the creation of a magnificent private estate. The Byron's unlimited wealth, impeccable taste and vision of a life of casual elegance led, two years later, to the completion of Prospect, a stately 20,000 square-foot Georgian mansion on six and one-half acres of terraced lawns. The brick mansion features a slate roof, Indiana limestone sills, copper spouting, decorative tile, oak flooring, double-curving wrought iron balustrades, scagliola columns and mahogany and chestnut paneling. The 250 year-old historic village of Mercersburg is the birthplace of President Buchanan and the home of the Mercersburg Academy.

Elegant Country Inn

RATES

15 rooms, $130/250 B$B.
Three with fireplaces, one with clawfoot whirlpool tub, three with antique baths. Kings and queens.
Open year-round except the 24th and 25th of December.

ATTRACTIONS

HERE: Skiing, hiking, biking, fly-fishing and cooking classes.
NEARBY: golf, tennis, antiquing, outlet shopping, malls, horseback riding, live theater, movie theaters, swimming and boating; 45 minutes to Gettysburg, Antietum and Harpers Ferry.

CUISINE

Full gourmet breakfast, evening refreshments, tea and scones on weekends. Candlelit dining on Thurs., Fri., Sat. evenings. We recommend that you make reservations. Wine dinners.

DIRECTIONS

I-81, PA exit 3 (Greencastle), W on 16; ten miles to Mercersburg. Located on E end of town at junction of 16 and 75.

Suitable for Children Over 7 • Non-Smoking Inn
Conference Facilities for 30 • Visa, MC, Disc Accepted
Reservations Accepted Through Travel Agents

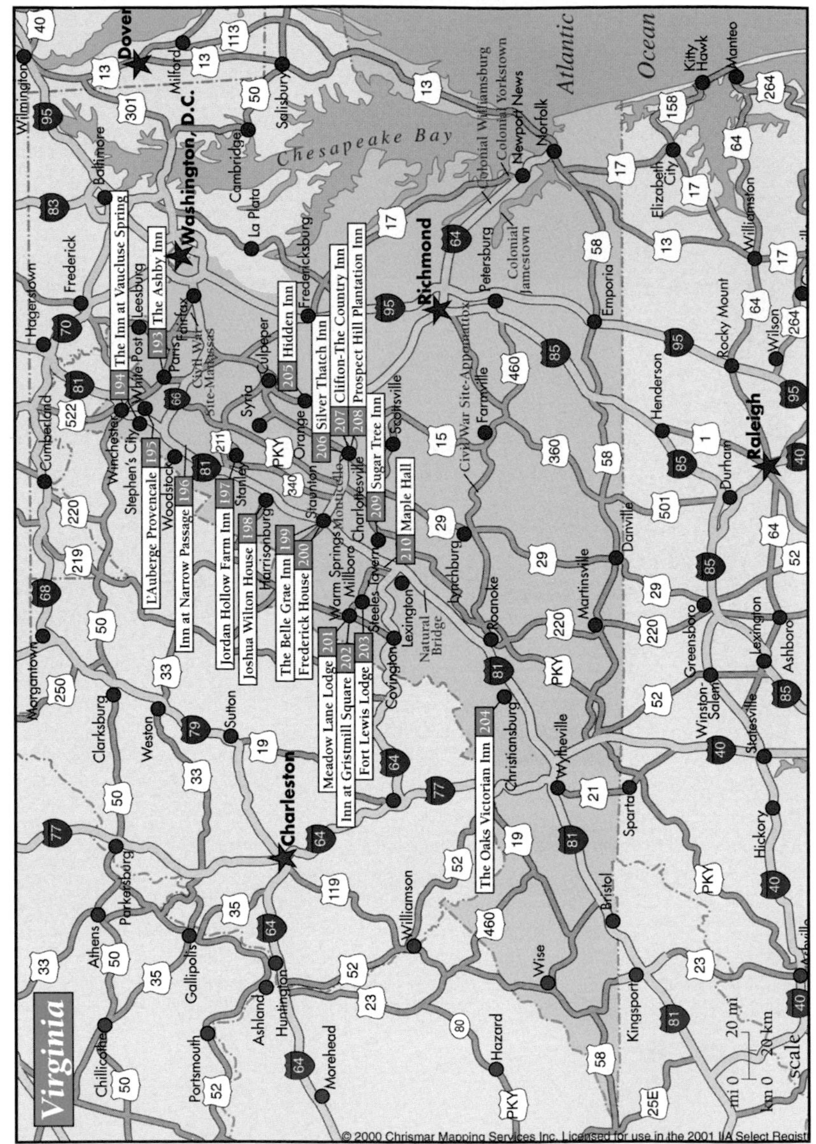

Virginia
194 The Inn at Vaucluse Spring
193 The Ashby Inn
195 L'Auberge Provencale
196 Inn at Narrow Passage
197 Jordan Hollow Farm Inn
198 Joshua Wilton House
199 The Belle Grae Inn
200 Frederick House
201 Meadow Lane Lodge
202 Inn at Gristmill Square
203 Fort Lewis Lodge
204 The Oaks Victorian Inn
205 Hidden Inn
206 Silver Thatch Inn
207 Clifton-The Country Inn
208 Prospect Hill Plantation Inn
209 Sugar Tree Inn
210 Maple Hall
Washington, D.C.
Richmond
Charleston
Raleigh
Dover
Chesapeake Bay
Atlantic
Ocean
Wilmington
Baltimore
Hagerstown
Frederick
Cumberland
Winchester
Stephen's City
White Post
Leesburg
Paris
Fairfax
Civil War Site-Manassas
Woodstock
Stanley
Harrisonburg
Staunton
Syria
Culpeper
Orange
Fredericksburg
Charlottesville
Monticello
Scottsville
Warm Springs
Millboro
Steeles Tavern
Lexington
Natural Bridge
Covington
Roanoke
Lynchburg
Christiansburg
Wytheville
Martinsville
Danville
Farmville
Civil War Site-Appomattox
Petersburg
Colonial Jamestown
Colonial Williamsburg
Colonial Yorktown
Newport News
Norfolk
Emporia
La Plata
Cambridge
Salisbury
Milford
Morgantown
Clarksburg
Weston
Sutton
Parkersburg
Athens
Gallipolis
Chillicothe
Portsmouth
Ashland
Huntington
Morehead
Williamson
Hazard
Wise
Bristol
Kingsport
Sparta
Winston-Salem
Greensboro
Lexington
Ashboro
Statesville
Hickory
Asheville
Henderson
Durham
Rocky Mount
Wilson
Williamston
Elizabeth City
Kitty Hawk
Manteo
mi 0 20 mi
km 0 20 km
scale
© 2000 Chrismar Mapping Services Inc. Licensed for use in the 2001 IIA Select Regist

Paris, VA

The Ashby Inn & Restaurant

540-592-3900
Fax 540-592-3781
www.ashbyinn.com
celebrate@ashbyinn.com
692 Federal Street, Paris, VA 20130

Select Registry Member *Since 1988*
Innkeepers/Owners
John and Roma Sherman

THIS 1829 INN finds its character in the small village of Paris and its heart in the kitchen. The menu is guided more by tradition than trend—with great attention paid to seasonal foods like asparagus, shad roe, softshell crabs and game. Much of the summer produce, herbs and flowers come from its gardens. Rooms (half with fireplaces and balconies) have views stretching beyond the formal perennial gardens to the hills of the Blue Ridge. Summer dining on the patio attracts a wide Washington following.

Traditional Village Inn

RATES

6 rooms, $145/$180 B&B.
4 suites, $250.
Sun.-Thurs. discounts on all rooms.
Open year-round.

ATTRACTIONS

Antiquing, vineyards, horseback riding, golf, tennis, hiking, seasonal point-to-point races, horse shows and stable tour.

CUISINE

Breakfast, dinner (Wed-Sat), Sunday brunch. On-site special event. Wine and liquor available.

DIRECTIONS

From Washington DC: Rte 66 W to exit 23, Rte 17 N, 7.5 miles L on Rte 701 for .5 miles or Rte 50 W thru Middleburg, L just after light at Rte 17.

Suitable for Children Over 12
Conference Facilities for 20 • Credit Cards Accepted

Stephens City, VA

The Inn at Vaucluse Spring

800-869-0525
540-869-0200 Fax 540-869-9546
www.vauclusespring.com
mail@vauclusespring.com
231 Vaucluse Spring Lane, Stephens City, VA 22655

SET AMIDST 100 SCENIC ACRES in the rolling orchard country of the northern Shenandoah Valley, this enclave of guest houses is the perfect setting for a romantic getaway or an executive retreat. Experience the elegance of a meticulously restored 200 year-old manor house or the warmth and charm of an 1850s log home. For the ultimate in peace and privacy, stay in the old mill or the gallery guest house. Relax beside Vaucluse Spring's cool, crystal-clear waters. Savor the bounty our region has to offer at our delicious three-course breakfasts or our candlelit Saturday night dinners. *Country Home* Magazine called it 'Paradise found'. Come discover why.

Select Registry Member *Since 2000*
Innkeepers/Owners
BARRY AND NEIL MYERS

TRADITIONAL COUNTRY BREAKFAST INN

RATES
12 rooms/suites, $140-285 B&B. Beautifully furnished, queen or king beds, all have fireplace, 11 w/Jacuzzi, some water/mtn views. *Open year-round.*

ATTRACTIONS
On-site: Vaucluse Spring, swimming pool, strolling gardens, bird-watching, xc-skiing, historic family cemetery. Nearby: Shenandoah Nat'l. Park, Shenandoah River, historic home and battlefield tours, antiquing, wineries, golf, horseback riding, caverns.

CUISINE
Three-course gourmet breakfast daily. Romantic four-course gourmet dinner for overnight guests on Saturday evenings by advance reservation. Wine and beer available.

DIRECTIONS
From I-66 W: Take exit 1B to I-81 N. Go 1 mile to exit 302. Turn L on Rte 627, go .5 mile. Turn R on Rte 11, go 2 miles. Turn L on Rte 638, go 1/2 mile to inn on L. Follow signs to check-in.

1 Guestroom Handicap Accessible • Suitable for Children Over 10
Non-Smoking Inn • Conference Facilities for 15 • Visa, MC Accepted
Reservations Accepted Through Travel Agents

White Post, VA

L' Auberge Provencale

800-638-1702
540-837-1375 Fax 540-837-2004
www.laubergeprovencale.com
cborel@shentel.net
Route 340, P.O. Box 190, White Post, VA 22663

Select Registry Member *Since 1988*
Innkeepers/Owners/Chef
ALAIN AND CELESTE BOREL

A WARM "SOUTH OF FRANCE" BREATH blows over this eclectic and sophisticated Country Inn with its renowned "Provencal Cuisine Moderne" by chef/owner Alain Borel. Orchards, herbs, flowers and vegetables grown by the innkeepers. Charming elegant guest rooms and suites, some with fireplaces, all romantic. Perfect for honeymoons and special getaways. Our new Villa La Campagnette offers swimming pool, luxury suites and privacy. The two inns, set in Virginia Hunt Country, offer a special experience for discerning guests, with exquisite food and courteous attentive service. AAA ◆◆◆◆-rated restaurant. Weddings and rehearsal dinners a specialty.

ELEGANT COUNTRY INN

RATES
10 rooms, $145/$225.
4 suites, $225/$295.
All private baths.
Closed January.

ATTRACTIONS
Canoeing, antiquing, vineyard tours, horseback riding, ballooning, golfing, tennis, Longbranch Plantation and Skyline Drive.

CUISINE
Dinner served Wednesday thru Sunday, breakfast, picnics. Full extensive wine list, liquor.

DIRECTIONS
1 hour W of DC Beltway. One mile S of Rte 50 on Rte 340, inn is on the R.

Suitable for Children Over 10 • Common Rooms Handicap Accessible
Conference Facilities for 20 • MC, Visa, AMEX, Disc, Diners Accepted
Non-Smoking Inn • Reservations Accepted Through Travel Agents

Woodstock, VA

The Inn at Narrow Passage

800-459-8002
540-459-8000 Fax 540-459-8001
www.innatnarrowpassage.com
innkeeper@innatnarrowpassage.com
P.O. Box 608, Route 11 South, Woodstock, VA 22664

Select Registry Member *Since 1990*
Innkeepers/Owners
ELLEN AND ED MARKEL

THIS HISTORIC 1740 LOG INN WITH FIVE ACRES on the Shenandoah River is a convenient place to relax and enjoy the beauty and history of the valley. In a country setting along the old Valley Pike, the inn's newer guest rooms open onto porches with views of the river and Massanutten Mountain. Early American antiques and reproductions, working fireplaces, queen-sized beds, original beams, exposed log walls and pine floors create a comfortable colonial atmosphere. Fine restaurants for lunch and dinner are nearby. AAA ◆◆◆ and Mobil ★★★.

RUSTIC COUNTRY
BREAKFAST INN

RATES
12 rooms, $95/$145.
Dbl, with full breakfast.
Open year-round.

ATTRACTIONS
Fishing and horseshoes on-site. Vineyards, caverns, hiking, antiquing, canoeing, horseback riding, Civil War sites, golf, skiing nearby.

CUISINE
Full breakfast daily; other meals by arrangement for groups. Wine and beer available.

DIRECTIONS
From Washington DC: I-66 W to I-81 S to exit 283 (Woodstock) and U.S. Rte 11 S for 2 miles. The inn is on the corner of Rte 11 and Rte 672 (Chapman Landing Rd.).

1 Guestroom Handicap Accessible • Suitable for ChildrenOver 5
Conference Facilities for 24 • Visa, MC, Disc Accepted
Designated Smoking Areas • Reservations Accepted Through Travel Agents

Stanley, VA

Jordan Hollow Farm Inn

888-418-7000
540-778-2285 Fax 540-778-1759
www.jordanhollow.com
jhf@jordanhollow.com
326 Hawksbill Park Road, Stanley, VA 22851

Select Registry Member *Since 1985*
Innkeepers/Owners
GAIL KYLE AND
BETSY MAITLAND

TRADITIONAL COUNTRY INN

SURROUND YOURSELF with spectacular mountain views, history, peace and serenity at our over 200 year-old horse farm. Centrally located in the Shenandoah Valley, you can relax in a rocking chair on a sunporch outside your room, or in front of a cozy fire. Explore the valley, vineyards, Civil War sites, historical villages, or take a hike on the miles of trails or in the nearby national park and forest. Begin and end each day with fabulous meals in our restored 1800s farmhouse restaurant. As we are a working horse farm, you are welcome to bring your own horse and enjoy our beauriful trails if you like. We have 150 gorgeous acres for you to enjoy!

RATES

15 rooms, $130-$195 B&B.
11 rooms with fireplaces, thermo-massage spas, whirlpool baths.
Open year-round.

ATTRACTIONS

Here: biking, hiking, birding, horseback riding with our horse. Nearby: Swimming, vineyards, antiquing, canoeing, golf, skiing, fishing, Civil War sites.

CUISINE

Full restaurant dinner, breakfast, American Regional features Virginia wines. Beer and wine available, service bar.

DIRECTIONS

Luray, VA Rte 340 Business S for 6 miles to L onto Rte 624 L on Rte 689 continue .5 mile and R on Rte 626 for .25 mile to inn on R.

---

1 Guestroom Handicap Accessible • Suitable for Children
Conference Facilities for 30 • Visa, MC, Diners Accepted
Designated Smoking Areas • Reservations Accepted Through Travel Agents

Harrisonburg, VA

Joshua Wilton House Inn and Restaurant

540-434-4464
Fax 540-432-9525
www.rica.net/jwhouse
jwhouse@rica.net
412 South Main Street, Harrisonburg, VA 22801

LOCATED IN AN ELEGANTLY RESTORED Victorian mansion, The Joshua Wilton House offers guests an oasis of quiet charm and gracious living in the heart of the Shenandoah Valley. The facility is within walking distance of historic downtown Harrisonburg and James Madison University. The restaurant offers a unique and extensive menu that changes with the season, along with an extensive list of the best wines and beer. The cafe presents a more casual environment for dining.

Select Registry Member *Since 1985*
Innkeepers / Owners
CRAIG AND ROBERTA MOORE

ELEGANT IN TOWN INN

RATES
5 rooms, $110/$150 B&B.
Open year-round.

ATTRACTIONS
Snow skiing, hiking, biking, antiquing, golfing and fishing all within 20 minutes of inn.

CUISINE
Breakfast seven days per week; Dining Tues. through Sat. Full bar, 100+ wines, microbrews.

DIRECTIONS
412 S Main St. I-81, exit 245, W on Port Rd. to Main St. N approx. 1 mile to Joshua Wilton House located on R.

Non-Smoking Inn • Suitable for Children Over 8
Conference Facilities for 20 • Visa, MC, AMEX, Diners, Disc Accepted
Reservations Accepted Through Travel Agents

Staunton, VA

The Belle Grae Inn and Restaurant

888-541-5151
540-886-5151 Fax 540-886-6641
www.bellegrae.com
bellegrae@sprynet.com
515 West Frederick Street, Staunton, VA 24401-3333

Select Registry Member *Since 1990*
Innkeeper/Owner
MICHAEL ORGAN

THIS ITALIANATE VICTORIAN HOUSE is the centerpiece of numerous restored 1890s homes transformed into comfortable lodging rooms in a quaint, architecturally rich residential district in Historic Staunton. The graciously furnished rooms, bistro bar, Azalea Courtyard and garden paths leading to the guest houses create a tasteful small hotel ambience. The inn is an easy walk to the shops and museums, and an easy drive to Colonial and Civil War History. Dining is a must at Belle Grae!

TRADITIONAL IN TOWN INN

RATES

Rooms, $99/$149.
Suites, $139/$209 B&B.
MAP available.
Honeymoon hideaway, $199.
Open year-round.

ATTRACTIONS

Nestled in the Shenandoah Valley where the Blue Ridge Parkway meets Skyline Drive—a gardener's paradise—an architecturally rich village and a great hub for exploring the homes of four presidents and Civil War heros, Jackson and Lee.

CUISINE

Breakfast is served daily 7:30-9 am. Dinner offered Wed.-Sun. 7:00 pm, is a delightful combination of taste and ambience. Seating is available in the old inn, casual garden room and azalea courtyard. Mon. and Tues. evening dinner baskets offered. Full ABC avail.

DIRECTIONS

I-81 exit 222 or 225. Follow signs to Woodrow Wilson Birthplace. W on East Frederick St. (Rte 250 W and 254 W) to 515 West Frederick (red brick mansion on R). Circle block for registration and off-street parking.

Handicap Access Available • Suitable for Children Over 12
Conference Facilities for 40 • AMEX, MC, CB Accepted
Designated Smoking Areas • Reservations Accepted Through Travel Agents

Staunton, VA

Frederick House

800-334-5575
540-885-4220 Fax 540-885-5180
www.frederickhouse.com
ejharman@frederickhouse.com
28 North New Street, Staunton, VA 24401

Select Registry Member *Since 1997*
Innkeepers/Owners
JOE AND EVY HARMAN

FREDERICK HOUSE encompasses six restored homes adjacent to Mary Baldwin College in historic Staunton. Rooms or suites have individual comfort controls, robes, remote TV, phones, reading and writing areas. Breakfast in Chumley's Tearoom includes ham and sausage pies, waffles, quiches, hot or cold cereal, home-baked breads. Restaurants, shops, museums and parks are available by easy walks through downtown Staunton. Frederick House is a convenient location from which to visit the Central Shenandoah Valley and Charlottesville. AAA ◆◆◆.

TRADITIONAL IN TOWN BREAKFAST INN

RATES
12 rooms, $85/$150 B&B.
11 suites, $125/$200 B&B.
Open year-round.

ATTRACTIONS
Shenandoah Valley, Blue Ridge Pkwy, Skyline Drive, Woodrow Wilson Birthplace, Museum of American Frontier Culture, Mary Baldwin College and antiquing.

CUISINE
Within walking distance of many restaurants.

DIRECTIONS
From I-81 exit 222 follow signs to Woodrow Wilson Birthplace. Turn L on Frederick St. We are two blocks on L. Off-steet parking in rear.

Suitable for Children • Non-Smoking Inn
Conference Facilities for 40 • Visa, MC, Diners, AMEX, Disc Accepted
Reservations Accepted Through Travel Agents

Warm Springs, VA

Meadow Lane Lodge

540-839-5959
Fax 540-839-2135
www.meadowlanelodge.com
meadowln@va.tds.net
HCR01 Box 110, Warm Springs, VA 24484

Select Registry Member *Since 1978*

Owners
HIRSH FAMILY

Innkeepers / Owners
CARTER AND MICHELLE ANCONA

TRADITIONAL COUNTRY INN

RATES

7 rooms, $105/$125 B&B.
3 suites, $115/$125 B&B.
3 cottages, $125 and up.
Open year-round.

ATTRACTIONS

Fly-fishing, tennis, golf, swimming, hiking, horseback riding, skiing, ice-skating, mountain biking, massage, and creative loafing.

CUISINE

Full breakfast daily. Picnic lunch and Saturday night dinners available. Beer and wine available.

DIRECTIONS

From Staunton: Rte 254 W to Buffalo Gap, Rte 42 S to Millboro Springs. Rte 39 W to Rte 220 continue on Rte 39 W 4.5 miles to Lodge entrance on R.

TWENTY MILES OF HIKING TRAILS and two miles of scenic Jackson River meander through this 1,600-acre farm of mountain forests and meadows where wildflowers, wildlife and domestic animals abound. Guests enjoy rooms and cottages with working fireplaces, sunny porches and roosters crowing wakeup calls to a country breakfast you will not soon forget. Caring for the land while preserving the past is a way of life here, as this unique country inn and estate has been placed under a conservation easement, guaranteeing an unspoiled refuge in perpetuity.

Suitable for Children
Conference Facilities for 25 • Credit Cards Accepted

Warm Springs, VA

The Inn at Gristmill Square

540-839-2231
Fax 540-839-5770
www.vainns.com/grist.htm
grist@va.tds.net
Box 359, Warm Springs, VA 24484

Select Registry Member *Since 1977*
Innkeepers/Owners
THE MCWILLIAMS FAMILY

THE INN WAS CREATED IN 1972 utilizing five original 19th-century buildings. A restored gristmill built in 1900 is the home of our Waterwheel Restaurant. A former blacksmith shop, a hardware store and two once-private homes house the guest rooms. Located in a picturesque little mountain village in the heart of Virginia Spa Country, guests come to enjoy the outdoors, relax and view the outstanding natural beauty.

TRADITIONAL VILLAGE INN

RATES
17 rooms,
$80/$140 EP. $155/$210 MAP.
Open year-round.

ATTRACTIONS
On premise: tennis and outdoor pool
1 mile: thermal pools.
3 miles: Hiking, fishing.
7 miles: Horseback riding.
5 miles: Skiing, ice-skating.
2 miles: Chamber music.

CUISINE
Continental breakfast served to room, dinner, brunch on Sunday. Wine and liquor served.

DIRECTIONS
Turn W from Rte 220 onto Rte 619 (Court House Hill), proceed 500 yds. to inn on R.

Suitable for Children• Designated Smoking Areas
Conference Facilities for 40 • MC, Visa, Disc Accepted
Reservations Accepted Through Travel Agents

Millboro, VA

Fort Lewis Lodge

540-925-2314
Fax 540-925-2352
www.fortlewislodge.com
ftlewis@tds.net
HCR 3 Box 21A, Millboro, VA 24460

Select Registry Member *Since 1990*
Innkeepers
John and Caryl Cowden

A FULL-SERVICE COUNTRY INN at the heart of a 3,200-acre mountain estate. Outdoor activities abound with miles of river trout and bass fishing, swimming, extensive hiking trails, mountain biking, magnificent views and abundant wildlife. Fort Lewis is a rare combination of unpretentious elegance and exceptional comfort with a variety of lodging choices where every room has a view. Three "in the round" silo bedrooms and two hand-hewn log cabins with stone fireplaces are perfect for a romantic getaway. Evenings are highlighted by contemporary American-style cuisine served in the historic Lewis Gristmill. A true country getaway. See us on the web. AAA ◆◆◆.

Rustic Mountain Inn

RATES

7 rooms, $150/$155 MAP.
4 family suites, $170 MAP.
2 log cabins, $210 MAP.
Open April - October. Closed November - March.

ATTRACTIONS

HERE: Miles of private river fishing (trout and smallmouth bass), extensive hiking trails with mountain views, swimming and inner-tubing, mountain biking, bird watching and wildlife viewing. Witness the wonders of the night sky from the "Star Deck." NEARBY: Jefferson Pools-historic thermal springs, horseback riding, sporting clays, antiquing, chamber music concerts, Lake Moomaw, scenic country drives.

CUISINE

Full dinner and breakfast daily; picnic lunch available. Beer and wine available.

DIRECTIONS

From Staunton: Rte 254 W to Buffalo Gap; Rte 42 to Millboro Springs; Rte 39 W for .7 mile to R onto Rte 678, 10.8 miles to L onto Rte 625, sign on L.

Handicap Access Available • Suitable for Children• Non-Smoking Inn
Conference Facilities for 30 • Visa, MC Accepted
Reservations Accepted Through Travel Agents

Christiansburg, VA

The Oaks Victorian Inn

800-336-6257
540-381-1500 Fax 540-381-3036
www.bbhost.com/theoaksinn

311 East Main Street, Christiansburg, VA 24073

WARM HOSPITALITY, comfortable, relaxed elegance and memorable breakfasts are the hallmark of The Oaks, a century-old Queen Anne Victorian on the National Register of Historic Places. Set on Christiansburg's highest hill in the beautiful mountain highlands of southwest Virginia, The Oaks delights and welcomes leisure and business travelers from around the world. Surrounded by lawn, perennial gardens and 300 year-old oak trees, the inn faces Main Street, once part of the Wilderness Trail blazed by Daniel Boone and Davy Crockett. Fireplaces and beautiful private baths with Jacuzzis for romantics, private telephone/computer jacks for business guests. Mobil ★★★ and AAA ◆◆◆◆.

Suitable for Children Over 12 • Non-Smoking Inn
Conference Facilities for 18 • AMEX, MC, Visa, Disc Accepted
Reservations Accepted Through Travel Agents

Select Registry Member *Since 1993*
Owners/Hosts
MARGARET AND TOM RAY

ELEGANT VILLAGE
BREAKFAST INN

RATES

7 rooms, $125/$165 B&B.
$85 corp. rate Sun. through Thu., sgl. only. Extended stay suites/7 days + (EP)(ck rates).
Open year-round except first two weeks in January.

ATTRACTIONS

Mountain winery tours, hiking, golf, tennis, antiquing and historic sites nearby.: Bikes for Two: explore our Rails to Trails bike paths (120 miles). Bikes w/gourmet picnic - $50.

CUISINE

Three-course breakfast by candlelight, good restaurants for dinner nearby.

DIRECTIONS

From I-81 exit 114 (Main St.) 2 miles. From Blue Ridge Pkwy.: Take Rte 8 (MP165) W 28 miles to The Oaks. Four blocks from US 460 and 38 miles N of I-77 and I-81 Interchange.

Orange, VA

Hidden Inn

800-841-1253
540-672-3625 Fax 540-672-5029
www.hiddeninn.com
hiddeninn@ns.gemlink.com
249 Caroline Street, Orange, VA 22960

Select Registry Member *Since 1991*
Innkeepers/Owners
BARBARA AND RAY LONICK

TRADITIONAL VILLAGE BREAKFAST INN

RATES
8 rooms, $99/$169 B&B.
Includes 2 cottages, B&B.
4 rooms have Jacuzzi tubs and private verandas.
Open year-round.

ATTRACTIONS
Monticello, Montpelier, tour wineries, antiquing, fishing, hiking, horseback riding, boating, biking and skydiving.

CUISINE
Full breakfast and afternoon tea. Optional candlelight picnic. Virginia wine and beer.

DIRECTIONS
From Washington DC: I-95 S, to exit 130B, to Rte 3 to Rte 20 to Rte 15 S. Inn on L.
From Richmond: I-64 W, exit 136 to Rte 15 N thru Gordonsville, to Orange Inn on R before traffic signal.

LACE AND FRESH-CUT FLOWERS accent this romantic Victorian farmhouse, surrounded by seven wooded acres and gardens, in the heart of historic Virginia's wine country. Enjoy a cup of tea before a crackling living room fire or sip lemonade on the veranda porch swing. A full country breakfast in the sunlit dining room starts the day, packed with fascinating things to do. Guests can visit Monticello, Ashlawn, Montpelier, tour several wineries, shop at local shops, art galleries and antique stores. Bicycling, horseback riding, golf, hiking and Civil War sites are nearby.

Suitable for Children • Non-Smoking Inn
Conference Facilities for 20 • AMEX, Visa, MC Accepted
Reservations Accepted Through Travel Agents

Charlottesville, VA

Silver Thatch Inn

804-978-4686
Fax 804-973-6156
www.silverthatch.com
info@silverthatch.com
3001 Hollymead Drive, Charlottesville, VA 22911

Select Registry Member *Since 1986*
Innkeepers/Owners
JIM AND TERRI PETROVITS

THIS HISTORIC INN began its life as a barracks built in 1780 by Hessian soldiers captured during the Revolutionary War. As wings were added in 1812 and 1937, it served as a boys' school, a tobacco plantation and a melon farm. It has been providing gracious lodging in antique-filled guest rooms and elegant candlelit dining since the 1970s. Relax and unwind in our intimate pub. Enjoy contemporary cuisine from our menu and wines from a list which has consistently won the *Wine Spectator* award of excellence. AAA ◆◆◆.

TRADITIONAL COUNTRY INN

RATES
7 rooms, $140/$175 B&B.
Open year-round.

ATTRACTIONS
ONSITE: summer swimming.
NEARBY: golf, horseback riding, jogging, biking, hiking, Blue Ridge Mountains, Monticello, U of Va, wineries and antiquing.

CUISINE
Breakfast for houseguests; Dinner Tues.-Sat. open to the public. Fine selection of liquor, wine and beer.

DIRECTIONS
From S: 6 miles N of intersection of US 29 and US 250 bypass, turn R on Rte 1520. From N: 1 mile S of Airport Rd., turn L on Rte 1520.

Suitable for Children Over 8 • Non-Smoking Inn
Conference Facilities for 20 • MC, Visa, AMEX, Diners Accepted

Charlottesville, VA

Clifton–The Country Inn

888-971-1800
804-971-1800 Fax 804-971-7098
www.cliftoninn.com

Select Registry Member *Since 1995*
General Manager
Michael Habony

1296 Clifton Inn Drive, Charlottesville, VA 22911

HISTORIC EIGHTEENTH-CENTURY manor house on a 40-acre country estate. Antique appointed rooms and suites, each with a wood-burning fireplace and the most modern amenities. Clifton offers romantic candlelit dining and award-winning American regional cuisine with classical French influences. Prix fixe seasonal menus feature the freshest local ingredients. Extensive wine cellar with selected vintages from all over the world. Deluxe recreational facilities on estate grounds. Located in the heart of Thomas Jefferson country.

Elegant Country Inn

RATES
7 rooms, $150/$340 B&B.
7 suites, $325/$495 B&B.
Open year-round.

ATTRACTIONS
Outdoor pool with cascading waterfall. Heated whirlpool, clay tennis court, lawn croquet, volleyball, horseshoes and private lake. Walking trails and picnic area. Monticello, Ashlawn-Highland, University of Virginia, antiquing and wine tours.

CUISINE
Early morning coffee tray, continental and full breakfast, prix fixe dining nightly. Full bar service with extensive award-winning wine list.

DIRECTIONS
From I-64 exit 124; turn E onto Rte 250. After 2 miles, turn R at traffic light onto Rte 729, 2nd drive on L past school. From Rte 29, take 250 E bypass 7 miles to Shadwell. Turn R at traffic light onto Rte 729, 2nd drive on L past school.

Handicap Access Available • Suitable for Children Over 12
Conference Facilities for 20 • Credit Cards Accepted
Reservations Accepted Through Travel Agents

Trevilians, VA

Prospect Hill Plantation Inn

800-277-0844
540-967-0844 Fax 540-967-0102
www.prospecthill.com
Michael@prospecthill.com
2887 Poindexter Road, Trevilians, VA 23093

Select Registry Member *Since 1979*
Second Generation Owners
MICHAEL AND LAURA SHEEHAN

AN AWARD-WINNING COUNTRY INN comprised of the 1732 manor house and authentic eighteenth century dependencies on 50 acres of lawns. Romantic five-course candlelit dining, breakfast-in-bed, working fireplaces, Jacuzzis, private balconies and swimming pool all located just 15 miles east of Charlottesville, VA, in the serenity of the countryside, add up to an inn that has been selected as one of America's most romantic getaways. Be sure to arrive early for informal afternoon tea and smell the aromas wafting from the kitchen as we prepare the evening dinner.

TRADITIONAL COUNTRY INN

RATES

13 rooms, suites and cottages, $190-275 B&B, $280-$365 MAP (some weekday discounts).
Open year-round.

ATTRACTIONS

Outdoor pool, peace and quiet, Jaccuzzis and fireplaces. Nearby historical sites of Monticello, Ashlawn, Montpelier, University of Virginia, Skyline Drive and the Blue Ridge Parkway, hiking, golf, wineries and antiques.

CUISINE

Wine on arrival, complete five-course romantic dinner daily, afternoon tea, full country breakfast-in-bed (or in the dining room) all included. Wines and beers available. Liquor for private functions only.

DIRECTIONS

Inn is 15 miles E of Charlottesville via I-64, exit #136. From Washington, DC (approx. 100 miles): Take I-66 W to Rte 29 S, to Rte 15 S to Zion Crossroads. Take L on 250 E for 1 mile and turn L on Rte 613. Inn is 3 miles down on L.

Designated Smoking Areas • Suitable for Children
Conference Facilities for 26 • Credit Cards Accepted
Reservations Accepted Through Travel Agents

Steeles Tavern, VA

Sugar Tree Inn

800-377-2197
Fax Call First
www.sugartreeinn.com
innkeeper@sugartreeinn.com
Highway 56, Steeles Tavern, VA 24476

Select Registry Member *Since 1998*
Innkeepers/Owners
TERRI AND HENRY WALTERS

VIRGINIA'S MOUNTAIN INN nestles in our serene private forest just off the Blue Ridge Parkway. Busy hummingbirds and 40-mile sunset views complement spring wildflowers, brilliant summer days with cool nights and dazzling fall foliage. Each rustically elegant room or suite has a woodburning fireplace; all are air-conditioned. Some rooms also offer a whirlpool and VCR. Full breakfast is served in a glass-walled dining room. Savor candlelit dining on weekends or weekday dinners by reservation. Nature is yours to discover on our own trails, or explore the historic Shenadoah Valley below.

RUSTIC MOUNTAIN INN

RATES
9 rooms, $105/$160 B&B.
2 suites, $160 B&B.
2 cottages, $140/$150
Open March - December.

ATTRACTIONS
Mountain hiking, touring, cycling, birding, wildflowers, fall foliage, antiquing, crafts, historic towns. Only five minutes to the Blue Ridge Parkway.

CUISINE
Gourmet regional dining by reservation Friday and Saturday evenings. Weekday dinner available by reservation.

DIRECTIONS
From I-81: Exit 205 to Steeles Tavern. Take Hwy 56 E up the mountain approx. 5 miles to sign. From Blue Ridge Parkway (milepost 27): W .9 mile on Hwy 56 to sign.

1 Guestroom Handicap Accessible • Suitable for Children
Conference Facilities for 22 • Visa, MC, Disc, AMEX Accepted
Reservations Accepted Through Travel Agents

Lexington, VA

Maple Hall

877-463-2044
540-463-6693 Fax 540-463-7262
www.selectregistry.com

3111 North Lee Highway, Lexington, VA 24450

A MEMBER OF THE HISTORIC COUNTRY INNS of Lexington, this 1850 plantation home on 56 rolling acres offers guests a lovely place to stay while exploring historic sites or attending college functions at VMI or W and L. The inn is located six miles north of Lexington, where one will find many specialty shops and museums. At Maple Hall, lovely gardens, verandas, spring wildflowers, fall leaves and fireplaces in rooms make each visit special. Small business conferences find our location convenient and our service attentive. Come and enjoy our inn.

Select Registry Member *Since 1987*
Owners
PETER MEREDITH FAMILY
Innkeeper
DON FREDENBURG

TRADITIONAL COUNTRY INN

RATES
16 rooms, $55-$135 B&B.
5 suites, $115-$180 B&B.
At Maple Hall.
Open year-round.

ATTRACTIONS
Walking trails, swimming pool, fishing pond, tennis court. Museums, Blue Ridge Parkway, canoeing, antiquing, Stonewall Jackson, Robert E. Lee, George C. Marshall, Cyrus McCormick historic sites. Lime Kiln Summer Theater.

CUISINE
Public invited nightly; three intimate dining rooms. Seasonal menus, nightly specials. Weddings, rehearsal dinner parties our specialties.

DIRECTIONS
Maple Hall from I-81 take exit 195 go N on Rte 11 (away from Lexington), large sign on Rte 11 Maple Hall.

Suitable for Children
Conference Facilities for 40 • Credit Cards Accepted
Reservations Accepted Through Travel Agents

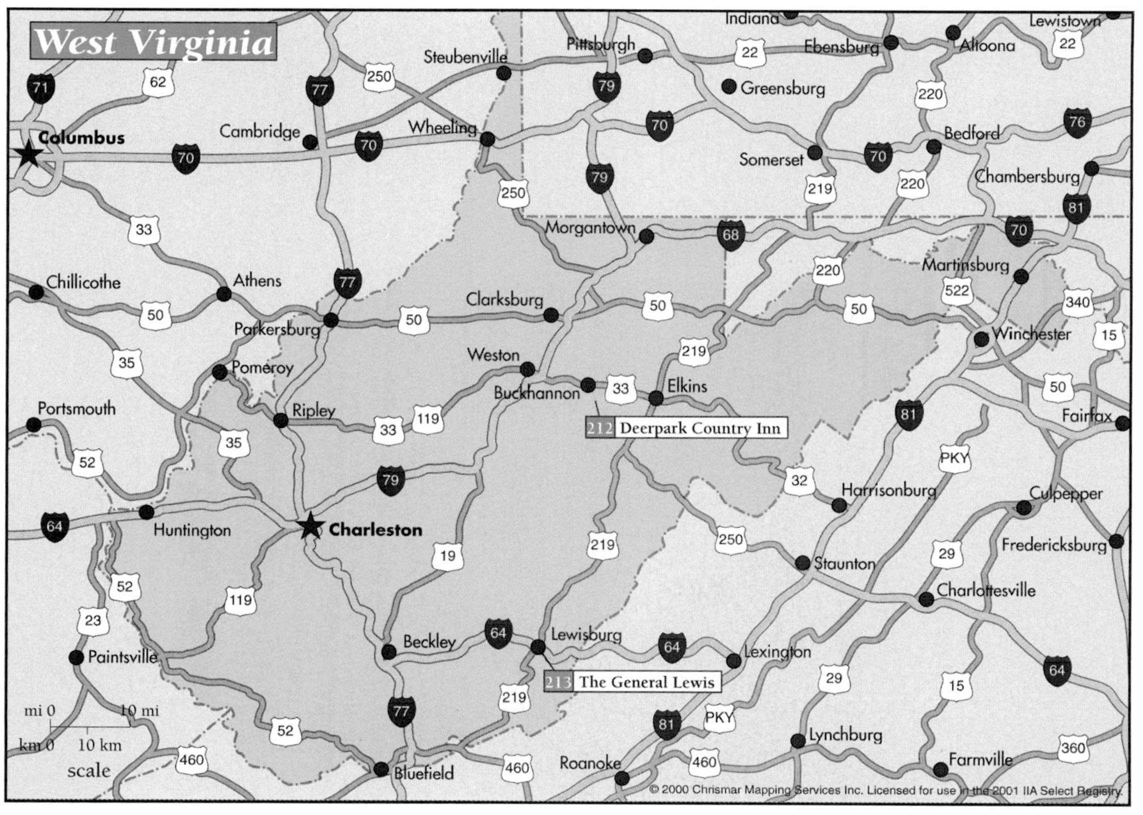
West Virginia
212 Deerpark Country Inn
213 The General Lewis
Columbus
Cambridge
Steubenville
Wheeling
Pittsburgh
Indiana
Ebensburg
Altoona
Lewistown
Greensburg
Somerset
Bedford
Chambersburg
Morgantown
Martinsburg
Winchester
Fairfax
Chillicothe
Athens
Parkersburg
Clarksburg
Weston
Buckhannon
Elkins
Pomeroy
Ripley
Portsmouth
Huntington
Charleston
Harrisonburg
Culpepper
Fredericksburg
Staunton
Charlottesville
Beckley
Lewisburg
Lexington
Paintsville
Lynchburg
Farmville
Roanoke
Bluefield
PKY
mi 0 10 mi
km 0 10 km
scale
© 2000 Chrismar Mapping Services Inc. Licensed for use in the 2001 IIA Select Registry.

Buckhannon, WV

Deerpark Country Inn

Voice 304-472-8400 Fax 304-472-5363
800-296-8430
www.deerparkcountryinn.com
deerpark@deerparkcountryinn.com
P.O. Box 817, Buckhannon, WV 26201

Select Registry Member *Since 1999*
Innkeepers/Owners
LIZ AND PAT HAYNES

SURROUND YOURSELF with 100 acres of the rejuvenating country ambiance of Deerpark. The Inn includes an eighteenth century log cabin and turn-of-the-century farmhouse. The lodge features wide verandas and a fireplace as large as a man is tall. Mist rises from ponds that invite you to fish under the watchful eye of resident geese. Be charmed by the hummingbirds in the English Gardens. The long, lazy day moves into the tranquil evening. Watch the fireflies. Listen to the frogs chirp. The stars are clear and bright. 'A truly wonderful Inn', writes the *Pittsburgh Gazette.* No matter what the season, you will want to return. We look forward to your visit. AAA ◆◆◆.

TRADITIONAL COUNTRY INN

RATES
Dble occupancy,
4 rooms, $135/185.
1 and 2-bedroom suites, $185/280.
All private baths, B&B, phone, TV, A/C. Packages available.
Open year-round.

ATTRACTIONS
Here: Private lakes, fishing, hiking trails, bird-watching, massage, lawn games, library, gift shop, special weekends. Near: WV Wildlife Center, festivals/workshops, antiquing, hot-air ballooning, historical sites, skiing, golf, horseback riding.

CUISINE
A fine dining restaurant featuring the superb creations of chef Dale Hawkins. Breakfast daily for lodging guests, dinner recommened by reservation, open 7 nights. Picnic lunches. Catered events for 2-400 guests.

DIRECTIONS
I-79, exit #99, US Rte 33 exit to County Rd. 151 E, 1 mile, R on Heavener Grove Rd., 1.3 miles to Deerpark sign at entrance.

Suitable for Children Over 8 • Non-Smoking Inn
Conference Facilities for 20 • Credit Cards Accepted
Reservations Accepted Through Travel Agents

Lewisburg, WV

The General Lewis Inn

304-645-2600
Fax 304-645-2601
www.generallewisinn.com
info@generallewisinn.com
301 East Washington Street, Lewisburg, WV 24901

Select Registry Member *Since 1973*
Innkeepers/Owners
THE MORGAN FAMILY

COME ROCK IN A CHAIR on the veranda of the Inn. On chilly days, dream by the fireplace, solve one of the puzzles or play a fascinating game. Don't miss Memory Hall's display of old tools for home and farm. Antiques furnish every room, including canopy, spool and poster beds. The dining room in the 1834 wing features Southern cooking. Nestled in beautiful Greenbrier County, the inn offers nearby walking tours. Explore the Historic District and browse specialty shops. Owned and operated by the same family since 1929. Featured in National Geographic Guide To Small Town Escapes. AAA ◆◆◆ and Mobil ★★★.

TRADITIONAL VILLAGE INN

RATES
23 rooms, $85/$126 EP.
2 suites, $126/$146 EP.
Open year-round.

ATTRACTIONS
Back roads and mountain biking, caverns, antique and specialty shops, live performance theatre, Civil War Cemetery and National Historic District, Greenbrier River Trail, arts and cultural center, golf, fishing, year-round chair rocking.

CUISINE
Breakfast, lunch and dinner. Wine and liquor available.

DIRECTIONS
I-64, Lewisburg exit 169, 219 S for 1.5 miles to 60 E, turn L, three blocks up on the R.

1 Guestroom Handicap Accessible • Suitable for Children
Non-Smoking Inn • MC, Visa, AMEX, Disc Accepted
Reservations Accepted Through Travel Agents

The South

Traveling through the South, a West Coast traveler found a small café on a back street in Savannah. Collard greens, sweet potatoes, black-eyed peas and Southern fried chicken—regional cuisine at its best. The skies are the blue of a cat's eye, and the slow drumbeat of summertime gladdens the avenues and parks and imbues this city with a particular festivity.

OPENING A COPY OF THE *Select Registry*, the traveler chooses a brownstone Inn built before the Civil War. The Inn is filled with the finest of American antiques. Rare paintings hang on the walls as in the vast majority of SELECT REGISTRY Inns, the decorating is splendid. The Innkeeper is friendly, charming, and personally responsible for the decor. The bedroom is exquisite, as comfortable and welcoming as the city itself. History oozes down the streets, and there—in one of the dozens of spectacular city squares—is the bench Forest Gump sequestered.

Many succumb to a tour of this city. As in so much of the South, history paints a rich picture.

A close cousin to Savannah, Charleston is an afternoon's drive away. A guest may revel in the colonial architecture, the regional cuisine or simply in the leisurely pace of the South's gracious citizens. The *Select Registry* is represented here. A traveler may choose to stay a day or two, then move on. Country or city—along the way, our Innkeepers anticipate your arrival. The *Select Registry* points the way.

Take some extra time to explore the rural and urban South. Sunshine and hospitality float like the cacophonies of songbirds wherever one ventures. From magnificent antebellum to rustic Country Inns, the SELECT REGISTRY is represented by nearly 50 Inns in the South, and its ten states featured in our *Registry,* including Kentucky, Tenessee, North and South Carolina, Georgia, Florida, Mississippi, Louisiana, Arkansas and Missouri. A visitor can stay overnight at any of dozens of our Inns and explore a diversity of food, culture and lifestyle that varies from region to region, state to state. Whether one chooses to eat simple, tasteful foods served in small cafés, or dines on elegant cuisine served with the formality and graciousness that has created a permanent image of a land and people from another time—a Southern time—a traveler will feel replenished. The Inns of SELECT REGISTRY simply do it better.

"This Inn is Heaven on Earth, whether one is on a romantic weekend, girls only reunion, mother/daughter retreat or get-away for all time."—Adrienne Urbach, Palm Springs, CA

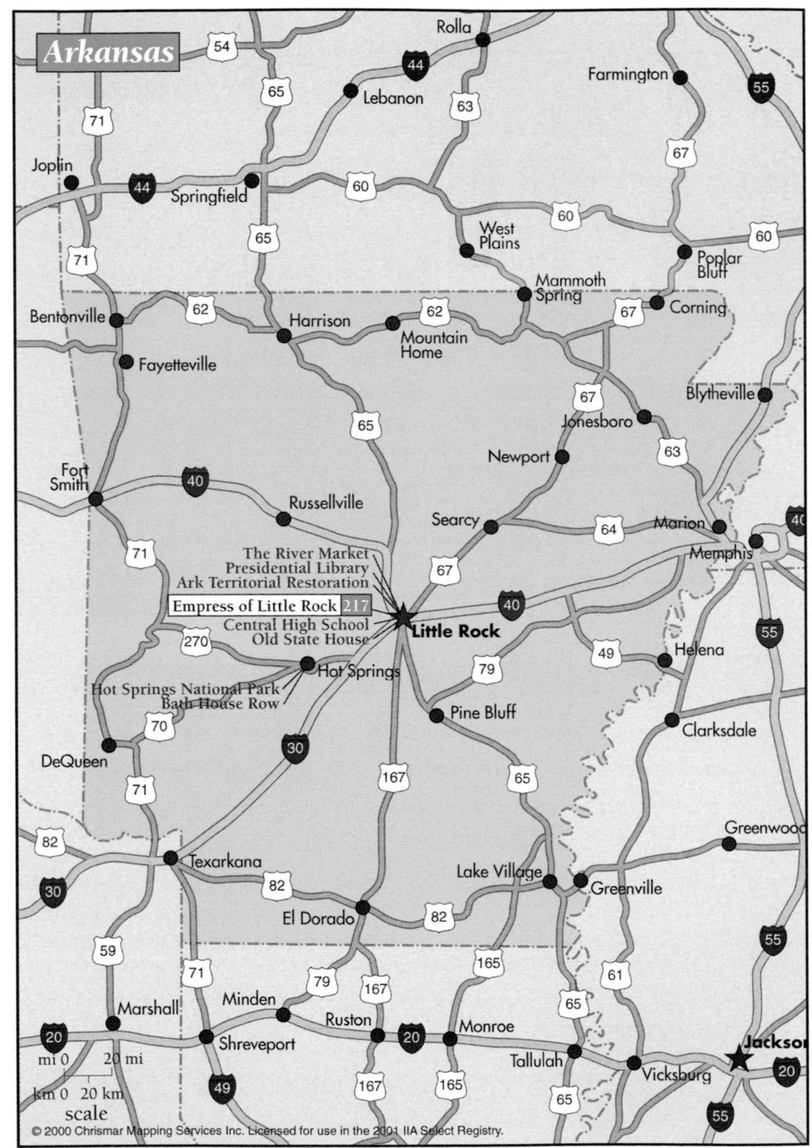
Arkansas
Rolla
Lebanon
Farmington
Joplin
Springfield
West Plains
Mammoth Spring
Poplar Bluff
Corning
Bentonville
Harrison
Mountain Home
Fayetteville
Blytheville
Jonesboro
Newport
Fort Smith
Russellville
Searcy
Marion
Memphis
The River Market
Presidential Library
Ark Territorial Restoration
Empress of Little Rock 217
Central High School
Old State House
Little Rock
Helena
Hot Springs
Hot Springs National Park
Bath House Row
Pine Bluff
Clarksdale
DeQueen
Greenwood
Texarkana
Lake Village
Greenville
El Dorado
Marshall
Minden
Ruston
Monroe
Shreveport
Tallulah
Vicksburg
Jackson
mi 0 20 mi
km 0 20 km
scale
© 2000 Chrismar Mapping Services Inc. Licensed for use in the 2001 IIA Select Registry.

Little Rock, AR

The Empress of Little Rock

Small Luxury Hotel

Reservations 877-374-7966 Fax 501-375-4537

501-374-7966

www.theempress.com

hostess@theempress.com

2120 Louisiana Street, Little Rock, AR 72206

IMAGINE AN EVENING IN THE FAMILY PARLOR at the Biltmore, surrounded by luxurious antiques, the warmth of the fire draining away the tension of a busy corporate day, stretched out in your smoking jacket or victorian dressing gown, and that special book you've been postponing for the "right time." Or as Scarlett, descending a magnificent double staircase, lighted by the rainbow hues of a 64 sq. foot stained glass skylight...breakfast smells beckon you to leisurely dining served by candlelight where unrushed conversation epitomize true southern hospitality. Now is the "right time." The Empress of Little Rock, *"The Forgotten Experience."* Historic tours available daily. AAA ◆◆◆◆.

Suitable for Children Over 10
Conference Facilities for 30 • Credit Cards Accepted
Reservations Accepted Through Travel Agents

Select Registry Member *Since 2001*

Innkeeper/Owners
ROBERT BLAIR AND SHARON WELCH-BLAIR

VICTORIAN IN TOWN
BREAKFAST INN

RATES

5 rooms
3 mini-suites, $125 to $195.
Period antiques, featherbeds, cable, phone, dataport, private baths, clock radio, luxury robes, fireplaces, antique soaking tub, Jacuzzi.
Open year-round.

ATTRACTIONS

Historic district, State Capitol, Territorial Restoration, Old State House, Presidential Library, arts center, Central High, Old Mill, Reperatory Theatre, Symphony, Tolec Indian archeological dig, River Market, antiquing, biking, birding, hiking, golf, tennis, fishing, nightlife.

CUISINE

Gourmet formal two-course breakfast by candlelight served "Before the Queen (portrait)" with all the formal Victorian pomp and circumstance - silver, china and an aproned maid. Plethora of excellent restaurants available.
Complimentary liquor.

DIRECTIONS

From I-30 take I-630 west. Exit Main St. Left on Main to 22nd St. Right on 22nd - one block. From Airport: I-440 W to I-30 E to I-630. Follow above directions. I-430: I-430 to I-630. Take Center St. exit thru light to Main to 22nd St.

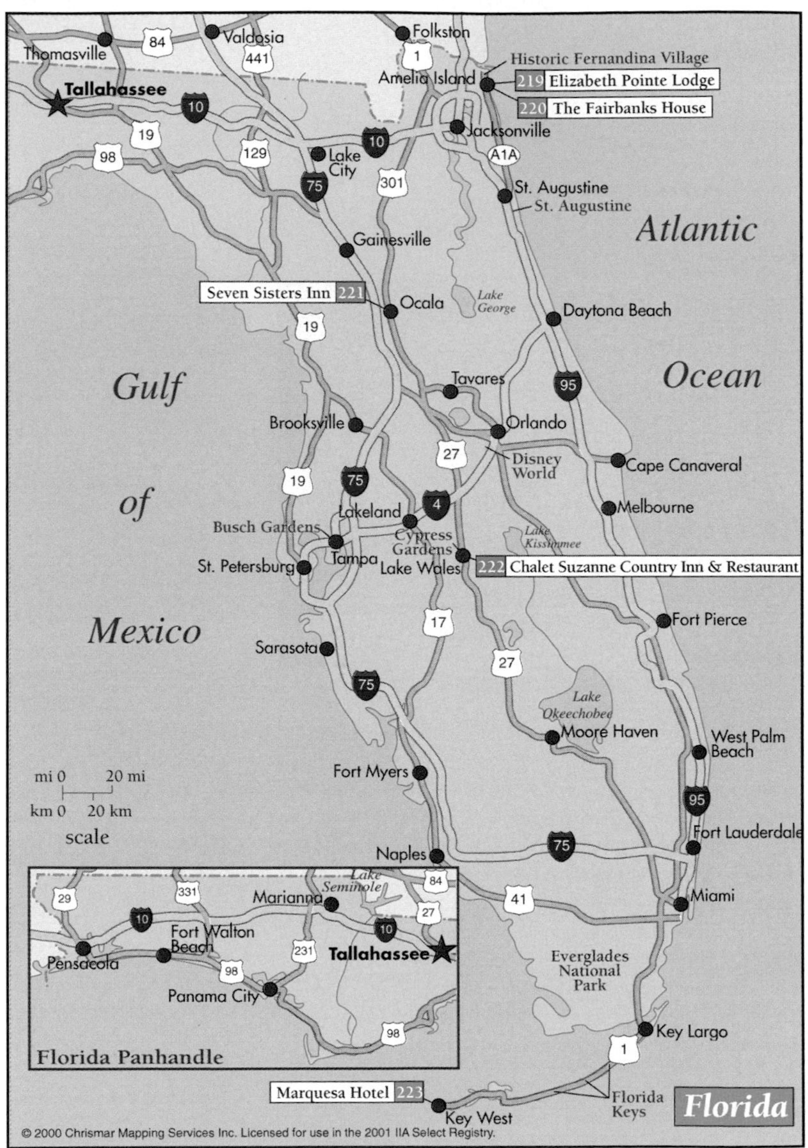
Thomasville
Valdosta
Folkston
84
441
1
Historic Fernandina Village
Amelia Island
219 Elizabeth Pointe Lodge
220 The Fairbanks House
Tallahassee
10
19
98
129
Lake City
Jacksonville
A1A
75
301
St. Augustine
St. Augustine
Atlantic
Gainesville
Seven Sisters Inn 221
Ocala
Lake George
Daytona Beach
Gulf
Tavares
95
Ocean
Brooksville
Orlando
27
Disney World
Cape Canaveral
of
4
Lakeland
Melbourne
Busch Gardens
Cypress Gardens
Lake Kissimmee
Tampa
St. Petersburg
Lake Wales
222 Chalet Suzanne Country Inn & Restaurant
Mexico
17
Fort Pierce
Sarasota
Lake Okeechobee
Moore Haven
West Palm Beach
Fort Myers
mi 0 20 mi
km 0 20 km
scale
Fort Lauderdale
Naples
41
Miami
Lake Seminole
29
331
Marianna
84
27
Fort Walton Beach
231
Tallahassee
Pensacola
98
Panama City
Everglades National Park
Key Largo
Florida Panhandle
Marquesa Hotel 223
Florida Keys
Key West
Florida
© 2000 Chrismar Mapping Services Inc. Licensed for use in the 2001 IIA Select Registry.

Amelia Island, FL

Elizabeth Pointe Lodge

800-757-1910
904-277-4851 Fax 904-277-6500
www.elizabethpointelodge.com
info@elizabethpointlodge.com
98 South Fletcher Avenue, Amelia Island, FL 32034

Select Registry Member *Since 1998*
Innkeepers/Owners
DAVID AND SUSAN CAPLES

RATED "ONE OF THE 12 BEST WATERFRONT INNS" in America, the Pointe sits overlooking the Atlantic Ocean. Focusing on individualized attention, the inn is Nantucket "shingle style" with an oversized soaking tub in each bath, robes, fresh flowers, morning newspaper, full seaside breakfast and a staff that wants to exceed your expectations. Light food, dessert and room service available all day. Only a short bike ride to the historic seaport of Fernandina. Horseback riding, tennis, golf and sailing nearby. AAA ◆◆◆.

TRADITIONAL WATERSIDE BREAKFAST INN

RATES
24 rooms, $160/$240 B&B.
1 cottage, $270 B&B.
Open year-round.

ATTRACTIONS
Historic touring, beach walking, fishing, sailing, golf, tennis, horseback riding, antiquing, biking, swimming, jet-ski rentals, biplane rides.

CUISINE
Full buffet breakfast, light fare all day. Complimentary social hour. Wine and beer available.

DIRECTIONS
From I-95 take exit 129 and follow Rte A1A to Amelia Island. Our address on A1A is 98 S Fletcher Ave., on ocean side.

20 Guestrooms Handicap Accessible • Suitable for Children
Conference Facilities for 20 • AMEX, Visa, MC, Disc Accepted
Designated Smoking Areas • Reservations Accepted Through Travel Agents

Amelia Island, FL

The Fairbanks House

888-891-9880
904-277-0500 Fax 904-277-3103
www.fairbankshouse.com
fairbanks@net-magic.net
227 South Seventh Street, Amelia Island, FL 32034

Select Registry Member *Since 1998*
Innkeepers/Owners
Bill and Theresa Hamilton

An elegant 1885 Italianate villa in the historic district of Fernandina Beach. The mansion, cottages and pool rest on a strikingly landscaped acre where guests enjoy a smoke-free stay. Rooms are romantically furnished with king or queen four poster or canopy beds and period antiques. The private guest baths have showers and offer Jacuzzi or Victorian soaking tubs. Movie channels, phones, hair dryers, irons and coffee are room amenities. Gourmet breakfast and social hour are served in our large public rooms and piazzas by the gardens. Off-street parking, complimentary bikes, walk to everything. "Top 10 Affordable Luxury Inns" - *Country Inns.*

Elegant In Town
Breakfast Inn

RATES
6 rooms.
3 cottages.
3 suites.
$150/$250 B&B.
Open year-round.

ATTRACTIONS
Historic walking tours, romantic carriage rides, sunset sails, art and antique galleries, nature hikes, birding, kayaking, watersports, horseback riding, golf, tennis, fishing, boating, bi-plane rides, civil war fort, 13 miles of pristine beaches.

CUISINE
Wonderful restaurants within easy walking distance. Complimentary social hour each day.

DIRECTIONS
Use exit 129 from I-95 and follow the signs for Fernandina Beach along Hwy A1A, 200 E. After bridge go 3.3 miles to Cedar. L onto Cedar and R onto 7th. 30 miles from JAX, FL airport.

Suitable for Children Over 12 • Non-Smoking Inn
Conference Facilities for 18 • MC, Visa, AMEX, Disc Accepted
Reservations Accepted Through Travel Agents

Ocala, FL

Seven Sisters Inn

800-250-3496
352-867-1170 Fax 352-867-5266
www.7sistersinn.com
sistersinn@aol.com
820 SE Fort King Street, Ocala, FL 34471

Select Registry Member *Since 2000*
Innkeepers/Owners
BONNIE MOREHARDT AND KEN ODEN

TRADITIONAL IN TOWN INN

THE SEVEN SISTERS INN chosen 'Inn of the Month' by *Country Inns* magazine, is located in historical Ocala, Florida. Built in 1888, this classic Victorian has been lovingly restored to its original elegance with beautiful period furnishings. The Inn was judged 'Best Restoration Project in Florida' and is listed on the National Register of Historic Homes. Morning newspaper, afternoon tea and treats, free bicycles, library and games room are provided for the guest. Business travelers will enjoy our corporate meeting room, in-room phones, fax facilities and executive retreat functions. Cinderella wedding packages are our specialty. AAA ◆◆◆ and Mobil ★★★.

RATES

8 rooms $115/$195.
Some rooms with Jacuzzi or Victorian soaking tub, others with romantic fireplace. All intended to pamper you during your stay.
Open year-round.

ATTRACTIONS

Popular day-trips include: Silver Springs Glass Bottom Boats, Appleton Art Museum, horse farm tours and golf. Ocala National Forest is nearby for canoe trips, hiking and bike trails. Antique shops tempt the discerning shopper with treasures galore.

CUISINE

Full breakfast daily. Afternoon tea with snacks. Candlelit dinners by our European chef or join other guests for family sit-down dining. Evening meals by reservation only. In-room coffee, tea and cocoa service.

DIRECTIONS

From I-75 take exit 69 Rte 40 E 3 miles into downtown Ocala. Turn R at 9th Ave. 1 block S to Ft. King St. From E take Hwy 40 into Ocala. 11th Ave. turn L 1 block, R onto Ft. King St. Inn is 1 1/2 blocks ahead.

Handicap Access Available • Suitable for Children Over 12
Conference Facilities for 30 • Credit Cards Accepted
Reservations Accepted Through Travel Agents

Lake Wales, FL

Chalet Suzanne Country Inn & Restaurant

800-433-6011
863-676-6011 Fax 863-676-1814
www.chaletsuzanne.com
info@chaletsuzanne.com
3800 Chalet Suzanne Drive, Lake Wales, FL 33853

IN THE HEART OF CENTRAL FLORIDA, a storybook Inn nestled among orange groves on small, sparkling Lake Suzanne. Around-the-world furnishings are enhanced by its fountains, courtyards, balconies and beautiful grounds. The essence of the Chalet's reputation is its award-winning cuisine served in a unique setting, winning 30 Golden Spoons and the *Wine Spectator* magazine Award of Excellence. Listed on the National Register of Historical Places, Chalet Suzanne receives Mobil's ★★★, AAA's ◆◆◆, ABBA's ★★★ Excellence Award, and the Ledger's ★★★★★ for dining.

Select Registry Member *Since 1973*
Innkeeper/Owner
VITA HINSHAW
FAMILY OWNED FOR 70 YRS

TRADITIONAL COUNTRY INN

RATES
26 rooms, $169/$229 B&B.
4 suites, $179/$229,
Summer packages.
Open daily year-round.

ATTRACTIONS
Gift shops, wedding garden, soup cannery, ceramic studio, airstrip, swimming, croquet, volleyball. Near Bok Tower Gardens, Cypress Gardens, Depot Museum.

CUISINE
American/continental. Breakfast, lunch and dinner. Intimate lounge. Award-winning wine list.

DIRECTIONS
From I-4 exit 23 take Hwy 27 S for 18.5 miles to Chalet Suzanne Rd. Turn L at the traffic light and go 1.5 miles to our entrance. From SR 60 go 4 mi N on US 27 to Chalet Suzanne Rd. Turn R at light.

3 Guestrooms Handicap Accessible • Suitable for Children
Conference Facilities for 40 +AMEX, Visa, MC, Disc, Diners, CB Accepted
Designated Smoking Areas • Reservations Accepted Through Travel Agents

Key West, FL

The Marquesa Hotel

800-869-4631
305-292-1919 Fax 305-294-2121
www.marquesa.com

600 Fleming Street, Key West, FL 33040

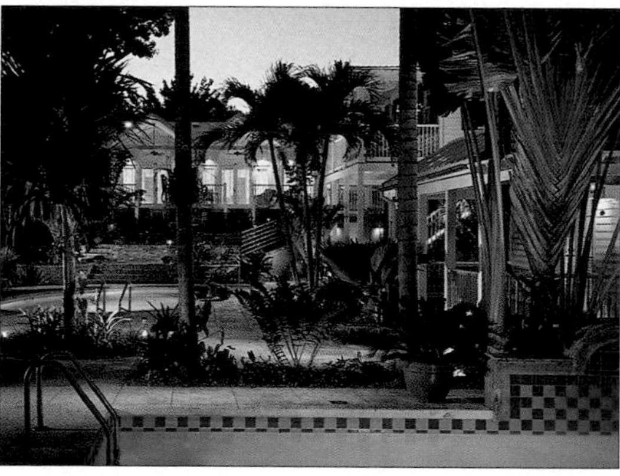

Select Registry Member *Since 1991*
Innkeeper/Owner
Carol Wightman
Owners
Richard Manley and
Erik DeBoer

ELEGANT IN TOWN HOTEL

RATES
14 rooms, $170/$295.
13 suites, $260/$395 .
Open year-round.

ATTRACTIONS
Heated pools, nearby snorkeling on coral reef, fishing, sailing, historic attractions and homes, theatre, galleries.

CUISINE
Poolside or room service dining for breakfast. Fine-dining in Cafe Marquesa with an inventive and delicious menu.

DIRECTIONS
US 1, R on N Roosevelt Blvd, becomes Truman Ave. Continue to Simonton, turn R, go 5 blks to Fleming. Turn R. Hotel on R.

IN THE HEART OF KEY WEST'S HISTORIC DISTRICT, the Marquesa Hotel and Cafe is a landmark 117-year-old home, restored to four-diamond status. Floor-to-ceiling windows, large bouquets of flowers, two shimmering pools and lush gardens are Marquesa trademarks. Rooms and suites are luxurious with private marble baths, bathrobes and fine furnishings. Located one block from Duval Street for shops, galleries, restaurants and night life. *The Miami Herald* rated it as one of Florida's top 10 Inns, and *Zagat's* rated it 17th in the U.S.A.

2 Guestrooms Handicap Accessible
Suitable for Children Over 12 • Visa, MC, AMEX, Diners Accepted
Reservations Accepted Through Travel Agents

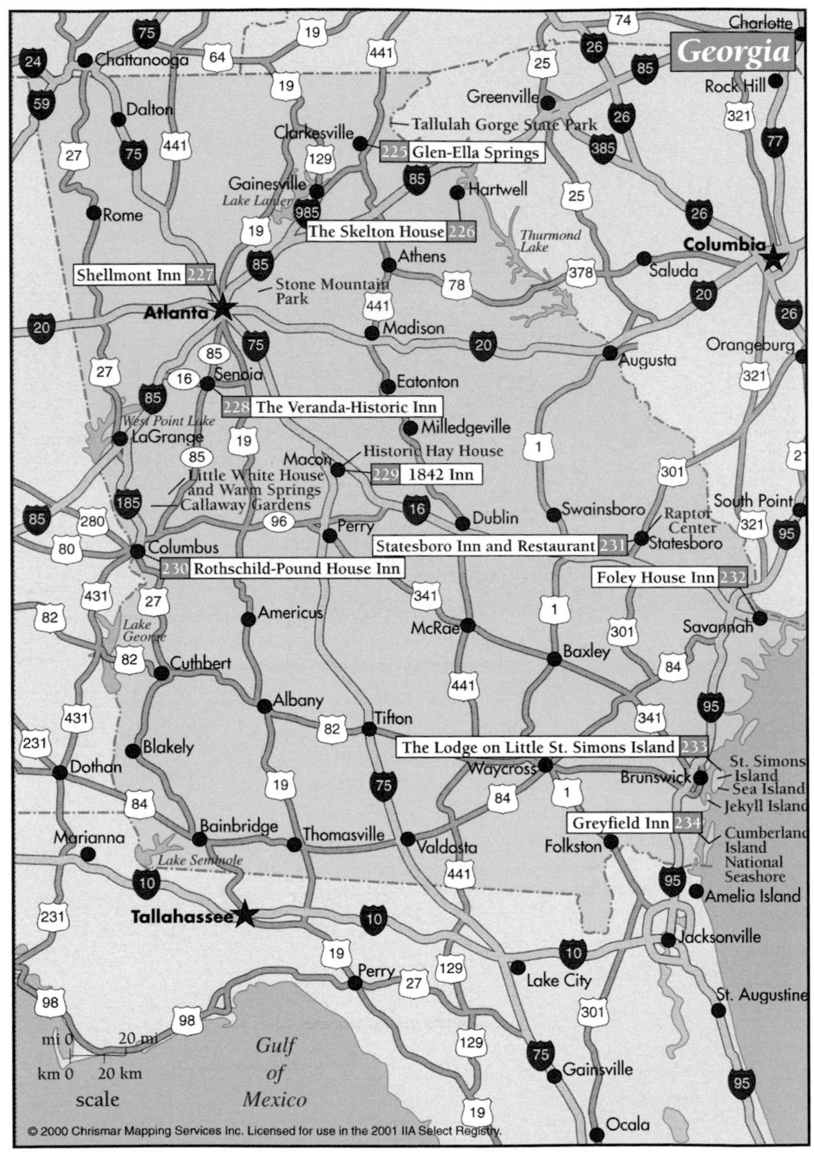
Georgia
Charlotte
Rock Hill
Chattanooga
Dalton
Greenville
Tallulah Gorge State Park
Clarkesville
225 Glen-Ella Springs
Gainesville
Lake Lanier
Hartwell
The Skelton House 226
Thurmond Lake
Columbia
Rome
Athens
Saluda
Shellmont Inn 227
Stone Mountain Park
Atlanta
Madison
Orangeburg
Augusta
Senoia
Eatonton
228 The Veranda-Historic Inn
West Point Lake
LaGrange
Milledgeville
Historic Hay House
Macon
229 1842 Inn
Little White House and Warm Springs
Callaway Gardens
Dublin
Swainsboro
Raptor Center
South Point
Perry
Statesboro Inn and Restaurant 231
Statesboro
Columbus
230 Rothschild-Pound House Inn
Foley House Inn 232
Americus
McRae
Savannah
Lake George
Baxley
Cuthbert
Albany
Tifton
Blakely
The Lodge on Little St. Simons Island 233
Dothan
Waycross
St. Simons Island
Sea Island
Brunswick
Jekyll Island
Greyfield Inn 234
Cumberland Island National Seashore
Marianna
Bainbridge
Thomasville
Valdosta
Folkston
Lake Seminole
Amelia Island
Tallahassee
Jacksonville
Perry
Lake City
St. Augustine
mi 0 20 mi
km 0 20 km
scale
Gulf of Mexico
Gainsville
Ocala
© 2000 Chrismar Mapping Services Inc. Licensed for use in the 2001 IIA Select Registry.

Clarkesville, GA

Glen-Ella Springs

888-455-8886
706-754-7295 Fax 706-754-1560
www.glenella.com
info@glenella.com
1789 Bear Gap Road, Clarkesville, GA 30523

Select Registry Member *Since 1990*
Innkeepers/Owners
BARRIE AND BOBBY AYCOCK

DOWN A GRAVEL ROAD at the edge of the Blue Ridge Mountains, this historic Inn listed on the National Register of Historic Places, is one of the few remaining examples of traditional small hotels which dotted the Northern Georgia mountains in the mid-1800s. The simple heart pine structure is tastefully decorated with great attention to detail and comfort. Eighteen acres of meadows and gardens, a large swimming pool and sun deck, outstanding food and a friendly attentive staff, all combine to make Glen-Ella Springs the perfect spot for a vacation or an executive retreat.

RUSTIC MOUNTAIN INN

RATES
16 rooms, $125/$200 B&B.
Open year-round.

ATTRACTIONS
Outdoor pool, 5 miles from Tallulah Gorge Park, hiking, trout fishing, white-water rafting, horseback, golf, great antiques and folk-art galleries.

CUISINE
Dinner most evenings by reservation. BYOB.

DIRECTIONS
3 miles off US 441 between Clarkesville and Clayton; go W on T. Smith Rd. at mile marker 18, then N on Historic Old 441 for 1/4 mile; turn L on Orchard Rd. and follow the signs.

4 Guestrooms Handicap Accessible • Suitable for Children Over 6
Conference Facilities for 25 • MC, Visa, AMEX, Disc Accepted
Designated Smoking Areas • Reservations Accepted Through Travel Agents

Hartwell, GA

The Skelton House

877-556-3790
706-376-7969 Fax 706-856-3139
www.theskeltonhouse.com
skeltonhouse@hartcom.net
97 Benson Street, Hartwell, GA 30643-1991

Select Registry Member *Since 2001*
Innkeepers/Owners
RUTH AND JOHN SKELTON

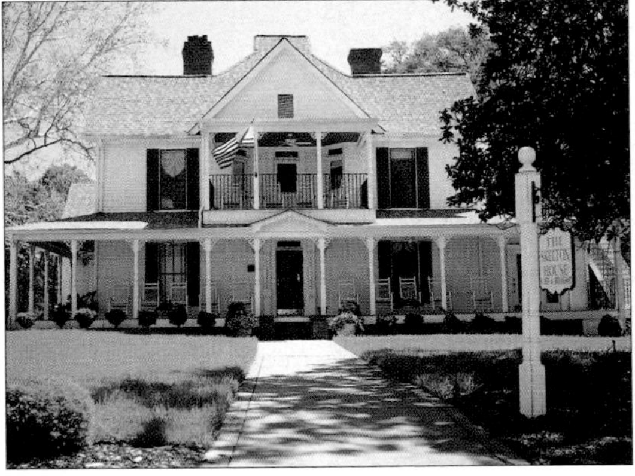

THE SKELTON HOUSE IS AN 1896 NATIONAL REGISTER VICTORIAN located in the small lake-side town of Hartwell. The charm, grace and hospitality of the original Skelton family and their grand home has been retained by today's generation of Skeltons as their recently restored home enjoys its new life as The Skelton House. Wrap yourself in luxury while enjoying the beauty of the Victorian period joined with the comfort and elegance today's discerning guests expect. Enjoy the beautiful Victorian parlor, the sunny morning room, the cozy receiving room, the spacious dining room, or one of the many porches or balconies. Located only 13 miles from I-85 in NE Georgia. AAA ◆◆◆.

VICTORIAN VILLAGE
BREAKFAST INN

RATES
7 rooms, $85/$125.
Each guestroom is furnished with antiques and includes amenities such as baths, TVs, phones with data ports and climate controls.
Open year-round.

ATTRACTIONS
Hartwell Dam and Lake Hartwell. Historic walking tour of downtown district. Community theater, Hart State Park, museum, antique shops, fishing and hunting, championship golf courses, art exhibits, bike races, regattas.

CUISINE
Full service gourmet breakfasts. Complimentary beverages and snacks. Casual but elegant fine dining restaurant nearby serving various entrees prepared with a southern flair. Extensive selection of beer and wine.

DIRECTIONS
I-85 to GA exit 177. 13 miles S on GA Hy. 77 to Hartwell. Turn R at 5th red light onto Carter St. and look for us on the immediate left next to the Presbyterian Church.

Handicap Access Available • Suitable for Children
Designated Smoking Areas • MC, Visa, AMEX, Disc, Diners Accepted
Reservations Accepted Through Travel Agents

Atlanta, GA

Shellmont Inn

404-872-9290
Fax 404-872-5379
www.shellmont.com
innkeeper@shellmont.com
821 Piedmont Avenue N.E., Atlanta, GA 30308

Select Registry Member *Since 1994*
Innkeepers/Owners
ED AND DEBBIE MCCORD

THE SHELLMONT INN is an impeccably restored 1891 National Register mansion in Midtown Atlanta's theater, restaurant and cultural district. The Inn is a treasure chest of stained, leaded and beveled glass, intricately-carved woodwork and hand-painted stenciling. Guestrooms are furnished with antiques, oriental rugs and period wall treatments. Wicker-laden verandas overlook manicured lawns and gardens-including a Victorian fishpond. The experience is unforgettable. City of Atlanta Landmark Building. Recipient of Mayor's Award for Excellence for Historic Preservation. AAA ◆◆◆.

TRADITIONAL IN TOWN BREAKFAST INN

RATES

5 rooms, $110/$175 B&B.
2 suites, $150/$275 B&B.
Smoking on verandas only.
Open year-round.

ATTRACTIONS

Botanical gardens, art museums, fine dining, theatres, historic tours, symphony, shopping, GA World Congress Center, Georgia Dome, Underground Atlanta, Margaret Mitchell House, Turner Field (Braves), Philips Arena, Atlanta History Center, Fox Theatre.

CUISINE

Gourmet breakfast, complimentary beverages, fresh fruit basket, evening chocolates.

DIRECTIONS

I-75/85 N, exit 248-C (International Blvd), turn L at 2nd traffic light (Ellis St.), turn R at next traffic light (Piedmont Ave.). Go N 1 1/2 miles. Located at the intersection of Piedmont Ave. and 6th St. on the R.

Suitable for Children Over 12 • Designated Smoking Areas
Visa, MC, Diners, Disc, AMEX, JCB Accepted
Reservations Accepted Through Travel Agents

Atlanta, GA

The Veranda–Historic Inn

770-599-3905
Fax 770-599-0806
www.selectregistry.com

252 Seavy Street, Box 177, Senoia, GA 30276

Select Registry Member *Since 1988*
Innkeepers/Owners
JAN AND BOBBY BOAL

WITH WRAPAROUND PORCH and rocking chairs, this elegant turn-of-the-century National Register Inn offers a quiet, relaxed Southern lifestyle just 37 miles south of bustling downtown Atlanta. Guests enjoy fresh flowers, books, games, puzzles, walking canes and historic memorabilia plus one of the finest collections of kaleidoscopes in the world. The Veranda is renowned for its lavish breakfasts and gourmet candlelit dinners. Local attractions include antiques, historic tours, Riverwood Studios (where "Fried Green Tomatoes," "The War," etc. were filmed) and The Veranda's unique gift shop. 1990 INN OF THE YEAR.

TRADITIONAL VILLAGE INN

RATES

9 rooms, $125/$175 B&B.
All rooms have queen beds (one king), tile baths, AC and feature in-room kaleidoscopes.
Open year-round.

ATTRACTIONS

HERE: Senoia boasts small-town charm with 113 places on the Historic Register. NEARBY: Callaway Gardens, FDR Little White House. Golf and pond fishing. Atlanta offers sports, arts, shopping, sightseeing, etc.

CUISINE

Breakfast daily. Dinners by reservation: 3-course Mon-Thu; 6 pm. 5-course Fri-Sat; 7 pm. Complimentary homemade snacks, drinks, fruit available anytime. No alcohol served or permitted in public rooms.

DIRECTIONS

From Atlanta I-85 S to exit 61; L, SE Hwy 74 16.7 miles; R, S Rockaway Rd. 3.3 miles. L, E at light to Inn. Ask for brochure and directions from other places.

---

2 Guestrooms Handicap Accessible • Limited Access For Children
Conference Facilities for 20 • Visa, MC, Disc, AMEX Accepted
Designated Smoking Areas • Reservations Accepted Through Travel Agents

Macon, GA

1842 Inn

800-336-1842
478-741-1842 Fax 478-741-1842
www.the1842inn.com
The1842INN@worldnet.att.net
353 College Street, Macon, GA 31201

Select Registry Member *Since 1994*
Innkeeper
NAZARIO FILIPPONI

MOBIL ★★★★, AAA ◆◆◆◆; *Zagat* top 50 US Inns and Resorts. The 1842 Inn boasts 21 luxurious rooms and public areas tastefully designed with fine English antiques, tapestries and paintings. A quaint garden courtyard and garden pool greet guests for cocktails or breakfast. Nightly turndowns, shoeshines and fresh flowers enhance many other gracious grand hotel amenities. Rooms available with whirlpool tubs and fireplaces. High level of service. Valet parking on request. Considered 'One of America's Top 100 Inns in the 20th Century' by the International Restaurant and Hospitality Rating Bureau.

ELEGANT IN TOWN BREAKFAST INN

RATES
21 guestrooms, $170/$260 B&B. (Rates subject to change without notice.)
Open year-round.

ATTRACTIONS
Walking distance to museum houses and historic districts with 5,500 structures on National Register. VIP access to country club and health club.

CUISINE
Breakfast and hors d'oeuvres included. Dinner in nearby private club. Full service bar.

DIRECTIONS
Exit 164 on I-75 turn L from N; R from S go 2 lights to College St.; turn L; Inn is 2 blks on L.

1 Guestroom Handicap Accessible • Suitable for Children Over 12
Conference Facilities for 20 • AMEX, Diners, Visa, MC Accepted • Pets Accepted
Designated Smoking Areas • Reservations Accepted Through Travel Agents

Columbus, GA

Rothschild-Pound House Inn

800-585-4075
706-322-4075 Fax 706-317-4989
www.awts.com/poundhouse
mpound@awts.com
201 Seventh Street, Columbus, GA 31901

Select Registry Member *Since 2000*
Owners
MAMIE AND GARRY POUND

THE INN SPEAKS OF 'OLD' COLUMBUS with warmth and casual charm. Travelers here will find inviting guest suites with period baths or Jacuzzi tubs, fireplaces, steam showers and beautiful hardwood floors. Every suite was designed with comfort and convenience in mind, cable TV, stocked mini-refrigerators, in-room coffee and tea, plush robes, private phone and fax make each suite inviting. Fresh flowers, original art, antique oriental rugs and fine antiques fill the Inn. Each evening cocktails and hors d'oeuvres are served in the main house. Breakfast is served in several courses. Guests enjoy the gourmet grits, homemade breads, quiches and preserves. Always created to please!

ELEGANT IN TOWN BREAKFAST INN

RATES

10 suites, $97/$165.
Guest suites furnished in antiques, 14-ft. ceilings, feather beds; all individually decorated.
Open year-round.

ATTRACTIONS

Riverwalk, downtown business district, fine restaurants, Performing Arts Center, historic Springer Opera House, Columbus Museum, Civil War and colonial sights tours.

CUISINE

Full breakfast, evening refreshments, honor bar. Membership for guests to Chattahoochee River Club (private dining club on the river).

DIRECTIONS

From Atlanta, take I-85 S to 185. Take the airport throughway exit, turning R. At the second light, turn L. Go 5 1/2 miles on Veteran's Pkwy. Turn R onto 7th St. the inn is 2 blocks up on R.

Handicap Access Available • Suitable for Children • Credit Cards Accepted
Reservations Accepted Through Travel Agents

Statesboro, GA
Historic Statesboro Inn and Restaurant

800-846-9466
912-489-8628 Fax 912-489-4785
www.statesboroinn.com
frontdesk@statesboroinn.com
106 South Main Street, Statesboro, GA 30458

Select Registry Member *Since 1998*
Innkeepers/Owners
Tony and Michele Garges; Melissa (daughter) and John Armstrong

Traditional In Town Inn

A 1905 HISTORIC REGISTER VICTORIAN OASIS where porches, rockers, gardens and ponds await guests. Fireplaces, whirlpool baths and a small pub add all the amenities of a European-style inn. Our style is eclectic, yet comfortable, with furnishings from three generations. Our service is attentive, just right for a relaxing getaway. Fireplaces, candlelight and music provide a romantic setting for a casual, but elegant, dining experience. The conference and banquet rooms make the Inn a natural setting for that special function or corporate retreat. Mobil ★★★.

RATES
17 rooms.
1 two-room suite, $85/$130 B&B.
Open year-round.

ATTRACTIONS
Savannah 45 miles, Georgia Southern University, botanical gardens, historical district, GSU Museum, Raptor Center, antiquing and nearby golf courses.

CUISINE
Breakfast, dinner and catering facilities. Wine and liquor available.

DIRECTIONS
From Savannah: I-16 W to exit 127 (Rt. 67) to Statesboro to 301 N (Main St.). From Atlanta: I-75 S to Macon I-16 E to exit 116, 301 N to Statesboro. (Do not take bypass).

1 Guestroom Handicap Accessible • Suitable for Children • Pets Allowed
Conference Facilities for 50 • MC, Visa, Disc, AMEX Accepted
Non Smoking Inn • Reservations Accepted Through Travel Agents

Savannah, GA

Foley House Inn

800-647-3708
912-232-6622 Fax 912-231-1218
www.foleyinn.com
foleyinn@aol.com
14 West Hull Street, Savannah, GA 31401

Select Registry Member *Since 1998*
Innkeeper/Owner
PHIL JENKINS AND RICHARD MEILS, M.D.

AN ELEGANT TOWNHOUSE MANSION on beautiful moss-draped Chipewa Square. An easy stroll to everything. Public and guestrooms decorated with saavy English and British Colonial decor. Gas fireplaces in most rooms, canopied and four-poster beds. Some rooms with oversized Jacuzzi baths. Our concierge will make dinner and tour reservations. Walk to restaurants, theaters, symphony, antique stores and art galleries from this perfect location. Complimentary video library. Some rooms have private balconies overlooking this lovely square, the site where "Forrest Gump" ate chocolate and waited for the bus.

ELEGANT IN TOWN BREAKFAST INN

RATES

19 rooms $185/$295-all year.
Open year-round.

ATTRACTIONS

Restaurants, symphony, jazz, theater, antiques, shopping, parks, carriage rides, museums within walking distance, golf and tennis can be arranged.

CUISINE

Wine for sale by glass or bottle. Enjoy a complimentary hot and cold breakfast, afternoon tea and coffee with sweets and hors d'oeuvres,with our cash wine bar in the evening.

DIRECTIONS

From I-95 to I-16 to end at Montgomery St. R at 2nd light onto Oglethorpe St., R onto Bull St., R onto Hull St. 1st red brick building on R.

1 Guestroom Handicap Accessible • Suitable for Children Over 12
Conference Facilities for 16 • AMEX, MC, Visa Accepted
Designated Smoking Areas • Reservations Accepted Through Travel Agents

Little St. Simons Island, GA

The Lodge on Little St. Simons Island

888-733-5774

912-638-7472 Fax 912-634-1811

www.LittleStSimonsIsland.com

lssi@mindspring.com

P.O. Box 21078

Little St. Simons Island, GA 31522-0578

Select Registry Member *Since 1993*

Resident Manager

MAUREEN AHERN

©Randall Perry Photography

NATURE PREVAILS ON THIS PRISTINE ISLAND where 10,000 acres are shared with no more than 30 overnight guests at a time. Accessible only by boat, Little St. Simons Island unfolds its secrets to those eager to discover a bounty of natural wonders. Seven miles of shell-strewn beaches meet acres of legendary moss-draped live oaks, glistening tidal creeks and shimmering salt marshes to provide an unparalleled setting for a host of activities or relaxation. Creature comforts include gracious accommodations, gourmet regional cuisine and Southern hospitality. Awarded *Condé Nast Traveler* magazine's "Best Small Hotel in North America," 2000 Readers' Choice Awards.

RUSTIC OCEANSIDE ISLAND RETREAT/LODGE

RATES

11 rooms, $350/$525 AP.
2 suites, $600/$900 AP.
Full island rental from $4,700.
Open year-round.
Children Over 8 Welcome Oct. - Apr., All Ages May - Sept.

ATTRACTIONS

7-mile beach, boating, canoeing, fishing, swimming, hiking, biking, kayaking, horseback riding, naturalist programs, birding and wildlife observation.

CUISINE

Gourmet regional cuisine served family style. Three meals daily. Snacks, personal picnics, oyster roasts, crab boils, cocktail cruises and full moon beach picnics.

DIRECTIONS

Accessible only by boat with departures twice daily from St. Simons Island. Airports: Savannah and Brunswick, GA., Jacksonville, FL.

1 Guestroom Handicap Accessible • Conference Facilities for 30
Suitable for Children at Designated Times • AMEX, Visa, MC, Disc Accepted
Smoking in Designated Areas • Reservations Accepted Through Travel Agents

Cumberland Island, GA

The Greyfield Inn

888-243-9238

904-261-6408 Fax 904-321-0666

www.greyfieldinn.com

seashore@greyfieldinn.com

P.O. Box 900, Fernandina Beach, FL 32035

Select Registry Member *Since 1982*

Owners
FERGUSON FAMILY
Innkeepers
BRYCEA MERRILL AND
ZACHARY Z. ZOUL

TRADITIONAL WATERSIDE RETREAT/LODGE

THIS TURN-OF-THE-CENTURY CARNEGIE MANSION is on Georgia's largest and southernmost coastal island. Miles of trails traverse the island's unique ecosystems along with a beautiful, undeveloped white sand beach for shelling, swimming, sunning and birding. Exceptional food, lovely, original furnishings, and a peaceful, relaxing environment provide guests with a step back into another era. Overnight rate includes an island outing with our naturalist, bicycles for exploring the island and round-trip boat passage on our private ferry.

RATES

17 rooms, $275/$450 AP.
Open year-round.

ATTRACTIONS

Guided Jeep tour with a naturalist, birding/wildlife observation, hiking, biking, 18-mile pristine beach, shelling, swimming, photography. Historic museum, ruins, library, river and ocean fishing.

CUISINE

Breakfast, picnic lunch, candlelit gourmet dinner. Full bar; wine, beer, liquor, cocktail hour with hors d'oeuvres.

DIRECTIONS

I-95 to Florida exit 129 (AIA) to Amelia Island 14.6 miles to Ash St. to waterfront park L in gravel lot. Meet at 'D' Dock.

Handicap Access Available • Suitable for Children Over 5
Conference Facilities for 22 • Credit Cards Accepted
Reservations Accepted Through Travel Agents

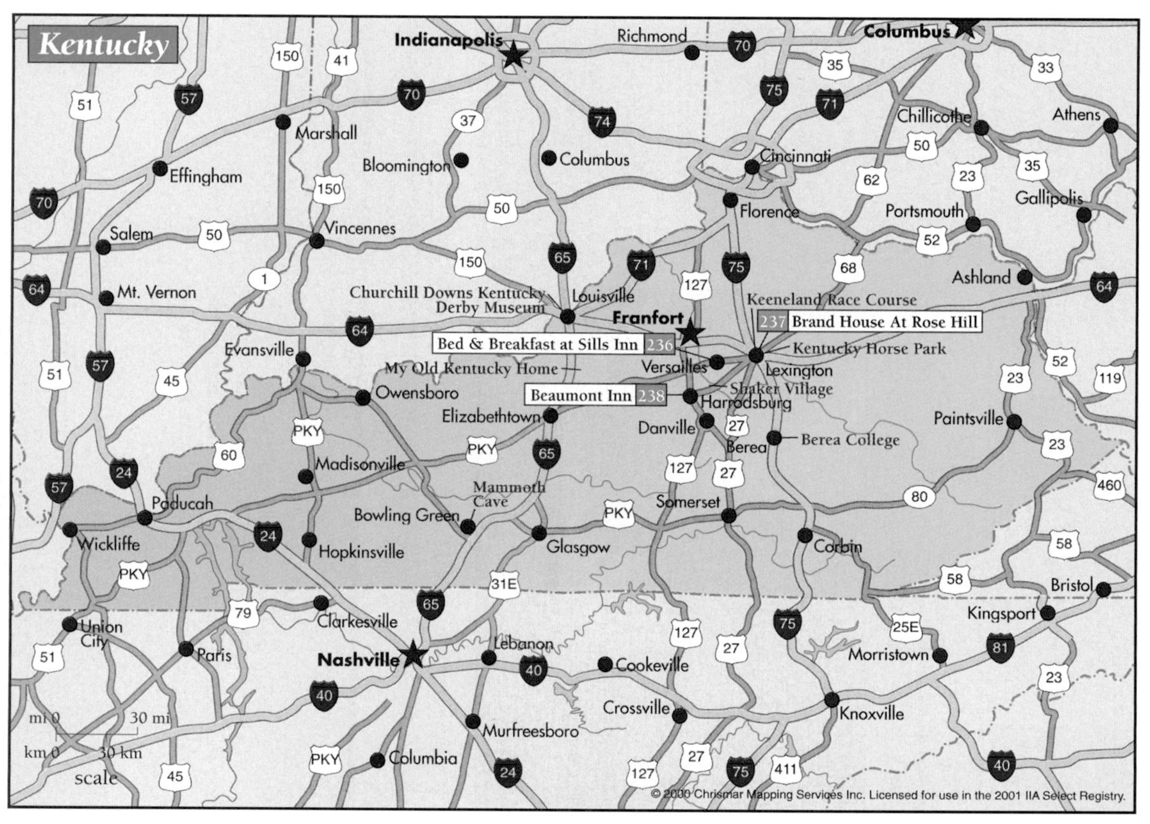
Kentucky
Indianapolis
Columbus
Nashville
Franfort
237 Brand House At Rose Hill
236 Bed & Breakfast at Sills Inn
238 Beaumont Inn
Keeneland Race Course
Kentucky Horse Park
Lexington
Shaker Village
Harrodsburg
Berea College
Berea
Versailles
Danville
Louisville
Churchill Downs Kentucky Derby Museum
My Old Kentucky Home
Elizabethtown
Mammoth Cave
Owensboro
Bowling Green
Glasgow
Somerset
Corbin
Paintsville
Ashland
Portsmouth
Chillicothe
Athens
Gallipolis
Cincinnati
Florence
Richmond
Columbus
Bloomington
Vincennes
Marshall
Effingham
Salem
Mt. Vernon
Evansville
Madisonville
Hopkinsville
Paducah
Wickliffe
Union City
Paris
Clarkesville
Columbia
Murfreesboro
Lebanon
Cookeville
Crossville
Knoxville
Morristown
Kingsport
Bristol
mi 0 30 mi
km 0 30 km
scale
© 2000 Chrismar Mapping Services Inc. Licensed for use in the 2001 IIA Select Registry.

Versailles, KY

Bed and Breakfast at Sills Inn

800-526-9801
606-873-4478 Fax 606-873-7099
www.SillsInn.com
sillsinn@aol.com
270 Montgomery Avenue, Versailles, KY 40383

Select Registry Member *Since 1998*
Innkeepers/Owners
TONY SILLS AND GLENN BLIND

ENJOY THE AMBIANCE OF SOUTHERN HOSPITALITY as you step into the 1911, three-storied restored Victorian Inn. The nearly 10,000 square feet are highly decorated and filled with Kentucky antiques. You can relax on the wraparound porch in a wicker swing or rocking chair, or step inside to enjoy a book from the library. The staff will be at your beck and call to help with travel plans, restaurants, reservations and any other needs. So make your reservations today with the Sills Inn for a memory cherished tomorrow. AAA ◆◆◆.

TRADITIONAL VILLAGE
BREAKFAST INN

RATES
2 rooms, $89/$99 B&B.
10 Jacuzzi suites,
$109/$179 B&B, yr. rates.
Open year-round.

ATTRACTIONS
Horse farms, historic distilleries, Keeneland Race Course, Shaker Village, state capitol, historic museums, Kentucky Horse Park and Lexington attractions.

CUISINE
Fine dining within walking distance or short drive. BYOB.

DIRECTIONS
Directions available upon making reservations.

Suitable for Children Over 12 • Non-Smoking Inn
Conference Facilities for 15 • All Major Credit Cards Accepted
Reservations Accepted Through Travel Agents

Lexington, KY

Brand House at Rose Hill

800-366-4942
859-226-9464 Fax 859-367-0470
www.brandhouselex.com
info@brandhouselex.com
461 North Limestone Street, Lexington, KY 40508

Select Registry Member *Since 1998*
Innkeepers/Owners
PAM AND LOGAN LEET

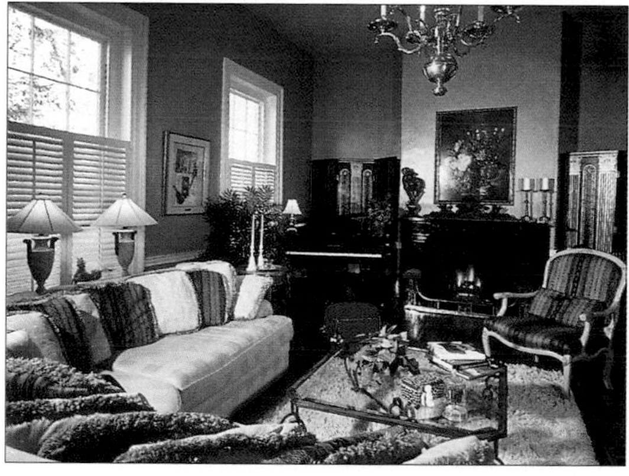

THIS NATIONAL REGISTER HOME (circa 1812), located in the center of the Bluegrass, is situated on 1.3 wooded acres adjacent to Lexington's Historic districts and only minutes from the legendary thoroughbred horse farms of central Kentucky. The casually elegant decor boasts large dining and drawing rooms, as well as a relaxing billiard room. Bountiful breakfast fare offers culinary delights to prepare you for a day of sightseeing or simply reading by the fountain on the brick terrace. Also listed with the Library of Congress, Brand House has been featured in numerous publications including *Country Inns, National Geographic, Gourmet* and *Southern Living.* AAA ◆◆◆◆.

ELEGANT IN TOWN BREAKFAST INN

RATES
5 rooms.
All with whirlpool tubs, private phones, TVs w/movie channels.
3 rooms w/fireplaces.
$109/$239 B&B.
Open year-round.

ATTRACTIONS
Kentucky Horse Park, Keeneland Race Course, University of KY, Transylvania University, Shaker Village, historic districts/homes, antiques, crafts, horseback riding, golf, relaxing and much more!

CUISINE
Bountiful breakfast. Snacks and beverages. 15 excellent restaurants within walking distance. BYOB.

DIRECTIONS
I-75/64, take exit 113. Go 2.7 miles S on Broadway, turn L on 3rd St. Go 2 blks, turn L on N Limestone, go 2 blks, house on L SW corner.

Suitable for Children Over 12 • Smoking Outside Only
Conference Facilities for 10 • Visa, MC, Disc, AMEX Accepted
Reservations Accepted Through Travel Agents

Harrodsburg, KY

Beaumont Inn

800-352-3992
859-734-3381 Fax 859-734-6897
www.beaumontinn.com
cmdedman@searnet.com
638 Beaumont Inn Drive, Harrodsburg, KY 40330

Select Registry Member *Since 1979*
Innkeepers/Owners
THE DEDMAN FAMILY

THE BEAUMONT INN has been owned and operated by four generations of the Dedman Family. The Inn, on the National Register of Historic Places, was built in 1845 as a school for young ladies. In the heart of Bluegrass Country, it is redolent of Southern history, brimming with beautiful antiques and fascinating memorabilia, while serving traditional Kentucky cuisine. Over 30 varieties of trees grace the grounds. The town of Harrodsburg, founded in 1774, is the first permanent English settlement west of the Allegheny Mountains. Located amid numerous historic sites and attractions. Experience a genuine Kentucky tradition.

TRADITIONAL VILLAGE INN

RATES
33 rooms, $85/$150 B&B (continental).
Open March - December..

ATTRACTIONS
Swimming pool, golf, fishing, historic attractions, antique galleries and summer theater.

CUISINE
Breakfast daily. Lunch Wednesday through Saturday, dinner Wednesday through Sunday. Sunday brunch buffet. Basket suppers available to overnight guests on Mondays and Tuesdays by prior request.

DIRECTIONS
In Harrodsburg at intersection with U.S. 68, take U.S. 127 S to Inn at S end of town on E side of U.S. 127.

Suitable for Children• Designated Smoking Areas
Conference Facilities for 24 • AMEX, MC, Visa, Disc Accepted
Reservations Accepted Through Travel Agents

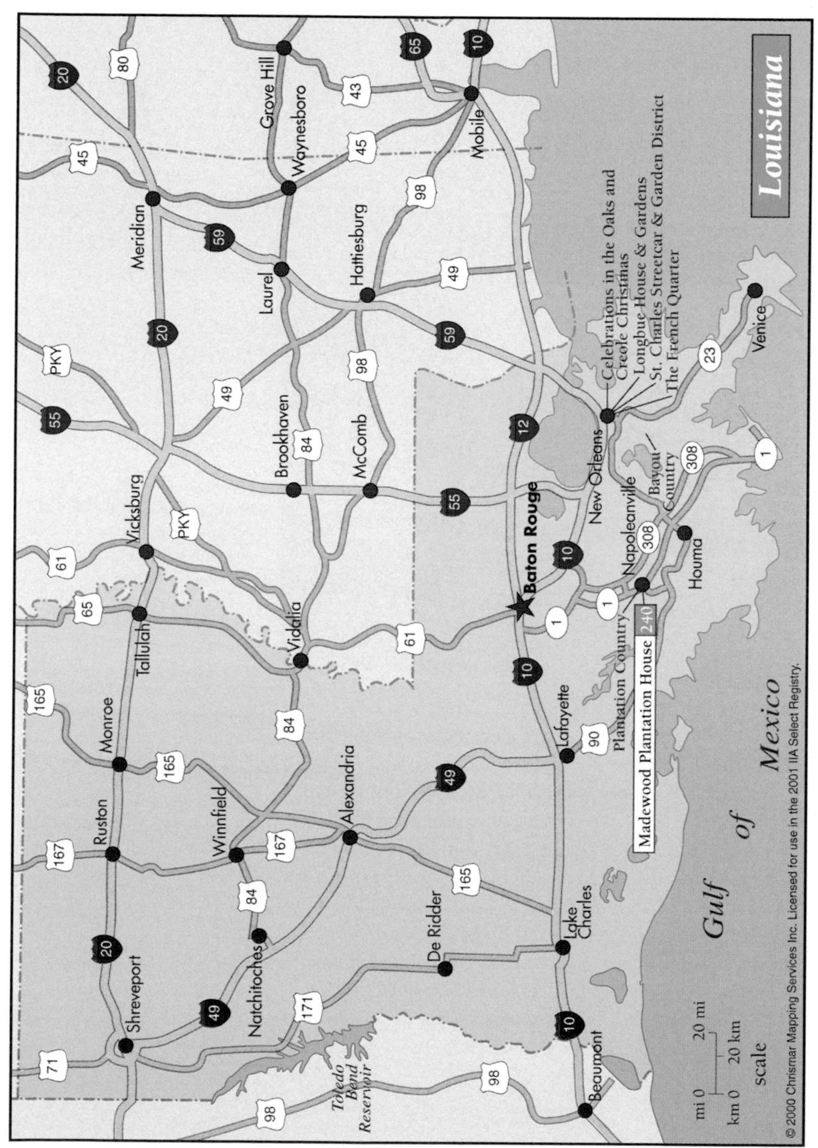
Louisiana
Celebrations in the Oaks and Creole Christmas
Longbue House & Gardens
St. Charles Streetcar & Garden District
The French Quarter
Madewood Plantation House 240
Plantation Country
Bayou Country
Baton Rouge
New Orleans
Napoleanville
Houma
Venice
Lafayette
Lake Charles
Beaumont
De Ridder
Alexandria
Natchitoches
Shreveport
Ruston
Monroe
Winnfield
Tallulah
Vicksburg
Vidalia
Brookhaven
McComb
Meridian
Laurel
Hattiesburg
Waynesboro
Grove Hill
Mobile
Toledo Bend Reservoir
Gulf of Mexico
mi 0 20 mi
km 0 20 km
scale
© 2000 Chrismar Mapping Services Inc. Licensed for use in the 2001 IIA Select Registry.

Napoleonville, LA

Madewood Plantation House

800-375-7151
504-369-7151 Fax 504-369-9848
www.madewood.com
madewoodpl@aol.com
4250 Highway 308, Napoleonville, LA 70390

Select Registry Member *Since 1993*
Innkeepers/Owners
KEITH AND MILLIE MARSHALL
Manager
CHRISTINE GANDET

TRADITIONAL COUNTRY INN

THE "QUEEN OF THE BAYOU," Madewood Plantation House offers elegant accommodations in a homelike atmosphere. The National Historic Landmark is lovingly maintained by its longtime staff, who provide the relaxed atmosphere for which Madewood is noted. Guests enjoy antique-filled rooms and canopied beds along with a house-party ambiance that includes a wine and cheese hour prior to a family-style candlelit dinner prepared by Madewood's cooks. Selected one of the top 12 Inns of 1993 by *Country Inns* magazine, featured in *National Geographic Traveler,* 1996, and named by NGT as one of the top 54 inns in US, '99. *Travel Holiday* magazine, 1998. French spoken.

RATES

6 rooms.
2 suites, $225 for two.
No seasonal rates MAP.
(Dinner, Breakfast)
Open year-round.

ATTRACTIONS

Swamp tours, historic homes, National Park Service museum on wetlands and Cajun culture, E.D. White House Museum.

CUISINE

Candelit Southern/Cajun dinner served with other guests in plantation dining room. Wine and cheese hour. Full service liquor.

DIRECTIONS

I-10 W from New Orleans to exit 182, Cross Sunshine Bridge and follow LA Hwy to Spur 70, then L on LA Hwy 308, 2.2 miles past Napoleonville.

Credit Cards Accepted
Reservations Accepted Through Travel Agents

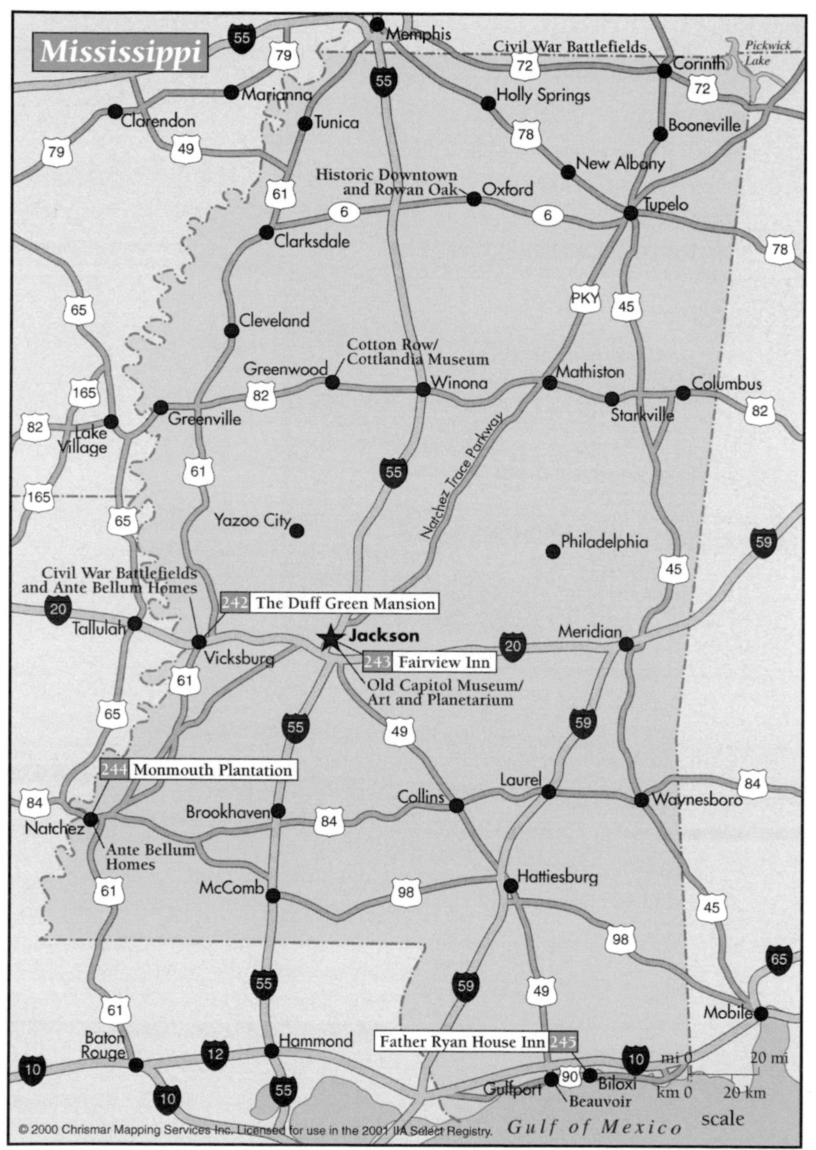

Mississippi
Memphis
Civil War Battlefields
Corinth
Pickwick Lake
Marianna
Holly Springs
Clarendon
Tunica
Booneville
New Albany
Historic Downtown and Rowan Oak
Oxford
Tupelo
Clarksdale
Cleveland
Cotton Row/ Cottlandia Museum
Greenwood
Winona
Mathiston
Columbus
Starkville
Greenville
Lake Village
Natchez Trace Parkway
Yazoo City
Philadelphia
Civil War Battlefields and Ante Bellum Homes
242 The Duff Green Mansion
Tallulah
Jackson
Meridian
Vicksburg
243 Fairview Inn
Old Capitol Museum/ Art and Planetarium
244 Monmouth Plantation
Laurel
Collins
Waynesboro
Brookhaven
Natchez
Ante Bellum Homes
Hattiesburg
McComb
Mobile
Baton Rouge
Hammond
Father Ryan House Inn 245
Gulfport
Biloxi
Beauvoir
Gulf of Mexico
mi 0 20 mi
km 0 20 km
scale

Vicksburg, MS

The Duff Green Mansion Inn

800-992-0037

601-636-6968 Fax 601-661-0079

www.SelectryRegistry.com
harrycsharp@cs.com

1114 First East Street, Vicksburg, MS 39180

Select Registry Member *Since 1991*
Innkeepers/Owners
HARRY AND ALICIA SHARP

ONE OF THE FINEST EXAMPLES of Palladian architecture in the state (National Register of Historic Places), this 1856 mansion was pressed into service as a hospital for Confederate, and later, Union soldiers during the famous siege of Vicksburg. The 12,000-square-foot mansion in the historic Old Town was restored in 1985 and is luxuriously furnished in period antiques and reproductions.

ELEGANT IN TOWN
BREAKFAST INN

RATES
6 rooms.
$95/$125
10% sales tax.
Open year-round.

ATTRACTIONS
Swimming pool on grounds, golf, tennis, fishing, hunting nearby. National military park, historic sites within walking distance, 6 blocks from Mississippi River. Massage therapy available.

CUISINE
Plantation breakfast. Wine, beer and liquor available. Complimentary cocktails 5:30-6:30 pm.

DIRECTIONS
From I-20 exit 4B to Clay St. Turn R on Adams. Go to First East St. Turn R and Duff Green is one block on the R.

2 Guestrooms Handicap Accessible • Suitable for Children
Conference Facilities for 80 • Visa, MC, AMEX, Disc Accepted
Pet Allowed • Reservations Accepted Through Travel Agents

Jackson, MS

Fairview Inn

888-948-1908
601-948-3429 Fax 601-948-1203
www.fairviewinn.com
fairview@fairviewinn.com
734 Fairview Street, Jackson, MS 39202

Select Registry Member *Since 1994*
Innkeepers./Owners
CAROL AND WILLIAM SIMMONS

THE FAIRVIEW INN is located in the Belhaven Historic District of Jackson, Mississippi, where its owners welcome guests in the hospitable tradition of the Old South. It offers luxury accommodations and fine dining in a quiet setting along with dataports and voice mail. Fairview Inn was named a Top Inn of 1994 by *Country Inns* magazine, and was awarded a certificate of excellence in the fields of hospitality and fine dining by *Country Inns* magazine and The James Beard Foundation in 1996. AAA ◆◆◆◆ Award. National Register of Historic Places.

ELEGANT IN TOWN BREAKFAST INN

RATES
3 rooms, $115 B&B.
15 suites, $165/$290 B&B.
Open year-round.

ATTRACTIONS
Walking and jogging. NEARBY: golf, Old Capitol Museum, Art Museum, New Stage Theatre, antiques, Agricultural Museum and the Governor's Mansion.

CUISINE
Breakfast, dinner by reservation. Wine and liquor available.

DIRECTIONS
I-55 exit 98A on Woodrow Wilson, L at second traffic light at North State, L one block past second traffic light at Fairview St., Inn is first on L.

1 Guestroom Handicap Accessible • Suitable for Children
Conference Facilities for 100 • Credit Cards Accepted
Non-Smoking Inn • Reservations Accepted Through Travel Agents

Natchez, MS

Monmouth Plantation

800-828-4531
601-442-5852 Fax 601-446-7762
www.monmouthplantation.com
luxury@monmouthplantation.com
36 Melrose Avenue, Natchez, MS 39120

Select Registry Member *Since 1993*
Owners
LANI AND RON RICHES

MONMOUTH PLANTATION, a National Historic Landmark (circa 1818), is a glorious return to the Antebellum South, rated "one of the ten most romantic places in the USA" by *Glamour* magazine and *USA Today*. It waits to enfold you in luxury and service. Walk our beautifully landscaped acres. Thirty-one rooms and suites in the mansion and the five other historic buildings hold priceless art and antiques while providing every modern comfort. Mornings begin with a delightful complimentary Southern breakfast. Nights sparkle under candlelight during 5-course dinners. AAA ◆◆◆◆.

ELEGANT IN TOWN INN

RATES

15 rooms, $150/$200.
16 suites, $190/$365.
Open year-round.

ATTRACTIONS
Croquet course, fishing and walking trails, golf and tennis 1/2 mile from property, gambling boat two miles away on Mississippi River.

CUISINE
Breakfast and dinner, lunch for private parties only. Wine, liquor and beer.

DIRECTIONS
E on State St., 1 mile from downtown Natchez on the corner of John Quitman Parkway and Melrose Ave.

Non-Smoking Inn • Suitable for Children Over 14
Conference Facilities for 50 • AMEX, Visa, Disc, CB Accepted
Reservations Accepted Through Travel Agents

Biloxi, MS

Father Ryan House Inn

800-295-1189
228-435-1189 Fax 228-436-3063
www.frryan.com
frryan@frryan.com
1196 Beach Boulevard, Biloxi, MS 39530

Select Registry Member *Since 1995*
Owner
Rosanne McKenney

A ROMANTIC 1841 BEACHFRONT INN located on the Gulf Coast of Mississippi. The one-time home of Father Abram Ryan, Poet Laureate and Chaplain of the Confederacy. You may choose to enjoy the spectacular view from the Jefferson Room and pamper yourself with a whirlpool bath or relax in the stately elegance and romance of the Father Ryan Rooms which are furnished with exquisitely hand-crafted beds and antiques dating back to the early 1800s. All rooms include a private bath, cable television, telephone, a full gourmet breakfast, Tea Time in the afternoon, bathrobes, and coffee service. Selected by *Travel and Leisure* magazine as one of 'The best beachfront resorts in the country.' AAA ◆◆◆.

TRADITIONAL IN TOWN BREAKFAST INN

RATES

10 rooms, \$100/\$150 B&B.
5 suites, \$165/\$225 B&B.
Open year-round.

ATTRACTIONS

On-site pool, beach across from Inn, golf, pool, historic sites, antique shops, local art galleries and museums nearby. Shrimpboat and schooner tours, charter boat and deep-sea fishing. Fine dining restaurants nearby. One mile from Casino Row.

CUISINE

Full gourmet breakfast, afternoon tea time and refreshments.

DIRECTIONS

Centrally located between New Orleans, LA and Mobile, AL. Take I-10 to exit 46-A, I-110 S to Hwy 90 W. Just 6 blocks W of I-110 off ramp.

2 Guestrooms Handicap Accessible
Conference Facilities for 35 • Visa, MC, Disc, AMEX Accepted
Non-Smoking Inn • Reservations Accepted Through Travel Agents

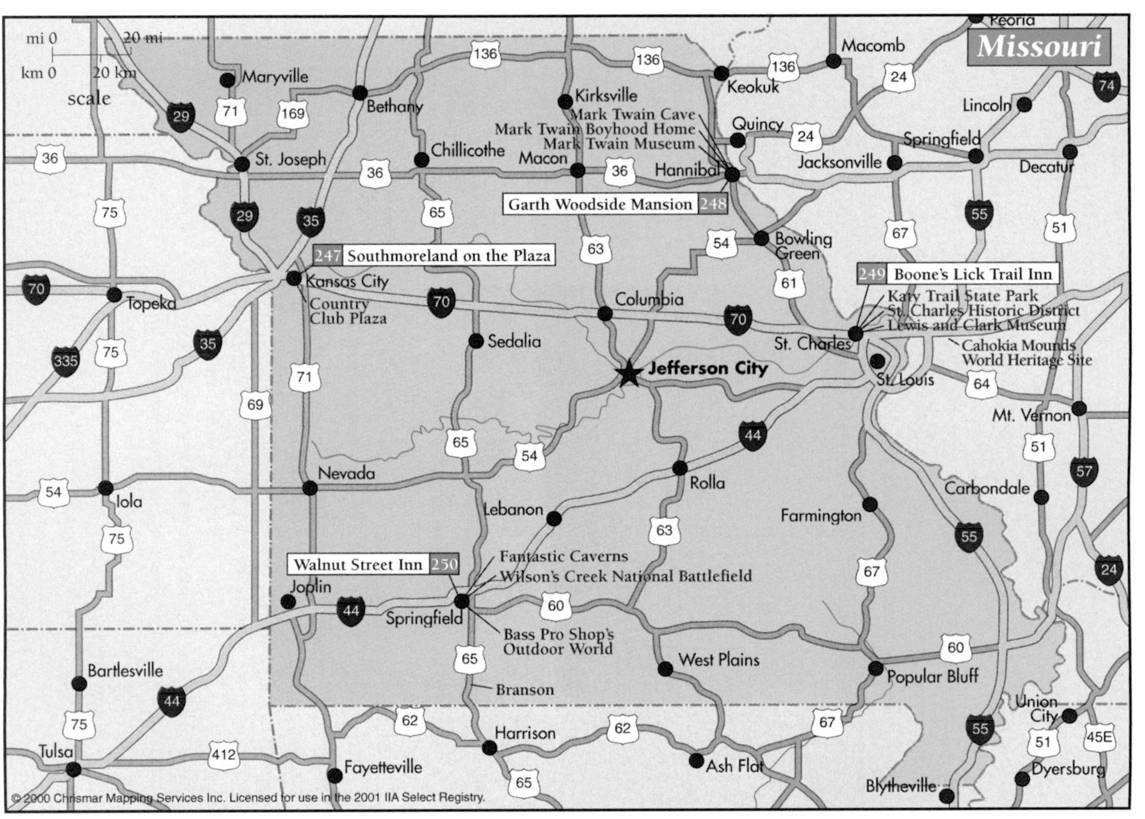
Missouri
mi 0 20 mi
km 0 20 km
scale
Maryville
Bethany
Kirksville
Mark Twain Cave
Mark Twain Boyhood Home
Mark Twain Museum
Keokuk
Macomb
Peoria
Lincoln
Quincy
Springfield
Jacksonville
Decatur
St. Joseph
Chillicothe
Macon
Hannibal
Garth Woodside Mansion 248
Bowling Green
247 Southmoreland on the Plaza
249 Boone's Lick Trail Inn
Katy Trail State Park
St. Charles Historic District
Lewis and Clark Museum
Cahokia Mounds World Heritage Site
Kansas City
Country Club Plaza
Topeka
Columbia
St. Charles
Sedalia
Jefferson City
St. Louis
Mt. Vernon
Nevada
Iola
Rolla
Carbondale
Lebanon
Farmington
Walnut Street Inn 250
Fantastic Caverns
Wilson's Creek National Battlefield
Joplin
Springfield
Bass Pro Shop's Outdoor World
West Plains
Popular Bluff
Bartlesville
Branson
Union City
Harrison
Ash Flat
Tulsa
Fayetteville
Blytheville
Dyersburg
© 2000 Chrismar Mapping Services Inc. Licensed for use in the 2001 IIA Select Registry.

Kansas City, MO

Southmoreland on the Plaza

816-531-7979
Fax 816-531-2407
www.southmoreland.com
southmoreland@earthlink.net
116 East 46th Street, Kansas City, MO 64112

AWARD-WINNING Southmoreland's 1913 Colonial Revival styling brings New England to the heart of Kansas City's historic, arts, entertainment and shopping district - The Country Club Plaza. Business and leisure guests enjoy individually decorated rooms offering decks, fireplaces or Jacuzzi baths. Business travelers find respite at Southmoreland with its rare mix of corporate support services: in room phones, fax, copier, message center, modem hookups, 24-hour access and switchboard. Six-time winner of Mobil ★★★★ Award. Visit us at www.southmoreland.com.

Select Registry Member *Since 1992*
Innkeepers/Owners
MARK REICHLE AND NANCY MILLER REICHLE

TRADITIONAL IN TOWN BREAKFAST INN

RATES
12 rooms/ 1 Carriage House Suite
$110/$170 Summer.
$105/$165 Winter.
$215 Carriage House
$20 add. for DBL. Discounted corp. rates for single travelers, Sunday - Thurs.
Open year-round.

ATTRACTIONS
Nelson-Atkins Museum of Art, Country Club Plaza, Kemper Museum, dining, shopping, theatre, UMKC, Royals baseball, Chiefs football, jazz.

CUISINE
Breakfast served daily. Complimentary afternoon wine and hors d'oeuvres, with hot beverages and sweets served in the evening. Courtyard breakfast barbeque served Saturdays, April - October.

DIRECTIONS
From I-70 or I-29 in downtown KC, take Broadway S to 47th St. L on 47th, L on Main, R onto E 46th St. About 1.5 blks down E 46th on the L. From I-35, take Main St. S to E 46th. Make L onto E. 46th-down 1.5 blks on L.

1 Guestroom Handicap Access Available • Suitable for Children Over 13
Conference Facilities for 18 • MC, Visa, AMEX Accepted
Non-Smoking Inn • Reservations Accepted Through Travel Agents

Hannibal, MO

Garth Woodside Mansion

888-427-8409
573-221-2789 Fax 573-221-9941
www.garthmansion.com
garth@nemonet.com
11069 New London Road, Hannibal, MO 63401

Select Registry Member *Since 2001*
Innkeepers/Owners
COL(RET.) JOHN AND JULIE ROLSEN

STEP BACK IN TIME in this beautifully restored 1871 Second Empire Victorian mansion, nestled in 33 acres of gardens, rolling meadows, ponds, and woodlands. Relax among original antiques that fill the parlors, library, sitting and dining rooms. Play the 1869 Steinway Square Grand Piano. Savor the solitude of natural surroundings or enjoy beautiful architecture including the "famed flying staircase." Stretch out on the grand porch or hide away on the romantic 2nd floor balcony. Afternoon treats with tea or your favorite beverage are complimentary upon check-in. Relish staying where Samuel Clemens opted to be a frequent overnight guest.

VICTORIAN COUNTRY BREAKFAST INN

RATES

8 rooms, $83/$150.
Many rooms w/original antiques. Hypo-allergenic feather beds-queen and full. All rooms feature private baths and central heat and air.
Open year-round.

ATTRACTIONS

Mark Twain boyhood home, Mark Twain Museum, Riverboat Dinner & Day cruise, Molly Brown birthplace & museum, Mark Twain Cave, fishing, boating, golfing, hiking trails, Becky Thatcher House, Outdoor theater and Mark Twain Dinner Theater.

CUISINE

Full breakfast; fresh baked chocolate chip cookies daily, complimentary beverages. Picnic lunch available upon request.

DIRECTIONS

From St. Louis N on SR 61, 75 miles N of I-70. Turn R on Warren-Barrett, R on New London, follow signs. From SR36 or I-72 S on SR61, L on Warren-Barrett, R on New London. Follow signs to Mansion.

Suitable for Children Over 12 • Designated Smoking Areas
Common Rooms Handicap Accessible • MC, Visa, AMEX Accepted
Reservations Accepted Through Travel Agents

Saint Charles, MO

Boone's Lick Trail Inn

636-947-7000
Fax 636-946-2637
www.booneslick.com
innkeeper@booneslick.com
1000 South Main Street, Saint Charles, MO 63301

Select Registry Member *Since 1992*
Innkeepers
V'ANNE AND PAUL MYDLER AND VENETIA MCENTIRE (DAUGHTER)

EXPLORE FOR YOURSELF this 1840s Federal-style inn with antiques where Daniel Boone and Lewis and Clark trekked along the wide Missouri River. In the heart of a colonial village setting of a National Register Historic District with over 100 shops, 30 restaurants, museums and Katy Trail State Park at our door. The old river settlement with its brick street, gas lamps and green spaces, is the start of the Boone's Lick Trail (8 miles to airport & 25 minutes to St. Louis' sights). V'Anne's delicate lemon biscuits, freshest fruits, and hot entrees are served amidst Paul's working duck decoy collection; a perfect escape for new inngoers, return guests and corporate seekers of a different style of lodging. Seasonal duck hunting available. AAA ◆◆◆ and Mobil ★★★.

2 Guest Rooms Handicap Accessible • Suitable for Children
Conference Facilities for 16 • Disc, Visa, MC, Diners, AMEX, CB Accepted
Designated Smoking Areas • Reservations Accepted Through Travel Agents

TRADITIONAL IN TOWN BREAKFAST INN

RATES

4 rooms, $105/$175.
1 attic loft, $115/175.
Open year-round.

ATTRACTIONS

HERE: National Register Historic District, shopping, dining, museums, wineries, antiques, Goldenrod Showboat, KATY Trail State Park, biking, hiking, birding. NEARBY: golfing, swimming, fishing, boating, Cahokia Mounds-World Heritage site.

CUISINE

Traditional full or continental-plus breakfast served in dining room. Breakfast brought to attic loft or master bedroom for extra fee.

DIRECTIONS

From downtown St. Louis: I-70 W to Exit 229 (St. Charles Fifth St.), go N 3 blocks to Boone's Lick Rd. R 4 blocks to Main St. Inn on SE corner of Main and Boone's Lick Rd. From I-70 E exit Fifth St. go N on Fifth to Boone's Lick Rd.

Springfield, MO

Walnut Street Inn

800-593-6346
417-864-6346 Fax 417-864-6184
www.walnutstreetinn.com
stay@walnutstreetinn.com
900 East Walnut Street, Springfield, MO 65806

ONE OF THE "Top Twelve Inns in the Country" and recommended by *Southern Living* magazine, this 14-room luxury urban inn is in Springfield's Historic District and 30 minutes from Branson. Enjoy fireplaces, Jacuzzis, steam showers, balconies, and feather beds. Business guests will appreciate cable TV, two-line room phones, stocked beverage bar, and access to copier and fax. Relax on the porch swing, read a book by the fire, walk to theaters, shops, fine dining or enjoy the Ozarks' natural beauty. Just five minutes from Bass Pro—Missouri's number one tourist attraction!

1 Guestroom Handicap Accessible • Suitable for Children
Designated Smoking Areas • AMEX, Visa, MC, Diners, Disc Accepted
Reservations Accepted Through Travel Agents

Select Registry Member *Since 1993*
Innkeepers/Owners
GARY & PAULA BLANKENSHIP

TRADITIONAL IN TOWN BREAKFAST INN

RATES
14 rooms, \$84/\$159 B&B.
Open year-round.

ATTRACTIONS
Walking distance to restaurants, theaters, conference center, SMSU, shops. Nearby: Bass Pro, Branson, Civil War Battlefield, golf, lakes and rivers.

CUISINE
Breakfast, home-baked cookies, beverages and snacks available. Wine and beer available.

DIRECTIONS
From I-44 take U.S. Hwy 65 S. Exit Chestnut Expressway W-R to Sherman Ave. Turn S-L and go 4 blocks to Walnut Street.

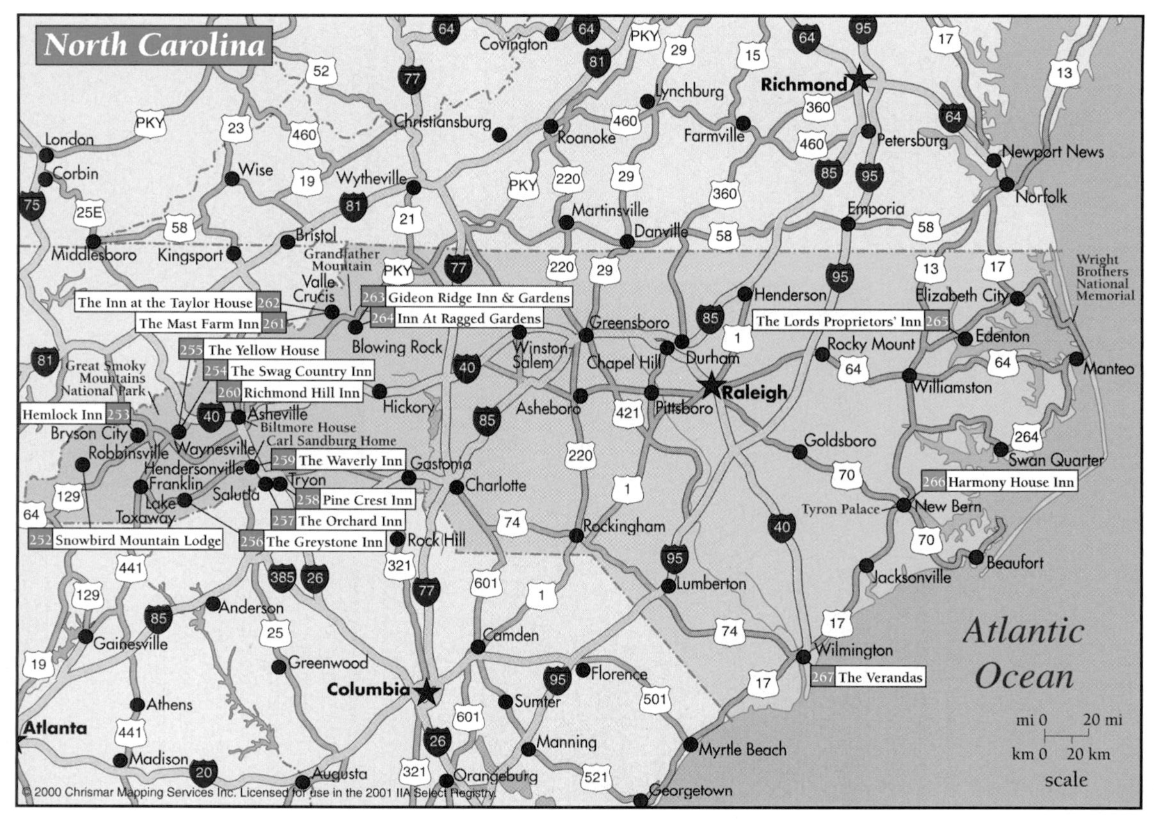

North Carolina
Atlantic Ocean
mi 0 20 mi
km 0 20 km
scale
262 The Inn at the Taylor House
261 The Mast Farm Inn
263 Gideon Ridge Inn & Gardens
264 Inn At Ragged Gardens
255 The Yellow House
254 The Swag Country Inn
260 Richmond Hill Inn
253 Hemlock Inn
259 The Waverly Inn
258 Pine Crest Inn
257 The Orchard Inn
256 The Greystone Inn
252 Snowbird Mountain Lodge
265 The Lords Proprietors' Inn
266 Harmony House Inn
267 The Verandas
Great Smoky Mountains National Park
Grandfather Mountain
Biltmore House
Carl Sandburg Home
Tyron Palace
Wright Brothers National Memorial
Richmond
Raleigh
Columbia
Atlanta
Covington
Christiansburg
Lynchburg
Roanoke
Farmville
Petersburg
Newport News
Norfolk
London
Corbin
Wise
Wytheville
Martinsville
Danville
Emporia
Bristol
Middlesboro
Kingsport
Valle Crucis
Blowing Rock
Winston-Salem
Greensboro
Chapel Hill
Durham
Henderson
Elizabeth City
Edenton
Rocky Mount
Williamston
Manteo
Hickory
Asheville
Asheboro
Pittsboro
Bryson City
Robbinsville
Waynesville
Hendersonville
Franklin
Lake Toxaway
Saluda
Tryon
Gastonia
Charlotte
Goldsboro
Swan Quarter
New Bern
Rock Hill
Rockingham
Beaufort
Jacksonville
Lumberton
Anderson
Gainesville
Camden
Wilmington
Greenwood
Florence
Athens
Sumter
Manning
Myrtle Beach
Madison
Augusta
Orangeburg
Georgetown
© 2000 Chrismar Mapping Services Inc. Licensed for use in the 2001 IIA Select Registry.

Robbinsville, NC

Snowbird Mountain Lodge

800-941-9290

828-479-3433 Fax 828-479-3473

www.snowbirdlodge.com

innkeeper@snowbirdlodge.com

275 Santeetlah Road, Robbinsville, NC 28771

Select Registry Member *Since 1973*

Innkeepers / Owners

KAREN AND ROBERT RANKIN

HIGH UP IN SANTEETLAH GAP, on the southern border of the Great Smoky Mountain National Park, lies this secluded, rustic yet elegant, historic lodge built of stone and huge chestnut logs. The view from the porch is one of the best in the mountains. An excellent library, huge stone fireplaces and award-winning gourmet cuisine make this lodge an exceptional retreat from the pressures of the world. Whether it's fly-fishing, hiking, biking, or just relaxing in front of the fire we can make your trip to the mountains picture-perfect.

RUSTIC MOUNTAIN RETREAT/LODGE

RATES

25 rooms, $175/$300 AP.
In-room fireplaces, whirlpool tubs and steam showers available.
Open April - November.

ATTRACTIONS

Hiking, mountain biking, white-water rafting, horseback riding, boating, lake fishing, trout streams, water skiing, historic Indian sites.

CUISINE

Buffet breakfast, picnic lunch and gourmet dinner. BYOB. Nearest package store 31 miles.

DIRECTIONS

From Robbinsville take Hwy 143 W 10.5 miles to the Snowbird Mountain Lodge.

---

1 Guestroom Handicap Accessible • Suitable for Children Over 12
Non-Smoking Inn • MC, Visa, Disc Accepted

North Carolina *The South*

Bryson City, NC

Hemlock Inn

828-488-2885
Fax 828-488-8985
hemlock@dnet.net
www..selectregistry.com
Galbraith Creek Road, Bryson City, NC 28713

Select Registry Member *Since 1973*
Innkeepers/Owners
MORT AND LAINEY WHITE

RUSTIC MOUNTAIN INN

HIGH, COOL, AND RESTFUL. This Inn is beautifully situated on 50-wooded acres on top of a small mountain on the edge of the Great Smoky Mountain National Park. There is a friendly informality in the family atmosphere and authenic country furniture. Honest-to-goodness home cooking and farm fresh vegetables are served family style from Lazy Susan tables. Come enjoy a change of pace, a change of scene and the simple pleasures. Get away from schedules as you walk in the Smokies, ride white-water rapids, ride the Great Smoky Mountain Train, or just sit and relax in a rocking chair on our front porch. AAA ◆◆◆.

RATES

22 rooms, $139/$159 MAP.
3 cottages, $145/$189 MAP.
Open mid-April – October.

ATTRACTIONS

Great Smoky Mountain National Park, Cherokee Indian Reservation, hiking, white-water rafting, tubing, fishing, horseback riding, mountain biking, Great Smoky Mountain Railway.

CUISINE

Breakfast, dinner included. Breakfast 8:30 am, daily dinner 6:00 pm Monday-Saturday, and 12:30 pm Sunday.

DIRECTIONS

Hwy 74 to exit 69-Hyatt Creek Rd., R on Hyatt Creek 1.5 miles, L on Hwy 19, 1.5 miles to Hemlock Inn sign, turn R at sign, Inn 1 mile on L.

Handicap Access Available • Visa, MC, Disc Accepted
Suitable for Children • Reservations Accepted Through Travel Agents

Waynesville, NC

The Swag Country Inn

800-789-7672
828-926-0430 Fax 828-926-2036
www.theswag.com
letters@theswag.com
2300 Swag Road, Waynesville, NC 28786

Select Registry Member *Since 1991*
Owner
DEENER MATTHEWS

RUSTIC COUNTRY INN

ANDREW HARPER DESCRIBES THE INN AS...'A peaceful, relaxing high-country sanctuary secluded on a breathtaking 5,000-foot ridge overlooking the Smoky Mountains.' *Town and Country* calls the meals at The Swag...'sophisticated.' The Swag is a paradise for nature lovers who seek the finest amenities in a romantic and natural setting. Exquisite guestrooms boast beautiful handcrafted interiors. Swag Country Inn is a retreat on 250 private acres with a private entrance into Great Smoky Mountains National Park. Full food service. Mobil ★★★★.

RATES
12 rooms, $265/$520 AP.
3 cabins, $395/$580 AP.
Open April through November out-of-season for corporate groups.

ATTRACTIONS
Hiking trails, racquetball, croquet, badminton, horseshoes, pond with boat and dock, spa, sauna, library and video library.

CUISINE
All meals, hors d'oeuvres, high tea at 5,000 feet, coffee beans and grinders in rooms. BYOB.

DIRECTIONS
NC I-40 exit 20 to Hwy 276 for 2.8 miles to Grindstone Rd. turn R at dead-end on Hemphill 4 miles up blacktopped road to Swag Rd. Turn L on gravel rd. 2.5 miles to end.

2 Guestrooms Handicap Accessible • Suitable for Children
Conference Facilities for 20 • MC, Visa, Disc, AMEX Accepted
Non-Smoking Inn • Reservations Accepted Through Travel Agents

Waynesville, NC

The Yellow House

800-563-1236
828-452-0991 Fax 828-452-1140
www.theyellowhouse.com
yelhouse@asap-com.com
89 Oakview Drive, Waynesville, NC 28786

The Yellow House on Plott Creek Road, is a European inn of casual elegance with a decor favoring the French Impressionists, and an accent on fine service in a romantic, intimate setting. We are located a mile outside the quaint town of Waynesville, North Carolina, at an approximate elevation of 3,000 feet. The 100-year-old home sits on a knoll surrounded by four acres of lawn and garden. There is a lily pond with a footbridge and deck. The main Inn has two rooms and four suites. Each have private baths, fireplaces, a wet bar or refrigerator and a mountain or lily pond view. The Inn boasts a quiet rural setting and piped in music with no cable TV or other distractions. The serenity provides relaxation and renewal.

Cottage Suitable for Children • Non-Smoking Inn
Conference Facilities for 14 • MC, Visa Accepted
Reservations Accepted Through Travel Agents

Select Registry Member *Since 1998*
Innkeepers/Owners
Sharon and Ron Smith

Elegant Mountain Breakfast Inn

RATES
$125/$250
2 rooms, 4 suites,
2-bedroom cottage.
Some suites have private balconies or terraces.
Open year-round.

ATTRACTIONS
Hiking, golfing, mountain biking, white-water rafting, horseback riding, fly-fishing, Biltmore Estate, Smoky Mountain National Park, Brevard Music Festival, Folkmoot International Dance Festival and loafing.

CUISINE
Gourmet breakfast each morning; appetizers each evening.

DIRECTIONS
From S: Take exit 100 off US 23/74. Proceed to the L for 1 1/2 miles on Plott Creek Rd.
From N: Exit 100 from US 23/74, turn R on Eagles Nest Rd., L on Will Hyatt, R on Plott Creek Rd.

Lake Toxaway, NC

The Greystone Inn

800-824-5766
828-966-4700 Fax 828-862-5689
www.greystoneinn.com

Greystone Lane, Lake Toxaway, NC 28747

WITH ALL THE DIVERSIONS of spectacularly beautiful Lake Toxaway at its doorstep, this intimate, historic (National Register), resort inn combines the lure of its panaromic mountain setting with comfort of modern luxuries and an exceptional cuisine. Romantic and tranquil. Excellent pampering spa, guided hikes on adventurous trails ranging from intermediate to advanced. Complimentary golf certain months. Daily champagne cruise. Mid-afternoon tea served with refreshments on the sun porch. Warm, friendly and personable service. Winner of many awards.

Select Registry Member *Since 1991*
Innkeepers/Owners
TIM AND BOO BOO LOVELACE

ELEGANT WATERSIDE RESORT

RATES
30 rooms, $285/$445 MAP.
3 suites, $395/$550 MAP, incl. boats and most recreational activities.
Open year-round.

ATTRACTIONS
ONSITE: spa, golf, tennis, fishing, water skiing, kayaks, sea cycle, champagne cruise, mountain bikes, croquet, pool, trails to waterfalls and mountain tops.

CUISINE
Includes gourmet dinner, high-country breakfast and afternoon tea. Good wine list; liquor available.

DIRECTIONS
I-40 to Ashville, I-26 E, 9 miles, Rte 280S 20 miles, US 64 W 20 miles to Lake Toxaway C.C./Greystone Inn sign R 3.5 miles to Inn. From I-85 N, SC 11 N 33 miles, SC 130 W, NC 281 N, US-64 E, 1.5 miles to sign.

Handicap Access Available • Suitable for Children
Conference Facilities for 35 • Credit Cards Accepted
Reservations Accepted Through Travel Agents

Saluda, NC

The Orchard Inn

800-581-3800

828-749-5471 Fax 828-749-9805

www.orchardinn.com

orchard@saluda.tds.net

Highway 176, P.O. Box 128, Saluda, NC 28773

Select Registry Member *Since 1985*

Innkeepers/Owners

KATHY AND BOB THOMPSON

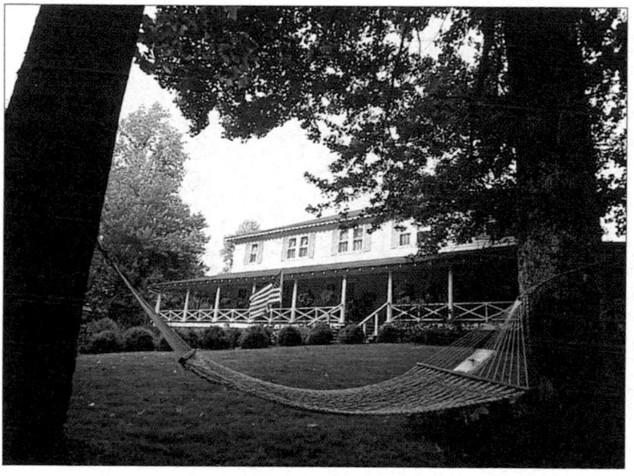

ASCENDING THE WINDING DRIVE, the rest of the world falls away as The Orchard Inn comes into view. Situated on a 12-acre mountaintop with stunning views, this historic structure, built in 1910, has long been a favorite retreat with its wraparound porches and large, inviting living room with stone fireplace. Guest quarters are furnished with period pieces and antiques. Cottages feature fireplaces, whirlpools and private decks. Enjoy fine dining on the glassed-in dining porch overlooking the gardens, vineyard and mountains. Guests explore nature trails, watch birds and experience the peace and tranquillity of this lovely retreat.

TRADITIONAL MOUNTAIN INN

RATES

9 rooms, $119/$189 B&B.
4 cottages, $169/$245 B&B.
Open year-round.

ATTRACTIONS

Biltmore Estate, Carl Sandburg's home, Flat Rock Playhouse, Chimney Rock Park, hiking, fishing, antiquing, or just nothing at all.

CUISINE

Dinner by reservation Tues-Sat. Fine wines and beer available.

DIRECTIONS

From I-26, exit 28 Saluda NC, head W up hill 1 mile to Rte 176, turn L on Rte 176, and the Inn will be 1/2 mile on R.

Suitable for Children Over 12 • Non-Smoking Inn
Conference Facilities for 15 • Visa, MC, Disc Accepted

Tryon, NC

Pine Crest Inn

800-633-3001

828-859-9135 Fax 828-859-9135

www.pinecrestinn.com

85 Pine Crest Lane, Tryon, NC 28782

SITUATED IN THE BLUE RIDGE FOOTHILLS, Pine Crest Inn has been a Tryon tradition since 1917 offering rustic elegance, fine cuisine and warm, caring service. Our thirty-five rooms, suites and cottages on 3.5 well-cared-for acres feature individual temperature controls, televisions, VCRs and robes; and most have fireplaces to warm you in the winter months. We are proud to hold AAA ◆◆◆◆ awards for both the Inn and restaurant, and we work hard to meet the high expectations which these create.

Select Registry Member *Since 1991*

Owners

BARNEY & DEBORAH DUBOIS

General Manager

RHONDA TEAT

ELEGANT MOUNTAIN INN

RATES

17 rooms, B&B $170/$230.
18 suites, B&B $190/$275.
Open year-round.

ATTRACTIONS

Golf, tennis, swimming, hiking, Biltmore House and Gardens, Blue Ridge Parkway, Fence Equestrian Nature Center, antiques and waterfalls.

CUISINE

Full breakfast served each day included in the guestroom rate. Monday through Saturday evenings, the restaurant at Pine Crest Inn offers gourmet, continental cuisine with regional accents.

DIRECTIONS

From I-26, exit 36 in Columbus, NC to Hwy 108. Follow Hwy 108 to town of Tryon. At intersection of Hwy 108 (Trade St.) and New Market Rd.; turn L onto New Market Rd. Proceed 1/8 mile to Pine Crest Ln. Turn L onto Pine Crest Ln., follow to Pine Crest Inn.

2 Guestrooms Handicap Accessible • Suitable for Children
Conference Facilities for 60 • AMEX, Visa, MC, Disc Accepted
Designated Smoking Areas • Reservations Accepted Through Travel Agents

Hendersonville, NC

The Waverly Inn

800-537-8195
828-693-9193 Fax 828-692-1010
www.waverlyinn.com
register@waverlyinn.com
783 North Main Street, Hendersonville, NC 28792

Select Registry Member *Since 1991*
Innkeepers/Owners
JOHN AND DIANE SHEIRY
DARLA OLMSTEAD

IN AN AREA RICH WITH HISTORY and natural scenery, this National Register Inn is the oldest inn in Hendersonville's historic district. Within walking distance to fine restaurants, exceptional shopping and antiquing. Polished wood, turn-of-the-century fittings, four-poster beds, wide porches and rocking chairs are only part of the picture that brings guests back to this comfortable, friendly place. Join us for our daily social hour between 5 and 6 pm or just raid the cookie jar for one of Darla's famous inn-house delectables, baked fresh each day.

TRADITIONAL VILLAGE BREAKFAST INN

RATES
13 rooms, $109/$159 B & B.
1 suite, $165/$215 B & B.
Open year-round.

ATTRACTIONS
Biltmore Estate, Flat Rock Playhouse, antiquing, golf, Blue Ridge Pkwy., hiking, fishing, horseback riding and Chimney Rock Park.

CUISINE
Full breakfast, refreshments, evening social hour and fresh-baked goods. BYOB.

DIRECTIONS
From I-26, NC exit 18 B, U.S.-64 W; go 2 miles W into Hendersonville, bear R onto Rte 25 N for 500 yds., Inn is on L at corner of 8th Ave. and Main St.

Suitable for Children • MC, Visa, AMEX, Disc, Diners, CB Accepted
Designated Smoking Areas
Reservations Accepted Through Travel Agents

Asheville, NC

Richmond Hill Inn

888-742-4550
828-252-7313 Fax 828-252-8726
www.richmondhillinn.com

Select Registry Member *Since 1991*
Innkeeper/Owner
SUSAN MICHEL

87 Richmond Hill Drive, Asheville, NC 28806

ROMANCE IS ENCOURAGED EVERY MOMENT. The 1889 mansion is perched on a hillside, and each room is uniquely decorated and furnished with antiques. Charming cottages surround a croquet court and feature fireplaces and porch rockers. Each of the spacious rooms in the Garden Pavilion offers beautiful views of the Parterre Garden, waterfall and mansion. Stroll through gardens by the cascading brook. Relax at afternoon tea in the stately Oak Hall. Read in the library. Savor an exquisite dinner in Gabrielle's, featuring an extensive wine list. Listen to our acclaimed pianist.

ELEGANT IN TOWN INN

RATES
33 rooms, $155/$395 B&B.
3 suites, $240/$450 B&B.
Open year-round.

ATTRACTIONS
Croquet, waterfall, gardens, walking trail, gift shop on-site. NEARBY: Biltmore Estate, Blue Ridge Parkway, Thomas Wolfe Home, Folk Art Center, Historic Asheville, craft and antique shopping, rafting, North Carolina Arboretum.

CUISINE
Full breakfast, afternoon tea. Gabrielle's fine dining in mansion. Extensive wine list and liquor.

DIRECTIONS
Take Hwy 251 exit on 19/23, three miles NW from downtown. Follow signs.

24 Guestrooms Handicap Accessible • Suitable for Children Over 8
Conference Facilities for 50 • MC, Visa, AMEX Accepted
Non-Smoking Inn • Reservations Accepted Through Travel Agents

Valle Crucis, NC

The Mast Farm Inn

888-963-5857
828-963-5857 Fax 828-963-6404
www.MastFarmInn.com
stay@MastFarmInn.com
2543 Broadstone Road, Valle Crucis, NC 28691

Select Registry Member *Since 1988*
Innkeepers
WANDA HINSHAW AND
KAY HINSHAW PHILIPP

RUSTIC MOUNTAIN INN

ON THE NATIONAL REGISTER of Historic Places, The Mast Farm Inn continues a century-long tradition of hospitality in the Blue Ridge. Choose from nine spacious guest rooms in our three-story 1880s farmhouse, four romantic getaway cottages crafted from the original 19th Century farm buildings, or two new cottages opened in April 2000 featuring a hot tub under the stars. The Inn's organic gardens supply flowers, herbs and vegetables for our tables. Relax with a glass of wine on our wraparound porch or in front of the fire in the parlour. Winner of 'Blue Ridge Country' Gold Award for Best Mountain Inn and 'Our State' 1st place award for Most Enjoyable Historic Inn.

RATES

9 spacious farmhouse rooms, $125/$195 B&B.
6 private cottages, $195/$360 B&B.
Open year-round.

ATTRACTIONS

Hiking, fly-fishing, golf, canoeing, white-water rafting, horseback riding, Blue Ridge Parkway, Grandfather Mountain, antiques and mountain crafts, Mast General Store, theater, skiing, ice-skating, Tweetsie Railroad.

CUISINE

Full two-course breakfast included with lodging. An a la carte menu featuring fresh, organic Contemporary Regional Cuisine is offered for dinner. Private parties. Wine and beer available.

DIRECTIONS

Boone/Blowing Rock/Banner Elk area. From E and S: Turn at V.C. sign on 105 between Boone and Linville. Inn is 2.5 miles from 105 on Broadstone Rd. From W and N: Take 194 from 321/421 W of Boone. In V.C., continue STRAIGHT on Broadstone to the Inn, 1/4 mile on the R.

Handicap Access Available • Suitable for Children
Conference Facilities for 14 • Credit Cards Accepted
Reservations Accepted Through Travel Agents

Valle Crucis, NC

The Inn at the Taylor House

828-963-5581
Fax 828-963-5818
www.highsouth.com/taylorhouse
#4584 Highway 194, P.O. Box 713
Valle Crucis, NC 28691

Select Registry Member *Since 1990*
Innkeeper
CHIP WILSON

A BIT OF EUROPE in the peaceful, rural heart of the Blue Ridge Mountains, this charming farmhouse is decorated with fine antiques, Oriental rugs, artwork and European goose-down comforters on all the beds. Bright fabrics, wicker furniture and flowering plants invite guests to rock on the wide wraparound porch, while the friendly hospitality and memorable breakfasts add to their pleasure.

ELEGANT COUNTRY INN

RATES
7 rooms, $150/$185.
3 suites, $200/$295 B&B.
Cabin $175 per night.
All private baths.
Smoking in gazebo.
Open April through December.

ATTRACTIONS
Canoeing, rafting, golf, horseback riding, hiking, antique shops, theater, fly-fishing and fine dining.

CUISINE
Breakfast. Arrangements may be made for private parties, weddings and family reunions.

DIRECTIONS
From Boone, take Hwy 105 S. towards Linville. R on Broadstone Rd. (State Rd. 1112). Go 2.8 miles. Turn L onto Hwy 194. Just under a mile on R side.

---

1 Guestroom Handicap Accessible • Suitable for Children
Designated Smoking Areas • MC, Visa Accepted
Reservations Accepted Through Travel Agents

Blowing Rock, NC

Gideon Ridge Inn & Gardens

828-295-3644
Fax 828-295-4586
www.gideonridge.com
Innkeeper@ridge-inn.com
202 Gideon Ridge Road, Blowing Rock, NC 28605

Select Registry Member *Since 1990*
Innkeepers/Owners
CINDY AND COBB MILNER

GIDEON RIDGE INN is ten delightful guest rooms with mountain breezes, French doors and stone terraces. Intimate walking paths through elegant gardens. Ceiling fans and wicker chairs. Antiques and good books. Fine breakfasts to linger over. Earl Grey Tea and fresh-baked shortbread cookies to savor. Bedrooms with warm fireplaces and comfortable sitting areas. Crisp cotton bed linens and well-appointed bathrooms. And in the library, a grand piano with a breathtaking view of the mountains. Really.

ELEGANT MOUNTAIN INN

RATES
11 rooms, including
1 deluxe suite, 3 terrace and
2 whirlpool rooms.
8 rooms have fireplaces.
All rooms B&B. \$115/\$260.
Open year-round.

ATTRACTIONS
Hiking, Blue Ridge Parkway, village and craft shops, golf, tennis, biking, fly-fishing, white-water rafting.

CUISINE
Full breakfast included, featuring cornmeal pancakes, blueberry-stuffed French toast or other signature entrees. Afternoon tea with fresh-made shortbread cookies or scones. BYOB. Wine delivery available. Great restaurants nearby.

DIRECTIONS
US 321, 1.5 miles S of Village of Blowing Rock, turn W on Rock Rd. and L on Gideon Ridge Rd. at fork. Go to top of the ridge.

Suitable for Children Over 12
Conference Facilities for 12 • Credit Cards Accepted
Reservations Accepted Through Travel Agents

Blowing Rock, NC

The Inn at Ragged Gardens

828-295-9703
www.ragged-gardens.com
innkeeper@ragged-gardens.com

203 Sunset Drive, Blowing Rock, NC 28605

Select Registry Member *Since 2001*
Innkeepers/Owners
LEE AND JAMA HYETT

BORDERED BY A ROCK WALL ACRE OF LUSH LAWN AND GARDENS is a bark sided manor whose curb appeal has welcomed guests for a century. Interior architectural highlights are virgin chestnut paneling, a granite staircase and hand-forged ironwork. Garden theme rooms tailored for guest's comfort feature fireplaces, whirlpool baths, thoughtful amenities, absence of TV and phone, sitting areas, balconies and patios. Gourmet breakfasts are a special occasion served gardenside in the sunlit dining room. Not to be overlooked is the Blue Ridge Mountain charm, attentive service and attention to detail of the innkeepers and their staff in this elegant village inn.

ELEGANT VILLAGE INN

RATES
5 rooms, $170/$220
7 suites, $220/$310 B&B
Rooms offer designer interiors, fine linens, whirlpool baths, air-conditioning, fireplaces, sitting areas indoors and out.
Open year-round, except Thanksgiving and December 23-25.

ATTRACTIONS
NEARBY: biking, hiking, golf, tennis, scenic day-trips, downhill and xc-skiing, day-spas, horseback riding, Blue Ridge Parkway, Grandfather Mountain, Linville Falls, The Blowing Rock Summer Theatre, music performances, fly-fishing, village shops, antiques.

CUISINE
Full gourmet breakfast, daily refreshments. Evening wine, hors d'oeuvres. Wine service available.

DIRECTIONS
Turn W at stoplight intersection of Hwy 321 by-pass and Sunset Dr. Inn two blocks on right. Or from village center 1 block E on Sunset Drive. inn on left.

Suitable for Children Over 12 • Non-Smoking Inn • MC, Visa Accepted
Reservations Accepted Through Travel Agents

Edenton, NC

The Lords Proprietors' Inn

800-348-8933
Fax 252-482-2432
www.edentoninn.com
stay@edentoninn.com
300 North Broad Street, Edenton, NC 27932

Select Registry Member *Since 1990*

Owners

ARCH AND JANE EDWARDS

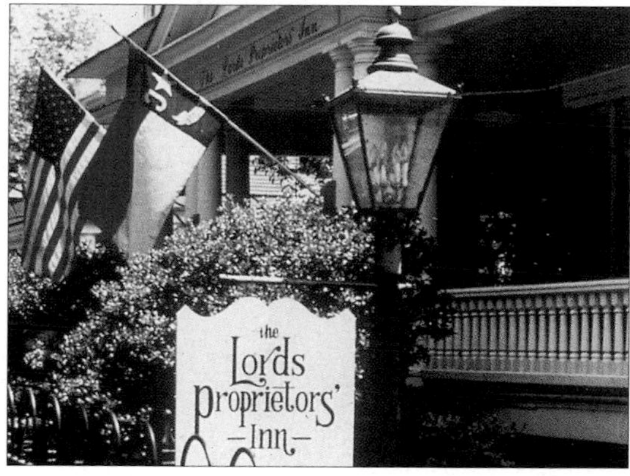

THE INN COMPRISES THREE RESTORED HOMES, a separate dining room building, and ample parking, all on two acres of property in Edenton's Historic district. In addition to the large Victorian house and the Pack House, both offering lovely rooms with private baths, the Satterfield House, c. 1801, has been newly renovated to offer guests two extremely spacious and elegant suites including sitting rooms with fireplaces, spa areas with double whirlpool tubs, plus bedrooms with king beds and bathrooms with large showers. Renowned chef, Kevin Yokely comtinues to delight guests with exceptional dinners Tuesdays through Saturdays. Prix-fixe or a la carte dining is available.

TRADITIONAL VILLAGE INN

RATES
16 rooms and 2 suites.
Daily $155/$225 B&B.
Tues.-Sat. $225/$295 MAP.
a la carte dining available.
Open year-round.

ATTRACTIONS
Guided walking tours of Edenton's Historic District daily. Other historical sites nearby. The Inn's Preservation Weekend programs feature tours of private historic homes. Swimming at owners' restored plantation home. Golf nearby.

CUISINE
Full breakfast daily. Exceptional dinner service Tues. through Sat. Complimentary Port and Sherry. Wine available with dinner.

DIRECTIONS
US 64 and US 17 from Raleigh. US 17 from Norfolk. I-95, US 460, VA/NC 32 from DC/Richmond. US 17 from Wilmington.

1 Guestroom and Dining Room Handicap Accessible • Suitable for Children
Visa, MC, Disc, AMEX Accepted • Conference Facilities for 20
Designated Smoking Areas • Reservations Accepted Through Travel Agents

New Bern, NC

Harmony House Inn

800-636-3113
Phone 252-636-3810
www.harmonyhouseinn.com
harmony@cconnect.net
215 Pollock Street, New Bern, NC 28560

Select Registry Member *Since 1990*
Innkeepers/Owners
ED AND SOOKI KIRKPATRICK

AS THE ELLIS FAMILY GREW, so did their home (circa 1850), with additions in 1860 and 1880. During the Civil War, the house was headquarters for Company K of the 45th Regiment, Massachusetts Volunteer Militia. Circa 1900, the house was sawed in half, moved apart and rejoined with a second front door, hallway and staircase, plus a front porch—a popular spot to relax on one of the swings or rockers. Located in the heart of the Historic District, this spacious inn is decorated with antiques, locally made reproductions and Sooki's collection of handmade crafts.

TRADITIONAL VILLAGE
BREAKFAST INN

RATES
3 suites, two with two person Jacuzzi; two-room suite w/queen canopy bed $150.
Seven rooms: $99/$109.
All rooms have private baths.
Open year-round.

ATTRACTIONS
Historic Tryon Palace and Gardens, Firemen's Museum, Civil War Museum and shop, two rivers nearby, Croatan National Forest, antique and specialty shops, near beaches and Cape Lookout Lighthouse, several golf courses, health club (nominal fee).

CUISINE
Full homemade breakfast included in rates. Early continental breakfast available. Several fine dining and casual restaurants within walking distance. Complimentary white wine served from 6-7 pm. Port or Sherry nightcap.

DIRECTIONS
From US 70 or Hwy 17 S: Exit E Front St. Cross bridge and turn L at second st. (Pollock).
From 17 N: Go through town until 17 ends. Turn R onto E Front St. At next street, turn R onto Pollock St.

Suitable for Children • Non-Smoking Inn
Conference Facilities for 12 • Visa, MC, Disc Accepted
Reservations Accepted Through Travel Agents

Wilmington, NC

The Verandas

910-251-2212
Fax 910-251-8932
www.verandas.com
verandas4@aol.com
202 Nun Street, Wilmington, NC 28401-5020

TOWERING ABOVE A QUIET TREE-LINED STREET in the historic district stands this grand antebellum mansion. Built in 1854, the award winning Inn is a blend of history, luxury, charm and hospitality. Guest space abounds with wonderful colors, original art, French and English antiques. Four verandas, garden terrace and cupola offer hideaways. Professionally decorated guestrooms have sitting areas, telephone, cable TV, PC jacks. Hand ironed linens dress comfortable beds. Baths have soaking tubs, showers, marble floors, luxury amenities and robes. French pressed coffee with a gourmet breakfast and evening social wine hour. "An Inn Second to Nun."

Suitable for Children Over 12 • Designated Smoking Areas
MC, Visa, AMEX, Disc Accepted
Reservations Accepted Through Travel Agents

Select Registry Member *Since 2001*
Owners
DENNIS MADSEN
CHUCK PENNINGTON

ELEGANT IN TOWN BREAKFAST INN

RATES

8 corner rooms, $135/$195 two night weekends.
Sunny rooms filled with antiques, original art and incredily comfortable beds, spacious sitting areas and individual a/c heat.
Open year-round, except Dec. 24-26.

ATTRACTIONS

Beautiful beaches, Cape Fear River, river boat rides, 6 museums, battleship, Fort Fisher, antique shops, walking tours, deep-sea fishing, fine dining, golf, aquarium and 2 fine southern gardens.

CUISINE

Included with the room is a full gourmet breakfast with French pressed coffee served in our beautiful dining room. Complimentary soft drinks and bottled water are always available and white wine is served each evening.

DIRECTIONS

I-40 to exit 8 L on Rt. 17 for 4.5 miles L on 3rd St. for 4 blocks R on Nun St. Next corner. Routes 17, 74, 76, going North cross drawbridge L on 3rd St. for 4 blocks L on Nun St. Next corner.

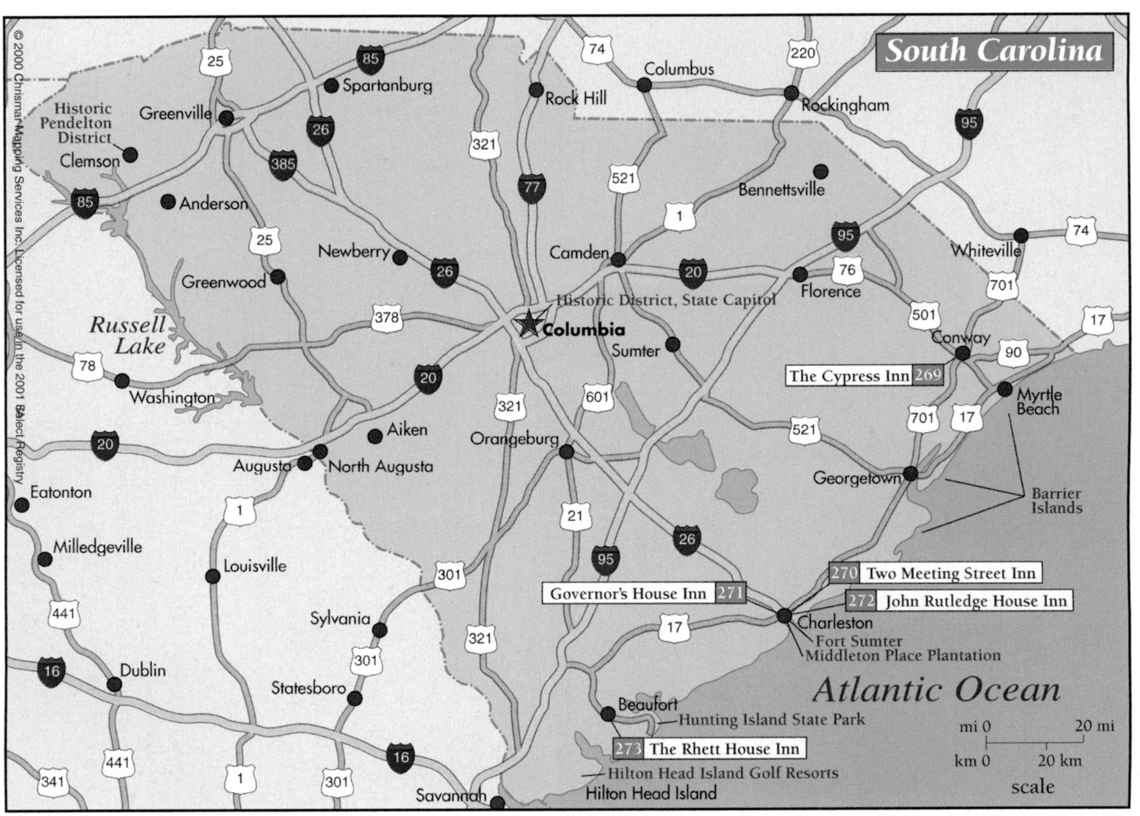
South Carolina
The Cypress Inn 269
270 Two Meeting Street Inn
272 John Rutledge House Inn
Governor's House Inn 271
273 The Rhett House Inn
Atlantic Ocean
Barrier Islands
Columbia
Historic District, State Capitol
Charleston
Fort Sumter
Middleton Place Plantation
Hunting Island State Park
Hilton Head Island Golf Resorts
Hilton Head Island
Beaufort
Myrtle Beach
Conway
Whiteville
Georgetown
Florence
Bennettsville
Rockingham
Columbus
Rock Hill
Sumter
Camden
Orangeburg
Greenville
Spartanburg
Historic Pendelton District
Clemson
Anderson
Newberry
Greenwood
Russell Lake
Washington
Aiken
North Augusta
Augusta
Eatonton
Milledgeville
Louisville
Sylvania
Statesboro
Dublin
Savannah
mi 0 20 mi
km 0 20 km
scale
© 2000 Chrismar Mapping Services Inc. Licensed for use in the 2001 Select Registry

Conway, SC (Myrtle Beach area)

The Cypress Inn

800-575-5307
843-248-8199 Fax 843-248-0329
www.acypressinn.com
info@acypressinn.com
16 Elm Street, P.O. Box 495, Conway, SC 29528

Select Registry Member *Since 2001*
Innkeepers/Owners
CAROL AND JIM RUDDICK

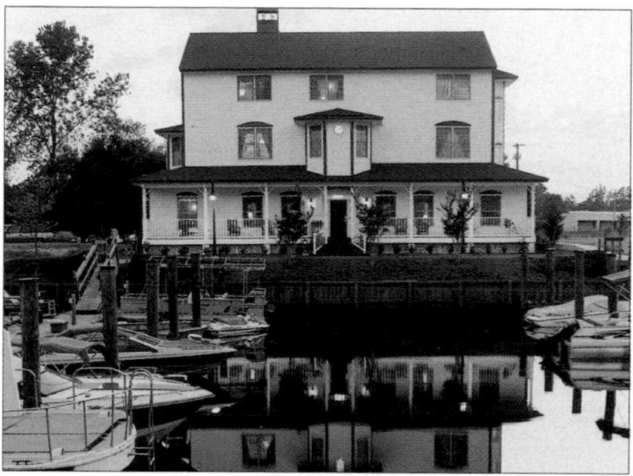

OVERLOOKING THE WACCAMAW RIVER in the historic town of Conway, this luxury Inn is near but distinctly apart from the golf mecca of Myrtle Beach. Twelve unique guestrooms, each with its own personality, offer charm and comforts such as plush robes and bed linens, climate control, Jacuzzis, TV/VCR with video library and some fireplaces. The Inn offers the privacy of a hotel with the personal service of a bed and breakfast. The excellence is in the details. Bicycle this quiet town or paddle the river just outside the door. Sample the many extras such as massages, a day at the spa, or hot-air balloon rides. AAA ◆◆◆◆.

TRADITIONAL IN TOWN BREAKFAST INN

RATES

12 rooms, $100/$175 B&B. Rooms are a gentle mix of old and new with amenitites for both the business and leisure traveler. *Open year-round.*

ATTRACTIONS

Brookgreen (sculpture) Gardens, hot-air balloon rides, horseback riding, outlet shopping, sea aquarium, butterfly pavilion, state parks, golf, tennis, history tours, entertainment theaters and the ocean.

CUISINE

A wonderful breakfast is served each morning. Picnic baskets available. Near many fine restaurants. A small guest refrigerator is stocked with lemonade, iced tea, bottled water. Complimentary sherry and cookies.

DIRECTIONS

From Hwy 501: Take Bus 501. W on 3rd Ave. L on Elm St. Inn is on L. From Charleston: Use Hwy 701. R on Elm St. Inn is on L. From Wilmington: Use Hwy 90. R on Bus 501. L on 3rd Ave. L on Elm St. Inn is on L.

1 Guestroom Handicap Accessible • Suitable for Children Over 12
Conference Facilities for 24 • AMEX, Visa, MC, Disc, Diners Accepted
Non-Smoking Inn • Reservations Accepted Through Travel Agents

Charleston, SC

Two Meeting Street Inn

843-723-7322

www.twomeetingstreet.com

Select Registry Member *Since 1992*

Innkeepers/Owners

Pete and Jean Spell

Karen Spell Shaw

2 Meeting Street, Charleston, SC 29401

Given as a wedding gift by a bride's loving father, this Queen Anne mansion welcomes all who are romantic at heart. From Southern rockers on the arched piazza, guests overlook the historic Charleston Battery. The Spell's collection of antiques and silver, Tiffany windows and canopy beds, create a most charming atmosphere. Upon awakening, join us in the courtyard for our fresh muffins and local fruits. End the day relaxing on the verandah enjoying afternoon tea with homemade treats. For 55 years, the Spell family has graciously welcomed guests.

Elegant In Town Breakfast Inn

RATES

9 guestrooms, $165/$310 B&B. Victorian rooms with 12' ceilings, canopy beds and private baths. *Open year-round, except Christmas.*

ATTRACTIONS

In the Historic District, enjoy antiquing, Southern homes and gardens and low-country cuisine. Pristine beaches and world-class golf courses nearby.

CUISINE

A gracious continental breakfast; afternoon tea; evening sherry. No bar in the home.

DIRECTIONS

From I-26, exit Meeting St./Visitor Center. Continue 2 miles S on Meeting St. When Meeting St. dead ends into the park, we're last house on the L.

Suitable for Children Over 12 • Non-Smoking Inn

Charleston, SC

Governor's House Inn

800-720-9812
Phone 843-720-2070
www.governorshouse.com
innkeeper@govhouse.com
117 Broad Street, Charleston, SC 29401

A NATIONAL HISTORIC LANDMARK (circa 1760), the Inn is one of Charleston's most elegant and historically significant homes. Its romantic 18th century grandeur is preserved with nine original fireplaces, 12-foot ceilings, crystal chandeliers, fresh flowers, family antiques and Southern afternoon tea on a sprawling double veranda. Guests may request king or queen four-poster bed, fireplace, whirlpool, wet bar and a private porch. A legacy of civility and service is part of the Inn's heritage. Located in the heart of the Historic District, the Inn is within walking distance of The Battery and Old Market.

Select Registry Member *Since 2000*
Innkeepers/Owners
KAREN SPELL SHAW AND ROBERT SHAW

ELEGANT IN TOWN BREAKFAST INN

RATES
9 guest rooms and suites $170/$345 in season. Elegant rooms with 12' ceilings and canopy beds. Private piazza, whirlpool baths, fireplaces available.
Open year-round, except Christmas.

ATTRACTIONS
Historic district sites, the Battery and Market, antique shopping, house and garden tours, museums and restaurants. Beaches and plantations nearby!

CUISINE
Southern continental breakfast in dining room or veranda, low-country afternoon tea.

DIRECTIONS
From I-26 or Hwy 17, take Meeting St./Visitor Center exit. Travel approximately 2 miles S to Broad St. Turn R on Broad, travel 2 blocks. Governor's House is on L, at corner of Orange St.

Non-Smoking Inn • Conference Facilities for 14

Charleston, SC

John Rutledge House Inn

800-476-9741
843-723-7999 Fax 843-720-2615
www.charminginns.com
jrh@charminginns.com
116 Broad Street, Charleston, SC 29401

Select Registry Member *Since 1992*
Owner
RICHARD WIDMAN
Innkeeper
LINDA BISHOP

ELEGANT IN TOWN
BREAKFAST INN

BUILT IN 1763 BY JOHN RUTLEDGE, a signer of the U.S. Constitution, this antebellum home is now an elegant B&B Inn. Located in the heart of the Historic District, the Inn is a reminder of a more gracious time. Guests enjoy afternoon tea, wine and sherry in the ballroom where patriots, statesmen and presidents have met, evening turn-down service with chocolates at bedside and pastries delivered to the room each morning. Charter member Historic Hotels of America, designated National Historic Landmark.

RATES
16 rooms, $185/$325 B&B.
3 suites, $290/$375 B&B.
Open year-round.

ATTRACTIONS
In historic and antique district, home and garden tours, walking distance to city market, near plantations, museums and restaurants.

CUISINE
Continental breakfast included, full breakfast available, afternoon tea with refreshments.

DIRECTIONS
From Charleston Visitor Center: R on John St., then L on King St., 1 mile, then R on Broad St. The John Rutledge House Inn is 4th house on R.

2 Guestrooms Handicap Accessible • Suitable for Children
Conference Facilities for 50 • AMEX, MC, Diners, Disc, Visa Accepted
Designated Smoking Areas • Reservations Accepted Through Travel Agents

Beaufort, SC

The Rhett House Inn

888-480-9530

843-524-9030 Fax 843-524-1310

www.rhetthouseinn.com

rhetthse@hargray.com

1009 Craven Street, Beaufort, SC 29902

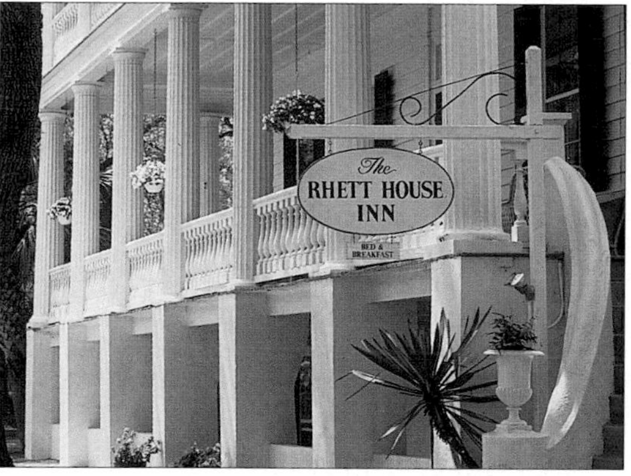

LOCATED IN HISTORIC BEAUFORT BY THE BAY, The Rhett House Inn is a beautifully restored 1820 plantation house, furnished with English and American antiques, oriental rugs, fresh flowers, fireplaces and spacious verandahs. Lush gardens provide the perfect setting for weddings and parties. Our Inn was the film site for "Forrest Gump," "Prince of Tides," "The Big Chill" and "White Squal." "Beach Music" due to be filmed in fall and spring 2001. History-laden Beaufort, Charleston and Savannah offer rich exploring. Mobil ★★★★ and AAA ◆◆◆◆.

Select Registry Member *Since 1991*

Owners
STEVE AND MARIANNE HARRISON

General Manager
STEPHANIE FAIRBANKS

ELEGANT IN TOWN BREAKFAST INN

RATES

17 rooms $150/$300.
8 with fireplaces and whirlpool baths.
Open year-round.

ATTRACTIONS

Low country history, packages including romantic, summer, and winter getaways. Antiques, historic antebellum mansions, moss-draped live oaks, Barrier Island beaches, golf, tennis, carriage and boat tours and lovely gardens.

CUISINE

Breakfast, afternoon tea, evening hors d'oeuvres, homemade dessert, picnic baskets. Beer, wine and liquor.

DIRECTIONS

From the N: Take I-95 to exit 33, then follow the signs to Beaufort. From the S: Take I-95 to exit 8 and follow the signs.

4 Guestrooms Handicap Accessible • Suitable for Children
Conference Facilities for 20 • Credit Cards Accepted
Designated Smoking Areas • Reservations Accepted Through Travel Agents

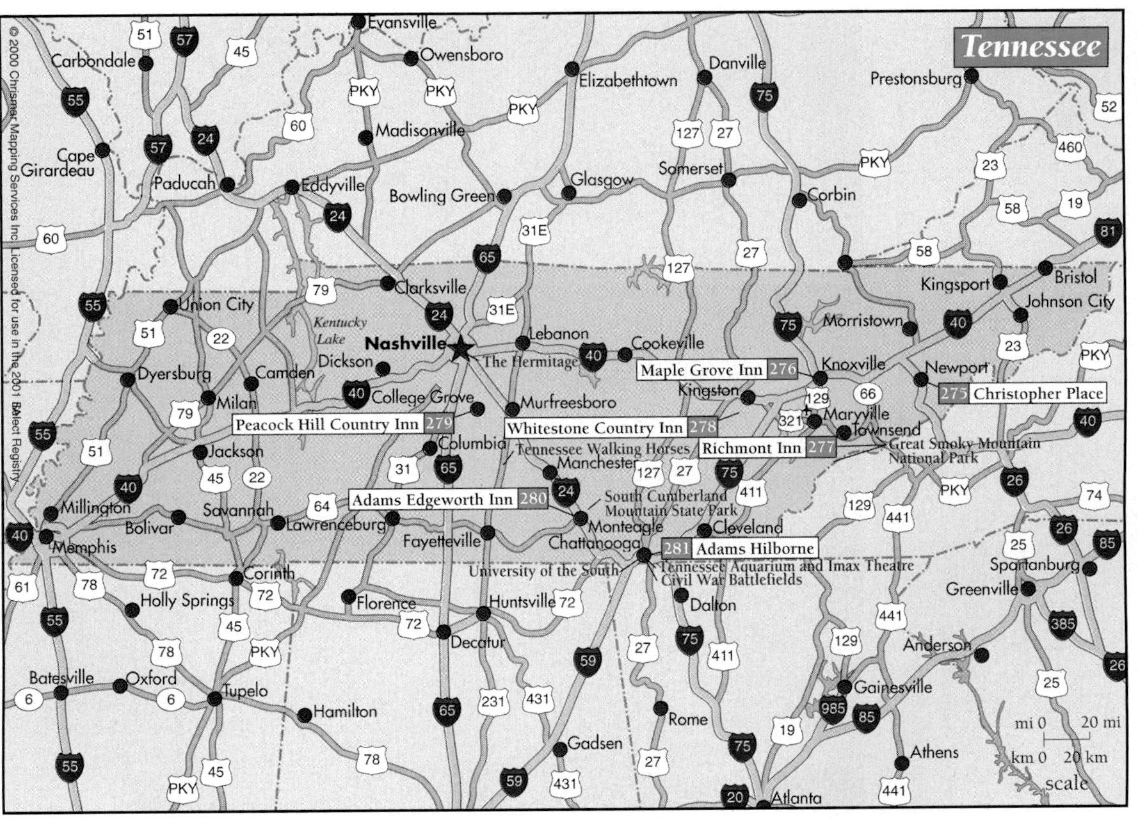

Tennessee
275 Christopher Place
276 Maple Grove Inn
277 Richmont Inn
278 Whitestone Country Inn
279 Peacock Hill Country Inn
280 Adams Edgeworth Inn
281 Adams Hilborne
Nashville
The Hermitage
Tennessee Walking Horses
Great Smoky Mountain National Park
South Cumberland Mountain State Park
Tennessee Aquarium and Imax Theatre
Civil War Battlefields
University of the South
Kentucky Lake
Knoxville
Chattanooga
Memphis
mi 0 20 mi
km 0 20 km
scale
© 2000 Chrismar Mapping Services Inc. Licensed for use in the 2001 Select Registry

Newport, TN

Christopher Place, An Intimate Resort

800-595-9441
423-623-6555 Fax 423-613-4771
www.christopherplace.com
TheBestInn@aol.com
1500 Pinnacles Way, Newport, TN 37821

Select Registry Member *Since 2000*
Owner
DREW OGLE
Innkeeper
TIM HALL

ELEGANT MOUNTAIN INN

SECLUDED IN THE SCENIC SMOKY MOUNTAINS on a 200-acre private estate, Christopher Place is the ideal inn for a romantic, relaxing getaway. An elegant setting is coupled with friendly, unpretentious service and unspoiled, panoramic views. The hosts know your name and greet you with a warm smile. You can fill your days with activities, or with none at all, for the inn is centrally located to most of the sights and attractions of the Smokies and offers many resort amenities of its own. Casual fine dining completes your romantic retreat. Above all else, special requests are encouraged. Featured on *The Travel Channel*, in *Time* magazine and *Country Inns*. AAA ◆◆◆◆. Named one of the ten most romantic inns in America.

Handicap Access Available • Suitable for Children Over 12
Conference Facilities for 10 • MC, Visa, AMEX, Disc Accepted
Reservations Accepted Through Travel Agents

RATES

4 rooms, $150.
4 suites, $250/$300.
Spacious and romantically appointed. Most have double whirlpools, woodburning fireplaces and/or scenic views.
Open year-round.

ATTRACTIONS

Swimming, tennis, hiking, sauna all on-site. Great Smoky Mountain National Park, Gatlinburg, rafting, golf, Dollywood, arts and crafts community, horseback riding, outlet shopping, music theatres, Pigeon Forge, wineries, Biltmore Estate all nearby.

CUISINE

Hearty mountain breakfast served at your leisure. Picnics. Intimate four-course candlelit dinners by reservation at tables set for two. Some seats available to non-inn guests. Light afternoon snacks in game room. BYOB.

DIRECTIONS

I-40 to exit 435. Go S 2 miles on Hwy 32. Turn R on English Mountain Rd. Go 2 miles. Turn R on Pinnacles Way. Follow to the top.

Knoxville, TN

Maple Grove Inn

800-645-0713
423-690-9565 Fax 423-690-9385
www.maplegroveinn.com
mginn@usit.net
8800 Westland Drive, Knoxville, TN 37923

Select Registry Member *Since 1998*
Contact
CURT LOCKETT

A FEW BLOCKS from Knoxville's main highways on 16 acres, Maple Grove Inn is one of Tennessee's most splendid inns. The house was built in 1799, yet features many modern amenities. Suites have fireplaces, TVs, VCRs, Jacuzzi tubs, decks and porches. Swimming and tennis are on the premises. Antiques, collectibles and fine art, combined with gourmet meals and warm hospitality, make all guests want to return. We are located near the Smoky Mountains and other area attractions. Conference center available. Whatever the reason for your stay—it will be most memorable.

ELEGANT COUNTRY INN

RATES

6 rooms. 2 suites, B&B.
Room rates-leisure travel
$125/$200.
Open year-round.

ATTRACTIONS

We are located at the foothills of the Smoky Mountains. Hiking, tennis, swimming, antiques, near mall, museum of art, historic city, near University of Tennessee.

CUISINE

Full breakfast, gourmet dinner served Thurs.-Sat. BYOB.

DIRECTIONS

Exit I-40 at West Hills; L off exit at light; at next light, turn R onto Morrell; pass through 5 lights; at 5th light, turn R onto Westland; go 2 miles. Drive on L.

Suitable for Children Over 12 • Designated Smoking Areas
Conference Facilities for 30 • AMEX, Visa, MC Accepted
Reservations Accepted Through Travel Agents

Townsend, TN – the peaceful side of the Smokies

Richmont Inn

866-267-7086 Toll Free
865-448-6751 Fax 865-448-6480
www.richmontinn.com
richmontinn@aol.com
220 Winterberry Lane, Townsend, TN 37882

Select Registry Member *Since 1997*
Innkeepers/Owners
SUSAN AND JIM HIND SR.
General Manager
JIM HIND JR.

TRADITIONAL MOUNTAIN INN

THE INN IS BUILT IN THE ARCHITECTURAL STYLE of the historic Appalachian cantilever barn and beautifully furnished with 18th century English antiques and French paintings in the living-dining rooms. Room names honor eminent Appalachian people, and the decor captures their mountain history and culture. Breathtaking views, private balconies, spa tubs and woodburning fireplaces are some of our special treats. Rated "Top Inn" by *Country Inns* magazine and awarded grand prize by *Gourmet Magazine* for our signature dessert. "...just might be the most romantic place in the Smokies"-*Southern Living* magazine. "A wonderful place to recharge your batteries"-*Country Magazine.* "Appalachia with style"-*National Geographic Traveler magazine.* "...a romantic getaway"-*HGTV*

1 Guestroom Handicap Accessible • Non-Smoking Inn
Suitable for Children Over 10 • Conference Facilities for 25
Reservations Accepted Through Travel Agents

RATES

9 rooms, $115/$150 B&B.
3 luxury suites $165/$225 B&B.
Most with king beds/spa tubs for two/wood-burning fireplaces/balconies/refreshment centers.
Closed Christmas Eve/Day..

ATTRACTIONS

Hiking, biking, fishing, picnicking, horseback riding, rafting, golf, swimming, historic tours, antique/crafts shopping, wildflower walks, theatre. Ten minutes to Great Smoky Mountains National Park.

CUISINE

Full breakfast. Gourmet desserts and flavored coffees by candlelight complimentary. BYOB. Dining most evenings by reservation.

DIRECTIONS

Enter Townsend (mile marker 26), from Maryville on US 321 N. 1st R on Old Tuckaleechee Rd., R on next paved rd. (Laurel Valley), .8 miles through stone wall entry. Crest hill, turn L.

Only 20 munites from McGhee-Tyson Airport for Metro Knoxville.

Kingston, TN

Whitestone Country Inn

888-247-2464
423-376-0113 Fax 423-376-4454
www.whitestoneinn.com
moreinfo@whitestoneinn.com
1200 Paint Rock Road, Kingston, TN 37763

Select Registry Member *Since 2000*
Owners
PAUL COWELL AND
JEAN COWELL

ELEGANT WATERSIDE INN

ON THE SHORES OF WATTS BAR LAKE with views of the Smoky Mountains, Whitestone's rolling hillsides and serene combination of natural woods and landscaped gardens soothe your soul and relax your spirit. The dining rooms overflow with delictable treats, serving three meals a day. Each room and suite is named for a bird in the neighboring Wildlife and Waterfowl Refuge. Stained-glass transoms at each suite's door depict the bird for which it is named. Perfect for vacations, retreats, meetings or honeymoons, Whitestone is one of only five AAA four-diamond inns in Tennessee, and was named one of the '10 Most Romantic Inns in America' in 1999.

RATES

20 rooms/suites, $125/$250 per night. Each room and suite has fireplace, king bed, spa tub, TV/VCR and refrigerator.
Open year-round.

ATTRACTIONS

ON SITE: Tennis, croquet, volleyball, hiking, biking, fishing, paddle boating, canoes and kayaking on our 360-acre estate. Eight miles of trails and 8000 feet frontage on Watts Bar Lake. NEARBY: visit the aquarium, historic sites, the Great Smoky Mountains, or play golf.

CUISINE

The very best classic cuisine. Enjoy elegant meals in one of our three dining rooms, two overlooking the lake. BYOB and setups available. For between-meal snacks, sample from the cookie jars in our great room.

DIRECTIONS

From I-75, exit 72. Turn W on Hwy 72, go 9 miles. R on Paint Rock Rd., just after Hwy 322 jct. Entrance is 4 miles on R. From I-40, exit 352 S on Hwy 58. Go 6 miles to L on Hwy 72 E, then 5 miles to L on Paint Rock Rd. 4 miles.

---

3 Guestrooms Handicap Accessible • Suitable for Children
Conference Facilities for 50 • Visa, MC, Disc, AMEX Accepted
Non-Smoking Inn • Reservations Accepted Through Travel Agents

College Grove, TN

Peacock Hill Country Inn

800-327-6663
615-368-7727
www.peacockhillinn.com

Select Registry Member *Since 2000*
Proprietors
ANITA AND WALTER OGILVIE

6994 Giles Hill Road, College Grove, TN 37046

THIS QUIET 1000-ACRE RETREAT nestled deep in rolling hills of Tennessee was in *Country Home*, Sept. '99, and among Top Affordable Luxuries in *Country Inns*, Feb. '99. The inn is on a cattle farm with peacocks, deer, wild turkey, a creek and trails in woods. The main farmhouse pampers guests in five rooms, each with its own distinct decor. Large comfortable common areas afford relaxing conversation. The rustic log cabin and grainery offer private hideaways for romance. The historic McCall House, one mile away in a hollow on the farm, has two guest rooms, screened porches and The Grand Suite with spacious log dining/living room. Nonsmoking. AAA ◆◆◆◆.

1 Guestroom Handicap Accessible • Suitable for Children in Suites
Conference Facilities for 15 • Visa, MC, AMEX, Disc Accepted
Non-Smoking Inn • Reservations Accepted Through Travel Agents

ELEGANT COUNTRY INN

RATES

7 rooms $125/$145.
3 suites $165/$225.
Luxurious rooms and suites have king beds and large private baths, some with woodburning fireplaces, whirlpools, European showers.
Open year-round.

ATTRACTIONS

HERE: Trails for hiking, bikes and horses. Horse stables for boarding your horses. NEARBY: Elegant 19th century antebellum homes, Civil War landmarks, antique and specialty shops, malls, golf, walking horse show farms, Grand Ole Opry and Nashville.

CUISINE

A full complimentary breakfast is served in the dining room or on the sun porch. Box lunches for picnics on the grounds or day trips, and delicious dinners at individual tables are available with advance reservations.

DIRECTIONS

From Nashville: I-65 S to Franklin exit #65, E on Hwy 96 1.5 miles, R on Arno Rd., 13.7 miles to Giles Hill Rd., R 2.8 miles to Peacock Hill Country Inn on the L.

Monteagle, TN

Adams Edgeworth Inn

87-RELAXINN

931-924-4000 Fax 931-924-3236

www.1896-edgeworth-mountain-inn.com
innjoy@blomand.net

Monteagle Assembly, Monteagle, TN 37356

Select Registry Member *Since 1992*
Owners
WENDY AND DAVID ADAMS

NESTLED IN AN HISTORIC Victorian Chautaugua atop the Cumberland Mountains, this 1896 National Register Inn is a 'Camelot' in a forest of brooks, vales and tall trestle footbridges. Summer cottage decor featuring colorful chintzes, art, antiques, wicker, collector quilts. This quaint Victorian retreat of over 165 historic homes is a 'spa for the spirit.' Fireside chats in winter, a Chautaugua summer program of music, literature and recreation for all ages. Full country breakfast and five-course candlelit dinners enhance the serenity of this magical inn. Two hundred feet of verandas with rocking chairs. Library of over two thousand books. Gift shop.

RUSTIC MOUNTAIN INN

RATES

12 rooms, $125/$295.
2 suites, $175/$295.
All private baths.
Open year-round.

ATTRACTIONS

Historic Chautaugua Victorian Village, mountain hiking, biking, caves. Tennis, swimming, five Jack Nicklaus Golf Courses, Jack Daniels, Sewanee University of the South, music, fairs, flea markets, Chautaugua Summer Program, Tennessee Williams Memorial Theatre, antiquing.

CUISINE

Intimate candlelit dining, five-course prix-fixe by reservation. Bring own wine. Picnic lunches pre-arranged. Monteagle winery nearby. Full country breakfast.

DIRECTIONS

I-24 exit 134, R 1/2 mile, L under "Monteagle Assembly" archway. Through stone gateway to private village. Follow signs to Adams Edgeworth Inn .2 mile from gate.

12 Guestrooms Handicap Accessible • Suitable for Children
Conference Facilities for 24 • Visa, MC, AMEX Accepted
Non-Smoking Inn • Reservations Accepted Through Travel Agents

Chattanooga, TN

Adams Hilborne Mansion Inn

888-I-INNJOY
423-265-5000 Fax 423-265-5555
www.innjoy.com
innjoy@worldnet.att.net
801 Vine Street, Chattanooga, TN 37403

Select Registry Member *Since 1996*
Owners
WENDY AND DAVID ADAMS

HUGE OAKS shelter this magnificent mayor's mansion built in 1889 in Chattanooga's opulent historic Fortwood District. The Inn is quiet, residential, yet close to all activities. Winner of the coveted National Trust for Historic Preservation Award, this massive stone Victorian architectural treasure features 16-foot coffered ceilings, carved pocket doors, hand-painted murals and a breathtaking staircase. Hidden among the oriental carpets, fine art and antiques are TVs, VCRs, modems and telephones. The Fortwood Ballroom and Tiffany Dining Room host fabulous fare of world-class chefs. Historic walking tours at Inn's entrance. Private parking. Views of mountains.

ELEGANT IN TOWN INN

RATES

4 suites, $175/$325.
6 rooms, $125/$195.
Open year-round.

ATTRACTIONS

Civil War sights, Aquarium, art district, museums, riverwalk, Southern Belle, TN River, mountains, hiking, river sports, hang gliding, shopping, antiques, rafting Ocoee, UTC, theatre, historic tours, auctions, Discovery Museum, IMAX Theatre, Rock City.

CUISINE

Fine dining, wines, liquors, brews, and spirits available. Home of Southern Gourmet Society. Professional Member Chaine des Rotisseurs. James Beard Society. Chef. A la carte menu. Weddings, corporate retreats, private parties.

DIRECTIONS

From Atlanta or Knoxville I-75 to I-24 W. 27 N to exit 1C. 1 mile straight, R on Palmetto St. 1 1/2 block to Inn. Turn L on Vine St and L into parking area. From Nashville I-24 E to 27 N, then same.

1 Guestroom, 4 Common Rooms Handicap Accessible
Conference Facilities for 75 • Visa, MC, AMEX, Diners Accepted
Children by Arrangement • Reservations Accepted Through Travel Agents

The Great Lakes Region and Ontario

Diversity is a cornerstone of the Select Registry. Shadowing the Great Lakes region and Iowa, one of our Inns was build from hand-hewed logs from the early nineteenth century. The building had been faithfully restored. Vegetables are picked daily from the garden. At this particular Inn, the faire is vegetarian. A guest can walk nature trails that twine throughout the sixty-acre property.

WE HAVE A STUNNING INN IN URBAN CHICAGO, award winning Inns in the rural countryside of Indiana, Ohio, and Wisconsin. One Country Inn in Minnesota serves superlative German cuisine. The appointments are heavenly. A favorite Innkeeper in Michigan is legendary for his warmth and compassion. Across the big water, Ontario beckons with dozens of quality Country Inns. Ontario is rich in style and custom. Our customers have come to expect a common denominator called excellence. Excellence is our motto. Excellence is our legacy. On either side of the border, the land holds steady, and so does our hospitality.

Driving along Lake Superior a traveler can lose himself in the richness of the place. Summer beams down upon the lucky travelers. The water is stunning with aqueous fields of royal blue, and the skies deep and handsome.

Many a lucky couple has stumbled upon the charming towns that border the Great Lakes. From an upstairs room they watch the sun kiss the water in flurries as delicate as dancing brushstrokes, or watch snow gust into divine whorls that suggest a state of grace. Later, dinner is a highlight with fillets of venison and rich demi-glace sauce reduced with wild berries with a splash of red wine and a dab of butter. But no matter how sublime the food, it is the Innkeepers who made the strongest impression. With humor and warmth unusual in its generosity, travelers feel nurtured as never before.

Traveling from Inn to Inn on either side of the border, a special quality runs like a river: after years of service, the Innkeepers continue to dote on their customers. Many are old friends.

Our guests are glad for the relationships, for the long lovely summers or the white-cloaked winters, for adventure textured in Select richness. Rarely has life felt so easy, so good.

"Possibly the finest Inn in North America! The staff is second to none. Highly recommended!"
—Mark C. Robins, Toronto, ONT

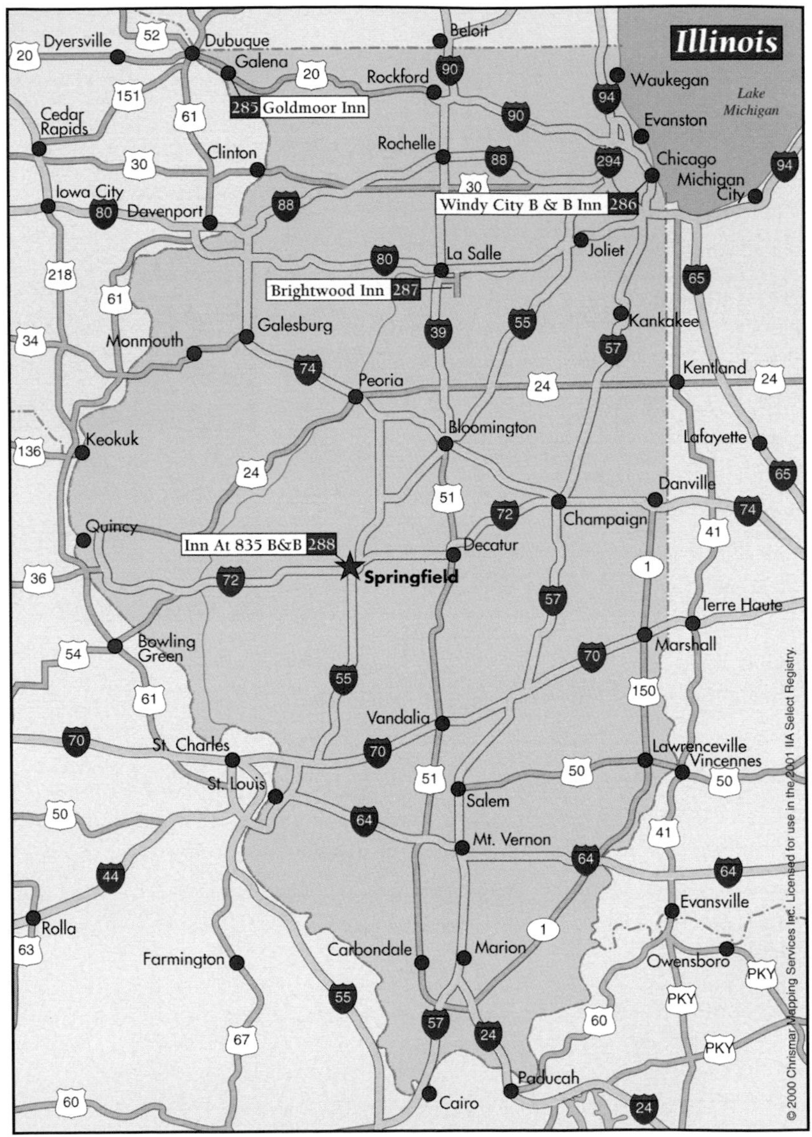
Illinois
Lake Michigan
285 Goldmoor Inn
Windy City B & B Inn 286
Brightwood Inn 287
Inn At 835 B&B 288
Springfield
Dyersville
Dubuque
Galena
Beloit
Rockford
Waukegan
Evanston
Chicago
Michigan City
Cedar Rapids
Clinton
Rochelle
Iowa City
Davenport
La Salle
Joliet
Galesburg
Monmouth
Kankakee
Peoria
Kentland
Bloomington
Keokuk
Lafayette
Danville
Champaign
Quincy
Decatur
Terre Haute
Marshall
Bowling Green
Vandalia
St. Charles
Lawrenceville
Vincennes
St. Louis
Salem
Mt. Vernon
Evansville
Rolla
Owensboro
Farmington
Carbondale
Marion
Paducah
Cairo
© 2000 Chrismar Mapping Services Inc. Licensed for use in the 2001 IIA Select Registry.

Galena, IL

Goldmoor Inn

800-255-3925
815-777-3925 Fax 815-777-3993
www.galena-il.com
goldmoor@galenalink.com
9001 Sand Hill Road, Galena, IL 61036-9341

A CONTEMPORARY LUXURY COUNTRY INN high atop the bluff overlooking the Mississippi River, 6 miles south of historic Galena. The Goldmoor features the perfect setting for romantic getaways, anniversaries, and honeymoons. Our grand deluxe suites and cottages feature fireplaces and whirlpools overlooking the Mississippi. We pamper you with first-class amenitites such as European terry robes, stereo systems with Bose surround sound, TVs with digital satellite system and multi-line phones with modem hook-ups. Complimentary mountain bikes and a full gourmet breakfast. "Top rated Inn in Illinois" from 1993 to present by ABBA.

2 Guestrooms Handicap Accessible • Suitable for Children
Conference Facilities for 24 • Visa, MC, Disc Accepted
Non-Smoking Inn • Reservations Accepted Through Travel Agents

Select Registry Member *Since 2001*
Innkeepers/Owners
PATRICIA AND JAMES GOLDTHORPE

ELEGANT COUNTRY BREAKFAST INN

RATES

2 rooms, $115/$145.
4 suites, $175/$265.
3 cottages $255/$295.
2 rooms with private baths, 1 fireplace suite, 3 fireplace/ whirlpool suites, 3 grand deluxe fireplace/whirlpool cottages.
Open year-round.

ATTRACTIONS

Complimentary bikes, hiking, shopping, dining, skiing, horseback riding, fishing, art galleries, museums, golf, landscaped grounds with gazebos, patio with grill. Historic Galena 6 minutes away. Dubuque, IA and its historic sites are just 15 minutes away.

CUISINE

Afternoon fresh gourmet cookies in room. Early morning tea, coffee and cocoa. Gourmet full breakfast served 8:30 to 10:00 overlooking the Mississippi River. Custom catering for groups or wedding receptions.

DIRECTIONS

Six miles south of Galena on Blackjack Road to Sand Hill Road, turn on Sand Hill and the Inn is first place on left.

Chicago, IL

Windy City B&B Inn

877-897-7091
773-248-7091 Fax 773-248-7090
www.chicago-inn.com
stay@chicago-inn.com
607 W. Deming Place, Chicago, IL 60614-2630

Select Registry Member *Since 2001*
Owners
Mary and Andy Shaw

THIS 1886 MANSION IS REBORN AS AN URBAN INN. Located in Lincoln Park on a quiet street of grand old homes just 2 miles north of Downtown Chicago and west of the park that runs along the lakefront. The main house has four rooms and the coach house in the back has three suites. In betweeen is an ivy covered garden. Large common spaces in the main house make this ideal for small meetings. All accommodations have eclectic, individual decor. The fabrics, wallpapers and colors are rich and interesting. Throughout there is a wealth of Chicago art and artifacts. Your innkeepers admit to being chauvinistic about their city and look forward to sharing their enthusiasm.

Contemporary In Town Breakfast Inn

RATES

4 rooms, $145/$225.
3 suites, $185/$325.
Main house-3 queens and 1 king, all private baths, 2 with Jacuzzis, two common rooms with fireplaces. Coach house suites have kitchens, fireplace, Jacuzzis and queen and king beds.
Open year-round.

ATTRACTIONS

World class museums, architecture, theater, symphony, opera, jazz, restaurants, shopping, sports teams, zoo, beach, lakefront, neighborhood fests, public transportation.

CUISINE

Continental buffet breakfast in main house. Snacks and beverages.

DIRECTIONS

Via I-90/I-94 exit at Fullerton. E 1 1/2 miles to Halsted. N/L 1 light to Wrightwood. E/R to dead end at Clark. S/R 1 block to Deming. W/R 1 1/2 blocks to Inn. Parking at 2515 N. Clark Street. Via Lake Shore Drive exit Fullerton. W 1/2 mile to Clark. N/R 1/4 mile to Deming. W/L to the Inn.

Suitable for Children Over 10 • Conference Facilities for 20
Designated Smoking Areas • MC, Visa, Diners, Disc, AMEX Accepted
Reservations Accepted Through Travel Agents

Oglesby, IL

Brightwood Inn

888-667-0600
815-667-4600 Fax 815-667-4727
www.starved-rock-inn.com
brtwood@starved-rock-inn.com
2407 North IL Route 178, Oglesby, IL 61348

NEWLY CONSTRUCTED IN 1996 and nestled on 14 acres of meadow within the confines of Matthiessen State Park, the Brightwood Inn was designed to resemble a vintage farmhouse complete with a veranda and rocking chairs. The Inn will provide you with a peaceful and luxurious stay amid the beauty of nature. All rooms have TV/VCR and phones with modem hookup. Six rooms have large Jacuzzi tubs and three have private balconies. Starved Rock State Park and the I&M Canal are located just two miles north. Intimate dining room with seasonally adjusted menu features herbs fresh-picked from our garden. AAA ◆◆◆.

Select Registry Member *Since 2000*
Innkeepers/Owners
JO AND JOHN RYAN
General Manager
KEVIN RYAN

TRADITIONAL COUNTRY INN

RATES

7 rooms, $90/$185.
1 suite, $190/$225.
Each of the eight rooms features its own unique personality and style. All rooms have gas fireplace, private bath and TV/VCR. $10 off each night if you stay 2 or more nights.
Open year-round.

ATTRACTIONS

Hiking, biking, horseback riding, canoeing, white-water, rafting, golfing, skydiving, fishing, antiquing, shopping, boating and cross-country skiing.

CUISINE

Full breakfast with room. Dinner Thurs.-Sun., full bistro-style menu. Beer, wine and liquor.

DIRECTIONS

From I-80: Take exit 81, go S on IL Rte 178 for 6 miles. Inn will be on R side. From I-39: Take Tonica exit. Go R second stop sign take L on IL Rte 178. Follow for 3 miles, Inn on L side.

1 Guestroom Handicap Accessible • Suitable for Children Over 8
Conference Facilities for 40 • Visa, MC,Disc,AMEX Accepted
Non-Smoking Inn • Reservations Accepted Through Travel Agents

Springfield, IL

The Inn at 835

217-523-4466
Fax 217-523-4468
www.innat835.com
theinnat835@worldnet.att.net
835 South Second Street, Springfield, IL 62704

Select Registry Member *Since 2001*
Innkeepers/Owners
COURT AND KAREN CONN

EXPERIENCE OLD WORLD CHARM and attention to detail while enjoying the conveniences of a modern European style Inn. Verandas, cozy fireplaces and Jacuzzis are just a few of the delights awaiting visitors to The Inn at 835. Each guestroom is individually decorated in period antiques. Located within easy walking distance to historic sites and fine dining. Our experienced staff will gladly assist you in handling catering arrangements, audio visual and entertainment requirements. We welcome you to review our exciting catering menu.

ELEGANT INTOWN BREAKFAST INN

RATES
2 luxury suites, 4 corporate suites, 8 rooms, $99/$189 B&B
Single person corporate discount available Sunday - Thursday.
Open year-round.

ATTRACTIONS
NEARBY: museum, library, Frank Lloyd Wright home, Lincoln historic sites, golf, historic parks, and swimming.

CUISINE
Full breakfast and daily refreshments. Dining available for private parties. Wine and liquor available.

DIRECTIONS
From I-55 take Clearlake Ave exit into town. Turn L onto Second Street, continue 7 blocks. Inn is on the right.

---

1 Guestroom Handicap Accessible • Suitable for Children Over 13
Conference Facilities for 40 • Credit Cards Accepted
Designated Smoking Areas • Reservations Accepted Through Travel Agents

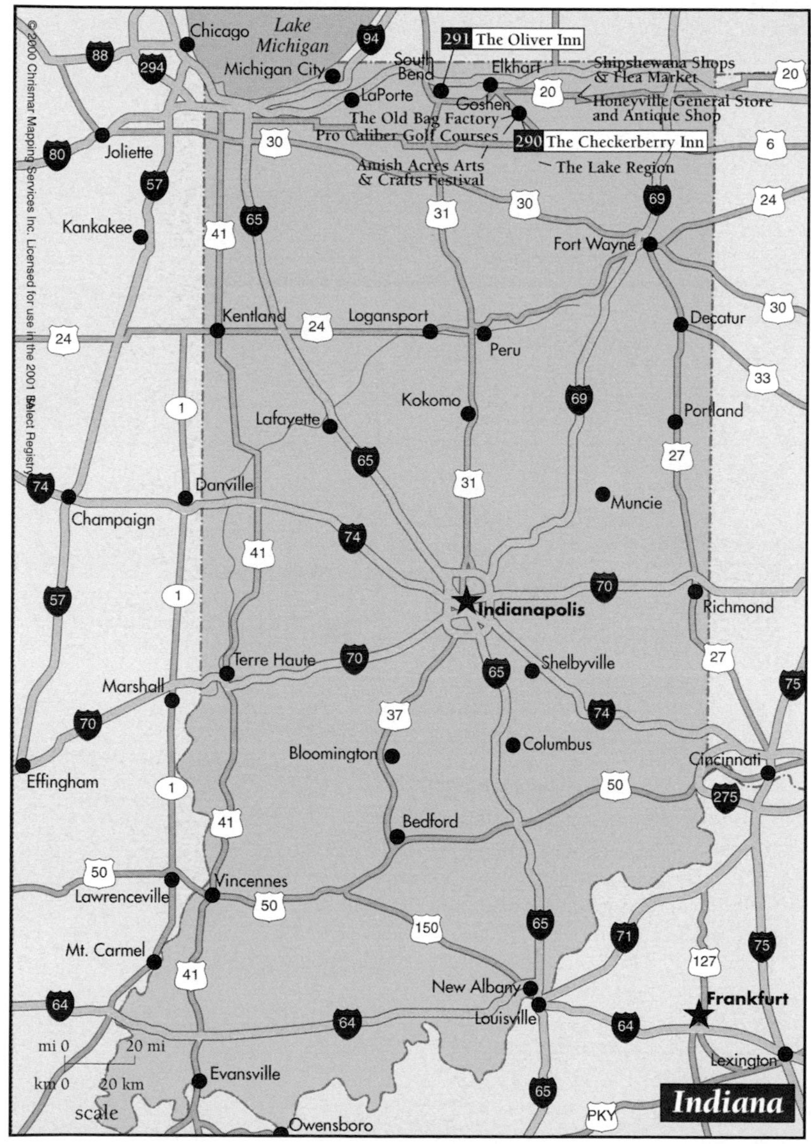

© 2000 Chrismar Mapping Services Inc. Licensed for use in the 2001 BA/Select Registry
Lake Michigan
Chicago
Michigan City
South Bend
Elkhart
LaPorte
Goshen
291 The Oliver Inn
Shipshewana Shops & Flea Market
Honeyville General Store and Antique Shop
The Old Bag Factory
Pro Caliber Golf Courses
290 The Checkerberry Inn
Amish Acres Arts & Crafts Festival
The Lake Region
Joliette
Kankakee
Fort Wayne
Kentland
Logansport
Peru
Decatur
Kokomo
Lafayette
Portland
Danville
Champaign
Muncie
Indianapolis
Richmond
Terre Haute
Shelbyville
Marshall
Columbus
Bloomington
Effingham
Cincinnati
Bedford
Vincennes
Lawrenceville
Mt. Carmel
New Albany
Louisville
Frankfurt
Lexington
Evansville
Owensboro
mi 0 20 mi
km 0 20 km
scale
Indiana

Goshen, IN

The Checkerberry Inn

219-642-4445
Fax 219-642-4445
www.checkerberryinn.com

62644 County Road 37, Goshen, IN 46528

WATCH FOR AMISH BUGGIES in this pastoral farmland. On a 100-acre wooded estate, the Inn offers breathtaking views of unspoiled rolling countryside from individually decorated rooms. While away the hours enjoying fields of wildflowers, massive beech trees, miles of country roads and grazing horses and sheep in nearby pastures. Browse the many antiques shops throughout the area. Restaurant and Inn featured in *Gourmet* and many national publications. Described by guests as "one of the last oases of genuine hospitality and tranquility."

Select Registry Member *Since 1990*
Owners
JOHN AND SUSAN GRAFF
General Managers
KELLY GRAFF, KAREN KENNEDY

ELEGANT COUNTRY INN

RATES
11 rooms, $130/$155 B&B.
3 suites, $160/$375 B&B.
Open Feb. - Dec.

ATTRACTIONS
Tennis, outdoor pool, croquet green; golf and lakes nearby. Goshen College and Notre Dame University within minutes.

CUISINE
Continental-plus breakfast, dinner Tuesday-Saturday (fine dining, reservations required.) Fine wines and beer.

DIRECTIONS
Exit 107, Toll Rd., S on State Rd. 13 to R on State Rd. 4, 1/2 mile, L on County Rd. 37, 1 mile to Inn. (15 min. from Toll Rd.).

3 Common Rooms Handicap Accessible • Suitable for Children Over 6
Conference Facilities for 80 • Visa, MC, AMEX Accepted
Non-Smoking Inn • Reservations Accepted Through Travel Agents

South Bend, IN

The Oliver Inn

888-697-4466
219-232-4545 Fax 219-288-9788
www.oliverinn.com
oliver@michiana.org
630 West Washington Street, South Bend, IN 46601

Select Registry Member *Since 2000*
Innkeepers/Owners
RICHARD AND VENERA MONAHAN

ELEGANT IN TOWN BREAKFAST INN

RATES
9 rooms/suites.
$95/$150-$145/$225.
King or queen beds with down blankets. Some feature fireplaces, balcony or Jacuzzi. All have telephone, cable TV.
Open year-round.

ATTRACTIONS
University of Notre Dame, Studebaker Mansion (Tippecanoe Place Restaurant), the Studebaker National Museum, the Oliver Mansion (Copshaholm House Museum), East Race Waterway, Amish area, 400 antique dealers, canoeing, kayaking and carriage rides.

CUISINE
Full candlelight breakfast by the fire to live piano music. Complimentary drinks, and snacks from Butler's Pantry. Dine at Tippecanoe Place Restaurant in the Studebaker Mansion right next door.

DIRECTIONS
From the N: Indiana Toll Rd. I-80/90, exit 77, turn S at light on Hwy 31/933, 2 miles to R on Washington St. From the S: N on Hwy 31 into downtown South Bend, L on Washington St.

THE OLIVER INN BED & BREAKFAST offers a 'turn-of-the-century' feeling with all of today's important amenities. Choose from nine beautifully furnished rooms, with air-conditioning, private baths, phone and cable TV. Several feature the warmth of a fireplace, balcony or Jacuzzi. Warm and inviting, The Oliver's richly decorated library is the perfect place for conversation with old friends and new. Keep warm around the fire while enjoying live piano music from the computerized baby grand. Come discover why The Oliver Inn was voted the Michiana area's 'Best Bed & Breakfast' and why Steve Thomas from "This Old House" stays at The Oliver Inn.

Suitable for Children • Conference Facilities for 20
Non-Smoking Inn • AMEX, Disc, Visa, MC Accepted
Reservations Accepted Through Travel Agents

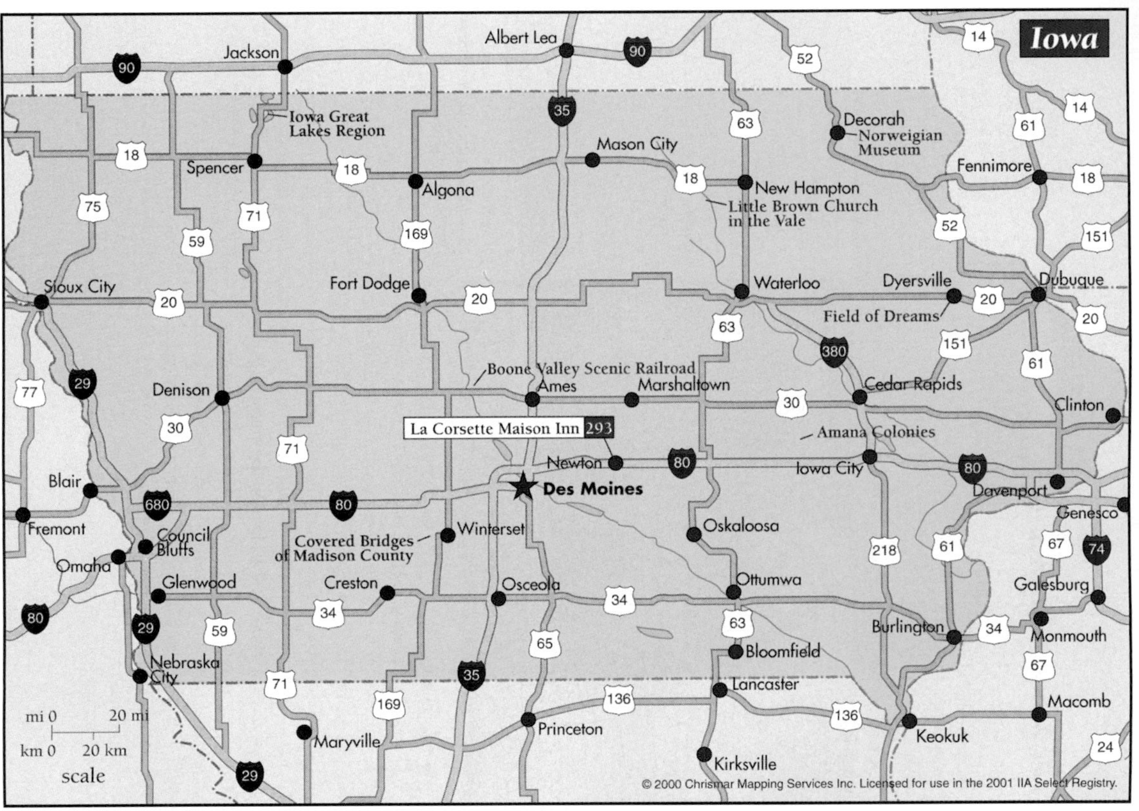
Iowa
Albert Lea
Jackson
Iowa Great Lakes Region
Spencer
Algona
Mason City
Decorah
Norweigian Museum
Fennimore
New Hampton
Little Brown Church in the Vale
Sioux City
Fort Dodge
Waterloo
Dyersville
Dubuque
Field of Dreams
Boone Valley Scenic Railroad
Ames
Marshaltown
Denison
Cedar Rapids
Clinton
La Corsette Maison Inn 293
Amana Colonies
Newton
Iowa City
Davenport
Blair
Des Moines
Genesco
Fremont
Winterset
Covered Bridges of Madison County
Oskaloosa
Council Bluffs
Omaha
Glenwood
Creston
Osceola
Ottumwa
Galesburg
Burlington
Monmouth
Bloomfield
Nebraska City
Lancaster
Macomb
Princeton
Keokuk
Maryville
Kirksville
mi 0 20 mi
km 0 20 km
scale
© 2000 Chrismar Mapping Services Inc. Licensed for use in the 2001 IIA Select Registry.

Newton, IA

LaCorsette Maison Inn

641-792-6833
Fax 641-792-6597
www.selectregistry.com

629 1st Avenue East, Newton, IA 50208

Select Registry Member *Since 1993*
Innkeeper/Owner
Kay Owen

Erected in 1909, LaCorsette Maison Inn is a mission-style mansion. The Inn is elegant, yet comfortable, with cozy nooks and alcoves. It is on the National Historic Register. Kay Owen, the innkeeper, is also a gourmet chef and specializes in continental food with a French flair. The Inn offers deluxe accommodations and exquisite meals to travelers.

Traditional In Town Inn

RATES
5 rooms, $70/$185 B&B.
2 suites, $95/$185 B&B.
Open year-round.

ATTRACTIONS
Nearby YMCA, tennis, swimming, cross-country skiing, parks, bicycle trails.

CUISINE
Breakfast, dinner by reservation. Wine available.

DIRECTIONS
On I-80 E of Des Moines, 7 blocks E of the city square on Hwy 6.

Suitable for Children by Pre-Arrangement • Limited Pet Policy
Conference Facilities for 10 • Visa, MC, AMEX Accepted
Non-Smoking Inn • Reservations Accepted Through Travel Agents

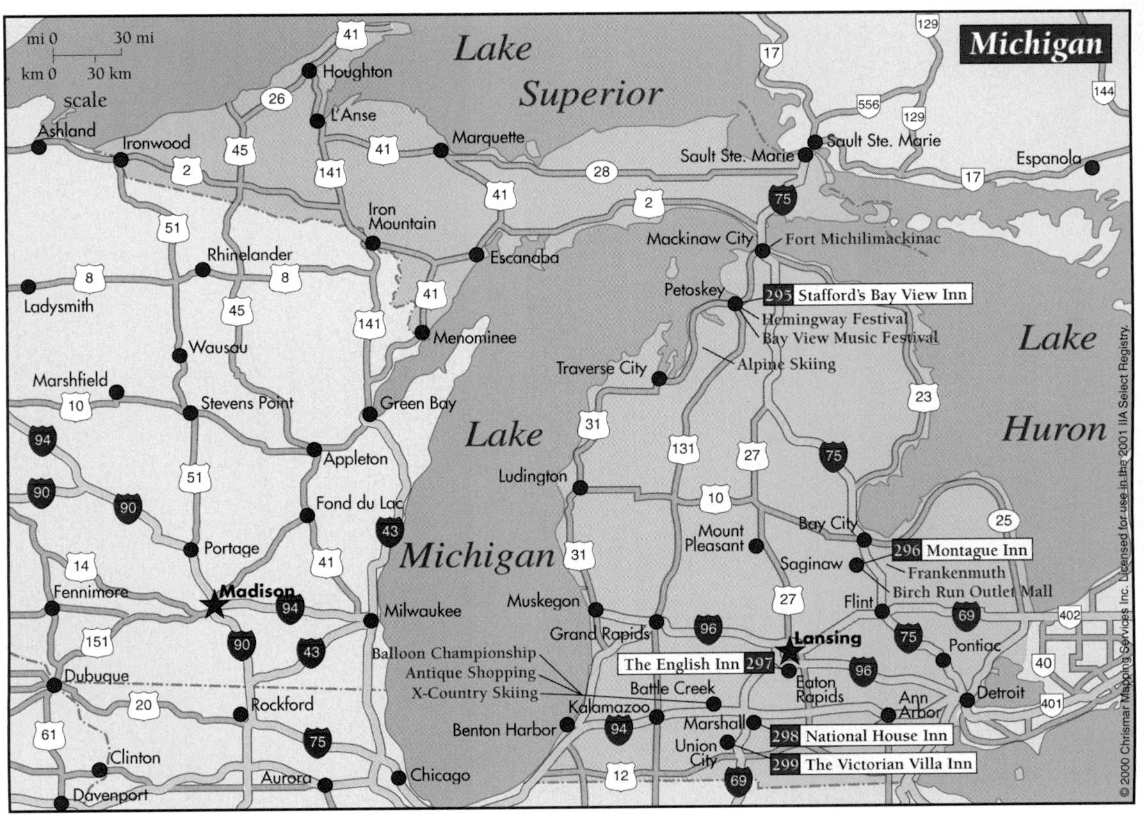

Michigan
mi 0 30 mi
km 0 30 km
scale
Lake Superior
Lake Huron
Lake Michigan
Houghton
L'Anse
Ashland
Ironwood
Marquette
Sault Ste. Marie
Sault Ste. Marie
Espanola
Iron Mountain
Escanaba
Mackinaw City
Fort Michilimackinac
Rhinelander
Ladysmith
Petoskey
295 Stafford's Bay View Inn
Hemingway Festival
Bay View Music Festival
Menominee
Wausau
Traverse City
Alpine Skiing
Marshfield
Stevens Point
Green Bay
Appleton
Ludington
Fond du Lac
Bay City
Mount Pleasant
296 Montague Inn
Portage
Saginaw
Frankenmuth
Birch Run Outlet Mall
Fennimore
Madison
Milwaukee
Muskegon
Flint
Grand Rapids
Lansing
Pontiac
Balloon Championship
Antique Shopping
X-Country Skiing
The English Inn 297
Eaton Rapids
Dubuque
Battle Creek
Detroit
Kalamazoo
Ann Arbor
Rockford
Benton Harbor
Marshall
298 National House Inn
Union City
299 The Victorian Villa Inn
Clinton
Aurora
Chicago
Davenport
© 2000 Chismar Mapping Services Inc. Licensed for use in the 2001 IIA Select Registry.

Petoskey, MI

Stafford's Bay View Inn

800-258-1886
231-347-2771 Fax 231-347-3413
www.staffords.com
bayview@staffords.com
2011 Woodland Avenue, P.O. Box 3
Petoskey, MI 49770

Select Registry Member *Since 1972*
Innkeepers
STAFFORD SMITH FAMILY

FOR 40 YEARS THE STAFFORD SMITH FAMILY has owned, operated and lovingly restored this 1886 grand dame Victorian Country Inn. Located on the shores of Lake Michigan's Little Traverse Bay, in the Historic Landmark District of Bay View, this Inn sets the standard in fine dining and gracious service with beautifully appointed bed chambers and public areas. Guests enjoy summer Chautauqua programs, fall color tours and winter ski packages, including sleigh rides through the historic cottage colony grounds. Petoskey's famous resort retail district and marina are located nearby. Named 'Michigan's Best Brunch' by *Michigan Living* magazine. Mobil ★★★ and AAA ◆◆◆.

TRADITIONAL COUNTRY INN

RATES
20 rooms, $84/$205 B&B.
11 spa-fireplace suites, $114/$295 B&B.
Open year-round.

ATTRACTIONS
Driving distance: ski and golf resorts, Mackinac Island, antiques, resort shops and boat tours. Walk to: summer theatre, concerts, tennis and waterfront-located on major bike path and historic trails; on-site bikes.

CUISINE
Breakfast/Dinner: May-Oct. and winter weekends. Lunch: June-Aug. Brunch: Holidays, June-Oct. House guests: BYOB. Full beverage service and dining at innkeeper-owned properties nearby.

DIRECTIONS
From Detroit: I-75 N to Gaylord Exit 282, Rte 32 W to US 131 N to Petoskey. From Chicago: I-94 to I-196 N to US 131 N to Petoskey.

Limited Handicap Access Available • Suitable for Children
Conference Facilities for 100 • Visa, MC, AMEX, Disc Accepted
Non-Smoking Inn • Reservations Accepted Through Travel Agents

Saginaw, MI

Montague Inn

517-752-3939
Fax 517-752-3159
www.montagueinn.com
montaguein@aol.com
1581 South Washington, Saginaw, MI 48601

Select Registry Member *Since 1989*
Innkeeper
WILLY SCHIPPER

THIS GEORGIAN MANSION ON LAKE LINTON, restored to its original splendor, is surrounded by spacious lawns and city parks. Summer evenings may be spent under trees watching the sun set over the lake. Enjoy winter evenings in front of a fire in our library. Fine cuisine is offered in our intimate dining room overlooking the beautiful grounds. The Montague Inn provides a peaceful and elegant oasis in the heart of the city.

ELEGANT IN TOWN INN

RATES
18 rooms, $65/$125.
1 suite, $160.
Gas log fireplaces in 3 rooms.
Open year-round.

ATTRACTIONS
Only minutes from Frankenmuth and the Birch Run shopping outlet. Golf, antiquing, art museums, Saginaw Children's Zoo, sculpture gallery and Japanese Tea House also nearby. The Inn features herbal luncheons, holiday buffets.

CUISINE
Breakfast included for all guests. Dining open to the public for lunch and dinner. Lunch Tuesday-Saturday 11:30-2:00. Dinner Monday-Saturday 6:00-10:00. Facilities for private parties, dinners, weddings and receptions.

DIRECTIONS
From I-75 exit 149 B on Holland Ave. W. Follow and stay R as Holland splits and becomes Remington. Continue on Remington to the stop light on Washington Ave., then L, S on Washington 1/4 mile to the Inn. Washington Ave. is also M-13.

1 Guestroom Handicap Accessible • Suitable for Children
Conference Facilities for 30 • Visa, MC, AMEX Accepted
Non-Smoking Inn

Lansing/Eaton Rapids, MI

The English Inn

517-663-2500
Fax 517-663-2643
www.englishinn.com
677 South Michigan Road
Lansing/Eaton Rapids, MI 48827

Select Registry Member *Since 1991*
Innkeepers / Owners
GARY AND DONNA NELSON

TRADITIONAL COUNTRY INN

A FORMER AUTO BARON'S RESIDENCE, this 1927 Tudor mansion will make you feel as though you've been transported to the English countryside. Perched on a hillside overlooking the Grand River, the Inn is part of a 15-acre estate that includes formal gardens and wooded nature trails. The main house has six well-appointed bedrooms named for English towns or the royal family, a cozy pub, library and a cottage includes a 3-bedroom suite, pool and fireplace sitting room. The Inn's award-winning 110 seat restaurant includes a wine list bestowed with the Award of Excellence by *Wine Spectator.* A perfect setting for get-aways, executive retreats and family gatherings. AAA ◆◆◆.

Handicap Access Available • Suitable for Children by prior arrangement
Conference Facilities for 50 • Visa, MC, AMEX, Disc Accepted
Non-Smoking Inn • Reservations Accepted Through Travel Agents

RATES

10 rooms, $75/$175 B&B.
Includes 6 Inn rooms, 2 cottages.
Open year-round.

ATTRACTIONS

Golf, fishing, canoeing, hiking, biking, cross-country skiing, antiquing.

CUISINE

110 seat fine-dining restaurant - lunch and dinner. Breakfast for overnight guests.

DIRECTIONS

From I-96 in Lansing, take M-99 S 8 miles. From I-94, take M-99 N 22 miles. Ninety miles W of Detroit, 15 miles S of State Capitol (Lansing), and Michigan State University.

Marshall, MI

National House Inn

616-781-7374
616-781-0027 Fax 616-781-4510
www.nationalhouseinn.com

102 South Parkview, Marshall, MI 49068

Select Registry Member *Since 1978*
Innkeeper
BARBARA BRADLEY

RUSTIC VILLAGE
BREAKFAST INN

RATES
16 rooms, \$68/\$105 B&B.
2 suites, \$136/\$145.
Open year-round.

ATTRACTIONS
National Historic Landmark tours, gift shops, antiquing, Golf pkgs., NHI & Schulers pkgs., Brooks Memorial Park, Great biking area.

CUISINE
Breakfast, afternoon tea, catered dinners for receptions.

DIRECTIONS
I-94 to exit 110 Rte. 27 S 2 miles to Michigan Ave. (SW corner of circle, located in downtown Marshall).

MARSHALL, with a National Historic Landmark District designation and home of Schuler's Restaurant, has many citations for its 850 structures of 19th-century architecture, including the National Register of Historic Places, on which this Inn is also listed. Michigan's oldest operating Inn, and first brick building in the county, has been restored as a warm, hospitable Inn, beautifully furnished, with lovely gardens. Afternoon tea, candlelight home tours and cooking classes.

Suitable for Children • Conference Facilities for 25 • Non-Smoking Inn
AMEX, Visa, MC Accepted • 3 Guestrooms Handicap Accessible
Reservations Accepted Through Travel Agents

Union City, MI

The Victorian Villa Inn

800-348-4552
517-741-7383 Fax 517-741-4002
www.avictorianvilla.com
info@avictorianvilla.com
601 North Broadway Street, Union City, MI 49094

A QUIET AND UNHURRIED REFLECTION of the 19th Century, the charming and romantic Victorian Villa Inn offers distinctively furnished guest chambers, delicious hearty breakfasts, afternoon English teas and seasonal lunches. The Victorian Villa Inn also offers 19th Century gourmet 7-course Victorian dining, which has achieved national recognition in *Victoria Magazine, Midwest Living* and *Wine Spectator.* Guests may also choose a special selection from over 200 wines from the Villa's own wine cellar, awarded *Wine Spectator's* "Best of Award of Excellence".

1 Guestroom Handicap Accessible • Suitable for Children Over 12
Conference Facilities for 30 • Visa, MC, Disc Accepted
Non-Smoking Inn • Reservations Accepted Through Travel Agents

Select Registry Member *Since 1990*
Innkeepers/Owners
RONALD GIBSON AND
CYNTHIA SHATTUCK

VICTORIAN VILLAGE INN

RATES

5 rooms, \$110/\$125 B&B,
(Weekly \$70/\$85).
5 suites, \$125/\$160 B&B,
(Weekly \$85/\$120).
Open year-round.

ATTRACTIONS

Antiquing, golf, canoeing, fishing, croquet, tandem bicycles, wineries, museums, zoo, outlet shopping, Amish settlements, Kellogg's Cereal City, Old Car Museums, fishing and boating, Victorian Christmas Weekends and Mystery Weekends.

CUISINE

Breakfast, afternoon tea, champagne dinners, picnic baskets, Victorian theme dinners. Full service—Best of Award of Excellence wine list, *Wine Spectator.*

DIRECTIONS

From I-69, exit M-60 (exit 25); 8 miles W to Union City, L on Broadway St., continue 3 blocks to Inn on R (601 N. Broadway).

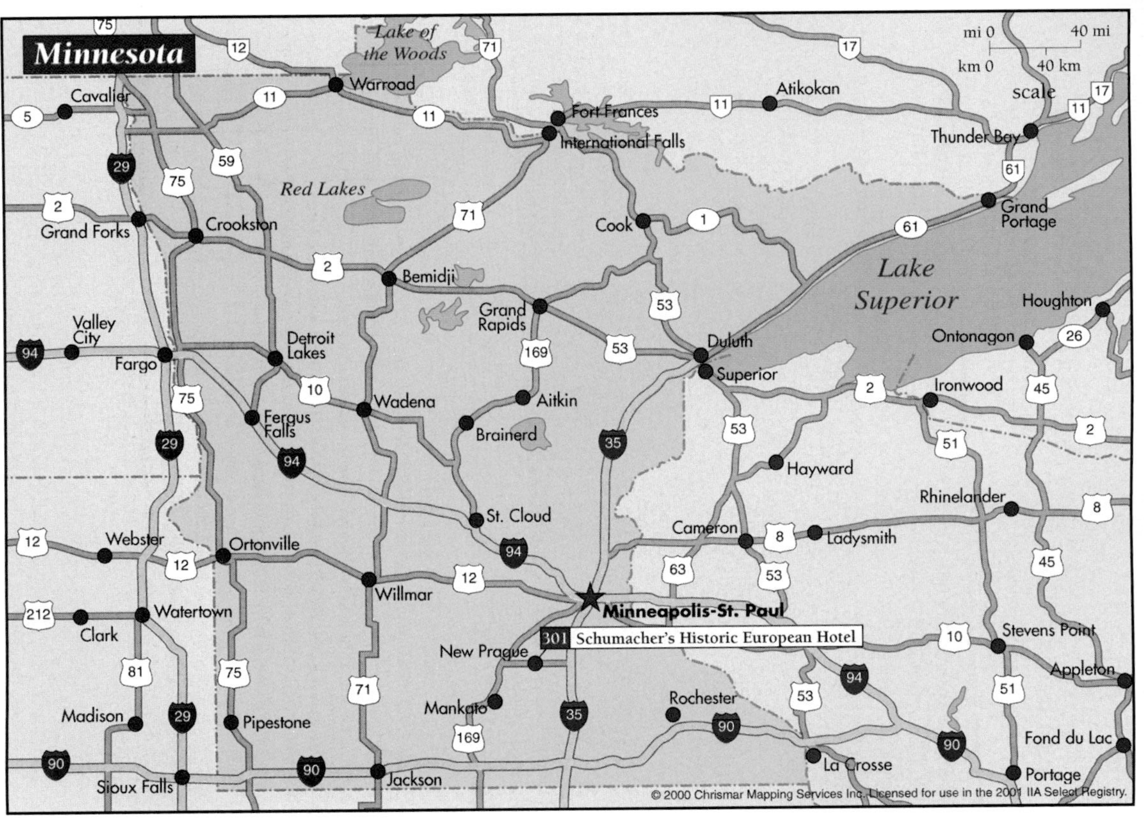
Minnesota
Lake of the Woods
Red Lakes
Lake Superior
mi 0
40 mi
km 0
40 km
scale
Cavalier
Warroad
Fort Frances
International Falls
Atikokan
Thunder Bay
Grand Portage
Grand Forks
Crookston
Cook
Bemidji
Grand Rapids
Duluth
Superior
Houghton
Ontonagon
Ironwood
Valley City
Fargo
Detroit Lakes
Fergus Falls
Wadena
Aitkin
Brainerd
Hayward
Rhinelander
St. Cloud
Cameron
Ladysmith
Webster
Ortonville
Willmar
Watertown
Clark
Minneapolis-St. Paul
301 Schumacher's Historic European Hotel
New Prague
Stevens Point
Appleton
Madison
Pipestone
Mankato
Rochester
Fond du Lac
La Crosse
Portage
Sioux Falls
Jackson
© 2000 Chrismar Mapping Services Inc. Licensed for use in the 2001 IIA Select Registry.

New Prague, MN

Schumacher's Hotel and Restaurant

800-283-2049
612-758-2133 Fax 612-758-2400
www.schumachershotel.com
SNPH@schumachershotel.com
212 West Main Street, New Prague, MN 56071

Select Registry Member *Since 1979*
Proprietors
JOHN AND KATHLEEN SCHUMACHER

ELEGANT VILLAGE INN

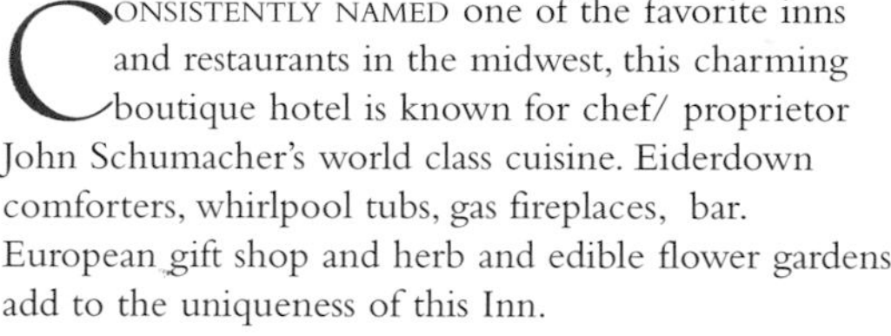

CONSISTENTLY NAMED one of the favorite inns and restaurants in the midwest, this charming boutique hotel is known for chef/ proprietor John Schumacher's world class cuisine. Eiderdown comforters, whirlpool tubs, gas fireplaces, bar. European gift shop and herb and edible flower gardens add to the uniqueness of this Inn.

RATES
3 rooms, $165 plus tax B&B.
3 rooms, $195 plus tax B&B.
3 rooms, $225 plus tax B&B.
7 rooms, $275 plus tax B&B.
Midweek and mini-vacations packages
Open year-round.

ATTRACTIONS
Several golf courses in town and nearby, Mall of America, casino, biking.

CUISINE
Sunday brunch, lunch, dinner. Full bar.

DIRECTIONS
From MPLS, I-35W, S to exit 76. County Rd. 2, W for 10 miles at 13, turn L follow 13 for 2 miles, merges w/19 W. Follow two Hwys into New Prague. W end city.

---

1 Guestroom Handicap Accessible • Suitable for Children Over 12
Conference Facilities for 16 • Visa, MC, AMEX, Disc, Diners Accepted
Designated Smoking Areas • Reservations Accepted Through Travel Agents

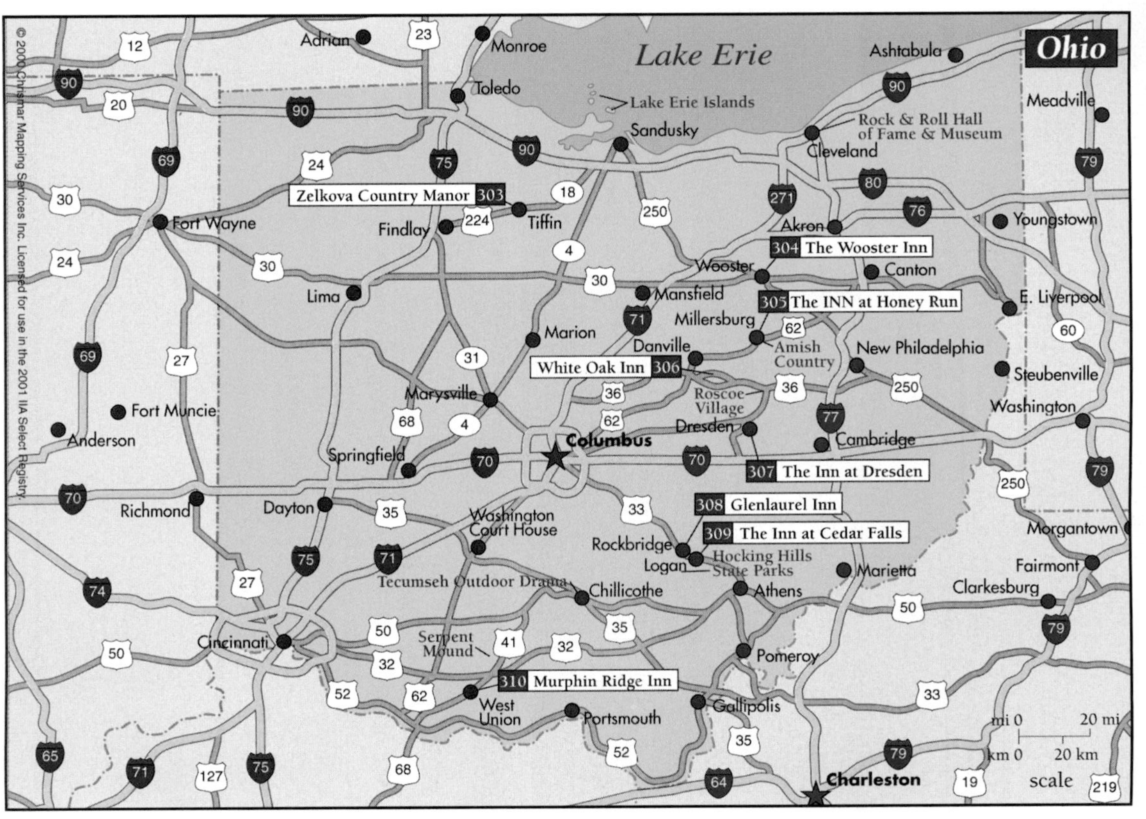

Ohio
Lake Erie
Lake Erie Islands
Adrian
Monroe
Toledo
Ashtabula
Meadville
Rock & Roll Hall of Fame & Museum
Cleveland
Sandusky
Zelkova Country Manor 303
Findlay
Tiffin
Fort Wayne
Akron
304 The Wooster Inn
Youngstown
Wooster
Canton
Lima
Mansfield
305 The INN at Honey Run
E. Liverpool
Millersburg
Marion
Amish Country
Danville
New Philadelphia
White Oak Inn 306
Steubenville
Roscoe Village
Marysville
Washington
Fort Muncie
Dresden
Anderson
Columbus
Cambridge
Springfield
307 The Inn at Dresden
Richmond
Dayton
Washington Court House
308 Glenlaurel Inn
309 The Inn at Cedar Falls
Morgantown
Rockbridge
Hocking Hills State Parks
Logan
Marietta
Fairmont
Tecumseh Outdoor Drama
Chillicothe
Athens
Clarkesburg
Cincinnati
Serpent Mound
Pomeroy
310 Murphin Ridge Inn
West Union
Gallipolis
Portsmouth
Charleston
mi 0 20 mi
km 0 20 km
scale
© 2000 Chrismar Mapping Services Inc. Licensed for use in the 2001 IIA Select Registry.

Tiffin, OH

Zelkova Country Manor

419-447-4043
419-447-6467 Fax 419-447-6473
www.zelkovacountrymanor.com
zelkova@bpsom.com
2348 South County Road 19, Tiffin, OH 44883

Select Registry Member *Since 1998*
Innkeeper
MICHAEL PINKSTON

ELEGANT COUNTRY INN

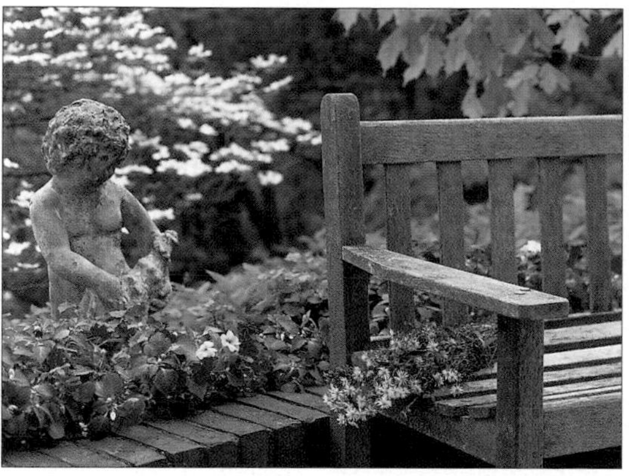

OUR ZELKOVA TREE-LINED DRIVE welcomes you to a world of country elegance and manor life. Tucked into Ohio's pastoral countryside is a romantic country retreat where goosedown pillows are still fluffed for guests, pure cotton sheets carry the faint scent of flowers from nearby perennials, and menus are inspired by fresh fruits and vegetables harvested from the Manor's bountiful gardens. A classic Georgian Revival house with a hillside view. The manor rests on 27 acres of sprawling green lawns, country gardens, lush woodland and wetlands.

RATES

8 rooms, $75/$150 B&B.
Open year-round.

ATTRACTIONS

Antiques, gardens, museums, bicycling, canoeing, Cedar Point Amusement Park, Lake Erie, Presidents Center, 1928 $5 Million Theatre and glass crafts.

CUISINE

Full English breakfast, gourmet dinner, afternoon tea, Manor Reception. Full service wine and liquor.

DIRECTIONS

Columbus, Rte 23 N to Rte 53 N to Tiffin. Cleveland Rte 80/90 W to exit 6 to Rte 53 S to Tiffin. Chicago, Turnpike to Ohio exit 6, Rte 53 S to Tiffin.

Handicap Access Available • Suitable for Children
Conference Facilities for 40 • Credit Cards Accepted
Reservations Accepted Through Travel Agents

Wooster, OH

The Wooster Inn

330-264-2341
Fax 330-264-9951
www.selectregistry.com

Select Registry Member *Since 1988*
Contact
Kathy A. Kruse

801 East Wayne Avenue, Wooster, OH 44691

Experience comfortable lodging and exquisite dining in a relaxed atmosphere at the gateway to Amish country. Enjoy chef Ken Edward's seasonal menu and innovative American style cuisine featuring farm-raised Atlantic salmon and steaks. Relax in our main dining room which overlooks a nine-hole golf course and driving range. Choose from a fine selection of wines and beers. Full menus for lunch and dinner available for house guests, as well as general public. Read, play bridge and board games, or meet other inn and dinner guests in our billiard room featuring a vintage pool table.

Traditional In Town Inn

RATES

13 rooms, $90/$100.
2 remodeled suites, $115/$135.
B&B; Phone, modem port, video conferencing, TV, A/C.

ATTRACTIONS

9-hole golf course and driving range on-site. Close by: outdoor track and tennis. Gateway to Amish country and home of Cat's Meow. Summer: Ohio Light Opera. Winter and Fall: college activities.

CUISINE

Continental breakfast and a full dinner menu served daily. Lunch served Monday through Friday. Sunday brunch buffet 11:00 to 2:00.

DIRECTIONS

I-71 S Exit Rte 83 S, 18 miles. Exit at Rte 585 S, R for 200 ft. R on Wayne Ave. Inn .7 miles on L. I-71 N exit U.S. 30 E 24 miles to Madison exit. Turn R and follow Bever to Wayne Ave. R on Wayne. Inn 2 blocks.

---

1 Guestroom Handicap Accessible • Suitable for Children • Pets Allowed
Conference Facilities for 50 • Credit Cards Accepted
Non-Smoking Inn • Reservations Accepted Through Travel Agents

Millersburg, OH

The INN at Honey Run

800-468-6639
330-674-0011 Fax 330-674-2623
www.innathoneyrun.com
innhoney@valkyrie.net
6920 County Road 203, Millersburg, OH 44654

A CONTEMPORARY SERENE COUNTRY INN located amidst the world's largest Amish community. Nestled in sixty acres of woods and pasture, the INN offers 25 rooms in its Main building, each individually decorated. The earth-sheltered Honeycombs has 12 rooms with stone fireplaces & patios. Our 3 guest cottages are ideal for honeymoon/anniversary getaways. Guests enjoy bird watching from picture windows, reading by blazing fireplaces & hiking our forest trails. Many guests like golfing at our local scenic courses or just exploring the backroads of Holmes County. Visiting Honey Run is truly an unforgettable experience.

Select Registry Member *Since 1984*
Innkeeper/Owner
MARGE STOCK

CONTEMPORARY
COUNTRY INN

RATES
40 rooms, $75/$280 B&B.
3 guest houses.
Open year-round.

ATTRACTIONS
Bird-watching, nature trails, game room, gift shop on-site. Amish country, cheese factories, craft shops, hiking trails, golf in area.

CUISINE
Breakfast for houseguests only, lunch and dinner reservations required.

DIRECTIONS
From Millersburg: Rtes 62/39 E for 2 blocks, L on Rte 241 N for 1.9 miles R, E on County Rd. 203 for 1.5 miles.

---

1 Guestoom Handicap Accessible
Conference Facilities for 55 • Credit Cards Accepted
Designated Smoking Areas

Danville, OH

The White Oak Inn

740-599-6107
www.whiteoakinn.com
Yvonne@ecr.net
29683 Walhonding Road (SR715)
Danville, OH 43014

Select Registry Member *Since 1989*
Innkeepers/Owners
YVONNE AND IAN MARTIN

WE INVITE YOU to visit our turn-of-the-century farmhouse in its quiet wooded country setting. The inn has ten comfortable, antique-filled guest rooms, three with fireplaces. Savor one of our generous country meals. Relax on the front porch rockers and gliders or in the common room with fireplace and square grand piano. Explore the surrounding area and shop for Amish quilts and cheeses, new and antique furniture, or Longaberger baskets. Enjoy outdoor activities such as canoeing, hiking and bird-watching. Murder mysteries and other packages are available. Our romantic guest house is perfect for honeymoons or anniversaries. The inn is ideal for business meetings and retreats.

Suitable for Children Over 12 • Non-Smoking Inn
Conference Facilities for 16 • AMEX, Visa, MC, Disc Accepted
Reservations Accepted Through Travel Agents

TRADITIONAL COUNTRY INN

RATES
10 rooms, $85/$140 B&B.
3 rooms have fireplaces.
Packages available.
Open year-round.

ATTRACTIONS
Hiking, cycling, canoeing, golf, tour Amish country, Roscoe Village, Longaberger basket tour, numerous gift, antique, quilt shops and wineries.

CUISINE
Full breakfast included, evening fine dining by advance reservation, lunches for groups. BYOB.

DIRECTIONS
From I-71: Rte 36 E or Rte 13 S to Mount Vernon. Then Rte 36 E 13 miles to Rte 715 E. From I-77: Rte 36 W 35 miles to Rte 206 N. 2 miles to Rte 715. 715 W for 4 miles.

Dresden, OH

The Inn at Dresden

800-373-7336
740-754-1122 Fax 740-754-9856
www.theinnatdresden.com
info@theinnatdresden.com
209 Ames Drive, Dresden, OH 43821

Select Registry Member *Since 2000*
Innkeeper/Owner
Patricia Lyall

TUCKED AWAY AMONG THE ROLLING HILLS of southeastern Ohio, The Inn at Dresden provides the perfect setting for a relaxing getaway with family and friends, or a quiet weekend with someone special. Originally built by Dave Longaberger, founder of Longaberger Baskets, this elegant Tudor home offers guests a panoramic view of Dresden and the surrounding countryside. Guests at the Inn enjoy an evening social hour and a full buffet breakfast. Individually decorated rooms feature VCRs, CD players and special ammenities such as wraparound private decks, two person Jacuzzi tubs and gas-log fireplaces.

Elegant Village Breakfast Inn

RATES

10 rooms, $85/$170 per night. Each room is individually decorated to depict the area. Many rooms have fireplaces, decks and Jacuzzi tubs. *Open year-round.*

ATTRACTIONS

Visit the famous Longaberger Basket Company and Homestead, nearby Roscoe Village; spend an afternoon at the Wilds. Guests enjoy visiting pottery outlets in Zanesville, and the quaint shops of Dresden. Local championship golf courses and Amish country nearby.

CUISINE

The Inn provides an evening social hour and full breakfast. Menus are available for all restaurants in the surrounding area.

DIRECTIONS

The Inn may be reached by state Rte 60. N from Zanesville, or state Rte 16 from Newark or Coshocton.

1 Guestroom Handicap Accessible
Conference Facilities for 12 • Visa, MC, AMEX, Disc Accepted
Non-Smoking Inn • Reservations Accepted Through Travel Agents

Rockbridge, OH

Glenlaurel-A Scottish Country Inn

800-809-REST
740-385-4070 Fax 740-385-9669
www.glenlaurelinn.com
Michael@Glenlaurelinn.com
14940 Mount Olive Road, Rockbridge, OH 43149

Select Registry Member *Since 1998*
Innkeeper/Owner
MICHAEL DANIELS

ANCHORED ATOP A RIDGE overlooking Camusfearna Gorge, the Glenlaurel Manor House, Carriage House and Cottages of Thistle Ridge have the look of the Scottish countryside and the feel of times gone by. Sumptuous fine dining in the European tradition. Music to melt the senses. Intimate fireside conversation. Lazy kidless afternoons. Hot tub sedation. Dozing after 7 am. Delightful breakfast choices. A morning walk in the gorge with ne'er a soul in sight. All in the Hocking Hills of southeastern Ohio. Glenlaurel—the anniversary remembered...

ELEGANT COUNTRY BREAKFAST INN

RATES

3 suites, 4 rooms, 10 cottages.
$154/$254 weekends.
$124/$204 weeknights; B&B.
Open year-round.

ATTRACTIONS

Whether you like to hike, bike, ride horses, fish, golf, canoe, antique or walk in nature's silent splendor, the Hocking Hills region fulfills.

CUISINE

Dinner is a leisurely 5- to 7-course experience. Full breakfast choices. No alcoholic beverages are sold.

DIRECTIONS

Rte 33 SE from Columbus through Lancaster, then 12 miles to exit 180/Laurelville, then R onto 180 for 4.8 miles, then L at Glenlaurel sign for .5 miles.

---

1 Guestroom, 3 Common Rooms Handicap Accessible
Conference Facilities for 20 • MC, Visa, AMEX, Disc Accepted
Non-Smoking Inn • Reservations Accepted Through Travel Agents

Logan, OH

The Inn At Cedar Falls

800-653-2557
740-385-7489 Fax 740-385-0820
www.innatcedarfalls.com
innatcedarfalls@hockinghills.com
21190 State Route 374, Logan, OH 43138

Select Registry Member *Since 1989*
Innkeeper
ELLEN GRINSFELDER

THE RESTORED AND COMFORTABLY RUSTIC 1840 log houses are an open kitchen-dining room, serving the most refined of American cuisine, prepared from home-grown produce. Antique appointed guestrooms in a barn-like structure have rockers and writing desks and offer sweeping views of meadows, woods and wildlife. Secluded, fully-equipped 19th century log cabins accommodate up to four. Two common rooms service small business retreats as well. The rugged and beautiful Hocking Hills State Parks with glorious caves and waterfalls flanks the Inn on three sides. Special events are scheduled year-round in the calendar of events. Midweek special packages.

RUSTIC COUNTRY INN

RATES
9 rooms, $75/$102 B&B.
6 cabins, $125/$205 B&B.
2 cabins with whirlpool tub, $160/$240 B&B
Open year-round, cabins only on Christmas.

ATTRACTIONS
The Inn's 60 acres provides a nature retreat. Outdoor enthusiasts, hikers, photographers and cyclists enjoy recreational activites. Swimming, canoeing, antiquing, golfing and artisan shops are nearby. Call for our calendar of events.

CUISINE
Watch meals being created in the open kitchen. Hearty country breakfasts, delectable brown bag lunches, sumptuous dinners by candlelight. Patio dining in the warm months.

DIRECTIONS
From Columbus: U.S. Rte 33 S to Logan-Bremen Exit 664 S, R on 664, 9.5 miles, L on St. Rte 374, Inn is 1 mile on L. From Cincy: 71 N to Washington CH at 35 E to 22 E. In Circleville, access 56 E to St. Rte 374, turn L, Inn is 2 1/2 miles on R.

---

2 Guestrooms Handicap Accessible • Suitable for Children
MC, Visa Accepted • Conference Facilities for 20
Designated Smoking Areas • Reservations Accepted Through Travel Agents

West Union, OH

Murphin Ridge Inn

937-544-2263
877-687-7446 Fax 937-544-8151
www.murphinridgeinn.com
murphinn@bright.net
750 Murphin Ridge Road, West Union, OH 45693

Select Registry Member *Since 1992*
Innkeepers / Owners
Sherry and Darryl McKenney

SELECTED BY *NATIONAL GEOGRAPHIC TRAVELER* as one of the top 54 Inns – this Revolutionary War land grant is the setting for this 142-acre prize-winning Inn. The brick 1828 farmhouse blends three dining rooms, original fireplaces and an art and antique gallery. Guests enjoy homegrown and deliciously prepared soups, salads, entrees and desserts. Our chef and kitchen staff make dining memorable. The guest house and woodland cabins are custom furnished by David T. Smith. Some rooms have fireplaces, some porches. Cabins all have fireplaces, whirlpools and porches. Relax on the front porch and view the Appalachian Highlands or sit by the campfire and enjoy the night sky. Journey to the local Amish shops, go hiking, birding or visit the Serpant Mound. Golf and ski close by. Perfect for retreats and conferences.

Handicap Access Available • Suitable for Children• Non-Smoking Inn
Conference Facilities for 20 • MC, Visa Accepted

Traditional Country Inn

RATES
10 rooms; all private baths, $85/$135 B&B.
NEW Woodland cabins $130/$175. All cabins with fireplaces and whirlpools.
Closed first 2 weeks in January.

ATTRACTIONS
On-site: swimming, hiking, tennis, shuffleboard, basketball, horseshoes, croquet, bird-watching, art and antique gallery, local Amish country.

CUISINE
Country Inn fine dining for Inn guests and by reservation. Full breakfast for overnight guests. BYOB guest house only.

DIRECTIONS
From Cincinnati: Rte 32 E R on Unity Rd. 2.4 miles to Wheat Ridge Rd. L at stop sign 2.6 miles to Murphin Ridge Rd. L.
From Columbus: Rte 23 to 32 W, L on 41 S to Dunkinsville R on Wheat Ridge Rd. 2.5 miles R on Murphin Ridge Rd.

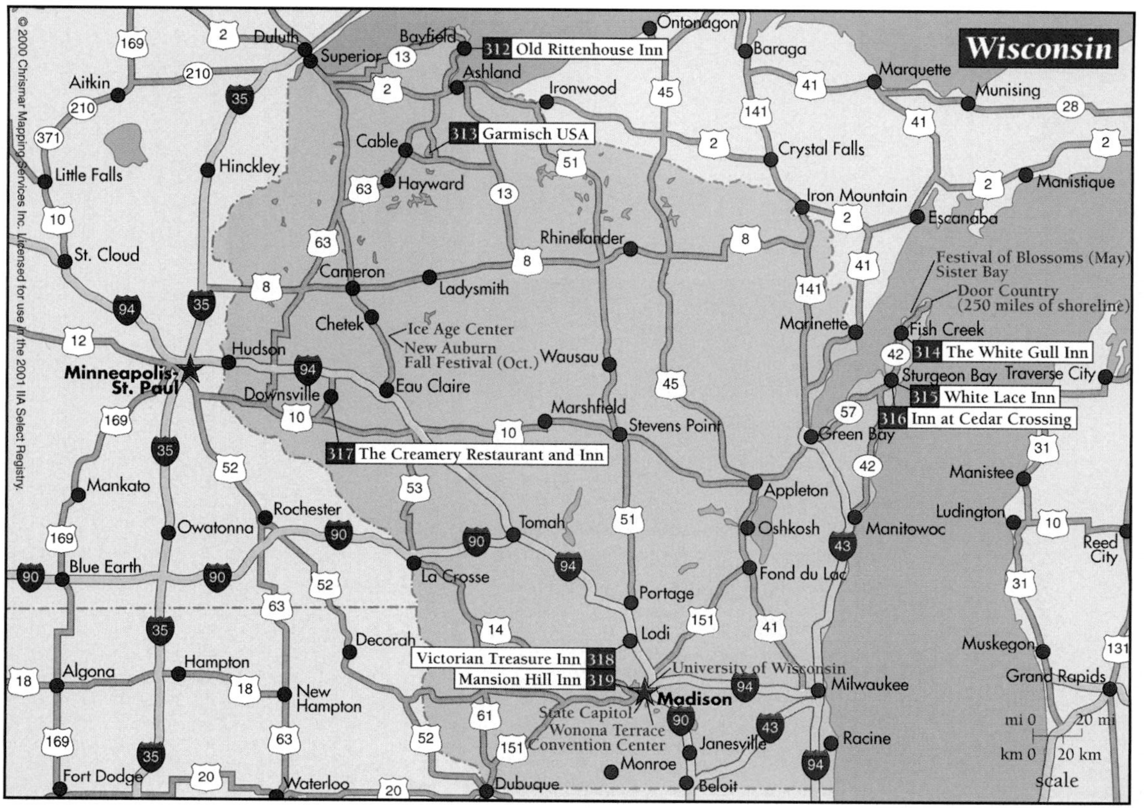
Wisconsin
312 Old Rittenhouse Inn
313 Garmisch USA
314 The White Gull Inn
315 White Lace Inn
316 Inn at Cedar Crossing
317 The Creamery Restaurant and Inn
Victorian Treasure Inn 318
Mansion Hill Inn 319
Festival of Blossoms (May)
Sister Bay
Door Country
(250 miles of shoreline)
Ice Age Center
New Auburn
Fall Festival (Oct.)
University of Wisconsin
State Capitol
Wonona Terrace
Convention Center
Madison
Minneapolis-St. Paul
Duluth
Superior
Bayfield
Ashland
Ontonagon
Baraga
Marquette
Munising
Aitkin
Ironwood
Cable
Hayward
Crystal Falls
Little Falls
Hinckley
Iron Mountain
Manistique
Escanaba
St. Cloud
Rhinelander
Cameron
Ladysmith
Chetek
Marinette
Fish Creek
Hudson
Wausau
Sturgeon Bay
Traverse City
Downsville
Eau Claire
Marshfield
Stevens Point
Green Bay
Manistee
Mankato
Appleton
Rochester
Tomah
Ludington
Owatonna
Oshkosh
Manitowoc
Reed City
Blue Earth
La Crosse
Fond du Lac
Portage
Lodi
Decorah
Muskegon
Hampton
Algona
New Hampton
Grand Rapids
Milwaukee
Janesville
Racine
Monroe
Fort Dodge
Waterloo
Dubuque
Beloit
mi 0 20 mi
km 0 20 km
scale
© 2000 Chrismar Mapping Services Inc. Licensed for use in the 2001 IIA Select Registry.

Bayfield, WI

Old Rittenhouse Inn

888-560-4667
715-779-5111 Fax 715-779-5887
www.rittenhouseinn.com
frontdsk@rittenhouseinn.com
301 Rittenhouse Avenue, Bayfield, WI 54814

©Don Albrecht

VICTORIAN LODGING AND DINING with guestrooms in two historic Queen Anne-style mansions and one private cottage. A stay at the Old Rittenhouse Inn combines an evening of romance and elegance with gourmet cuisine and comfortable lodging. Guestrooms are beautifully appointed with period antique furnishings. Amenities include wood-burning fireplaces, private baths, breath-taking views of Lake Superior, and luxury whirlpools. Open all year offering romantic winter get-aways, wine and beer tasting weekends, wassail dinner concerts and murder mystery weekends.

2 Guestrooms Handicap Accessible • Suitable for Children
Conference Facilities for 30 • Visa, MC Accepted
Non-Smoking Inn • Reservations Accepted Through Travel Agents

Select Registry Member *Since 1980*
Innkeepers/Owners
JERRY AND MARY PHILLIPS

TRADITIONAL VILLAGE INN

RATES

7 rooms, $99/$159 B&B.
7 rooms, $159/$179 whirlpool.
3 suites, $179/$249 whirlpool.
1 cottage, $229 whirlpool.
All have private baths.
Open year-round.

ATTRACTIONS

Apostle Island's National Lakeshore, sailing, sea kayaking, island tours, summer music/theater, Big Top Chautauqua, shopping, golfing, downhill and cross-country skiing. Fine dining restaurant on location serving breakfast, lunch, and dinner. Weddings, corporate retreats, private parties.

CUISINE

Seasonally fresh, gourmet cuisine with an emphasis on the freshest available regional delicacies. Breakfast, lunch and dinner. Full bar and extensive wine list. Open to the public.

DIRECTIONS

Duluth E Hwy 2 for 60 miles, to N on Hwy 13 for 20 miles, to Bayfield. Located on Hwy 13 (Rittenhouse Ave.), in the heart of Bayfield.

Garmisch USA

800-794-2204
715-794-2204 Fax 715-794-2205
www.garmischresort.com
garmisch@win.bright.net
HC73 Box 700, Cable, WI 54821

Select Registry Member *Since 2000*
Managers/Owners
BRUCE AND SHELBY NIEBERGALL

NESTLED QUIETLY IN THE MIDST of the Chequamagon National Forest on Lake Namakagon, this historic Inn offers rooms, each uniquely charming with its own warm fireplace and many with a breathtaking lake view. The architecture is old-world, handcrafted by local artisans in the 1920s as a wealthy family's northwoods vacation retreat. The Inn provides luxury accommodations with an extensive art collection and impresive fish and wildlife mounts. The spectacular lake view from the dining room provides the perfect setting to enjoy a hearty breakfast or lunch or watch a glorious sunset while enjoying your favorite American or German cuisine.

RUSTIC WATERSIDE RESORT

RATES

12 rooms/suites, $85/$135.
11 guest homes, $675/$1200.
Uniquely different. Each have private bath, telephone, color TV, fireplace, many with deck.
Open May to mid March.

ATTRACTIONS

Beautiful Lake Namakagon is one of the best all-around fishing lakes in Wisconsin. In summer enjoy hiking, biking, boating, swimming, canoeing. Fall brings legendary colors of the northwoods. In winter, experience the best in xc-skiing, snowmobiling, snowshoeing.

CUISINE

Breakfast, lunch and dinner. Full liquor and wine service available. The Bierstube Lounge provides casual food service daily.

DIRECTIONS

Eau Claire Hwy 53 N to Trego, then Hwy 63 N to Cable (47 miles), then R on Hwy M for 8 1/2 miles then L on Garmisch Rd. for 2 miles to resort entrance.

Pets Accepted • Suitable for Children • Conference Facilities for 15
Designated Smoking Areas • Visa, MC, Disc, CB, Diners Accepted

Fish Creek, WI

White Gull Inn

920-868-3517
Fax 920-868-2367
www.whitegullinn.com
innkeeper@whitegullinn.com
4225 Main Street, P.O. Box 160
Fish Creek, WI 54212

Select Registry Member *Since 1979*
Innkeepers
ANDY AND JAN COULSON

ESTABLISHED IN 1896, this white clapboard Inn is tucked away in the scenic bayside village of Fish Creek, on Wisconsin's Door Peninsula. Turn-of-the-century antiques, fireplaces and meticulously restored and decorated rooms and cottages, several with whirlpools, provide a warm, hospitable atmosphere. Famous for hearty breakfasts, lunches and candlelit dinners, the Inn is renowned for its unique, traditional Door County fish boils, featuring locally caught whitefish cooked outside over an open fire.

TRADITIONAL VILLAGE INN

RATES
6 rooms, $115/$175 EP.
7 suites, $175/$275 EP.
4 cottages, $185/$300 EP.
All private baths.
Open year-round.

ATTRACTIONS
Golf, tennis, swimming, sailing, hiking, biking, cross-country skiing, antique shops, art galleries, theatre, music festival.

CUISINE
Breakfast, lunch, dinner. Wine and beer available.

DIRECTIONS
Milwaukee I-43 for 98 miles to Green Bay, then Rte 57 N for 39 miles to Sturgeon Bay; N on Rte 42 for 25 miles to Fish Creek, L at stop sign for 3 blks.

1 Guestroom Handicap Accessible • Non-Smoking Inn
Suitable for Children in Cottages • MC, Visa, AMEX, Disc, Diners Accepted
Reservations Accepted Through Travel Agents

Sturgeon Bay, WI

White Lace Inn

877-948-5223

920-743-1105 Fax 920-743-8180
www.WhiteLaceInn.com
romance@whitelaceinn.com

16 North 5th Avenue, Sturgeon Bay, WI 54235

Select Registry Member *Since 1988*
Innkeepers / Owners
DENNIS AND BONNIE STATZ

TRADITIONAL IN TOWN
BREAKFAST INN

RATES
13 rooms, $119/$199.
5 suites, $199/$239.
Nov.-April weeknights $58/$150.
Open year-round.

ATTRACTIONS
Gardens on-site. State parks, beaches, biking, cross-country skiing, summer theatre, art galleries, shops, golf, tennis and sailing.

CUISINE
Breakfast, refreshments and evening treats included.

DIRECTIONS
Hwy 42 or 57 N to Sturgeon Bay. Business Rte 42/57 into town across Old Bridge. L on 5th Ave. 1/2 block on 5th Ave. to Inn on R.

ROMANCE AND RELAXATION IN DOOR COUNTY begin as you follow a winding garden pathway that links this charming inn's four historic homes. Guestrooms are furnished for a special getaway with period antiques, an oversized whirlpool and/or an inviting fireplace, and down comforters on wonderfully ornate beds. Suites include whirlpool and fireplace, CD stereo, TV/VCR. A warm welcome awaits as guests are greeted with lemonade or hot chocolate and cookies. Mornings start with a delicious full breakfast. Bonnie and Dennis and their staff invite you to enjoy their Door County hospitality.

---

1 Guestroom Handicap Accessible • Non-Smoking Inn
Suitable for Children Over 6 • Visa, MC, Disc, AMEX Accepted
Reservations Accepted Through Travel Agents

Sturgeon Bay, WI

Inn at Cedar Crossing

920-743-4200
Fax 920-743-4422
www.innatcedarcrossing.com
innkeeper@innatcedarcrossing.com
336 Louisiana Street, Sturgeon Bay, WI 54235

Select Registry Member *Since 1990*
Innkeeper/Owner
TERRY SMITH

TRADITIONAL IN TOWN INN

WARM HOSPITALITY, elegant antique-filled guest rooms and creative regional cuisine are tradition at this Door County Inn, National Register of Historic Places. Cozy fireplaces, room service and evening refreshments await pampered guests. Exceptional furnishings include oversized canopied beds, double whirlpool tubs, private porches, inviting fireplaces. Acclaimed dining features fresh seasonal ingredients, enticingly prepared entrees, scratch bakery, sinful desserts, select wines, casual pub. Set in the beauty and culture of Wisconsin's Door peninsula.

RATES
9 rooms (6 with fireplaces), $110/$180 B&B.
Winter dinner pkgs. $129/$199.
Open year-round.

ATTRACTIONS
Sailing, hiking, skiing, beaches, five state parks, galleries, shops, summer theatre, golf, historic districts, maritime museum, restored waterfront.

CUISINE
Breakfast, lunch, dinner, evening refreshments, scratch bakery. Wine service, pub and full liquor.

DIRECTIONS
From Green Bay: Hwy 57 N to Sturgeon Bay, Bus. Rte 42/57 into town. Cross old bridge then L on 4th and L on Louisiana St. to Inn.

---

1 Common Room Handicap Accessible • Children Access Limited
Conference Facilities for 25 • Visa, MC, AMEX, Disc Accepted
Non-Smoking Inn

Downsville, WI

The Creamery Restaurant and Inn

715-664-8354
Fax 715-664-8353
www.creameryrestaurant-inn.com
visit@creameryrestaurant-inn.com
P.O. Box 22, Downsville, WI 54735

Select Registry Member *Since 1991*
Contact
JANE THOMAS DEFLORIN, BRUCE, JOHN, DAVID AND RICHARD THOMAS

CONTEMPORARY VILLAGE INN

THE REMODELED TURN-OF-THE-CENTURY Downsville Cooperative Creamery building, set in the hills of western Wisconsin, contains twelve large guest rooms featuring cherry woodwork, handmade tiles, and roomy jacuzzis. Its woodland setting adjacent to the Red Cedar River, along with a reputation for exceptional cuisine, a large selection of fine wines and friendly staff make for a relaxing and pleasurable stay. Two fully-equipped executive conference rooms are also available. The adjacent Gift Shop and Bakery feature local hand-crafted items and unique gifts, along with fresh breads, cookies and pies.

RATES
11 rooms.
$115/$130 per night B&B.
1 suite, $160 per night B&B.
Open year-round.

ATTRACTIONS
Hiking, biking, skiing, canoeing and bird-watching on the adjacent Red Cedar State Trail. Golfing, historic sites and museums, antique shops and local trout farm nearby. Many seasonal events in the local communities of the Chippewa Valley.

CUISINE
Continental breakfast included with your room. Luncheons, appetizers and dinners available in restaurant, lounge or on the outdoor garden terrace during the summer. Picnic lunches available. All meals, desserts and breads are handmade on-site for guests.

DIRECTIONS
From I-94, exit 41 at Menomonie, Hwy 25 S 10 miles, L at CTH"C". 1/3 mile on R (70 miles E of St. Paul, MN).

Handicap Access Available • Suitable for Children
Conference Facilities for 30 • Credit Cards Accepted

Lodi, WI

Victorian Treasure Inn

608-592-5199
Fax 608-592-7147
www.victoriantreasure.com
innkeeper@victoriantreasure.com
115 Prairie Street, Lodi, WI 53555

Select Registry Member *Since 1998*
Innkeepers / Owners
TODD AND KIMBERLY SEIDL

TUCKED AWAY in the scenic Wisconsin River Valley, you will find a true Victorian Treasure—a luxury inn discovery. Gracious hospitality and casual elegance in two 1890s Queen Anne Victorians; all rooms individually decorated in lovely antiques, florals and lace. Romantic whirlpool suites with fireplaces, canopy beds. Caring owner innkeepers fuss over details—meticulous rooms, luxurious amenities, attentive service. Featured on national PBS, called 'One of America's truest and finest bed and breakfast inns' by Gail Greco. Only three hours from Chicago Loop, four hours from Minneapolis. Visit our website, then come discover a treasure. AAA ◆◆◆.

ELEGANT VILLAGE BREAKFAST INN

RATES
7 rooms.
5 suites with whirlpools.
4 with fireplaces, $95/$195.
Includes full breakfast.
Weekday packages.
Open year-round.

ATTRACTIONS
Nestled between the Capitol City of Madison and Baraboo, Devils Lake/Dells, close to Spring Green/Taliesen/APT. Quiet, Victorian town in the heart of South-Central Wisconsin, yet close to major attractions. On Nat'l Scenic Ice Age Trail in the Wisconsin River Valley.

CUISINE
Enjoy a memorable, full breakfast as featured on PBS "Country Inn Cooking with Gail Greco." Complimentary evening wine and Wisconsin cheese reception provided. Casual room service menu available.

DIRECTIONS
20 miles N of Madison on I-90/94, Exit Hwy 60/Lodi W. Four miles to Main St./Hwy 113, continue straight on 60 one block, the first R turn is Prairie St.

Non-Smoking Inn • Credit Cards Accepted
Reservations Accepted Through Travel Agents

Madison, WI

Mansion Hill Inn

800-798-9070
608-255-3999 Fax 608-255-2217
www.mansionhillinn.com

Select Registry Member *Since 1997*
General Manager
ANKE CRAMBLIT

424 North Pinckney Street, Madison, WI 53703

MANSION HILL INN is an 1858 Romanesque Revival mansion located in the historic district. Our guest rooms are filled with select period antiques, hand-carved marble fireplaces and floor-to-ceiling arched windows. Rooms have sumptuous baths with whirlpool tubs or steam showers. You'll be greeted with complimentary spirits and refreshments upon arrival, given evening turndown service, and in the morning, a silver service continental-plus breakfast will be delivered to your door.

ELEGANT IN TOWN INN

RATES
11 rooms including 2 suites, $120/$340 B&B.
Open year-round.

ATTRACTIONS
Four blocks to State Capitol, shopping, theater, museums, downtown, historic district. One block from Lake Mendota, farmers' market and restaurants.

CUISINE
Many fine restaurants within walking distance. Complimentary refreshments.

DIRECTIONS
Hwy 151 to State Capitol, turn R on Wisconsin, 4 blocks to R on Gilman 1 block to R on Pinckney.

Suitable for Children Over 13 • Non-Smoking Inn
Conference Facilities for 20 • Visa, MC, AMEX Accepted
Reservations Accepted Through Travel Agents

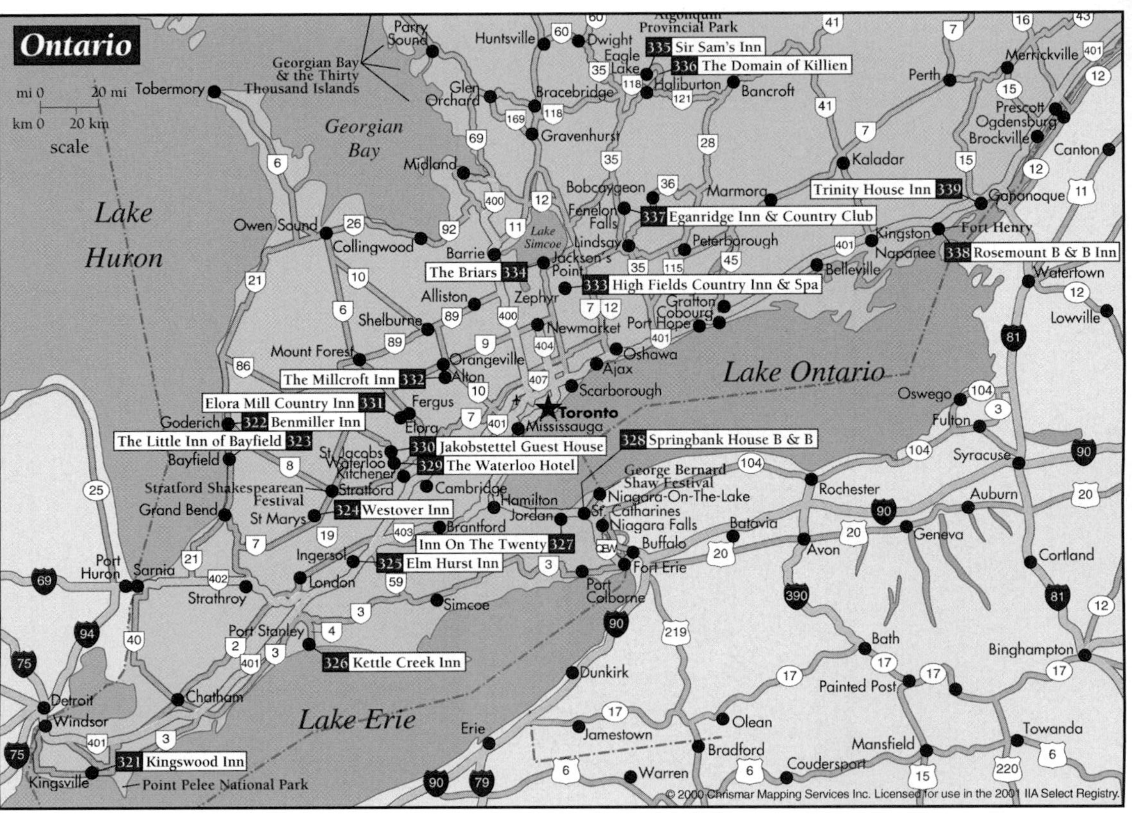

Ontario
mi 0 20 mi
km 0 20 km
scale
Lake Huron
Georgian Bay
Lake Ontario
Lake Erie
Lake Simcoe
Georgian Bay & the Thirty Thousand Islands
Algonquin Provincial Park
Point Pelee National Park
321 Kingswood Inn
322 Benmiller Inn
323 The Little Inn of Bayfield
324 Westover Inn
325 Elm Hurst Inn
326 Kettle Creek Inn
327 Inn On The Twenty
328 Springbank House B & B
329 The Waterloo Hotel
330 Jakobstettel Guest House
331 Elora Mill Country Inn
332 The Millcroft Inn
333 High Fields Country Inn & Spa
334 The Briars
335 Sir Sam's Inn
336 The Domain of Killien
337 Eganridge Inn & Country Club
338 Rosemount B & B Inn
339 Trinity House Inn
Toronto
George Bernard Shaw Festival
Stratford Shakespearean Festival
© 2000 Chrismar Mapping Services Inc. Licensed for use in the 2001 IIA Select Registry.

Kingsville, ONT Canada

Kingswood Inn

519-733-3248
Fax 519-733-8734
www.lsol.com/kingswood
kingswd@mnsi.net
101 Mill Street W, Kingsville, Ontario N9Y 1W4

Located in the heart of Victorian Kingsville, the Kingswood Inn is the perfect romantic getaway. Once you enter the gate, the tranquility of the three-acre grounds surrounds you. Beautiful gardens, mature trees and garden swings encourage you to unwind inside the walled park-like setting. Built in 1859, in the octagonal style, the Inn is architecturally unique. Lovingly preserved and luxuriously furnished, it boasts hardwood flooring, antiques, fine art and personal treasures. Relax in the spacious drawing room, or curl up in front of the fireplace in the cozy library. Warm hospitality keeps guests coming back. Canada Select ★★★★.

Select Registry Member *Since 2001*
Innkeepers / Owners
HELEN AND JAY KOOP
BARB AND BOB DICK

ELEGANT IN TOWN
BREAKFAST INN

RATES
5 rooms, $95/$280 CDN
Immaculate guestrooms feature fine linens, robes, phones, central air-conditioning and private baths. *Open February - the middle of December.*

ATTRACTIONS
HERE: outdoor pool, bikes available, gift shop, croquet. NEARBY: wineries, golf, nature trails, birdwatching, antiques, historic sites, caneoing, Point Pelee National Park, Colasanti Tropical Gardens, casino, Jack Miner's Bird Sanctuary, xc-skiing.

CUISINE
An abundant breakfast is served in elegant style. Refreshments are always available. Fine dining within walking distance of the inn.

DIRECTIONS
From Toronto: 401W to Hwy 77 exit, S to Leamington, R onto Hwy 3 W to Rd. 29, turn L to Kingsville.
From Detroit: Hwy 3 E to Rd. 29, turn R to Kingsville.

Suitable for Children Over 12 • Non-Smoking Inn • Visa, MC Accepted
Reservations Accepted Through Travel Agents

Goderich, ONT Canada

Benmiller Inn

800-265-1711

519-524-2191 Fax 519-524-5150

www.benmiller.on.ca

benmillerinn@odyssey.on.ca

R.R. #4, Goderich, ONT Canada N7A 3Y1

NESTLED IN THE ROLLING HILLS of the Maitland River Valley, Benmiller Inn is housed in four beautifully restored pioneer mills and their owners' homes. Each guest room is uniquely furnished with antiques and offers an incredible view of our flowing rivers or wooded hillsides. Some rooms have a fireplace or double Jacuzzi. Our exceptional dining room features creative local cuisine. Indulge in a wide array of spa services. Three theaters nearby offer acclaimed performances. Great golf courses, wonderful fishing sites, delightful galleries, museums and excellent shopping. Come, relax and enjoy our hospitality. AAA ◆◆◆◆.

Select Registry Member *Since 1995*
Innkeeper
RANDY STODDART
Director of Operations
SUE MURRAY

TRADITIONAL COUNTRY INN

RATES
47 rooms.
$115/$312 B&B.
$173/$350 MAP, CDN.
Open year-round.

ATTRACTIONS
Full service spa, indoor pool, fishing, cycling, nature/ski trails, snowshoeing, golfing, three theaters nearby, theme weekends, art galleries, museums, specialty shopping, fireside lounge, patio, afternoon tea.

CUISINE
Excellent wine list, liquor with good choice of single malt whisky to sample. All meals available including afternoon tea and bountiful Sunday brunch.

DIRECTIONS
From Provincial Hwy #8 between Clinton and Goderich, turn onto Huron Rd. #1 (at Benmiller sign) 3 kms. to Benmiller Inn.

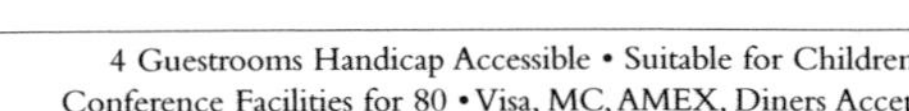

4 Guestrooms Handicap Accessible • Suitable for Children
Conference Facilities for 80 • Visa, MC, AMEX, Diners Accepted
Designated Smoking Areas • Reservations Accepted Through Travel Agents

Bayfield, ONT Canada

The Little Inn of Bayfield

800-565-1832
519-565-2611 Fax 519-565-5474
www.littleinn.com
innkeeper@littleinn.com
P.O. Box 100, Main Street
Bayfield, ONT Canada N0M 1G0

Select Registry Member *Since 1991*
Innkeepers
PATRICK AND GAYLE WATERS

A N ORIGINAL COUNTRY INN ON A GREAT LAKE, with an impeccable pedigree dating back to the 1830s; a landmark in the heart of a heritage village. With up-to-the-minute amenities, the Inn offers distinctive guest rooms, individually and attractively decorated with an emphasis on comfort, most with double whirlpools, fireplaces and private verandas. The snug bar displays the *Wine Spectator* Award of Excellence and the kitchen produces justifiably famed regional and seasonal dishes. Enjoy county roads and trails, a guided wilderness walk, a fly-fishing expedition, a maple syrup festival, a trip to Stratford. An ideal place for rest or romance. AAA ◆◆◆◆.

TRADITIONAL VILLAGE INN

RATES
29 en suite rooms—many with double whirlpools, verandas and fireplaces, AC.
Doubles: $145/$275 EP.
Doubles from $225/$350 MAP.
CDM.
Open year-round.

ATTRACTIONS
Fly-fish, cycle, golf, wilderness walks, swim, horseback ride, tennis, xc-skiing, shop, theatres, picnics, gourmet cooking classes, wine tastings, Christmas and New Year's galas, single malt tastings, or just sit in the gardens with a good book.

CUISINE
Four Diamond Award restaurant, *Wine Spectator* Award of Excellence, extensive cellar open for tours and tastings. Chef Jean Jacques Chappuis' acclaimed kitchen presents dishes from local fields, forests, streams and lakes.

DIRECTIONS
From Port Huron, MI: Hwy 402 E to Hwy 21 N to Bayfield. From Toronto: Hwy 401 W to Hwy 8 W. In Seaforth, follow signs to Bayfield. From Windsor: Hwy 401 E to Hwy 21 N to Bayfield.

---

1 Guestrooms Handicap Accessible • Suitable for Children • Pets Allowed
Conference Facilities for 80 • Visa, MC, AMEX, Diners Accepted
Designated Smoking Areas • Reservations Accepted Through Travel Agents

St. Marys, ONT Canada

Westover Inn

519-284-2977
Fax 519-284-4043
www.westoverinn.com
innkeeper@westoverinn.com
300 Thomas Street, P.O. Box 280
St. Marys, ONT Canada N4X 1B1

Select Registry Member *Since 1995*
Innkeepers
JULIE DOCKER-JOHNSON AND STEPHEN MCCOTTER

THE INN BEGAN as a limestone Victorian mansion built in 1867, and now offers 19 acres of landscaped grounds, three unique buildings housing 22 charming guest rooms, a licensed outdoor patio and two dining rooms serving award-winning regional cuisine. Private facilities available for conferences, meetings and weddings. One of 64 restaurants in Canada to receive two stars in Anne Hardy's *Where to Eat in Canada.* Our guests describe us best-"Unparalleled." 'When Christopher Plummer is performing at the Stratford Festival, he will only stay at the Westover Inn.' AAA ◆◆◆◆(Dining). AAA ◆◆◆(Accommodations).

TRADITIONAL VILLAGE INN

RATES
19 rooms, $115/$200 CDN.
3 suites, $185/$250 CDN.
Open year-round.

ATTRACTIONS
Historic walking tours, Stratford Festival, antiquing, cross-country skiing, outdoor swimming pool, bicycling, golf, tennis and tube sliding.

CUISINE
Open daily for breakfast, lunch, dinner. Four Diamond CAA/AAA dining. Licensed under the LLBO.

DIRECTIONS
Hwy 401 exit Hwy 8 W to Kitchener, take Hwy 7/8 to Stratford, turn L onto Erie St. (Hwy 7) follow to St. Marys Perth Line 9, turn R, go thru town turn L on Thomas St.

Suitable for Children • Conference Facilities for 40
Non-Smoking Inn • Visa, AMEX, MC, Diners/ EN Accepted
Reservations Accepted Through Travel Agents

Ingersoll, ONT Canada

Elm Hurst Inn

800-561-5321
519-485-5321 Fax 519-485-6579
www.elmjurstinn.com
accommodations@elmhurstinn.com
Highway 401 and Plank Line Rd., P.O. Box 123
Ingersoll, ONT Canada N5C 3K1

Select Registry Member *Since 1996*
Innkeeper
Patrine Frey

Traditional Country Inn

OUR COUNTRY INN is nestled amongst century-old maple trees. Our spacious guest rooms are uniquely decorated with picturesque views and some have a fireplace or a Jacuzzi. The Elm Hurst Inn also offers dining in its famous Victorian Mansion and is an ideal setting for any occasion. Enjoy our full-service spa with reflexology, aromatherapy, esthetic services, sauna, steam room and whirlpool. We are perfectly situated for great shopping, sightseeing and tourist attractions. We have a putting green, skating rink, interpretive trail, woodlands, a flowing creek and a picturesque pond on our 37 acres of land.

RATES

43 rooms, $126 CDN, B&B.
6 suites, $150/$189 CDN, B&B.
Open year-round.

ATTRACTIONS

Spa, games room, fitness room, gift shop, walking trail, putting green, croquet, horseshoes, badminton, golf, skating, live theatre, racetrack, swimming, volleyball, cross-country skiing.

CUISINE

Breakfast, lunch and dinner in our Victorian Mansion Restaurant. Alcoholic beverages available in restaurant.

DIRECTIONS

One hour W of Toronto, Ontario, and 30 minutes E of London, Ontario, on Hwy 401 at Plank Line Rd. exit 218.

Handicap Access Available • Suitable for Children
Conference Facilities for 200 • Credit Cards Accepted
Reservations Accepted Through Travel Agents

Port Stanley, ONT Canada

Kettle Creek Inn

519-782-3388
Fax 519-782-4747
www.kettlecreekinn.com
kci@webgate.net
216 Joseph Street
Port Stanley, ONT Canada N5L 1C4

Select Registry Member *Since 1997*
Innkeepers / Owners
JEAN STRICKLAND AND
GARY VEDOVA

TRADITIONAL VILLAGE INN

NESTLED IN THE HEART of a small fishing village on Lake Erie, our 1849 inn offers unique accommodations and incredible cuisine. Cozy parlour with fireplace, intimate English pub, three dining rooms, outside patio, gazebo and gardens for fair weather dining. Five luxury suites with whirlpools, gas fireplaces in living room and private balconies, ten charming guest rooms. Each room features the paintings of local artists. Discover sandy beaches, world-class pickerel fishing, sailing and birding. Art galleries, boutiques and summer theatre…our tourist train. But don't forget the peace and romance of wintertime.

RATES
10 rooms, $110 B&B.
5 suites, $175/$195 CDN B&B.
Open year-round.

ATTRACTIONS
Hiking, swimming, sailing, golfing, tennis, cross-country skiing, biking, birding, summer theatre.

CUISINE
Breakfast, lunch and dinner. Fully licensed.

DIRECTIONS
Traveling E on Hwy 401 or 3, exit at Hwy 20; traveling W on Hwy 401 or 3, exit at Hwy 4, proceed S to Port Stanley. Inn located at main intersection.

---

2 Guestrooms Handicap Accessible • Suitable for Children Over 2
Conference Facilities for 26 • AMEX, Visa, MC, Diners/EN Accepted
Designated Smoking Areas • Reservations Accepted Through Travel Agents

Jordan, ONT Canada

Inn on the Twenty (formerly Vintner's Inn)

800-701-8074
905-562-5336 Fax 905-562-0009
www.innonthetwenty.com
vintners@niagara.net
3845 Main Street, Jordan, ONT Canada L0R 1S0

Select Registry Member *Since 1998*
Innkeeper/Owner
HELEN YOUNG

ELEGANT VILLAGE INN

THIS IS THE HEART OF ONTARIO'S WINE COUNTRY! Renovated winery building boasts twenty-six suites, all with fireplaces and Jacuzzi tubs; antiques and unique art abound. The Inn is located in a charming village with artisans and antique shops. Great golf, walking and bicycling opportunities, as well as the sophistication of Niagara's famous Shaw Theatre and the not-to-be-missed Falls. Our restaurant, On the Twenty, is a DiRoNa award winner and a leader in regional cuisine. Cave Spring Cellars, one of Canada's most prestigious wineries is our partner. The wine route beckons!

RATES
26 suites, 7 two-story, 19 one-level. 5 with private garden. $219/$325, CDN, May-Nov. *Open year-round.*

ATTRACTIONS
Wineries and vineyards of Niagara, close to Niagara Falls, Niagara-on-the-Lake, Shaw Theatre Festival. Great biking, hiking and golf.

CUISINE
On the Twenty is a DiRoNa Award restaurant with regional focus. Ontario wines and beers. Full bar.

DIRECTIONS
QEW Hwy to Victoria Ave. (Vineland Exit 57). L off Service Rd., S to Regional Rd. 81. Turn L and go through valley; first L at top of hill onto Main St.

17 Guestrooms Handicap Accessible • Suitable for Children Over 10
Conference Facilities for 130 • AMEX, Visa, MC, Diners Accepted
Non-Smoking Inn • Reservations Accepted Through Travel Agents

St. Catharines, ONT Canada

Springbank House Bed and Breakfast Inn

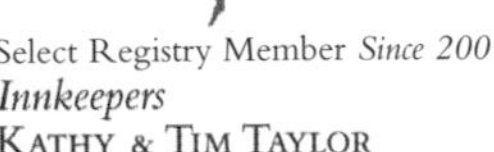

905-641-1713
Fax 905-641-7557
www.springbankhouse.com
kathyt@springbankhouse.com
68 Yates Street, St. Catharines, ONT Canada L2R 5R8

SPRINGBANK HOUSE is in the heart of one of the finest residential areas of Niagara, just minutes from all of the cultural and natural attractions of the region. Built 100 years ago, this grand stone home offers intimate, professional hospitality. Inside the massive oak front door, the house unfolds into a variety of special common areas - formal dining room, parlor, conservatory, inglenook and leather-paneled library. The air-conditioned bedrooms are adorned with the furnishings of five generations of the innkeepers' families. Walk to award-winning restaurants. Complete silver-service English breakfast, afternoon tea, and cookies at bedtime! Secluded garden swimming pool.

Non-Smoking Inn • Suitable for Children Over 12
Credit Cards Accepted
Reservations Accepted Through Travel Agents

Select Registry Member *Since 2001*
Innkeepers
KATHY & TIM TAYLOR

ELEGANT IN TOWN
BREAKFAST INN

RATES

3 rooms, $99/$145 CDN.
1 suite, $225 CDN.
Centrally air-conditioned. All bathrooms ensuite. Each room uniquely decorated with antiques and family treasures. Two king, one queen and one double.
Open year-round.

ATTRACTIONS

HERE: Swimming pool, historic walking tours, cycling.
NEARBY: Niagra Falls, Shaw Festival Theatre, golf, Niagara Wine Country, Welland Canal and Museum, day-trips to Buffalo and Toronto.

CUISINE

Complete silver-service English Breakfast highlighting the produce of one of North America's finest tender fruit and grape-growing regions. Afternoon tea and lemonade.

DIRECTIONS

Queen Elizabeth Way to Hwy 406 (exit 49). S to Westchester exit. Turn R to St. Paul St. W. Turn L to Yates St. R onto Yates to Inn.

Waterloo, ONT Canada

Waterloo Hotel

877-885-1890
519-885-2626 Fax 519-885-4774
www.waterloohotel.com
waterloohotel@aol.com
2 King St. N, Waterloo, ONT Canada N2J 2W7

Select Registry Member *Since 2001*
Innkeepers
BILL & MARION WEBER

EXPERIENCE THE BEST OF TOWN AND COUNTRY in an 1890 heritage hotel. Completely restored in 1997, the Waterloo Hotel has fourteen elegant rooms with fireplaces and fine antique furnishings. The decor is updated Victorian, with high ceilings, faux paint finishes, pine floors, lovely fabrics, carved walnut queen-sized beds and feather duvets. Amenities include data-port phones, air-conditioning, television and en-suite tiled Victorian bathrooms.

ELEGANT IN TOWN HOTEL

RATES
14 rooms
$130/$155 CDN
Full-service spa is adjacent to hotel. Spa program includes couples package.
Open year-round.

ATTRACTIONS
Specialty shops, including Waterloo County farmers' markets. Traditional Mennonite countryside. Village of St. Jacobs. Antiquing, country tours, theater, and Kitchener - Waterloo's annual Octoberfest.

CUISINE
Continental breakfast with espresso coffees and pastries served in the European-style cafe in the hotel. Fine dining to bistros and pubs within walking distance.

DIRECTIONS
From Hwy 401, exit at Hwy 8 W to Kitchener - Waterloo. Exit at Hwy 86 to Waterloo. Drive W on Bridgeport Rd. Turn L at King St. and drive 2 blocks S to the Hotel at Erb St. Turn L at Erb St. and enter parking area at the rear of Hotel.

Non-Smoking Inn

St. Jacobs, ONT Canada

Jakobstettel Guest House

519-664-2208
Fax 519-664-1326
www.selectregistry.com

16 Isabella Street, St. Jacobs, ONT Canada N0B 2N0

Select Registry Member *Since 1995*
Innkeeper
Ella Brubacher

THIS VICTORIAN INN HAS STYLE—with casual hospitality. Property of five treed acres is two blocks from the main street. Open kitchen, lounge and library. Staff available for planning activities, dining choices, museums, theatre and seasonal happenings. One meeting room where lunch is available to these groups only. When booking the entire house, private dinner can be arranged. We are steps away to fabulous shopping, dining, and theater. A visitors' village featuring artifact stores, specialty food items, unique gifts and antiques is nearby.

Traditional Village
Breakfast Inn

RATES
12 rooms, $125 to $190 B&B.
Mid-week specials.
Open year-round.

ATTRACTIONS
Outdoor pool, tennis court, bikes, walking trail, horseshoes, rose garden, antique shops, summer theatre, museums and visitors' shopping village.

CUISINE
Lunch and dinner served to groups only when pre-arranged. Not licensed.

DIRECTIONS
From Hwy 401 exit Hwy 8 W to Kitchener then Hwy 86 N through Waterloo, choose Rd. 15 or Rd. 17 exit; in St. Jacobs turn W on Albert St.

Suitable for Children Over 6 • Non-Smoking Inn
Conference Facilities for 12 • Visa, MC, AMEX, Diners/ EN Accepted

Elora, ONT Canada

The Elora Mill Country Inn & Restaurant

519-846-5356

Fax 519-846-9180

www.eloramill.com

information@eloramill.com

77 Mill Street West, Elora, ONT Canada N0B 1S0

Select Registry Member *Since 1991*

Innkeeper

JENNIFER SMITH

TRADITIONAL COUNTRY INN

PERCHED OVERLOOKING the spectacular Elora Gorge and Grand River Falls this historic renovated grist Mill is set in the tranquility of small town Ontario. Many of the inn's charming guestrooms overlook the extraordinary view of the Gorge and Grand River as do the Gorge Dining Room and Penstock Lounge. The distinguished, relaxed dining room serves an elegant fine dining menu of traditionally Canadian food with an international flair. A casual fare is served in the lounge in the winter in front of a warm crackling fire or in the summer on the balcony with a breathtaking view. The quaint village of Elora has a relaxing country atmosphere, wealth of outdoor activities, unique shops and boutiques and so much more.

Handicap Access Available • Suitable for Children
Conference Facilities for 100 • Visa, MC Accepted
Designated Smoking Areas • Reservations Accepted Through Travel Agents

RATES

31 rooms, from $160.
Suites, $220/$250.
Packages available. Some rooms w/fireplaces, water views, lofted beds or private deck.
Open year-round.

ATTRACTIONS

Hiking, cycling, canoeing, craft and antique shopping, cross-country skiing, golf, tennis, squash, music and Scottish Festivals, theaters, fly-fishing.

CUISINE

Dining room overlooks the Elora Gorge and offers fireside dining. Breakfast, lunch and dinner served daily. Cart service is available for dinner. Wine and liquor available. Our Penstock lounge also overlooks the water.

DIRECTIONS

From Hwy 401 exit 295, N on Hwy 6. Merge R on Woodlawn Rd. for 2 km to Woolwich St. Turn L (still Hwy 6). 4 km to County Rd. 7. Turn L and follow into Elora. Turn R at first stop light. Turn L at stop sign. Turn L at stop light (Mill St.)

Alton, ONT Canada

The Millcroft Inn

800-383-3976
519-941-8111 Fax 519-941-9192
www.millcroft.com spa website: spa.millcroft.com
millcroft@millcroft.com
55 John Street, Alton, ONT Canada L0N 1A0

Select Registry Member *Since 1995*
Innkeeper
WOLFGANG STICHNOTHE

NESTLED IN THE ROLLING CALEDON HILLS, only 40 minutes from Toronto, The Millcroft Inn offers understated elegance. With its 52 elegantly appointed guest rooms and 100 acres of magnificent outdoor trails, The Millcroft Inn is truly the definitive country retreat. Savour the Inn's Four Diamond Cuisine and vintage wine cellar in our exquisite Dining Room or in the glass pod overlooking the falls. Choose from one of the Inn's exciting packages, relax in our Spa and give yourself an excuse to revel in the ultimate combination of luxury and hospitality, all in a country inn.

TRADITIONAL COUNTRY INN

RATES
52 rooms, $230/325 CDN per person, depending on rate of exchange. B&B. Many pkgs. avail. Four Diamonds from CAA/AAA. *Open year-round.*

ATTRACTIONS
ON-SITE: cross-country skiing, bikes, trails, outdoor pool, hot tub, games room, spa facilities-massage and esthetic treatments.
OFF-SITE: golf, theater, art galleries and antiques.

CUISINE
Continental cuisine available for breakfast, lunch and dinner. Four Diamonds CAA/AAA. Selection of wines and spirits available.

DIRECTIONS
From Toronto: Hwy 401 W to Hwy 410, N to Mayfield Rd., W, L to Hwy 10, N to Caledon, L on Hwy 24 (Charleston Sideroad) 3 km to Peel Regional Rd. 136 (Main St.) R (3 km) to stop sign then L on Queen St.

1 Guestroom Handicap Accessible • Suitable for Children
Conference Facilities for 65 • Visa, MC, AMEX, Diners Accepted
Designated Smoking Areas • Reservations Accepted Through Travel Agents

Zephyr, ONT Canada

High Fields Country Inn & Spa

888-809-9992
905-473-6132 Fax 905-473-1044
www.highfields.com
norma@inforamp.net
11568-70 Concession 3
Zephyr, ONT Canada L0E 1T0

HIGH FIELDS IS ONE OF AMERICA'S Great Inn and Spa Resorts, offering peace, tranquility and elegant comfort. It's truly a haven for those seeking wellness within quiet, natural surroundings. The Inn is situated on 175 acres of rolling fields and woodlands less than an hour northeast of downtown Toronto. This luxurious adult retreat is smoke-free and provides an essential respite from the effects of modern everyday living. Whether your pleasure is a soothing visit to the day spa or an overnight stay in the guest quarters, your well-being is of foremost importance. Whatever the season, High Fields offers you a rewarding escape.

Select Registry Member *Since 2000*

Innkeepers / Owners

NORMA DANIEL AND JOHN DANIEL

TRADITIONAL COUNTRY BREAKFAST INN

RATES

9 accommodations from $130-$350 CDN.
King or twin beds. Decorated in calming country motifs. En suite bathrooms with whirlpool tub. Personal amenities provided.
Open year-round.

ATTRACTIONS

Outdoor pool, hot tub, tennis court, hiking trails, horseback riding, snowshoeing, snowmobiling, sauna, gym, very unique spa on premises. Golf, skiing, mountain biking, Lake Simcoe, live theater, Canada's wonderland nearby.

CUISINE

Unlicensed, you may bring your own alcoholic beverages. A continental breakfast is complimentary. Our Executive Chef offers fresh market cuisine in a fine dining atmosphere as well as picnic lunches. Reservations are necessary for both lunch and dinner.

DIRECTIONS

From Toronto: Hwy 404 N to Davis Dr.—16.5 km E on Davis Dr. 7.5 km N on 3rd concession. High Fields is on the W side.

Conference Facilities for 32 • Non-Smoking Inn
AMEX, Visa, MC, Diners Accepted
Reservations Accepted Through Travel Agents

Jackson's Point, ONT Canada

The Briars

800-465-2376

905-722-3271 Fax 905-722-9698

www.briars.ca

briars@ils.net

55 Hedge Road, R.R. #1

Jackson's Point, ONT Canada L0E 1L0

Select Registry Member *Since 1980*

Innkeepers / Owners

JOHN AND BARBARA,
HUGH AND ANDREW SIBBALD

THE BRIARS IS A LOVELY HISTORIC INN with lush lawns, gardens and hedges, on sparkling Lake Simcoe an hour from Toronto. Our 160 year-old Regency manor house, with adjoining wings, dining rooms, lounges and lakeside cottages welcomes you. Play The Briars 6,300-yard championship Scottish woodlands golf course. We are known for our fine country fare. Couples, families, reunions and social gatherings have appreciated our traditional Canadian hospitality for years. We are an Ontario Heritage property.

TRADITIONAL WATERSIDE RESORT

RATES

46 rooms, $115/$195 CDN. PP MAP; 4 suites and cott. $119/$195 CDN. PP MAP. *Open year-round.*

ATTRACTIONS

Golf, tennis, spa, lake, boating, nature trails, indoor and outdoor pools, whirlpool, sauna, exercise and game rooms, live theatre. Nearby internationally known attractions.

CUISINE

Breakfast, lunch, and dinner in dining rooms. Lounge menu all day. Licensed dining rooms, lounges, patios, lawns.

DIRECTIONS

From Toronto, 404 N to Davis Dr.,R, E 6 miles to 48; L, N 15 miles to Sutton; L on High St., follow signs to Jackson's Point and Briars. To avoid Toronto traffic, take ETR 407 to 404.

Suitable for Children• Non-Smoking Inn
Conference Facilities for 160 • MC, Visa, AMEX, Diners Accepted
Reservations Accepted Through Travel Agents

Eagle Lake, ONT Canada

Sir Sam's Inn

800-361-2188
705-754-2188 Fax 705-754-4262
www.sirsamsinn.com
sirsamsinn@cybernet.on.ca
Eagle Lake P.O.
Eagle Lake, ONT Canada K0M 1M0

Select Registry Member *Since 1995*
Innkeeper
JAMES T. ORR

TRADITIONAL WATERSIDE RESORT

RATES
22 rooms, from $125 per person/day; MAP.
3 suites with kitchen facilities.
Open year-round.

ATTRACTIONS
Haliburton Forest and Wildlife, Algonquin Park, Minden White Water Park, golf.

CUISINE
Candlelit fireside dining by the lake offering creative fresh menus that tempt and delight everyday.

DIRECTIONS
2.5 hours NE of Toronto, 15 minutes from Haliburton. Follow Hwy 118 to Eagle Lake Rd.

ORIGINALLY SIR SAMUEL HUGHES' HALIBURTON estate, the Inn offers historic charm and classic elegance. Magnificently situated on Eagle Lake, we celebrate nature through a host of activities—waterskiing, windsurfing, sailing, canoeing or kayaking. There is tennis, mountain biking, hiking and more. In winter, exciting downhill and Nordic skiing. Year-round our superb candlelit dining is complemented by our unique wine cellar. Intimate rooms (most with whirlpool and fireplace). At Sir Sam's, what nature does not offer...we do.

Conference Facilities for 35 • Credit Cards Accepted
Reservations Accepted Through Travel Agents

Haliburton, ONT Canada

Domain of Killien

705-457-1100
Fax 705-457-3853
www.domainofkillien.com
killien@halhinet.on.ca
P.O. Box 810, Haliburton, ONT Canada K0M 1S0

Select Registry Member *Since 1995*
Contact
JEAN-EDOUARD DE MARENCHES

NEAR THE SOUTHERN TIP OF ALGONQUIN PARK, there is a small and intimate Inn on the shores of a serene lake. Set within a private 5,000-acre estate of forests, hills and lakes, the Domain offers regional French cuisine and wines, quiet comfort and hospitality, all in the tradition of the finest European Inns. Throughout the seasons, enjoy outdoor silent sports or simply, 'Master the Art of Doing Nothing...Beautifully.'

TRADITIONAL WATERSIDE INN

RATES
5 rooms, $150/$182.
CDN PP MAP.
1 suite.
6 chalets, $142/$206 PP MAP.
Open year-round.

ATTRACTIONS
On-site stocked lakes, beaches, sailing, canoeing, fly-fishing, hiking trails, biking, tennis, skiing, snowshoeing, and skating. Golf and downhill skiing nearby.

CUISINE
Breakfast and dinner. Picnic lunches available. Liquor served.

DIRECTIONS
From Toronto Hwy 401 East to 115/35 N. 35 N to Minden, 121 R, N to Haliburton L, W on 118, R N on Harburn Rd. 12 km to Carroll Rd.

Conference Facilities for 16 • Credit Cards Accepted
Reservations Accepted Through Travel Agents

Fenelon Falls, ONT Canada

Eganridge Inn

888-452-5111
705-738-5111 Fax 705-738-5111
www.eganridge.com
info@eganridge.com

RR #3, Fenelon Falls, ONT Canada K0M 1N0

Select Registry Member *Since 1991*
Innkeepers / Owners
JOHN AND PATRICIA EGAN

A LOVINGLY RESTORED ENGLISH MANOR HOME combining the perfect blend of century heritage and modern luxury on Sturgeon Lake in the heart of the Trent Severn Waterway. Set amongst towering pines and acres of professionally groomed grounds, this two-story, hand-hewn log home built in 1837 is unique in North America. Challenging golf; award-winning continental cuisine from a seasoned kitchen of Swiss experts; and the ultimate in understated luxury throughout, fulfills guests' highest expectations. The only AAA ◆◆◆◆ award recipient in the Kawartha region.

ELEGANT COUNTRY INN

RATES
5 cottages, $190/$225 CDN B&B.
6 suites, $175 CDN B&B.
May thru October.

ATTRACTIONS
On-site: golf, tennis, beach, boating. Nearby: theatre, antiquing, galleries, shopping, nature trails, hiking and biking.

CUISINE
Breakfast, lunch and dinner. Room service. MAP rates. Wine and liquor available.

DIRECTIONS
From Toronto: Hwy 401 E to Hwy 115/35 exit. Follow to Hwy 35 N towards Lindsay. Once in Lindsay turn R on Hwy 7 to Hwy 36 N towards Bobcaygeon. Once in Bobcaygeon turn L on Duke St. which turns into County Rd. 8. Proceed 5 km on County Rd. 8 to the Eganridge sign.

Handicap Access Available • Suitable for Children • Non-Smoking Inn
Conference Facilities for 25 • Visa, MC, AMEX, Diners Accepted
Reservations Accepted Through Travel Agents

Kingston, ONT Canada

Rosemount Bed & Breakfast Inn

888-871-8844
613-531-8844 Fax 613-544-4895
www.rosemountinn.com
rosemt@kingston.net
46 Sydenham Street South
Kingston, ONT Canada K7L 3H1

Select Registry Member *Since 1993*
Innkeepers/Owners
HOLLY DOUGHTY AND
JOHN EDWARDS

STEP THROUGH the original cast-iron swinging gates into the quiet charm of an 1850 limestone Tuscany villa in the heart of Historic Kingston. Let us pamper you—your room is exquisitely appointed with Victorian antiques, fine linens and down duvets! Each morning we will treat you to a special gourmet breakfast as you share in lively conversation with other guests. For total relaxation, experience Aromatherapy massage in "The Gazebo Room!" For private retreats—The Coach House! Fully equipped kitchen, loft bedroom with whirlpool bath, corner fireplace in living room and antique pine floors.

TRADITIONAL IN TOWN BREAKFAST INN

RATES
8 rooms and coach house.
$119/$275 CDN, includes gourmet breakfast.
Open year-round, except Christmas and New Years.

ATTRACTIONS
Historic museums and forts, art galleries, antiquing, riverboat cruises, stage productions, farmers' market. Aromatherapy massage and reflexology on-site.

CUISINE
Brew pubs, wine bars, fine dining—just a short stroll away.

DIRECTIONS
Hwy 401 to exit 619 (Montreal St.) South 5 km to Brock St. Turn R; take first L onto Sydenham St. S Proceed 2 1/2 blks.

Suitable for Children Over 13 • Designated Smoking Areas
Conference Facilities for 10 • Visa, MC, AMEX Accepted
Reservations Accepted Through Travel Agents

Gananoque, ONT Canada

Trinity House Inn

613-382-8383
Fax 613-382-1599
www.trinityinn.com
trinity@kingston.net

90 Stone Street South
Gananoque, ONT Canada K7G 1Z8

IN THE HEART OF FAMOUS 1,000 ISLANDS, the Trinity House Inn (1859), offers award-winning hospitality, superior accommodations and dining excellence, complemented with an atmosphere of casual elegance. Renowned for exceptional service and detail, the Inn has been completely restored adding fine antiques, artwork and manicured Victorian waterfall gardens. Enjoy fireside candlelit dinners or relax in our sofa lounge or sun terrace. Experience the beauty of the islands aboard one of the many boat tours and savour the scenery. Selected "Best Canadian Inn" as voted in North American Country Inns *Bed & Breakfast* Magazine's 2000 Readers' Choice Survey.

Suitable for Children Over 10 • Designated Smoking Areas
Conference Facilities for 16 • Visa, MC Accepted

Select Registry Member *Since 1995*
Innkeepers/Owners
JACQUES O'SHEA AND
BRAD GARSIDE

ELEGANT IN TOWN INN

RATES
6 rooms, $100/$165 CDN B&B.
2 suites, $165/$200 CDN B&B.
Brief seasonal closure in Winter. Call the Inn for dates.

ATTRACTIONS
1,000 Island cruises, Boldt Castle, live theater, cycling, antiques, historic sites, national parks, fishing, boat and cycle rentals and nature trails.

CUISINE
Breakfast (guests), dinner: a la carte menu, fully licensed (wine, beer and liquor), two dining rooms and veranda, seating 42, El Fresco Garden Patio, seating 30+, cocktail lounge. Classical cuisine.

DIRECTIONS
Hwy 401 to Gananoque (E of Kingston) exit 645 S on Hwy 32 (Stone St.) past first traffic light at King St.

The Rocky Mountains

The Rockies are stunning in the evening alpine glow. Our guests discover that right away. Here, highways snake through the most rugged and magnificent terrain in the country. Mountaintops loom before you. A visitor can follow the Select Registry like a road map. Like the landscape itself, quality refuses to be compromised.

A TRAVELER MIGHT REMEMBER THE WORDS from a song from the '70s, especially the line that proclaims, "Meet me in Boulder and live forever." The Rockies attract like music that rings in the back of your mind, over and over, until you find it and own it. Here, the mountains call.

If you love American history, the landscape is rich with lore: Native American fur trappers, early pioneers. If you could interrupt your busy life for a few days, where else might you choose to travel? Where else might you remember how lucky you are? Adventure awaits you.

Love to fish? This region is alive with trophy trout. Our guests have filled more than one creel with fat, bright trout. A helpful Innkeeper might fire up a batch for dinner. Many of our Innkeepers offer fine wine cellars, and a happy traveler most certainly will splurge. A basket of morel mushrooms graces the counter in an Innkeeper's handsome kitchen. Cous cous, trout, and wild mushrooms: Can't top that meal anywhere. The smile on a guest's face is as broad as the snow-capped mountains that lace the landscape.

After dinner a traveler might meander along a trail that shadows a fast mountain stream. An earth song criss-crosses the rugged property. The river has a music, and that sound gladdens.

Hand in hand a couple plans out an adventure for the next several days. The *Selet Registry* leads the way. An ivory moon dangles just above the lofty mountain peaks. Here is John Denver's "Rocky Mountain High."

"This luxury Inn is beautiful, opulent, cozy, comfortable and in every detail impeccable – simply wonderful."—
Patti Anderson, Lafayette, CA

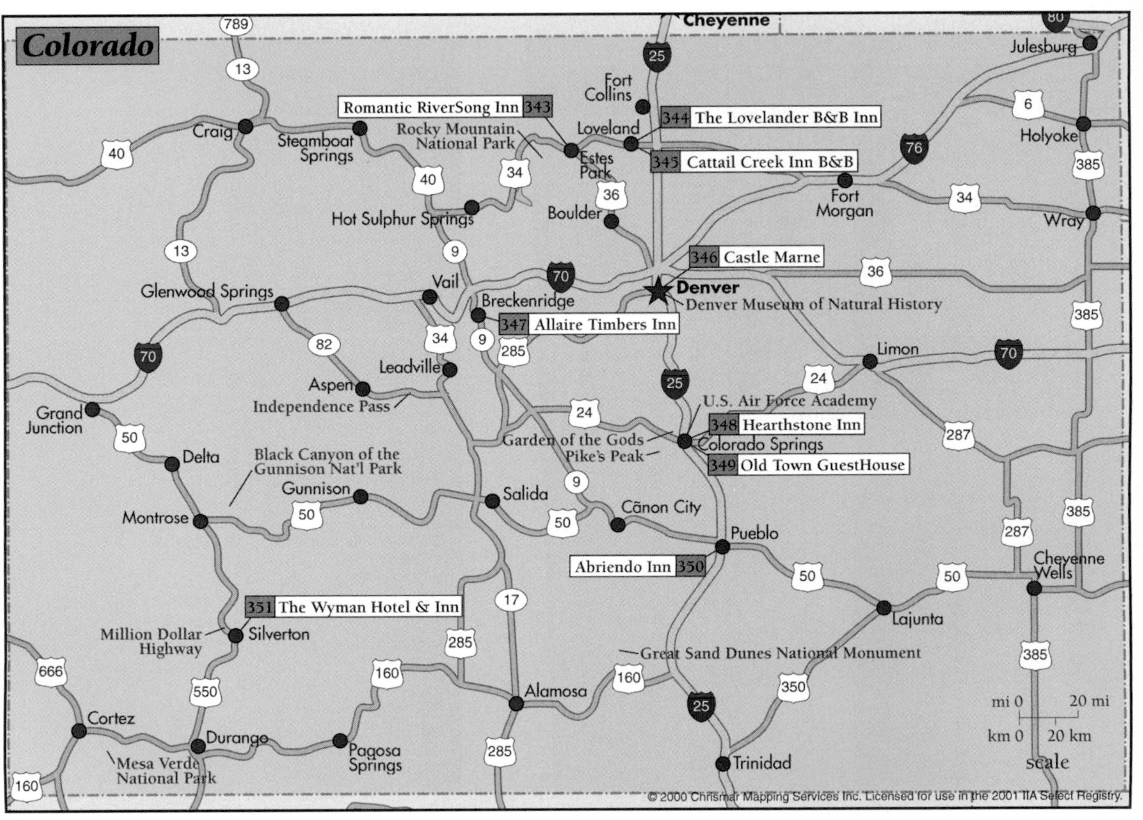

Colorado
Cheyenne
Julesburg
Fort Collins
Romantic RiverSong Inn 343
344 The Lovelander B&B Inn
345 Cattail Creek Inn B&B
Holyoke
Craig
Steamboat Springs
Rocky Mountain National Park
Loveland
Estes Park
Fort Morgan
Hot Sulphur Springs
Boulder
Wray
346 Castle Marne
Denver
Denver Museum of Natural History
Glenwood Springs
Vail
Breckenridge
347 Allaire Timbers Inn
Limon
Leadville
Aspen
Independence Pass
U.S. Air Force Academy
348 Hearthstone Inn
Grand Junction
Garden of the Gods
Pike's Peak
Colorado Springs
349 Old Town GuestHouse
Delta
Black Canyon of the Gunnison Nat'l Park
Gunnison
Salida
Cãnon City
Montrose
Pueblo
Abriendo Inn 350
Cheyenne Wells
351 The Wyman Hotel & Inn
Lajunta
Million Dollar Highway
Silverton
Great Sand Dunes National Monument
Alamosa
mi 0 20 mi
km 0 20 km
Cortez
Durango
Pagosa Springs
Trinidad
scale
Mesa Verde National Park
© 2000 Chrismar Mapping Services Inc. Licensed for use in the 2001 IIA Select Registry.

Estes Park, CO

Romantic RiverSong Inn

970-586-4666
Fax 970-577-0699
www.coloradogetaways.com
riversng@frii.com
P.O. Box 1910, Estes Park, CO 80517

Select Registry Member *Since 1987*
Innkeepers/Owners
SUE AND GARY MANSFIELD

IMAGINE LYING IN A MAGNIFICENT ANTIQUE BED, the glaciers of Rocky Mountain National Park looming just over the tops of your toes, seeing the stars through the skylights above your brass bed. Thrill to feeding a gentle fawn outside your door or be lulled to sleep by the melody of our mountain stream. After a great hike or snowshoeing in the park, come home to your own romantic fireside whirlpool tub for two. Enjoy dining by firelight, picnic backpacks and directions to that special place for lunch. Elopement and snowshoe weddings. TREAT YOURSELF! Relax! AAA ◆◆◆ and Mobil ★★★.

TRADITIONAL MOUNTAIN RETREAT/LODGE

RATES

4 rooms, $155/$175 B&B.
5 suites, $195/$295 B&B.
4 rooms-main house and 5 cottages.
Open year-round.

ATTRACTIONS

On the edge of Rocky Mountain National Park - tops in scenery and wildlife, outstanding park trail system, golfing, horseback riding, fishing, birding, hiking, and galleries.

CUISINE

Inn dinners w/prior reservations, fireside dining, picnic basket dinners. Guests invited to bring their own wine.

DIRECTIONS

Hwy 36 through midtown of Estes, Hwy 36 to Mary's Lk. Rd; L at Mary's Lk. Rd.; Go 1 blk. cross bridge. Turn R immed., take Country Rd. following river to Rd. end.

3 Guestrooms Handicap Accessible • Non-Smoking Inn
Suitable for Children Over 12 • Visa, MC, Disc Accepted
Reservations Accepted Through Travel Agents

Loveland, CO

The Lovelander Bed & Breakfast Inn

800-459-6694
970-669-0798 Fax 970-669-0797
www.lovelander.com
love@ezlink.com
217 West 4th Street, Loveland, CO 80537

Select Registry Member *Since 1990*
Innkeepers/Owners
LAUREN AND GARY SMITH

A WARM CUP OF TEA, the aroma of freshly-baked desserts and a cozy fire welcome you to The Lovelander. Built in 1902, the essence of Victorian style is combined with contemporary convenience to make The Lovelander a haven for recreational and business travelers alike. Each of our 11 rooms have their own private bath, several with amenities such as whirlpool tubs, steam shower or fireplace. Our delectable breakfasts feature such things as Black Forest Stuffed French Toast or Lovelander Chef's Torte. Each evening enjoy a tempting dessert such as Chocolate Decadence or Key Lime Cheesecake. We guarantee you will have a memorable stay or your next stay is on us!

1 Guestroom Handicap Accessible • Suitable for Children Over 10
Conference Facilities for 35 • Visa, MC, Disc, AMEX Accepted
Non-Smoking Inn • Reservations Accepted Through Travel Agents

TRADITIONAL IN TOWN BREAKFAST INN

RATES
11 rooms, $105/$155 B&B.
Open year-round.

ATTRACTIONS
Rocky Mountain National Park, Benson Sculpture Park, galleries and Big Thompson Canyon.

CUISINE
Full breakfast, beverages and snacks, complimentary evening dessert, and liquor available.

DIRECTIONS
I-25 to 257B to U.S. Hwy 34 W for 5 miles to Garfield Ave. Turn L. Go 10 blks to 4th St. R to 2nd house on R.

Loveland, CO

Cattail Creek Inn B&B

800-572-2466
970-667-7600 Fax 970-667-8968
www.cattailcreekinn.com
ccinn@oneimage.com
2665 Abarr Drive, Loveland, CO 80538

Select Registry Member *Since 2000*
Innkeepers/Owners
SUE AND HAROLD BUCHMAN

YOU WILL SENSE THE FEELING of casual elegance and warmth the minute you enter the grand foyer of this luxurious inn. From the finely crafted cherry woodwork, the golden-glazed hand-plastered walls to the fine art and the world-class bronze sculpture, this unique inn is truely an artistic experience! Located on the seventh tee box of the Cattail Golf Course, guests have peaceful views of Lake Loveland and majestic views of the Rocky Mountains. The Inn is across the lagoon from Columbine Art Gallery and is within walking distance to Benson Sculpture Park.

CONTEMPORARY IN TOWN BREAKFAST INN

RATES
8 rooms, $105/$170.
The inn's eight guest rooms have distinctive individual features and are situated for optimal privacy.
Open year-round.

ATTRACTIONS
Rocky Mountain National Park, walking distance to Benson Sculpture Park and Columbine Art Gallery, three golf courses, Big Thompson Canyon.

CUISINE
Full gourmet breakfast, snacks, B&B liquor license.

DIRECTIONS
I-25 to exit 257B to US Hwy 34 W for 6 miles to Taft. Turn R 3/4 mile to 28th. Turn L on 28th one block to Abarr Dr. Turn L on Abarr Dr.

1 Guestroom, 3 Common Rooms Handicap Accessible
Non-Smoking Inn • MC, Visa, AMEX, Disc Accepted
Reservations Accepted Through Travel Agents

Denver, CO

The Historic Castle Marne, An Urban Inn

800-92-MARNE
303-331-0621 Fax 303-331-0623
www.castlemarne.com
themarne@ix.netcom.com
1572 Race Street, Denver, CO 80206

DENVER'S GRANDEST HISTORIC MANSION (National & Local Historic Register). Built in 1889, designed by famous architect, William Lang. Features hand-hewn rhyolite, hand-rubbed woods, balconies, three-story tower and stained glass "Peacock Window". It all blends beautifully with period antiques and family heirlooms to create a charming Victorian atmosphere. Game room and English garden. Full gourmet breakfast served in original dining room. Complimentary afternoon tea served in the parlour. Whirlpool spas and private outdoor hot tubs. Private candlelight dinner by reservation. National Register Landmark in Denver's Wyman Historic District. Near museums and shopping.

Suitable for Children Over 10 • Non-Smoking Inn
Conference Facilities for 12 • Credit Cards Accepted
Reservations Accepted Through Travel Agents

Select Registry Member *Since 1991*
Owners
THE PEIKER FAMILY-
DIANE, JIM, MELISSA AND LOUIE

ELEGANT IN TOWN
BREAKFAST INN

RATES
7 rooms, $95/$245,
2 suites w/Jacuzzi tubs, $195/$245.
3 rooms w/hot tubs for 2.
Open year-round.

ATTRACTIONS
Museums, Zoo, Botanic Gardens, Historic Sites, Elitches, Lodo, Coors Field, Downtown, Cherry Creek, Shopping, Fine Dining, Convention Center, The Plex.

CUISINE
Dinner and luncheons available by reservation. No liquor license, set-ups available.

DIRECTIONS
From DIA, Pena Blvd to I-70 W to Quebec. S to 17th Ave. R to York St. L to 16th Ave. R to Race St.

Breckenridge, CO

Allaire Timbers Inn

800-624-4904
970-453-7530 Fax 970-453-8699
www.allairetimbers.com
allairetimbers@worldnet.att.net
9511 Highway 9, P.O. Box 4653
Breckenridge, CO 80424

Select Registry Member *Since 1995*
Innkeepers / Owners
JACK AND KATHY GUMPH

THIS CONTEMPORARY LOG B&B is the perfect Rocky Mountain Hideway. Guest rooms are named and decorated for Colorado Mountain passes. Each offers private bath and private deck with mountain views, TV, telephone, fluffy robes and an attention to detail that makes you feel special and welcome. Elegant suites offer a special touch of romance with private hot tub and fireplace. Relax by a crackling fire in the great room, enjoy the serenity of the sunroom and loft, or unwind in the outdoor hot tub with spectacular views. Featured on the Travel Channel's *Romantic Inns of America* and CNN's *Travel Guide.* Mobil ★★★ and AAA ◆◆◆.

CONTEMPORARY MOUNTAIN BREAKFAST INN

RATES
8 rooms, $145/$250.
2 suites, $215/$380.
All private baths.
Open year-round.

ATTRACTIONS
Alpine & cross-country skiing, historic tours, snowmobiling, fishing, golf, bicycling, hiking and music festivals.

CUISINE
Hearty full breakfast, afternoon social hour, evening desserts.

DIRECTIONS
From Denver, I-70 W to exit 203. Take Hwy 9 S to Breckenridge. Through town past light at gas station. Take next R, bear R.

1 Guestroom Handicap Accessible • Suitable for Children Over 13
Non-Smoking Inn • MC, Visa, Disc, AMEX Accepted
Reservations Accepted Through Travel Agents

Colorado Springs, CO

Hearthstone Inn

719-473-4413
www.hearthstoneinn.com
hearthstone@worldnet.att.net

506 North Cascade Avenue
Colorado Springs, CO 80903

Select Registry Member *Since 1979*
Innkeepers / Owners
DAVID AND NANCY OXENHANDLER

VICTORIAN DECOR, friendly people, delightful breakfasts and period antiques create a welcome change of pace. Rooms with wood-burning fireplaces or private porches are especially popular. Walk to quaint shops, coffee houses, book stores, restaurants (brew pub to elegant dining) or enjoy the nearby four-mile jogging trail and neighborhood stately mansions. With all the activities of the Pikes Peak area, you'll find exciting things to see and do for several days! Our conference center, dining room and entire Inn are available for meetings, weddings and special events. May through October is 'high' season—so advance reservations are advised! We are happy to assist in planning your activities. Welcome! Mobil ★★★ and AAA ◆◆◆.

Handicap Access Available • Suitable for Children
Conference Facilities • Credit Cards Accepted
Reservations Accepted Through Travel Agents

TRADITIONAL IN TOWN BREAKFAST INN

RATES

22 rooms, $69/$159 B&B.
3 suites, $199 B&B.
Open year-round.

ATTRACTIONS

On-site: croquet, puzzles and games, rocking chairs on the veranda. Nearby: downtown shops and restaurants, jogging path, tennis, golf, Pikes Peak (road and train), museums, U.S. Air Force Academy, Colorado College, Garden of the Gods, US Olympic Training Center.

CUISINE

Full gourmet breakfast included with room. Restaurant with French and Continential cuisine is open for breakfast, lunch, dinner and Sunday brunch. Full liquor license.

DIRECTIONS

From I-25, exit 143 E (Uintah St.) away from mountains 3 blocks to Cascade Ave. Turn R-S 7 blocks to corner of Cascade and St. Vrain.

Colorado Springs, CO

Old Town GuestHouse

888-375-4210
719-632-9194 Fax 719-632-9026
www.bbonline.com/co/oldtown
oldtown@rmi.net
115 South 26th Street, Colorado Springs, CO 80904

Select Registry Member *Since 2001*
Innkeepers/Owners
KAYE AND DAVID CASTER

THE THREE STORY BRICK GUESTHOUSE, built as a B&B, is in perfect harmony with the 1859 period of the surrounding historic Old Town. The urban Inn offers upscale amenities for discerning adult leisure and business travelers. The foyer elevator allows the entire Inn to be accessible. The soundproof, uniquely decorated guestrooms have private porches overlooking Pikes Peak. Relax on the umbrella covered patio for afternoon wine and hors d'oeuvres. The innkeepers are Pikes Peak area concierges. The elegance and hospitality of the GuestHouse was awarded AAA's 4 Diamond Award for Excellence.

ELEGANT IN TOWN BREAKFAST INN

RATES

8 rooms, $95/$195 B&B. Corporate rates available. Architecturally designed rooms offer hot tubs, steam showers, fireplaces, private porches, TV/VCR, ISDN lines, air conditioned. *Open year-round.*

ATTRACTIONS

Walk to historic Old Town restaurants, boutiques, galleries, and antique shops. Pikes Peak area offers natural mountain beauty, a cograil train, Garden of the Gods, horses, rafting, bike and hiking trails, fishing, Air Force Academy, Olympic Training Center.

CUISINE

Wine and hors d'oeuvres, sherry and chocolate, full sit-down breakfast.

DIRECTIONS

From I-25, exit 141 West. W to 26th St. N on 26th S, 2 blocks to corner of Cucharra and 26th St. Private parking in lot N of B&B.

Handicap Access Available • Suitable for Children Over 16
Conference Facilities for 26 • Credit Cards Accepted
Non-Smoking Inn • Reservations Accepted Through Travel Agents

Pueblo, CO

Abriendo Inn

719-544-2703
Fax 719-542-6544
www.bedandbreakfastinns.org/abriendo
abriendo@rmi.net
300 West Abriendo Avenue, Pueblo, CO 81004

Select Registry Member *Since 1992*
Innkeeper/Owner
KERRELYN M. TRENT

FROM THE SPIRAL STAIRCASE to the curved stained-glass windows and parquet floors, you know that you are entering a special place. *The Essential Guide to Favorite Places, Colorado's Best* proclaimed the Abriendo Inn "The best bed and breakfast" for the entire Colorado front range. Feel like you belong at the Inn and absorb the tranquility while strolling the park-like grounds or walking through the tree-lined neighborhoods and the nearby historic Union Avenue. Delight in a beautiful full breakfast, warm hospitality and personal attention. Restaurants, shops, galleries and other attractions are within five minutes of the Inn. All rooms have a king or queen bed, air-conditioners, TV and telephone. Some rooms have two-person jetted tubs.

Suitable for Children • AMEX, Visa, MC, Diners Accepted
Designated Smoking Areas • Reservations Accepted Through Travel Agents

TRADITIONAL IN TOWN
BREAKFAST INN

RATES
9 rooms, $69/$125.
1 suite, $89 B&B.
Open year-round.

ATTRACTIONS
Historic walking tour, museums, nature, bike trails, rafting, fishing, golf, swimming, galleries, boutiques, shops and scenic drives.

CUISINE
Full breakfast, 24-hour beverage and snack center. BYOB.

DIRECTIONS
I-25 to exit 97B, then W 1 mile.

Silverton, CO

The Wyman Hotel & Inn

800-609-7845
970-387-5372 Fax 970-387-5745
www.thewyman.com
thewyman@frontier.net
1371 Greene Street, PO Box 780, Silverton, CO 81433

COME HOME TO THE WYMAN HOTEL & INN, Silverton's finest B&B, which is nestled in the heart of the San Juan Mountains. Listed on the National Register of Historic Places and featured on the Travel Channel, The Wyman is an historic jewel of Colorado. Spend your days hiking and spend your nights relaxing and rejuvenating. Curl up under a goose down comforter or indulge in a two-person whirlpool. All rooms are individually decorated with one-of-a-kind antiques and many have floor to ceiling windows with spectacular views of the mountains. Costa Rican coffee, Mozart and a gourmet breakfast start the day off right!

1 Guestroom Handicap Accessible • Suitable for Children
Pets Allowed • Non-Smoking Inn • Visa, MC, AMEX, Disc Accepted
Reservations Accepted Through Travel Agents

Select Registry Member *Since 2001*
Innkeeper/Owner
LORRAINE LEWIS
Chef
TOM LEWIS

TRADITIONAL IN TOWN BREAKFAST INN

RATES

17 rooms, $95/$180, lower rates in winter; higher rates for holidays/festivals/special events. Rooms range from cozy and intimate to large and luxurious. All have a Colorado theme and are furnished with exceptional antiques.
Open December 28 to February 18 and May 1 to October 28.

ATTRACTIONS

Durango and Silverton Narrow Gauge Railroad, gold mine tour, hiking, horseback riding, mountain biking, rafting, museum and mill-tour, jeep tours of ghost towns and backcountry, music festivals, xc-skiing, alpine skiing, snowshoeing, and ice skating.

CUISINE

A full gourmet breakfast includes souffles, fresh fruits and homemade breads. Afternoon tea with our "famous" cookies. Champagne basket, romantic picnic basket and breakfast in bed by special arrangement.

DIRECTIONS

From North or South, you must take the Million Dollar Highway (Rte 550). Upon arrival in Silverton, you will be on Greene St. The Wyman is on the corner of Greene and 14th Sts., across from City Hall.

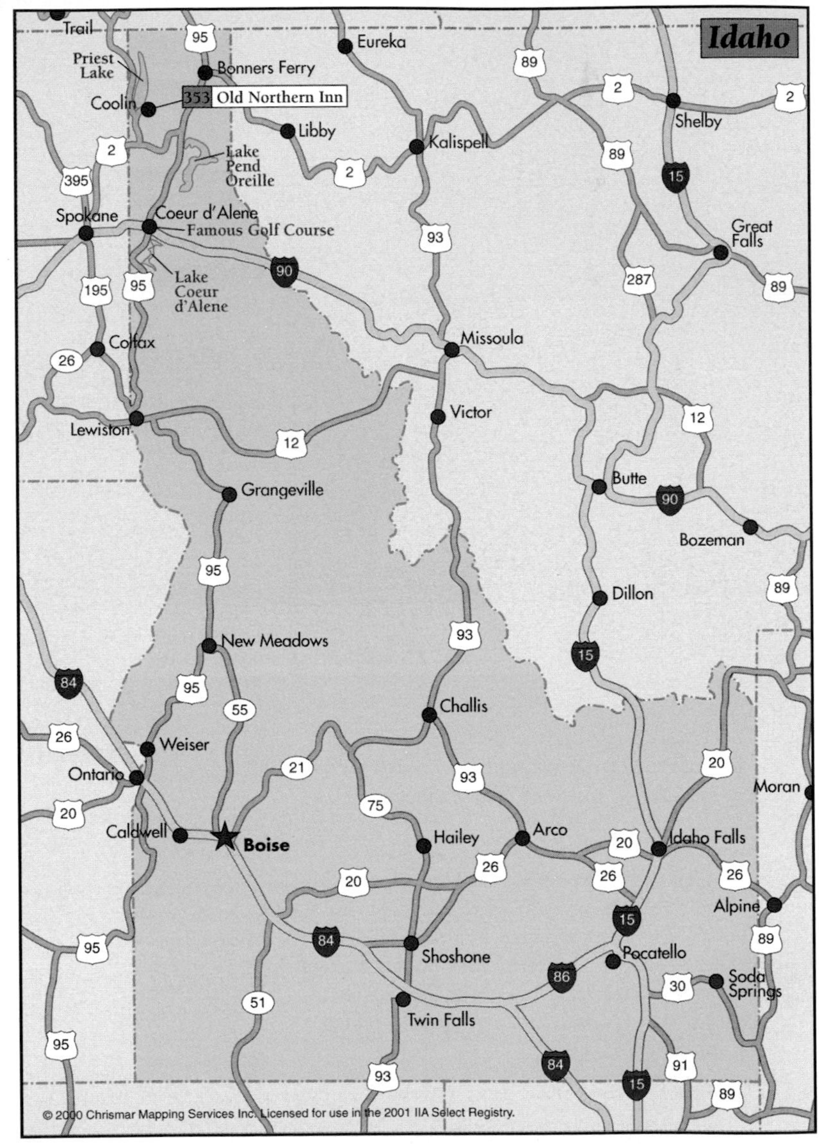
Idaho
Trail
Priest Lake
Coolin
Bonners Ferry
353 Old Northern Inn
Eureka
Libby
Kalispell
Shelby
Lake Pend Oreille
Spokane
Coeur d'Alene
Famous Golf Course
Lake Coeur d'Alene
Great Falls
Missoula
Colfax
Lewiston
Victor
Grangeville
Butte
Bozeman
Dillon
New Meadows
Challis
Weiser
Ontario
Moran
Caldwell
Boise
Hailey
Arco
Idaho Falls
Alpine
Shoshone
Pocatello
Soda Springs
Twin Falls
© 2000 Chrismar Mapping Services Inc. Licensed for use in the 2001 IIA Select Registry.

Coolin, ID

The Old Northern Inn

208-443-2426
208-443-3856 Fax 208-443-3856
www.oldnorthern inn.com

Select Registry Member *Since 1998*
Owner/Manager
The Phil Battaglia Family

220 Bayview Drive, Coolin, ID 83821

SITUATED IN THE VILLAGE OF COOLIN on the shores of Priest Lake, the Old Northern Inn harkens back to a grand but unpretentious style of the Great Northwest, at the turn of the century. The Battaglia Family restored the classic two-story hotel and filled it with antiques of the era, including brass bath fixtures, antique checkerboards and flour-sack pillows, a spacious but intimate lounge including a stone fireplace, bookshelves and picture windows overlooking the lake. The separate dining area also has its own fireplace where delicious full breakfasts of fresh fruit, German Huckleberry pancakes and fresh-baked breads are served.

Rustic Waterside Breakfast Inn

RATES

Individual rooms and suites, all with private baths and European down comforters and Ralph Lauren towel-robes & amenities.
Open Memorial Day weekend through mid-October each year.

ATTRACTIONS

Priest Lake is the main attraction—boating and water sports, excellent hiking and mountain biking. The area is home to woodland caribou, moose, bear, elk, lynx and mountain goats. Guided fishing excursions for trophy cutthroat and rainbow trout, and the lakes.

CUISINE

Numerous restaurants on the lake & several within walking distance.

DIRECTIONS

Take Hwy 2 to the town of Priest River, then N on Hwy 57 to Priest Lake. Take Coolin/Dickensheet, turn off and go five miles to Coolin. Inn is on L as you enter Coolin.

Handicap Access Available
Suitable for Children Over 12 • Credit Cards Accepted
Reservations Accepted Through Travel Agents

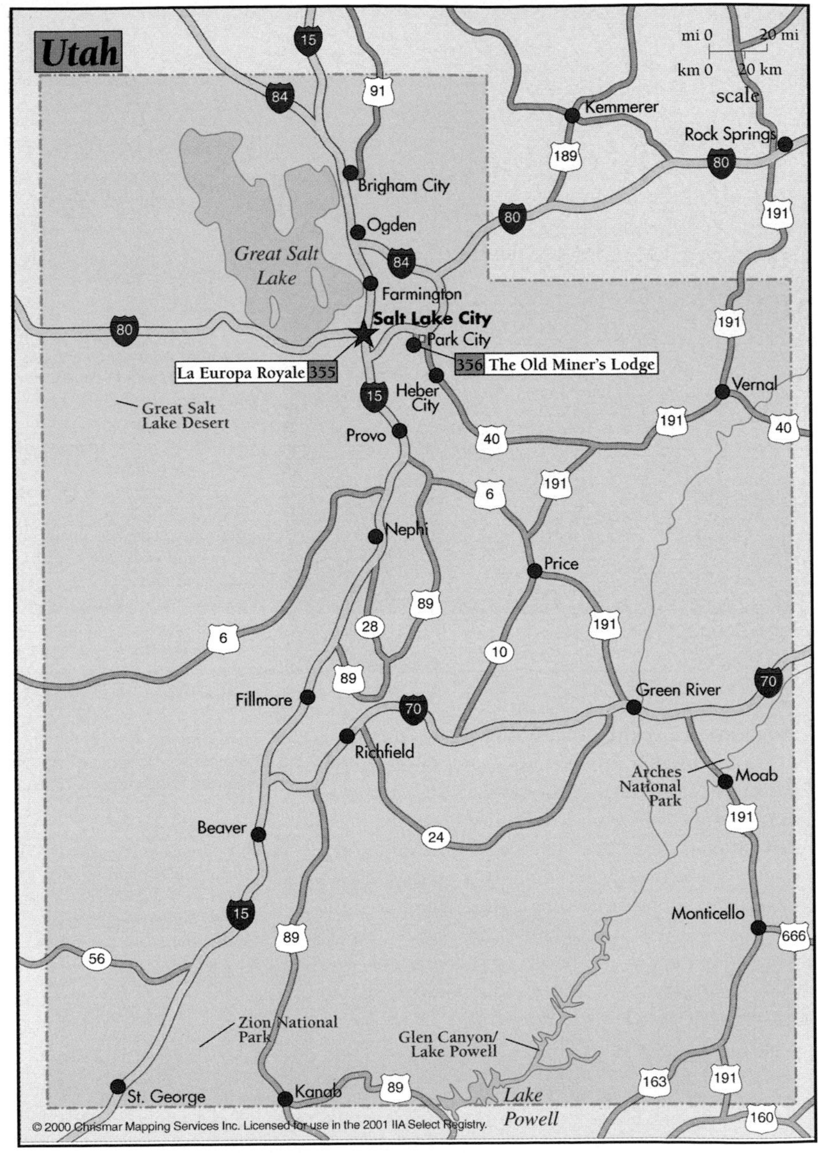
Utah
mi 0
20 mi
km 0
20 km
scale
Kemmerer
Rock Springs
Brigham City
Ogden
Great Salt Lake
Farmington
Salt Lake City
Park City
La Europa Royale 355
356 The Old Miner's Lodge
Heber City
Vernal
Great Salt Lake Desert
Provo
Nephi
Price
Fillmore
Green River
Richfield
Arches National Park
Moab
Beaver
Monticello
Zion National Park
Glen Canyon/ Lake Powell
St. George
Kanab
Lake Powell
© 2000 Chrismar Mapping Services Inc. Licensed for use in the 2001 IIA Select Registry.

Salt Lake City, UT

La Europa Royale

800-523-8767
801-263-7999 Fax 801-263-8090
www.laeuropa.com
tflynn@laeuropa.com
1135 East Vine Street, Salt Lake City, UT 84121

Select Registry Member *Since 1999*
Owners
TOM AND FRANCES FLYNN

LA EUROPA ROYALE, a small elegant European style hotel, newly built in 1995, provides full hotel services to include airport pickup, room service, full breakfast, same-day cleaning and laundry and exercise room. Each guest room is elegantly appointed with a sitting area, desk, data grade telephone, fireplace, oversized Jacuzzi, separate shower, TV/VCR and made quiet by 14-inch walls and solid core doors. La Europa Royale is a spectacularly landscaped two-acre site with trees, ponds and a lovely walking path that encircles the grounds. Breakfast on our flower-laden patio is a favorite. We are strategically located between downtown and the mountain recreation.

ELEGANT IN TOWN HOTEL

RATES
$159/$235 including breakfast. Corporate rates available to qualified business guests.
Open year-round.

ATTRACTIONS
Skiing from Thanksgiving to May 1. Hiking and mountain biking from May through October. Boating and fishing all year.

CUISINE
Room rates include breakfast. Seven fine-dining restaurants are located in close proximity to the hotel. Shuttle service available.

DIRECTIONS
Just N of the I-215 loop at 6000 S and 1135 E.

Handicap Access Available • Conference Facilities for 25
MC, Visa, AMEX, Diners, Disc, CB Accepted
Suitable for Children • Reservations Accepted Through Travel Agents

Park City, UT

Old Miners' Lodge

800-648-8068
435-645-8068 Fax 435-645-7420
www.oldminerslodge.com
stay@oldminerslodge.com
615 Woodside Avenue, Park City, UT 84060-2639

Select Registry Member *Since 1998*
Innkeepers
SUSAN WYNNE AND
LIZA SIMPSON

THE OLD MINERS' LODGE is located in the National Historic District of the colorful resort town of Park City, Utah. This charming bed and breakfast inn was established in 1889 as a boarding house for miners seeking their fortune in Park City's ore-rich mountains. Today, the spirited warmth and hospitality of Park City's illustrious past remains in this building, which has been lovingly restored to its original splendor. A full hearty breakfast is included, along with evening beverages. An outdoor hot tub welcomes guests back from a day of winter skiing or summer sports. The Old Miners' Lodge is a non-smoking inn, that accepts children, but not pets.

TRADITIONAL MOUNTAIN BREAKFAST INN

RATES
9 guest rooms and 3 suites, $70/$275 (seasonal).
Open year-round.

ATTRACTIONS
'Alpine heart of the 2002 Winter Olympic Games' and an all-season mountain resort with skiing, snowboarding, galleries, historic district, museum, golf, tennis, fishing, biking, shopping, and ballooning all close to the lodge.

CUISINE
Park City boasts over one hundred eating establishments from deli's and pizza, to regional and gourmet cuisine, most within walking distance of the inn. Your innkeepers will help with menus, suggestions and reservations.

DIRECTIONS
Take exit 145 from I/S 80 (Park City/Utah Hwy 224 exit), approximately 6 miles into town. Stay on 224 (now Park Ave.), to 8th St. (ski chair lift overhead), R on 8th one short block, then L on Woodside Ave. 150 yards up on R.

Non-Smoking Inn • Suitable for Children • Conference Facilities for 20
Visa, MC, AMEX, Disc, CB, Diners Accepted
Reservations Accepted Through Travel Agents

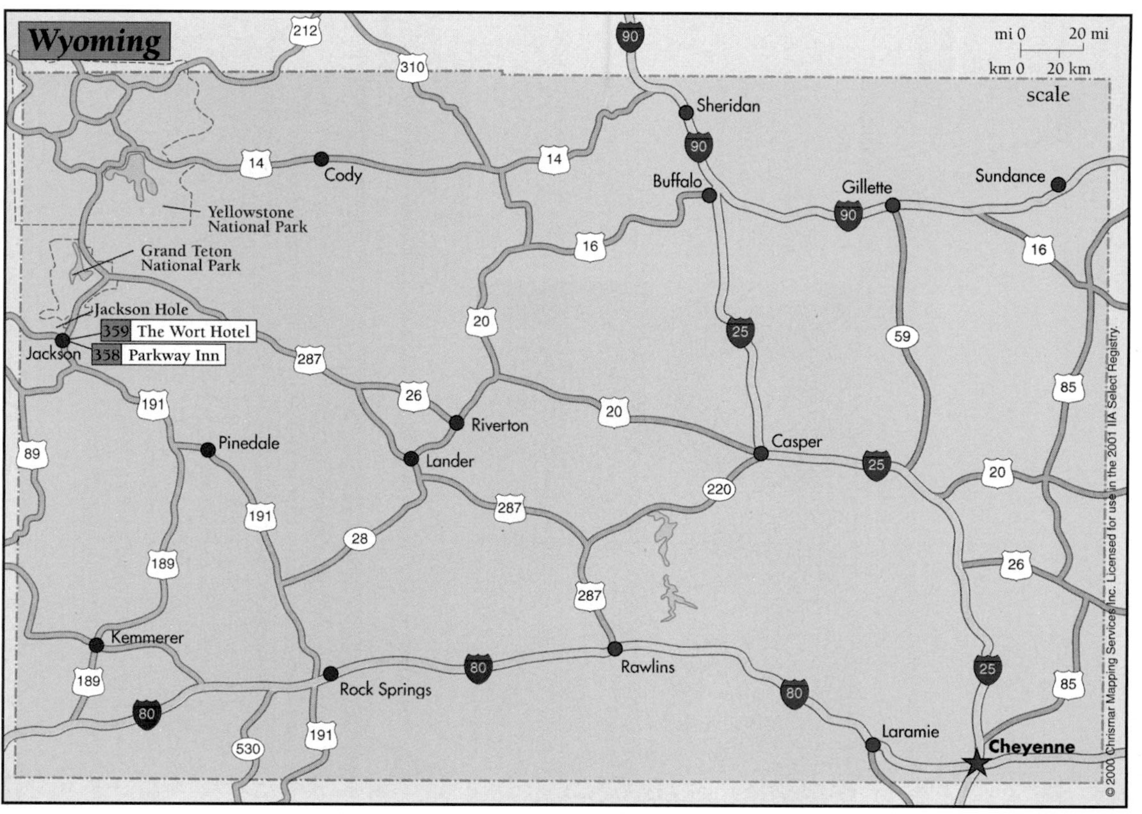
Wyoming
mi 0 20 mi
km 0 20 km
scale
Cody
Sheridan
Buffalo
Gillette
Sundance
Yellowstone National Park
Grand Teton National Park
Jackson Hole
359 The Wort Hotel
358 Parkway Inn
Jackson
Riverton
Lander
Casper
Pinedale
Kemmerer
Rock Springs
Rawlins
Laramie
Cheyenne
© 2000 Chrismar Mapping Services Inc. Licensed for use in the 2001 IIA Select Registry.

Jackson, WY

Parkway Inn

800-247-8390
307-733-3143 Fax 307-733-0955
www.parkwayinn.com
info@parkwayinn.com
125 Jackson Street,P.O. Box 494, Jackson,WY 83001

A WARM WESTERN WELCOME awaits you at the Parkway Inn, the perfect haven from which to explore Jackson Hole, long noted for its spectacular natural beauty, its National Parks and exceptional skiing. The charming rooms and suites are complemented by a fitness center that includes lap pool, saunas, spas and gym. We are perfectly located just a few short blocks from the center of the old west town of Jackson, which offers a variety of art galleries, shops and restaurants. We offer the personality of a Bed & Breakfast and the privacy and amenities of a fine country inn, along with a friendly staff to help you make the most of your visit to the last of the old west.

Select Registry Member *Since 1999*
Innkeepers/Owners
TOM AND CARMEN ROBBINS
Manager
MARK LAJUDICE

TRADITIONAL IN TOWN BREAKFAST INN

RATES
37 rooms, queen or king beds with fireplace, $89/$179 B&B;
8 suites, $90/$195 B&B;
4 cottage suites, $99/$199 B&B.
Open year-round.

ATTRACTIONS
Ski Jackson Hole, xc-skiing, dog sled, National Elk Refuge, Grand Teton National Park, Yellowstone Park, fishing, hiking, biking, golf, tennis, bird/wildlife viewing, river rafting, National Museum Wildlife Art, Grand Teton Music Festival, Fall Art Festival.

CUISINE
Continental breakfast, afternoon lemonade in summer, hot cider and cookies in winter. Fine selection of restaurants nearby.

DIRECTIONS
Three blocks W of town square. From S I-89: turn L on Jackson St., 1 block. From N I-89: turn R on Deloney St. 3 blocks. The Inn is located on the corner of Jackson St. and Deloney St.

Suitable for Children Over 6 • Non-Smoking Inn
3 Common Rooms Handicap Accessible • Visa, MC, AMEX, Disc Accepted
Reservations Accepted Through Travel Agents

Jackson Hole, WY

The Wort Hotel

800-322-2727
307-733-2190 Fax 307-733-2067
www.worthotel.com
info@worthotel.com
50 North Glenwood, Jackson Hole, WY 83001

Select Registry Member *Since 2000*
Proprietor
LEE RILEY

THE WORT HOTEL, built in 1941 as Jackson's first luxury hotel, is 1/2 block from the Town Square amid boutiques, galleries, shops and museums. The atmosphere offers the warmth and charm of a western lodge, while specializing in old-fashioned western hospitality. Guest rooms feature all the amenities expected from a fine hotel including luxurious monogrammed bathrobes and a cuddle Teddy named 'Sam'. The Wort Hotel was named one of the '50 Great Inns of America' by *National Geographic Traveler* (April 1999) and is on the National Register of Historic Places.

TRADITIONAL IN TOWN HOTEL

RATES

57 rooms, 3 suites $140/$485. Luxurious and spacious 'New West' guest rooms are decorated with tapestry fabrics, down comforters and Lodgepole pine.
Open year-round.

ATTRACTIONS

Hiking, white-water rafting, horseback riding, Yellowstone & Grand Teton Nat'l Parks, shopping, golf, fly-fishing, mountain biking, museums, galleries, skiing, xc-skiing, snowmobiling, skating, dogsledding, sleighing in the Nat'l Elk Refuge, fine dining.

CUISINE

Home of the famous Silver Dollar Bar & Grille. Full American breakfast October 16-May 15. Western Regional Cuisine serving breakfast, lunch and dinner.

DIRECTIONS

From I-15 N past Idaho Falls, Hwy 26, L on Hwy 31, R at Victor Hwy 22 L on Broadway, L on Glenwood. From Hwy 89 S from National Parks to Jackson, R on Broadway, R on Glenwood.

3 Guestrooms Handicap Accessible • Suitable for Children
Conference Facilities for 125 • AMEX, MC, Visa, Diners, CB Accepted
Non-Smoking Inn • Reservations Accepted Through Travel Agents

The Southwest

The Southwest landscape touches a traveler's soul with mystery and awe. Here is a melding of cultures: Hopi and Navaho, Mexican, Europeans, pioneers, explorers and American fur trappers tracing back to the 17th century. The famous cuisine stands on its own. Nowhere in America is food more colorful, more alive with hot, exotic tastes and rich diversity.

THE CURRENT HOLDS STEADY—standards remain consistent: Here are some of the finest Inns of the *Select Registry*. Southwest colors brighten up the bedrooms and dining rooms and bleed into the horizon. The sunshine is intense.

Chose a *Select Registry* Inn as you cross New Mexico, Arizona or Oklahoma. Styles vary but quality is constant. Our innkeepers are the best in the business.

The Southwest generates rich soul medicine. Here is what the doctor ordered. Here are the sunsets, sweeping vistas and the ruins of the Anasazi. One can easily imagine the awe on the faces of the Spanish conquistadors as they stumbled across this Big Land, or the strong stern eyes of the famous Apache chief Geronimo as he appraised his beloved homeland.

Along the highways, wildflowers are in bloom. The road stretches across painted deserts alive with sandstone monuments. The landscape is enchanting.

Spend a few days at a ranch in New Mexico. Go horseback riding for the first time in your life. Descend into the terra-cotta canyons. Marvel at the cactus, the gangly mesquite and high-sculpted buttes.

Travel into Texas and remember romance. The state is vast, but the quality of the SELECT REGISTRY never disappoints. New friendships will certainly flourish. This is one of the benefits of SELECT REGISTRY Inns, at the breakfast table or in the common room. Our customers are special. We guarantee it.

"Most outstanding B&B we've been in! The extras and attention to details are incredible – and the food...mmmmmm!"
—Sarah Fiash, Chester, VA

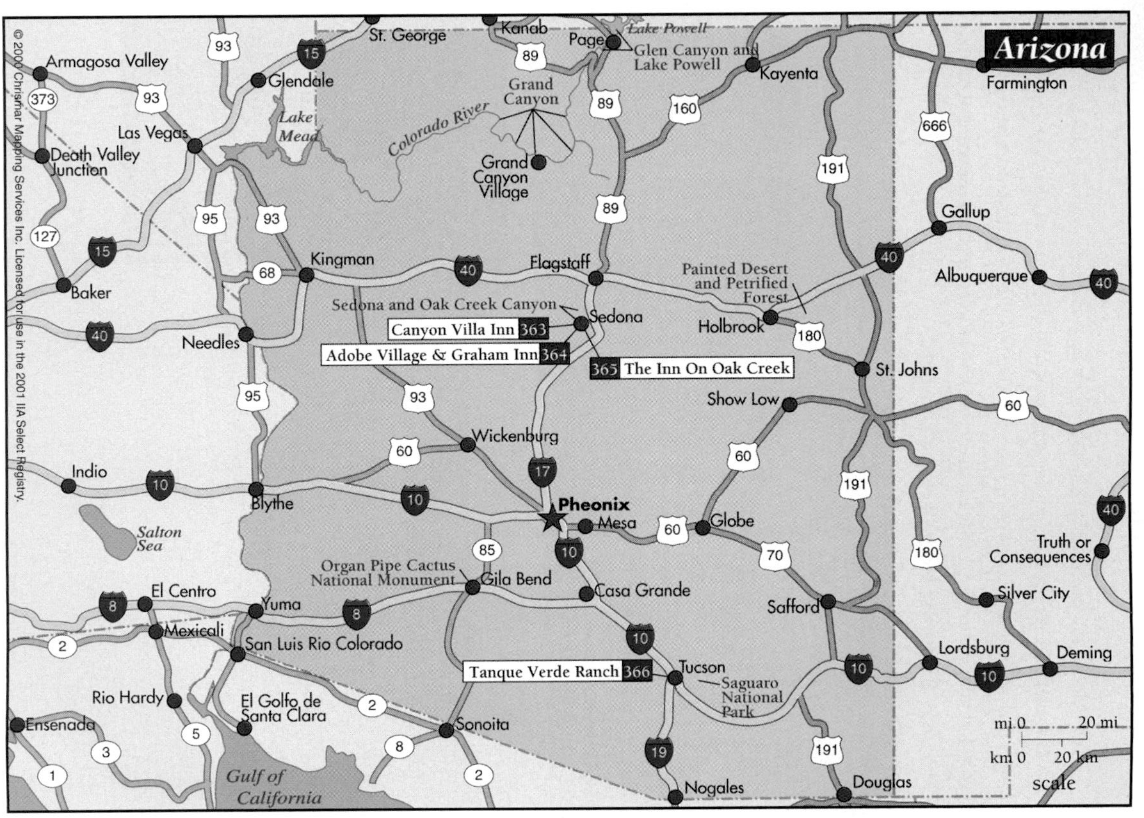

Arizona
St. George
Kanab
Lake Powell
Page
Glen Canyon and Lake Powell
Kayenta
Farmington
Armagosa Valley
Glendale
Lake Mead
Colorado River
Grand Canyon
Grand Canyon Village
Las Vegas
Death Valley Junction
Gallup
Baker
Kingman
Flagstaff
Painted Desert and Petrified Forest
Albuquerque
Sedona and Oak Creek Canyon
Sedona
Canyon Villa Inn 363
Adobe Village & Graham Inn 364
365 The Inn On Oak Creek
Holbrook
Needles
St. Johns
Show Low
Wickenburg
Indio
Blythe
Pheonix
Mesa
Globe
Salton Sea
Truth or Consequences
Organ Pipe Cactus National Monument
Gila Bend
Casa Grande
El Centro
Yuma
Safford
Silver City
Mexicali
San Luis Rio Colorado
Lordsburg
Deming
Tanque Verde Ranch 366
Tucson
Saguaro National Park
Rio Hardy
El Golfo de Santa Clara
Ensenada
Sonoita
Gulf of California
Nogales
Douglas
mi 0 20 mi
km 0 20 km
scale

Sedona, AZ

Canyon Villa Inn

800-453-1166

520-284-1226 Fax 520-284-2114

www.canyonvilla.com

canvilla@sedona.net

125 Canyon Circle Drive, Sedona, AZ 86351

Select Registry Member *Since 1995*

Innkeepers / Owners

Les and Peg Belch

Elegant Village Inn

TWO HOURS SOUTH OF THE GRAND CANYON, this mission-style inn affords spectacular red rock views. French doors in individually decorated guest rooms open onto scenic patios or balconies fronting a lush walled garden centerpieced by an inviting swimming pool. Stylish, comfortable rooms offer TV, radio, CD player and some have fireplaces. Ceramic-tiled baths feature whirlpool tubs and luxurious lounging robes. Guests indulge in early morning coffee, homemade cinnamon rolls served daily with bountiful breakfasts, sumptuous afternoon hors d'oeuvres and nightly sweet dreams. Enjoy the Inn's many special touches and friendly hospitality. AAA ◆◆◆◆ and Mobil ★★★★.

RATES
11 rooms, $160/$250 B&B.
Open year-round.

ATTRACTIONS
Heated swimming pool on premises, nearby golf, tennis, hiking, jeep tours, ballooning, horseback riding, galleries, 2.5 hours to Grand Canyon.

CUISINE
Full, gourmet breakfast, evening hors d'oeuvres. BYOB.

DIRECTIONS
From I-17, turn W on SR179 8 mi, L on Bell Rock Blvd 1 blk, R on Canyon Circle Dr. Inn on R. Please call for information.

---

1 Guestroom Handicap Accessible • Non-Smoking Inn
Suitable for Children Over 11 • AMEX, Visa, MC Accepted
Reservations Accepted Through Travel Agents

Sedona, AZ

Adobe Village & Graham Inn

800-228-1425
520-284-1425 Fax 520-284-0767
www.SedonasFinest.com
graham@sedona.net
150 Canyon Circle Drive, Sedona, AZ 86351

Select Registry Member *Since 2000*
Innkeepers/Owners
STUART AND ILENE BERMAN

BED & BREAKFAST AS ORIGINAL ART. This impressive AAA ◆◆◆◆ inn offers a peaceful setting with breathtaking red rock views and southwest art, rugs, and tiles. All guest rooms are individual theme rooms. The 850 sq. ft. Adobe Village casitas are built around a brick paved courtyard and are surrounded by an adobe wall. Beautifully landscaped grounds with shaded veranda, pool, hot tub, and fountain invite enjoyment of the outdoors. Mountain bikes are provided and hiking/biking trails are close. Experience comfortable elegance and memorable breakfasts. Alone Together. Find a Special Place in you Heart... "the most romantic new guest rooms in America..." *Honeymoon Magazine*.

Suitable for Children Over 8 • Visa, MC, Disc, AMEX Accepted
Designated Smoking Areas • Reservations Accepted Through Travel Agents

ELEGANT VILLAGE
BREAKFAST INN

RATES

6 rooms in main inn, $169/$369. 4 luxury casitas, $339/$499. Spacious and distinctive theme rooms with fireplace, Jacuzzi tub, TV/VCR, CD player, balcony. Casitas-waterfall shower, breadmaker, bath fireplace, kitchenette.
Open year-round.

ATTRACTIONS

Heated swimming pool, hot tub, mountain bikes on premises, nearby golf, tennis, hiking, Indian ruins, jeep tours, ballooning, horseback riding, art galleries, the Chapel of the Holy Cross. Grand Canyon is 2 1/2 hours, a perfect day-trip.

CUISINE

Early AM coffee. Full, gourmet breakfast. Afternoon refreshments. Evening cookie jar. Casitas have bread makers allowing guests to come in to the aroma of fresh-baked bread each day. Dinner is served on Thanksgiving. BYOB.

DIRECTIONS

From Hwy 179, turn W onto Bell Rock Blvd. Drive two blocks passing the first Canyon Circle Dr. You will see us on the R, on the corner of Bell Rock Blvd and Canyon Circle Dr. You're home.

Sedona, AZ

The Inn on Oak Creek

800-499-7896
520-282-7896 Fax 520-282-0696
www.sedona-inn.com
theinn@sedona.net
556 Hwy 179, Sedona, AZ 86336

Select Registry Member *Since 2001*
Owner/Manager
Rick and Pam Morris

Initially built in 1972 as an art gallery then totally refurbished and transformed in 1995, the Inn perches on a bluff overlooking Oak Creek, one of Arizona's premier year-round spring fed streams. Within easy walking distance are Sedona's best art galleries, boutique shops, and several fine restaurants. Yet almost as close are National Forest trails that will take you to the heart of red rock country. So while our guests are constantly surprised that an inn so centrally located in Sedona can offer such privacy, the luxurious AAA Four Diamond accommodations, professional staff, and culinary delights are what really please them.

Elegant In Town Breakfast Inn

RATES

9 rooms, $165/$260 night dbl.
2 suites, $195/$250
$20 for each additional person.
All feature private baths, whirlpool tubs, gas fireplces, and TV/VCRs. Creek side rooms have decks with dramatic views.
Open year-round.

ATTRACTIONS

Hike scores of trails with our private guide. Rent a mountain bike or a horse. Take a jeep ride. Fly over it all in balloons, biplanes, or helicopters. Enjoy great nearby restaurants, galleries and shops, or just relax in our creek side park.

CUISINE

Full breakfast and afternoon hor d'oeuvres. Guests are welcome to bring their own adult beverages.

DIRECTIONS

In Sedona on Hwy 179 just 0.4 mile south of the intersection of Hwy 179 and 89A.

---

1 Guestroom Handicap Accessible • Suitable for ChildrenOver 10
Designated Smoking Areas • MC, Visa, Disc, AMEX Accepted
Reservations Accepted Through Travel Agents

Tucson, AZ

Tanque Verde Ranch

800-234-3833
520-296-6275 Fax 520-721-9426
www.tanqueverderanch.com
Dude@tvgr.com
14301 E Speedway, Tucson, AZ 85748

FOUNDED ON SPANISH LAND GRANT IN 1868 in the spectacular Sonoran Desert, Tanque Verde Ranch has evolved into one of the Southwest's most complete vacation destinations. A Mobil ★★★★ star resort, it maintains the cowboy traditions and spirit unique to this western cattle ranch. Sonoran-style with adobe walls, high saguaro rib ceilings, beehive fireplaces and mesquite corrals, the Ranch setting provides expansive desert and mountain views. The facilities are just as remarkable, with 130 horses, tennis courts, indoor/outdoor pools, saunas, spa, guided hiking and mountain biking, outdoor BBQ's and breakfast rides, in a casual relaxed atmosphere. The supervised children's program offers a fantastic ranch experience for kids ages 4-11.

2 Guestrooms Handicap Accessible • Suitable for Children
Conference Facilities for 150 • Visa, MC, Disc, AMEX Accepted
Reservations Accepted Through Travel Agents

Select Registry Member *Since 1970*
Contact
ROBERT AND RITA COTE

TRADITIONAL COUNTRY RANCH

RATES
51 guest rooms.
23 suites, american plan, meals, riding, all activites.
Rates vary by room type and season; please call for details.
Open year-round.

ATTRACTIONS
Tucson Environs, Arizona/Sonora Desert Museum, San Xavier Mission, Kitt Peak Observatory, Biosphere II, Old Tucson, Pima Air Museum, Tombstone, Mexico, Saguaro National Park and Karthner Caverns.

CUISINE
Three meals and all activities are included in rate. Meals are served daily 8-9 am, 12-1:30 pm and 6:30-8 pm.

DIRECTIONS
From Tucson, drive East on Speedway Blvd all the way to the dead-end, where the driveway begins.

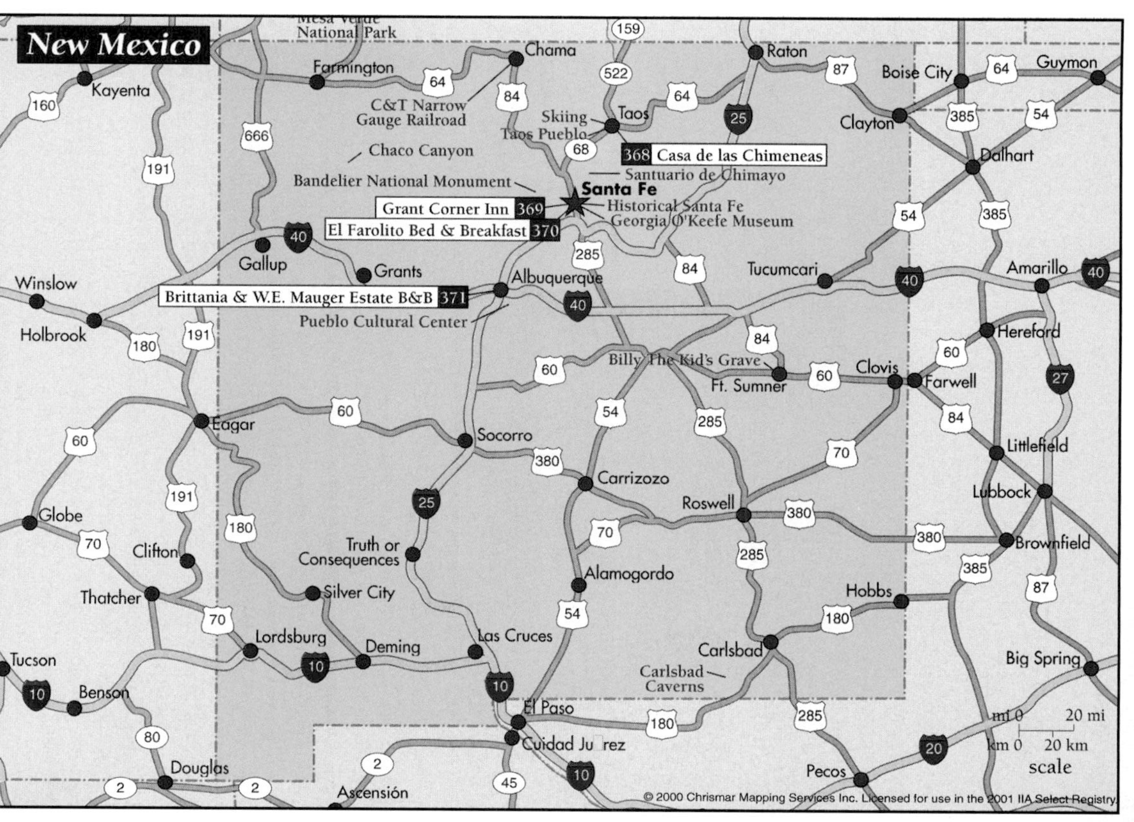

New Mexico
368 Casa de las Chimeneas
369 Grant Corner Inn
370 El Farolito Bed & Breakfast
371 Brittania & W.E. Mauger Estate B&B
Santa Fe
Santuario de Chimayo
Historical Santa Fe
Georgia O'Keefe Museum
Skiing
Taos Pueblo
Bandelier National Monument
Pueblo Cultural Center
Chaco Canyon
C&T Narrow Gauge Railroad
National Park
Billy The Kid's Grave
Carlsbad Caverns
Kayenta
Farmington
Chama
Taos
Raton
Boise City
Guymon
Clayton
Dalhart
Gallup
Grants
Albuquerque
Tucumcari
Amarillo
Winslow
Holbrook
Hereford
Ft. Sumner
Clovis
Farwell
Eagar
Socorro
Carrizozo
Littlefield
Lubbock
Roswell
Brownfield
Globe
Clifton
Truth or Consequences
Alamogordo
Thatcher
Silver City
Hobbs
Lordsburg
Deming
Las Cruces
Carlsbad
Big Spring
Tucson
Benson
El Paso
Cuidad Ju rez
Douglas
Ascensión
Pecos
mi 0 20 mi
km 0 20 km
scale
© 2000 Chrismar Mapping Services Inc. Licensed for use in the 2001 IIA Select Registry

Taos, NM

Casa de las Chimeneas

877-758-4777
505-758-4777 Fax 505-758-3976
www.VisitTaos.com
casa@newmex.com
405 Cordoba Road, Taos, NM 87571

Select Registry Member *Since 1998*
Innkeeper
SUSAN VERNON

CONVERTED TO AN INN from a luxurious home, Casa de las Chimeneas ('House of Chimneys') retains its regal air with expanded guest facilities—fitness room, massage and sauna, outdoor hot tub under the stars, and three separate gardens. Surrounded by a high wall flanked by 17 towering trees, the Inn is 2 1/2 short blocks from historic Taos Plaza. The Innkeeper is an award-winning cook and her hearty cuisine has been featured in *Gourmet* and *Bon Appetit*. There are many special touches such as in-room bars, beverages, fireplaces and jetted tubs. 'Everything—from the fine linens to the corner fireplaces—invites cozying up with someone you love.'—*New Mexico's Best*. AAA ♦♦♦♦.

1 Guestroom Handicap Accessible • Suitable for Children
Non-Smoking Inn • Visa, MC, AMEX, Disc, Diners Accepted
Reservations Accepted Through Travel Agents

TRADITIONAL VILLAGE
BREAKFAST INN

RATES
6 rooms, $175/$290 B&B.
2 suites, $325/$615 B&B.
Open year-round.

ATTRACTIONS
1000-year-old Indian pueblo, downhill/xc-skiing at five ski areas, historic Spanish colonial churches, Kit Carson's home, art galleries, shops, scenic Enchanted Circle Byway, river rafting, hiking, seven museums, hot air ballooning, horseback riding.

CUISINE
Two-course breakfast with hot entree, ample afternoon hors d'oeuvres, hearty soup suppers in winter, complimentary in-room bars with juices, sodas, mineral waters, complimentary in-room coffee, tea, cocoa, etc.

DIRECTIONS
From Santa Fe on Hwy 68: Turn R onto Los Pandos, go 1 block & turn R on Cordoba at the four-way stop. The inn is the first L off Cordoba.

Santa Fe, NM

Grant Corner Inn

800-964-9003
505-983-6678 Fax 505-983-1526
www.grantcornerinn.com

Select Registry Member *Since 1988*
Innkeeper/Owner
LOUISE STEWART

122 Grant Avenue, Santa Fe, NM 87501

TRADITIONAL IN TOWN
BREAKFAST INN

RATES
8 rooms, $115/$225 B&B.
Hacienda, $130/$145 B&B.
10 private baths.
Open year-round.

ATTRACTIONS
Cross-country and downhill skiing, hiking, fishing, golf, tennis, swimming and spa (fee).

CUISINE
Daily breakfast and Sunday brunch included in room rates and served to the public. Special dinners, picnic lunches, weddings and catered events.

DIRECTIONS
From Albuquerque, I-25 N exit St. Francis L-N 4.5 miles to R-W at Alameda. 6 blks., L-N on Guadalupe, 2 blks., R-W on Johnson, 2 blks., park on L.

THIS DELIGHTFUL INN HAS AN IDEAL LOCATION just two blocks from the historic plaza of downtown Santa Fe, among intriguing shops, galleries and restaurants. The world reknowned Georgia O'Keeffe Museum is next door to the Inn. Lush gardens, beautifully appointed guest rooms, fabulous gourmet breakfasts and the gracious hospitality of Louise and her staff make this an experience not to be missed. Open to the public daily for breakfast, Sunday brunch and special occasion dinners. Ample parking for houseguests on premises.

1 Guestroom Handicap Accessible • Suitable for Children Over 9
Conference Facilities for 20 • Visa, MC, AMEX Accepted
Non-Smoking Inn • Reservations Accepted Through Travel Agents

Santa Fe, NM

El Farolito Bed & Breakfast Inn

888-634-8782
505-988-1631 Fax 505-989-1323
www.farolito.com
innkeeper@farolito.com
514 Galisteo Street, Santa Fe, NM 87501

Select Registry Member *Since 2001*
Innkeepers / Owners
Walt Wyss
Wayne Mainus

SURROUND YOURSELF WITH THE RICHNESS OF SANTA FE'S art and history in an authentic adobe compound. The Inn offers you award winning private casitas, showcasing exquisite southwestern art and furnishings. The Inn is conveniently located in the historic district, a short walk to galleries, shops, museums, fine dining and the central plaza. In the warm sunshine, savor a leisurely breakfast on the back portal and relax on your garden patio. In the winter, enjoy a fireside breakfast in the brightly decorated dining room and the coziness of a fireplace in each room. "Most beautifully decorated B&B ever! Great hospitality - great breakfasts!" AAA ◆◆◆.

Southwestern In Town Breakfast Inn

RATES

7 rooms, $100/$170 B&B
1 suite, $140/$210 B&B
Rooms feature handcrafted furnitue, private baths, fireplaces, quality linens, air conditioning, coffee service and patios.
Open year-round.

ATTRACTIONS

Art galleries, museums, world class shopping, great restaurants, historic sites, Indian ruins and pueblos, outdoor activities including hiking, skiing, rafting, horseback riding, ballooning, golf, fishing. Performing arts - opera, theater, symphony, spas.

CUISINE

Expanded continental breakfast featuring quality home baked goods, fresh fruit plate and ample accompaniment. In-room coffee service. Extensive selection of nearby world-class fine dining.

DIRECTIONS

From Albuquerque: I-25 N, exit 282 St. Francis N to Cerrillos, R on Cerrillos, R at Paseo de Peralta, L at Galisteo to 514. From Taos: S on 84/285, bear L to downtown, L on Paseo de Peralta, R on Galisteo.

Suitable for Children • Conference Facilities for 20
Designated Smoking Areas • MC, Visa, AMEX, Disc Accepted
Reservations Accepted Through Travel Agents

Albuquerque, NM

Brittania & W.E. Mauger Estate B&B

800-719-9189
505-242-8755 Fax 505-842-8835
www.maugerbb.com
maugerbb@aol.com
701 Roma Avenue NW, Albuquerque, NM 87102

THIS 1897 VICTORIAN is ideally located downtown, just four blocks walking distance from the convention center/business district, and one mile from Old Town. The Inn is centrally located to enjoy the best of Albuquerque's attractions. Listed on the National Register of Historic Places, the Inn has enjoyed kind restoration with attention to detail. Guests delight in a sumptuous breakfast, while admiring the hummingbirds and roses on the big old front porch, or relax over wine and cheese in the evening by the fireplace in the main parlor. Business travelers enjoy the convenience of in-room phones with voice-mail and dataports. AAA ◆◆◆ and Mobil ★★★.

Select Registry Member *Since 2000*
Innkeepers / Owners
MARK BROWN AND KEITH LEWIS

TRADITIONAL IN TOWN BREAKFAST INN

RATES
9 rooms/1 suite, \$89/\$179/\$169/\$209.
Rooms include down comforters, television, small fridge, coffee maker, snack basket, phone with voice mail and dataport.
Open year-round.

ATTRACTIONS
Near Old Town, Rte 66 District, zoo, Biopark, Rio Grande Nature Center, Aerial Tramway, ballooning, Indian Pueblo Cultural Center, Acoma Sky City Pueblo, gaming casinos, Turquoise Trail, llama hiking, wineries and many museums.

CUISINE
Full breakfast with hot entree, late afternoon hors d'oeuvres, evening sweets, complimentary beverages and in-room coffee.

DIRECTIONS
From Airport take I-25 N. From I-40, take I-25 S. Exit Martin Luther King Blvd. Turn W, through downtown, to 7th St. Turn R one block to Roma. The B&B is located on the corner of 7th St. and Roma.

Suitable for Children • Pets Allowed
Conference Facilities for 15 • MC, Visa, AMEX, Disc, Diners Accepted
Reservations Accepted Through Travel Agents

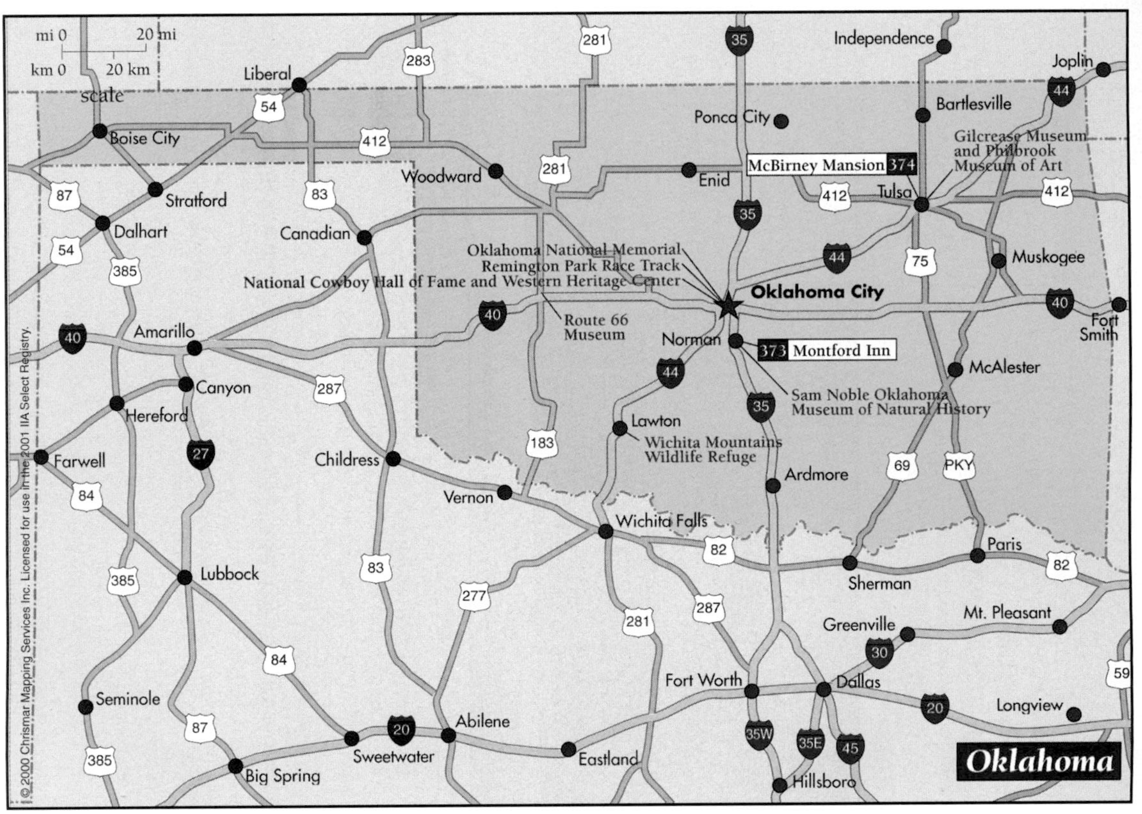
Oklahoma
Oklahoma City
McBirney Mansion 374
373 Montford Inn
Gilcrease Museum and Philbrook Museum of Art
Sam Noble Oklahoma Museum of Natural History
Oklahoma National Memorial
Remington Park Race Track
National Cowboy Hall of Fame and Western Heritage Center
Route 66 Museum
Wichita Mountains Wildlife Refuge
Independence
Joplin
Bartlesville
Ponca City
Enid
Tulsa
Muskogee
Fort Smith
Norman
McAlester
Lawton
Ardmore
Wichita Falls
Sherman
Paris
Mt. Pleasant
Greenville
Fort Worth
Dallas
Longview
Hillsboro
Eastland
Abilene
Sweetwater
Big Spring
Seminole
Lubbock
Farwell
Hereford
Canyon
Amarillo
Childress
Vernon
Canadian
Woodward
Liberal
Boise City
Stratford
Dalhart
mi 0 20 mi
km 0 20 km
scale
© 2000 Chrismar Mapping Services Inc. Licensed for use in the 2001 IIA Select Registry.

Norman, OK

Montford Inn

800-321-8969
405-321-2200 Fax 405-321-8347
www.montfordinn.com
innkeeper@montfordinn.com
322 West Tonhawa, Norman, OK 73069

Select Registry Member *Since 1997*
Innkeepers / Owners
PHYLLIS AND RON MURRAY
WILLIAM AND GINGER MURRAY

TRADITIONAL IN TOWN
BREAKFAST INN

RATES
10 rooms, $75/$155 B&B.
6 cottage suites, $120/$200 B&B.
Open year-round.

ATTRACTIONS
Health club privileges, golf, tennis, hiking, horseback riding, sailing and fishing nearby, University of Oklahoma sporting and cultural events.

CUISINE
Breakfast. Complimentary wine and refreshments early evening.

DIRECTIONS
20 minutes S of Oklahoma City. From I-35, take Main St., Downtown exit 109. Turn L on University (about 2.2 miles from I-35). Go 2 blocks, turn R block on Tonhawa.

NESTLED IN THE HEART of Norman's Historic District, this prairie-style inn envelopes travelers in a relaxing atmosphere. Antiques, family heirlooms and Native American art accent the individually decorated guest rooms and suites. Awaken to rich coffees and a gourmet country breakfast served in the beautifully appointed dining room or in the more intimate setting of the suites. Relax in private hot tubs. Escape in luxurious whirlpool bathtubs. Unwind in elegant cottage suites. Stroll through beautiful gardens. Find your heart...at the Montford Inn! AAA ◆◆◆ and Mobil ★★★.

1 Guestroom Handicap Accessible • Suitable for Children
Conference Facilities for 20 • Visa, MC, AMEX, Diners, Disc Accepted
Non-Smoking Inn • Reservations Accepted Through Travel Agents

Tulsa, OK

McBirney Mansion

918-585-3234
Fax 918-585-9377
www.mcbirneymansion.com

1414 South Galveston, Tulsa, OK 74127

Select Registry Member *Since 2001*
Co-Owners
Kathy Collins and Renita Shofner

Elegant In Town Inn

Situated on a crest overlooking the Arkansas River, McBirney Mansion offers three acres of beautiful grounds. The estate is adjacent to Tulsa's River Parks with 12 miles of biking and jogging trails. McBirney Mansion is a treasured historic dwelling offering the discriminating traveler all the comforts of a country estate in a quiet residential neighborhood. Curl up in the library with a good book, enjoy the music room's grand piano, and savor afternoon refreshments in the sunroom or elegant living room. When the need for privacy or sleep overtakes you, retire to the comfort of your own graciously appointed room complete with fresh flowers.

RATES
8 guest rooms, $119/$225.
All rooms include private bath, individul phones, and cable TV. Two luxurious suites with sitting rooms. *Open year-round.*

ATTRACTIONS
Philbrook Museum, Gilcrease Museum, Utica Square shopping center, Cherry St. antiques, Performing Arts Center, Tulsa RiverParks.

CUISINE
Full American breakfast is included with your room. Morning coffee on the upstairs landing. Late afternoon refreshments served in the sunroom and elegant living room.

DIRECTIONS
At 15th Street, Riverside Drive and Galveston, go N on Galveston for one block. Entrance is located on the W side through stone pillars.

5 Common Rooms Handicap Accessible • Conference Facilities for 200
Non-Smoking Inn • Visa, AMEX, MC, Disc Accepted
Reservations Accepted Through Travel Agents

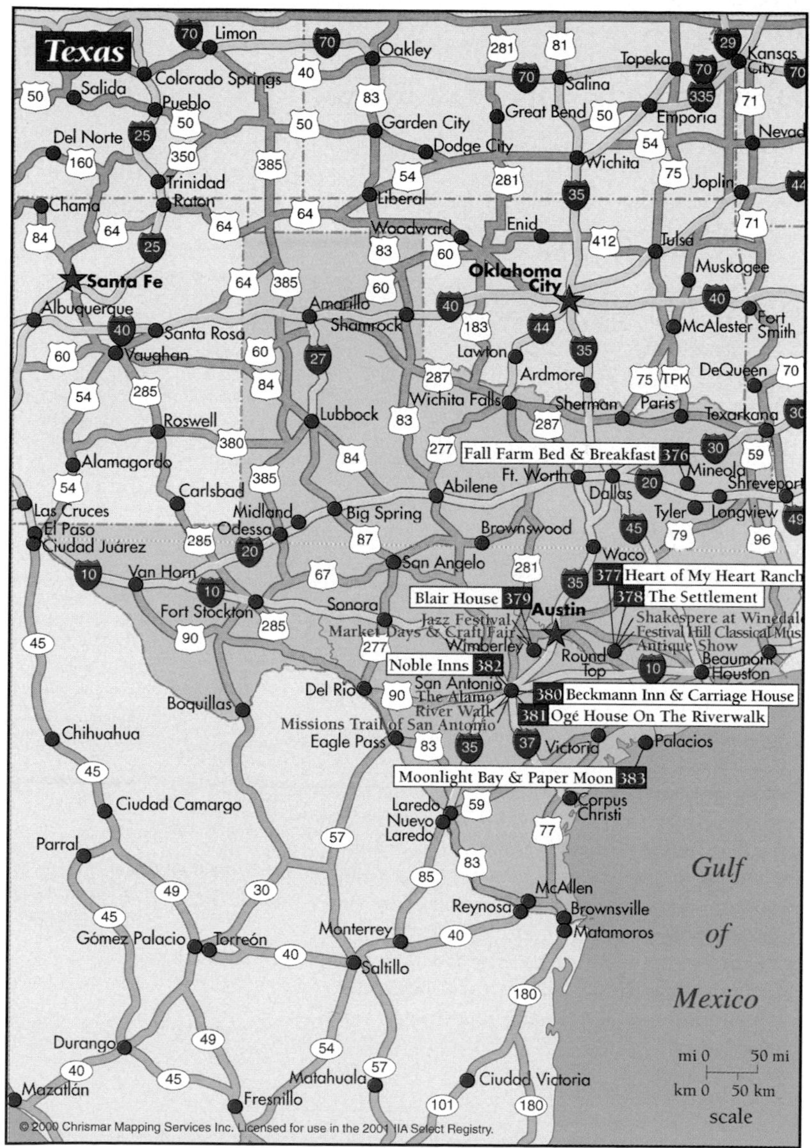

Texas
Fall Farm Bed & Breakfast 376
377 Heart of My Heart Ranch
378 The Settlement
Blair House 379
380 Beckmann Inn & Carriage House
381 Ogé House On The Riverwalk
Noble Inns 382
Moonlight Bay & Paper Moon 383
Austin
Oklahoma City
Santa Fe
Gulf of Mexico
© 2000 Chrismar Mapping Services Inc. Licensed for use in the 2001 IIA Select Registry.

Mineola, TX

Fall Farm Bed & Breakfast Retreat

903-768-2449
Fax 903-768-2079
www.fallfarm.com
info@fallfarm.com
2027 FM 779, Mineola, TX 75773-3287

Select Registry Member *Since 2000*
Innkeepers/Owners
MIKE AND CAROL FALL

ESCAPE TO THIS TRANQUIL, TEN-ACRE RETREAT in the scenic piney woods of East Texas and be drawn into a luxurious country farmhouse with a unique personality, reflecting Mike and Carol's history and welcoming spirit. The inviting atmosphere conveys a familiar feeling of home, yet transforms you with beautifully decorated rooms filled with color and whimsical details. Sun worshippers will enjoy the sparkling pool in the afternoon, as well as romantic stargazing in the soothing spa after dark. A bountiful breakfast assures that no one leaves hungry. Quiet moments and total relaxation are inevitable...our hospitality awaits!

TRADITIONAL COUNTRY BREAKFAST INN

RATES
5 rooms/suites, $110/$165.
2 cottages, $200/$250.
Each guestroom's individual personality includes sitting areas, oversized or multiple beds, ceiling fans, robes, CD players.
Open year-round.

ATTRACTIONS
Antiquing, art galleries, theatres. Massage, swimming, golf, historic attractions. Dogwood, Azalea, Rose and Autumn trails. NEARBY: Canton's 'First Monday Trade Days,' Lake Fork, 'Big Bass' capital of Texas. Tournaments and fishing guides year-round.

CUISINE
Full gourmet breakfast, afternoon refreshments, fresh fruit and cold drinks provided.

DIRECTIONS
Mineola is approximately 80 miles from both Dallas and Shreveport. From I-20, take Hwy 69 N to Mineola. When Hwy 69 forks, take Hwy 37 N for 6 miles and turn L on FM 779. Fall Farm is 2 miles on L.

4 Common Rooms Handicap Accessible
Designated Smoking Areas • Visa, MC, Disc, AMEX Accepted
Reservations Accepted Through Travel Agents

Round Top, TX

Heart of My Heart Ranch

800-327-1242
979-249-3171 Fax 979-249-3193
www.heartofmyheartranch.com
heart17@cvtv.net
403 Florida Chapel Road, Round Top, TX 78954

Select Registry Member *Since 1998*
Innkeepers/Owners
BILL AND FRANCES HARRIS

LOCATED ON 200 WOODED ACRES one mile from historic Round Top, the Inn is a cluster of six houses with a stocked fishing lake with boats and lighted pier. There's a stone swimming pool, wrap-around porches with rockers, where breakfast is served and stories are told. The houses are furnished with family antiques. Bill's grandmother's house is a museum nearby. Some rooms have fireplaces, some king-sized beds, some in-room Jacuzzi tubs. Families, lovers, and business associates all enjoy the relaxed, informal, open kitchen and delicious snacks, the donkeys, horses, cats, dogs and congenial hosts. Honeymoon packages available. AAA ◆◆◆ and Mobil ★★★.

TRADITIONAL COUNTRY BREAKFAST INN

RATES

8 rooms, $135/$195.
2 suites, $135/$225 B&B.
2 cottages, $150/$175.
Open year-round.

ATTRACTIONS

Fishing lake, hiking trails, horseback riding, pool, hot tub, biking, storytelling, driving range, classical music concerts, antiquing, Shakespeare theatre and historic tours.

CUISINE

Breakfast buffet, picnic basket, other meals available for conferences. Complimentary wine, lemonade and cookies.

DIRECTIONS

From Houston or Austin: take Hwy 290 to 237 S to Round Top to 1 mile S. Turn L on Florida Chapel Rd. First gate on the L.

1 Guestroom Handicap Accessible • Suitable for Children
Conference Facilities for 25 • Visa, MC, AMEX, Disc Accepted
Non-Smoking Inn • Reservations Accepted Through Travel Agents

The Settlement at Round Top

888-ROUNDTOP
979-249-5015 Fax 979-249-5587
www.thesettlement.com
stay@thesettlement.com
P.O. Box 176, Round Top, TX 78954

Select Registry Member *Since 1999*
Innkeepers / Owners
KAREN AND LARRY BEEVERS

THIS DELIGHTFUL INN WILL ENCHANT YOU with the comforts of today combined with the charms of yesterday within a fully restored pioneer era complex of log cabins, German cottages and character houses on a peaceful 35-acre setting, complete with wildflowers, deer, antique roses, miniature horses, split rail fences and towering oaks. All rooms and suites have private baths, heat and air-conditioning, porches with rockers, original art and fine linens, some with private whirlpools for two and/or fireplaces. The stars twinkle seductively over the romantic open-air spa. Fantastic full country breakfasts served under the trees in a restored civil-war era barn. Featured in *Country Living* magazine.

Conference Facilities for 26 • Visa, MC, AMEX, Novus Accepted
Non-Smoking Inn • Reservations Accepted Through Travel Agents

RUSTIC COUNTRY
BREAKFAST INN

RATES

Ten rooms total.
4 rooms, $110/$145.
3 suites, $185/$225.
2 cottages, $145/$175.
All B&B, single or double occupancy. Honeymoon packages available.
Closed Christmas Eve/Day.

ATTRACTIONS

HERE: Rocking, hiking, bicycling, croquet, board games, books, cassette library, outdoor spa, wildflowers, bird-watching, miniature horses and antique roses. NEAR: Music Institute, painted churches, lakes, antiques, monastery, herb show, Shakespeare.

CUISINE

Full Texas country breakfast buffet, afternoon beverage and snacks. Picnic lunches and dinners available upon advance request. 'Worth the drive just for the breakfast!' C.M., Kingwood, Texas. BYOB.

DIRECTIONS

Conveniently located half-way between Austin and Houston. Round Top is eight miles S of U.S. Hwy 290 on FM 237. Continue S 1 1/2 miles, W on Hartfield Rd. 1/2 mile to ranch on R. Guest entrance second gate; enter to a warm country welcome.

Blair House

877-549-5450
512-847-1111 Fax 512-847-8820
www.blairhouseinn.com
info@blairhouseinn.com
100 Spoke Hill Road, Wimberley, TX 78676

Select Registry Member *Since 1998*
Innkeeper/Owner/Chef
JONNIE STANSBURY

TRADITIONAL COUNTRY INN

BLAIR HOUSE IS A "LITTLE BIT OF HEAVEN" with your own private Walden Pond on 90 serene acres of Texas Hill Country. Meticulous service, warm hospitality, delectable food and luxury amenities provide the "ultimate" comfort. Consistently listed in the top Country Inns by *Conde Nast Traveler, Nat'l Geographic Traveler, Southern Living, Dallas Morning News, Houston Chronicle* and *Austin Chronicle*. The Inn is light and airy, the ambiance refreshing and inviting. A stay at Blair House will 'revive your spirit, and fill your heart and mind with peace'.

RATES
8 rooms, $145/$225.
Special business single rates.
Open year-round.

ATTRACTIONS
Lakes/rivers, water sports, hike 90 acres, golf, historic sightseeing 50 minutes to Austin/San Antonio Alamo. Sauna, massage, art, videos, CDs, library.

CUISINE
Full breakfast, 5-course Sat. evening dining. Other times by request, special occasions. Complimentary wine.

DIRECTIONS
From Austin take I-35 S to Kyle Exit. Continue W to Wimberley. 1.6 miles S of Wimberley Square on E side of Ranch Rd. 12.

1 Guestroom Handicap Accessible • Suitable for Children Over 12
Conference Facilities for 24 • Visa, MC, AMEX, Disc, Diners, CB Accepted
Non-Smoking Inn • Reservations Accepted Through Travel Agents

A. Beckmann Inn and Carriage House

800-945-1449
210-229-1449 Fax 210-229-1061
www.beckmanninn.com
beckinn@swbell.net
222 East Guenther Street, San Antonio, TX 78204

Select Registry Member *Since 1997*
Innkeepers / Owners
Betty Jo and Don Schwartz

Experience warm and gracious hospitality at its very best, in a beautiful Victorian home and carriage house in the picturesque, downtown, King William Historic District. The perfect location for business or leisure travel. The 'hidden treasure' of San Antonio, across the street from the Riverwalk and minutes to the Alamo by trolley. The wonderful wrap-around porch welcomes guests to spacious, antique-filled rooms, ornately carved, high back, queen-sized beds, private baths, lush robes, TVs, phones and guest refrigerators. A gourmet breakfast, with a breakfast dessert, is served in the formal dining room with china, crystal and silver. AAA ◆◆◆ and Mobil ★★★.

Elegant In Town Breakfast Inn

RATES
3 rooms, $99/$130 B&B.
2 suites, $120/$150 B&B.
Open year-round.

ATTRACTIONS
Riverwalk, Alamo, missions, Mexican market, zoo, botanical gardens, Sea World, Six Flags-Fiesta Texas, golf, museums, theatres, art galleries, antiquing, shopping, dining, dancing, convention center, day-trips into the hill country and much more.

CUISINE
Full gourmet breakfast, with a breakfast dessert.

DIRECTIONS
From airport, 281 S to 37 S, exit R on Durango Alamodome, L on S St. Mary's St., then immediately take R on King William St., L on E Guenther St.

Suitable for Children Over 12 • Designated Smoking Areas
Conference Facilities for 10 • MC, Visa, AMEX, Disc, Diners Accepted
Reservations Accepted Through Travel Agents

The Ogé Inn on the Riverwalk

800-242-2770
210-223-2353 Fax 210-226-5812
www.ogeinn.com
ogeinn@swbell.net
209 Washington Street, San Antonio, TX 78204-1336

Select Registry Member *Since 1994*
Innkeepers / Owners
SHARRIE AND PATRICK MAGATAGAN

ELEGANT IN TOWN INN

©Tom Jenkins

PRIVATELY LOCATED ON 1.5 LANDSCAPED ACRES along the famous Riverwalk in the King William Historic District. This 1857 Antebellum Mansion with its grand verandas is known for its elegance, quiet comfort and luxury. Furnished in European and American antiques, all rooms have a king or queen bed, private baths, TVs, phones with voicemail and guest refrigerators. Seven with fireplaces and porches. Conveniently located downtown, 4-6 blocks to the Alamo, Convention center, Alamodome, shopping, dining and entertainment. Business travelers-Fax, voicemail, copier, *Wall Street Journal, NY Times.* Local papers complimentary. Mobil ★★★.

Suitable for Children Over 16
12 Conference Facilities • MC, Visa, AMEX, Diners, CB Accepted

RATES
10 rooms, $145/$225 B&B.
Corp. weekday rates for single travelers Sun. thru Thurs.
Open year-round.

ATTRACTIONS
Riverwalk, Alamo, missions, museums, zoo, botanical gardens, Sea World, Six Flags, art galleries, antiquing, shopping, dining, convention center.

CUISINE
Full gourmet breakfast. BYOB.

DIRECTIONS
From airport: Hwy 37 S to Durango. Alamodome exit turn R. Go thru 3 stoplights; turn L on Pancoast. Inn is 1st house on R. Historic marker.

San Antonio, TX

Noble Inns

800-221-4045
210-225-4045 Fax 210-227-0877
www.nobleinns.com
innkeeper@nobleinns.com
107 Madison Street, San Antonio, TX 78204

Select Registry Member *Since 2001*
Owners
LIESL AND DON NOBLE

DON AND LIESL NOBLE, sixth-generation San Antonians, invite guests to experience the rich history and ambience of San Antonio. Noble Inns comprises The Jackson House(JH) and Pancoast Carriage House(PCH), two 1890s-era historic landmarks, located four houses apart in the King William Historic District. Both provide Victorian elegance with modern luxuries for the discerning traveler, and are just off the Riverwalk near all downtown sites. Antiques, sumptuous fabrics and wallpapers adorn common areas and guestrooms. Two-person whirlpool tub in bath, and transportation in our classic 1960 Rolls Royce Silver Cloud are available. AAA ◆◆◆ and Mobil ★★★.

1 Guestroom Handicap Accessible • Suitable for Children at PCH
Conference Facilities for 15 • MC, Visa, AMEX, Disc Accepted
Designated Smoking Areas • Reservations Accepted Through Travel Agents

ELEGANT IN TOWN
BREAKFAST INN

RATES

7 rooms, $125/$180.
2 suites, $175/$200.
Special weekday rates.
All feature antiques, private marble bath, gas fireplace, cable TV, phone with dataport and voicemail, robes, fresh flowers.
Open year-round.

ATTRACTIONS

HERE: Swimming pool and heated spa, relax on porch or patios shaded by century-old trees. NEARBY: RiverWalk, Alamo, Convention Center, Spanish Missions, zoo, golf, Six Flags, Sea World, shopping, dining, universities. Texas Hill Country is a short drive away.

CUISINE

The Jackson House features a full gourmet breakfast, complimentary beverages, afternoon refreshments and evening sherry. Pancoast Carriage House features expanded continental breakfast and full kitchens en suite.

DIRECTIONS

From airport: to JH-US 281 S to Durango/Alamodome exit. R on Durango. L on S. St. Mary's. R on Madison. To PCH-same as above, then continue R on Turner. L on Washington.

Moonlight Bay & Paper Moon B&B

877-461-7070
361-972-2232 Fax 361-972-0463
www.bbhost.com/moonlightbaybb
grogers@wcnet.net
506 South Bay Boulevard., Palacios, TX 77465

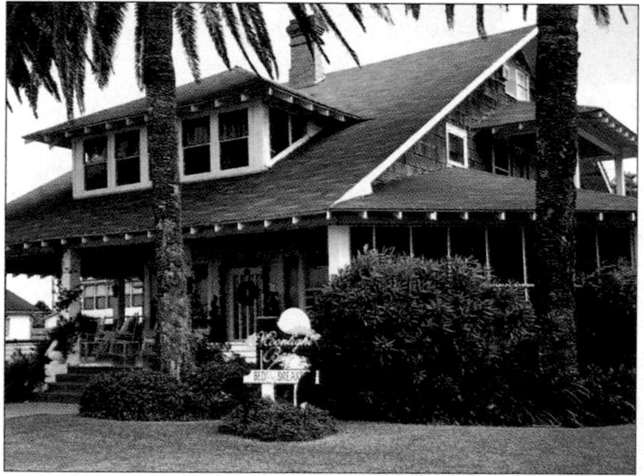

MOONLIGHT BAY is a 1910 Craftsman Bungalow home. This registered Texas historical landmark invites you to share its spectacular view of the bay from its splendid front porch. Your escape to casual elegance by the sea is reflected in the music of the 1940s. Most rooms are upstairs and include in-room coffee, refrigerators, robes and slippers. Paper Moon Guest House invites you to share literary interpretations of some of the owner's favorite selections. Trompe l'oeil murals grace every room. This unhosted property features art deco from the 1930s. Afternoon tea is served in the parlor on Saturday at 4 pm featuring live piano music of the 1940s.

Select Registry Member *Since 2000*
Proprietors
GAYE AND EARL HUDSON

ELEGANT WATERSIDE BREAKFAST INN

RATES

7 rooms, $95/$200 D.
4 rooms w/music themes- Moonlight and Roses, Moonglow, Ebbtide and Moonlight Serenade.
3 w/literary-Sandpiper, The Great Gatsby and A Gift From the Sea.
Open year-round.

ATTRACTIONS

View of the sea, dolphins, coastal birds, shrimping fleets, uncommercialized beach, golf, fishing, boating, sailing, regattas, State of Texas Marine, Education Center. Monarch trail, music and books.

CUISINE

Full gourmet breakfast; prix fixe, 5-course candlelit dining by advanced reservation available. BYOB.

DIRECTIONS

From Houston: Hwy 59 to El Campo. Take Hwy 71 to Hwy 35. Turn R on Bus. Hwy 35 to the first red light. Turn L at 4th and Main. Go 2 blks, turn R on South Bay Blvd. Go 1 blk and see Moonlight Bay on the R.

2 Guestrooms Handicap Accessible • Non-Smoking Inn
Conference Facilities for 14 • AMEX, Visa, MC, Disc, CB, Diners Accepted
Reservations Accepted Through Travel Agents

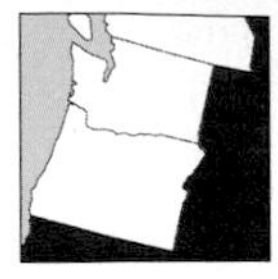

The Pacific Northwest and British Columbia

The first heavy rains fall in early October in the Pacific Northwest. In a handsome Country Inn, a couple snuggles beside a log fire. The next day the forest is as green as a moss-backed rock, spangled with silver and gold and the promise of autumn. In an evergreen copse, thirty varieties of wild mushroom push aside a millennium of duff and nettle. That very morning, a breakfast omelet is resplendent with forest mushrooms: chanterelles, chicken-of-the-woods, or the famous Boletus edulis, the "King." The land is verdant and wild, and the sun smites it in brilliant forays of intricate patterned light.

THIS IS YOUR DAY, YOURS ALONE. Hike up a mountain trail that unravels 30 miles into a pristine National Park. Fall in love with the verdant terrain, or with your lover, all over again. You might choose to stay at a Country Inn in a historic town that sits on a lofty perch above the Pacific Ocean or on one of the many saltwater inlets that lace the Northwest. Choose an Inn, the food exquisite and the hospitality superlative. The SELECT REGISTRY is here.

A ferry ride across the water is British Columbia, the jewel in the Canadian crown. Cultures cross here: Native American, British and French Canadian pioneers, Asian Americans. Here is a mixing bowl of remarkable tastes and colors, a kaleidoscope of knowledge and customs. By European standards this civilization is young, but the contribution of thousand of years of the First Peoples shines like light through a dense forest. Totems abound along the way, as do carved ceder masks and beautiful weavings. British Colombia speaks of this remarkable culture, speaks of craftsmanship and artists, to a way of life that embraces the land.

The weather is fair. Move down the Washington and Oregon Coast. There, you will find several more SELECT REGISTRY Inns. You are surrounded by a salmon culture. Feast on the red flesh or dabble in succulent oysters, on a cornucopia of mushrooms, wild greens or berries. Indigenous products are the calling card of Northwest Inns.

Streams are swollen with sparkling silver water. Dally and watch the miracle of the returning salmon. The whole landscape spells out a lush dream-like vista. A day in the forest, an evening feasting on Northwest delectable, a bedroom that overlooks the Pacific Ocean—The land romances. Come rain or shine, the Pacific Northwest is splendid to behold.

"Can't say enough good things about this Inn, including food, staff, and a wonderful destination. We will go back."
—Mr. & Mrs. William H. (Buddy)Kane, Jacksonville, FL

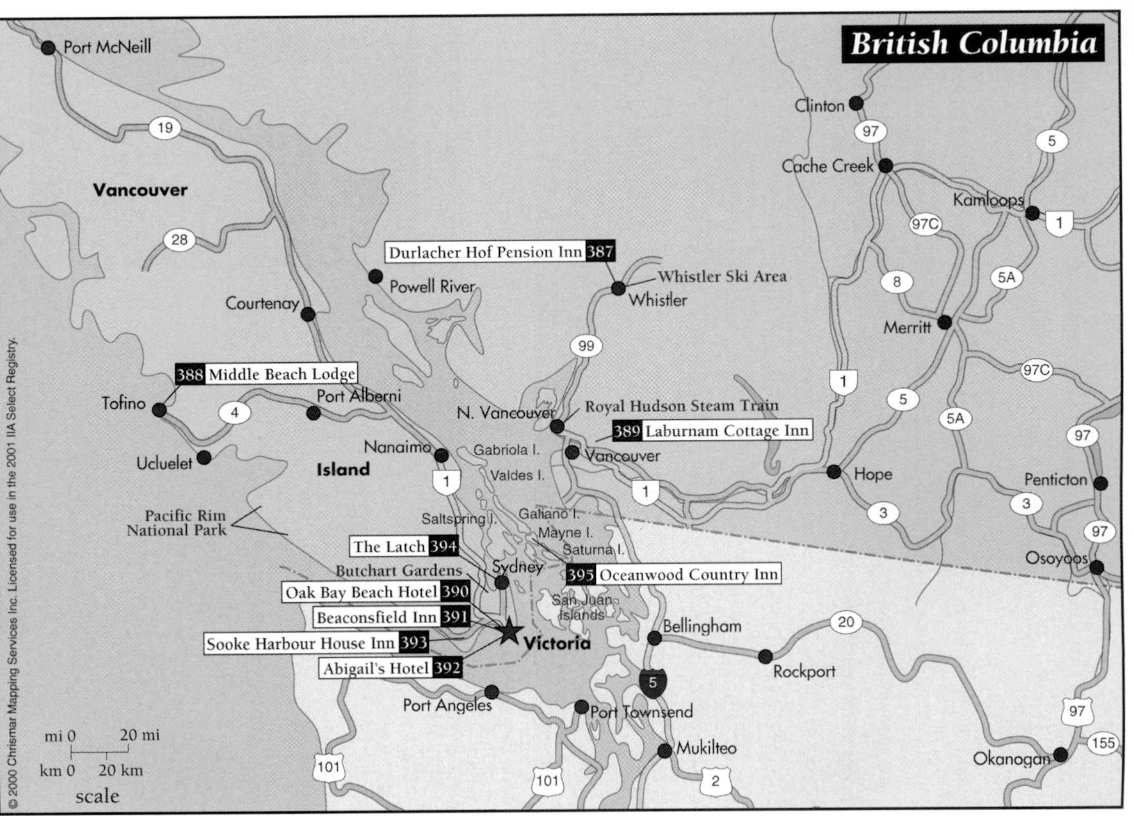
British Columbia
Port McNeill
Vancouver
Island
Tofino
Ucluelet
Pacific Rim National Park
Courtenay
Port Alberni
Nanaimo
Powell River
Whistler
Whistler Ski Area
N. Vancouver
Vancouver
Royal Hudson Steam Train
Gabriola I.
Valdes I.
Galiano I.
Mayne I.
Saturna I.
Saltspring I.
Sydney
San Juan Islands
Victoria
Butchart Gardens
Port Angeles
Port Townsend
Mukilteo
Bellingham
Rockport
Hope
Merritt
Kamloops
Clinton
Cache Creek
Penticton
Osoyoos
Okanogan
387 Durlacher Hof Pension Inn
388 Middle Beach Lodge
389 Laburnam Cottage Inn
390 Oak Bay Beach Hotel
391 Beaconsfield Inn
392 Abigail's Hotel
393 Sooke Harbour House Inn
394 The Latch
395 Oceanwood Country Inn
1
2
3
4
5
5A
8
19
20
28
97
97C
99
101
155
mi 0 20 mi
km 0 20 km
scale
© 2000 Chismar Mapping Services Inc. Licensed for use in the 2001 IIA Select Registry.

Whistler, BC Canada

Durlacher Hof Alpine Inn

604-932-1924
Fax 604-938-1980
www.durlacherhof.com
peterika@direct.ca
7055 Nesters Rd., Whistler, BC Canada VON 1BO

Select Registry Member *Since 1998*
Innkeepers / Owners
PETER AND ERIKA DURLACHER

AN ENCHANTING MOUNTAIN HIDEAWAY at Whistler Resort. Durlachers' reputation as Whistler's most welcoming and generous innkeepers is legendary. The Hof serves up the complete authentic Austrian experience from ornate exterior trimmings to the Kaiserschmarren served at breakfast. Painstaking attention to detail is evident in the cozy guest lounge and the immaculate pretty rooms all with mountain views, down duvets and ensuite baths. Durlacher Hof is part of a place that mixes charm with romance and a natural beauty with inviting warmth and hospitality. Rating ★★★★ 1/2 Canada Select Inn. AAA ◆◆◆.

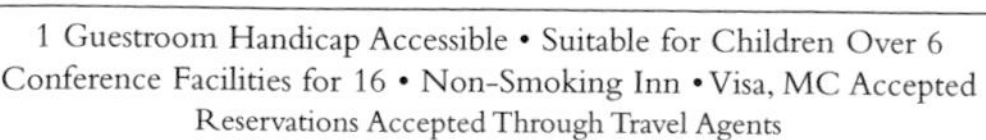

1 Guestroom Handicap Accessible • Suitable for Children Over 6
Conference Facilities for 16 • Non-Smoking Inn • Visa, MC Accepted
Reservations Accepted Through Travel Agents

TRADITIONAL MOUNTAIN BREAKFAST INN

RATES

8 guest rooms.
Jacuzzi/sauna/balconies.
Summer $130/$195 CDN.
Winter $165/$260 CDN.
Singles $20 less. Call for US rates.
7 days summer, 30 days winter cancellation policy, minimal
Ski, golf and summer adventure packages available. German spoken.
Open year-round with seasonal closure spring and fall.

ATTRACTIONS

Whistler Resort has it all. Rated #1 ski resort in North America, four championship golf courses, a charming Alpine village, intriguing shops, cozy bistros and excellent fine dining. Mountain bike, hike, kayak, fish. Activities for everyone; from spirited adventurer to the faint of heart.

CUISINE

Guest lounge. Licensed. Full country breakfast and afternoon tea, social hour. Dinners on select evenings in winter, picnic baskets in summer. Special culinary and classical music events in spring and fall. "Best Place to Kiss" - *US Travel*

DIRECTIONS

75 miles/125 kilometres N of Vancouver on Hwy 99. L after1km N of Whistler Village or 5th traffic lights on Hwy 99 from the 'Welcome to Whistler' sign.

Tofino, BC Canada

Middle Beach Lodge

250-725-2900
Fax 250-725-2901
www.middlebeach.com
lodge@middlebeach.com
400 Mackenzie Beach Road
Tofino, BC Canada V0R 2Z0

Select Registry Member *Since 1996*
Contact:
JEFF HALE

MIDDLE BEACH LODGE is situated on its own private wilderness headland and warm sandy bay. Our lodges and cabins provide a blend of fine rustic West Coast architecture, coupled with warm coastal interiors, highlighted by recycled timbers, and two lodges—one adult-oriented, the other for families. Accommodations include lodge suites, rooms and private self-contained oceanfront cabins with kitchenettes, fireplaces and hot tubs. Magnificent oceanfront lounges with massive stone fireplaces provide wonderful places to relax. The headlands lodge is open year-round, so think wild winter storm-watching. Corporate and group retreats welcome. AAA ◆◆◆.

RUSTIC WATERSIDE
BREAKFAST INN

RATES
34 rooms, $75/$250 B&B.
19 cabins, $110/$370 B&B.
11 suites, $110-$325 B&B.
"Beach House" Deluxe Six Plex Suites; Ocean facing, beachfront, full kitchen, gas fireplace, Jacuzzi tubs or soaker tubs, balcony.
Open year-round.

ATTRACTIONS
Whale watching, day-trips to the hot springs, hiking through the rain forest, kayaking, fishing, beachcombing, surfing and nature exploration. Fitness room, massage room, and outdoor BBQ area.

CUISINE
Breakfast (included in room rates), dinner five nights a week in summer, Saturdays only during winter. Full-service bar during dinner nights.

DIRECTIONS
4 1/2 hours N of Victoria, 3 hours W of Nanaimo. Take the Port Alberni turn-off, a scenic drive through Mountain Pass, Middle Beach Lodge is 3 km. S of Tofino, B.C.

2 Guestrooms Handicap Accessible • Suitable for Children
Conference Facilities for 30 • Visa, MC, AMEX Accepted
Non-Smoking Inn • Reservations Accepted Through Travel Agents

North Vancouver, BC Canada

Laburnum Cottage Bed & Breakfast Inn

888-207-8901
604-988-4877 Fax 604-988-4877
www.vancouver-bc.com/LaburnumCottageBB/
laburnum@home.com
1388 Terrace Avenue
North Vancouver, BC Canada V7R 1B4

Select Registry Member *Since 1999*
Innkeeper/Owner
DELPHINE MASTERTON

RESTFUL, PEACEFUL, SECLUSION far from the "madding" crowd. This elegant country home is set off by an award-winning English Garden surrounded by virgin forests. The Inn features four beautifully decorated, charming rooms with queen beds, private baths and garden views. The Summer House cottage, accessible by a foot bridge that crosses a small creek, is a Rosamund Pilcher novel come-to-life. Perfect for a couple on their honeymoon. The Carriage House is romantic or suitable for a small family stay. Delphine's gift for welcoming and her ability to weave strangers into friends, over the cheerful breakfast tables, make a stay here all it should be.

ELEGANT VILLAGE BREAKFAST INN

RATES

4 romantic rooms all with private bath and garden views, $110/$175 CAN.
2 enchanting cottages, $175/$250 CAN.
Extra person $30.00.
Open year-round.

ATTRACTIONS

Walking, hiking, golf, tennis, shopping, dining, gardens, theatre, skiing, antiquing. Featured in 1999 "Best Places to Kiss" from *US Travel* channel and publication and "Fifty Romantic Getaways - Weekends for in Pacific Northwest" by Bill Gleeson.

CUISINE

Full breakfast prepared by gourmet chef, Karin; afternoon tea upon request.

DIRECTIONS

From Vancouver: Take Georgia St. through Stanley Park, across the Lions Gate Bridge. R on Marine Dr., L on Capilano Rd. for one mile, R on Paisley Rd., R on Philip Ave., R on Woods Dr., L on Terrace Ave. and '1388'.

Suitable for Children • Non-Smoking Inn • Visa, MC Accepted
Reservations Accepted Through Travel Agents

Victoria, BC Canada

Oak Bay Beach Hotel & Marine Resort

800-668-7758
250-598-4556 Fax 250-598-6180
www.oakbaybeachhotel.bc.ca
reservations@oakbaybeachhotel.bc.ca
1175 Beach Drive, Victoria, BC Canada V8S 2N2

IN A BEAUTIFUL SEASIDE LOCATION, you will find warm and gracious hospitality, crackling fireplaces and first-class accommodation in an atmosphere of old-world charm. This prestigious, family-owned hotel in the residential area of Oak Bay is a significant part of the history and heritage of the city of Victoria. Magnificent lawns and gardens rolling to the ocean with islands and mountains in the distance providing wonderful views. The Tudor-style architecture is complemented by antiques and period pieces. Meals, service and hospitality are the best. Canada Select Four Star Award.

3 Guesrtooms Handicap Accessible • Suitable for Children
Conference Facilities for 130 • Visa, MC, AMEX, Diners Accepted
Designated Smoking Areas • Reservations Accepted Through Travel Agents

Select Registry Member *Since 1979*
Owner/General Manager
KEVIN WALKER

TRADITIONAL IN TOWN HOTEL

RATES
50 rooms and suites.
$155/$450 CDN. B&B.
Open year-round.

ATTRACTIONS
Whale watching/marine wildlife adventure cruises and sunset dinner cruises (seasonal). Jogging, golf, tennis, fishing & centre with pool nearby. Whale watching, Roche Harbour Ferry, guided kayak tours, Botanical Garden tour. Guided out island hiking. Complimentary shuttle.

CUISINE
Breakfast, lunch, dinner. High tea (seasonal). Liquor available.

DIRECTIONS
From Airport and Ferries: S on Hwy 17, L on Hillside E, which becomes Lansdowne. R on Beach Dr. to hotel.

Victoria, BC Canada

Beaconsfield Inn

250-384-4044
Fax 250-384-4052
www.beaconsfieldinn.com
beaconsfield@islandnet.com
998 Humboldt Street, Victoria, BC Canada V8V 2Z8

VICTORIA'S PREMIER BED & BREAKFAST INN. A 1905 Edwardian Manor set in an English garden, is a luxurious, retreat in the residential heart of Victoria. Step back in time when you come to this award-winning class 'A' heritage Sammuel Mcclure Mansion. Admire English antiques and oriental carpets, enjoy sunshine reflected through stained glass windows, luxuriate in feather beds with down comforters, sip champagne in a Jacuzzi tub, snuggle before roaring fireplaces. Winner of "Andrew Harper's Hideaway Report" B&B of the year. Highest ★★★★★ rating by Canada Select. Featured in *Country Inns*. This is the ultimate in charm and luxury.

Visa, MC Accepted • Non-Smoking Inn
Reservations Accepted Through Travel Agents

Select Registry Member *Since 1994*
Innkeepers/Owners
JAMES AND EMILY YUNGKANS

ELEGANT IN TOWN
BREAKFAST INN

RATES

10 rooms and suites
High, $140/$280 US.
Low, $90/$215 US.
Fireplaces, Jacuzzi tubs, private bathrooms.
Special vacation packages available.
Open year-round.

ATTRACTIONS

Golfing, whale watching, sailing, or stroll through Butchart Gardens and stay for the Saturday night fireworks (summer season). Antique stores and theatres. Horse-drawn carriages will pick you up at the Beaconsfield for a romantic tour of Victoria.

CUISINE

Gourmet breakfasts served in the dining room or conservatory, afternoon high tea with sherry hour in the library and a midnight snack of tea and cookies is included. Special packages can be arranged by our expert staff.

DIRECTIONS

From N: Hwy 17 to City Centre, L on Humboldt St.; From Inner Harbor: Government St. N to Humboldt St. turn R for 4 blocks.

Victoria, BC Canada

Abigail's Hotel

800-561-6565
250-388-5363 Fax 250-388-7787
www.abigailshotel.com
innkeeper@abigailshotel.com
906 McClure Street, Victoria, BC Canada V8V 3E7

Select Registry Member *Since 2000*

Owners

Daniel and Frauke Behune

Experience the charm of Victoria's beautiful heritage inn, rated five stars. Elegantly decorated with warm soft colors, all 22 rooms have antique country furnishings, cozy goose down duvets, bouquets of fresh flowers and private ensuite bathrooms. Many suites have woodburning fireplaces and Jacuzzi tubs for relaxation. A perfect place for a romantic getaway. Abigail's Hotel, with its classic Tudor architecture and colorful English gardens, evokes the true spirit of Victoria. Each morning enjoy one of our famous gourmet breakfasts. Complimentary hors d'oeuvres are served every evening. Discover why so many fall in love with our very special charm!

Elegant In Town Breakfast Inn

RATES

22 rooms, $199/$329 CDN. Celebration Suites, king beds, fireplaces, Jacuzzi tubs. Charming sunflower and country rooms. Queen beds with soaker tubs or shower. *Open year-round.*

ATTRACTIONS

Our friendly staff are always pleased to recommend Victoria's most facinating attractions, favorite restaurants and intriguing shops. Enjoy fine parks and the spectacular ocean views. Hike, bike or golf in any season. It is a pleasant walk anywhere!

CUISINE

We are famous for our gourmet breakfasts. Other meals are available at one of Victoria's fine restaurants only a few blocks in any direction. Evening social hour with appetizers is available every night in the library.

DIRECTIONS

From Airport: S on Hwy 17, L on Fort St., R on Vancouver St. and R on McClure St. From Downtown: E on Fort St., R on Vancouver St. and R on McClure St.

Suitable for Children Over 10 • Non-Smoking Inn
Conference Facilities for 18 • Visa, MC, AMEX Accepted
Reservations Accepted Through Travel Agents

Sooke, BC Canada

Sooke Harbour House

800-889-9688
250-642-3421 Fax 250-642-6988
www.sookeharbourhouse.com
info@sookeharbourhouse.com
1528 Whiffen Spit Road
Sooke, BC Canada V0S 1N0

Select Registry Member *Since 1988*
Innkeepers
SINCLAIR AND FREDERIQUE PHILIP

COZY AND ELEGANT WITH HOMELIKE ATMOSPHERE, it was rated the best restaurant in the world for authentic local cuisine, one of the top five for romance and honeymoons and one of the top twenty-five hotels in the world in the May, 1997, *Gourmet* magazine. Its restaurant specializes in West Coast Canadian cuisine, especially seafood, and much of its produce comes from the Inn's gardens. The Inn offers secluded, romantic rooms with spectacular views of the ocean and mountains. Each room features fireplaces, some jetted tubs for two, as well as antique and modern furnishings and original artwork. Mobil ★★★★ 1999 Award and *Wine Spectator* 1999 Best Award of Excellence.

ELEGANT WATERSIDE RETREAT/LODGE

RATES
28 guest rooms $125/$365 U.S. Includes breakfast and lunch during full and high seasons.
Open year-round.

ATTRACTIONS
Beautiful beaches, hiking, salmon fishing, golfing, biking, cross-country skiing, whale watching and kayaking.

CUISINE
Specializing in West Coast Canadian Cuisine, menu changes daily, according to which foods are in season. Rated #1 in world, *Gourmet* May '97. Extensive wine list consisting of both Canadian and international wines.

DIRECTIONS
23 miles W of Victoria. Follow Hwy 1 to exit 10 (Hwy 14 W junction). Follow Hwy 14 to Sooke. Turn L 1 mile past Sooke's only traffic light onto Whiffen Spit Rd. Follow to end of road. Inn on the R.

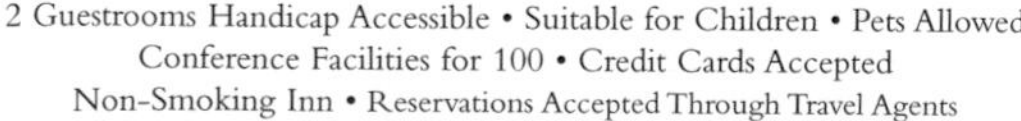

2 Guestrooms Handicap Accessible • Suitable for Children • Pets Allowed
Conference Facilities for 100 • Credit Cards Accepted
Non-Smoking Inn • Reservations Accepted Through Travel Agents

Sidney, BC Canada

The Latch Country Inn

250-656-6622
877-956-6622 Fax 250-656-6212
www.latchinn.com
latch@latchinn.com
2328 Harbour Road, Sidney, BC Canada V8L 2P8

Select Registry Member *Since 1999*
Owners & General Managers
BERND AND HEIDI RUST

ELEGANT VILLAGE INN

THE LATCH COUNTRY INN is an Original British Columbia Heritage Log Home, built in 1920 for the Lieutenant-Governor of British Columbia, by the famous Canadian Architect, Samuel Maclure. Canadian and European antiques abound, and the Inn has seven romantic guest suites. For your enjoyment we have a sailing yacht on the premises, and offer intimate and romantic wedding facilities. The 'Best kept travel secret of the year' - Travel Holiday Insiders Award, 1998. We are in a quiet location near the yacht harbor, close to airport, ferries, BUTCHARD GARDENS, and 25 minutes from downtown Victoria.

RATES

7 suites.
CDN $129/$299.
US $87/$205.
Diamond Golf Package Available
Open year-round.

ATTRACTIONS

Sailing and lunch cruises on property owned 32' sailing vessel, three golf courses nearby, whale watching. Visit the famous Butchard Gardens, museums, arts and craft shops, antique stores, trips to Gulf Islands and beaches.

CUISINE

Renowned, everything fresh, 'Euro-Pacific' cuisine, romantic candlelit dining rooms, sundown terrace, menu with fresh fish, meat, vegetarian dishes, fully-licensed 'Romancing Gourmet' packages (MAP).

DIRECTIONS

From Swartz Bay ferry: Take McDonald Park Rd. (first exit to your R), to Resthaven Rd. to Harbour Rd. From Victoria: Take Hwy 17 N to Sidney, turn R on Beacon Ave., L on Resthaven to Harbour Rd. (turn R).

Handicap Access Available • Designated Smoking Areas
Conference Facilities for 75 • Visa, MC, AMEX, Diners Accepted
Reservations Accepted Through Travel Agents

Mayne Island, BC Canada

Oceanwood Country Inn

250-539-5074
Fax 250-539-3002
www.oceanwood.com
oceanwood@gulfislands.com
630 Dinner Bay Road,
Mayne Island, BC Canada V0N 2J0

Select Registry Member *Since 1994*
Innkeeper/Owner
JONATHAN CHILVERS

ON THE WATERFRONT in Canada's spectacularly beautiful Gulf Islands, Oceanwood is like a cozy and civilized English Country House. Twelve individually decorated guest rooms, all with private baths, many with fireplaces. Comfortable living room, well-stocked library, plant-filled garden room and cozy games room. Charming dining room overlooking Navy Channel features Pacific Northwest cuisine and West Coast wines. Island activities include ocean kayaking, cycling, tennis, country walks and the infinite pleasure of peace and quiet. Canada Select ★★★★ award.

TRADITIONAL WATERSIDE RETREAT/LODGE

RATES
12 rooms, many with fireplaces, big tubs, decks facing the sea. $119/$329 CDN B&B and tea. *Closed December through February.*

ATTRACTIONS
Bicycling, hiking, beachcombing, ocean kayaking, tennis, sailing, wildlife marine tours, hot tub, sauna.

CUISINE
Breakfast, afternoon tea included in the basic room rate. Romantic, gourmet dinners also available in our beautiful ocean-view dining room. Fully licensed with extensive West Coast wine list.

DIRECTIONS
BC ferries from either Tsawwassen (Vancouver), or Swartz Bay (Victoria). Reservations possible from mainland. Float plane service also available.

Suitable for Children Over 16 • Non-Smoking Inn
Conference Facilities for 12 • Visa, MC Accepted
Reservations Accepted Through Travel Agents

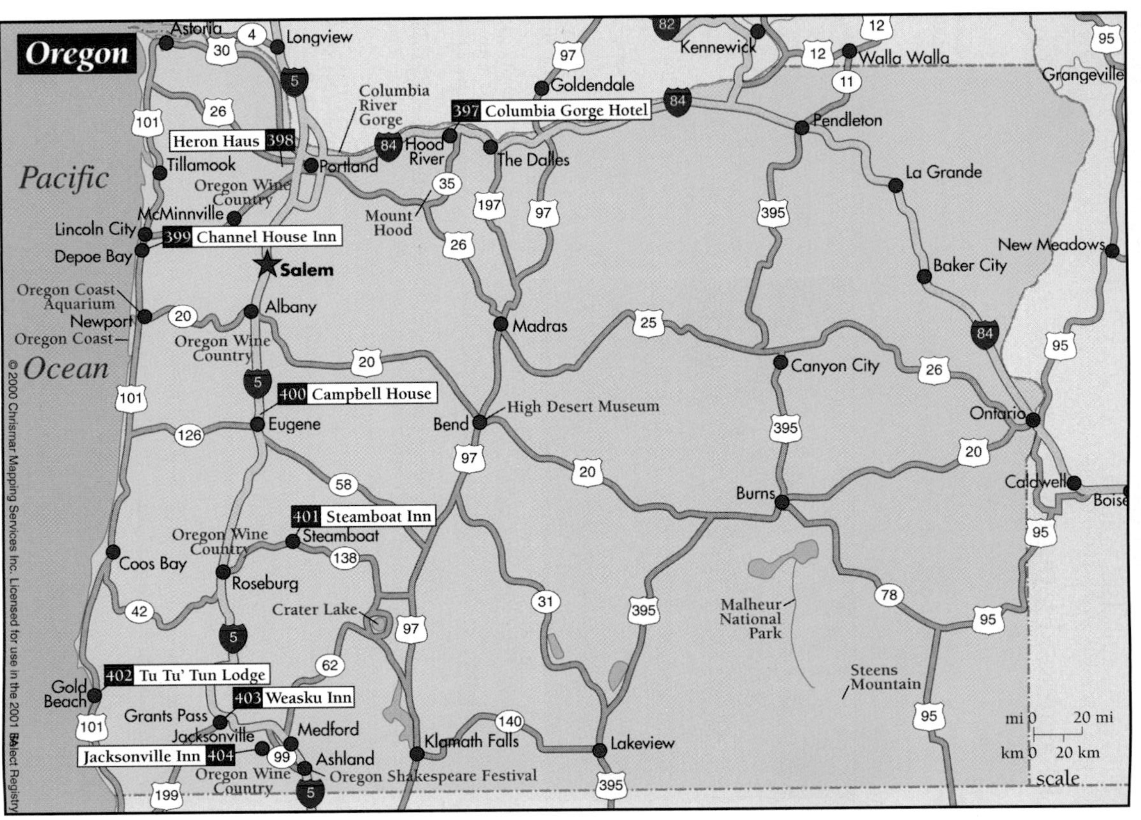
Oregon
Pacific Ocean
Astoria
Longview
Tillamook
Heron Haus 398
Portland
Columbia River Gorge
Hood River
397 Columbia Gorge Hotel
Goldendale
The Dalles
Kennewick
Walla Walla
Grangeville
Pendleton
La Grande
Oregon Wine Country
McMinnville
Lincoln City
399 Channel House Inn
Depoe Bay
Mount Hood
Salem
Baker City
New Meadows
Oregon Coast Aquarium
Newport
Oregon Coast
Albany
Madras
Canyon City
Ontario
400 Campbell House
Eugene
Bend
High Desert Museum
Caldwell
Boise
Burns
401 Steamboat Inn
Steamboat
Coos Bay
Roseburg
Crater Lake
Malheur National Park
Steens Mountain
402 Tu Tu' Tun Lodge
Gold Beach
403 Weasku Inn
Grants Pass
Jacksonville
Medford
Jacksonville Inn 404
Ashland
Oregon Shakespeare Festival
Klamath Falls
Lakeview
mi 0 20 mi
km 0 20 km
scale
© 2000 Chrismar Mapping Services Inc. Licensed for use in the 2001 Select Registry

Columbia Gorge Hotel

800-345-1921
541-386-5566 Fax 541-387-5414
www.ColumbiaGorgeHotel.com
cghotel@gorge.net
4000 Westcliff Drive, Hood River, OR 97031

Select Registry Member *Since 1998*
Innkeeper
CHAVALLA LOPEZ

THE COLUMBIA GORGE HOTEL, 60 miles east of Portland, was built in 1921 as a gracious oasis for travelers along the, then new, Columbia River Gorge Highway. Situated at the top of a 210-foot waterfall on the banks of the majestic Columbia River, the hotel gained a national reputation for fine cuisine and elegant surroundings. Restored and reopened by the Graves family in the late '70s, the Hotel boasts 40 unique guest rooms, an award-winning dining room, and exquisite wedding and meeting facilities on eleven beautifully landscaped acres.

ELEGANT WATERSIDE HOTEL

RATES
40 rooms, $159/$275.
2 rooms with fireplace.
Open year-round.

ATTRACTIONS
Located in Columbia Gorge National Scenic Area. Close to golf, river rafting, hiking, windsurfing, skiing, fly-fishing and museums. Massage therapists on site.

CUISINE
Fine Northwest continental dining, 'World Famous Farm Breakfast'®. Full-service lounge, wine list, piano.

DIRECTIONS
One hour E of Portland on I-84. Take exit 62, turn L. Take next L, hotel on R.

Non-Smoking Inn • Pets Allowed • Conference Facilities for 200
Visa, MC, Disc, AMEX, CB, Diners Accepted
Reservations Accepted Through Travel Agents

Portland, OR

Heron Haus

503-274-1846
Fax 503-248-4055
www.heronhaus.com

Select Registry Member *Since 1994*
Owner
JULIE BEACON KEPPELER

2545 NW Westover Road, Portland, OR 97210

THIS ELEGANT, three-story, turn-of-the-century tudor sits high in the hills, offering accommodations for both the business traveler and romantic getaways for couples. Each room has sitting areas, work areas, phones with computer hook-ups and TVs, all have fireplaces. All have queen- or king-size beds. The baths offer special extras—one has a spa on a windowed porch; another has a shower with seven shower heads. Off-street parking is provided. Two and one-half blocks down the hill is the Nob Hill area with boutiques, specialty shops and some of the best eating places in Portland.

ELEGANT IN TOWN
BREAKFAST INN

RATES
6 rooms, all w/fireplaces, private baths, TV, sitting areas, phones, work areas, parking, A/C.
$95/$185 Single.
$135/$350 Double.
Open year-round.

ATTRACTIONS
Columbia River, Mt. Hood, Mt. St. Helens, coast, wine country, city sights, rose test garden, Japanese Garden Omsi!

CUISINE
Continental breakfast.

DIRECTIONS
On brochure.

Suitable for Children Over 10 • Non-Smoking Inn
Visa, MC Accepted

Depoe Bay, OR

Channel House Inn

800-447-2140

541-765-2140 Fax 541-765-2191

www.channelhouse.com

cfinseth@channelhouse.com

35 Ellingson Street, Depoe Bay, OR 97341

Select Registry Member *Since 1997*

Owners

CARL AND VICKI FINSETH

AMID THE OREGON COAST'S most magnificent scenery, Channel House combines the comforts of a first-class hotel with the congeniality of a small Country Inn. Imagine fresh ocean breezes, sweeping panoramic views, unbelievable sunsets and whales within a stone's throw. Nestled on an oceanfront perch, guestrooms have an elegant contemporary decor including gas log fireplaces and whirlpools on oceanfront decks. One of the West Coast's most renowned and romantic Inns, it's the ideal honeymoon, anniversary or special couple's getaway.

CONTEMPORARY VILLAGE BREAKFAST INN

RATES

5 rooms, $175 B&B.
9 oceanfront suites, $235.
Open year-round.

ATTRACTIONS

Fishing, beachcombing, whale watching, hiking, golfing, antiques, museums, galleries, lighthouses, covered bridges, Marine Science Center, Oregon Coast Aquarium.

CUISINE

Buffet-style breakfast featuring fresh-baked goods.

DIRECTIONS

Just off Hwy 101, one block S of Depoe Bay Bridge. Turn W onto Ellingson St.

Credit Cards Accepted • Non-Smoking Inn
Reservations Accepted Through Travel Agents

Eugene, OR

Campbell House, A City Inn

800-264-2519
541-343-1119 Fax 541-343-2258
www.campbellhouse.com
campbellhouse@campbellhouse.com
252 Pearl Street, Eugene, OR 97401

Select Registry Member *Since 1997*
Proprietor
MYRA PLANT

BUILT IN 1892 and restored in the tradition of a fine European hotel, the Campbell House is surrounded by beautiful gardens. It is located in the historic district, within walking distance of downtown, restaurants and the theater. Hike Skinner's Butte or use over ten miles of riverside jogging and bicycle paths. Elegant guest rooms have private bathrooms, hidden TV with VCR, telephones and luxury amenities. Luxury rooms feature gas fireplaces, four-poster beds and Jacuzzi tubs. Enjoy complimentary wine in the evening and a full breakfast with newspaper in the morning. "Top 25 Inns in the nation," *American Historic Inns.* Weddings, receptions, meetings. AAA ◆◆◆◆.

ELEGANT IN TOWN BREAKFAST INN

RATES
18 rooms total.
12 rooms, $79/$149.
1 two-room suite FP/Jacuzzi, $229/$349.
5 luxury FP/Jacuzzi, $189/$269.
B&B.
Open year-round.

ATTRACTIONS
Walk historic neighborhood, hiking, riverside bike/jogging paths, two blocks to boutique and antique shops, performing arts theater. Winery tours, fishing and rafting.

CUISINE
Complimentary full breakfast in dining room (room service available). 10 restaurants within walking distance (2-3 blocks). Also, Pony Express Delivery Room Service from over 12 restaurants in the area. Lunch delivery times: 11-2 pm and dinner 5-10 pm.

DIRECTIONS
From Airport: Hwy 99 becomes 7th Ave., L on High, L on 5th, R on Pearl. From I-5: Take I-105 to Eugene (exit 194B), to Coburg Rd. (exit 2), stay L, merge onto Coburg Rd., cross over river, take the Downtown exit, R on High, L on 5th, R on Pearl.

1 Guestroom Handicap Accessible • Suitable for Children
Conference Facilities for 150 • Credit Cards Accepted
Designated Smoking Areas • Reservations Accepted Through Travel Agents

Steamboat, OR

Steamboat Inn

800-840-8825

541-498-2230 Fax 541-498-2411

www.thesteamboatinn.com

stmbtinn@rosenet.net

42705 North Umpqua Highway
Steamboat, OR 97447-9703

Select Registry Member *Since 1984*
Innkeepers
JIM AND SHARON VANLOAN
General Manager
PATRICIA LEE

TRADITIONAL WATERSIDE INN

NESTLED AMONG TOWERING FIRS, along one of the Northwest's premier rivers, guests may choose from cozy streamside cabins, cottages in the woods, luxurious suites or fully-furnished three bedroom houses. You may want a picnic for a days outing to Crater Lake, local waterfalls, swimming holes, hiking trails or the wineries of Douglas County. Be sure to be back for the evening dinner. This creative meal featuring fresh local ingredients and Oregon wine, will add the perfect finish to an already perfect day! Or just spend the day enjoying the Inn's gardens!

RATES
8 cabins, $135.
5 cottages, $170.
2 suites, $250.
4 houses, $175 EP.
Closed January and February.

ATTRACTIONS
Crater Lake, hiking, waterfalls, summer steelhead fishing and swimming, mt. biking.

CUISINE
Day restaurant serving breakfast and lunch. Evening dinner by reservation, $37. Extensive wine list. Guest chef/winemaker dinners.

DIRECTIONS
I-5: Roseburg City Center Exit. Inn is 38 mi E on Rte 138, 70 mi W of Crater Lake; 40 mi W of Diamond Lake.

Handicap Access Available • Suitable for Children • Non-Smoking Inn
Conference Facilities for 40 • Visa, MC Accepted
Reservations Accepted Through Travel Agents

Gold Beach, OR

Tu Tu' Tun Lodge

800-864-6357
541-247-6664 Fax 541-247-0672
www.tututun.com
tututun@harborside.com
96550 North Bank Rogue, Gold Beach, OR 97444

Select Registry Member *Since 1989*
Innkeepers / Owners
DIRK AND LAURIE VAN ZANTE

NESTLED ON THE BANKS OF THE ROGUE RIVER, Tu Tu' Tun Lodge combines the comforts of a first-class resort with the congeniality of a small hideaway. Guests enjoy hors d'oeuvres around the large stone fireplace, gourmet dining overlooking the river, and madrone wood fires on the terrace at dusk. Come, partake in the serious challenge of the steelhead and salmon, experience the excitement of a white-water excursion, or simply enjoy some solitude.
Mobil ★★★★ and AAA ◆◆◆◆.

CONTEMPORARY
WATERSIDE INN

RATES
16 rooms.
2 suites.
1 garden house.
1 river house.
Rates: $95/$400.
Open year-round.

ATTRACTIONS
White-water boat trips, guided fishing for salmon and steelhead, heated lap pool, 4-hole pitch and putt, pool table, riverfront walking, old growth forest hikes and seashore adventures.

CUISINE
Hors d'oeuvres served around stone fireplace. Gourmet four-course dinner. Full-service bar. Exceptional wines.

DIRECTIONS
From N: Hwy 101 S 6 hrs. from Portland. 7 miles E along N bank of Rogue River. Follow hwy signs. From S: Hwy 101 N. 8 hrs. from S.F. Follow hwy signs.

Handicap Access Available • Suitable for Children
Conference Facilities for 20 • Credit Cards Accepted
Reservations Accepted Through Travel Agents

Grants Pass, OR

Weasku Inn

800-493-2758

541-471-8000 Fax 541-471-7038

www.weasku.com

info@weasku.com

5560 Rogue River Hwy, Grants Pass, OR 97527

Select Registry Member *Since 2001*

Innkeeper

DAYLE SEDGMOR

THE WEASKU INN was recently named as "one of the countries greatest inns" by *Travel and Leisue* and rests on the banks of the famous Rogue River, in Southern Oregon. This secluded fishing lodge was a favorite vacation spot of Clark Gable during the 1920s and 30s. A complete remodeling took place in 1998, restoring the Inn to its former glory. The warm log exterior, surrounded by towering trees and 10 private acres provides a tranquil setting ideal for an intimate getaway or corporate retreat. The lodge houses 5 guestrooms and there are an additional 12 riverside cabins. A wine and cheese reception and continental breakfast is served each day.

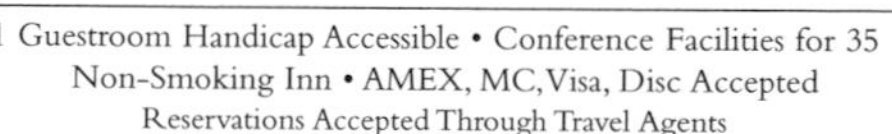

1 Guestroom Handicap Accessible • Conference Facilities for 35
Non-Smoking Inn • AMEX, MC, Visa, Disc Accepted
Reservations Accepted Through Travel Agents

RUSTIC WATERSIDE RETREAT/LODGE

RATES

5 lodge rooms, $85/$150.
Jacuzzi suites, $295
12 river cabins, $195
River cabins have fireplaces. All with private baths and modern conveniences several with Jacuzzi tubs.
Open year-round.

ATTRACTIONS

Fishing, white water rafting, jet-boating, golfing, antique shopping, hiking, wine tasting, Oregon Monument Caves, Wildlife Images, Applegate Trail Interpretive Center, Oregon Shakespeare Festival, Peter Britt Festival, Ashland Ski Resort, Crater Lake.

CUISINE

Complimentary wine and cheese reception and continental breakfast are provided each day. A BBQ is offered on the lodge deck for a minimum fee, weekends, May through September. Several restaurants are within minutes.

DIRECTIONS

Located 51 miles north from the California and Oregon border. Take I-5 exit 48. Turn W, go across the bridge to the stop sign, *Rogue River Hwy*, and turn R. Go 3 miles. The Inn is on your right.

Jacksonville Inn

800-321-9344
541-899-1900 Fax 541-899-1373
www.jacksonvilleinn.com
jvinn@mind.net
P.O. Box 359, Jacksonville, OR 97530

Select Registry Member *Since 1991*
Innkeepers/Owners
JERRY AND LINDA EVANS

THE INN OFFERS ITS GUESTS LUXURY and opulence, and its honeymoon cottages cater to romance and privacy of special occasions. Each has a king-sized canopy bed, whirlpool tub, steam shower, entertainment center, wet bar, fireplace, sitting room and private patio. The Jacksonville Inn is nestled in a National Historic Landmark town and was featured on CNN and the Learning Channel's 'Great Country Inns.' The restaurant is one of Oregon's most award-winning restaurants. Connoisseurs' Wine Cellar Award of Excellence from *Wine Spectator.* Five-star Diamond Academy Award of Restaurant Industry, ◆◆◆ AAA and ★★★ Mobil.

ELEGANT IN-TOWN INN

RATES

8 rooms, $125/$169 B&B.
3 honeymoon cottages, $224/$260 B&B.
Open year-round.

ATTRACTIONS

Museum, antiques, hiking, wineries, swimming, white-water river rafting, shopping, Shakespeare Festival, Britt Music Festival. Perfect setting for small weddings and receptions.

CUISINE

Complimentary full breakfast in dining room. Restaurant, bistro, Sunday brunch, lounge, garden patio dining. Wine and liquor available.

DIRECTIONS

From I-5 N: Take exit 40; go S on Old Stage Rd. to Jacksonville. Turn L on California St. to 175 E California. From I-5 S: Take S Medford exit. L on Barnett Rd., R on Riverside, L on Main St. to Jacksonville. Turn R on California St.

---

3 Guestrooms Handicap Accessible • Conference Facilities for 100
Suitable for Children • Visa, MC, Diners, Disc, AMEX, CB Accepted
Non-Smoking Inn • Reservations Accepted Through Travel Agents

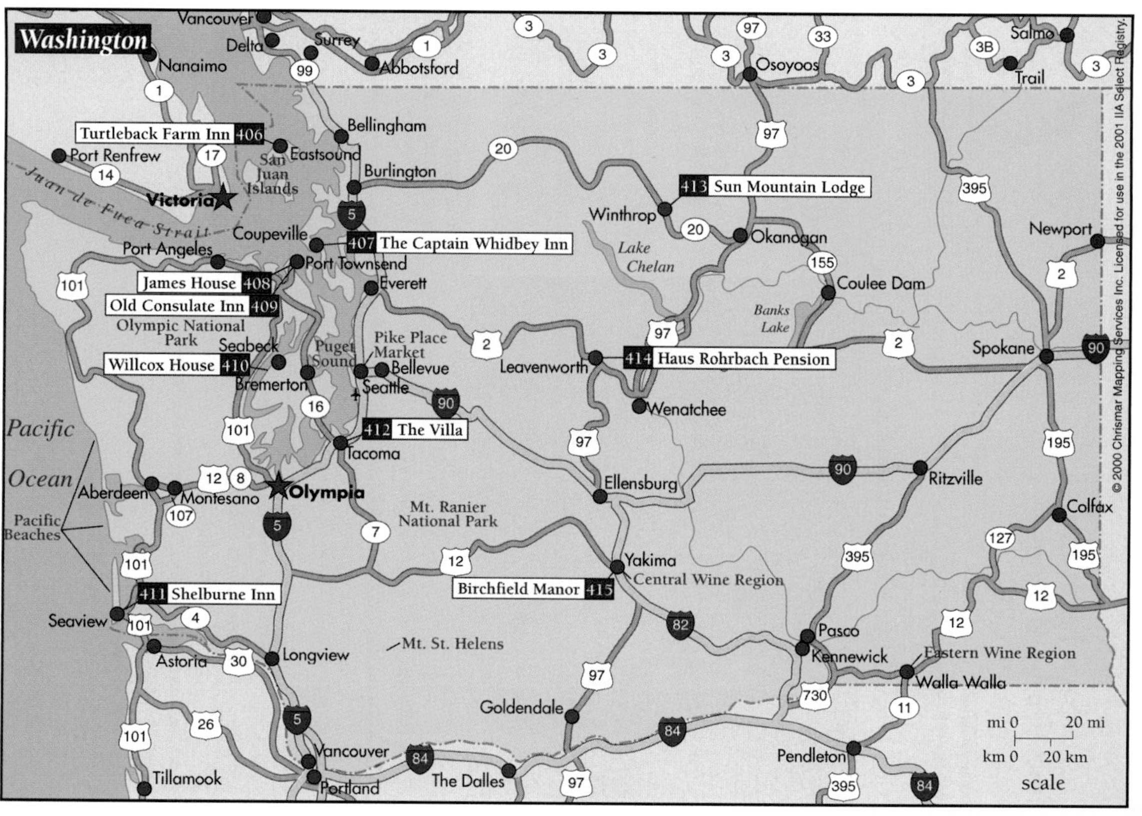
Washington
Vancouver
Delta
Surrey
Abbotsford
Nanaimo
Turtleback Farm Inn 406
Port Renfrew
Eastsound
San Juan Islands
Victoria
Juan de Fuca Strait
Bellingham
Burlington
Coupeville
Port Angeles
407 The Captain Whidbey Inn
Port Townsend
James House 408
Old Consulate Inn 409
Everett
Olympic National Park
Seabeck
Puget Sound
Pike Place Market
Willcox House 410
Bellevue
Bremerton
Seattle
412 The Villa
Tacoma
Pacific Ocean
Aberdeen
Montesano
Olympia
Pacific Beaches
Mt. Ranier National Park
411 Shelburne Inn
Seaview
Astoria
Longview
Mt. St. Helens
Vancouver
Portland
Tillamook
The Dalles
Goldendale
Osoyoos
Trail
Salmo
413 Sun Mountain Lodge
Winthrop
Okanogan
Lake Chelan
Coulee Dam
Banks Lake
Newport
Leavenworth
414 Haus Rohrbach Pension
Spokane
Wenatchee
Ellensburg
Ritzville
Colfax
Yakima
Central Wine Region
Birchfield Manor 415
Pasco
Kennewick
Eastern Wine Region
Walla Walla
Pendleton
mi 0 20 mi
km 0 20 km
scale
© 2000 Chismar Mapping Services Inc. Licensed for use in the 2001 IIA Select Registry.

Eastsound, WA

Turtleback Farm Inn and Orchard House

800-376-4914 U.S.
360-376-4914 Fax 360-376-5329
www.turtlebackinn.com
turtleback@interisland.net
Orcas Island, 1981 Crow Valley Rd, Eastsound, WA 98245

A COUNTRY FARMHOUSE located on Orcas Island, the loveliest of the San Juan Islands of Puget Sound. This graceful and comfortable inn is considered one of the most romantic places in the country. The addition of the very private Orchard House adds to this description. Highlighted by a spectacular setting, detail-perfect restoration, spotless maintenance and award-winning breakfasts, a haven for those who enjoy breathtaking scenery, varied outdoor activities, unique shopping and fine food. Turtleback Farm is the perfect spot for discriminating travelers. AAA ◆◆◆ and Mobil ★★★.

Select Registry Member *Since 1991*
Innkeepers / Owners
WILLIAM AND SUSAN C. FLETCHER

TRADITIONAL COUNTRY BREAKFAST INN

RATES
11 rooms, $80/$210 B&B.
Open year-round.

ATTRACTIONS
Hiking, whale watching, golf, bicycling, salt & fresh-water fishing, sea kayaking, sailing, tennis, swimming, boating, bird-watching, varied fine dining, arts and crafts.

CUISINE
Full breakfast, beverages anytime, fruit and complimentary sherry. BYOB.

DIRECTIONS
From Orcas Ferry Landing: Follow Horseshoe Hwy N 2.9 mi. Turn L, .9 mi to first R, continue N on Crow Valley Rd. 2.4 mi. to Inn.

1 Guestroom Handicap Accessible • Suitable for Children Over 8
Conference Facilities for 15 • Visa, MC, Disc Accepted
Non-Smoking Inn • Reservations Accepted Through Travel Agents

Coupeville, WA

The Captain Whidbey Inn

800-366-4097

360-678-4097 Fax 360-678-4110

www.captainwhidbey.com
info@captainwhidbey.com

2072 West Captain Whidbey Inn Road
Coupeville, WA 98239

Select Registry Member *Since 1973*
Innkeeper
FRANK J. PUSTKA
Proprietor
CAPTAIN JOHN COLBY STONE

RUSTIC WATERSIDE INN

THIS ROMANTIC, RUSTIC LOG INN dates from 1907 and overlooks the waters of Penn Cove. We offer featherbeds, down comforters, antiques, and artwork in every room, Superb Northwest coastal cuisine and wines are enjoyed by guests. Sail the cove aboard the 52-foot ketch *Cutty Sark* with the proprietor, Capt. John Colby Stone, read by the fireplace or walk the beach to spot eagles and herons. A gracious welcome and profound relaxation await you.

RATES

25 rooms, $95/$155.
7 cabins and cottages, $160/$225 B&B.
Full country breakfast included in rate.
Open year-round.

ATTRACTIONS

Beaches, kayaks, sailing charters, motorboats, five state parks, hiking, historic town, antique shops, golf, horseback riding, carriage rides, winery, galleries, museum, gardens.

CUISINE

Full country breakfast daily; lunch and dinner daily, July-September; weekends only, October-June. Wine, beer and liquor available.

DIRECTIONS

From N: I-5 S Exit 230 to Hwy 20 to Whidbey Island to Coupeville. Turn on Madrona Way. From S: Mukilteo Ferry, Hwy 525-Hwy 20. From W: Port Townsend Ferry, Hwy 20 to Madrona Way.

Suitable for Children • Conference Facilities for 25
Credit Cards Accepted
Reservations Accepted Through Travel Agents

Port Townsend, WA

The James House

800-385-1238

360-385-1238 Fax 360-379-5551

www.jameshouse.com

innkeeper@jameshouse.com

1238 Washington Street, Port Townsend, WA 98368

©Lawrence N. Padgett

THIS GRAND VICTORIAN MANSION sits high on the bluff with unsurpassed water and majestic mountain views. Impeccably maintained inside and out, The James House is just a short stroll from the charming historic Victorian village of Port Townsend. Each distinctive room is nicely furnished with period antiques, comfortable and cozy beds, and most have expansive water views. Beautiful perennial English gardens offer a wonderful setting to watch the ferries and sailing vessels come and go. We pride ourselves in gracious hospitality and invite you to come see why *Northwest Best Places* calls us "one of the best places to stay in the entire state."

Non-Smoking Inn • Conference Facilities for 12

Visa, MC, AMEX, Disc Accepted

Select Registry Member *Since 1996*

Innkeeper/Owner

CAROL MCGOUGH

ELEGANT WATERSIDE BREAKFAST INN

RATES

12 rooms, $120/$225 B&B.
2 double suites, master/bridal suite, gardener's cottage, private bungalow on the bluff.
Open year-round.

ATTRACTIONS

Walking, hiking, bicycling, kayaking, fishing, whale watching, golf, antiquing, art, music, Olympic National Park. Port Townsend is located on the Olympic Peninsula, surrounded on three sides by water with a backdrop of the Olympic Mountains!

CUISINE

Cookies baked daily in late afternoon. Evening cordials, delicious full breakfast included. Excellent restaurants within walking distance.

DIRECTIONS

From Seattle: Take Bainbridge Island ferry. Follow signs to Hood Canal Bridge to Hwy 19. Follow signs to Port Townsend. Inn is located on bluff overlooking Whidbey Island ferry. Please check out http://www.jameshouse.com for more specific directions and map.

Port Townsend, WA

Old Consulate Inn

800-300-6753
360-385-6753 Fax 360-385-2097
www.oldconsulateinn.com
anyone@oldconsulateinn.com
313 Walker at Washington, Port Townsend, WA 98368

Select Registry Member *Since 1996*
Innkeeper/Owner
MICHAEL DELONG

STEP BACK TO A QUIETER MORE ROMANTIC TIME. Visit Port Townsend's award-winning founding family mansion-on-the-bluff. Warm hospitality greets you at every turn. Indulge your senses and refresh your spirit in the beauty of sweeping views of the bay and snowcapped Olympics. Old-fashioned porch swings on the veranda offer views of the flower-filled gardens. Curl up with a good book by the fire-side, relax in the gazebo hot tub. Enjoy afternoon tea and fresh-baked treats, evening desserts and cordials. Share a friendly game of billiards. At day's end, retire to your king bed with sweet turndowns. Awaken well rested to our renowned Banquet Breakfast. Come join us! AAA.

Suitable for Children Over 12 • Non-Smoking Inn
Conference Facilities for 18 • MC, Visa Accepted
Reservations Accepted Through Travel Agents

ELEGANT WATERSIDE BREAKFAST INN

RATES

5 king bedrooms.
2 king suites/ 1queen suite.
$106/$160 B&B Full.
$160/$210.
All private baths. All B&B banquet.
Open year-round.

ATTRACTIONS

Bicycling, golf, tennis, fresh/saltwater fishing, clamming, sailing, kayaking, antiquing, art and music festivals. Historic tours close to Olympic National Park and Forest, whale watching.

CUISINE

Complimentary afternoon tea, cocoa and fresh baked treats. Evening desserts and cordials. Early morning coffee, tea and cocoa. Banquet breakfast at 9 am with consideration to special dietary needs. Custom catering for groups available.

DIRECTIONS

From Seattle: Bainbridge Ferry, take Hood Canal Bridge to Hwy 19 to P.T. From Tacoma: I-5 to Hwy 16\3 to Hood Canal Bridge (etc). From N: Hwy 20 to Keystone Ferry to P.T. On the bluff by the historic courthouse.

Seabeck, WA

Willcox House Country Inn

800-725-9477

360-830-4492 Fax 360-830-0506

www.willcoxhouse.com

2390 Tekiu Road NW, Seabeck, WA 98380

Select Registry Member *Since 1993*

Innkeepers / Owners

CECILIA AND PHILLIP HUGHES

WITH SPECTACULAR VIEWS of Hood Canal and the Olympic Mountains, this waterfront Country House Inn is situated in a forest setting beween Seattle and the Olympic Peninsula. The historic 1930s mansion estate offers park-like grounds, fish ponds, private pier, and an oyster-laden saltwater beach. Period pieces and antiques are featured in guest rooms, the great room, billiard room, pub, library, theater, and dining room. Award winning chef. *Country Inns* magazine award: One of the top twelve inns in North America. Featured on *Great Country Inns* TV series. AAA ◆◆◆.

ELEGANT WATERSIDE INN

RATES
5 rooms, $129/$199 B&B.
Open year-round.

ATTRACTIONS
Private beach and pier, floating dock, hiking, golf nearby, antiquing, gardens and museums.

CUISINE
Breakfast, wine and cheese social hour included. Prix fixe dinner available. Large selection of fine wines.

DIRECTIONS
17 miles W of Bremerton on Hood Canal, near Holly.

Suitable for Children Over 15 • Visa, MC, Disc, AMEX Accepted
Non-Smoking Inn • Conference Facilities for 10
Reservations Accepted Through Travel Agents

Seaview, WA

Shelburne Inn

800-INN-1896
360-642-2442 Fax 360-642-8904
www.theshelburneinn.com
innkeeper@theshelburneinn.com
4415 Pacific Way, P.O. Box 250, Seaview, WA 98644

Select Registry Member *Since 1988*
Innkeepers / Owners
DAVID CAMPICHE AND
LAURIE ANDERSON

TRADITIONAL VILLAGE INN

AN UNSPOILED 28-MILE STRETCH of wild Pacific seacoast is just a 10-minute walk through rolling sand dunes from this inviting Country Inn, built in 1896. Restoration and refurbishing of the award-winning Inn has included the addition of Art Nouveau stained glass windows, along with antique furnishings. A sumptuous breakfast featuring the best of the Northwest is complimentary with your room. Innovative cuisine has brought international recognition to the restaurant and pub. Selected as 'Best Bed & Breakfast in the Northwest', *NW Palate Readers' Favorites.* 'One of 25 Great American Inns with Super Chefs.' *Conde Nast Traveler,* April, 1999.

RATES
13 rooms, $109/$159 B&B.
2 suites, $189 B&B.
Newly-acquired off-site waterside B&B.
2 rooms $199, 1 Suite $239.
Open year-round.

ATTRACTIONS
Beachcombing, bicycling, golf, horseback riding, antiquing, hiking, galleries, historical museums nearby, bird-watching and kayaking.

CUISINE
Breakfast, lunch and dinner available. Wine and liquor available.

DIRECTIONS
From Seattle: I-5 S to Olympia, Hwy 8 and 12 to Montesano and Hwy 107, then 101S to Seaview. From OR coast: U.S. 101 N across Astoria Bridge L to Seaview.

1 Guestroom Handicap Accessible • Suitable for Children
Conference Facilities for 35 • Visa, MC, AMEX Accepted
Non-Smoking Inn • Reservations Accepted Through Travel Agents

Tacoma, WA

The Villa

888-572-1157

253-572-1157 Fax 253-572-1805

www.villabb.com

villabb@aol.com

705 North 5th Street, Tacoma, WA 98403

Select Registry Member *Since 2000*

Innkeepers/Owners

BECKY AND GREG ANGLEMYER

BEAUTIFULLY APPOINTED AND SPOTLESS, this Italian Renaissance mansion on the Historic Register is attractively furnished in Italian Country decor. From a quiet byway The Villa overlooks the congenial Stadium Historic District with views expanding to Puget Sound and the majestic Olympic Mountains. Amenities include Belgian linen sheets, Egyptian cotton robes and plush towels. En suite dinners or massage may be arranged. Truly a place to relax your body and revive your spirit, yet located centrally to the most popular NW attractions. Rated 'excellent' by *Mobil, NW Best Places.* and *Best Places to Kiss NW* travel guides. Full business services.

---

1 Guestroom, 6 Common Rooms Handicap Accessible
Suitable for Children Over 12 • Visa, MC, AMEX Accepted
Conference Facilities for 18 • Reservations Accepted Through Travel Agents

TRADITIONAL IN TOWN BREAKFAST INN

RATES

6 rms/suites, k/q, $115/$210 B&B. Fireplace, TV/CD/stereo, soaking/spa tub, shower, veranda, mtn/water view, phone.
Open year-round.

ATTRACTIONS

Mt. Rainier, Mt. St. Helen and Olympic Natl. Park, Seattle, Victoria, BC; Portland, OR; history/art museums, theater, opera and ballet, wineries, zoos and aquariums, summer, winter and water sports, arboretums and conservatories, racetrack and casino.

CUISINE

Three-course breakfast featuring NW fare and Seattle's Best Coffee 7-9 am weekdays, 8-10 am weekends. Complimentary fine WA wines, beer, ale, pop, cookies and snacks. Award-winning waterfront restaurants nearby.

DIRECTIONS

From I-5 N or S: Take exit 133, follow I-705 N, Exit to Schuster Parkway, then exit Stadium Way. At first light R on Stadium Way. At next light R on Tacoma Ave. N, then L on N 5th St. 1 block on R.

Winthrop, WA

Sun Mountain Lodge

800-572-0493

509-996-2211 Fax 509-996-3133

www.sunmountainlodge.com

sunmtn@methow.com

P.O. Box 1000, Patterson Lake Road,
Winthrop, WA 98862

Select Registry Member *Since 1998*
General Manager
BRIAN CHARLTON

RUSTIC MOUNTAIN RESORT

SUN MOUNTAIN LODGE has achieved international acclaim with awards for the hotel, guest rooms, cuisine and wine list. Our greatest compliments, however, come from the guests who return to us again and again. Set on 3,000 acres, Sun Mountain's combination of privacy, tranquility and serenity balanced by the highest standard of excellence in service and guest amenities makes this an unmatched experience. Whether you're here to remove yourself from the routine or try your hand at our long list of activities, we will make your visit a peak experience. AAA ◆◆◆◆.

RATES
Lodge $120/$325.
Cabins $120/$210.
Suites, $215/$625; EP.
Open year-round.

ATTRACTIONS
Horseback riding, mountain biking, river rafting, golf, tennis, hiking, fishing, full-service spa, cross-country skiing, ice-skating, sleigh rides, and two swimming pools.

CUISINE
Full-service dining room, Northwest cuisine, cafe, room service. Full-service lounge. *Wine Spectator* award.

DIRECTIONS
9 miles SW of Winthrop, WA, just off the North Cascades Hwy. From Seattle: I-5 N to Burlington. Rte 20 E to Winthrop, 190 miles.

---

6 Guestrooms Handicap Accessible. • Suitable for Children
Conference Facilities for 150 • Visa, MC, AMEX, Diners Accepted
Designated Smoking Areas • Reservations Accepted Through Travel Agents

Leavenworth, WA

Haus Rohrbach Pension

800-548-4477

509-548-7024 Fax 509-548-6455

www.hausrohrbach.com

info@hausrohrbach.com

12882 Ranger Road, Leavenworth, WA 98826

Select Registry Member *Since 1994*

Innkeepers / Owners

CAROL AND MIKE WENTINK

HUGGING A MOUNTAINSIDE in the Cascades, Haus Rohrbach, fashioned after the pensions of Europe, offers guests the experience of "Gemutlichkeit," meaning coziness, joviality and kindness. The Inn enjoys spectacular valley views. Close-up, the fragrant flower boxes and well-maintained gardens soothe the soul. Guests are pampered with a welcoming common area, suites designed for romance, down comforters, and home-made desserts. Whatever your whim-shopping, recreation, or relaxation-the richness of our four seasons makes your stay a time to remember.

RUSTIC MOUNTAIN BREAKFAST INN

RATES

5 rooms, $85/$110 B&B.
5 suites, $140/$175 B&B.
Open year-round.

ATTRACTIONS

Pool, hot tub, sledding, hiking, biking, skiing, horseback riding, sleigh rides, fishing, shopping, art galleries, golf, rafting and museums.

CUISINE

Breakfast. Other meals available for groups. Picnic lunches by request.

DIRECTIONS

From Seattle: I-5 N to Everett, Wenatchee exit stay on Hwy 2 to Leavenworth. L on Ski Hill Dr. for 1/2 mi. Turn L on Ranger Rd. to end of road.

---

2 Guestrooms Handicap Accessible • Suitable for Children
Conference Facilities for 20 • Credit Cards Accepted
Non-Smoking Inn • Reservations Accepted Through Travel Agents

Yakima, WA

Birchfield Manor Country Inn

800-375-3420
509-452-1960 Fax 509-452-2334
www.selectregistry.com
2018 Birchfield Road, Yakima, WA 98901

Select Registry Member *Since 1993*
Innkeepers / Owners
WIL AND SANDY MASSET

YAKIMA'S TRUE COUNTRY INN only two miles from town. We offer a relaxing getaway with dinners prepared by professional chef/owners served in the casual warm atmosphere of a gracious home. Park-like grounds surround the outdoor pool. Choose from the wonderful Washington wines-and you may find your favorite winemaker at the next table! Some rooms w/fireplace, two-person tub, panoramic views. We can personalize a tour of local wineries, direct you to roadside stands for fresh fruit and vegetables, or you may talk to Brad or Tim for tee times at the best golf courses. Mobil and AAA ◆◆◆.

TRADITIONAL COUNTRY INN

RATES
11 rooms, $99/$199 B&B.
Open year-round.

ATTRACTIONS
Tour the wineries or play golf in the sun. Pick up fresh fruit and vegetables at the source, or fly-fish in the Yakima River.

CUISINE
Award-winning Northwest cuisine in a casual relaxed atmosphere. Wine and microbrewery beers.

DIRECTIONS
I-82 to Yakima, exit 34. Go E 2 miles, turn R-S on Birchfield Rd. First house on R.

1 Guestroom Handicap Accessible • Suitable for Children Over 8
Conference Facilities for 50 • Visa, MC, AMEX, Disc, Diners Accepted
Non-Smoking Inn • Reservations Accepted Through Travel Agents

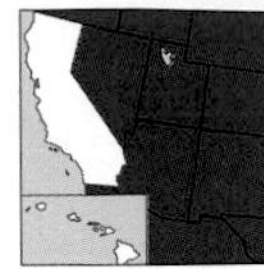

Pacific Coastline

California. In Napa and Sonoma the wines are deep with ruby color, fat and fruity in the mouth, luscious in the bouquet. Travelers can eat like royalty, sleep late into the morning. The mood is easy. California can consummate an infatuation as few other states can.

PICNIC ON A PACIFIC BEACH, then drive east. Your car appears to have a mind of its own; it keeps stopping at the Inns of the SELECT REGISTRY. Traveling through the Redwoods, a traveler can't see enough. Even the most gifted writer has trouble describing the mood that the great Redwoods stir, the magnificence of their size, and something intangible about an evergreen that reigns for a thousand years or more. The giants seem cloaked in a spirit that remains intimidating but nurturing. We are awestruck by the majesty.

In a small rural town in Northern California, one couple discovered a suite that they proclaimed to be the most romantic they had ever seen. To prove a point, they stayed. That Inn is a member of the SELECT REGISTRY. That came as no surprise. They had discovered the best, and the best displays the sign of the SELECT REGISTRY. The Innkeeper was a big, gentle man. The travelers were taken with him. His kindness shone like the big amber sun.

Our Inns are plentiful here. The sunshine supreme. When the rains come, the land turns a rich verdant green overnight. In California, menus suggest state-of-the-art. Hauté cuisine dominates everywhere. Big Inns and small ones—the standard is consistent. Hospitality holds constant. The sign beside the front door proclaims, SELECT REGISTRY.

Eat a splendid meal in St.Helena, Healdsburg or Elk—there are more than 30 of our Inns in Northern California alone. You are staying at a SELECT REGISTRY Inn, and the accommodations remain superlative. The thought of traveling on can produce a soulful mood; you might choose to extend your vacation. The choices are many, and our guidebook leads the way.

Here in the land of big sunshine, of red wines and floral bouquets, an enchanting mood reaches through cerulean skies and beckons seductively. The bronze plaque promises distinction: this Inn belongs to the SELECT REGISTRY.

We exist to please.

"We fell in love with this Inn at first sight and were not disappointed—everything about the Inn and people were wonderful – Yes, we will return again soon!"—Len Lambert, Clarksburg, WV

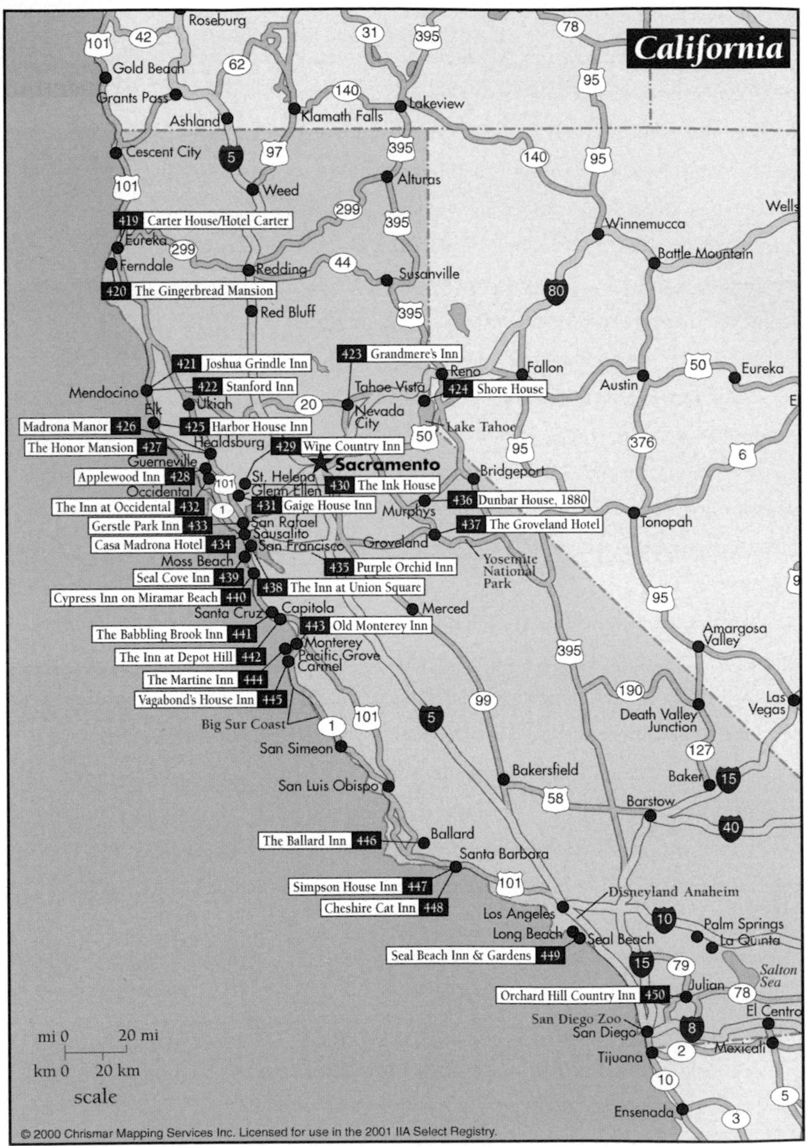
California
419 Carter House/Hotel Carter
420 The Gingerbread Mansion
421 Joshua Grindle Inn
422 Stanford Inn
423 Grandmere's Inn
424 Shore House
425 Harbor House Inn
Madrona Manor 426
The Honor Mansion 427
Applewood Inn 428
429 Wine Country Inn
430 The Ink House
431 Gaige House Inn
The Inn at Occidental 432
Gerstle Park Inn 433
Casa Madrona Hotel 434
435 Purple Orchid Inn
436 Dunbar House, 1880
437 The Groveland Hotel
438 The Inn at Union Square
Seal Cove Inn 439
Cypress Inn on Miramar Beach 440
The Babbling Brook Inn 441
The Inn at Depot Hill 442
443 Old Monterey Inn
The Martine Inn 444
Vagabond's House Inn 445
The Ballard Inn 446
Simpson House Inn 447
Cheshire Cat Inn 448
Seal Beach Inn & Gardens 449
Orchard Hill Country Inn 450
Sacramento
mi 0 20 mi
km 0 20 km
scale
© 2000 Chrismar Mapping Services Inc. Licensed for use in the 2001 IIA Select Registry.

Eureka, CA

Carter House Hotel Carter

707-444-8062

707-445-1390 Fax 707-444-8067

www.carterhouse.com

reserve@carterhouse.com

301 L Street, Eureka, CA 95501

Select Registry Member *Since 1988*
Innkeepers / Owners
MARK AND CHRISTI CARTER

LOCATED ON THE NORTHERN BORDER of Eureka's historic Old Town, The Carter House Victorians and Restaurant 301 have been welcoming travelers to The Redwood Empire with world-class accommodations and cuisine since 1981. An enclave of four unique, magnificent Victorians perched alongside Humboldt Bay, we greet our guests with a special brand of hospitality imbued with the friendly, easy-going style of the North Coast. Our accommodations and service are unparalleled; our cuisine and wine list, award-winning. Restaurant 301 is one of only 83 dining establishments worldwide to hold a *Wine Spectator* Grand Award.

ELEGANT IN TOWN HOTEL

RATES
31 rooms.
19 $145/$195 B&B.
12 suites, $195/$500 B&B.
Open year-round.

ATTRACTIONS
Golf, beach, tennis, antiquing, hiking, horseback riding, bird-watching, redwood forests, camping, swimming, kayaking, rafting, night life, microbreweries.

CUISINE
Full service award-winning restaurant open nightly, full breakfast. Full bar, wine shop – 3000 vintages.

DIRECTIONS
Take 101 N to Herrick Rd, just S of Eureka, turn R. Herrick Rd becomes Fairway Dr. Fairway Dr. becomes F Street. R on Oak Street. L on H Street. R on Harris Street. L on I Street. I Street will intersect 3rd Street, R on 3 Street. Hotel Carter is on corner of 3rd and L Street.

Handicap Access Available • Suitable for Children
Conference Facilities for 35 • Credit Cards Accepted
Reservations Accepted Through Travel Agents

Ferndale, CA

Gingerbread Mansion Inn

800-952-4136
707-786-4000 Fax 707-786-4381
www.gingerbread-mansion.com
innkeeper@gingerbread-mansion.com
400 Berding Street, P.O. Box 40, Ferndale, CA 95536

EXQUISITELY TURRETED AND GABLED, the Gingerbread Mansion Inn is truly a visual masterpiece. Located in the Victorian village of Ferndale, the Inn is surrounded by lush English gardens. Featuring two of the West Coast's most luxurious suites—the 'Empire Suite' and 'Veneto'. Garden views, and old-fashioned tubs and fireplaces for fireside bubble baths are featured. Amenities include a morning tray service, full breakfast, afternoon high tea, turn-down service with bedside chocolates, bathrobes. Ferndale is close to the Giant redwood parks and ocean beaches. AAA ♦♦♦♦.

Select Registry Member *Since 1988*
Innkeeper
KEN TORBERT

ELEGANT VILLAGE
BREAKFAST INN

RATES
11 rooms and suites, $150/$385.
Open year-round.

ATTRACTIONS
Victorian village shops, galleries, historic walking tours, wilderness trails, giant redwood forests and beaches.

CUISINE
Full gourmet breakfast with hot entree and side dish with many other items and English high tea service.

DIRECTIONS
101 4 1/2 hours N of S.F. Ferndale exit, 5 miles to town, L at Bank, 1 block to Inn. From Oregon: 20 minutes S of Eureka. Ferndale exit.

Suitable for Children • Designated Smoking Areas
MC, Visa, AMEX Accepted
Reservations Accepted Through Travel Agents

Mendocino, CA

Joshua Grindle Inn

800-474-6353
707-937-4143
www.joshgrin.com
stay@joshgrin.com
44800 Little Lake Road,P.O. Box 647, Mendocino, CA 95460

Select Registry Member *Since 1996*
Proprietors
JIM AND ARLENE MOOREHEAD

EXPERIENCE MENDOCINO AT ITS BEST. Our welcoming home sits atop a two-acre knoll overlooking the village and ocean. Park and forget about your car, as galleries, shops, restaurants and hiking trails are just a short stroll away. Tastefully decorated, comfortable, and exceptionally clean rooms await you. Our friendly staff will attend to your every need, and serve a full gourmet breakfast. Enjoy chatting with fellow guests over evening refreshments in our parlor, or escape to a private, quiet nook in our gardens. Relax on our front veranda and watch the whales spout in the distance. Recommended by prestigious *Andrew Harper's Hideaway Report*. AAA ◆◆◆ and Mobil ★★★.

Suitable for Children Over 12 • Visa, MC Accepted
Non-Smoking Inn

TRADITIONAL VILLAGE BREAKFAST INN

RATES

10 rooms in Main House, Cottage, Water Tower, $125/$250 B&B. Ocean-view luxury Grindle Guest House $250/$400 EP.
Open year-round, except December 24 & 25. Lower rates mid-week, November through May.

ATTRACTIONS

Hiking, mountain biking, canoeing, kayaking, whale watching, horseback riding, tide-pooling, redwoods, wineries, art galleries and live theater. Visit the beautiful Mendocino Coast Botanical Gardens. Ride the Skunk Train through the redwoods.

CUISINE

Excellent nearby restaurants specializing in fresh local ingredients. The highly regarded Cafe Beaujolais is just a two-block stroll from the Inn.

DIRECTIONS

From San Francisco: Take Hwy 101 N to Hwy 128 W to Hwy 1 N. From Hwy 1: Turn W onto Little Lake Rd. First driveway on your R.

Mendocino, CA

The Stanford Inn By The Sea

800-331-8884
707-937-5615 Fax 707-937-0305
www.stanfordinn.com
stanford@stanfordinn.com
P.O. Box 487, Mendocino, CA 95460

Select Registry Member *Since 1995*
Innkeepers/Owners
JOAN AND JEFF STANFORD

ELEGANT COUNTRY INN

ELEGANT, RUSTIC INN, embodying the best of the Mendocino Coast. The lodge sits atop beautifully landscaped grounds including an organic nursery and llamas. The hillside perch provides sweeping views over the gardens and pastures to the bay and Mendocino village. Accommodations are furnished with antiques and sofas for evenings in front of wood-burning fireplaces. Combining the best of hotels and pensions, all have telephones and TVs, VCRs, stereos, refrigerators and more. A large pool with sauna and spa are protected from the fog by a solaruim. An exercise room, in-room massage, kayaking, canoeing and mountain biking are also available. AAA ◆◆◆◆.

RATES

23 rooms, $215/$265 B&B.
5 one-bedroom suites, $275/$365 B&B.
5 two-bedroom suites, $515/$640 B&B.
Open year-round.

ATTRACTIONS

Canoeing and kayaking on Big River—California's longest undeveloped estuary. Complimentary use of our mountain bikes. Organic gardens and nurseries. Garden tours and seminars. Solarium enclosed pool, spa and sauna. Exercise room.

CUISINE

Exquisite complimentary breakfasts, prepared to order. Meet other guests over afternoon tea and cake or over hors d'oeuvres and wine. For dinner, experience one of California's finest vegetarian dining rooms—The Ravens.

DIRECTIONS

1/4 mile S of historic village center. On Coast Hwy One at Comptche-Ukiah Rd.

Handicap Access Available • Suitable for Children • Pets Allowed
Conference Facilities for 50 • Credit Cards Accepted
Reservations Accepted Through Travel Agents

Grandmere's Inn

530-265-4660
Fax 530-265-4416
www.nevadacityinns.com
grandmere@nevadacityinns.com
449 Broad Street, Nevada City, CA 95959

Select Registry Member *Since 2000*
Innkeepers/Owners
RUTH ANN AND RICHARD RIESE

A GOLD COUNTRY LANDMARK, this beautiful Inn is well-known for warm hospitality, spacious rooms, elegant style and formal gardens. The estate, built in 1856 by Aaron Sargent, U.S. Senator and early Nevada City settler, is on the National Register of Historic Places. Comfortable rooms feature French country decor, high ceilings, four-poster beds, American folk art and tiled baths. Bountiful breakfasts and afternoon cookies get rave reviews from guests. Grandmere's is one block from the Historic District of shops, museums, live theatre and dining. Set in the beautiful Sierra foothills, the Inn is perfect for a relaxing getaway or special occasion. Voted "The Best of Nevada County."

TRADITIONAL VILLAGE
BREAKFAST INN

RATES

3 rooms, $115/$145.
3 suites, $160/$240.
All rooms have queen beds, private baths, central heat/air, sitting areas and modem jacks. Two rooms with private entrances.
Open year-round.

ATTRACTIONS

Historic District with shops, galleries, antiques, wine-tasting. Empire Mine State Park nearby. Hiking, cycling, fly-fishing, swimming, golf, gold panning. Live theatres, seasonal special events.

CUISINE

Delicious full breakfast, afternoon tea and cookies. 16 restaurants within walking distance.

DIRECTIONS

From Sacramento: I-80 E to Hwy 49 N (Auburn). In Nevada City turn L on Broad St. From Reno: I-80 W to Hwy 20. In Nevada City turn L onto Coyote St., R on Broad.

Non-Smoking Inn • Conference Facilities for 12
Visa, MC, AMEX Accepted
Reservations Accepted Through Travel Agents

Tahoe Vista, CA

Shore House at Lake Tahoe

800-207-5160

530-546-7270 Fax 530-546-7130

www.tahoeinn.com

shorehouse@tahoeinn.com

7170 North Lake Boulevard, Tahoe Vista, CA 96148

Select Registry Member *Since 2000*

Innkeepers/Owners

BARB AND MARTY COHEN

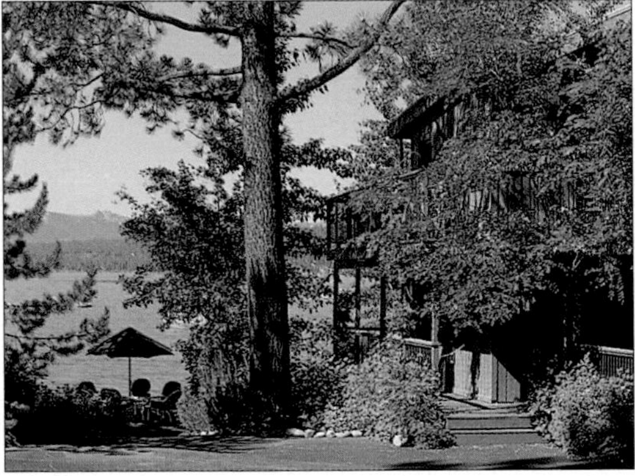

THE SHORE HOUSE is the ultimate romantic getaway on spectacular Lake Tahoe, with lakefront gardens, lawns, pier and adjoining sandy beach. Each floor is surrounded by decks offering fabulous views of our pristine lake and snow-capped mountains. A large outdoor lakefront hot tub offers relaxation with spectacular vistas. Fine lakefront restaurants, quaint shops, museums, art galleries and top-name entertainment at casinos are only steps away, or a short drive. Wedding packages for small intimate lakefront weddings. Honeymoon cottage. Your hosts, Barb, Marty and Jake Cohen, have lived at Lake Tahoe for 27 years.

CONTEMPORARY WATERSIDE BREAKFAST INN

RATES

9 rooms, including 2 cottages, $160/$315. Each room has a private bath, gas log fireplace, knotty pine walls, custom-built log furniture, down comforters and feather beds.

Open year-round.

ATTRACTIONS

Winter: Ski, snowboard or xc-ski at 29 ski areas within an hours drive. Try snowshoeing, ice-skating, and snowmobiling. Summer: Hiking to mountain tops, cruises on Shore House yacht, bicycling, tennis, golf, rafting, horseback riding, parasailing, kayaking and boating.

CUISINE

Breakfast includes fresh fruit and award-winning gourmet entrees served to your table in our lakefront dining room. We serve wine each afternoon, and freshly-baked treats to your room each day. Extraordinary restaurants nearby.

DIRECTIONS

Take Hwy 80 E from San Francisco or 80 W from Reno. Exit at Hwy 267 towards North Lake Tahoe. Turn R at Hwy 28, or N Lake Blvd. Go 3/4 mile to the Shore House at 7170 N Lake Blvd.

Designated Smoking Areas • Visa, MC, Disc Accepted
Reservations Accepted Through Travel Agents

Elk, CA

Harbor House Inn By The Sea

800-720-7474
707-877-3203 Fax 707-877-3452
www.theharborhouseinn.com
harborhs@mcn.org
P.O. Box 369, Elk, CA 95432

BUILT IN 1916, the Harbor House is the Grand Dame of the Redwood Empire standing vigil on a cliff overlooking Greenwood Cove with its spectacular rock formations and powerful, ever-changing sea. Pathways meander through magnificent gardens and lead to the beach below. The drama continues throughout the Inn's ten guest rooms, its stately sitting room and breathtaking ocean-view dining room. Newly refurbished with luxury in mind, the Inn features antique and classic appointments throughout. California cuisine with inspirations from Tuscany and Provence. Extensive wine cellar. Dinner included. Distinctive lodging, fine dining and timeless luxury only three hours from San Francisco.

7 Guestrooms Handicap Accessible • Non-Smoking Inn
Conference Facilities for 20 • MC, Visa, AMEX Accepted

Select Registry Member *Since 1975*
Innkeepers / Owners
ELLE AND SAM HAYNES

ELEGANT COUNTRY INN

RATES

10 rooms, $205/$400 MAP.
Open year-round.

ATTRACTIONS

Private beach, enchanting gardens, wineries, galleries, golf, riding, tennis, kayaking, canoeing, hiking, whale watching, and Redwood forests.

CUISINE

Dramatic ocean-view dining. Full breakfast and highly rated four-course gourmet dinner included in rates. Extensive wine cellar featuring local and international selections.

DIRECTIONS

From San Fancisco: Take 101 N, in Cloverdale take Hwy 128 W to Hwy 1, S 5 miles to Elk.

The Madrona Manor, A Wine Country Inn

800-258-4003
707-433-4231 Fax 707-433-0703
www.madronamanor.com
madronaman@aol.com
1001 Westside Road, Healdsburg, CA 95448

Select Registry Member *Since 1987*
Proprietors
William and Trudi Konrad
Innkeepers
Joseph and Maria Hadley

Elegant Country Inn

THIS MAJESTIC VICTORIAN MANOR, on the National Register of Historic Places, conveys a sense of elegance and gracious hospitality. Guests enjoy tantalizing mountain views in the surrounding Sonoma wine country. Landscaped romantic grounds, eight acres with heated pool. All 22 rooms individually decorated with king/queen beds. No TV by popular romantic demand. Live music on beautiful veranda Friday and Saturday evenings seasonally. An internationally inspired restaurant serves superb dinners by candlelight. Extensive gold-medal wine list.

RATES

22 rooms.
4 suites, $220/$425 B&B.
18 rooms, most w/fireplace and king beds.
Open year-round.

ATTRACTIONS

Visit wineries, explore local farms, hike, bike or jog, see the ocean, shop for antiques, listen to concerts in the plaza, water sports, ballooning, lounge poolside.

CUISINE

Relax in the country while enjoying the urban pleasure of fine romantic dining. Full licensed bar.

DIRECTIONS

From Hwy 101 N take the Central Healdsburg exit. At second stop light make a sharp L onto Westside Rd. Go under the freeway traveling W .7 mile until you see the manor arches straight ahead.

1 Guestroom Handicap Accessible • Suitable for Children
Non-Smoking Inn • Conference Facilities for 30 • Visa, MC Accepted
Reservations Accepted Through Travel Agents

Healdsburg, CA

The Honor Mansion

800-554-4667
707-433-4277 Fax 707-431-7173
www.honormansion.com
innkeeper@honormansion.com
14891 Grove Street, Healdsburg, CA 95448

Select Registry Member *Since 1998*
Innkeepers
STEVE AND CATHI FOWLER

A LUXURY INN. From mints on your pillow…to a full gourmet breakfast…come let us pamper you! Built in 1883, completely restored in 1994, this elegant yet comfortable Inn awaits your arrival. World-class amenities with hometown hospitality complete with pool, decks, fountains, and walking gardens are situated on more than an acre of landscaped grounds, yet a mere ten-minute walk to downtown. More than 100 wineries nearby. AAA ◆◆◆◆.

ELEGANT COUNTRY BREAKFAST INN

RATES
8+ rooms, king and queen, several fireplaces, afternoon refreshments. VISA, MC, Discover. Two people per room.
Open year-round.

ATTRACTIONS
Wineries, antiquing, ballooning, canoeing, boating, waterskiing, river, bicycling, hiking, art galleries, ocean nearby.

CUISINE
Full gourmet breakfast, evening wine and sherry, complimentary cappuccino machine.

DIRECTIONS
From the S: Take Hwy 101 N to Healdsburg. Take the Dry Creek exit to the R for 1 block, turn R on Grove St. We are the first white picket fence on the R. From the N: Take Hwy 101 S to the Dry Creek exit; go L.

1 Guestroom Handicap Accessible • Suitable for Children Over 16
Conference Facilities for 16 • Visa, MC, Disc Accepted
Non-Smoking Inn • Reservations Accepted Through Travel Agents

Guerneville, CA

Applewood Inn & Restaurant

707-869-9093
Fax 707-869-9170
www.applewoodinn.com
stay@applewoodinn.com
13555 Highway 116, Guerneville, CA 95446

PEOPLE WITH A TASTE FOR WINE and bucolic sanctuary have their own favorite wine country hideaway—or at least they should. Nestled on six lush acres in the Russian River Valley, Applewood is a California Mission Revival-Style villa surrounded by Redwoods and apple and pear orchards (guests are encouraged to pick their own snacks). The retreat blends the deluxe with the comfortable in peaceful pocket canyon, and it's only 20 minutes from the Sonoma Coast. If a bottle of wine was purchased at every winery within a half-hour drive, a visitor would have an impressive cellar of outstanding vintages. Applewood is laid-back luxury at its best.

1 Guestroom Handicap Accessible • Non-Smoking Inn
Conference Facilities for 20 • AMEX, Visa, MC, Disc Accepted
Reservations Accepted Through Travel Agents

Select Registry Member *Since 1998*
Innkeepers/Owners
JIM CARON AND
DARRYL NOTTER

ELEGANT COUNTRY INN

RATES
16 rooms in 3 villas, $165/$295.
Open year-round.

ATTRACTIONS
The courtyard and bubbling fountain beckon readers, dozers and weary wine-tasters returning from the scores of wineries nearby. Roses, azaleas and rhododendrons invite garden walks and a heated pool and spa suggest relaxation amid the Redwoods.

CUISINE
Sophisticated California Provencal cuisine offered on an ever-changing, dinner menu enhanced by exceptional Russian River Valley wines on an award-winning list.

DIRECTIONS
Hwy 101 N from San Francisco to Hwy 116 at Cotati W 22 miles to the Inn.

St. Helena, CA

The Wine Country Inn

707-963-7077
Fax 707-963-9018
www.winecountryinn.com
romance@winecountryinn.com
1152 Lodi Lane, St. Helena, CA 94574

Select Registry Member *Since 1978*
Innkeeper
JIM SMITH

TRADITIONAL COUNTRY INN

PERCHED ON A SMALL HILL, overlooking the manicured vineyards and nearby hills of the Napa Valley, this Inn is known for its casual and quiet atmosphere. The intimate rooms boast family-made quilts, private balconies, fireplaces and pine antiques. Famous restaurants and winery tours round out the Napa Valley experience. AAA ◆◆◆.

RATES
21 rooms and 3 suites.
Rates are $176/$345 B&B.
Off-season discounts.
Open year-round.

ATTRACTIONS
Pool and Jacuzzi on property. World -class wineries and restaurants abound. Hot air ballon rides, antique shopping, excellent golf and great specialty shopping.

CUISINE
Full buffet breakfast included in rate. Menus of lunch and dinner spots. Afternoon wine and appetizers served.

DIRECTIONS
From San Francisco: Take I-80 E to Hwy 37 follow signs to Napa Hwy 29 N 18 miles N to St. Helena. 2 miles N to Lodi Ln. R on Lodi 1/3 mile.

Suitable for Children • Credit Cards Accepted
Reservations Accepted Through Travel Agents

St. Helena, CA

The Ink House

707-963-3890

Fax 707-968-0739
www.inkhouse.com
inkhousebb@aol.com

1575 St. Helena Highway, St. Helena, CA 94574

Select Registry Member *Since 1998*
Innkeeper/Owner
DIANE DEFILIPI

ELEGANT COUNTRY BREAKFAST INN

RATES
5 rooms, $105/$190 B&B.
2 suites, $210 B&B.
Open year-round.

ATTRACTIONS
Wineries, tennis, golf, hiking, horseback riding, spas, ballooning, picnic table, pool table and 18-speed bikes.

CUISINE
Full gourmet breakfast, wine and appetizers. Wine, brandy and port.

DIRECTIONS
From S.F.: 80 N to Hwy 37 exit to Hwy 29 N to St. Helena. L at Whitehall or 101 N to Hwy 37 E to Hwy 121 to Hwy 29 N. L at Whitehall.

BUILT IN 1884 BY THERON H. INK, this landmark home is listed on the National Register of Historic Places. The Inn offers Victorian elegance in the midst of Napa Valley's world-famous wine-growing region. Each room offers antiques from the world over, family heirlooms, original artwork, as well as views of two acres of Victorian Gardens, groves, vineyards, hillsides and grandfather redwoods and pines. Guests indulge and treat themselves to the fourth floor glass observatory which offers a 360-degree panoramic view high among the treetops.

Designated Smoking Areas • MC, Visa Accepted
Reservations Accepted Through Travel Agents

Glen Ellen/Sonoma, CA

Gaige House Inn

800-935-0237
707-935-0237 Fax 707-935-6411
www.gaige.com
gaige@sprynet.com
13540 Arnold Drive
Glen Ellen/Sonoma, CA 95442-9305

©Richard Jung

IN JUNE 2000, The Gaige House Inn was named the #1 B&B in America by *Travel & Leisure* Magazine. This follows last year's accolade from the *A&E Channel*, which honored the inn as one of the "top 10 most romantic getaways in the world." Less than an hour from San Francisco, the inn is in the heart of Napa/Sonoma Wine country. Gently influenced Asian and West Indian decor helps create sophisticated yet comfortable environment. Breakfst are outrageously good," according to *Random House's Guide to The Wine Country*. Relax by the pool, or walk to nearby restaurants. Noting all of this, *Frommer's* calls The Gaige House the "Best B&B in the wine country."

1 Guestroom Handicap Accessible
Non-Smoking Inn • Visa, MC, AMEX, Disc, Diners Accepted
Reservations Accepted Through Travel Agents

Select Registry Member *Since 1998*
Innkeepers / Owners
KEN BURNET AND
GREG NEMROW

ELEGANT VILLAGE
BREAKFAST INN

RATES
12 rooms, 6 w/fireplace.
3 suites w/fireplace.
15 pvt. baths, 5 w/Jacuzzi.
TV, AC, TEL, Dataports.
$150/$495 B&B.
2 cottages off-site.
Open year-round.

ATTRACTIONS
Heated pool and whirlpool spa. Near Napa and Sonoma wineries. Jack London, Sugar Loaf and Annadel State Parks nearby for hiking and horseback. Three golf courses, tennis, day spas, cycling, ballooning. Near Historic Sonoma Plaza. Massage services in room or by pool.

CUISINE
Professional chef gourmet breakfasts served w/Peet's Coffee and fresh-squeezed juice. Evening wine service w/light appetizers. Complimentary water and snacks all day. Walk to four excellent restaurants for dinner.

DIRECTIONS
From San Fran.: Rte 101 N to Rte 37 exit. Follow Rte 37 to Rte 121 exit. Follow Rte 121 N to Rte 116. Take right-hand exit onto Arnold Dr./Glen Ellen. Proceed N and pass through village of Glen Ellen.

Occidental, CA

The Inn At Occidental

of Sonoma Wine Country

800-522-6324

707-874-1047 Fax 707-874-1078

www.innatoccidental.com

innkeeper@innatoccidental.com

3657 Church Street, Occidental, CA 95465

WORLD-CLASS ELEGANCE in a wine country setting, one hour north of the Golden Gate, just minutes from the Sonoma Coast and Redwoods, there's a place where time stands still. A Victorian bed and breakfast with the perfect mix of comfort, charm and elegance. Restored by innkeeper, Jack Bullard, it is furnished with antiques, family heirlooms and original art. The Inn offers guests bedrooms with feather beds, private baths, fireplaces, private decks, spa tubs for two and one room with a hot tub. The Inn's food and wine make your visit a memorable one, but nothing is more special than the hospitality you feel. AAA ◆◆◆◆.

1 Guestroom Handicap Accessible • Suitable for Children Over 12
Conference Facilities for 48 • Visa, MC, AMEX, Disc Accepted
Reservations Accepted Through Travel Agents

Select Registry Member *Since 1995*
Innkeepers / Owners
JACK BULLARD
BILL AND JEAN BULLARD

ELEGANT COUNTRY INN

RATES

2 suites: fireplaces, sitting rooms, spa tubs, $270.
14 rooms: sitting areas, fireplaces, 9 spa tubs, 1 outdoor hot tub, $175-$270.
Vacation rental cottage, $540/$600.
Open year-round.

ATTRACTIONS

Wine tasting, Osmosis Enzyme bath and massage, coastal beaches, redwoods, breath-taking scenery, horseback riding, tennis, biking, nurseries, hot-air ballooning, antiquing, rocking on the porch, relaxing with a good book—rejuvenation!

CUISINE

Gourmet full breakfasts, afternoon refreshments, wine and hors d'oeuvres in the evening, wonderful dining nearby, sometimes at The Inn. Special functions: Weddings, reunions, gatherings of friends.

DIRECTIONS

From SF: Cross Golden Gate Bridge 101 N to Rhonert Park Rte 116 W to Sebastopol 7.4 miles L Bodega Hwy 6.4 miles to Freestone R Bohemian Hwy to Occidental 3.7 miles R stop sign to Inn.

San Rafael, CA

Gerstle Park Inn

800-726-7611
415-721-7611 Fax 415-721-7600
www.gerstleparkinn.com
innkeeper@gerstleparkinn.com
34 Grove Street, San Rafael, CA 94901

JUST TWELVE MILES NORTH OF SAN FRANCISCO, the Inn was once the site of an English-style estate built in 1895. Located on one-half acre in a quiet and historic neighborhood, giant cedar, oak and redwood trees lend ample shade to terraced gardens and green lawns. In the evening, relax on the veranda during wine hour, play croquet or pick fruit from the orchard. In the morning, enjoy a full breakfast at leisure on the veranda. Spacious rooms are plush in comfort and color, with fine fabrics, antiques, parlor areas and private decks or patios with beautiful views. The inn offers a quiet private retreat that soothes the soul.

Select Registry Member *Since 1998*
Owners
JIM AND JUDY DOWLING

ELEGANT VILLAGE
BREAKFAST INN

RATES
12 rooms $169/$240 B&B
4 w/Jacuzzi tubs.
Cottages and Carriage House suites w/kitchens.
Open year-round.

ATTRACTIONS
Here: Hiking, croquet.
Nearby: Hiking, fishing, golf, tennis, wine-tasting, antiquing, sightseeing.

CUISINE
Accommodations include full breakfast during a two-hour period. Wine hour in the evening and all day kitchen privileges which include cookies, fruit, popcorn, sodas, juice, milk and tea.

DIRECTIONS
Hwy 101, exit Central San Rafael, W on 4th St., L on D St., R on San Rafael Ave., L on Grove St.

1 Guestroom Handicap Accessible • Suitable for Children
Conference Facilities for 20 • Visa, MC, AMEX, Disc Accepted
Reservations Accepted Through Travel Agents

Sausalito, CA

Casa Madrona Hotel

800-567-9524
415-332-0502 Fax 415-332-2537
www.casamadrona.com
casa@casamadrona.com
801 Bridgeway, Sausalito, CA 94965

Select Registry Member *Since 1998*
General Manager
KEVIN JOHNSON

NESTLED ON THE HILLSIDE overlooking the bay, Casa Madrona is a casually elegant blend of a 19th Century Victorian hotel (circa 1885), and a New England style deluxe inn. Rooms cascade down the hillside offering bay views with fireplaces and decks. Decorated in individual themes, rooms range from La Posada with its century-old Portuguese charm to the Artists Loft complete with antique easel and art supplies. Brick pathways guide you through scented gardens to the award-winning restaurant. Rates include buffet breakfast and a wine and cheese hour.

TRADITIONAL WATERSIDE HOTEL

RATES
34 rooms.
Until April:
$188/$300 weekdays.
$215/$340 weekends.
May 1-Nov. 1:
$215/$400 weekdays.
$240/$450 weekends.
72-hr cancellation policy.
Open year-round.

ATTRACTIONS
Sailing, rowing, kayaking or yachting on the bay, ferry rides, local art walk, hiking and biking on Mt. Tamalpais, visit Muir Woods Drive, Highway 1 and golf.

CUISINE
Mikayla Restaurant serves American cuisine; panoramic view, award-winning. Beer and wine only

DIRECTIONS
101 N over the Golden Gate Bridge, take the Alexander exit, follow until you come to Bridgeway; 101 S take Marin City/Sausalito exit 2 miles S on Bridgeway.

Suitable for Children • 22 Conference Facilities • Credit Cards Accepted
Reservations Accepted Through Travel Agents

Livermore, CA

Purple Orchid Inn Resort & Spa

800-353-4549

925-606-8855 Fax 925-606-8880

www.purpleorchid.com

info@purpleorchid.com

4549 Cross Road, Livermore, CA 94550

THIS DISTINCTIVE SOUTH LIVERMORE VALLEY INN offers fabulous views, gardens, a beach entry pool with adjoining hot tubs and a full-service spa. Accommodations presented with an understated natural elegance; food service is creative gourmet and made to order; staff embody a genuinely gracious, discerning attitude. Achieve a restful balanced harmony as you catnap near the waterfall with a rich Merlot in hand. Enjoy the estate's 21-acre olive orchard, views of thousands of acres of vineyards, championship golf courses, hiking and equestrian event areas.

Select Registry Member *Since 2000*

Owner
KAREN HUGHES
Property Manager
JESSICA TORRY

ELEGANT COUNTRY RESORT

RATES

4 rooms $150/$195.
4 suites/retreats $235/$260.
All rooms have Jacuzzi tubs, FP/TV/VCR/voicemail, concierge service until 9:00 pm, q/k beds, views from all rooms.
Open year-round.

ATTRACTIONS

Pamper yourself in the spa, go wine-tasting, bird-watching, hiking, horseback riding, antiquing, only 50 minutes to San Francisco shopping, museums, Del Valle State recreational park, golf at championship courses, take private golf lessons at the Inn.

CUISINE

Hearty gourmet made-to-order breakfast, complimentary evening wine and cheese reception, beer and wine available for purchase.

DIRECTIONS

From S.F. Int'l Airport: Take Hwy 101 S approx 5 miles to Hwy 92 E to I-880 N approx. 5 miles to I- 580 E approx. 25 miles to exit Vasco Rd. S until it ends at Tesla Rd. Turn L on Tesla Rd. approx. 2 miles. Turn L on Cross Rd. The Inn is on the L.

1 Guestroom Handicap Accessible • Non-Smoking Inn
Conference Facilities for 450 • Visa, MC Accepted
Reservations Accepted Through Travel Agents

Murphys, CA

Dunbar House, 1880

800-692-6006
209-728-2897 Fax 209-728-1451
www.dunbarhouse.com
innkeep@dunbarhouse.com
271 Jones Street, Murphys, CA 95247

Select Registry Member *Since 2001*
Innkeepers/Owners
BOB AND BARBARA COSTA

ARRIVE AT THE INN AND BEGIN A VISIT WITH HISTORY. Located two hours east of San Francisco between Lake Tahoe and Yosemite in the Sierra foothills. Murphys remains much the same as it was during the Great Gold Rush. The village is just steps across the bridge over Murphys Creek and offers fine dining, galleries, wineries, seasonal events and live theater. Water fountains and birdhouses abound in the lovingly tended historic rose garden surrounded by a white picket fence with many private sitting areas. A suite may offer such indulgences as English towel warmer, balcony in the trees, fine linen, stereo system, champagne and a whirlpool bath for two.

TRADITIONAL VILLAGE BREAKFAST INN

RATES

3 rooms, $145/$165.
2 suites, $185/$205
Designer decor, private baths, TV, refrigerators, Norwegian fire-stoves, down comforters, queen or king beds, air-conditioned.
Open year-round.

ATTRACTIONS

Antiquing, wine tasting, hiking, picnicing at nearby lakes, Big Trees State Park. Five excellent golf courses, downhill and xc-skiing at nearby Bear Valley Ski Resort. Unique shops and galleries grace Murphys tree lined historic Main Street.

CUISINE

Appetizer plate and bottle of wine await in each guest's room. Candlelit breakfast endowed with edible flowers served in dining room by the fire, in the rose garden or in the privacy of the guest's room.

DIRECTIONS

From San Francisco: 580 E to Tracy to 205 E to 99 N to Stockton, exit on Hwy 4 E (Farmington exit) to Angels Camp. 49 S to Hwy 4 E again. 9 miles to Murphys. L at Main St. L at Jones St.

Suitable for Children Over 10 • Non-Smoking Inn
AMEX, MC, Visa Accepted
Reservations Accepted Through Travel Agents

Groveland, CA

The Groveland Hotel

800-273-3314
209-962-4000 Fax 209-962-6674
www.groveland.com
peggy@groveland.com
18767 Main Street, P.O. Box 481
Groveland, CA 95321

Select Registry Member *Since 1993*
Innkeepers / Owners
PEGGY AND GROVER MOSLEY

TRADITIONAL MOUNTAIN HOTEL

RATES
17 rooms, including 3 two-room suites with fireplaces and spa tubs. $135/$155 DO B&B. $210 for suites. $25 for each additional adult and $15 children to 12.
Open year-round.

ATTRACTIONS
Yosemite National Park, golf, tennis, fly-fishing, white-water rafting, historic area, gold panning, horseback riding, lake, swimming and hiking.

CUISINE
Gourmet restaurant, featuring California seasonal fresh cuisine. Award-winning wines and beer. Saloon. Received the *Wine Spectator* Award of Excellence for our wine list.

DIRECTIONS
On Hwy 120, the Northern Yosemite Hwy Oakland Airport is 2.5 hours. San Jose, San Francisco and Sacramento are 3 hours. Local airport is Pine Mt. Lake - Q59. One-half hour from Yosemite National Park.

SOUTHERN HOSPITALITY in the heart of the Sierra. An 1849 adobe and 1914 Queen Anne, each listed on the National Register. European antiques, down comforters, robes, in-room coffee service, phones with data ports and upscale decor. Our restaurant features California seasonal fresh cuisine and award-winning wine list. The courtyard is open in summer. Special events include murder mysteries, living history with Mark Twain, etc. Conference facilities for groups to 25. Complete wedding facilities. Our professional staff can arrange and direct all your events with food and beverage, flowers, music, religious services, etc. *Country Inns* magazine's 'Top 10 Inns,' February, 1997.

Handicap Access Available • Suitable for Children • Pets Allowed
Conference Facilities for 25 • Credit Cards Accepted
Reservations Accepted Through Travel Agents

San Francisco, CA

The Inn At Union Square

800-288-4346
Fax 415-989-0529
www.unionsquare.com
inn@unionsquare.com
440 Post Street, San Francisco, CA 94102

Select Registry Member *Since 1998*
Owners
NORM AND NAN ROSENBLATT
General Manager
SUSAN D. PLATT

TRADITIONAL IN TOWN HOTEL

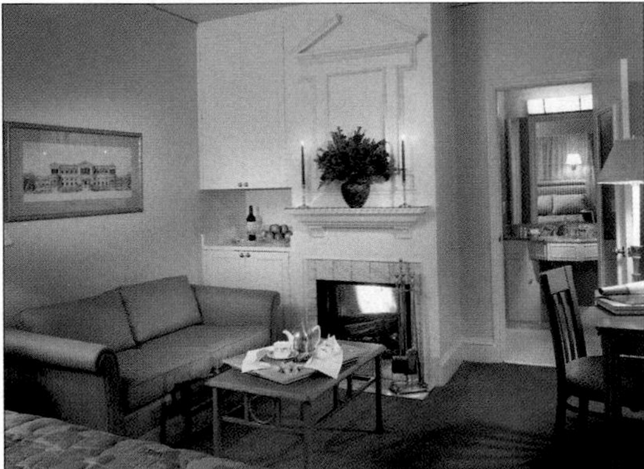

AT THE INN AT UNION SQUARE, your room feels like a private apartment. Along with all you'd expect to find at a superior small hotel, you'll discover goosedown pillows on the bed and fresh flowers on your work desk. It's a quiet urban retreat. When we serve wine and hors d'oeuvres in the early evening, guests gather to trade itineraries in the cozy fireplace lobby on each floor. Enjoy the croissants from your complimentary, continental breakfast with your *Wall Street Journal* and *New York Times.* The Inn is entirely non-smoking, and our staff—the most personable and professional in San Francisco—does not accept tips.

RATES

6 suites, $230.
1 Penthouse, $350.
30 rooms,
$185/$210/$220/$230 EP.
Specialties: Free massage, no tipping.
Open year-round.

ATTRACTIONS

Shopping, theater and restaurants in Union Square, Museum of Modern Art, Golden Gate Bridge and Park, cable cars, Moscone Convention Center, San Francisco Opera, symphony and ballet, Fisherman's Wharf, Alcatraz and Chinatown.

CUISINE

Room service, breakfast buffet and wine and hors d'oeuvres. Full bar and fine wines by the glass.

DIRECTIONS

From S: Hwy 101 to SF. Follow signs for GGB. Exit 9th St., cross Market to Larkin, R on Post. From E: Bay Bridge to 5th St. exit. Take 6th, cross Market to Taylor, R on Post. From N: GGB to Lombard. R on Van Ness, L on Bush, R on Mason, L on Post.

Handicap Access Available • Suitable for Children
Conference Room • Non-Smoking Inn • Credit Cards Accepted
Reservations Accepted Through Travel Agents

Moss Beach, CA

Seal Cove Inn

800-995-9987
650-728-4114 Fax 650-728-4116
www.sealcoveinn.com
sealcove@coastside.net
221 Cypress Avenue, Moss Beach, CA 94038

Select Registry Member *Since 1998*
Innkeepers/Owners
KAREN BROWN HERBERT AND RICHARD CRAIG HERBERT

SPECTACULARLY SET AMONGST WILDFLOWERS and bordered by towering cypress trees, Seal Cove Inn looks out to the ocean over acres of county park; an oasis where you can enjoy secluded beaches, explore tidepools, watch frolicking seals and follow the tree-lined path tracing the windswept ocean bluffs. Each bedroom is its own private haven with a fireplace and doors opening onto a private deck or patio with views to the distant ocean. Country antiques, lovely water-colors, rich fabrics and grandfather clocks all create a perfect romantic ambiance. Children welcome down-stairs. Three person maximum per room. AAA ◆◆◆◆.

ELEGANT COUNTRY BREAKFAST INN

RATES
2 suites, 8 guestrooms, $200/$280, includes breakfast and evening hors d'oeuvres.
Closed for Christmas.

ATTRACTIONS
Tidepools, bluff walks, biking, whale watching, fishing, golf and seals.

CUISINE
Full breakfast in dining room, continental offered in guestrooms. Complimentary wine and hors d'oeuvres.

DIRECTIONS
From Hwy 101 or 280 take Hwy 92 W to Half Moon Bay. Travel N from Half Moon Bay 6 miles on Hwy 1, turn W on Cypress Ave.

---

1 Guestroom Handicap Accessible • Conference Facilities for 16
Children Under 12 in Garden-level Rooms • Visa, MC, AMEX, Disc Accepted
Non-Smoking Inn • Reservations Accepted Through Travel Agents

Half Moon Bay, CA

Cypress Inn On Miramar Beach

800-83-BEACH

650-726-6002 Fax 650-712-0380

www.cypressinn.com
lodging@cypressinn.com

407 Mirada Road, Half Moon Bay, CA 94019

THIS CONTEMPORARY BEACH HOUSE is just steps from a five-mile stretch of white sand beach. Breathtaking ocean views, a palette of colors from the sea, sky and earth, Mexican folk art and hand-carved wooden animals contribute to the colorful celebratory embrace of nature. Natural Pine and wicker furniture, saltillo-tiled floors, dramatic skylights and gentle seabreezes through open windows blend freshly creating a peaceful serenity. Fall asleep listening to waves roll onto shore. In a separate home behind the Inn, called the 'Beach House', four luxurious new rooms named after area beaches have been added. Conference room available. In-house masseuse.

1 Guestroom Handicap Accessible • Non-Smoking Inn
Conference Facilities for 16 • Visa, MC, AMEX, Disc Accepted
Reservations Accepted Through Travel Agents

Select Registry Member *Since 2000*
Owners
DAN FLOYD AND SUZIE LANKES
Innkeeper
KELLY ROBINSON

CONTEMPORARY WATERSIDE BREAKFAST INN

RATES

12 rooms, $215/$325.
Penthouse, $345.
Most rooms have decks with view of ocean. All have fireplace, phone, TV. Some with 2-person tub. Queen/King, or twin beds.
Open year-round.

ATTRACTIONS

Beachcombing, gallop horseback in the surf, lighthouses, whales and elephant seals, abalone and mussel gathering, boating, fishing, tidepools with 200 species. Golf, archery, Coastal Bluff Bike Trail, nurseries, plays, shop Main St., plane rides.

CUISINE

Complimentary full gourmet breakfast in the dining room or brought to your room. Evening wine and hors d'oeuvres and homemade dessert served fireside in the lobby. Wine, champagne and non-alcoholic drinks. Conferences catered.

DIRECTIONS

One half-hour drive S of San Francisco off Hwy 1 between Princeton Harbor and Half Moon Bay. From Hwy 1: Take Medio towards the ocean. Last building on the L, on Miramar Beach.

Santa Cruz, CA

Babbling Brook Inn

800-866-1131

831-427-2437 Fax 831-427-2457

www.babblingbrookinn.com
lodging@babblingbrookinn.com

1025 Laurel Street, Santa Cruz, CA 95060

Select Registry Member *Since 1990*
Contact
Dan Floyd and
Suzie Lankes

Traditional In-Town Inn

Cascading waterfalls, a meandering brook, and a romantic garden gazebo grace an acre of gardens, pines and redwoods, surrounding this urban Inn, yet it is close to dining, shops, mall and beach. Built in 1909 on the foundation of a 1790 gristmill and 2000-year-old Indian fishing village, it's on the National Register of Historic Places. Rooms in Country French decor with four jet bathtubs, private entrances, decks overlooking the gardens. All have fireplaces. Gazebo is popular for weddings. Luxurious newly completed room has large deck with recessed hot tub overlooking the beautiful gardens.

RATES
13 rooms, $160/$220.
Open year-round.

ATTRACTIONS
Beaches, boating, fishing, golf, tennis, redwoods, parks, narrow-gauge railroad, boardwalk, Pacific Garden Mall, local artists, wineries, antiques.

CUISINE
Gourmet breakfast, afternoon tea and cookies. Evening wine and cheese.

DIRECTIONS
Hwy 17 take exit to Hwy 1 N continue on Mission St. to L on Laurel 1.5 blks downhill on R. From S on Hwy 1: Turn R on Laurel 1.5 blks on R.

1 Guestroom Handicap Accessible • Suitable for Children
Conference Facilities for 12 • Visa, MC, AMEX, Disc, Diners Accepted
Designated Smoking Areas • Reservations Accepted Through Travel Agents

Capitola-by-the-Sea, CA

Inn At Depot Hill

800-572-2632
831-462-3376 Fax 831-462-3697
www.innatdepothill.com
lodging@innatdepothill.com
250 Monterey Avenue
Capitola-by-the-Sea, CA 95010

Select Registry Member *Since 1992*
Innkeepers/Owners
SUZIE LANKES AND
DAN FLOYD

NEAR A SANDY BEACH in a quaint, Mediterranean-style resort, this award-winning Inn was named one of the top 10 Inns in the country. A decorator's delight, upscale rooms resemble different parts of the world: Cote d' Azur, a chic auberge in St. Tropez; Paris, a romantic French hideaway; Portofino, an Italian coastal villa; Kyoto, classic Japanese; and Sissinghurst, a traditional English garden room, to name a few. Fireplaces, TV/VCR, stereos, phones and modem connections, robes, feather beds and flowers. Most have hot tubs in private garden patios. Mobil ★★★★ and AAA ◆◆◆◆.

ELEGANT WATERSIDE
BREAKFAST INN

RATES

6 rooms, $210/$295 B&B.
King/Queen/Twin beds.
6 suites, $225/$295 B&B.
Open year-round.

ATTRACTIONS

Beach, 17 restaurants, shops, art galleries, antiques, water sports and golf. Wineries, redwoods, parks. Drive to Carmel/Monterey, Boardwalk.

CUISINE

Full gourmet breakfast, evening wine and hors d'oeuvres, tea and dessert. Wine, champagne, sherry, port.

DIRECTIONS

From Hwy 1: Exit Park Ave., turning towards the ocean for 1 mile. L on Monterey Ave. and immediately L into Inn's driveway. Look for white columns and flags.

Handicap Access Available • Designated Smoking Areas
Conference Facilities for 10 • Visa, MC, AMEX, Disc Accepted
Reservations Accepted Through Travel Agents

Monterey, CA

Old Monterey Inn

800-350-2344
831-375-8284 Fax 831-375-6730
www.oldmontereyinn.com
omi@oldmontereyinn.com
500 Martin Street, Monterey, CA 93940

Select Registry Member *Since 1993*
Innkeepers / Owners
ANN AND GENE SWETT
PATTI KREIDER

ELEGANT IN TOWN INN

SET AMIDST AN ACRE of spectacular gardens on a quiet, oak-studded Monterey hillside, the Old Monterey Inn exudes romance and warmth. The 1929 half-timbered English Tudor Inn's rooms all overlook the uniquely beautiful gardens. Inside, guests find the attention to detail, which is the hallmark of the Inn. Memorably fluffy feather beds and tasty breakfasts, the owners imbue every element with the extra touches that help the Inn achieve near perfection. "The level of service and accommodations here would rival most any inn or hotel we've visited," says *The San Francisco Chronicle*. Recommended by prestigious *Andrew Harper's Hideaway Report*. AAAA ◆◆◆◆ and Mobil ★★★★ Travel.

RATES
1 cottage, K, fireplace, sitting room, spa tub for two, $425.
1 suite, K, fireplace, sitting room, $350.
8 rooms w/sitting areas.
7 fireplaces, K/Q, 2 spa tubs, $220/310 B&B.
Open year-round.

ATTRACTIONS
17-Mile Dr. and world-class Pebble Beach Golf within minutes. Walk to Monterey Bay Aquarium, Cannery Row, wine tasting, shopping in Carmel. Explore Big Sur Coast.

CUISINE
Full gourmet breakfast served bedside or in our Heritage dining room, weather permitting in our gardens. 24-hour access to mineral waters, juices, tea and coffee. Evening wine and hors d'oeuvres. Extaordinary restaurants nearby.

DIRECTIONS
S Hwy 1: Exit Soledad-Munras Ave., cross Munras, R on Pacific, L on Martin. N Hwy 1: Exit Munras Ave., L to Soledad, R on Pacific, L on Martin.

Non-Smoking Inn • Visa, MC Accepted
Reservations Accepted Through Travel Agents

Pacific Grove, CA

The Martine Inn

800-852-5588

831-373-3388 Fax 831-373-3896

www.martineinn.com

P.O. Box 330, Pacific Grove, CA 93950

Select Registry Member *Since 1992*
Innkeeper
DON MARTINE

THIS 1890S FAMILY COMPOUND overlooks the rocky coastline of Pacific Grove on Monterey Bay. Watch sea otters, whales and sailboat races from our parlor, dining and sitting rooms, or many guest bedrooms. Each of our 23 rooms has a private bath, authentic American antique bedroom set, a fresh rose, a silver Victorian bridal basket filled with fresh fruit, a refrigerator and a private telephone. Your room may look directly at the waves crashing against the rocks and/or a wood-burning fireplace with wood provided. Awake to the newspaper placed outside your door and savor a full breakfast served on old Sheffield Silver, Victorian-style china, crystal and lace.

ELEGANT WATERSIDE BREAKFAST INN

RATES
23 rooms.
4 suites, $165/$300.
Rooms w/ fireplaces $200 and up.
Partial ocean view $240 and full ocean view $265/$300.
Open year-round.

ATTRACTIONS
Spa, pool table, courtyard, vintage auto collection, library, bike riding, bird, otter, whale watching, walking, kayaking, shopping, sightseeing, Monterey Bay Aquarium, 17-Mile Drive, Carmel, Big Sur, wine tasting, Cannery Row, Fisherman's Wharf.

CUISINE
Breakfast only. Wine and hors d'oeuvres in the evening, afternoon snacks, (lunch and dinners prearranged from 20 to 50), Victorian dinners up to 12 courses.

DIRECTIONS
Hwy 1 to Pebble Beach Pacific Grove exit. Turn onto Hwy 68 toward Pacific Grove. Stay in R lane on Forest Ave., at the water turn R on Ocean View Blvd turn R at 255 Ocean View Blvd.

---

6 Guestrooms Handicap Accessible • Suitable for Children
Conference Facilities for 50 • AMEX, Visa, MC, Disc Accepted
Designated Smoking Areas • Reservations Accepted Through Travel Agents

Carmel, CA

Vagabond's House Inn

800-262-1262
831-624-7738 Fax 831-626-1243
www.vagabondhouseinn.com

4th and Dolores, P.O. Box 2747, Carmel, CA 93921

THE STONE COURTYARD here is almost a magical experience, with the great oak and cascading waterfalls surrounded by award-winning flower gardens. Around the courtyard are unique rooms with fireplaces, antiques, designer fabrics and fresh flowers. All the natural beauty and fascinating shops of Carmel are just around the corner.

Select Registry Member *Since 1976*
Innkeeper/Owner
DAWN DULL AND
DENNIS LEVETT

ELEGANT VILLAGE INN

RATES
11 rooms, $115/$250, B&B.
Open year-round.

ATTRACTIONS
Carmel Beach, Aquarium, Monterey Bay, golf courses, Big Sur, Point Lobos, galleries, shops, fine restaurants.

CUISINE
Breakfast tray brought to your room.

DIRECTIONS
Hwy 1 (Carmel) R on Ocean Ave. to Dolores, turn R three blocks to 4th and Dolores.

Suitable for Children Over 12 • Pets Allowed
Non-Smoking Inn • AMEX, MC, Visa Accepted
Reservations Accepted Through Travel Agents

Ballard, CA

The Ballard Inn

800-638-2466

805-688-7770 Fax 805-688-9560

www.ballardinn.com

innkeeper@ballardinn.com

2436 Baseline Avenue, Ballard, CA 93463

Select Registry Member *Since 1993*

Contact

CHRISTINE FORSYTH

COMFORTABLY ELEGANT ACCOMMODATIONS in the heart of the Santa Barbara wine country. Just 40 minutes from Santa Barbara, yet nestled in a country neighborhood of orchards and vineyards, the Ballard Inn offers an intimate retreat. Each of the 15 rooms possesses its own special charm and character reflecting local history. Our own Café Chardonnay located in The Ballard Inn features creative wine country cuisine. Visit championship golf courses nearby, or drop by any of the award-winning wineries. AAA ◆◆◆◆.

ELEGANT COUNTRY INN

RATES
15 rooms, $175/$265.
Closed Christmas Day.

ATTRACTIONS
Wineries, antiques, mountain biking, art galleries, hiking, theatrefest, horseback riding, award-winning golf and glider rides.

CUISINE
Café Chardonnay (on the property) serving creative wine country cuisine. Beer and wine only.

DIRECTIONS
From Hwy 101: Take Solvang exit, follow Rte 246 E through Solvang to Alamo Pintado; turn L. Drive 3 miles to Baseline Ave. turn R. The Inn is on your R.

---

1 Guestroom Handicap Accessible
Non-Smoking Inn • Visa, MC, AMEX Accepted

Santa Barbara, CA

Simpson House Inn

800-676-1280

805-963-7067 Fax 805-564-4811

www.simpsonhouseinn.com

reservations@simpsonhouseinn.com

121 East Arrellaga, Santa Barbara, CA 93101

THIS ELEGANTLY RESTORED 1874 Historic Landmark Victorian estate is North America's highest rated historic Inn. The home is secluded in an acre of beautifully landscaped English gardens, yet just a five-minute walk from the historic downtown, restaurants, shopping, theater and a pleasant walk to the beach. For your enjoyment, a delicious full gourmet breakfast is served on the veranda, in your room or private garden patio. Each evening a lavish Mediterranean hors d'oeuvres buffet and local wines are served on the veranda overlooking the gardens. Guest rooms feature antiques and fine art, oriental carpets, wood-burning fireplaces and whirlpools are available. AAA ◆◆◆◆◆ and Mobil ★★★★.

1 Guestroom Handicap Accessible • Suitable for Children Over 12
Conference Facilities for 25 • Visa, MC, AMEX, Disc Accepted
Non-Smoking Inn • Reservations Accepted Through Travel Agents

Select Registry Member *Since 1993*
Proprietors
GLYN AND LINDA SUE DAVIES
Managing Partner
DIXIE ADAIR BUDKE

ELEGANT IN TOWN
BREAKFAST INN

RATES

7 rooms, $195/$395.
4 garden cottages, $485/$500.
4 suites, $475/$500.
Open year-round.

ATTRACTIONS

Historic sites, bicycling, hiking, ocean sports, pool and spa, golf, winery tours, horseback riding, sailing, tennis, croquet and theater.

CUISINE

Full breakfast, lavish Mediterranean hors d'oeuvres buffet, all inclusive. Complimentry local wine in afternoon.

DIRECTIONS

From San Francisco: Mission St. exit, R Anacapa St., R Arrellaga St., L From Los Angeles: Garden St. exit, R Cota St., L Santa Barbara St., R Arrellaga St., L.

Santa Barbara, CA

Cheshire Cat Inn & Spa

805-569-1610
Fax 805-682-1876
www.cheshirecat.com
cheshire@cheshirecat.com
36 West Valerio Street, Santa Barbara, CA 93101

Select Registry Member *Since 1999*
Owner
Christine Dunstan
Managers
Amy Taylor and Bharti Singh

Elegant In Town Inn

THREE GRACEFUL AND ELEGANT Queen Anne Victorians and three California craftsman cottages surrounded by flower-filled gardens, brick patios, gazebo with spa, located just one block from Santa Barabara's main shopping street and historic downtown centre. British antiques, Laura Ashley furnishings and Wedgewood china give a distinctly English atmosphere purposely created by the owner, Christine Dunstan, originally from Cheshire. Romantic suites and cottages feature fireplaces, hot tubs, or in-room Jacuzzis for two. Full spa services on premises. Amenities include: full breakfast, served either in the privacy of your room, or on the garden deck and afternoon wine and hors d'oeuvres.

RATES
15 rooms, $140/$220.
3 suites, $220/$300.
3 cottages, $300/$350.
Open year-round.

ATTRACTIONS
Spanish Mission, courthouse, Natural History Museum, Lotusland, golf, tennis, hiking, horseback riding, fishing, ocean sports, wine tours, whale watching, excursions, International Film Festival, Old Spanish Days. Full spa services on premises.

CUISINE
Full breakfast. Afternoon wine and hors d'oeuvres.

DIRECTIONS
From San Francisco: Mission St. exit L, State St. R, Valerio St. R.
From Los Angeles: Arrellaga St. exit R, Chapala St. L, Valerio St. R.

Limited Handicap Access Available • Suitable for Children
Conference Facilities for 20 • MC, Visa, Disc, AMEX Accepted
Reservations Accepted Through Travel Agents

Seal Beach, CA

The Seal Beach Inn & Gardens

1-800-HIDEAWAY

562-493-2416 Fax 562-799-0483

www.sealbeachinn.com

hideaway@sealbeachinn.com

212 5th Street, Seal Beach, CA 90740

Select Registry Member *Since 1981*

Contacts

MARJORIE BETTENHAUSEN SCHMAEHL AND HARTY SCHMAEHL

ELEGANT WATERSIDE INN

INTERNATIONALLY HONORED elegant country inn one block from the California seaside and pristine beaches. Elegant rooms and suites. Pool, library, tea-room and colorful intimate small garden nooks provide a soothing welcome in a classic French Mediterranean ambience. Brick courtyard, blue canopies, fountains, stately street lamps and antique ironwork. The inn radiates peaceful old-world charm and historic California elegance with quality handsome antiques and artifacts, lavish food, amenities and caring staff.

RATES

Renovated historic inn with rooms and suites exquisitely appointed. Call for specifics.
Open year-round.

ATTRACTIONS

Charming old town, Seal Beach shopping and antique shopping. Close to Queen Mary ship, Aquarium of the Pacific, historic sites, Disneyland, Knotts Berry Farm, Universal Studios, Getty Museum.

CUISINE

18 Restaurants within walking distance. Dinner at inn by advance arrangement. Many other restaurants a short drive away.

DIRECTIONS

405 Freeway S exit Seal Beach Blvd, go L to Pacific Coast Hwy R on PCH. L on 5th St., 2 blocks.

Non-Smoking Inn • AMEX, Disc, Diners, Visa, MC Accepted
Reservations Accepted Through Travel Agents

Julian, CA

Orchard Hill Country Inn

800-71-ORCHARD
760-765-1700 Fax 760-765-0290
www.orchardhill.com
information@orchardhill.com
2502 Washington Street, Julian, CA 92036

Select Registry Member *Since 1998*
Proprietors
DARRELL AND PAT STRAUBE AND FAMILY

ELEGANT COUNTRY INN

ORCHARD HILL, an award-winning premiere inn, in the heart of the Julian Historic District, features magnificent hilltop vistas, colorful gardens, meadows and hiking trails leading to abandoned gold mines. Visitors will love our deluxe rooms with private porches or patios, and in some rooms, dual-sided fireplaces serving both bed and bathrooms. Common rooms in our lodge are reminiscent of America's great national park lodges. Our dining room, with impeccable service and amenities, features a gourmet menu, changing with the seasons. Orchard Hill Country Inn is the ultimate in a secluded getaway destination. AAA ◆◆◆◆.

RATES

12 deluxe cottage rooms, $245/$285.
10 lodge rooms, $185/$245, B&B.
Seasonal specials available.
Open year-round.

ATTRACTIONS

Charming year-round vacation spot famous for fall apple harvest and spring wildflowers. Historic townsite, museum, wineries, shopping, boating, golf, riding, hiking, incredible birdwatching and stargazing.

CUISINE

Full breakfast, hors d'oeuvres. Dinner select nights. Picnic lunches available. Select wines and beers.

DIRECTIONS

60 miles NE of San Diego. Hwy 79 turns in to Main St. in Julian. Take Main to Washington. Turn R and travel two blocks to entrance.

2 Guestrooms Handicap Accessible • Non-Smoking Inn
Conference Facilities for 25 • AMEX, Visa, MC Accepted
Reservations Accepted Through Travel Agents

Pacific Coastline

HONEYMOON IN HAWAII. *Hand in hand, a couple walks the beaches. Many hike the nature trails that skirt the Islands. The abundance of wildlife and blossoming exotic plants stuns.*

EACH NIGHT OUR INN beckon like an oasis. Young or old, romantic couples dance to beach time. Here, the setting is among the most beautiful in the world. Where else might one choose to spend a honeymoon, retreat for that special anniversary or a well-deserved getaway? Where better to spoil yourself?

Your suite offers another retreat into romance. Breakfast is served at your leisure on Wedgewood china in your bedroom, or with other guests around a common table in a lavish dining room.

Above all else, the guests are treated as if each and every one is special. You'll find that commitment in all of our nearly 400 Inns throughout the United States and Canada. Our customers remain our raison-d'être.

The Innkeepers will give you space if that is your wish. They will lavish attention if that is your desire. We are the Innkeepers of the SELECT REGISTRY and we aim to please. We serve to please.

Surf's up. Come to Hawaii and discover romance. Under fair ocean skies, our promise beckons.

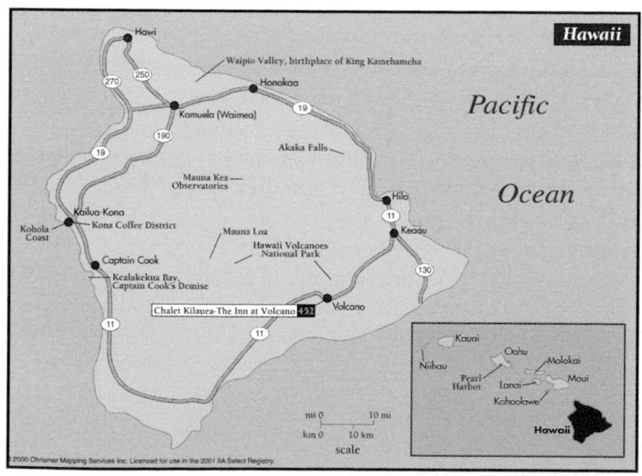

Volcano Village, HI

The Inn At Volcano

The Chalet Kilauea Collection

800-937-7786 Fax 800-577-1849 (reservations)
808-967-7786 Fax 808-967-8660
www.volcano-hawaii.com
reservations@volcano-hawaii.com
Box 998 Wright Road, Volcano Village, HI 96785

Select Registry Member *Since 1998*
Innkeepers/Owners
LISHA AND BRIAN CRAWFORD

TUCKED AWAY IN THE FERN FOREST BY Volcanoes National Park is Hawaii's first 3-Diamond Inn. This enchanting vision was created by world travelers Lisha and Brian Crawford. Fascinating theme rooms and luxurious suites are decorated with treasures from their extraordinary journeys. Enjoy a candlelit three-course gourmet breakfast and afternoon tea in front of the fireplace. Wrap up in a cozy robe to stargaze from the garden Jacuzzi. Marble baths with whirlpool tubs and tropical flowers are some of the extra touches. TV/VCR/Phone. Treehouse and Hapu'u Forest suites. AAA ◆◆◆.

TRADITIONAL VILLAGE INN

RATES
$129/$399.
12 units.
2 rooms.
4 suites.
6 vacation homes.
Open year-round.

ATTRACTIONS
Hawaii Volcanoes National Park, lava viewing, hiking, bird-watching, Black Sand Beach, winery, galleries, golf, botanical gardens and waterfalls.

CUISINE
Gourmet candlelit breakfast, international afternoon tea service. Complimentary kona coffee liqueur.

DIRECTIONS
Hwy 11 to Volcano Village. Turn off Hwy onto Wright Rd. (between 26 & 27 mile markers). Go 3/4 mile to driveway on R.

Suitable for Children • Conference Facilities for 25
Credit Cards Accepted
Reservations Accepted Through Travel Agents

Index

SELECT REGISTRY
DISTINGUISHED INNS OF NORTH AMERICA

Thank you for choosing a Select Registry Inn. You will be helping our members to uphold their standards of excellence if you take a moment to fill out this card and drop it in the mail.

It is difficult for the innkeepers to know the "real" problem if you just check the boxes and do not elaborate with any additional comments. Both the Select Registry office and the Inn will make every attempt to address your concerns or your praise. It is imperative, however, that you provide your name, address and phone number so that we can respond in a timely fashion.

Name of Inn: ....State or Province: ....Date of visit: ....

Your name and address (please print and be aware that we require a name): ....

....

....Your phone number: ....

Please check ONE box in each category:	Excellent	Good	Disappointing	Poor	Would not return
Bedrooms/comfort/décor	☐	☐	☐	☐	☐
Public rooms/aesthetics/furnishings	☐	☐	☐	☐	☐
Food/restaurant quality	☐	☐	☐	☐	☐
Service quality	☐	☐	☐	☐	☐
Welcome/friendliness	☐	☐	☐	☐	☐
Personality/character of the Inn	☐	☐	☐	☐	☐

Additional comments: ....

....

....

As a discriminating traveler who wants to go to the best Country Inns and B&Bs, I recommend the following inns (please include name, city and state/province, and tell us why): ....

....

....

Thank you for visiting our Select Registry Inn. We hope you will let the Registry be your guide in future travels.

The Vacation of a Lifetime

You are eligible to enter this contest because you have this guidebook and have submitted a comment (see reverse side) card on one of our Select Registry Inns.

Please send this card with your name and address filled out completely to the address below.

The lucky winner will be awarded a one-night stay at each one of our 380 Inns listed in this guidebook (subject to availability and restrictions). Please call (toll-free) 866-442-7353 if you have any questions.

Please check www.SelectRegistry.com for date of drawing and the results.

Name ______________________ Phone number ______________________

Address ____

At what Select Registry Inn did you see this card? ______________________

Select Registry employees, Innkeepers and staff are not eligible to enter this contest. Illegible entries will be eliminated. Some restrictions may apply.

Detach and Return

NO POSTAGE
NECESSARY
IF MAILED
IN THE
UNITED STATES

BUSINESS REPLY MAIL

FIRST-CLASS MAIL PERMIT NO. 150 MARSHALL, MI

POSTAGE WILL BE PAID BY ADDRESSEE

SELECT REGISTRY
DISTINGUISHED INNS OF NORTH AMERICA
PO BOX 150
MARSHALL MI 49068-9928